4th Edition

파고다
토익 RC

기본 완성

4th Edition

**파고다
토익** RC
기본 완성

초 판 1쇄 발행	2016년	5월	2일
개정 2판 1쇄 발행	2016년	12월	26일
개정 3판 1쇄 발행	2019년	1월	5일
개정 4판 1쇄 인쇄	2025년	1월	3일
개정 4판 1쇄 발행	2025년	1월	10일

지 은 이 | 파고다교육그룹 언어교육연구소, 김나래
펴 낸 이 | 박경실
펴 낸 곳 | **PAGODA Books** 파고다북스
출판등록 | 2005년 5월 27일 제 300-2005-90호
주   소 | 06614 서울특별시 서초구 강남대로 419, 19층(서초동, 파고다타워)
전   화 | (02) 6940-4070
팩   스 | (02) 536-0660
홈페이지 | www.pagodabook.com

저작권자 | ⓒ 2025 파고다아카데미, 파고다에스씨에스

ISBN 978-89-6281-905-2 (13740)

파고다북스	www.pagodabook.com
파고다 어학원	www.pagoda21.com
파고다 인강	www.pagodastar.com
테스트 클리닉	www.testclinic.com

▌ 낙장 및 파본은 구매처에서 교환해 드립니다.

파고다 토익 RC

4th Edition

파고다교육그룹 언어교육연구소 김나래 | 저

RC

기본 완성

PAGODA Books

파고다 토익 프로그램

독학자를 위한 다양하고
풍부한 학습 자료

각종 학습 자료가 쏟아지는

파고다 토익 공식 온라인 카페
http://cafe.naver.com/pagodatoeicbooks

교재 Q&A
교재 학습 자료
나의 학습 코칭
정기 토익 분석 자료
기출 분석 자료
예상 적중 특강
논란 종결 총평

온라인 모의고사 2회분
받아쓰기 훈련 자료
단어 암기장
단어 시험지
MP3 기본 버전
추가 연습 문제 등 각종 추가 자료

파고다 토익 기본 완성 LC/RC
토익 기초 입문서
토익 초보 학습자들이 단기간에 쉽게 접근할 수
있도록 토익의 필수 개념을 집약한 입문서

파고다 토익 실력 완성 LC/RC
토익 개념&실전 종합서
토익의 기본 개념을 확실히 다질 수 있는
풍부한 문제 유형과 실전형 연습 문제를 담은 훈련서

파고다 토익 고득점 완성 LC/RC
최상위권 토익 만점 전략서
기본기를 충분히 다진 토익 중상위권들의 고득점
완성을 위해 핵심 스킬만을 뽑아낸 토익 전략서

600+   700+   800+

파고다 토익 입문서 LC/RC
기초와 최신 경향 문제 완벽 적응 입문서
개념-핵심 스킬-집중 훈련의 반복을 통해 기초와
실전에서 유용한 전략을 동시에 익히는 입문서

파고다 토익 종합서 LC/RC
중상위권이 고득점으로 가는 도움닫기 종합서
고득점 도약을 향한 한 끗 차이의 간격을 좁히는 종합서

이제는 인강도 밀착 관리!

체계적인 학습 관리와 목표 달성까지 가능한

파고다 토익 인생 점수반
www.pagodastar.com

최단기간 목표 달성 보장
X10배속 토익

현강으로 직접 듣는 1타 강사의 노하우

파고다 토익 점수 보장반
www.pagoda21.com

파고다 토익 적중 실전 LC/RC

최신 경향 실전 모의고사 10회분
끊임없이 변화하는 토익 트렌드에 대처하기 위해
적중률 높은 문제만을 엄선한 토익 실전서

900+   VOCA+

파고다 토익 실전 1000제 LC/RC

LC/RC 실전 모의고사 10회분(1000제)
문제 구성과 난이도까지 동일한 최신 경향 모의고사
와 200% 이해력 상승시키는 온라인 및 모바일
해설서 구성의 실전서

파고다 토익 VOCA

LC, RC 목표 점수별 필수 어휘 30일 완성
600+, 700+, 800+, 900+ 목표 점수별,
우선순위별 필수 어휘 1500

목차

PART 5
GRAMMAR

PART 5
VOCA

PART 6

PART 7

MINI TEST 5회분 & ACTUAL TEST 1회분 문제 및 해설은 www.pagodabook.com에서 무료로 다운로드 가능합니다.

이 책의 구성과 특징

>> **PART 5** GRAMMAR 토익 입문자들에게 꼭 필요한 기초 토익 문법과 핵심 기본 문제 유형을 학습한다.
VOCA Part 5, 6, 필수 동사, 명사, 형용사, 부사 어휘를 핵심 어휘 문제로 정리한다.

>> **PART 6** Part 5에서 학습한 어법 적용 문제, 어휘 문제, 글의 흐름상 빈칸에 알맞은 문장을 고르는 문제에도 충분히 대비한다.

>> **PART 7** 문제 유형별 해결 전략과 지문의 종류 및 주제별 해결 전략을 학습한다.

OVERVIEW

본격적인 학습의 준비 단계로, 각 Part별 출제 경향 및 문제 유형, 그에 따른 접근 전략을 정리하였다.

기본 개념 이해하기

해당 Part의 기본 개념을 예문과 함께 익히고, 정답에 쉽게 접근할 수 있는 풀이 전략을 제시하였다.

핵심 문제 유형

기본 개념 이해하기 코너에서 학습한 내용을 바로 적용해 볼 수 있도록 해당 문제 유형의 대표 문제들을 제시하였다.

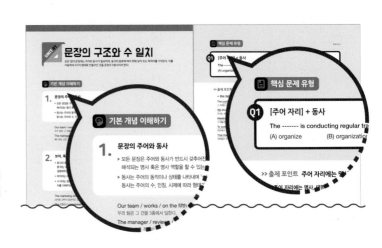

Practice

다양한 토익 실전 문제를 접할 수 있도록 해당 유형의 대표 문제들을 각 Part별로 골고루 구성하였다.

PART 5 GRAMMAR 20문항
        VOCA 20문항
PART 6 16문항
PART 7 지문 유형별 4지문

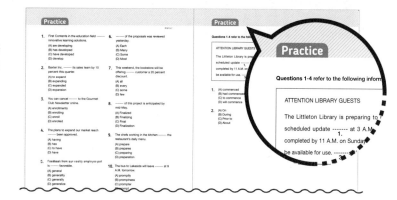

REVIEW TEST

각 Part별 학습한 내용을 마무리할 수 있도록 토익과 동일한 유형과 난이도로 구성하였다.

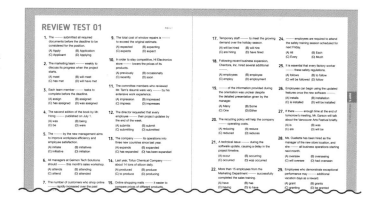

MINI TEST

실전 모의고사를 학습하기에 앞서 총 30문항으로 구성되어있는 MINI TEST 5회분을 먼저 학습해볼 수 있도록 구성하였다.
(www.pagodabook.com에서 무료로 다운로드 가능)

ACTUAL TEST

토익 시험 전 학습한 내용을 점검할 수 있도록 실제 정기 토익과 가장 유사한 형태의 모의고사 1회분을 제공하였다.
(www.pagodabook.com에서 무료로 다운로드 가능)

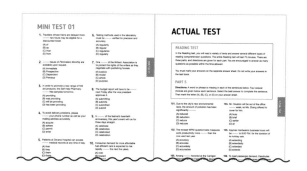

토익이란?

TOEIC(Test of English for International Communication)은 영어가 모국어가 아닌 사람들을 대상으로 일상생활 또는 국제 업무 등에 필요한 실용 영어 능력을 평가하는 시험입니다.

상대방과 '의사소통할 수 있는 능력(Communication ability)'을 평가하는 데 중점을 두고 있으므로 영어에 대한 '지식'이 아니라 영어의 실용적이고 기능적인 '사용법'을 묻는 문항들이 출제됩니다.

TOEIC은 1979년 미국 ETS(Educational Testing Service)에 의해 개발된 이래 전 세계 160개 이상의 국가 14,000여 개의 기관에서 승진 또는 해외 파견 인원 선발 등의 목적으로 널리 활용하고 있으며 우리나라에는 1982년 도입되었습니다. 해마다 전 세계적으로 약 700만 명 이상이 응시하고 있습니다.

▶▶토익 시험의 구성

	파트	시험 형태		문항 수	시간	배점
듣기 (LC)	1	사진 묘사		6	45분	495점
	2	질의응답		25		
	3	짧은 대화		39		
	4	짧은 담화		30		
읽기 (RC)	5	단문 공란 메우기 (문법/어휘)		30	75분	495점
	6	장문 공란 메우기		16		
	7	독해	단일 지문	29		
			이중 지문	10		
			삼중 지문	15		
계		7 Parts		200문항	120분	990점

1979 첫 토익

2006 NEW 토익

2016 신 토익

Present

토익 시험 접수와 성적 확인

토익 시험은 TOEIC 위원회 웹사이트(www.toeic.co.kr)에서 접수할 수 있습니다. 본인이 원하는 날짜와 장소를 지정하고 필수 기재 항목을 기재한 후 본인 사진을 업로드하면 간단하게 끝납니다.

보통은 두 달 후에 있는 시험일까지 접수 가능합니다. 각 시험일의 정기 접수는 시험일로부터 2주 전에 마감되지만, 시험일의 3일 전까지 추가 접수할 수 있는 특별 접수 기간이 있습니다. 그러나 특별 추가 접수 기간에는 응시료가 4,800원 더 비싸며, 희망하는 시험장을 선택할 수 없는 경우도 발생할 수 있습니다.

성적은 시험일로부터 12~15일 후에 인터넷이나 ARS(060-800-0515)를 통해 확인할 수 있습니다.

성적표는 우편이나 온라인으로 발급받을 수 있습니다. 우편으로 발급 받을 경우는 성적 발표 후 대략 일주일이 소요되며, 온라인 발급을 선택하면 유효 기간 내에 홈페이지에서 본인이 직접 1회에 한해 무료 출력할 수 있습니다.

시험 당일 준비물

시험 당일 준비물은 규정 신분증, 연필, 지우개입니다. 허용되는 규정 신분증은 토익 공식 웹사이트에서 확인하시기 바랍니다. 필기구는 연필이나 샤프펜만 가능하고 볼펜이나 컴퓨터용 사인펜은 사용할 수 없습니다. 수험표는 출력해 가지 않아도 됩니다.

시험 진행 안내

시험 진행 일정은 시험 당일 고사장 사정에 따라 약간씩 다를 수 있지만 대부분 아래와 같이 진행됩니다.

≫ 시험 시간이 오전일 경우

AM 9:30~9:45	AM 9:45~9:50	AM 9:50~10:05	AM 10:05~10:10	AM 10:10~10:55	AM 10:55~12:10
15분	5분	15분	5분	45분	75분
답안지 작성에 관한 Orientation	수험자 휴식 시간	신분증 확인 (감독 교사)	문제지 배부, 파본 확인	듣기 평가(LC)	읽기 평가(RC) 2차 신분증 확인

* 주의: 오전 9시 50분 입실 통제

≫ 시험 시간이 오후일 경우

PM 2:30~2:45	PM 2:45~2:50	PM 2:50~3:05	PM 3:05~3:10	PM 3:10~3:55	PM 3:55~5:10
15분	5분	15분	5분	45분	75분
답안지 작성에 관한 Orientation	수험자 휴식 시간	신분증 확인 (감독 교사)	문제지 배부, 파본 확인	듣기 평가(LC)	읽기 평가(RC) 2차 신분증 확인

* 주의: 오후 2시 50분 입실 통제

파트별 토익 소개

PART 5

INCOMPLETE SENTENCES
단문 공란 메우기

PART 5는 빈칸이 포함된 짧은 문장과 4개의 보기를 주고 빈칸에 들어갈 가장 알맞은 보기를 고르는 문제로, 총 30문제가 출제된다. 크게 문장 구조/문법 문제와 어휘 문제로 문제 유형이 나뉜다.

문항 수	30문항(101~130번에 해당합니다.)
문제 유형	- 문장 구조/문법 문제: 빈칸의 자리를 파악하여 보기 중 알맞은 품사나 형태를 고르는 문제와 문장의 구조를 파악하고 구와 절을 구분하여 빈칸에 알맞은 접속사나 전치사, 또는 부사 등을 고르는 문제 - 어휘 문제: 같은 품사의 4개 어휘 중에서 정확한 용례를 파악하여 빈칸에 알맞은 단어를 고르는 문제
보기 구성	4개의 보기

▶▶ 시험지에 인쇄되어 있는 모양

어형 문제
▶▶

101. The final due date for ------- of all budget reports has been pushed back for three days.

(A) complete   (B) completing

(C) completion   (D) completely

어휘 문제
▶▶

102. After being employed at a Tokyo-based technology firm for two decades, Ms. Mayne ------- to Vancouver to start her own IT company.

(A) visited   (B) returned

(C) happened   (D) compared

문법 문제
▶▶

103. ------- the demand for the PFS-2x smartphone, production will be tripled next quarter.

(A) Even if   (B) Just as

(C) As a result of   (D) Moreover

정답 **101.**(C) **102.**(B) **103.**(C)

PART 6

TEXT COMPLETION
장문 공란 메우기

Part 6는 4개의 지문에 각각 4개의 문항이 나와 총 16문제가 출제되며, Part 5와 같은 문제이나, 맥락을 파악해 정답을 골라야 한다. 편지, 이메일 등의 다양한 지문이 출제되며, 크게 문장 구조/문법을 묻는 문제, 어휘 문제, 문장 선택 문제로 문제 유형이 나뉜다.

문항 수	4개 지문, 16문항(131~146번에 해당합니다.)
지문 유형	설명서, 편지, 이메일, 기사, 공지, 지시문, 광고, 회람, 발표문, 정보문 등
문제 유형	- 문장 구조/문법 문제: 문장 구조, 문맥상 어울리는 시제 등을 고르는 문제 - 어휘 문제: 같은 품사의 네 개 어휘 중에서 문맥상 알맞은 단어를 고르는 문제 - 문장 선택 문제: 앞, 뒤 문맥을 파악하여 네 개의 문장 중에서 알맞은 문장을 고르는 문제
보기 구성	4개의 보기

▶▶ 시험지에 인쇄되어 있는 모양

Questions 131-134 refer to the following e-mail.

To: sford@etnnet.com
From: customersupprt@interhostptimes.ca
Date: July 1
Subject: Re: Your Subscription

Congratulations on becoming a reader of *International Hospitality Times*. ---131--- the plan you have subscribed to, you will not only have unlimited access to our online content, but you will also receive our hard copy edition each month. If you wish to ---132--- your subscription preferences, contact our Customer Support Center at +28 07896 325422. Most ---133--- may also make updates to their accounts on our website at www.interhosptimes.ca. Please note that due to compatibility issues, it may not be possible for customers in certain countries to access their accounts online. ---134---. Your business is greatly appreciated.

International Hospitality Times

문법 문제
▶▶
131. (A) Besides
(B) As if
(C) Under
(D) Prior to

어휘 문제
▶▶
132. (A) purchase
(B) modify
(C) collect
(D) inform

어형 문제
▶▶
133. (A) read
(B) readable
(C) readers
(D) reading

문장 삽입 문제
▶▶
134. (A) We have branches in over 30 countries around the globe.
(B) We provide online content that includes Web extras and archives.
(C) We are working to make this service available to all readers soon.
(D) We would like to remind you that your contract expires this month.

정답 131.(C) 132.(B) 133.(C) 134.(C)

PART 7

READING COMPREHENSION
독해

Part 7은 단일·이중·삼중 지문을 읽고 그에 딸린 2~5개의 문제를 푸는 형태로, 총 15개 지문, 54문제가 출제되어 RC 전체 문항의 절반 이상을 차지한다. 같은 의미의 패러프레이징된 표현에 주의하고, 문맥을 파악하는 연습을 한다. 키워드 파악은 문제 해결의 기본이다.

문항 수	54문항(147~200번에 해당합니다.)
지문 유형	- **단일 지문**: 이메일, 편지, 문자 메시지, 온라인 채팅, 광고, 기사, 양식, 회람, 공지, 웹페이지 등 - **이중 지문**: 이메일/이메일, 기사/이메일, 웹페이지/이메일 등 - **삼중 지문**: 다양한 세 지문들의 조합
문제 유형	- **핵심 정보**: 주제 또는 제목과 같이 가장 핵심적인 내용을 파악하는 문제 - **특정 정보**: 세부 사항을 묻는 문제로, 모든 질문이 의문사로 시작하며 지문에서 질문의 키워드와 관련된 부분을 읽고 정답을 찾는 문제 - **NOT**: 지문을 읽는 동안 보기 중에서 지문의 내용과 일치하는 보기를 대조해서 소거하는 문제 - **추론**: 지문의 내용을 바탕으로 전체 흐름을 이해하며 지문에 직접 언급되지 않은 사항을 추론하는 문제 - **화자 의도 파악**: 화자의 의도를 묻는 문제로, 문자 메시지나 2인 형태의 대화로 출제되며 온라인 채팅은 3인 이상의 대화 형태로 출제 - **동의어**: 주어진 단어의 사전적 의미가 아니라 문맥상의 의미와 가장 가까운 단어를 고르는 문제 - **문장 삽입**: 지문의 흐름상 주어진 문장이 들어갈 적절한 위치를 고르는 문제로, 세부적인 정보보다 전체적인 문맥 파악이 중요한 문제
보기 구성	4개의 보기

▶▶ 시험지에 인쇄되어 있는 모양

Questions 151-152 refer to the following text message chain.

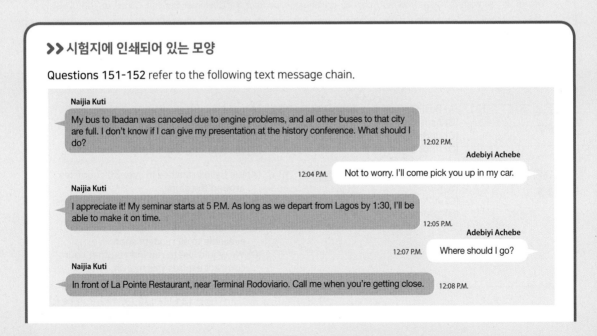

Naijia Kuti
My bus to Ibadan was canceled due to engine problems, and all other buses to that city are full. I don't know if I can give my presentation at the history conference. What should I do?
12:02 P.M.

Adebiyi Achebe
12:04 P.M. Not to worry. I'll come pick you up in my car.

Naijia Kuti
I appreciate it! My seminar starts at 5 P.M. As long as we depart from Lagos by 1:30, I'll be able to make it on time.
12:05 P.M.

Adebiyi Achebe
12:07 P.M. Where should I go?

Naijia Kuti
In front of La Pointe Restaurant, near Terminal Rodoviario. Call me when you're getting close. 12:08 P.M.

151. At 12:04 P.M., what does Mr. Achebe most likely mean when he writes, "Not to worry"?
(A) He has a solution to Ms. Kuti's problem.
(B) He can reschedule a presentation.
(C) He knows another bus will arrive soon.
(D) He is happy to cover Ms. Kuti's shift.

152. What is implied about Ms. Kuti?
(A) She has a meeting at a restaurant.
(B) She is going to be late for a seminar.
(C) She plans to pick up a client at 1:30 P.M.
(D) She is within driving distance of a conference.

정답 **151.**(A) **152.**(D)

Questions 158-160 refer to the following Web page.

http://www.sdayrealestate.com/listing18293

Looking for a new home for your family? This house, located on 18293 Winding Grove, was remodeled last month. It features 2,500 square feet of floor space, with 5,000 square feet devoted to a gorgeous backyard. Also included is a 625 square feet garage that can comfortably fit two mid-sized vehicles. —[1]—. Located just a five-minute drive from the Fairweather Metro Station, this property allows for easy access to the downtown area, while providing plenty of room for you and your family. —[2]—. A serene lake is just 100–feet walk away from the house. —[3]—. A 15 percent down payment is required to secure the property. —[4]—. For more detailed information or to arrange a showing, please email Jerry@sdayrealestate.com.

158. How large is the parking space?
(A) 100 square feet
(B) 625 square feet
(C) 2,500 square feet
(D) 5,000 square feet

159. What is NOT stated as an advantage of the property?
(A) It has a spacious design.
(B) It has been recently renovated.
(C) It is in a quiet neighborhood.
(D) It is near public transportation.

160. In which of the positions marked [1], [2], [3], and [4] does the following sentence best belong?

"A smaller amount may be accepted, depending on the buyer's financial circumstances."

(A) [1]
(B) [2]
(C) [3]
(D) [4]

정답 **158.**(B) **159.**(C) **160.**(D)

학습 플랜

4주 플랜

DAY 1	DAY 2	DAY 3	DAY 4	DAY 5
[PART 5 GRAMMAR] UNIT 01. 문장의 구조와 수 일치 UNIT 02. 시제 UNIT 03. 능동태와 수동태 REVIEW TEST 01	UNIT 04. 명사 UNIT 05. 대명사 UNIT 06. 형용사	UNIT 07. 부사 UNIT 08. 전치사 REVIEW TEST 02	UNIT 09. 접속사 UNIT 10. 명사절 접속사 UNIT 11. 형용사 접속사 REVIEW TEST 03	UNIT 12. to부정사 UNIT 13. 동명사 UNIT 14. 분사 UNIT 15. 비교 REVIEW TEST 04

DAY 6	DAY 7	DAY 8	DAY 9	DAY 10
[PART 5 VOCA] UNIT 01. 동사 어휘 UNIT 02. 명사 어휘 UNIT 03. 형용사 어휘 UNIT 04. 부사 어휘 REVIEW TEST	**[PART 6]** UNIT 01. 시제 UNIT 02. 대명사 UNIT 03. 연결어	UNIT 04. 어휘 선택 UNIT 05. 문장 선택 REVIEW TEST	UNIT 01. 주제·목적 문제 UNIT 02. 세부사항 문제 UNIT 03. 사실확인 문제	UNIT 04. 암시·추론 문제 UNIT 05. 문장 삽입 문제 UNIT 06. 동의어 문제

DAY 11	DAY 12	DAY 13	DAY 14	DAY 15
UNIT 07. 문자 대화문과 화자의도 UNIT 08. 편지·이메일 UNIT 09. 광고	UNIT 10. 공지·회람 UNIT 11. 기사 UNIT 12. 양식	UNIT 13. 이중 지문 UNIT 14. 삼중 지문	REVIEW TEST	MINI TEST 01

DAY 16	DAY 17	DAY 18	DAY 19	DAY 20
MINI TEST 02	MINI TEST 03	MINI TEST 04	MINI TEST 05	ACTUAL TEST

8주 플랜

DAY 1	DAY 2	DAY 3	DAY 4	DAY 5
[PART 5 GRAMMAR] UNIT 01. 문장의 구조와 수 일치 UNIT 02. 시제	UNIT 03. 능동태와 수동태 REVIEW TEST 01	UNIT 04. 명사 UNIT 05. 대명사 UNIT 06. 형용사	UNIT 07. 부사 UNIT 08. 전치사 REVIEW TEST 02	REVIEW TEST 01&02 다시보기 - 틀린 문제 다시 풀어보기 - 모르는 단어 체크해서 암기

DAY 6	DAY 7	DAY 8	DAY 9	DAY 10
UNIT 09. 접속사 UNIT 10. 명사절 접속사	UNIT 11. 형용사절 접속사 REVIEW TEST 03	UNIT 12. to부정사 UNIT 13. 동명사 UNIT 14. 분사	UNIT 15. 비교 REVIEW TEST 04	REVIEW TEST 03&04 다시보기 - 틀린 문제 다시 풀어보기 - 모르는 단어 체크해서 암기

DAY 11	DAY 12	DAY 13	DAY 14	DAY 15
PART 5 GRAMMAR 복습	**[PART 5 VOCA]** UNIT 01. 동사 어휘 UNIT 02. 명사 어휘	UNIT 03. 형용사 어휘 UNIT 04. 부사 어휘 REVIEW TEST	PART 5 VOCA 복습	**[PART 6]** UNIT 01. 시제 UNIT 02. 대명사

DAY 16	DAY 17	DAY 18	DAY 19	DAY 20
UNIT 03. 연결어 UNIT 04. 어휘 선택	UNIT 05. 문장 선택 REVIEW TEST	PART 6 복습	UNIT 01. 주제·목적 문제	UNIT 02. 세부사항 문제

DAY 21	DAY 22	DAY 23	DAY 24	DAY 25
UNIT 03. 사실확인 문제	UNIT 04. 암시·추론 문제	UNIT 05. 문장 삽입 문제	UNIT 06. 동의어 문제	UNIT 07. 문자 대화문과 화자의도

DAY 26	DAY 27	DAY 28	DAY 29	DAY 30
UNIT 08. 편지·이메일	UNIT 09. 광고	UNIT 10. 공지·회람	UNIT 11. 기사	UNIT 12. 양식

DAY 31	DAY 32	DAY 33	DAY 34	DAY 35
UNIT 13. 이중 지문	UNIT 14. 삼중 지문	REVIEW TEST	PART 7 복습	MINI TEST 01

DAY 36	DAY 37	DAY 38	DAY 39	DAY 40
MINI TEST 02	MINI TEST 03	MINI TEST 04	MINI TEST 05	ACTUAL TEST

PAP

GRAMMAR

RT 5

단문 빈칸
채우기

OVERVIEW

Part 5는 빈칸이 있는 문장이 하나 나오고, 4개의 선택지 중 빈칸에 가장 적절한 단어나 구를 고르는 문제로, 총 30문항이 출제된다.

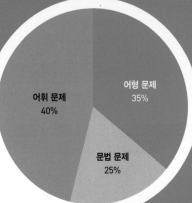

어형 문제
35%

어휘 문제
40%

문법 문제
25%

문제 유형 분석

어형 문제 ㅣ 빈칸의 자리를 파악하여 선택지 중 알맞은 품사나 형태를 고르는 문제
어휘 문제 ㅣ 같은 품사의 네 개 어휘 중 정확한 용례를 파악하여 알맞은 단어를 고르는 문제
문법 문제 ㅣ 문장의 구조 파악과 구와 절을 구분하여 접속사나 전치사, 부사 등을 고르는 문제

최신 출제 경향

- 문법적 지식과 어휘력을 동시에 묻는 문제들이 증가하고 있다.
  ⋯ 명사 자리인데 선택지에 비슷하게 생긴 명사가 두 개 이상 나오는 문제가 출제된다.
- 두 가지 이상의 문법 포인트를 묻는 문제들이 출제되고 있다.
  ⋯ 동사의 문장 형식을 이해하고 태를 결정하는 문제가 출제된다.
- 다양한 품사의 선택지로 구성된 문제들이 출제되고 있다.
  ⋯ 부사 문제이지만 전치사, 접속사, 관용 표현 등으로 선택지가 구성된다.

핵심 학습 전략

- 무조건 해석부터 하지 말고 선택지를 보고 [어형 문제/어휘 문제/문법 문제] 중 어떤 문제인 지부터 파악한다. 어형 문제는 해석 없이도 답이 나오는 문제가 대부분이므로 최대한 시간을 절약할 수 있는 방법으로 풀어나가야 한다.

- 고득점을 얻기 위해서는 한 단어를 외우더라도 품사, 파생어, 용법을 함께 암기해야 한다. 예를 들어, announce와 notify를 똑같이 '알리다'라고 외워두면 두 단어가 같이 선택지로 나 오는 어휘 문제는 풀 수 없다. notify 뒤에는 사람만이 목적어로 나온다는 사실을 꼭 알아 두어 야 한다.

단계별 문법 학습 전략
(1) 문장의 구조를 결정하는 5형식 동사와 품사별 문장 성분의 역할과 문법을 학습한다.
(2) 구와 절을 연결하여 문장을 확장시켜주는 전치사와 접속사의 역할을 학습한다.
(3) 동사의 시제와 태, 가정법, 분사 구문 등의 다소 까다로운 문법 지식을 습득한다.

문제 풀이 전략

1. 어형 문제

아래 문제처럼 한 단어의 네 가지 형태가 선택지로 나오는 문제를 어형 문제 또는 자리 찾기 문제라고 한다. 어형 문제는 빈칸이 [주어, 동사, 목적어, 보어, 수식어] 중에 어떤 자리인지를 파악해서 선택지 중 알맞은 품사나 형태를 고르는 문제이다.

> Our focus group will make direct ------- between several competing brands of carbonated drinks.
>
> (A) comparisons　　　　　　　(B) comparable
> (C) compare　　　　　　　　　(D) comparing

빈칸은 이 문장의 목적어 자리이며, 보기 중 목적어 자리에 들어갈 수 있는 품사는 명사 (A) 뿐이다.

2. 어휘 문제

아래 문제처럼 같은 품사의 네 가지 다른 단어가 선택지로 나오는 문제를 어휘 문제라고 한다. 어휘 문제는 최소한 빈칸 주변을 해석해야만 풀 수 있고, 어려운 문제의 경우에는 가산/불가산 명사의 구분, 자/타동사의 구분과 같은 문법 사항까지 같이 포함되어 출제되기도 한다.

> I have enclosed a copy of my résumé for your ------- and look forward to hearing from you soon.
>
> (A) explanation　　　　　　　(B) participation
> (C) reference　　　　　　　　　(D) consideration

빈칸은 전치사 for의 목적어 자리에 어떤 명사 어휘를 넣으면 가장 자연스러운지를 고르는 문제인데 '당신의 고려를 위해 제 이력서를 첨부합니다' 정도는 해석해야만 정답 (D)를 고를 수 있는 문제로 어형 문제보다는 훨씬 난도가 높다.

3. 문법 문제

아래 문제처럼 종속접속사, 등위접속사, 전치사, 부사 등이 선택지에 같이 나오는 문제를 문법 문제라고 한다. 문법 문제는 그 문장의 구조를 파악하여 구와 절을 구분하고 절이라면 여러 가지 절 중 어떤 절인지를 파악해야 하는 어려운 문제들로 대부분 해석까지도 필요하다.

> We need more employees on the production line ------- production has increased by 60 percent.
>
> (A) although　　　　　　　　　(B) since
> (C) because of　　　　　　　　(D) so

빈칸은 두 개의 절을 연결하는 종속접속사 자리이다. 전치사인 (C)와 등위접속사인 (D)는 답이 될 수 없고, 접속사 (A)와 (B) 중에서 '생산이 증가했기 때문에 추가 직원을 고용해야 한다'는 의미에 맞는 (B)를 답으로 고르는 문제이다.

문장의 구조와 수 일치

모든 영어 문장에는 주어와 동사가 필요하며, 동사의 종류에 따라 뒤에 보어 또는 목적어를 가져온다. 이를 이용하여 5가지 형태로 만들어진 것을 문장의 5형식이라 한다.

 기본 개념 이해하기

1. 문장의 주어와 동사

▶ 모든 문장은 주어와 동사가 반드시 갖추어진 절이다. 주어는 동작이나 상태의 주체로 '~은 / ~는 / ~이 / ~가'로 해석되는 명사 혹은 명사 역할을 할 수 있는 대명사, 동명사, 명사절의 형태를 갖는다.

▶ 동사는 주어의 동작이나 상태를 나타내며 '~이다 / ~하다'라고 해석되는 be동사 / have동사 / 일반동사를 말한다. 동사는 주어의 수, 인칭, 시제에 따라 형태가 달라지며, 뒤에 목적어의 유무에 따라 자동사와 타동사로 구별된다.

Our team / works / on the fifth floor of the building. 주어 + 동사 + 전치사구(수식어)
우리 팀은 그 건물 5층에서 일한다.

The manager / reviews / the performance / of all employees. 주어 + 동사 + 목적어 + 전치사구(수식어)
매니저는 모든 직원의 성과를 검토한다.

2. 보어, 목적어, 수식어의 자리

▶ 동사의 종류에 따라 보어나 목적어의 사용 여부가 결정된다. 보어는 주어나 목적어를 보충해주는 말로 '주어를 보충'하는 주격 보어와 '목적어를 보충'하는 목적격 보어로 구분해서 쓰인다. 보어 자리에는 주어나 목적어의 상태를 설명해주는 형용사 또는 동격을 나타내는 명사가 온다.

▶ 목적어는 타동사 뒤에서 동작의 대상이 되는 말로 '~을 / 를'로 해석되며 명사 또는 대명사가 쓰인다.

▶ 수식어는 문장에서 반드시 필요한 것이 아닌 부가적인 역할이며 문장의 필수성분(주어, 동사, 목적어, 보어)에 의미를 더해주는 역할을 한다. 수식어는 문장 내 다양한 자리에 나올 수 있다.

The marketing strategy / proved / **effective**. 주어 + 동사 + 주격 보어(형용사)
마케팅 전략이 효과적인 것으로 판명되었다.

The CEO / considered / the solution / **innovative**. 주어 + 동사 + 목적어 + 목적격 보어(형용사)
최고 경영자는 그 솔루션이 혁신적이라고 여겼다.

The IT team / designed / **the system** / innovatively. 주어 + 동사 + 목적어 + 부사(수식어)
IT 팀은 시스템을 혁신적으로 설계했다.

Over the last month, / Mr. Ford / has **successfully** negotiated / a key deal / **for his company**.
전치사구(수식어) + 주어 + 부사(수식어) + 동사 + 목적어 + 전치사구(수식어)
지난 한 달 동안, 포드 씨는 그의 회사를 위한 중요한 거래를 성공적으로 성사시켰다.

3. 1형식 문장 『주어 + 동사』

▶ 주어와 동사로 이루어진 기본적인 문장 구조이며, 1형식 자동사는 목적어를 취할 수 없으므로 부사나 전치사구 등의 수식어구와 함께 쓰인다.

대표적인 1형식 동사			
work 일하다	rise 오르다	fall 떨어지다	go 가다
come 오다	depart 출발하다	arrive 도착하다	start 시작하다
begin 시작하다	travel 여행가다	exist 존재하다	function 작동하다
happen 발생하다	take place 발생하다	occur 발생하다	appear 나타나다
emerge 나타나다	respond 반응하다	speak 말하다	differ 다르다
vary 다르다	last 지속하다	proceed 진행하다	expire 만료되다

The product launch / **went** / smoothly. 주어 + 동사 + 부사(수식어) 제품 출시가 순조롭게 진행되었다.

Ms. Ross / **works** / in the field of environmental research. 주어 + 동사 + 전치사구(수식어)
로스 씨는 환경 연구 분야에 종사한다.

☑ **문법 포인트** 동사 뒤에 목적어(~을/를)가 오지 않는 동사를 자동사라하고, 목적어가 오는 동사를 타동사라고 한다. 1형식 자동사 뒤에 부사를 고르는 문제가 자주 출제되므로 대표적인 자동사는 숙지해두자.

4. 2형식 문장 『주어 + 동사 + 주격 보어』

▶ 2형식 동사도 자동사이며 목적어는 없어도 되지만 보어는 꼭 있어야 하는 동사이다. 이때 주어의 상태를 설명해 주는 형용사나 주어와 동일한 대상(동격)을 나타내는 명사 보어가 올 수 있다.

대표적인 2형식 동사			
be ~이다	become ~되다	seem ~처럼 보이다	appear ~처럼 보이다
remain ~채로 남다	stay 여전히 ~하다	prove ~로 판명되다	turn out ~로 판명되다
look ~처럼 보이다	sound ~하게 들리다	feel ~한 느낌이 들다	taste ~한 맛이 나다

Our team members / **are** / innovative. 주어 + 동사 + 주격 보어(형용사) 우리 팀원들은 혁신적이다.

The startup / **became** / a market leader. 주어 + 동사 + 주격 보어(명사) 그 신생 업체가 시장 주도 기업이 되었다.

☑ **문법 포인트** 주격 보어 자리에 명사와 형용사 중 어느 것을 취할지는 의미상 구분해야 하나, 토익 시험에서는 동격을 나타내는 명사보다는 형용사를 고르는 문제가 자주 출제된다. 특히, 형용사 보어 자리에 부사를 쓰지 않도록 주의한다.

5. 3형식 문장 『주어 + 동사 + 목적어』

▶ 3형식 동사는 동작의 대상이 되는 목적어(~을 / 를)를 필요로 하는 동사이다.

The quality control team / **inspected** / the products / thoroughly. 주어 + 동사 + 목적어 + 부사(수식어)
품질관리팀이 제품을 철저히 검사했다.

6. 4형식 문장 『주어＋동사 + 간접 목적어 + 직접 목적어』

▶ 4형식 동사는 목적어를 2개 취할 수 있는 동사이다. 간접 목적어는 주로 사람(~에게)이 오며 직접 목적어는 주로 사물(~을/를)이 온다. 4, 5형식 동사들은 기본적으로 3형식으로도 쓰인다.

대표적인 4형식 동사 (수여동사)				
give 주다	offer 제공하다	award 수여하다	grant 수여하다	send 보내다
show 보여주다	win 얻게 해주다	assign 할당하다	charge 청구하다	

The company / **offered** / employees / yearly bonuses. 주어＋동사＋간접 목적어＋직접 목적어 **4형식**
회사는 직원들에게 연례 보너스를 제공했다.
The company / **offered** / yearly bonuses / (to employees). 주어＋동사＋직접 목적어＋간접 목적어 **3형식**

7. 5형식 문장 『주어 + 동사 + 목적어 + 목적격 보어(형용사/명사)』

▶ 5형식 동사는 목적어와 목적격 보어를 필요로 하는 동사이다. 목적격 보어 자리에는 목적어의 상태를 설명해주는 형용사와 동일한 대상(동격)을 나타내는 명사가 올 수 있다.

대표적인 5형식 동사 (목적격 보어로 형용사/명사를 취하는 동사)		
keep ~을 ~하도록 유지하다	find ~를 ~하다고 여기다 / 알다	목적어 + 형용사
consider ~을 ~하다고 여기다	make ~을 ~하게 만들다	
leave ~을 ~한 채로 두다		
name ~을 ~로 부르다 / 임명하다	appoint ~을 ~로 임명하다	목적어 + 명사
vote ~을 ~로 선출하다	elect ~을 ~로 선출하다	
call ~을 ~로 부르다	consider ~을 ~로 여기다	

The supervisor / **kept** / the workplace atmosphere / collaborative. 주어＋동사＋목적어＋목적격 보어(형용사)
상사는 작업장 분위기를 협력적으로 유지했다.
The sales team / **considered** / cost reduction / a top priority. 주어＋동사＋목적어＋목적격 보어(명사)
영업팀은 비용 절감을 최우선사항으로 여겼다.

8. 5형식 문장 『주어 + 동사 + 목적어 + 목적격 보어(to부정사/원형부정사)』

▶ 5형식 동사로는 보어 자리에 형용사나 명사 외에도 목적어의 동작을 설명하는 to부정사 또는 원형부정사를 동반하는 사역동사가 있다. 이때, 해석은 '(누가) ~하기를 ~하다'로 해석한다.
▶ help는 준사역동사로 목적격 보어 자리에 to부정사 또는 원형부정사가 둘 다 올 수 있다.

대표적인 5형식 동사 (목적격 보어로 to부정사/동사원형을 취하는 동사)			
ask 요청하다	request 요청하다	require 요구하다	
advise 조언하다	allow 허가하다	permit 허가하다	
encourage 권장하다	urge 촉구하다	force 강요하다	목적어 + to부정사
instruct 지시하다	expect 예상하다	remind 상기하다	
enable 가능하게 하다	cause 야기하다	help 돕다	
help ~가 ~하도록 돕다	have ~가 ~하도록 시키다		목적어 + 원형부정사
make ~가 ~하도록 만들다	let ~가 ~하도록 허락하다		

The CEO / **expected** / the team / **to meet** the deadlines. 주어 + 동사 + 목적어 + 목적격 보어(to부정사)
최고 경영자는 그 팀이 마감일을 맞출 것으로 예상했다.

The customer feedback / **helped** / the company / **improve** product quality.
주어 + 동사 + 목적어 + 목적격 보어(원형부정사)
고객 피드백은 회사가 제품 품질을 개선하도록 도왔다.

✓ **문법 포인트** 토익 시험에서는 주로 목적격 보어 자리에 알맞은 성분을 고르는 문제가 출제되므로, 목적격 보어 자리에 무엇이 오는가를 동사에 따라 구분해주도록 한다.

9. 주어와 동사의 수 일치

▶ 셀 수 있는 명사인 경우 단수와 복수 형태가 있다. 명사와 동사는 『주어 + 동사』의 관계에 놓이기 때문에 동사에도 단수와 복수 형태가 있다. 주어가 단수 명사인 경우 단수 동사를, 복수 명사이면 복수 동사로 수 일치를 맞춘다.

단수 주어 + 단수 동사 N + Vs	An employee works hard.
복수 주어 + 복수 동사 Ns + V	Employees work hard.

✓ **문법 포인트** 명사의 경우 복수형일 때 -(e)s의 형태가 붙지만, 반대로 동사의 경우는 -(e)s가 붙은 형태가 단수 동사이니 유의하도록 하자.

10. be동사와 일반동사의 단수형과 복수형

▶ 보통, 현재 시제에만 단수와 복수를 표시하지만 be동사는 과거(was / were)도 형태가 변한다. 일반동사의 과거와 미래는 수 일치와 상관이 없다.

	단수	복수	과거
be동사	is 이다	are 이다	was / were 였다
have동사	has 가지다	have 가지다	had 가졌다
do동사	does 하다	do 하다	did 했다
일반동사	offers 제공하다	offer 제공하다	offered 제공했다

A manager [conducts / conducted / will conduct] team meetings to discuss the agenda.
단수 주어 + [현재 / 과거 / 미래 시제]
관리자는 안건을 논의하기 위해 팀 회의를 [한다 / 했다 / 할 것이다].

Managers [conduct / conducted / will conduct] team meetings to discuss the agenda.
복수 주어 + [현재 / 과거 / 미래 시제]
관리자들은 안건을 논의하기 위해 팀 회의를 [한다 / 했다 / 할 것이다].

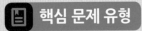
Q1 [주어 자리] + 동사

The ------- is conducting regular training programs to develop employees' skills.

(A) organize　　(B) organization　　(C) organizing　　(D) organizational

>> 출제 포인트　주어 자리에는 명사 또는 명사 역할을 하는 것이 온다.

● 주어 자리에는 명사, 대명사, 동명사, to부정사, 명사절 등이 올 수 있다.

The conference is happening tomorrow at the hotel downtown. 주어: 명사
그 학회는 내일 시내에 있는 호텔에서 열릴 것이다.

We should analyze the financial reports in detail. 주어: 대명사
우리는 재무 보고서를 상세히 분석해야 한다.

Meeting with clients provides valuable feedback. 주어: 동명사
고객들과의 만남은 가치 있는 피드백을 제공한다.

To work abroad is a unique opportunity for personal growth. 주어: to부정사
해외에서 일하는 것은 개인 성장을 위한 특별한 기회이다.

That the employees work in harmony ensures a productive environment. 주어: 명사절
직원들이 한마음으로 일하는 것은 생산적인 환경을 보장한다.

Q2 주어 + [동사 자리]

We ------- the presentation into three sections to cover each topic thoroughly.

(A) broke   (B) broken   (C) breaking   (D) to break

>> **출제 포인트** **to부정사, 동명사, 현재분사(-ing), 과거분사는 동사로 쓰일 수 없다.**

❶ 하나의 문장에는 주어가 생략되더라도 동사는 반드시 있어야 한다. 명령문은 주어(You)를 생략하고 동사원형으로 시작한다.

Please (you) <u>update</u> your contact information in the employee directory.
(Please) <u>update</u> your contact information in the employee directory.
직원 명부에 당신의 연락처를 업데이트해 주세요.

❷ **조동사 뒤에는 주어와 상관없이 동사원형이 온다.**

can / could ~할 수 있다 will / would ~할 것이다 may / might ~할지도 모른다 should / must / have to ~해야 한다 do / does / did not ~않는다	+ 동사원형

Vendors <u>can submit</u> their invoices electronically for faster processing.
판매업체들은 보다 빠른 처리를 위해 송장을 온라인으로 제출할 수 있다.

❸ **문장의 필수 성분(주어, 동사, 목적어, 보어) 외에 꼭 없어도 되는 수식어 역할을 하는 것들이 있다.**

부사	(Efficiently) manage your time to enhance productivity. 생산성을 높이기 위해 당신의 시간을 효율적으로 관리하시오.
전치사구	The training session will take place (in the conference room). 교육 세션이 회의실에서 열릴 것이다.
관계대명사절	The employee (who completed the training program) will lead the new project. 교육 프로그램을 이수한 직원이 새 프로젝트를 이끌 것이다.
부사절	(As the demand for the product grows,) the company plans to hire more staff. 제품 수요가 늘어나면서, 회사는 직원을 더 채용할 계획이다.

Q3 **주어와 동사의 수 일치**

Johnson Cosmetics ------- a new line of eco-friendly packaging.

(A) launching   (B) is launching   (C) are launching   (D) to launch

>> 출제 포인트 **동사는 반드시 문장의 주어와 수를 일치시켜야 한다.**

❶ **고유명사(사람 이름, 회사 명칭)는 -s가 붙어 복수 명사로 보이더라도 단수 취급한다.**

Mr. Jones is known for his business strategy.
존스 씨는 그의 비즈니스 전략으로 유명하다.

TechInnovators has introduced a new technology.
테크이노베이터는 새로운 기술을 도입했다.

❷ **「There + 동사(be) + 명사」 '~이 있다' 구조에서는 뒤에 오는 명사가 주어이므로, 명사에 수 일치를 해야 한다.**

There [**is** / are] a problem with the new software.
새로운 소프트웨어에 문제가 있다.

There [is / **are**] problems with the inventory management.
재고 관리에 문제가 있다.

❸ **문장의 주어로 동명사, to부정사, 명사절이 오면 동사는 단수를 쓴다.**

Attending the client meeting [**is** / are] mandatory. 동명사 주어
고객 회의에 참석하는 것은 의무이다.

To gather customer feedback [**improves** / improve] product satisfaction. to부정사 주어
고객 피드백을 수집하는 것은 제품 만족도를 향상시킨다.

That the team has exceeded its sales targets [**demonstrates** / demonstrate] its efficiency. 명사절 주어
팀이 영업 목표를 초과 달성했다는 것은 그들의 효율성을 입증한다.

Q4 주어 뒤에 오는 수식어

The company founded by several engineers ------- innovative software.
(A) developing (B) has developed (C) have developed (D) to develop

>> **출제 포인트** **주어 뒤에 오는 수식어구는 수 일치에 영향을 주지 않는다.**

● 주어 뒤에 바로 동사가 오지 않고, 주어를 수식하는 수식어구가 쓰였을 때 주어와 동사의 수 일치에 유의해야 한다. 특히, 수식어구에 속한 단어를 주어로 혼동하지 않도록 주의해야 한다.

주어	형용사	동사
	전치사 + 명사	
	분사(현재분사 / 과거분사)	
	to부정사	
	관계사절	

The **marketing team** (responsible for email campaigns) [**conducts** / conduct] surveys once a week.
주어 + (형용사 구) + 동사
이메일 캠페인을 담당하는 마케팅팀은 매주 1회 설문조사를 실시한다.

All **applicants** (from the education sector) [is / **are**] encouraged to highlight their teaching experience in their resumes. 주어 + (전치사 + 명사) + 동사
교육 부분의 모든 지원자는 이력서에 강의 경력을 강조하도록 권장된다.

The **employees** (working in the IT department) [maintains / **maintain**] the company's technological infrastructure. 주어 + (분사구) + 동사
IT 부서에서 근무하는 직원들은 회사의 기술 인프라를 유지관리한다.

Mr. Kim's **ability** (to handle technical issues) [**was** / were] crucial in maintaining the company's operational efficiency. 주어 + (to부정사) + 동사
기술적인 문제들을 처리하는 김 씨의 능력은 회사의 운영 효율성을 유지하는 데 결정적이었다.

The **customers** (who provide feedback) [helps / **help**] us improve our products and services.
주어 + (관계사절) + 동사
피드백을 제공하는 고객들은 우리가 제품과 서비스를 개선하는 데 도움을 준다.

✔ **문법 포인트** 토익 시험에서는 주어와 동사 사이의 수식어구를 하나로 묶고 동사의 수 일치를 묻는 문제가 주로 출제되지만, 동사의 수에 맞는 주어를 찾는 문제가 가끔 출제되기도 한다.

Q5 부정형용사 + 명사의 단 / 복수

------- manager conducts performance evaluations to assess employee productivity.

(A) Many   (B) Every   (C) All   (D) Most

>> **출제 포인트** 부정형용사는 뒤에 오는 명사가 단 / 복수인지를 구별해서 푼다.

● 부정형용사는 단 / 복수의 쓰임이 다르므로 뒤에 오는 명사에 따라 동사의 수를 일치시킨다.

a(n)(= one) 하나 / this 이것 / that 저것 / each 각각 / every 모든 / another 또다른 하나	+ 가산 단수 명사	+ 단수 동사
these 이것들 / those 저것들 / many 많은 / a few 조금 있는 / few 거의 없는 / all 모든 / most 대부분 / some 몇몇의	+ 가산 복수 명사	+ 복수 동사
this 이것 / that 저것 / much 많은 / a little 조금 있는 / little 거의 없는 / all 모든 / most 대부분 / some 약간의	+ 불가산 명사	+ 단수 동사
the 그 / my, your, his, her, its, our, their	+ 가산 / 불가산 명사	+ 단수 / 복수 동사

Every candidate is encouraged to ask questions.
모든 지원자는 질문을 하도록 권장된다.

A few people were selected for the leadership training.
리더십 연수를 위해 몇 명이 선발되었다.

Much information is available on the company website.
많은 정보는 회사 웹사이트에서 이용할 수 있다.

All customer complaints are addressed promptly.
모든 고객 불만사항은 신속하게 처리된다.

Q6 부정대명사 + of the + 명사의 단 / 복수

All of the employees ------- undergoing evaluations this month.

(A) is   (B) are   (C) was   (D) being

>> **출제 포인트** 『**부정대명사 + of the 명사**』의 구조로 쓰일 때, 단 / 복수의 짝이 정해져 있다.

❶ 부정형용사와 부정대명사 두 가지 쓰임이 있는 것들도 있다. 수 일치는 부정형용사의 수일치와 같다.

many a few few	+ of the 복수 명사	+ 복수 동사	~중 많은 ~중 약간 ~중 거의 없는
much a little little	+ of the 불가산 명사	+ 단수 동사	~중 많은 ~중 약간 ~중 거의 없는
all most some any	+ of the 복수 명사 of the 불가산 명사	+ 복수 동사 단수 동사	~의 전부 ~의 대부분 ~의 일부 ~의 아무도, 어느 것도 (아닌)

Some of the **managers are** attending a leadership seminar. 매니저들 중 일부가 리더십 세미나에 참석할 예정이다.

Some of the **equipment needs** maintenance. 장비 중 일부가 유지보수를 필요로 한다.

❷ each, one, either, neither는 바로 뒤에 명사가 올 경우 단수 명사와 어울려 쓰이지만, of the 뒤에는 복수 명사가 오므로 수 일치에 주의해야 한다.

each one either neither	+ of the 복수 명사	+ 단수 동사	~중의 각각 ~중의 하나 ~중의 하나(둘 중 하나) ~(둘 중) 어느 것도 아닌

One employee was promoted to a managerial position. 한 직원이 관리직으로 승진했다.

One of the strategies proves to be highly effective. 전략들 중 하나가 매우 효과적인 것으로 입증되었다.

✓ **문법 포인트** everything, everybody, everyone은 의미상 복수이지만 단수 취급한다. 특히, every는 뒤에 단수 명사를 취하지만 every of the 명사의 형태로 쓰이지는 않으므로 주의한다.

Everyone contributes to the success of the project.
모두가 프로젝트의 성공에 기여한다.

Every employee receives an annual performance review.
모든 직원은 매년 성과 평가를 받는다.

Every of the employees has their own strengths and responsibilities. ❌
모든 직원은 각자의 강점과 책임을 가지고 있습니다.

1. First Contents in the education field ------- innovative learning solutions.

(A) are developing
(B) has developed
(C) have developed
(D) develop

2. Baxter Inc. ------- its sales team by 15 percent this quarter.

(A) to expand
(B) expanding
(C) expanded
(D) expansion

3. You can cancel ------- to the Gourmet Club Newsletter online.

(A) enrollments
(B) enrolling
(C) enroll
(D) enrolled

4. The plans to expand our market reach ------- been approved.

(A) having
(B) has
(C) to have
(D) have

5. Feedback from our weekly employee poll is ------- favorable.

(A) general
(B) generality
(C) generally
(D) generalize

6. ------- of the proposals was reviewed yesterday.

(A) Each
(B) Many
(C) Some
(D) Most

7. This weekend, the bookstore will be offering ------- customer a 20 percent discount.

(A) all
(B) every
(C) some
(D) few

8. ------- of this project is anticipated by mid-May.

(A) Finalized
(B) Finalizing
(C) Final
(D) Finalization

9. The chefs working in the kitchen ------- the restaurant's daily menu.

(A) prepare
(B) prepares
(C) preparing
(D) preparation

10. The bus to Lakeside will leave ------- at 9 A.M. tomorrow.

(A) promptly
(B) promptness
(C) prompter
(D) prompt

11. Ms. Park, the store supervisor, frequently ------- new products.

(A) designs
(B) design
(C) to design
(D) designing

12. Requests made on the Budget Shop portal generally ------- three days to complete.

(A) requires
(B) requiring
(C) require
(D) to require

13. Please ------- the guide thoroughly before setting up your new application.

(A) examine
(B) examines
(C) examining
(D) to examine

14. Eco Fashion Ltd. ------- stores with sustainable and stylish apparel.

(A) supplying
(B) supply
(C) have supplied
(D) has been supplying

15. All staff members should ------- the security course by next week.

(A) finish
(B) finished
(C) finishes
(D) finishing

16. There ------- several luggage pieces in the airport lounge today.

(A) be
(B) being
(C) was
(D) were

17. Each of the attendees at this season's Tech Expo ------- excited about the new product launches.

(A) are
(B) is
(C) were
(D) being

18. Travelers can effortlessly ------- the downtown area by using the Blue Metro Line.

(A) accessing
(B) access
(C) accesses
(D) to access

19. One of the applicants ------- some incorrect data in his application.

(A) inserting
(B) insert
(C) inserted
(D) to insert

20. Some of the damaged items ------- scheduled to be sent to the central depot.

(A) is
(B) being
(C) were
(D) was

시제

동사의 때를 표현하는 시제에는 가장 기본적인 현재, 과거, 미래를 포함해 총 12가지 형태로 시간을 나타낼 수 있다.

💬 기본 개념 이해하기

1. 시제의 형태

	과거	현재	미래
단순	worked	works / work	will work
진행	was / were working	is / are working	will be working
완료	had worked	has / have worked	will have worked
완료 진행	had been working	has / have been working	will have been working

2. 단순 시제

▶ 특정 시간에 일어난 동작이나 상황을 나타낸다.

현재	동사원형-(e)s	'~이다 / ~한다'라고 해석되며 현재의 일반적인 사실을 나타내거나 습관적인 동작을 표현한다.
과거	동사원형-(e)d / 불규칙 동사	'였다 / ~했다'라고 해석되며 이미 끝난 과거의 동작이나 상태를 표현한다.
미래	will + 동사원형	'일 것이다 / ~할 것이다'라고 해석되며 미래 특정 시점에 행해질 사실이나 상태를 표현한다.

We **receive** monthly reports from our sales team.
우리는 영업팀으로부터 월별 보고서를 받는다.

We **received** approval for our budget proposal last week.
우리는 지난주에 예산안에 대한 승인을 받았다.

We **will receive** training on the new software next month.
우리는 다음 달에 새로운 소프트웨어에 대한 교육을 받을 것이다.

3. 진행 시제

▶ 현재, 과거, 미래 한 시점에 동작이 계속 진행되고 있는 것을 나타내며 『be + -ing』 형태를 취한다.

현재 진행	is / are + -ing	'~하는 중이다'라고 해석되며 현재 시점에 진행되고 있는 일을 표현한다. 또한, 가까운 미래의 예정된 계획을 나타낼 수도 있다.
과거 진행	was / were + -ing	'~하는 중이었다'라고 해석되며 특정한 과거 시점에 진행되고 있던 일을 표현한다.
미래 진행	will be + -ing	'~하는 중일 것이다'라고 해석되며 특정한 미래 시점에 진행되고 있을 일을 표현한다.

The customers **are browsing** through our online catalog.
고객들이 우리의 온라인 카탈로그를 살펴보고 있다.

The customers **were examining** the merchandise on display at the store.
고객들이 매장에 진열된 상품을 살펴보고 있었다.

The customers **will be participating** in the customer satisfaction survey.
고객들이 고객 만족도 조사에 참여할 것이다.

4. 완료 시제

▶ 완료 시제는 어떤 특정 시점부터 동작이나 상황이 일정 기간 계속 되는 것을 나타내며 『have + p.p.』형태를 취한다.

현재 완료	has / have + p.p.	'~해 왔다'라고 해석되며 과거에 시작된 일이 현재까지 계속되어 온 동작이나 상태를 표현한다.
과거 완료	had + p.p.	과거의 특정 시점 이전에 먼저 발생한 일을 표현한다.
미래 완료	will have + p.p.	미래 특정 시점 이전에 발생한 사건이나 동작이 미래의 특정 시점에 완료될 때를 표현한다.

The company **has expanded** to international markets.
그 회사는 해외 시장으로 확장했다.

The company **had completed** the merger last year.
그 회사는 작년에 합병을 (이미) 완료했다.

The company **will have launched** its new campaign by the end of the year.
회사는 연말쯤에 새로운 캠페인을 시작할 것이다.

 **핵심 문제 유형**

Q1 단순 시제

The sales team ------- regularly to discuss project updates.

(A) meet   (B) meets   (C) met   (D) will meet

>> **출제 포인트 문장에 쓰인 특정한 시간을 나타내는 부사구와 어울리는 시제를 고른다.**

● 단순 시제와 함께 자주 쓰이는 시간 부사 표현들이 있다.

현재	currently 현재 routinely 일상적으로 normally / typically 보통 regularly / periodically 정기적으로	always 항상 generally 일반적으로 frequently / often 자주, 종종	usually 대개 every / each ~마다 occasionally / sometimes 가끔
과거	yesterday 어제 last + 시간 표현 지난~ 시간 표현 + ago ~전에	recently 최근에 in + 과거 ~에	previously 이전에 once 한때
미래	tomorrow 내일 soon / shortly 곧 starting / beginning + 미래 ~부터	next / following + 시간 표현 다음의 upcoming 곧 있을	by the end of ~의 말에 as of + 미래 ~부터

The IT team **frequently updates** the company's website.
IT 팀은 회사 웹사이트를 자주 업데이트한다.

The HR department **conducted** interviews **yesterday**.
인사부는 어제 면접을 진행했다.

The finance team **will focus** on reducing costs **starting this quarter**.
재무팀은 이번 분기부터 비용 절감에 주력할 예정이다.

✔ **문법 포인트** 토익 시험에서는 문장 안에 시제를 나타내는 시간 단서를 찾아 어울리는 동사 시제를 선택하는 문제가 주로 출제되나 반대로, 문장 속 동사를 보고 선택지에 시제 부사를 선택하는 고난도 어휘 문제도 출제된다.

The CEO will announce the acquisition deal [**shortly** / ~~previously~~].
최고 경영자가 곧 인수 계약을 발표할 것이다.

주의 과거 시제와 현재 완료 시제를 나타내는 recently는 해석상 현재 시제와 어울린다고 오해하기 쉽기 때문에 유의한다.

Our company **recently launched** a new product line. ◎
우리 회사는 최근에 새로운 제품 라인을 출시했다.

Our company **has recently launched** a new product line. ◎
우리 회사는 최근에 새로운 제품 라인을 출시했다.

Our company **recently launches** a new product line. ✘
우리 회사는 최근에 새로운 제품 라인을 출시한다.

Q2 완료 시제

The software company ------- significantly over the past decade.

(A) grow
(B) grows
(C) grew
(D) has grown

>> **출제 포인트** 현재 완료 시제를 나타내는 부사구에 맞춰 동사의 시제를 결정한다.

● 완료 시제와 함께 자주 쓰이는 시간 부사 표현들이 있다.

현재 완료	for / during / over / past + 기간 지난 ~동안 in the last + 기간 지난 ~동안 since + 과거 시점 ~이후로 recently / lately 최근에 so far 지금까지 until now 지금까지
과거 완료	Before + 주어 + 과거 시제, 주어 + had p.p. ~하기 이전에, 이미 ~했었다 After + 주어 + had p.p., 주어 + 과거 시제 이미 ~한 후에, ~했다 By the time + 주어 + 과거 시제, 주어 + had p.p. ~했을 때쯤, 이미 ~했었다
미래 완료	By the time + 주어 + 현재 시제, 주어 + will have p.p. ~할 때쯤 이면, ~하게 될 것이다 By + 미래 시점, 주어 + will have p.p. ~까지, ~하게 될 것이다

Employee turnover **has been** higher **for the last six months**.
지난 6개월 동안 직원들의 이직률이 높았다.

By the time the new product **was launched**, the marketing team **had conducted** extensive research.
신제품이 출시될 무렵 마케팅팀은 광범위한 시장 조사를 진행했다.

By the time the meeting **starts**, the sales team **will have reviewed** the proposal.
고객 미팅이 시작될 때쯤이면 영업팀에서 제안서를 검토하게 될 것이다.

☑ **문법 포인트** since의 경우 전치사일 때는 뒤에 명사가, 접속사일 때는 뒤에 『주어 + 동사』를 갖춘 절이 올 수 있다. since 바로 뒤에는 과거 시점이나 과거 시제가 오지만, since 앞 절(주절)은 현재 완료 시제를 쓰는 것을 주의하자. 토익 시험에서는 since 앞 절에 현재 완료 시제를 묻는 문제가 출제되거나, since 바로 뒤에 과거 시제를 묻는 문제가 주로 출제된다.

Customer satisfaction levels **have risen** consistently **since 2020**.
고객 만족도가 2020년부터 꾸준히 상승했다.

Our market share **has expanded** significantly **since the merger was finalized**.
합병이 마무리된 후에 우리의 시장 점유율이 크게 확대되었다.

Q3 시간, 조건절의 시제 일치의 예외

If the shipment ------- on time, we will be able to meet our deadlines.
(A) arrive   (B) arrives   (C) arrived   (D) will arrive

>> 출제 포인트 **시간이나 조건의 부사절에서는 현재 시제가 미래 시제를 대신한다.**

● 문장에 접속사가 쓰여 동사의 개수가 두 개가 되면 동사들의 시제는 주절의 동사를 기준으로 일치해야 한다. 즉, 주절이 과거 시제이면 부사절도 과거 시제로 일치한다. 하지만, 시간이나 조건을 나타내는 부사절에서는 주절이 미래일지라도 종속절에는 현재 시제를 쓰므로 유의한다.

시간 부사절 접속사	when ~할 때 until ~까지	before ~전에 as soon as ~하자마자	after ~후에 while ~동안
조건 부사절 접속사	if ~라면 as long as ~하는 한	unless ~아니라면	once 일단 ~하면

When the sales report **was released**, it **exceeded** our expectations.
접속사 + 주어 + 과거 동사, 주어 + 과거 동사
매출 보고서가 발표되었을 때 우리의 예상을 뛰어넘었다.

The vendor **refused** to provide additional services **until** the contract **was renegotiated**.
주어 + 과거 동사 + 접속사 + 주어 + 과거 동사
공급업체는 계약이 재협상될 때까지 추가 서비스 제공을 거부했다.

As soon as the meeting **starts**, the project manager **will outline** the agenda.
접속사 + 주어 + 현재 시제, 주어 + 미래 시제
회의가 시작되는 대로 프로젝트 매니저가 안건의 개요를 설명할 것이다.

The contract **will be renewed if** the service quality **meets** the client's expectations.
주어 + 미래 시제 + 접속사 + 주어 + 현재 시제
서비스 품질이 고객의 기대에 부합하면 계약이 갱신될 것이다.

Q4 제안 및 요청의 동사와 should의 생략

The director requested that the team ------- the project by the end of the month.

(A) completes   (B) completed   (C) complete   (D) will complete

>> **출제 포인트** 제안이나 요청을 의미하는 동사 뒤 접속사 that절에는 「should + 동사원형」을 쓰는데 이때 should는 생략 가능하다.

● 주절에 제안·요청·의무를 의미하는 동사 또는 형용사가 나오면, 문맥상 당위성(~해야 한다)을 나타내므로 그 뒤 that절의 동사는 should가 생략된 경우 동사원형을 쓴다. 즉, that절의 동사는 주어의 수나 시제와 상관없이 항상 동사원형을 쓴다.

제안 · 요청 · 의무를 나타내는 동사	
suggest / propose / recommend 제안하다 ask / request 요청하다 require / demand 요구하다 order 명령하다 insist 주장하다	+ that + 주어 + (should) + 동사원형

당위성 형용사	
important 중요한 necessary 필요한 imperative / essential / vital 필수적인 mandatory 의무적인	+ that + 주어 + (should) + 동사원형

The analyst **suggested** that the IT team [**upgrade** / ~~upgrades~~] the company's software systems.
그 분석가는 IT 팀이 회사의 소프트웨어 시스템을 업그레이드할 것을 제안했다.

It is important that every employee [**be** / ~~is~~] aware of their responsibilities.
모든 직원들은 자신들의 직무를 알고 있어야 하는 것이 중요하다.

✓ **문법 포인트** 제안·요청·의무를 나타내는 동사가 주절에 나올 땐, that절에 동사원형을 선택하는 문제가 주로 출제된다. 단, 해당 동사가 제안·요청·의무를 의미하지 않는다면 that절에는 동사원형을 쓰지 않으니 유의하자.

Market research **suggests** that there **is** growing demand for eco-friendly products.
시장 조사는 친환경 제품에 대한 수요가 증가하고 있음을 시사한다.

Practice

1. Mr. Kim ------- the presentation last week.

(A) finalized
(B) finalizes
(C) finalizing
(D) to finalize

2. Mr. Lee ------- that the company introduce the new software immediately.

(A) recommended
(B) informed
(C) notified
(D) reminded

3. Mr. Johnson has been overseeing the project timelines since he ------- promoted to team leader.

(A) is
(B) was
(C) being
(D) be

4. Dr. Johnson, an authority in economics, was ------- appointed department head.

(A) frequently
(B) seldom
(C) recently
(D) now

5. Many cafes ------- guests loyalty cards since last year.

(A) have offered
(B) are offering
(C) has offered
(D) to offer

6. The council's project to develop the park ------- soon.

(A) has been completed
(B) has been completing
(C) will be completed
(D) is completed

7. Patrons generally ------- to Luigi's Bistro because of its great ambiance and tasty meals.

(A) has come back
(B) have been coming back
(C) comes back
(D) come back

8. We typically ------- your efforts to enhance service standards.

(A) will acknowledge
(B) are acknowledging
(C) acknowledge
(D) have acknowledged

9. Ever since Ms. Jones started at the firm, revenues ------- by nearly 25 percent.

(A) have improved
(B) had improved
(C) has improved
(D) improve

10. Smith's Emporium ------- operational for more than two decades, still providing excellent service.

(A) was
(B) is
(C) has been
(D) have been

11. ------ the last three months, the number of attendees at Dr. Lee's seminars has risen significantly.

(A) Around
(B) From
(C) Over
(D) Above

12. Before Ms. Lee ------- to the Seoul office, she will oversee the Thompson project.

(A) moves
(B) move
(C) moved
(D) moving

13. Mr. Brown managed to get a ticket to the musical because he ------- ahead of time.

(A) reserves
(B) has reserved
(C) reserving
(D) had reserved

14. Mr. Clark ------- management of the new plant when it starts next March.

(A) will supervise
(B) supervised
(C) supervises
(D) had supervised

15. The HR Department ------- applications for the new training program until the end of this month.

(A) will accept
(B) accepts
(C) has accepted
(D) had accepted

16. Mr. Thompson ------- a new inventory system over the last three months.

(A) is creating
(B) was creating
(C) has been creating
(D) will be creating

17. Beginning next Tuesday, the Lumina Mall ------- its closing time to 11 P.M.

(A) are changing
(B) will change
(C) changes
(D) was changing

18. Inquiries made after 7 P.M. to the customer support line ------- the next business day.

(A) address
(B) is addressed
(C) addressed
(D) will be addressed

19. Nexon Corporation will ------- expand its production capabilities in Dallas.

(A) shortly
(B) normally
(C) lately
(D) frequently

20. Both Mr. Kim and Mr. Park ------- at Zenith Corp for nearly a decade up to now.

(A) are employed
(B) have been employed
(C) were employed
(D) will be employed

능동태와 수동태

동사는 능동태와 수동태인 2가지의 태를 가지고 있다. 주어 자리에 행위의 주체가 오면 능동태, 행위를 당하는 대상이 나오면 수동태이다. 이 둘의 가장 큰 차이점은 동사 뒤의 '목적어 유무'이다.

 기본 개념 이해하기

1. 능동태: 「주어(행위의 주체) + 동사」

▶ 주어가 행위의 주체가 되어 어떤 동작을 할 때 사용하며, 일반적으로 동사 뒤에 목적어가 오며 '주어가 ~을 하다'라고 해석한다.

The employees **work** at the manufacturing plant.
직원들은 제조 공장에서 일한다.

The employees **have worked** together to resolve complaints efficiently.
직원들은 불만 사항을 효율적으로 해결하기 위해 함께 일해 왔다.

The employees **prepared** detailed reports for the board meeting.
직원들은 이사회를 위해 상세한 보고서를 준비했다.

The employees **have prepared** the agenda for the brainstorming session.
직원들은 브레인스토밍 세션을 위한 안건을 준비했다.

2. 수동태: 「주어(행위의 대상) + be동사 + 과거분사(p.p.)」

▶ 주어가 행위의 대상이 되어 어떤 동작을 당할 때 사용한다. 능동태 문장의 목적어가 주어 자리로 이동하며, 일반적으로 동사 뒤에 목적어가 없고 '주어가 ~이 되다'라고 해석된다. 수동태의 동사 형태는 『주어 + be + p.p. + (by 명사)(행위의 주체)』의 모양이다.

The company launched the new product last month.
주어(행위의 주체) + 능동태 동사 + 목적어(행위의 대상)
⋯▶ The new product was launched (by the company) last month.
주어(행위의 대상) + 수동태 동사 + (by 행위의 주체)

✔ **문법 포인트** 능동태의 목적어가 수동태 문장의 주어로 이동하기 때문에, 반드시 목적어를 가지는 타동사만 수동태 형태가 될 수 있다. 즉, 자동사는 수동태가 될 수 없다.
Housing prices [**have risen** / have been risen] steadily over the past few years.
주택 가격이 지난 몇 년 동안 꾸준히 상승했다.

3. 수동태의 형태

▶ 수동태도 시제에 따라 8가지 형태가 있으며 미래 진행과, 완료 진행은 수동태 형태가 없다.

종류		형태
현재	현재 수동태	am / is / are p.p.
	현재 진행 수동태	am / is / are being p.p.
	현재 완료 수동태	has / have been p.p.
과거	과거 수동태	was / were p.p.
	과거 진행 수동태	was / were being p.p.
	과거 완료 수동태	had been p.p.
미래	미래 수동태	will be p.p.
	미래 완료 수동태	will have been p.p.

A charity event **has been organized** to raise funds for the local community.
지역 사회를 위한 기금을 조성하기 위해 자선 행사가 조직되었다.

The customer survey **was being analyzed** to improve efficiency.
효율성을 개선하기 위해 고객 설문이 분석되고 있었다.

The new product **will be promoted** through social media campaigns.
신제품이 소셜 미디어 캠페인을 통해 홍보될 것이다.

4. 수동태 동사 + 전치사

▶ 수동태에서 by 이외의 전치사를 쓰는 관용적인 표현들도 있다.

with	be pleased with ~을 기뻐하다	be satisfied with ~에 만족하다
	be equipped with ~로 갖춰져 있다	be associated with ~에 연관되어 있다
	be covered with ~로 덮이다	be filled with ~로 가득 차다
in	be interested in ~에 관심이 있다	be involved in ~에 관련되다
	be engaged in ~에 관여하다	be indulged in ~에 빠지다
to	be related to ~에 관련되어 있다	
	be committed / dedicated / devoted to ~에 헌신, 전념하다	
	be exposed to ~에 노출되다	be entitled to ~에 대한 자격이 있다
기타	be known for ~로 알려져 있다	be reimbursed for ~에 대해 상환 받다
	be based on ~에 근거하다	be surprised at ~에 놀라다
	be worried about ~에 대해 걱정하다	be concerned about ~에 대해 걱정하다
	be made of ~로 만들어지다	

The client is satisfied [to / **with**] the quality of the service.
그 고객은 서비스의 질에 만족하고 있다.

The company is committed [**to** / in] providing excellent customer service.
그 회사는 훌륭한 고객 서비스를 제공하는 데 최선을 다하고 있다.

Q1 능동태와 수동태의 구별

The marketing team ------- the new campaign successfully.

(A) launched   (B) was launched   (C) launching   (D) were launching

>> **출제 포인트** **3형식 동사 뒤에 목적어가 있으면 능동태를, 목적어가 없으면 수동태를 선택한다.**

● 능동태 문장에서는 동사 뒤에 목적어가 올 수 있지만, 수동태 문장에는 동사 뒤에 목적어가 올 수 없으므로 부사, 전치사구 등 수식어가 뒤따라온다.

The management **announced** new initiatives to enhance product quality.
경영진은 제품 품질을 향상시키기 위한 새로운 계획을 발표했다.

New initiatives **were announced** to enhance product quality.
제품 품질을 향상시키기 위한 새로운 계획이 발표되었다.

✓ **문법 포인트** 시간을 나타내는 다음 표현 및 단어들은 부사 취급하니 목적어(명사)로 혼동하지 않아야 한다.

시간 부사	yesterday 어제 tomorrow 내일 three years ago 3년 전 this summer 올해 여름	today 오늘 last month 지난달 this morning 오늘 아침 once a year 1년에 한번
기타 부사	online 온라인으로 worldwide 전세계적으로 overseas 해외로	companywide 전사적으로 abroad 해외로

A new performance evaluation system [implemented / **was implemented**] companywide.
새로운 성과 평가 제도가 전사적으로 시행되었다.

Q2 주의해야 할 수동태 구문 : 4형식 동사의 수동태

The employees ------- new assignments by the manager.

(A) give   (B) were given   (C) gave   (D) have given

>> **출제 포인트** **목적어를 2개 취하는 4형식 동사 수동태 뒤에는 목적어가 한 개 남겨질 수 있다.**

● 목적어가 2개 있는 4형식 동사의 수동태 문장에는 동사 뒤에 목적어가 하나 남겨질 수 있으므로, 이를 능동태 문장으로 혼동해서는 안 된다.

주요 4형식 동사	give / offer / grant / award 주다, 수여하다 send 보내다 show 보여주다 assign 맡기다 win 얻게 해주다
능동태	주어 + 동사 + 사람 목적어 + 사물 목적어
수동태	사람 목적어 + be p.p. + 사물 목적어 + (by 행위자)

The team leader gave **the interns** valuable training.
팀장은 인턴들에게 귀중한 교육을 제공했다.

The interns were given valuable training (by the team leader).
인턴들은 팀장으로부터 귀중한 교육을 받았다.

✓ **문법 포인트** 모든 4형식 동사는 3형식 동사로도 쓰이기 때문에 3형식으로 쓰였을 경우에도 뒤에 목적어를 취할 수 있으며, 위와 같이 수동태 문장일 경우에도 뒤에 목적어가 올 수 있다. 따라서, 4형식 동사의 태를 결정할 때는 해석으로 판단한다.

Q3 주의해야 할 수동태 구문 : 5형식 동사의 수동태

The report ------- accurate by the committee.

(A) finds   (B) found   (C) was found   (D) were found

>> **출제 포인트** 5형식 동사 수동태 뒤에는 목적격 보어가 남겨질 수 있다.

● 목적어와 목적격 보어를 가지는 5형식 동사의 수동태 뒤에는, 목적격 보어(명사 / 형용사 / to부정사 / 분사)가 수동태 동사 뒤에 남는다. 특히, 목적격 보어로 명사가 오는 경우 능동태 문장으로 혼동하기 쉬우니 주의해야 한다.

• 목적격 보어가 명사인 경우의 수동태

`능동태` The committee elected John **the new chairman**. 위원회는 존을 새로운 의장으로 선출했다.

`수동태` John was elected **the new chairman** by the committee. 존은 위원회에 의해 새로운 의장으로 선출되었다.

• 목적격 보어가 형용사인 경우의 수동태

`능동태` The results made everyone **happy**. 결과는 모두를 행복하게 만들었다.

`수동태` Everyone was made **happy** by the results. 모두가 결과로 인해 행복하게 되었다.

• 목적격 보어가 to부정사인 경우의 수동태

`능동태` The manager asked the staff **to attend** the meeting. 매니저는 직원들에게 회의에 참석하라고 요청했다.

`수동태` The staff were asked **to attend** the meeting by the manager.
직원들은 매니저에 의해 회의에 참석하라고 요청받았다.

✓ **문법 포인트** 토익 시험에서는 목적격 보어 자리에 to부정사를 취하는 5형식 동사의 수동태를 완성하는 문제가 주로 출제된다. 자주 나오는 5형식 동사의 수동태 모양인 『be + p.p. + to부정사』 표현들을 기억해두자.

「be p.p. to부정사」	
be expected to부정사 ~할 것으로 예상되다	be scheduled to부정사 ~할 예정이다
be prepared to부정사 ~할 준비가 되다	be asked to부정사 ~하라고 요청받다
be requested to부정사 ~하라고 요청받다	be required to부정사 ~하라고 요구받다
be urged to부정사 ~하도록 요구받다	be invited to부정사 ~하라고 요청받다
be advised to부정사 ~하도록 조언받다	be encouraged to부정사 ~하라고 권장받다
be allowed to부정사 ~하도록 허가받다	be permitted to부정사 ~하도록 허가받다
be told to부정사 ~하라는 말을 듣다	be intended to부정사 ~을 위한 목적이다
be supposed to부정사 ~하기로 되어있다.	

All participants **are encouraged to provide** feedback on the new process.
모든 참가자들은 새로운 절차에 대한 피드백을 제공하도록 권장된다.

The candidates **are expected to arrive** at the venue an hour before the interview.
후보자들은 인터뷰 한 시간 전에 행사장에 도착할 것으로 예상된다.

Q4 주의 해야 할 수동태 구문 : 자동사의 수동태

The ceremony ------- at the town hall every year.

(A) takes place　　　(B) is taken place　　　(C) take place　　　(D) was taken place

>> **출제 포인트** 목적어가 없는 자동사는 수동태가 될 수 없다.

● 목적어가 있는 타동사만 수동태 문장을 만들 수 있다. 즉, 목적어가 없는 자동사는 수동태 문장으로 바꿀 수 없다. 해석상 수동태로 착각하기 쉽기 때문에 대표적인 자동사들은 꼭 기억해야 한다.

1형식 자동사			
arrive 도착하다	depart 출발하다	occur 일어나다	happen 발생하다
take place 개최되다	appear 나타나다	emerge 나타나다	exist 존재하다
expire 만기되다	last 지속되다	proceed 진행하다	rise 오르다

2형식 자동사		
become ~가 되다	seem ~인 것처럼 보이다	remain ~한 채로 남아있다

The old contract **expired** last month.
오래된 계약은 지난달에 만료되었다.

Alice **appears** happy with her new job.
앨리스는 새 직업에 만족하는 것처럼 보인다.

☑ **문법 포인트** 구동사라고 불리는 「자동사 + 전치사」 표현은 하나의 타동사처럼 취급하여 뒤에 목적어를 취할 수 있으므로 수동태로 표현할 수 있다.

수동태로 표현되는 「자동사 + 전치사」 표현		
be accounted for ~로 설명되다	be referred to ~로 참고되다	be dealt with ~로 다뤄지다
be disposed of ~로 처리되다	be relied on ~을 믿을 수 있다	be agreed upon ~에 합의되다

All customer complaints **are dealt with** promptly by the support team.
모든 고객 불만은 지원팀에 의해 신속하게 처리된다.

The old documents **were disposed of** according to company policy.
오래된 문서들은 회사 정책에 따라 처리되었다.

1. All photos in the brochure were ------- provided by the ABC Foundation.

(A) kindness
(B) kind
(C) kinder
(D) kindly

2. The engineering team ------- the task on time.

(A) completes
(B) completing
(C) to be completed
(D) is completed

3. The monthly project meeting is generally ------- in the afternoon.

(A) held
(B) holds
(C) holding
(D) holder

4. A huge office building ------- near Central Park.

(A) constructed
(B) construction
(C) will construct
(D) will be constructed

5. Adjustments to the delivery times ------- with the logistics coordinator directly.

(A) have discussed
(B) should be discussing
(C) should be discussed
(D) has been discussed

6. Akira Enterprises ------- economic issues for many months.

(A) encounters
(B) have been encountering
(C) has encountered
(D) has been encountered

7. The Top Performer ------- by the CEO last month.

(A) was announced
(B) announced
(C) announcing
(D) announcement

8. Hikers are advised ------- the park's information desk in order to get trail maps.

(A) to call
(B) call
(C) calling
(D) be called

9. This prescription should ------- with plenty of fluids.

(A) be consumed
(B) consume
(C) to consume
(D) consumes

10. All sensitive data collected from our customers will be kept ------- under our strict privacy policy.

(A) confidentially
(B) confidentiality
(C) confide
(D) confidential

11. All new recruits should ------- a mentor by the final day of August.

(A) offered
(B) be offered
(C) offer
(D) offering

12. The Greenwood Towers' cooling system ------- by the maintenance team now.

(A) checks
(B) is checking
(C) checked
(D) is being checked

13. All staff can request a raise after they ------- with the company for twelve months.

(A) have been
(B) are
(C) being
(D) were

14. All meals at the bistro were ------- by famous chef Robert Smith.

(A) cooked
(B) cook
(C) cooking
(D) cookery

15. Dr. Kim will ------- all meeting arrangements during Mr. Lee's absence.

(A) organize
(B) be organized
(C) being organized
(D) organization

16. Employees will be ------- to work remotely two days a week.

(A) permitted
(B) suggested
(C) liked
(D) noticed

17. The primary reason for the train delay was attributed ------- technical issues.

(A) with
(B) in
(C) at
(D) to

18. Any applications for leave must be ------- to the manager at least ten days in advance.

(A) sent
(B) sending
(C) send
(D) sends

19. The clinical trial outcomes ------- that the procedure was effective.

(A) were shown
(B) be shown
(C) has shown
(D) show

20. The event coordinators ------- accommodation for the guests.

(A) have booked
(B) have been booked
(C) was booking
(D) is booking

REVIEW TEST 01

해설서 p.7

1. The ------- submitted all required documents before the deadline to be considered for the position.
   - (A) Apply
   - (B) Application
   - (C) Applicant
   - (D) Applying

2. The marketing team ------- weekly to discuss its progress when the project starts.
   - (A) meet
   - (B) will meet
   - (C) has met
   - (D) will have met

3. Each team member ------- tasks to complete before the deadline.
   - (A) assign
   - (B) assigned
   - (C) has assigned
   - (D) was assigned

4. The second edition of the book by Mr. Hong ------- published on July 1.
   - (A) was
   - (B) being
   - (C) be
   - (D) were

5. The ------- by the new management aims to improve workplace efficiency and employee satisfaction.
   - (A) initiate
   - (B) initiatives
   - (C) initiative
   - (D) initiation

6. All managers at Geimon Tech Solutions should ------- this month's sales workshop.
   - (A) attends
   - (B) attending
   - (C) attend
   - (D) attended

7. The number of customers who shop online ------- rapidly increased over the past decade.
   - (A) have
   - (B) has
   - (C) was
   - (D) were

8. The technical specifications for the computer ------- in the user manual.
   - (A) were detailing
   - (B) are detailed
   - (C) to detai
   - (D) will detail

9. The total cost of window repairs is ------- to exceed the original estimate.
   - (A) expected
   - (B) expecting
   - (C) expects
   - (D) expect

10. In order to stay competitive, HI Electronics store ------- lowers the prices of its products.
    - (A) previously
    - (B) occasionally
    - (C) recently
    - (D) soon

11. The committee members who reviewed Mr. Tam's résumé were very ------- by his extensive work experience.
    - (A) impression
    - (B) impressed
    - (C) impress
    - (D) impresses

12. The director requested that every employee ------- their project updates by the end of the week.
    - (A) submits
    - (B) submit
    - (C) submitting
    - (D) submitted

13. The company ------- its operations into three new countries since last year.
    - (A) expands
    - (B) expanded
    - (C) has expanded
    - (D) has been expanded

14. Last year, Tofuo Chemical Company ------- about 14 tons of silicon daily.
    - (A) produced
    - (B) produce
    - (C) to produce
    - (D) producing

15. Online shopping malls ------- it easier to compare prices of different products.
    - (A) making
    - (B) make
    - (C) are made
    - (D) to make

16. Perstrom Corporation ------- electronic goods for over 30 years.
    - (A) has manufactured
    - (B) is manufacturing
    - (C) manufacture
    - (D) has been manufactured

17. Temporary staff ------- to meet the growing demand over the holiday season.

(A) will be hired
(B) will hire
(C) are hiring
(D) have hired

18. Following recent business expansion, Chentora, Inc. hired several additional -------.

(A) employees
(B) employee
(C) employ
(D) employment

19. ------- of the information provided during the orientation was unclear despite the detailed presentation given by the manager.

(A) Many
(B) Some
(C) One
(D) Either

20. The recycling policy will help the company ------- operating costs.

(A) reducing
(B) reduce
(C) reduced
(D) reduces

21. A technical issue ------- during the software update, causing a delay in the project timeline.

(A) occur
(B) occurring
(C) occurred
(D) was occurred

22. More than 15 employees from the Marketing Department ------- successfully completed the sales training.

(A) have
(B) has
(C) having
(D) to have

23. Employees who registered for the workshop will ------- monthly newsletters.

(A) receives
(B) receiving
(C) receive
(D) to receive

24. ------- employees are required to attend the safety training session scheduled for next Friday.

(A) All
(B) Each
(C) Every
(D) Much

25. It is essential that every factory worker ------- these safety regulations.

(A) follows
(B) to follow
(C) will be followed
(D) follow

26. Employees can begin using the updated features once the new software -------.

(A) installs
(B) installation
(C) is installed
(D) will be installed

27. If there ------- enough time at the end of tomorrow's meeting, Mr. Garson will talk about the Vancouver Arts Festival briefly.

(A) is
(B) was
(C) are
(D) will be

28. Ms. Ouellette has been hired as the manager of the new store location, and she ------- all business operations starting next month.

(A) oversaw
(B) overseeing
(C) will oversee
(D) had overseen

29. Employees who demonstrate exceptional performance may ------- additional vacation days as a reward.

(A) grant
(B) grants
(C) granting
(D) be granted

30. The results from the staff satisfaction survey were ------- positive by the management.

(A) considering
(B) consider
(C) consideration
(D) considered

명사

명사는 문장에서 주어, 목적어, 보어의 역할을 하며, 크게 셀 수 있는 가산 명사와 셀 수 없는 불가산 명사로 나뉜다.

 기본 개념 이해하기

1. 명사의 형태

▶ -tion, -sion, -ty, -ce, -ment, -ture, -sure, -dure로 끝나는 대부분의 단어는 사물 명사이다.

▶ -er, -ee, -or, -ist, -ant, -ian으로 끝나는 대부분의 단어는 사람 명사이다.

-tion, -sion	investigation 조사	division 부서	
-ty, -cy	productivity 생산성	efficiency 효율	
-se, -ce	expense 비용	experience 경험	
-ment, -th	advertisement 광고	length 길이	
-ness, -i(a)sm, -ship	awareness 인식	enthusiasm 열정	relationship 관계
-ture, -sure, -dure	feature 특징	measure 조치	procedure 절차
-er, -ee, -or, -ist, -ian, -ant	employer 고용주 specialist 전문가	employee 직원 technician 기술자	instructor 강사 accountant 회계사

2. 명사의 종류

▶ 명사는 셀 수 있는 가산 명사와 셀 수 없는 불가산 명사로 나뉜다.

▶ 가산 명사는 홀로 쓰일 수 없고 반드시 단수 또는 복수 형태로 써야 한다. 즉, 가산 명사 앞에 한정사(a / an / the)가 없을 경우, 복수 형태(-s)로 써야 한다.

▶ 불가산 명사는 셀 수 없는 명사이므로 단수와 복수의 개념이 없고, 단수 취급을 한다. 즉, 앞에 단수를 나타내는 한정사인 (a / an)과 쓰일 수 없으며 복수 형태도 없다.

가산 명사	discount 할인 profit 수익 fund 자금	price 가격 refund 환불 request 요청	complaint 불만사항 permit 허가증	approach 접근법 opening 공석
불가산 명사	money 돈 information 정보 permission 허가	work 업무 assistance 지원 furniture 가구	advice 조언 equipment 장비	access 접근 merchandise 상품

The company received (complaint / **a complaint** / **complaints**) from customers.
그 회사는 고객들로부터 불만사항을 접수받았다.

The office needs more (**equipment** / an equipment / equipments). 새 사무실은 장비가 더 필요하다.

3. 명사의 한정사

▶ 한정사란 명사 앞에 놓여 명사의 의미를 한정시켜주는 단어로 관사, 소유격, 수량형용사, 지시형용사 등이 있다.

▶ 한정사 뒤에 어떤 성격의 명사가 오는지 반드시 구분해서 외워 두어야 한다.

a(n) = one 하나	each 각각	every 모든	another 또 다른	+ 가산 단수 명사
many 많은 numerous 수많은	a few 몇 개의 various 다양한	few 거의 없는 multiple 다수의	several 몇몇의	+ 가산 복수 명사
much 많은	a little 약간의	little 거의 없는		+ 불가산 명사
all 모든 other 다른	most 대부분의	some 약간의	more 더 많은	+ 복수 명사 / 불가산 명사
the 그 any 어느 ~든지	소유격 my, your, his, her, its, their, our, 명사's			+ 가산 단수 / 복수 명사 / 불가산 명사

✓ 문법 포인트 토익 시험에서는 빈칸 앞 한정사를 보고 알맞은 명사를 선택하는 문제가 주로 출제된다. 이때, 해석으로 만 접근하면 오답을 선택하기 쉬우니 꼭 한정사의 성격을 구분해서 외워 두도록 해야 한다.

(**All**, Every, Each) **employees** must wear their ID badges.
전 직원은 신분증을 착용해야 한다.

4. 형태를 주의해야 할 명사

▶ 명사형 어미로 끝나지 않는 명사 단어들에 주의하도록 한다.

-al	approval 승인 rental 임대.대여 potential 잠재력	disposal 처분 withdrawal 인출	renewal 갱신 referral 추천	arrival 도착 proposal 제안
-tive	initiative 계획	alternative 대안	representative 대표자	objective 목적
-ing	planning 기획 parking 주차 boarding 탑승 catering 음식 납품	opening 공석.개막 advertising 광고업 housing 주택 hiring 고용	accounting 회계 seating 좌석 funding 자금 지원	training 훈련 dining 식사 staffing 직원 채용
기타	estimate 견적서 architect 건축가 analysis 분석 assembly 조립	delegate 대표자 inventory 재고 coverage (보상) 범위	candidate 후보자 complaint 불만사항 entry 출입, 출품작	critic 비평가 emphasis 강조 characteristic 특성

✓ 문법 포인트 토익 시험에서 명사 자리가 출제되는 경우, 위 명사들은 다른 품사로 착각하기 쉽기 때문에 반드시 기억 해두자.

The (**proposal** / propose) to expand the marketing team was finally approved.
마케팅 팀을 확대하자는 제안이 마침내 승인되었다.

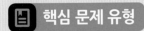
Q1 명사의 자리

The ------- was held in the main auditorium.

(A) presentation   (B) present   (C) presenting   (D) presented

---

>> **출제 포인트** 관사, 소유격, 형용사 다음은 명사 자리이다.

❶ 명사는 주어, 목적어, 보어 역할을 하고 또한 전치사 및 준동사의 목적어 역할을 한다.

주어	**The presentation** was well-received by the audience. 발표는 청중들에게 좋은 반응을 얻었다.
목적어	The manager reviewed **the report** thoroughly before the meeting. 매니저는 회의 전에 보고서를 철저히 검토했다.
보어	The main goal of the project is **efficiency**. 프로젝트의 주요 목표는 효율성이다.
전치사의 목적어	We are looking forward to **the conference** next month. 우리는 다음 달에 있을 회의를 기대하고 있다.
준동사의 목적어	Cindy decided to accept **the job offer** after careful consideration. 신디는 신중한 고민 끝에 직업 제안을 수락하기로 결정했다.

❷ 명사는 관사, 소유격, 형용사 / 분사, 명사 다음에 올 수 있다.

관사 + 명사	a supervisor 감독관 the department 부서
소유격 + 명사	my report 나의 보고서 your report 너의 보고서 his report 그의 보고서 her report 그녀의 보고서 its report 그것의 보고서 their report 그들의 보고서 our report 우리의 보고서 Mr. Park's report 박 씨의 (명사's) 보고서
형용사 + 명사 분사 + 명사	an innovative approach 혁신적인 접근법 a rising price 오르는 가격 a designated area 지정된 구역
명사 + 명사 [복합 명사]	office supplies 사무용품

✔ **문법 포인트** 토익 시험에서는 명사 앞에 형용사가 수식해주는 문제를 주로 출제하지만 명사 앞에 또 다른 명사가 와서 하나의 단어로 쓰이기도 한다. 이때, 이 두 가지는 해석으로 구별해야 한다.

The [**productivity** / productive] levels have increased this quarter.
이번 분기에 생산성 수준이 증가했다.

Q2 형태와 해석이 비슷한 가산 명사와 불가산 명사

Successful ------- is crucial for achieving our business goals.

(A) plan   (B) planning   (C) plans   (D) planner

>> **출제 포인트** 가산 명사는 반드시 앞에 한정사가 오거나 복수형으로 쓰여야 한다.

- 형태와 의미가 비슷하여 혼동하기 쉬운 가산 명사와 불가산 명사는 구분해서 외워 두도록 해야 한다.

가산 명사	불가산 명사
a permit 허가증	permission 허가
a certificate 증명서	certification 증명
a market 시장	marketing 마케팅
a fund 자금	funding 자금 조달
a plan 계획	planning 기획
a seat 좌석	seating 좌석 (배치)
a ticket 표	ticketing 발권
an advertisement 광고	advertising 광고업
a process 과정	processing 처리
an account 계좌	accounting 회계
a diner 식사하는 사람	dining 식사
a cloth 천	clothing 의류
an opening 공석, 개막	openness 개방성

☑ **문법 포인트** 비슷한 의미의 명사들이 함께 제시되어 해석으로 판단하기 어려울 땐, 한정사의 유무를 통해 가산 명사와 불가산 명사를 파악해야 한다.

This project requires [fund / **funding**] to proceed.
이 프로젝트를 진행하려면 자금 조달이 필요하다.

Mr. Oliver received **a [certificate** / certification] upon completing the course.
올리버 씨는 과정을 마치자마자 증명서를 받았다.

Q3 사람 명사 VS. 사물 / 추상명사

The task needs careful ------- to be finished on time.

(A) delegate (B) delegation (C) delegating (D) to delegate

>> **출제 포인트** 사람 명사는 가산 명사이므로 단수 또는 복수 형태로 써야 한다.

● 보통의 명사는 동사에서 파생이 되는데 어떤 동사는 사물 명사와 사람 명사 두 개를 파생한다. 이때 형태가 비슷한 사람 명사와 사물 / 추상 명사를 구분하는 문제가 출제된다. 선택지에 명사가 두 개 이상 같이 있다면, 한정사 유무 및 해석을 통해 잘 구분해야 한다.

사람 명사	사물 명사
accountant 회계사	account 계좌 accounting 회계
applicant 지원자	application 지원
attendant 수행원 attendee 참가자	attendance 참석
assistant 비서	assistance 지원
architect 건축가	architecture 건축
authority 권위자, 당국	authority 권한 authorization 승인
beneficiary 수혜자	benefit 혜택
consultant 상담가	consultation 상담
competitor 경쟁업체	competition 경쟁
contributor 공헌자	contribution 공헌
correspondent 특파원, 기자	correspondence 서신왕래, 서신
delegate 대표자	delegation 대표단, 위임
distributor 배급업자	distribution 분배
employer 고용주 employee 직원	employment 고용
manufacturer 제조사	manufacture 제조
producer 생산자	productivity 생산성 production 생산 product 제품
supplier 공급자	supply 공급품
supervisor 감독관	supervision 감독

✔ **문법 포인트** 선택지에 명사가 2개 이상이고 가산 / 불가산 명사의 차이로 구분할 수 없을 땐, 해석상 적절한 명사를 골라야 한다.

The HR department contacted several [**applicants** / applications] for interviews.
인사부는 여러 지원자에게 면접을 위해 연락했다.

Q4 명사 + 명사 = 복합 명사

Employees are encouraged to attend the keynote ------- on productivity improvements.

(A) speaker   (B) speaking   (C) speak   (D) speech

>> **출제 포인트** 명사 앞에는 또 다른 명사가 올 수 있다.

❶ 복합 명사는 「명사 + 명사」의 형태로 명사 두 개가 함께 어울려 하나의 단어처럼 쓰이는 것을 말한다. 이때 명사의 상태를 설명해주는 형용사와는 다르게 명사와 다른 하나의 명사가 동등하게 연결된 것을 의미한다.

❷ 복합 명사의 가산 / 불가산 또는 단수 / 복수 여부는 마지막 명사에 따라 결정되므로 수 일치는 뒤의 명사에 맞춘다. 복합 명사의 복수 형태는 마지막 명사에 -(e)s를 붙인다.

「명사 + 명사」: 복합 명사	
account number 계좌 번호	clearance sale 창고 정리
keynote speaker 기조 연설가	account information 계좌 정보
employee productivity 직원 생산성	maintenance work 정비 작업
application form 신청서	employee performance 직원 성과
office supply 사무용품	admission fee 입장료
entrance fee 입장료	parking permit 주차 허가증
assembly line 조립라인	expiration date 만료일
performance evaluation 직무 평가	bank transaction 은행 거래
exchange rate 환율	reference letter 추천서
budget estimates 예산 견적서	feasibility study 예비 조사
return policy 반품 정책	baggage allowance 수하물 허용량
growth rate 성장률	interest rate 금리
contingency plan 비상 대책	customer satisfaction 고객 만족
travel expense / itinerary 여행 경비 / 일정표	living expense 생활비
job opening 공석	safety regulation / inspection / precaution 안정 규정 / 검사 / 예방책

✓ **문법 포인트** 해석으로는 복합 명사를 찾기 어려울 수 있으니 토익에 나오는 빈출 복합 명사는 하나의 단어처럼 익혀 두도록 하자.

The company implemented new [**security** / secure] measures.
그 회사는 새로운 보안 조치를 시행했다.

1. Dr. Thompson's ------- to interact with his patients is remarkable.

(A) skill
(B) skilled
(C) skillfully
(D) skillful

2. Greenway Supermarket will offer ------- for all Eco Beauty Products bought during the sale .

(A) discount
(B) discounts
(C) discounting
(D) discounted

3. The newest smartphone is anticipated to be a market -------.

(A) lead
(B) leader
(C) leaders
(D) leading

4. The design team received ------- for the construction plan from the city council.

(A) propose
(B) proposals
(C) proposing
(D) propose

5. We are exploring an ------- to our current software system.

(A) alter
(B) alternate
(C) alternation
(D) alternative

6. ------- by renowned artists pulled in large crowds at the event.

(A) Exhibits
(B) Exhibited
(C) Exhibiting
(D) Exhibit

7. Because of the ongoing dry spell, water ------- for farming will rise.

(A) consumption
(B) consumed
(C) consumes
(D) consume

8. The ------- regarding the new safety measures has been postponed.

(A) discussion
(B) discuss
(C) discussing
(D) discussions

9. To finish the assignment promptly, we will employ an -------.

(A) expert
(B) expertise
(C) expertly
(D) experts

10. The workshop will cover how firms can improve their --------- of components.

(A) assemble
(B) assembler
(C) assembling
(D) assembly

11. It is advised that ------- update their subscriptions before the month's end.

(A) customers
(B) customary
(C) customs
(D) customized

12. We have allocated a budget specifically for ------- of our new product.

(A) advertise
(B) advertisement
(C) advertising
(D) advertised

13. We are negotiating new terms with our ------- to ensure better pricing.

(A) supplies
(B) suppliers
(C) supplying
(D) supplied

14. You need to obtain a ------- before starting any construction work on the property.

(A) permit
(B) permitting
(C) permitted
(D) permission

15. Chalden Corporation's latest ------- with Brimstone Ltd. enhanced its market share.

(A) merger
(B) merging
(C) merges
(D) merge

16. We have a job ------- for a marketing manager at our New York office.

(A) open
(B) opening
(C) opener
(D) openness

17. ------- of the Bridgestone initiative is anticipated to boost the company's revenue.

(A) Implements
(B) Implement
(C) Implementation
(D) Implemented

18. ------- at the yearly tourism seminar must present their passes at the entrance.

(A) Participants
(B) Participate
(C) Participated
(D) Participation

19. The Footway Footwear Outlet provides special discount vouchers to new-------.

(A) shoppers
(B) shopping
(C) shopped
(D) shopper

20. We need to provide all necessary documents to open an ------- with the new bank.

(A) account
(B) accounts
(C) accounting
(D) accountant

대명사

UNIT 05

대명사란 반복되는 명사를 피하기 위해 명사를 대신해서 쓰는 역할을 하므로 명사처럼 문장에서 주어, 목적어, 보어의 역할을 한다. 대명사는 쓰임에 따라 크게 인칭대명사, 재귀대명사, 지시대명사, 부정대명사로 나뉜다. 인칭대명사는 가장 출제율이 높으며 난이도는 낮은 편이다. 자리의 역할에 따라 형태가 다르므로 구분해서 익혀 둔다.

🧠 기본 개념 이해하기

1. 인칭대명사의 종류

▸ 인칭대명사는 대신하는 명사와 자리의 역할에 따라 주격, 소유격, 목적격의 형태가 있다. 형태가 같은 것들이 있으니 주의하도록 해야 한다.

▸ 주격은 주어 자리에 사용한다.

▸ 소유격은 다른 격과 달리 단독으로 사용할 수 없으며, 명사 앞에 쓰여 '~의'로 해석한다.

▸ 목적격은 타동사의 목적어, 전치사의 목적어 자리에 사용한다.

	주격	소유격	목적격
1인칭	I 나는	my 나의	me 나를
	we 우리는	our 우리의	us 우리를
2인칭	you 당신은	your 당신의	you 당신을
3인칭	he 그는	his 그의	him 그를
	she 그녀는	her 그녀의	her 그녀를
	they 그들은	their 그들의	them 그들을
	it 그것은	its 그것의	it 그것을

He works for a multinational company.
그는 다국적 회사에서 일한다.

Your application has been approved.
귀하의 신청서가 승인되었다.

The manager explained **it** to us.
매니저가 그것을 우리에게 설명했다.

The report was compiled **by her**.
그 보고서는 그녀에 의해 작성되었다.

2. 소유대명사

▶ 소유대명사는 『소유격 + 명사』를 대신해 쓰이며 '~의 것'으로 해석한다. 명사를 대신해서 쓰이므로 명사처럼 주어, 목적어, 보어 자리에 올 수 있다.

▶ 3인칭 단수 it의 소유대명사 형태는 없으며, 소유대명사 뒤에는 명사가 절대 나올 수 없다.

소유격	my 나의	our 우리의	your 당신(들)의	his 그의	her 그녀의	their 그들의
소유대명사	mine 나의 것	ours 우리의 것	yours 당신(들)의 것	his 그의 것	hers 그녀의 것	theirs 그들의 것

Ours was the only proposal that received approval.
우리 것만 유일하게 승인을 받은 제안서였다.

The director approved our suggestion and rejected **theirs**.
이사는 우리 제안을 받아들이고 그들의 것을 거절했다.

The laptop on the desk is **hers**.
책상 위의 노트북은 그녀의 것이다.

A colleague of **mine** recommended a software program for our project.
제 동료 중 한 명이 우리 프로젝트를 위해 소프트웨어 프로그램을 추천했다.

3. 재귀대명사

▶ 재귀대명사는 주어와 목적어가 의미상으로 동일한 대상을 나타낼 때 쓰이며, -self가 붙은 형태로, '~자신'이라고 해석한다.

▶ 재귀 용법은 목적어가 주어와 동일한 사람 / 사물을 의미할 때 목적어 자리에 재귀대명사를 사용하며 '~자신'이라고 해석한다. 이때 재귀대명사는 목적어 자리에 오므로 생략할 수 없다.

▶ 강조 용법은 주어나 목적어를 강조하기 위해서 강조하는 말 바로 뒤에 오거나 문장 끝에 올 수 있으며 '직접, 스스로'라고 해석한다. 이때 강조하기 위해 쓴 것이므로 생략할 수 있다.

1인칭	myself 나 자신	ourselves 우리들 자신	
2인칭	yourself 너희 자신	yourselves 너희들 자신	
3인칭	himself 그 자신	herself 그녀 자신	themselves 그들 자신

Our team leader prepared **herself** for the presentation. 생략 불가
팀장은 스스로 발표를 준비했다.

The technician fixed the issue **himself**. 생략 가능
그 기술자는 문제를 직접 해결했다.

The employee prefers to work **by himself**.
그 직원은 혼자 일하는 것을 선호한다.

4. 지시대명사

▶ 지시대명사 중 that / those는 앞에 언급된 명사를 반복할 때 쓰이며 단수 명사를 대신하면 that, 복수 명사를 대신하면 those를 쓴다.

▶ those는 '~한 사람들'이란 의미로도 쓰이며, those 뒤에 수식어인 관계사(who), 분사(-ing / p.p.), 전치사구의 형태가 올 수 있다.

The report you submitted today is more detailed than **that** (= the report) from last week.
당신이 오늘 제출한 보고서는 지난주에 제출한 것보다 더 자세하네요.

The suggestions from the meeting were better than **those** (= the suggestions) from last month.
회의에서 나온 제안들이 지난달의 것보다 더 좋았습니다.

Those who meet the qualifications will be invited for an interview next week.
자격을 갖춘 분들이 다음 주에 있을 면접에 초대될 것입니다.

5. 부정대명사

▶ one, all, most, some, any, each 등의 부정대명사는 정해져 있지 않은 불특정한 사람이나 사물을 가리킬 때 쓴다.

▶ 『부정대명사 + of + the 명사』의 형태로 쓰일 수 있으며, 전체 모두와 가리키는 대상의 수에 따라 형태가 다양하다.

▶ 명사를 수식하는 부정형용사의 역할도 할 수 있는 부정대명사들이 있다.

Some are interested in the new project.
몇몇은 새로운 프로젝트에 관심이 있다.

Most of the employees are satisfied with the new policy.
대부분의 직원들은 새로운 정책에 만족하고 있다.

The customer finished his coffee and ordered **another**.
그 손님은 커피를 다 마시고 하나 더 주문했다.

The pupil wanted to read **another book**.
그 학생은 또 다른 책을 읽고 싶었다.

Q1 인칭대명사의 자리

Please submit ------- application form by Friday.

(A) you　　　　　(B) your　　　　　(C) yours　　　　　(D) yourself

>> **출제 포인트** 문장에서 주어진 역할에 따라 주격, 목적격, 소유격을 쓴다.

● 인칭대명사는 자리에 따라 주격, 목적격, 소유격의 형태가 있다. 특히, 소유격(~의)은 다른 격들과 달리 단독으로 쓰일 수 없으며 항상 명사 앞에 쓰인다. 소유격과 함께 쓰일 수 있는 own(자신의)은 소유격의 의미를 강조할 수 있다.

He submitted the report on time. 주격 대명사
그는 보고서를 제시간에 제출했다.

The director invited **them** to the meeting. 목적격 대명사
감독은 그들을 회의에 초대했다.

The committee agreed with **him** on the decision. 목적격 대명사
위원회는 그 결정에 대해 그와 동의했다.

The department head praised the employee for **his own** effort. 소유격 대명사
부서장은 그 직원 본인이 한 노력에 대해 칭찬했다.

✓ **문법 포인트** 빈칸 앞에 타동사나 전치사만 보고 바로 목적격을 쓰지 않도록 주의해야 한다.

The team thanked [him / **his**] contributions.
팀은 그의 기여에 감사했다.

Q2 재귀대명사의 자리

The CEO presented the new strategy -------.

(A) she   (B) her   (C) hers   (D) herself

>> **출제 포인트** 강조하고자 하는 말 바로 뒤나, 문장 맨 뒤에 재귀대명사를 쓴다.

❶ '주어가 목적어로 돌아온다'라는 의미의 재귀 용법은 주어와 목적어가 같은 대상을 지칭할 때 목적어 자리에 목적격 대신에 재귀대명사를 쓴다. 이때 '~자신'이라고 해석하며 필수 성분인 목적어 자리이므로 생략할 수 없다.

New staff introduced **themselves** at the meeting.
신입 직원들은 회의에서 자신들을 소개했다.

❷ 주어나 목적어를 강조하기 위해서 강조하고자 하는 명사 바로 뒤나, 문장 맨 뒤 재귀대명사를 쓴다. 이때 '직접, 스스로'라고 해석하며 부사 자리이므로 생략할 수 있다.

The CEO **herself** announced the new policy.
최고 경영자가 직접 새로운 정책을 발표했다.

The CEO announced the new policy **herself**.
최고 경영자가 새로운 정책을 직접 발표했다.

❸ 재귀대명사에는 전치사와 함께 숙어처럼 쓰이는 관용 표현들이 있다.

by oneself (= on one's own) 혼자 힘으로, 혼자서	for oneself 혼자 힘으로

The marketing team completed the project **by themselves**.
마케팅 팀은 그 프로젝트를 자체적으로 완료했다.

Jane decided to live **on her own** (= by herself).
제인은 자립하기로 결심했다.

I often travel **on my own** (= by myself).
나는 종종 혼자 여행을 한다.

The employees need to see the results **for themselves**.
직원들은 직접 결과를 확인해야 한다.

Q3 ## 지시대명사 that / those

The salary offered by the new company is higher than ------- offered by the old company.

(A) this   (B) those   (C) that   (D) these

>> **출제 포인트** 지시대명사 that / those는 앞에 나온 명사를 대신해서 사용한다.

❶ 지시대명사 that / those는 앞서 언급한 명사를 반복하는 대신에 쓸 수 있다. 이때 비교 대상이 단수이면 that으로, 복수이면 those로 쓴다.

The efficiency of this new system is better than **that** (= the efficiency) of the old one.
이 새로운 시스템의 효율성은 이전 시스템의 효율성보다 더 좋다.

The requirements for this position are different from **those** (= the requirements) for the previous one.
이 직책의 요구 사항은 이전 직책의 요구 사항과 다르다.

❷ those는 일반적인 사람들인 people을 의미하기도 하며, 이때 those 뒤에는 수식어(관계절 / 분사 / 전치사구)가 올 수 있다.

Those who + 복수 동사 ~하는 사람들	Those (who are) interested in the workshop should register for it in advance.
Those + -ing / p.p. / 전치사구 ~하는 사람들	Those interested in the workshop should register for it in advance. Those with the computer experience can apply for the company.

✓ **문법 포인트** 토익 시험에서는 대명사 those와 anyone을 구분하는 문제가 출제된다. anyone도 '~한 사람 누구나'라는 해석으로 사람을 의미하며, those와 마찬가지로 뒤에 수식어(관계절 / 분사 / 전치사구)가 올 수 있다. 하지만, 복수 동사를 취하는 those와는 달리 단수 동사로 수를 일치시키는 점에 유의해야 한다.

[Those / **Anyone**] who **has** completed the survey will receive a discount coupon.
설문조사를 완료한 사람 누구나 할인 쿠폰을 받을 것이다.

Q4 부정대명사 / 부정형용사

Among the four proposals, one was accepted, and ------- were rejected.

(A) another   (B) others   (C) the other   (D) the others

>> **출제 포인트** **부정대명사는 문맥과 가리키는 대상의 단수와 복수를 고려하여 결정한다.**

● 부정대명사의 의미와 쓰임에 맞게 구별해서 외워 두도록 해야 한다. 특히, 부정대명사와 부정형용사 둘 다의 쓰임이 있는 단어들은 유의해야 한다.

부정형용사	another 또 다른 하나의	+ 가산 단수명사
	the other (정해진 수 중에서) 나머지 하나의	+ 가산 단수명사
	other 다른	+ 가산 복수 명사 / 불가산 명사
부정대명사	one 하나	단수 취급
	another 또 다른 하나	단수 취급
	the other (정해진 수 중에서) 나머지 하나	단수 취급
	the others (정해진 수 중에서) 나머지 전부	복수 취급
	others (정해지지 않은) 다른 것들	복수 취급
기타	each other (둘 사이에) 서로	주어 자리에 복수 명사를 지칭
	one another (셋 이상에서) 서로	

Moving from **one** job to **another** can be challenging.
한 직장에서 다른 직장으로 옮기는 것은 어려울 수 있다.

We need to consider **other** options before making a decision.
결정을 내리기 전에 다른 옵션들을 고려해야 한다.

The two colleagues helped **each other** with their tasks.
두 동료는 서로의 업무를 도왔다.

✓ **문법 포인트** 토익 시험에서는 부정대명사의 쓰임에 맞게 구별하는 문제가 주로 출제되니 성격을 꼭 구분해서 외워야 한다. 특히, other는 부정형용사이므로 단독으로 쓸 수 없으며 반드시 뒤에 가산 복수 명사 또는 불가산 명사와 함께 쓰여야 한다. 또한 each other와 one another는 '서로'라는 의미의 관용 표현으로 주어 자리에 올 수 없고 타동사나 전치사의 목적어로만 쓰인다.

1. While Mr. Johnson is away, please contact ------- personal assistant.

(A) he
(B) his
(C) him
(D) himself

2. Ms. Lee requires all employees to coordinate directly with ------- regarding the new sales strategy.

(A) she
(B) her
(C) hers
(D) herself

3. Any staff members with remaining leave days should utilize ------- before December 31.

(A) it
(B) its
(C) themselves
(D) them

4. Zenith Corp. plans to take over ------- chief rival, Maxon Inc., next quarter.

(A) it
(B) its
(C) itself
(D) it's

5. The employees presented ------- final report to the management.

(A) their
(B) them
(C) they
(D) theirs

6. ------- of the recently shipped XR30 tablets were broken in transit.

(A) These
(B) Every
(C) Many
(D) One

7. Once the report had been evaluated by several directors, ------- was ultimately approved.

(A) their
(B) they
(C) its
(D) it

8. Most of the devices used by our team members are not ------- but are provided by the organization.

(A) they
(B) their
(C) theirs
(D) themselves

9. Ms. Park has shown ------- to be a dedicated and valuable asset to the Marketing Team.

(A) she
(B) herself
(C) her
(D) hers

10. The technician was unable to fix the printer since ------- components were out of stock.

(A) their
(B) his
(C) her
(D) its

11. ------- who has questions about the project should contact the manager directly.

(A) Those
(B) Every
(C) They
(D) Anyone

12. Even though Luxure Skincare and PureGlow Cosmetics suffered losses this year, ------- predict better sales next year.

(A) one
(B) another
(C) either
(D) both

13. Ms. Johnson completed her presentation, but Mr. Smith is still working on -------.

(A) he
(B) his
(C) him
(D) himself

14. The company's profits have significantly improved compared to ------- of the previous year.

(A) this
(B) those
(C) that
(D) these

15. Despite the challenge, Mr. Kim was able to assemble the complicated furniture by -------.

(A) his own
(B) himself
(C) he
(D) him

16. The team members collaborated well and supported ------- throughout the project.

(A) other
(B) the other
(C) another
(D) one another

17. Many graduates from Levinson College take on internships before beginning ------- initial full-time employment.

(A) they
(B) themselves
(C) them
(D) their

18. Please let Ms. Chen know that ------- trip to the Tokyo branch has been postponed.

(A) we
(B) our
(C) ourself
(D) ours

19. Please review the document and let me know if you need ------- information.

(A) other
(B) another
(C) each other
(D) one another

20. ------- participants joined the outdoor concert even with the rain.

(A) Another
(B) Others
(C) The others
(D) Most

형용사

형용사란 명사 앞에서 명사를 수식하며 수식 받는 명사의 상태를 설명한다. 또한, 주어와 목적어의 상태를 설명하는 보어 역할도 한다. 2형식과 5형식 문장에서 보어 자리에 형용사를 넣는 문제가 자주 출제된다.

💬 기본 개념 이해하기

1. 형용사의 형태

일반 형용사	effect**ive** 효과적인 respons**ible** 책임감 있는 length**y** 긴	expen**sive** 비싼 cauti**ous** 주의 깊은 profession**al** 전문적인	comfort**able** 편안한 success**ful** 성공적인 dramat**ic** 극적인
분사형 형용사(-ing / p.p.)	promis**ing** 유망한 experienc**ed** 노련한	ri**sing** 오르는 qualif**ied** 자격을 갖춘	
명사 + -ly형 형용사	time**ly** 시기 적절한 cost**ly** 값비싼 week**ly** 매주의 year**ly** 매년의	friend**ly** 친절한 hour**ly** 매시간의 month**ly** 매달의	order**ly** 질서 정연한 dai**ly** 매일의 quarter**ly** 분기마다의

The **rising** demand for electric vehicles has increased production.
전기차에 대한 수요 증가가 생산을 늘렸다.

The company is seeking a **qualified** applicant for the new position.
회사는 새로운 직책에 자격을 갖춘 지원자를 찾고 있다.

The project was completed in a **timely** manner.
프로젝트는 시기 적절하게 완료되었다.

✓ **문법 포인트** 『명사 + ly』는 형용사이므로, 부사 『형용사 + ly』로 혼동하지 않도록 유의해야 한다.

2. 명사를 수식하는 형용사

▶ 형용사는 대부분 명사를 앞에서 수식할 수 있다. 만약, 명사 앞에 관사나 소유격 대명사 등이 있을 경우 『관사 / 소유격대명사 / 지시형용사 + 일반 형용사 + 명사』의 순서로 온다.

▶ 형용사와 전치사구가 함께 쓰여 수식어구가 길어질 땐, 명사 뒤에서 꾸미기도 한다. 주로 -able, -ible로 끝나는 형용사들이 명사를 뒤에서 수식한다.

The new policy was implemented last week.
그 새로운 정책은 지난주에 시행되었다.

Her recent achievements were recognized by the company.
그녀의 최근 성과들이 회사에 의해 인정받았다.

The manager gave **a very detailed** presentation.
매니저는 매우 상세한 발표를 했다.

The equipment **available** for rent is listed on the website.
대여 가능한 장비는 웹사이트에 나와 있다.

✔️ **문법 포인트** 형용사는 -one / -body / -thing 으로 끝나는 부정대명사를 뒤에서 수식할 수 있다. 일반적으로 형용사는 대명사를 수식할 수 없으니 예외적으로 기억해두자!

There is **something important** you need to know.
당신이 알아야 할 중요한 것이 있다.

3. 보어 역할을 하는 형용사

▶ 2형식 동사(be / become / seem / remain) 뒤에 주어를 보충 설명하는 주격 보어 역할을 한다.

▶ 5형식 동사(keep / find / consider / make) 뒤에 목적어를 보충 설명하는 목적격 보어 역할을 한다.

The proposal **seems promising**. 주어 + 동사 + 주격 보어(형용사)
그 제안은 유망해 보인다.

Our partner company **found** the report **satisfactory**. 주어 + 동사 + 목적어 + 목적격 보어(형용사)
우리 협력사는 그 보고서를 만족스럽다고 여겼다.

4. 형용사와 명사의 형태가 같은 경우

▶ 형용사 어미로 끝나지만 형용사와 명사 두가지로 쓰일 수 있는 단어에 유의해야 한다. 이때 문장 속 자리와 해석을 통해 역할을 파악한다.

	형용사	명사
individual	개인적인, 각각의	개인
potential	잠재적인	잠재력
representative	대표하는	대표자, 직원
alternative	대안적인, 대체 가능한	대안
professional	전문적인	전문가
commercial	상업적인	광고
objective	객관적인	목적
original	원래의	원본

Each **individual** member contributed to the project. 형용사
각 개인의 구성원이 프로젝트에 기여했다.

The survey was completed by 100 **individuals**. 명사
설문조사는 100명의 응답자가 참여했다.

5. 수량형용사

▶ 수량형용사는 명사 앞에서 명사의 수나 양을 나타낸다. 가산 명사와 불가산 명사 앞에 오는 수량 표현을 구분해서 외워 두어야 한다.

one 하나의 every 모든	each 각각의	another 또 다른 하나의	+ 가산 단수 명사
many 많은 several 몇몇의 a number of 많은	a few 조금의 various 다양한 multiple 많은	few 거의 없는 a variety of 다양한	+ 가산 복수 명사
much 많은 less 더 적은	a little 조금의	little 거의 없는	+ 불가산 명사
all 모든 other 다른 plenty of 많은	most 대부분의 a lot of 많은	some 몇몇의 lots of 많은	+ 가산 복수 명사 + 불가산 명사
any 어느 ~든지	no 어떤 ~도 아니다		+ 가산 단수 명사 + 가산 복수 명사 + 불가산 명사

Each employee must complete the training.
모든 직원은 교육을 완료해야 한다.

Much information is available on the website.
많은 정보가 웹사이트에 있다.

Some equipment needs to be replaced.
일부 장비는 교체되어야 한다.

✓ **문법 포인트** every와 another은 뒤에 둘 이상의 수와 함께하면 복수 명사를 쓸 수 있다. 이때 해석은 every '~마다', another '~더'라고 해석한다.

The software is updated **every** six **weeks**.
소프트웨어는 6주마다 업데이트된다.

The company expanded its operations by adding **another** two **branches**.
그 회사는 지점을 두 개 더 추가하여 운영을 확장했다.

Q1 형용사의 자리

We need to buy an ------- printer for the office.

(A) add   (B) addition   (C) additional   (D) additionally

>> **출제 포인트** 형용사는 명사를 앞에서 수식할 수 있다.

❶ 명사를 앞에서 수식하는 형용사

한정사 + 형용사 + 명사	The manager approved **a conservative budget** for the next quarter. 매니저는 다음 분기를 위한 보수적인 예산을 승인했다.
부사 + 형용사 + 명사	The report provided a **highly detailed analysis** of the market trends. 그 보고서는 시장 동향에 대한 매우 상세한 분석을 제공했다.
전치사 + 형용사 + 명사	We are looking for a solution **to** the **current problem**. 우리는 현재 문제에 대한 해결책을 찾고 있다.
형용사 + 복합 명사	The company offers **excellent employee benefits**. 그 회사는 훌륭한 직원 혜택을 제공한다.
형용사 + 형용사 + 명사	The team developed a **comprehensive strategic plan** for the project. 팀은 그 프로젝트를 위한 포괄적인 전략 계획을 개발했다.

✅ **문법 포인트** 토익 시험에서는 형용사 앞에 대부분 부사가 출제되지만, 뒤의 명사를 수식하는 두 개 이상의 형용사가 연속해서 나올 수도 있다. 다만, 형용사가 두 개 이상 오는 경우는 반드시 뒤에 수식을 받는 명사가 있어야 한다.

❷ 명사를 뒤에서 수식하는 형용사

명사 + -able / -ble	We need to hire **personnel capable** of handling complex tasks. 우리는 복잡한 작업을 처리할 수 있는 인원을 고용해야 한다.

Q2 형용사의 자리

The manager found the report -------.

(A) accurate   (B) accurately   (C) accuracy   (D) accurateness

>> **출제 포인트** 형용사는 주어나 목적어의 상태를 설명해주는 보어 자리에 온다.

❶ 2형식 동사 뒤 주격 보어 자리에는 형용사가 온다.

be ~이다	become ~되다	seem ~하게 보이다	
remain ~인 채로 남다	stay ~한 상태로 남아있다	appear ~하게 보이다	+ 주격 보어(형용사)
prove ~임이 판명되다			

The results **seem promising**.
결과가 유망해 보인다

The new software **appears user-friendly**.
새로운 소프트웨어는 사용자 친화적으로 보인다.

✓ **문법 포인트** 토익 시험에서는 2형식 주격 보어 자리에 주어의 상태를 설명하는 형용사가 주로 출제되지만, 주어와 동격을 나타낼 경우에는 명사가 온다.

His job is **a sales manager**.
그의 직업은 영업 관리자이다.

❷ 5형식 동사 뒤 목적격 보어 자리에는 형용사가 온다.

keep ~한 상태로 유지하다	find ~라고 생각하다	consider ~라고 여기다	+ 목적어 + 목적격 보어(형용사)
make ~로 만들다	leave ~한 상태로 두다		

The manager **kept** the meeting **short** to save time.
매니저는 시간을 절약하기 위해 회의를 짧게 유지했다.

The committee **found** the proposal **acceptable**.
위원회는 그 제안이 수용 가능하다고 생각했다.

✓ **문법 포인트** 토익 시험에서는 2형식과 마찬가지로 목적어의 상태를 설명하는 형용사가 주로 보어 자리에 출제되지만, 목적어와 동격을 나타낼 경우에는 명사가 온다.

appoint, name, vote, elect ~로 임명/선출하다	+ 목적어 + 목적격 보어(명사)

The company **elected** Jane **president** of the organization.
회사는 제인을 그 조직의 회장으로 선출했다.

Q3 **수량형용사**

The company received ------- applications for the job opening.

(A) much　　　　　(B) many　　　　　(C) little　　　　　(D) less

>> **출제 포인트** **수량 표현 뒤에 오는 명사의 성격을 구분해서 외워 두어야 한다.**

● 다음 수량형용사들이 명사를 수식하는 경우 뒤에는 반드시 복수 명사를 동반해야 한다.

many 많은	a number of 많은	numerous 많은	
a few 몇몇의	few 거의 없는	both 둘 다의	+ 가산 복수 명사
several 몇몇의	various 다양한	a variety of 다양한	
multiple 많은	a diverse of 다양한	a wide range of 다양한	

A number of customers have complained about the service.
많은 고객이 서비스에 대해 불만을 제기했다.

The company offers **a variety of benefits** to its employees.
회사는 직원들에게 다양한 혜택을 제공한다.

✓ **문법 포인트** 토익 시험에서는 명사 앞에 알맞은 수량형용사를 묻는 문제가 주로 출제된다. 반대로, 수량형용사 뒤 알맞은 명사를 묻는 문제도 출제되니 그 성격을 반드시 구분해서 외워야 한다.

[**Several** / Every] **managers** should attend the meeting.
여러 명의 매니저가 회의에 참석해야 한다.

The company has **various** job [opening / **openings**] available.
그 회사는 지원 가능한 다양한 채용 공고가 있다.

Q4 혼동하기 쉬운 형용사

The manager made a ------- decision that pleased the employees.

(A) considerable   (B) considering   (C) considerate   (D) consider

>> 출제 포인트 **형태가 비슷하게 생겼지만 의미는 서로 다른 형용사를 주의해야 한다.**

● 다음의 형용사들은 형태가 비슷하나 의미가 다르므로 해석으로 구분해야 한다.

considerable 상당한	considerate 사려 깊은
confidential 기밀의	confident 자신감 있는
complimentary 무료의, 칭찬하는	complementary 보충의
comprehensive 종합적인, 포괄적인	comprehensible 이해할 수 있는
comparable 비슷한	comparative 비교의
dependable 신뢰할 만한	dependent 의존하는
extensive 폭넓은	extended 연장된
favorable 호의적인	favorite 가장 좋아하는
impressive 인상적인	impressed 감명받은
informative 유익한	informed 정통한, 알고있는
profitable 이익이 있는	proficient 능숙한
reliable 신뢰할 만한	reliant 의존적인
responsible 책임이 있는	responsive 반응하는
variable 변동이 심한	various 다양한
successful 성공적인	successive 연속적인

[Complementary / **Complimentary**] breakfast is offered to all hotel guests.
모든 호텔 손님에게 무료 아침 식사가 제공된다.

We need [**dependable** / dependent] employees for this critical project.
우리는 이 중요한 프로젝트를 위해 신뢰할 수 있는 직원이 필요하다.

Practice

해설서 p.14

1. Crystal Cove is a favored vacation spot for budget-conscious tourists because of its ------- lodging.

(A) economical
(B) economy
(C) economize
(D) economically

2. Professor Lee is eager to gather student feedback on this ------- approach.

(A) innovates
(B) innovation
(C) innovative
(D) innovatively

3. Nowadays, numerous individuals are too ------- to focus on their nutrition.

(A) laze
(B) lazily
(C) lazy
(D) laziness

4. Following extended discussions, the parties seemed ------- with the conditions of the partnership.

(A) accept
(B) acceptance
(C) accepts
(D) acceptable

5. Mr. Smith intends to hold a workshop for ------- employees in the marketing department.

(A) every
(B) each
(C) several
(D) a little

6. The heated debate was settled in a ------- fashion.

(A) prompt
(B) promptly
(C) prompting
(D) prompts

7. Thoroughly analyzing feedback from ------- client will enhance our service quality.

(A) every
(B) several
(C) most
(D) all

8. When the plant becomes completely -------, it will require more employees.

(A) functioning
(B) function
(C) functional
(D) functionally

9. Gofirst Travels hired Ms. Johnson due to her ------- knowledge of the hospitality industry.

(A) broadth
(B) broad
(C) broadly
(D) broaden

10. According to the feedback, the majority of clients considered Zandro's latest collection of shoes extremely -------.

(A) appealing
(B) appeal
(C) appeals
(D) appealed

11. The backpacks produced by EcoCarry are both ------- and fashionable.

(A) sturdy
(B) sturdiness
(C) sturdily
(D) sturdiest

12. Trinity Consulting Firm offers a ------- range of business solutions.

(A) diverse
(B) diversify
(C) diversely
(D) diverseness

13. Several of the Northridge Railway lines require ------- maintenance.

(A) thorough
(B) thoroughness
(C) thoroughly
(D) thoroughest

14. We need a ------- supplier to meet our production deadlines.

(A) rely
(B) reliance
(C) reliant
(D) reliable

15. The files should be organized in an ------- manner before the meeting.

(A) order
(B) ordering
(C) ordered
(D) orderly

16. All employees at the conference recognized that security was one of the most ------- aspects.

(A) significant
(B) significantly
(C) significance
(D) signification

17. The marketing strategy was ------- in boosting the organization's revenue.

(A) effectiveness
(B) effective
(C) effectively
(D) effect

18. The store carries a variety of ------- to cater to different tastes.

(A) product
(B) products
(C) production
(D) productive

19. GreenTech Solutions has been ------- in supporting sustainability projects for more than two decades.

(A) instrumental
(B) instruments
(C) instrumentation
(D) instrumentalize

20. Numerous traffic collisions are ------- through strategic planning and driver training.

(A) avoidable
(B) avoidance
(C) avoiding
(D) avoids

부사

부사는 명사를 제외한 형용사, 부사, 동사 및 구, 절, 문장 전체를 꾸며주는 만능 수식어 역할을 한다. 부사의 자리는 출제율이 높은 편이니, 다양한 부사의 자리를 기억하도록 한다.

기본 개념 이해하기

1. 부사의 형태

▶ 부사는 주로 『형용사 + -ly』 형태이지만 그 외에도 시간, 장소, 빈도를 나타내는 다양한 형태가 있다.

시간 부사	early 일찍 tomorrow 내일	yesterday 어제 already 이미	now 지금 still 여전히
빈도 부사	once 한번 usually 보통	almost 거의 sometimes 가끔	often 자주
부정 부사	hardly / rarely / seldom / scarcely / barely 거의 ~않는		never 결코 ~않는
기타 부사	so 매우 also 또한 too 너무	very 매우 again 다시	quite 매우 instead 대신에

Our team / works / **diligently**. 주어 + 동사 + 부사
우리 팀은 성실히 일한다.

The manager / reviews / the performance / **carefully**. 주어 + 동사 + 목적어 + 부사
매니저는 성과를 신중히 검토한다.

2. 형용사와 부사를 수식하는 부사

▶ 부사는 형용사와 다른 부사 앞에서 수식해줄 수 있다.

The presentation was **extremely informative**. 부사 + 형용사
그 발표는 매우 유익했다.

Natalya completed the project **very quickly**. 부사 + 부사
나탈리아는 프로젝트를 매우 빠르게 완료했다.

3. 동사를 수식하는 부사

▶ 주어와 동사 사이에 동사를 수식하는 부사가 올 수 있다.

▶ 자동사의 경우는 자동사 바로 뒤에서 수식하고, 타동사는 타동사와 목적어 뒤 문장 맨 끝에 부사가 온다.

▶ 동사를 수식하기 때문에 동사의 중간 자리인 조동사와 동사 사이, 진행형과 수동태에서는 be동사와 분사(-ing / p.p.) 사이, 현재 완료에서는 have / has와 과거분사(p.p.) 사이에 올 수 있다.

▶ 부사는 준동사(to부정사 / 동명사 / 분사)를 수식할 수 있다.

Our boss **always** reviews the reports carefully. 부사＋동사
상사는 항상 보고서를 신중하게 검토한다.

The sales figures increased **significantly** last quarter. 동사＋부사
지난 분기에 매출 수치가 크게 증가했다.

The engineer explained the problem **thoroughly**. 동사＋목적어＋부사
그 엔지니어는 문제를 철저히 설명했다.

Our company is **currently** expanding its operations. be동사＋부사＋현재분사
우리 회사는 현재 사업을 확장하고 있다.

The project was **successfully** completed ahead of schedule. be동사＋부사＋과거분사
그 프로젝트는 예정보다 일찍 성공적으로 완료되었다.

The team has **already** finished the report. have＋부사＋과거분사
팀은 이미 보고서를 끝냈다.

The board of directors plans to **quickly** address the issue. to＋부사＋동사원형
이사회는 그 문제를 빠르게 해결할 계획이다.

Regularly training employees can enhance their performance. 부사＋동명사
직원을 정기적으로 훈련시키는 것은 성과를 향상시킬 수 있다

Confidently presenting, the sales representative impressed the audience. 부사＋분사
자신감 있게 발표하면서, 그 영업사원은 청중을 감명시켰다.

4. 문장 전체를 수식하는 부사

▶ 부사는 문장 맨 앞에서 문장 전체를 수식한다.

Unfortunately, the meeting was canceled due to unforeseen circumstances. 부사＋명사구
불행하게도, 회의는 예상치 못한 상황으로 인해 취소되었다.

Interestingly, the survey results showed a surprising trend. 부사＋전치사구
흥미롭게도, 설문조사 결과는 놀라운 경향을 보였다.

5. 명사구와 전치사구를 수식하는 부사

▶ 부사는 전치사구와 명사구 앞에 위치하여 수식할 수 있다.

Among all the participants, John is **clearly** the winner.
모든 참가자 중에서, 존이 분명히 우승자이다.

The success of the project was **largely** due to the team's dedication.
그 프로젝트의 성공은 주로 팀의 헌신 덕분이었다.

6. 시간 부사

▶ already는 '이미, 벌써'라는 의미로 보통 긍정문에서 쓰인다.

▶ still은 '여전히, 아직'이라는 의미로 긍정문, 부정문에서 쓰인다.

▶ yet은 '아직'이라는 의미로 부정문의 문장 맨 끝에서 쓰인다.

The tickets for the concert are **already** sold out.
콘서트 티켓은 이미 매진되었다.

The colleague **still** works at the same company.
그 동료는 여전히 같은 회사에서 일하고 있다.

The customer **still** has not received the package.
그 고객은 아직도 그 패키지를 받지 못했다.

The report is not finished **yet**.
그 보고서는 아직 끝나지 않았다.

✔ **문법 포인트** 부정문에서 still과 yet은 '아직'이라는 의미로 같지만, not을 기준으로 그 위치가 다르니 꼭 구분해야 한다. 또한 yet을 이용한 관용 표현인 「have / be yet to do」 '아직 ~하지 못했다' 표현도 기억해두자.

The issue is **still not** resolved.
그 문제는 아직 해결되지 않았다.

The issue is **not yet** resolved.
그 문제는 아직 해결되지 않았다.

They **have yet to** make a decision.
그들은 아직 결정을 내리지 못했다.

Q1 부사의 자리

The company introduced a ------- new product line last month.

(A) complete   (B) completely   (C) completion   (D) completes

>> **출제 포인트** 부사는 관사와 형용사 사이에 올 수 있다.

❶ 부사는 명사를 제외한 품사들과 동사, 형용사, 부사를 수식한다.

부사 + 동사	The director **frequently meets** with investors. 그 감독은 자주 투자자들과 만난다.
부사 + 형용사	The conference was an **incredibly successful** event. 그 회의는 믿을 수 없을 정도로 성공적인 행사였다.
부사 + 부사	The presentation was delivered **quite effectively**. 발표는 꽤 효과적으로 전달되었다.

❷ 다양한 동사 형태(조동사 + 동사원형, 진행형, 수동태, 현재 완료) 사이에도 부사가 들어간다.

자동사 + 부사	The performance **improved significantly**. 실적은 상당히 개선되었다.
조동사 + 부사 + 동사원형	The team **should definitely consider** the new proposal. 팀은 새 제안을 반드시 고려해야 한다.
be동사 + 부사 + -ing	The company **is currently developing** a new product. 그 회사는 현재 신제품을 개발하고 있다.
be동사 + 부사 + p.p.	The building was **completely** renovated last year. 그 건물은 작년에 완전히 개조되었다.
have / has + 부사 + p.p.	The engineer **has finally submitted** the report. 그 엔지니어는 마침내 보고서를 제출했다.

✓ **문법 포인트** 3형식 동사의 수동태 뒤에는 수식어 역할을 하는 부사가 온다. 즉, 수동태 동사 사이와 수동태 동사 바로 뒤에는 부사가 정답이다.

The report was reviewed **thoroughly** by the manager.
그 보고서는 매니저에 의해 철저하게 검토되었다.

Q2 부사의 자리

The company is dedicated to ------- enhancing its customer service.

(A) careful   (B) carefully   (C) care   (D) carefulness

>> **출제 포인트** 전치사와 동명사 사이에는 부사가 온다.

❶ 부사는 준동사(to부정사 / 동명사 / 분사)를 수식할 수 있다.

to + 부사 + 동사원형	The team needs **to quickly resolve** the issue. 팀은 그 문제를 빠르게 해결할 필요가 있다.
전치사 + 부사 + 동명사	The project was delayed **due to unexpectedly finding** new complications. 프로젝트는 예상치 못한 새로운 문제를 발견하여 지연되었다.
부사 + 분사 + 명사	The **newly appointed manager** has implemented several changes. 새로 임명된 매니저는 몇 가지 변화를 시행했다.

☑ **문법 포인트** 명사를 수식하는 것은 형용사이지만, 동명사를 수식해주는 것은 부사라는 점에 유의하자.

Before [thorough / **thoroughly**] starting the project, they conducted extensive research. 프로젝트를 시작하기 전에 철저하게 광범위한 조사를 실시했다.

❷ 부사는 구(명사구 / 전치사구)와 절을 수식할 수 있다.

부사 + 명사구	**Nearly all employees** attended the meeting. 거의 모든 직원들이 회의에 참석했다.
부사 + 전치사구	The event was postponed **primarily due to** scheduling conflicts. 그 행사는 주로 일정 충돌로 인해 연기되었다.
부사 + 절	**Unfortunately**, the event was canceled due to bad weather. 불행히도, 그 행사는 악천후로 인해 취소되었다. The marketing team launched the campaign **successfully**. 마케팅 팀은 캠페인을 성공적으로 시작했다.

☑ **문법 포인트** 다음은 명사구 수식이 가능한 부사이다.

formerly / previously 이전에	clearly 분명히	once 한때
simply / only / just 단지	mainly / largely 주로	even 심지어(~조차)
originally 원래		

주의 빈칸 뒤에 『a / the + 명사』 형태의 명사구가 있을 때 형용사를 넣지 않도록 주의하자.

Dr. Smith was **formerly** a professor at the university. 스미스 박사는 이전에 대학 교수로 재직했다.

Q3 숫자와 양을 수식하는 부사

The project will take ------- six months to complete.

(A) approximately   (B) slowly   (C) quietly   (D) carefully

>> **출제 포인트 숫자 앞에는 부사가 수식한다.**

● 숫자 표현은 형용사로 취급하므로 그 앞에는 부사가 수식한다.

approximately / about / around / roughly 대략		
nearly / almost 거의		
more than ~이상	over ~이상	**+ 숫자 + 명사**
less than ~이하	under ~이하	
up to 최대 ~까지	at least 적어도	
just 딱	only 오직	

The company has **approximately 500** employees working in its main office.
그 회사는 본사에서 일하는 대략 500명의 직원이 있다.

The seminar lasted for **just three** hours but was very informative.
그 세미나는 딱 세 시간 동안 진행되었지만 매우 유익했다.

Q4 주의해야 할 부사

The team developed a ------- innovative solution to the problem.

(A) highly   (B) high   (C) height   (D) highest

>> **출제 포인트**   형태가 비슷하지만 의미가 다른 부사들을 주의해야 한다.

- 형태가 비슷하지만 의미가 다른 부사이기 때문에 주의해야 한다. 이때, 해석으로 구별을 해야 한다.

short 형 짧은 부 짧게 shortly 부 곧	end **short** 짧게 끝내다 reply **shortly** 곧 답장하다
hard 형 근면한 부 열심히 hardly 부 거의 ~않다	study **hard** 열심히 공부하다 **hardly** notice 거의 알아차리지 못하다
high 형 높은 부 높게 highly 부 매우	fly **high** 높이 날다 **highly** recommend 매우 추천하다
late 형 늦은 부 늦게 lately 부 최근에	arrive **late** 늦게 도착하다 have been busy **lately** 최근에 바빴다
close 형 가까운 부 가깝게 closely 부 긴밀히	sit **close** 가깝게 앉다 examine **closely** 면밀히 조사하다
near 형 가까운 부 가까이 nearly 부 거의	stand **near** 가까이 서다 **nearly** finish 거의 끝내다

1. Nearly 150 staff members have ------- finished their introductory training.

(A) effective
(B) effectively
(C) effect
(D) efficiency

2. The Downtown Café on Main Avenue ------- holds special promotion weeks.

(A) regular
(B) regularly
(C) regulate
(D) regulation

3. The development of TechWave's encryption protocol has been ------- assisted by Ms. Lee.

(A) complete
(B) completely
(C) completion
(D) completes

4. One of the most ------- acclaimed classical music festivals takes place in Vienna.

(A) high
(B) higher
(C) highly
(D) height

5. By reducing the number of staff, output decreased ------- at Brighton Technologies.

(A) somehow
(B) quietly
(C) randomly
(D) considerably

6. Davenport Inc. has acquired Nova Tech for ------- $15 million.

(A) loudly
(B) shortly
(C) nearly
(D) lately

7. The advanced medical scanner aims to ------- reduce diagnostic errors.

(A) considerable
(B) considerably
(C) consider
(D) consideration

8. Assembly line workers are prohibited from using that equipment for safety -------.

(A) reasons
(B) reasoning
(C) reasonable
(D) reasonably

9. Client reactions to the updated product wrapping remain ------- favorable.

(A) uniform
(B) uniformity
(C) uniformly
(D) uniformed

10. A promotional strategy created by NOVA Promotions will make your services more ------- to clients.

(A) desirable
(B) desire
(C) desires
(D) desirably

11. The board members were not ------- happy with the updated marketing strategy.

(A) full
(B) filling
(C) fully
(D) filled

12. Applicants for the customer service position need to convey information -------.

(A) clarity
(B) clear
(C) clearly
(D) clearness

13. Breakable objects need to be packed ------- to prevent damage during shipment.

(A) individually
(B) individual
(C) individualize
(D) individualized

14. Team members are required to work ------- to finish tasks on schedule.

(A) effect
(B) effectate
(C) effective
(D) effectively

15. Tech Innovators seeks to boost revenue by ------- engaging with their clients.

(A) continue
(B) continuous
(C) continually
(D) continuity

16. Participants are requested to leave the conference hall ------- after the discussion concludes.

(A) calmly
(B) calmer
(C) calm
(D) calmest

17. ------- 500 people signed up for the latest Tech Trends Newsletter.

(A) Often
(B) More than
(C) Rarely
(D) Briefly

18. The meeting was ended ------- after an unexpected issue was discovered.

(A) short
(B) shortly
(C) shorten
(D) shorted

19. -------, Mr. Kim has been staying late to finish the report on time.

(A) Recently
(B) Recent
(C) Recency
(D) Recentness

20. Adding more public transport options has been shown to be ------- in cutting city air pollution.

(A) beneficial
(B) benefit
(C) benefitting
(D) beneficially

UNIT 08 전치사

전치사는 명사나 명사 역할을 하는 성분과 함께 쓰여야 하며 장소, 시간, 이유 등을 나타낸다. 전치사의 기본적인 의미와 용법을 기억해둔다.

🗨 기본 개념 이해하기

1. 전치사의 자리

▶ 전치사 뒤에는 명사 역할(명사, 대명사, 동명사, 명사절)이 와야 하며 『전치사 + 명사』의 구 형태를 '전치사구'라고 한다.

▶ 전치사구는 문장에서 명사를 꾸미는 형용사 역할이나 동사를 꾸미는 부사 역할을 할 수 있다.

Customers will arrive on time **despite the heavy traffic.** 전치사 + 명사 = 부사구
고객들은 교통 체증에도 불구하고 제시간에 도착할 것이다.

The document explains the process **of receiving a family discount.** 전치사 + 동명사 = 형용사구
이 문서는 가족 할인을 받는 절차를 설명한다.

We made adjustments based **on what we learned from the feedback.** 전치사 + 명사절 = 부사구
우리는 피드백에서 배운 것을 바탕으로 조정을 했다.

2. 시간 전치사

▶ 시간 전치사

in + 월 / 연도 / 계절 / 시기	~에	**in** January 1월에 **in** 2025 2025년에 **in** summer 여름에 **in** the morning 아침에
on + 날짜 / 요일 / 특정일	~에	**on** March 5th 3월 5일에 **on** Monday 월요일에 **on** Christmas 크리스마스에
at + 시각 / 시점	~에	**at** 7 o'clock 7시에 **at** noon 정오에

▶ 시점을 나타내는 전치사

before(= prior to) + 시점	~전에	**before** 8 A.M. 오전 8시 전에
after(= following) + 시점	~후에	**after** lunch 점심 후에
since + 과거 시점	~이후로	**since** last year 작년 이후로
by + 완료 시점	~까지	**by** the end of the month 이달 말까지
until + 지속되는 시점	~까지	**until** next week 다음 주까지
from + 시점	~로부터	**from** the beginning 처음부터

▶ 기간을 나타내는 전치사

for + 숫자 기간	~동안	**for** two weeks 2주 동안
during + 특정 기간	~동안	**during** the meeting 회의하는 동안
over + 기간	~동안	**over** the weekend 주말 동안
in + 기간	~동안 / ~후에	**in** a few minutes 몇 분 후에
within + 기간	~이내에	**within** 24 hours 24시간 이내에
throughout + 기간	~내내	**throughout** the year 연중 내내

3. 장소 전치사

▶ 장소 전치사

in + 큰 공간의 안 / 국가 / 도시	~안에	**in** the park 공원 안에 **in** Korea 한국 안에 **in** Seoul 서울 안에
on + 표면 위 / 도로	~위에	**on** the table 테이블 위에 **on** the road 도로 위에
at + 지점 / 번지	~에	**at** the bus stop 버스 정류장에 **at** 123 Main Street 메인 스트리트 123번지에

▶ 위치를 나타내는 전치사

above	~위쪽에	**above** the clouds 구름 위쪽에
over	~바로 위에	**over** the table 테이블 바로 위에
below	~아래쪽에	**below** the surface 표면 아래쪽에
under	~바로 밑에	**under** the bridge 다리 바로 밑에
behind	~뒤에	**behind** the house 집 뒤에
in front of	~앞에	**in front of** the school 학교 앞에
beside	~옆에	**beside** the river 강 옆에
next to	~옆에	**next to** the store 가게 옆에
by	~옆에	**by** the window 창문 옆에
near	~가까이	**near** the station 역 가까이에
around	근처에	**around** the corner 모퉁이 근처에
between A and B	A와 B 사이에	**between** the two buildings 두 건물 사이에
among + 복수 명사	셋 이상 사이에	**among** the trees 나무들 사이에
within	~이내에	**within** the building 건물 내에
throughout	~걸쳐서	**throughout** the country 전국에 걸쳐서
past	~을 지나	**past** the museum 박물관을 지나

▶ 방향을 나타내는 전치사

from + 출발지	~로부터	**from** the airport 공항으로부터
to + 목적지	~쪽으로	**to** the office 사무실 쪽으로
towards	~을 향하여	**towards** the north 북쪽을 향하여
into	~안으로	**into** the room 방 안으로
out of	~밖으로	**out of** the building 건물 밖으로
across	~을 건너, ~의 전역에 걸쳐	**across** the river 강을 건너
for	~을 향해	**for** the station 역을 향해
through	~을 통과하여	**through** the tunnel 터널을 통과하여
along	~을 따라	**along** the street 길을 따라

4. 이유, 양보, 추가, 제외, 목적을 나타내는 전치사

because of due to owing to on account of	~때문에	**because of** the high cost 높은 비용 때문에 **due to** bad weather 악천후 때문에 **owing to** his illness 그의 병 때문에 **on account of** the delay 지연 때문에
in spite of despite notwithstanding	~에도 불구하고	**in spite of** the difficulties 어려움에도 불구하고 **despite** the warnings 경고에도 불구하고 **notwithstanding** the challenges 도전에도 불구하고
in addition to besides	~에 더해서	**in addition to** his job 그의 직업에 더해서 **besides** her qualifications 그녀의 자격조건에 더해서
except (for)	~을 제외하고	**except for** the final exam 마지막 시험을 제외하고
excluding	~을 제외하고	**excluding** weekends 주말을 제외하고
apart from	~외에도	**apart from** his duties 그의 임무 외에도
aside from	~외에도	**aside from** the main topic 주요 주제 외에도
instead of	~대신에	**instead of** coffee 커피 대신에
for	~을 위해	**for** the project 프로젝트를 위해

5. -ing 형태 전치사

regarding	~에 관해서	**regarding** your request 귀하의 요청에 관해서
concerning	~에 관해서	**concerning** the meeting 회의에 관해서
pertaining to	~에 관해서	**pertaining to** the policy 정책에 관해서
about	~에 관해서	**about** the issue 문제에 관해서
on	~에 관해서	**on** this matter 이 문제에 관해서
including	~을 포함하여	**including** tax 세금을 포함하여
excluding	~을 제외하고	**excluding** holidays 공휴일을 제외하고
barring	~없이	**barring** any delays 지연이 없다면
following / after	~후에	**following / after** the announcement 발표 후에

6. 기타 주요 전치사

by	~의해서, ~함으로써	**by** working hard 열심히 일함으로써
with	~와 함께, ~을 가지고	**with** his colleagues 그의 동료와 함께
without	~없이	**without** permission 허가 없이
as	~로서	**as** a teacher 교사로서
like unlike	~처럼 ~와 달리	**like** a professional 전문가처럼 **unlike** his friends 그의 친구들과 달리
for	~을 위해서	**for** the team 팀을 위해
of	~의, ~중에서	**of** all the options 모든 옵션 중에서
against	~에 기대어, ~에 반대하여	**against** the wall 벽에 기대어
alongside	~와 함께	**alongside** his peers 그의 동료와 함께
on / upon	~하자마자	**on** arrival 도착하자마자
beyond	~을 넘어서는	**beyond** the limits 한계를 넘어

7. 전치사 숙어 표현

「동사 + 전치사」	
account for ~을 설명하다	correspond with ~에 일치하다 / ~와 서신왕래하다
apply for / to ~에 지원하다 / ~에 적용되다	deal with ~을 다루다
agree to / with ~에 동의하다	depend / rely on ~에 의존하다
adhere to ~을 준수하다	enroll in ~에 등록하다
benefit from ~로부터 혜택을 얻다	participate in ~에 참여하다
comply with ~을 준수하다	proceed to / with ~을 진행하다
consist of ~로 구성되다	refrain from ~을 삼가다
contribute to ~에 공헌하다	respond / reply / react to ~에 응답하다
complain about ~에 관해 불평하다	refer to ~을 참조하다
come into effect 효력이 발생하다	succeed to / in ~을 계승하다 / ~을 성공하다
collaborate / cooperate with ~와 협력하다	specialize in ~을 전문으로 하다
compensate for ~에 대해 보상하다	take advantage of ~을 이용하다

「be동사 + 형용사 + 전치사」	
be aware / conscious of ~을 인식하다	be equipped with ~을 갖추고 있다
be accessible to ~을 이용하다	be equal to ~와 동등하다
be affiliated with ~와 제휴하다	be entitled to ~에 대한 자격이 있다
be appreciative of ~에 감사하다	be eligible for ~할 자격이 있다
be capable of ~을 할 수 있다	be famous for ~로 유명하다
be concerned about ~에 관해 염려하다	be familiar with ~에 익숙하다
be compliant with ~을 준수하다	be involved in ~에 연관되다
be compatible with ~와 호환되다	be responsible for ~에 책임이 있다
be consistent with ~와 일관되다	be satisfied with ~에 만족하다
be dependent / reliant on ~에 의존하다	be similar to ~에 비슷하다
be dedicated / committed / devoted to ~에 헌신하다	be subject to ~하기 쉽다

「명사 + 전치사」	
increase / rise in ~의 증가	in honor of ~에게 경의를 표하며
decrease / drop in ~의 감소	in operation 가동 중인
experience in ~에 대한 경험	in compliance with ~을 준수하여
advance in ~의 진보	in accordance with ~일치하여
demand for ~에 대한 수요	in the event of ~의 경우에
request for ~에 대한 요구	in preparation for ~을 준비하여
standard for ~에 대한 기준	in favor of ~을 찬성하여
commitment to ~에 헌신	in response to ~에 응하여
contribution to ~에 대한 기여	in terms of ~에 관해서
approach to ~에 대한 접근법	in observance of ~을 준수하여
access to ~에 접근	in charge of ~을 책임지고 있는
information on / about ~에 대한 정보	by means of ~을 수단으로

PART 5 UNIT 08

Q1 시점 vs. 기간 전치사

The meeting will start ------- 5 o'clock.

(A) in   (B) on   (C) at   (D) for

>> **출제 포인트** 시간 전치사는 시점과 기간을 나타내는 전치사를 구분해서 풀어야 한다.

● 같은 시간 전치사라고 하더라도 시점과 기간을 나타내는 전치사를 구분해야 한다. 시점 전치사는 뒤에 특정 시점을 나타내는 표현이 나오며, 기간 전치사는 기간을 나타내는 표현들과 함께 쓰인다.

시점	from A to B A에서 B까지 before / after ~이전에 / ~이후에 since ~이래로 until / by ~까지	+ 시점 표현 (May 30, 5 o' clock, March, Monday)
기간	for / during / over ~동안 through(out) ~내내 within ~이내에	+ 기간 표현 (five years, two hours, the month of March)

The meeting will be held [**before** / ~~during~~] 5 o'clock.
회의는 5시 이전에 열릴 것이다.

The project must be completed [**within** / ~~by~~] two weeks.
프로젝트는 2주 이내에 완료되어야 한다.

✅ **문법 포인트** by와 until은 해석상 같아 보이나 차이점을 구분해야 한다. until은 '동작이나 상태가 특정 시점까지 계속'되는 것을 의미한다. 반면에, by는 '특정 시점까지 완료되는 동작'을 강조할 때 사용한다.

You need to submit the report (~~until~~ / **by**) Friday.
금요일까지 보고서를 제출해야 한다.

Please wait here [**until** / ~~by~~] 2:30 p.m.
여기서 오후 2시 30분까지 기다리세요.

Q2 장소 전치사

The researcher found her keys ------- the dozens of books on the library shelf.

(A) between   (B) among   (C) within   (D) next to

>> **출제 포인트** 위치를 나타내는 전치사들은 해석으로 서로 구별해야 한다.

● **주요 장소 및 방향 전치사**

in + 넓은 장소 ~안에	**in** the city 도시 내에 **in** Korea 한국에 **in** the building 빌딩 안에
on + 표면 / 거리 ~위에	**on** the shelf 선반 위에 **on** the third floor 3층에
at + 번지 / 회사 / 특정 지점 ~에서	**at** Jamison Company 제미슨 사에서 **at** the intersection 교차로에서
between (둘) 사이에	**between** the desk and the chair 책상과 의자 사이에 **between** two buildings 두 빌딩 사이에
among (셋 이상) 사이에	**among** the textile companies 섬유 회사들 중에서
within ~이내에	**within** walking distance 도보거리 이내에
throughout / across ~걸쳐, 곳곳에	**throughout / across** the country 전국에 걸쳐
along ~을 따라	**along** the street 길을 따라
through ~을 통해서	run **through** the city 도시를 관통하여 달리다
for + 목적지 ~로 향하는	a train heading **for** New York 뉴욕으로 향하는 기차

✔ **문법 포인트** 위치를 나타내는 전치사들은 서로 해석으로 구별하는 문제가 주로 출제되지만 숙어 표현을 묻는 문제도 출제되므로 『전치사 + 명사』를 덩어리째 기억해두자.

There are 10 parking lots **within** walking distance.
도보거리 이내에 10개의 주차장이 있다.

Q3 **구 전치사**

We will make a decision ------- to the meeting.

(A) prior   (B) after   (C) during   (D) before

>> **출제 포인트** **구 전치사의 해석뿐만 아니라 어울리는 전치사 짝을 함께 기억해 두어야 한다.**

● 구 전치사란 두 가지 이상의 단어들이 하나의 전치사로 쓰이는 것을 의미한다.

구 전치사	
prior to (= before) ~전에	except for ~을 제외하고
instead of ~대신에	regardless of ~와 상관없이
according to ~에 따르면	as a result of ~의 결과로
in addition to (= on top of) ~에 더하여	such as ~와 같은
based on ~을 바탕으로	up to (최대) ~까지
as to (= as for, pertaining to) ~에 관해서	thanks to ~덕분에
depending on ~에 따라	along with (= alongside) ~와 함께
as of + 시간 ~부터	apart / aside from ~외에도

Everyone was present **except for** John, who was sick.
병가 중인 존을 제외하고 모두 참석했다.

According to the report, sales have increased by 20%.
보고서에 따르면 매출이 20% 증가했다.

Q4 전치사의 숙어 표현

The new office building is currently ------- construction.

(A) in   (B) at   (C) on   (D) under

>> **출제 포인트** 특정 동사, 명사, 형용사와 함께 쓰이는 전치사의 표현을 함께 기억한다.

● 기타 주요 전치사 숙어 표현

under the construction 공사 중인 under warranty 보증 기간 중에 under the supervision 감독 하에	with no exception 예외없이 with experience 경험을 가진 without approval / permission 허가 없이
out of stock 재고가 없는 out of order 고장 난 out of print 절판된 out of date 구식인, 시대에 뒤쳐진	in operation 가동 중인 in transit 이송 중인 in writing 서면으로 in advance 미리
at no cost (= charge) 무료로 at all times 항상 at once 즉시 at one's convenience 편리한 때에 at one's expense ~의 비용으로	on vacation 휴가 중인 on duty 근무 중인 on call 대기 중인 (up)on arrival 도착하는 즉시 (up)on request 요청하는 즉시

The policy will be enforced **with no exception**.
정책은 예외없이 시행될 것이다.

The book has been **out of print** for years.
그 책은 몇 년간 절판된 상태이다.

☑ **문법 포인트** 토익 시험에서는 해석을 통해 문맥에 맞는 전치사를 선택하는 문제 뿐만 아니라, 숙어 표현을 완성하는 문제도 출제
되므로 덩어리째 암기하자.

1. The Sunset Diner will be shut on Wednesday, August 15, ------- a special occasion.
   (A) over
   (B) due to
   (C) because
   (D) about

2. Blaze Pharmaceuticals acquired new research equipment ------- the additional budget support.
   (A) by
   (B) to
   (C) through
   (D) on

3. Drivers can help reduce traffic congestion ------- using public transit.
   (A) to
   (B) without
   (C) from
   (D) by

4. Enrollments at Miranda Technical Institute are accepted at any time ------- the month.
   (A) while
   (B) throughout
   (C) with
   (D) across

5. The Harmony Hotel is ideally situated ------- driving distance of popular landmarks.
   (A) next to
   (B) within
   (C) beside
   (D) near

6. Due to the frigid weather and heavy snowfall, the school semester will be extended ------- the end of March.
   (A) during
   (B) until
   (C) by
   (D) on

7. The proposal was submitted ------- the budget report.
   (A) according to
   (B) based on
   (C) such as
   (D) along with

8. The meeting room is situated ------- the main door of the facility.
   (A) beside
   (B) next
   (C) close
   (D) towards

9. The client sent a confirmation email right ------- receiving the contract.
   (A) across
   (B) after
   (C) through
   (D) along

10. Mr. Kim has been employed at TechCorp ------- over a decade.
    (A) since
    (B) while
    (C) around
    (D) for

11. We received an email ------- the upcoming project deadline.

(A) without
(B) following
(C) besides
(D) regarding

12. The quotation for your office refurbishment will be delivered ------- three business days.

(A) by
(B) until
(C) within
(D) throughout

13. The design team will not alter the layout ------- the client's prior agreement.

(A) though
(B) with
(C) without
(D) except for

14. The itinerary might change from the plan in the booklet ------- the number of participants.

(A) according to
(B) in
(C) based on
(D) with

15. Prior to moving to Seoul, Mr. Jack had been employed ------- a branch supervisor.

(A) by
(B) as
(C) at
(D) on

16. Kindly be aware that messages sent ------- 9 A.M. will be reviewed later in the afternoon.

(A) prior
(B) under
(C) through
(D) before

17. Staff members who are in charge ------- maintaining the conference room should inspect the space twice daily.

(A) with
(B) about
(C) regarding
(D) of

18. Make sure to save all your documents ------- backing them up to your computer.

(A) except
(B) concerning
(C) against
(D) following

19. ------- the last few weeks, the enrollment at Maplewood College has risen sharply.

(A) Over
(B) Following
(C) Behind
(D) At

20. ------- a power outage, Green Bistro will remain closed until additional notification.

(A) Prior to
(B) Due to
(C) Because to
(D) Since to

REVIEW TEST 02

해설서 p.19

1. Jorcom Advertising aims to hire salespeople with ------- skills.

(A) organizational   (B) organize
(C) organizations   (D) organizes

2. Mr. Lee completed the entire project by ------- without any assistance from the team.

(A) he   (B) him
(C) his   (D) himself

3. Dreambird Furniture offers a money-back guarantee on all -------.

(A) purchase   (B) purchaser
(C) purchasers   (D) purchases

4. Security cameras have been installed ------- the building to ensure the safety of all employees.

(A) onto   (B) under
(C) throughout   (D) towards

5. The HR manager reminded employees to bring completed forms with ------- to the meeting.

(A) they   (B) them
(C) their   (D) theirs

6. The IT manager is known for being ------- of her team's needs, always ensuring a supportive work environment.

(A) considerable (B) considerate
(C) considered   (D) considering

7. The new policy changes ------- with additional training sessions will be implemented next month.

(A) along   (B) aside
(C) over   (D) beyond

8. The company's sales figures this year exceeded ------- of its main competitor, showing strong market growth.

(A) this   (B) these
(C) that   (D) those

9. Jassom Ltd. welcomes your ------- concerning new products.

(A) suggests   (B) suggest
(C) suggested   (D) suggestions

10. The company is dedicated to improving customer satisfaction and ------- avoiding any potential complaints.

(A) complete   (B) completed
(C) completion   (D) completely

11. The air conditioner may be returned ------- six months of the purchase date free of charge.

(A) by   (B) until
(C) within   (D) on

12. The company's new Web site will make product information more ------- accessible to consumers.

(A) ready   (B) readily
(C) readied   (D) readier

13. The quality control team monitors production ------- to ensure that all products meet the company's standards.

(A) close   (B) closed
(C) closely   (D) closeness

14. As a result of increasing -------, the company is offering its employees incentives.

(A) producer   (B) produces
(C) productive   (D) productivity

15. Due to high demand, there are only a few seats ------- for the upcoming workshop.

(A) avail   (B) availability
(C) available   (D) availablely

16. The CEO encouraged open communication ------- team members to foster a collaborative work environment.

(A) between
(B) among
(C) across
(D) beside

17. Ryan submitted his report yesterday, and Susan will do ------- by the end of the day.

(A) her
(B) hers
(C) herself
(D) she

18. The finance department reported that a few ------- had not been updated properly, requiring immediate attention.

(A) account
(B) accounts
(C) accounting
(D) accountants

19. Workers at the factory should wear hearing ------- devices.

(A) protect
(B) protection
(C) protected
(D) protects

20. Ms. Lee will interview the top candidates for the marketing position -------.

(A) she
(B) her
(C) hers
(D) herself

21. ------- who want to attend the seminar should contact Mr. Chang.

(A) Those
(B) Anyone
(C) Other
(D) Themselves

22. Ms. Smythe had to work overtime to finish the design as the team had only two designers, and ------- designer was away on vacation.

(A) the other
(B) others
(C) the others
(D) other

23. Many colleagues stay in touch with ------- after they've left their companies.

(A) one another
(B) another
(C) other
(D) each

24. ------- students are expected to attend Professor Kumar's history lecture.

(A) Another
(B) Much
(C) Every
(D) Many

25. Several employees found the noise from the road repairs ------- to their work.

(A) disruptive
(B) disrupt
(C) disruptions
(D) disruptively

26. The spokesperson clarified that the incident was simply a ------- and not a serious concern.

(A) mistake
(B) mistook
(C) mistaking
(D) mistaken

27. Security guards are required to remain on ------- at all times to ensure the safety of the premises.

(A) task
(B) duty
(C) transit
(D) post

28. All the office computers are now working ------- with the updated software.

(A) correcting
(B) correction
(C) corrects
(D) correctly

29. All employees are expected to attend the training session ------- their level of experience.

(A) regardless of
(B) except for
(C) according to
(D) as to

30. The Garrison Law Center has served the local community for ------- two decades.

(A) between
(B) over
(C) from
(D) during

접속사 (상관·등위·부사절접속사)

접속사란 두 개의 단어, 구, 절을 연결해 주는 역할을 하는 품사이다. 문법적으로 동등한 것들을 연결하는 등위접속사와 상관접속사가 있으며 주절과 종속절을 연결하는 종속접속사가 있다. 종속절은 유형에 따라 크게 3가지인 부사절, 명사절, 형용사절로 나뉜다.

기본 개념 이해하기

1. 등위접속사

▶ 등위접속사는 단어와 단어, 구와 구, 절과 절처럼 문법적으로 동등한 것을 연결해주는 역할을 하며 이를 병렬 구조라고 한다.

▶ 등위접속사는 문장 맨 앞에 쓰지 않는다. 등위접속사 중 so는 절과 절만 연결한다.

등위접속사	and 그리고 or 또는 but / yet 그러나 nor 또한 ~도 아닌 so 그래서

The company offers bonuses **and** incentives. 단어 – 단어
회사는 보너스와 인센티브를 제공한다.

The meeting was scheduled for 3 PM, **but** it started at 3:30 P.M. 절 – 절
회의는 오후 3시에 예정되어 있었으나, 3시 30분에 시작되었다.

The budget was reduced, **so** the department had to cut costs. 절 – 절
예산이 삭감되어서 그 부서는 비용을 절감해야 했다.

2. 상관접속사

▶ 상관접속사는 등위접속사들과 서로 짝을 이루어 함께 쓰이는 접속사이다.

▶ 등위접속사와 마찬가지로 단어와 단어, 구와 구, 절과 절을 대등하게 연결해주는 역할을 한다.

상관접속사	both A and B A와 B 둘 다	not A but B A가 아니라 B
	either A or B A나 B 둘 중 하나	neither A nor B A도 B도 아닌
	not only A but (also) B A뿐만 아니라 B도 (= B as well as A)	

Both managers **and** employees attended the meeting.
매니저들과 직원들 모두 회의에 참석했다.

The company offers **not only** competitive salaries **but also** excellent benefits.
회사는 높은 급여뿐만 아니라 우수한 복리후생도 제공한다.

Either the team will complete the task by Friday, **or** they will need to request an extension.
그 팀은 금요일까지 과제를 완료하거나 연장을 요청해야 한다.

3. 부사절 접속사

▶ 부사절이란 종속절인 『접속사 + 주어 + 동사』 형태가 문장에서 시간, 조건, 이유 등의 의미를 가지며 부사 역할을 하는 절을 말한다.

▶ 부사절 접속사가 이끄는 부사절은 주절의 앞에 오거나 뒤에 온다.

부사절 접속사의 위치	부사절 접속사 + 주어 + 동사, 주어 + 동사. 주어 + 동사 + 부사절 접속사 + 주어 + 동사.

시간	when ~할 때 until ~까지 as ~할 때, ~하면서 by the time ~까지	before ~전에 while ~동안에 as soon as ~하자마자	after ~후에 since ~이후로 once ~하고 나서
이유	because / as / since ~때문에 now that ~이므로		
양보	though / although 비록 ~에도 불구하고 even though / if 비록 ~에도 불구하고		
대조	whereas / while 반면에		
조건	if / providing (that) / provided (that) / assuming (that) ~라면 unless (= if ~ not) 만일 ~이 아니라면 in case (that) ~의 경우 in the event (that) ~의 경우		as long as ~하는 한 once 일단 ~하면
목적	so (that) ~하기 위해서 in order that ~하기 위해서		
결과	so + 형용사 / 부사 + that 너무 ~해서~하다 such + 명사 + that 너무 ~해서 ~하다		
기타	given / considering (that) ~을 고려해 볼 때 as if / though 마치 ~인 것처럼 except (that) ~을 제외하고		

The meeting will start **when** all participants arrive.
모든 참가자가 도착하면 회의가 시작될 것이다.

As the company expanded, new employees were hired.
회사가 확장되었기 때문에 신입 직원들이 채용되었다.

Even though the prices increased, customers continued to buy the products.
가격이 인상되었는데도 고객들은 그 제품을 계속 구매했다.

If you finish the project early, you can leave for the day.
프로젝트를 일찍 끝내면 그날은 퇴근해도 된다.

☑ 문법 포인트 in order that의 that은 다른 접속사와 다르게 생략할 수 없다. 또한, 같은 의미의 in order to는 뒤에 동사원형이 온다.

The manager extended the deadline **in order that** the team could complete the project.
매니저는 팀이 프로젝트를 완성할 수 있도록 기한을 연장했다.

Employees attended the training session **in order to** improve their skills.
직원들은 능력을 향상시키기 위해 교육 세션에 참석했다.

4. 접속부사

▶ 접속부사는 접속사가 아니라 부사이므로 절과 절을 연결할 수 없다. 대신 앞뒤 절의 의미를 자연스럽게 연결해주는 역할을 한다.

▶ 접속부사는 콤마와 함께 문장 맨 앞에 위치하거나 두 문장을 연결할 때는 접속사 and나 세미콜론(;)과 함께 쓰인다.

접속부사의 위치	주어 + 동사 ~. 접속부사, 주어 + 동사 ~. 주어 + 동사 ~ 접속사 and + 접속부사, 주어 + 동사 ~. 주어 + 동사 ~; 접속부사, 주어 + 동사 ~. * 『접속사 + 접속부사』 and also 또한, and then 그리고 나서, and therefore 그러므로

The new regulations were implemented **therefore** all employees must follow the updated guidelines. ✖
The new regulations were implemented. **Therefore**, all employees must follow the updated guidelines. ⭕
새 규정이 시행되었다. 그러므로, 모든 직원은 업데이트된 지침을 따라야 한다.

The meeting was canceled, **and therefore**, everyone returned to their offices.
회의가 취소되었고, 그래서, 모두 사무실로 돌아갔다.

The software update was successful; **therefore**, users can now access the new features.
소프트웨어 업데이트가 완료되었다; 따라서, 사용자들은 이제 새로운 기능을 이용할 수 있다.

 **핵심 문제 유형**

해설서 p.21

> **Q1** 등위·상관접속사
>
> The new policy will not only improve employee satisfaction ------- reduce turnover rates.
>
> (A) but also   (B) and   (C) nor   (D) yet

>> **출제 포인트** 상관접속사는 어울리는 짝끼리 쓰여야 한다.

❶ 등위접속사는 성격이 동일한 단어, 구, 절을 이어주는 역할로 문맥에 맞는 것을 선택해야 한다.

The team leader wanted to hold the meeting at 9 A.M., [**but** / and] some employees preferred a later time.
팀장은 오전 9시에 회의를 열려고 했지만, 일부 직원들은 더 늦은 시간을 원했다.

The company offers excellent benefits, [but / **and**] many employees are satisfied.
회사는 훌륭한 복리후생을 제공하며 많은 직원이 만족하고 있다.

❷ 상관접속사는 등위접속사와 짝을 이루어 함께 쓰이기 때문에 어울리는 짝끼리 기억해야 한다.

The manager needs to address **both** the staff's concerns [**and** / or] the customers' complaints during the meeting.
매니저는 회의 중에 직원들의 우려와 고객들의 불만을 모두 해결해야 한다.

Invited guests can **either** take a taxi [and / **or**] walk to the meeting venue.
초대받은 손님들은 택시를 타거나 회의 장소까지 걸어갈 수 있다.

✔ **문법 포인트** 상관접속사가 주어 자리에 있는 단어를 연결하는 경우, 주어와 동사의 수 일치에 주의해야 한다. 「both A and B」는 항상 복수 동사를 쓰며, 나머지 상관접속사는 명사 B(동사에 더 가까운 주어)를 기준으로 동사의 수를 맞춘다.

Both the proposal **and** the budget report <u>have</u> been submitted to the board for review.
제안서와 예산 보고서가 모두 이사회에 검토를 위해 제출되었다.

Either the plan to expand the business **or** <u>the strategies</u> for cost reduction <u>need</u> to be revised before the meeting.
회의 전에 사업 확장 계획이나 비용 절감 전략을 수정해야 한다.

Q2 두 가지 이상의 의미를 가진 접속사

The meeting was postponed ------- the CEO was unavailable.

(A) before   (B) while   (C) since   (D) after

>> **출제 포인트** 여러 가지 의미로 쓰이는 접속사들은 문맥에 어울리는 것을 선택해야 한다.

● 의미가 한 가지인 접속사도 있지만, 두 가지 이상의 의미를 가진 접속사들도 있다.

while	**While** the company focuses on expanding its product line, it continues to improve its existing offerings. 회사가 제품 라인 확장에 집중하는 동안 기존 제품 개선을 계속한다. **While** the new software is user-friendly, it lacks advanced features. 새로운 소프트웨어는 사용자 친화적인 반면 고급 기능이 부족하다.
since	**Since** the new product was launched, sales have increased significantly. 새로운 제품이 출시된 이후로 매출이 많이 증가했다. The project was delayed **since** the team encountered unforeseen issues. 팀이 예상치 못한 문제에 직면했기 때문에 프로젝트가 지연되었다.
as	**As** the CEO announced the new policy, the employees began to ask questions. 최고 경영자가 새로운 정책을 발표할 때 직원들이 질문을 하기 시작했다. The customer left a positive review **as** the service exceeded expectations. 서비스가 기대를 뛰어넘었기 때문에 고객이 긍정적인 리뷰를 남겼다.

✔ **문법 포인트** 접속사 since가 '~이후로'라고 해석이 될 때는 주절에 현재 완료 「have + p.p.」 시제와 함께 쓰여야 한다.

Mr. Johnson **has worked** in the marketing department since he **graduated** from college.
존슨 씨는 대학 졸업 후 마케팅 부서에서 근무해왔다.

Q3 같은 의미의 전치사와 접속사

------- Ms. Lyuba was tired, she continued working on the project until late at night.

(A) Despite　　　　(B) In spite of　　　　(C) Although　　　　(D) Even

>> **출제 포인트** 빈칸 뒤의 구조를 보고 전치사와 접속사의 자리를 구별해야 한다.

● 부사절 접속사 뒤에는 『주어 + 동사』가 포함된 절이 오고, 전치사 뒤에는 명사(구)가 와야 한다. 특히, 같은 의미의 혼동되는 접속사, 전치사, 접속부사가 함께 출제되니 품사와 의미를 정확하게 기억해야 한다.

	전치사	접속사	접속부사
~때문에	because of due to owing to	because as since now that	
~동안에	during for	while	meantime meanwhile
~임에도 불구하고	despite in spite of	although though even though even if	nonetheless nevertheless
~후에	after following	after	afterward(s) and thereafter

✔ **문법 포인트** 접속사와 전치사로 둘 다 쓰이는 단어들이므로 뒤의 구조를 보고 역할을 파악하는 것이 중요하다.

	접속사	전치사
before	~전에	~전에
after	~후에	~후에
until	~까지	~까지
since	~이후로 / ~때문에	~이후로
as	~할 때 / ~때문에	~로서
except	~을 제외하고	~을 제외하고

Before the meeting starts, please review the agenda. 접속사 + 주어 + 동사
회의가 시작되기 전에 의제를 검토해 주세요.

The report was completed **before** the deadline. 전치사 + 명사
그 보고서는 마감일 전에 완료되었다.

The traffic was heavy; -------, participants arrived on time for the meeting.

(A) because of   (B) although   (C) despite   (D) however

>> 출제 포인트   접속부사는 접속사가 아니라 부사 자리에 들어가야 한다.

❶ 접속부사는 부사이기 때문에 절과 절을 연결해줄 수 없고, 두 개의 절의 의미만 자연스럽게 연결해주는 역할을 한다. 주로 문장 맨 앞에 콤마와 함께 오거나 세미콜론(;)과 함께 쓰인다.

The company plans to expand its operations next year **therefore** it is seeking new investment opportunities. ✗
회사는 내년에 운영을 확장할 계획이다. 따라서 새로운 투자 기회를 찾고 있다.

The new policy has been well received by employees; **moreover**, it has improved overall productivity. ◎
새로운 정책은 직원들에게 호응을 얻었다; 게다가 전체적인 생산성을 향상시켰다.

The new policy has been well received by employees. **Moreover**, it has improved overall productivity. ◎
새로운 정책은 직원들에게 호응을 얻었다. 게다가 전체적인 생산성을 향상시켰다.

❷ 접속부사의 종류

양보	nevertheless / nonetheless 그럼에도 불구하고		
대조	however 그러나 on the contrary 반대로	in contrast 반대로 on the other hand 반면에	
시간	meanwhile / meantime 그 동안, 그 사이에		
첨가	in addition 게다가	additionally / moreover / furthermore / besides 게다가	
결과	therefore / thus 그러므로	as a result 그 결과	consequently 그 결과
기타	otherwise 그렇지 않으면 in fact 사실은 afterward(s) 그 다음에 accordingly 그에 따라	likewise 마찬가지로 if so 그렇다면 namely 즉	for example / instance 예를 들어 thereafter 그러고나서 rather 차라리

✔ **문법 포인트**   토익 시험에서 문맥에 알맞은 접속부사를 선택하는 문제가 파트 6에서 주로 출제되니 뜻을 정확하게 외워주도록 하자.

1. ------- offering free shipping, the store gives customers an additional 10% off on large orders.

   (A) In spite of
   (B) Besides
   (C) And
   (D) In addition

2. ------- becoming a part of our team, Mr. Johnson was employed at a competitor.

   (A) As
   (B) Before
   (C) During
   (D) Since

3. Brookside is a famous holiday spot, ------- promotes international tourism.

   (A) but
   (B) if
   (C) so
   (D) and

4. You won't be able to access the online course ------- you complete the registration process.

   (A) as
   (B) because
   (C) unless
   (D) once

5. Staff members can participate in the training session ------- they register beforehand.

   (A) unless
   (B) If
   (C) even though
   (D) because

6. ------- staff members had to leave by 5, several frequently worked overtime.

   (A) Despite
   (B) In spite of
   (C) Since
   (D) Although

7. The recently opened restaurant was so successful ------- it needed to recruit more employees.

   (A) that
   (B) because
   (C) as a result
   (D) in the event

8. The library will be inaccessible ------- it is being remodeled.

   (A) over
   (B) during
   (C) once
   (D) while

9. The customer management software was enhanced ------- staff could locate data more efficiently.

   (A) while
   (B) so that
   (C) otherwise
   (D) now that

10. The new energy-saving initiative will be implemented ------- it proves to reduce costs.

    (A) once
    (B) even if
    (C) unless
    (D) in the case of

11. We can't share our clients' data ------- their approval.

(A) regarding
(B) without
(C) if
(D) owing to

12. Employees will qualify for a reward ------- they achieve or surpass their performance targets.

(A) nevertheless
(B) providing that
(C) in order to
(D) moreover

13. The air conditioning system will be replaced ------- its ineffective performance.

(A) because of
(B) therefore
(C) in order to
(D) provided that

14. Participants who win the competition will receive ------- a gift voucher and money.

(A) not only
(B) both
(C) either
(D) neither

15. ------- completing the training program, John applied for several positions in the marketing field.

(A) Once
(B) Now that
(C) After
(D) Since

16. You can borrow the company car ------- you return it by 8 PM.

(A) unless
(B) as long as
(C) even if
(D) in case of

17. The project budget was adjusted ------- cover the costs of extra equipment.

(A) so as to
(B) for
(C) in order that
(D) moreover

18. Every staff member must join the upcoming workshop ------- they attended it the previous year.

(A) although
(B) regardless of
(C) as though
(D) in spite of

19. The cost estimated for the maintenance was incorrect, ------- therefore, we have included a revised bill.

(A) yet
(B) and
(C) or
(D) plus

20. ------- Milltek, Ltd. has achieved great success in San Francisco, it plans to establish a new office in Tokyo.

(A) As well as
(B) Because
(C) Thus
(D) So

명사절 접속사

명사절 접속사란 『접속사 + 주어 + 동사』 형태가 명사 자리인 주어, 목적어, 보어 자리에 쓰인다고 해서 붙여진 이름으로, 크게 that, whether / if, what, 의문사, 복합관계대명사 등이 이끄는 명사절이 있다. 명사절 접속사는 문장에서 명사 역할을 하며 부사절 접속사와 구별하도록 한다.

 기본 개념 이해하기

1. 명사절의 자리

▶ 명사절은 『접속사 + 주어 + 동사』 형태가 문장 내에서 명사 자리인 주어, 목적어, 보어 역할을 하는 것을 의미한다.

Whether the meeting will be held next week is still uncertain. 주어
회의가 다음 주에 열릴지 여부는 아직 불확실하다.

The manager explained **that the project deadline had been extended.** 동사의 목적어
매니저는 프로젝트 마감일이 연장되었다고 설명했다.

We are interested in **what the survey results indicate.** 전치사의 목적어
우리는 설문조사 결과가 무엇을 나타내는지에 관심이 있다.

The main concern is **that the budget will not be approved.** 보어
가장 큰 걱정은 예산이 승인되지 않을 것이라는 점이다.

2. 명사절 접속사 that '~것'

▶ 『that + 주어 + 동사』 형태가 명사처럼 주어, 목적어, 보어 자리에 들어갈 수 있다. 단, 전치사의 목적어 자리에는 쓰지 않는다.

That the product launch was successful surprised everyone. 주어
제품 출시가 성공적이었다는 것이 모두를 놀라게 했다.

It is clear **that the company will achieve its goals.** 가주어 it – 진주어 that
회사가 목표를 달성하리라는 것은 분명하다.

The team believes **(that) the new strategy will improve sales.** 목적어
팀은 새로운 전략이 매출을 개선할 것이라고 확신한다.

The biggest challenge is **that the market is highly competitive.** 보어
가장 큰 어려움은 시장 경쟁이 매우 치열하다는 점이다.

The success of the plan depends on **that everyone cooperates.** ❌
계획의 성공은 모두가 협력한다는 것에 달려 있다.

3. 명사절 접속사 what '~것'

▶ 주어, 목적어, 보어 자리에 들어갈 수 있다. what 뒤에는 불완전한 구조의 절이 온다.

What the committee decides will impact the entire company. 주어
위원회가 결정하는 것이 회사 전체에 영향을 미칠 것이다.

4. 명사절 접속사 whether/if '~인지 아닌지'

▶ whether 명사절은 주어, 목적어, 보어, 전치사 뒤 등 명사 역할을 하는 모든 자리에 쓰일 수 있지만, 같은 의미의 if 명사절은 타동사의 목적어로만 쓰인다.

▶ whether는 『whether A or B』, 『whether or not』, 『whether to부정사』의 형태로 자주 쓰인다.

Whether the client will accept the proposal remains uncertain. 주어
고객이 제안을 받아들일지 여부는 불확실하다.

The manager wondered **whether the team could meet the deadline**. 동사의 목적어
매니저는 팀이 마감일을 맞출 수 있을지 궁금해했다.

The key issue is **whether the new policy will be effective**. 보어
핵심 문제는 새로운 정책이 효과적일지 여부이다.

We are concerned about **whether the event will be canceled**. 전치사의 목적어
우리는 행사가 취소될지 여부에 대해 걱정하고 있다.

We need to decide **whether to attend the conference or not**. whether + to부정사
우리는 회의에 참석할지 여부를 결정해야 한다.

5. 명사절 접속사로 쓰이는 의문사

▶ 『의문사 + 주어 + 동사』의 형태가 문장의 주어, 목적어, 보어 자리에 들어갈 수 있다.

▶ 『의문사 + to부정사』의 축약 형태는 명사절 자리에 올 수 있으나 why는 축약 형태로 쓰이지 않는다.

how to do ~하는 법 what to do ~하는 것 where to do ~하는 곳 when to do ~하는 때

How the new software works is still a mystery to many employees. 주어
새 소프트웨어가 어떻게 작동하는지는 많은 직원에게 여전히 미스터리다.

The CEO asked **what the next steps in the project are**. 목적어
최고 경영자는 프로젝트의 다음 단계가 무엇인지 물었다.

The main concern is **where the company will open its new branch**. 보어
가장 큰 관심사는 회사가 새로운 지점을 어디에 열 것인가이다.

He explained **how to use the new equipment**. how + to부정사
그는 새로운 장비를 사용하는 법을 설명했다.

6. 복합관계대명사

▶ 『관계대명사 + ever』의 형태로 문장에서 주어와 목적어로 쓰이며, '~든지'라고 해석한다.

▶ 관계대명사와 마찬가지로 뒤에는 불완전한 구조의 절이 온다.

whoever (= anyone who) ~하는 사람 누구든지   whichever (= anything that) ~하는 것은 어느 것이든지
whatever (= anything that) ~하는 것은 무엇이든지

Whoever finishes the report first will receive a bonus. 주어
누구든지 보고서를 가장 먼저 끝낸 사람은 보너스를 받을 것이다.

The company will support **whichever project seems the most promising**. 목적어
회사는 가장 유망해 보이는 프로젝트라면 어떤 것이든 지원할 것이다.

 **핵심 문제 유형**

해설서 p.23

Q1 명사절 접속사 that

The manager announced ------- the project deadline had been extended by a week.

(A) when   (B) if   (C) that   (D) what

>> **출제 포인트** 명사절 접속사는 명사 자리에 들어가야 한다.

● 명사절 접속사 that과 함께 쓰이는 표현들

「동사 + that 절」	
announce (that) ~을 발표하다	recommend (that) ~을 권장하다
indicate (that) ~을 나타내다	suggest (that) ~을 제안하다
note (that) ~을 언급하다	ensure (that) 확실히 ~하다
state (that) ~을 명시하다	make sure (that) 확실히 ~하다

The report **indicated that** customer satisfaction had significantly improved.
보고서는 고객 만족도가 크게 향상되었음을 나타냈다.

✓ **문법 포인트** '알리다'라는 의미의 announce는 뒤에 that절이 바로 나오지만, 같은 의미의 inform이나 notify는 뒤에 사람(~에게) 목적어가 반드시 나와야 하므로 이 두 단어를 구분하는 문제가 주로 출제된다.

Mr. Kim has [announced / **informed**] us that the project deadline has been extended.
김 씨는 우리에게 프로젝트 마감일이 연장되었음을 알려주었다.

「명사 + that 동격절」	
fact that ~라는 사실	news that ~라는 소식
rumor that ~라는 소문	confirmation that ~라는 확인

The news that the company will be relocating its headquarters has surprised many employees.
회사가 본사를 이전할 것이라는 소식에 많은 직원들이 놀랐다.

「형용사 + that절」	
be aware that ~을 알고 있다	be sure that ~을 확신하다
be glad / happy / pleased that ~해서 기쁘다	be convinced that ~을 확신하다
be sorry that ~해서 유감이다	be afraid that 미안하지만 ~이다

The team **is convinced that** the new marketing strategy will increase sales significantly.
팀은 새로운 마케팅 전략이 매출을 많이 증가시킬 것이라고 확신한다.

Q2 명사절 접속사 that vs. what

The study shows ------- the company is planning to launch next quarter.

(A) what   (B) that   (C) if   (D) which

>> **출제 포인트** 뒤의 문장 구조를 보고 알맞은 명사절 접속사를 선택해야 한다.

● 명사절 접속사 that은 뒤에 완전한 구조의 절이 오지만, what은 불완전한 구조의 절이 온다.

that '~것'	주어, 동사의 목적어, 보어 역할	+ 완전한 문장
what '~것'	주어, 동사의 목적어, 전치사의 목적어, 보어 역할	+ 불완전한 문장

The department head explained **that the new policy would be implemented next month.** 동사의 목적어
부장은 새로운 정책이 다음 달에 시행될 것이라고 설명했다.

The report shows **that the sales have increased significantly this quarter.** 동사의 목적어
보고서는 이번 분기에 매출이 많이 증가했다고 보여준다.

What the customer requested was a refund for the defective product. 주어
고객이 요청한 것은 결함이 있는 제품에 대한 환불이었다.

We are unsure about **what the future holds for the organization.** 전치사의 목적어
우리는 조직의 미래가 어떻게 될지 확신하지 못한다.

Q3 명사절 접속사 whether

The decision about ------- stakeholders will invest in the new project will be made tomorrow.

(A) what   (B) whether   (C) if   (D) how

>> **출제 포인트** **명사절 접속사 if는 타동사의 목적어 역할만 할 수 있다.**

❶ 명사절 접속사 whether와 if는 '~인지 아닌지'를 의미하며, 불확실성(wonder / doubt)이나 결정을 의미하는 동사(determine / decide / choose)와 함께 쓰인다.

We are still **wondering whether** the event should be postponed due to the weather conditions.
우리는 여전히 기상 조건 때문에 행사를 연기해야 할지 고민 중이다.

The management team has not **decided whether** to implement the new policy next quarter.
경영진은 다음 분기에 새로운 정책을 시행할지 여부를 결정하지 않았다.

❷ 명사절 접속사 whether는 주어, 동사의 목적어, 전치사의 목적어, 보어 등 모든 명사 자리에 쓰일 수 있다. 반면에, 명사절 접속사 if는 타동사의 목적어로만 쓰인다.

Whether the project will be completed on time depends on the team's efficiency.
프로젝트가 제시간에 완료될지는 팀의 효율성에 달려 있다

The manager doesn't know **whether / if the report has been submitted**.
매니저는 보고서가 제출되었는지 여부를 알 수 없다.

The main question is **whether the new policy will be effective**.
주요 질문은 새로운 정책이 효과가 있을지 여부이다

❸ 명사절 접속사 whether의 다양한 형태

whether (or not) + 완전한 문장 / whether + 완전한 문장 + (or not) ~인지 아닌지
whether A or B A든지 B든지
whether to부정사 ~할지 말지

Q4 명사절 접속사로 쓰이는 의문사

The manager did not know ------- would be available for the meeting tomorrow.

(A) whom   (B) who   (C) where   (D) when

>> **출제 포인트** 동사의 목적어로 사용된 명사절을 이끄는 알맞은 의문사를 묻는다.

● 명사절 접속사로 쓰인 알맞은 의문사를 선택하기 위해선 뒤의 구조와 문맥을 보고 결정한다.

의문대명사 + 불완전한 절	who	누가 ~하는지
	what	무엇을 ~하는지, 무엇이 ~하는지
	which	어떤 것을 ~하는지, 어떤 것이 ~하는지
의문부사 + 완전한 절	when	언제 ~하는지
	where	어디서 ~하는지
	how	어떻게 ~하는지
	why	왜 ~하는지
의문형용사 + 명사	which + 명사	어떤 명사
	what + 명사	무슨 명사
	whose + 명사	누구의 명사

The committee will decide **what needs to be done next**.
그 위원회는 다음에 무엇을 해야 할지를 결정할 것이다.

Please let me know **where the conference will be held**.
회의가 어디에서 열릴 것인지 알려주세요.

The survey asks **which features are most important to users**.
그 설문조사는 어떤 기능이 사용자에게 가장 중요한지를 묻는다.

☑ **문법 포인트** 빈칸 뒤에 『형용사 / 부사 + 주어 + 동사』의 구조가 있을 때는 how가 정답이다.

The report shows **how well the new product has been received** by customers.
그 보고서는 새로운 제품이 고객들에게 얼마나 잘 받아들여졌는지를 보여준다.

1. ------- the company invested in was innovative technology to improve efficiency.

(A) That
(B) What
(C) If
(D) While

2. The board will determine ------- to collaborate with the organization.

(A) that
(B) unless
(C) whether
(D) if

3. The latest research ------- that many tourists prefer to reserve their accommodations with an app.

(A) indicated
(B) informed
(C) notified
(D) reminded

4. The committee needs to determine ------- will be responsible for organizing the annual conference.

(A) what
(B) who
(C) when
(D) how

5. The outcome of the proposal depends on ------- the team members can collaborate with one another.

(A) that
(B) what
(C) how
(D) during

6. The employees are afraid ------- they will have to interview with management on a certain date.

(A) of
(B) because of
(C) that
(D) whom

7. Gleaming Gem offers customers 30% off their total bill ------- they purchase five or more items.

(A) when
(B) so that
(C) that
(D) in that case

8. The purpose of the meeting is to determine ------- the new policy will be implemented or not next quarter.

(A) whether
(B) that
(C) when
(D) because

9. Considering her outstanding performance, ------- is no wonder that Ms. Rebecca was appointed head of department.

(A) it
(B) they
(C) this
(D) that

10. Please make sure ------- all tags are attached to the packages correctly before delivering them to the storage.

(A) if
(B) what
(C) that
(D) where

11. The policy ensures ------- the device will be exchanged if it has issues.

(A) whether
(B) why
(C) what
(D) that

12. The manager announced ------- the construction has been postponed due to unforeseen circumstances.

(A) what
(B) so that
(C) now that
(D) that

13. The marketing team is discussing ------- the campaign will succeed or not in the current market.

(A) when
(B) whether
(C) because
(D) although

14. ------- the manager gives permission by the end of the week, the team will start the project.

(A) What
(B) Whether
(C) That
(D) If

15. ------- Frenex Corp. establishes a new plant could change depending on future demand.

(A) If
(B) What
(C) Since
(D) Whether

16. ------- the company did not receive the updated address, the package was delivered on time.

(A) Even though
(B) Despite
(C) What
(D) That

17. Ms. Nataliya told us ------- she would be away for a week at a conference.

(A) while
(B) there
(C) what
(D) that

18. The manager will ------- the team members that the project deadline has been extended by one week.

(A) suggest
(B) inform
(C) notice
(D) request

19. The engineer will find out precisely ------- led to the system's shutdown.

(A) what
(B) how
(C) that
(D) why

20. The committee ------- that multiple adjustments be applied to the firm's policy.

(A) suggested
(B) mentioned
(C) stated
(D) indicated

형용사절 접속사

흔히 관계대명사를 의미하며 명사를 꾸며주는 형용사 역할을 한다고 해서 붙여진 이름이다. 관계대명사는 일반 대명사와 달리 대명사와 접속사의 역할을 동시에 할 수 있다.

 기본 개념 이해하기

1. 관계대명사의 역할

▶ 관계대명사는 『접속사 + 대명사』의 형태로 명사를 수식하는 형용사 역할을 한다. 이때 수식하는 앞 명사를 선행사라고 한다.

The man works at the company. He is very friendly.
그 남자는 그 회사에서 일한다. 그는 매우 친절하다.

⋯▸ The man works at the company, **and he** is very friendly.
그 남자는 그 회사에서 일하는데 매우 친절하다.

⋯▸ The man **who** works at the company is very friendly.
그 회사에서 일하는 남자는 매우 친절하다.

2. 관계대명사의 종류

▶ 선행사가 사람이면 who(m), 사물이나 동물이면 which를 쓴다. that은 사람과 사물을 모두 수식할 수 있다.

▶ 관계대명사도 대명사와 마찬가지로 격이 존재하며 주격, 목적격, 소유격이 있다. 관계대명사 that은 선행사와 상관없이 주격과 목적격으로는 쓸 수 있으나 소유격으로는 쓰이지 않는다.

선행사(명사)	주격	목적격	소유격
사람	who / that	whom / that	whose
사물	which / that	which / that	whose

The employee **who** manages the sales team is very competent. 주격 관계대명사
영업 팀을 관리하는 직원은 매우 능숙하다.

The project **that** the team completed was a huge success. 목적격 관계대명사
그 팀이 완료한 프로젝트는 큰 성공을 거두었다.

The employee **whom** the manager recommended received a promotion. 목적격 관계대명사
매니저가 추천한 직원은 승진되었다.

The company **whose** products are popular is expanding rapidly. 소유격 관계대명사
제품이 인기가 많은 그 회사는 빠르게 확장하고 있다.

3. 관계대명사의 한정적 용법과 계속적 용법

▶ 한정적 용법: 관계대명사절이 앞의 명사를 수식하면서 의미를 한정해준다.

▶ 계속적 용법: 관계대명사절이 콤마 뒤에서 앞의 명사에 대해 보충 설명을 해준다. 단, 관계대명사 that은 콤마 뒤에서 계속적 용법으로 쓰이지 않는다.

The candidate **that** the company hired is very experienced. 한정적 용법
회사가 고용한 후보자는 매우 경험이 많다.

The employee received a bonus, [**who** / that] organized the event. 계속적 용법
그 직원은 보너스를 받았는데, 그는 행사를 조직했다.

4. 관계대명사 that vs. 명사절 접속사 that

▶ 관계대명사 that은 앞의 명사를 수식해줘야 하며 뒤의 불완전한 절을 이끈다.

▶ 명사절 접속사 that '～것'은 뒤에 완전한 절을 이끌며 문장에서 명사 역할인 주어, 목적어, 보어로 쓰인다.

The report that was submitted yesterday received positive feedback. 관계대명사 that
어제 제출된 보고서는 긍정적인 피드백을 받았다.

The client **requested that** the company send the invoice by the end of the week. 명사절 접속사 that
고객은 회사가 주말까지 송장을 보내줄 것을 요청했다.

5. 관계부사

▶ 관계부사는 『접속사 + 부사』의 역할을 하며 선행사의 종류에 따라 when, where, why, how를 쓴다.

▶ 관계부사는 『전치사 + 관계대명사』로 바꾸어 쓸 수 있으며 뒤에는 완전한 절이 온다.

The year **when** the company was founded is 1998.
= The year **in which** the company was founded is 1998.
회사가 설립된 해는 1998년이다.

Let me show you **how** this feature works.
= Let me show you **the way** this feature works.
이 기능이 어떻게 작동하는지 보여드리겠습니다.

 **핵심 문제 유형**

해설서 p.25

Q1 관계대명사의 종류

The applicant ------- received the highest score will be offered the position.
(A) who　　　　　(B) which　　　　　(C) whose　　　　　(D) whom

>> **출제 포인트** 선행사와 뒤의 어순을 확인한 후 알맞은 관계대명사를 선택한다.

- 관계대명사가 수식하는 선행사(사람 / 사물)를 확인한 후, 뒤의 어순에 따라 관계대명사의 격을 결정한다.

선행사 + 주격 관계대명사 + 동사	주어가 빠진 불완전한 문장
선행사 + 목적격 관계대명사 + 주어 + 타동사 (목적격 관계대명사는 생략 가능)	목적어가 빠진 불완전한 문장
선행사 + 소유격 관계대명사 + 주어 + 동사 + 목적어 / 보어	완전한 문장

The woman **who** gave the presentation is our new manager. 주격 관계대명사
발표 한 그 여자는 우리 회사의 새로운 매니저이다.

The equipment **(which)** the technicians installed is functioning properly. 목적격 관계대명사
기술자들이 설치한 장비는 제대로 작동하고 있다.

The employee **whose** ideas improved the company's sales was promoted. 소유격 관계대명사
아이디어로 회사의 매출을 향상시킨 그 직원은 승진했다.

✔ **문법 포인트** 소유격 관계대명사 뒤에는 한정사가 붙지 않은 명사가 오며 이때 해석은 '(선행사)의 명사'라고 해석한다.

The company hired an engineer **whose** expertise is in renewable energy.
그 회사는 전문 지식이 재생 에너지에 있는 엔지니어를 고용했다.

Q2 선행사 + 주격 관계대명사 + 동사

The new policy which ------- by the management aims to improve employee satisfaction.

(A) was implemented   (B) implement   (C) to implement   (D) implementing

>> **출제 포인트** 주격 관계대명사 뒤의 동사는 선행사와 수 일치가 되어야 한다.

❶ 주격 관계대명사 뒤의 동사는 선행사와 수, 시제, 태를 일치시켜야 한다.

The employee who [work / **works**] in the marketing department is organizing the event.
마케팅 부서에서 일하는 직원이 행사를 준비하고 있다.

The team discussed the project that [is complete / **was completed**] last week.
그 팀은 지난주에 완료된 프로젝트에 대해 논의했다.

The proposal which [prepared / **was prepared**] by the intern received excellent reviews.
인턴이 준비한 제안서는 훌륭한 평가를 받았다.

❷ 주격 관계대명사 뒤에 be동사가 오는 경우 『주격 관계대명사 + be동사』를 함께 생략할 수 있으며 뒤에는 분사, 형용사, 전치사구 등이 남게 된다.

Those **(who are)** interested in the seminar should register by Friday. 분사구
세미나에 관심 있는 사람들은 금요일까지 등록해야 한다.

Anyone **(who is)** responsible for the project must attend the meeting. 형용사구
프로젝트를 책임지고 있는 사람은 회의에 참석해야 한다.

The parking lot **(which is)** next to the building is under construction. 전치사구
건물 옆 주차장은 공사 중이다.

Q3 관계대명사 that vs. what

This is exactly ------- I needed to solve the problem.

(A) that   (B) what   (C) which   (D) whose

>> 출제 포인트 **what은 앞에 선행사가 필요 없다.**

● 관계대명사 that과 what은 불완전한 절을 이끌지만, 가장 큰 차이는 '선행사의 유무'이다.

that	선행사가 있음 + 불완전한 문장
what (= the thing which)	선행사가 없음 + 불완전한 문장

The company offers a service **that** meets customer needs. 선행사가 있음
그 회사는 고객의 요구를 충족하는 서비스를 제공한다.

The company offers **what** the customer needs. 선행사가 없음
그 회사는 고객이 요구하는 것을 제공한다.

Q4 관계대명사 vs. 관계부사

The conference room ------- we held the meeting yesterday is located on the third floor.

(A) where   (B) which   (C) what   (D) who

>> **출제 포인트** 관계부사는 완전한 절을 이끈다.

● 관계부사는 선행사(장소, 시간, 이유, 방법)를 꾸며주며 뒤에 완전한 문장이 온다. 또한 『전치사 + 관계대명사』의 형태로 바꾸어 쓸 수 있다.

This is the park. I jog in the park every morning. 이곳은 내가 매일 아침 조깅하는 공원이다.
= This is the park which I jog in every morning.
= This is the park in which I jog every morning.
= This is the park where I jog every morning.

선행사	관계부사	전치사 + 관계대명사
장소(the place, the company)	where	at / on / in which
시간(time, day, year)	when	at / on / in which
이유(the reason)	why	for which
방법(the way)	how	in which

☑ **문법 포인트**   선행사가 the way일 경우 관계부사 how를 함께 쓰지 못하며 둘 중 하나만 쓴다.

The guide described **how** the route passes through scenic areas.
= The guide described **the way** the route passes through scenic areas.
그 가이드는 경치 좋은 지역을 어떻게 지나가는지 설명했다.

1. The list of technicians who ------- the system is posted on the notice board.

   (A) operate
   (B) operates
   (C) is operating
   (D) are being operated

2. The document ------- we examined will be presented to the management team.

   (A) that
   (B) what
   (C) whose
   (D) who

3. The report that ------- the new sales strategy will be sent to you by the end of this week.

   (A) outline
   (B) outlines
   (C) to outline
   (D) outlining

4. A number of the candidates ------- applied for the position were highly competent.

   (A) whom
   (B) whose
   (C) what
   (D) who

5. Bluewave Ltd., ------- commercials are often seen on the internet, is introducing a new service.

   (A) that
   (B) which
   (C) who
   (D) whose

6. The warehouse is the place ------- all the products are stored before shipping.

   (A) which
   (B) where
   (C) what
   (D) who

7. An orientation for staff members ------- will operate the new machines is planned for 7 October.

   (A) that
   (B) whom
   (C) whose
   (D) they

8. Greenwood Factory, ------- produces reusable packaging materials, has moved to Northwood.

   (A) which
   (B) what
   (C) where
   (D) that

9. ------- who would like to unsubscribe should contact the support team by 20 July.

   (A) Those
   (B) They
   (C) Them
   (D) Every

10. The survey was conducted by a company ------- has earned recognition in the field of sociology.

    (A) whose
    (B) that
    (C) whom
    (D) what

11. The shipment was delayed because the courier couldn't find the person ------- address was missing on the label.

(A) who
(B) whom
(C) that
(D) whose

12. Mr. Brown is curious about the date ------- Ms. Nicole submitted her assignment late.

(A) when
(B) that
(C) why
(D) which

13. VIP Club members ------- account expires this month are asked to renew before the 30th.

(A) that
(B) whose
(C) whom
(D) who

14. All of the new employees our company recruited ------- showing outstanding performance.

(A) has been
(B) be
(C) is
(D) are

15. Ms. Cassandra, ------- currently oversees JH Corporation's facility in Edinburgh, will be appointed the operations manager next quarter.

(A) who
(B) whose
(C) which
(D) where

16. The costs of electricity have risen gradually for weeks, most of ------- are predicted to decrease in October.

(A) which
(B) who
(C) whom
(D) them

17. All of the belongings that ------- not retrieved within seven days will be thrown away.

(A) is
(B) are
(C) has
(D) been

18. Terranova Construction reported ------- the planning for the Eagle Heights project is almost finished.

(A) that
(B) what
(C) since
(D) whose

19. The renovated LX Event Center, ------- can hold large numbers of attendees, is scheduled to open in November.

(A) which
(B) that
(C) where
(D) it

20. The organization recently hired an employee ------- performance has been outstanding.

(A) whose
(B) that
(C) who
(D) which

REVIEW TEST 03

해설서 p.27

1. The new software is easy to use, ------- it needs higher system requirements to run smoothly.

   (A) so
   (B) but
   (C) and
   (D) or

2. ------- various efforts to boost sales, the company's revenue did not increase.

   (A) Even
   (B) Despite
   (C) Although
   (D) Because

3. Ms. Wilson, ------- is retiring soon, will be presented with an outstanding employee award.

   (A) she
   (B) who
   (C) her
   (D) which

4. The steak dish at Jackie's Diner comes with a side of either rice ------- sweet potatoes.

   (A) neither
   (B) or
   (C) but
   (D) and

5. Stores that ------- heavily on younger workers are struggling to find suitable candidates.

   (A) relying
   (B) relies
   (C) reliant
   (D) rely

6. The new marketing strategy has been successful in increasing brand awareness; -------, it has also boosted sales significantly.

   (A) and
   (B) moreover
   (C) however
   (D) thus

7. The conclusion of the tax consulting firm was ------- the company needed to improve its budgeting.

   (A) whose
   (B) what
   (C) that
   (D) which

8. The lease agreement will be official ------- the tenant and the landlord sign it.

   (A) once
   (B) despite
   (C) but
   (D) until

9. Go Aid is an organization ------- goal is to improve living conditions across Asia.

   (A) who
   (B) which
   (C) whose
   (D) what

10. ------- FG Advertising offers reasonable rates, DTO Ads has a better reputation.

    (A) As soon as
    (B) And
    (C) However
    (D) While

11. At the 10th Landscaping Conference, Ms. Petal will present the gardening plan ------- designed last month.

    (A) she
    (B) herself
    (C) her own
    (D) hers

12. The Purchasing Department will decide ------- to purchase the new photocopier from Adalet Corp.

    (A) whether
    (B) neither
    (C) that
    (D) even if

13. The law which ------- international trade has been changed.

    (A) regulate
    (B) regulates
    (C) regulating
    (D) is regulated

14. ------- we requested immediate replacement of the parts, it took several days to book a service appointment.

    (A) However
    (B) Although
    (C) Otherwise
    (D) Yet

15. The manager needs to determine ------- the most cost-effective option for the project is.

    (A) that
    (B) what
    (C) where
    (D) how

16. ------- Ms. Kang nor Ms. Lee was appointed to the planning committee.
(A) None
(B) Both
(C) Neither
(D) Not only

17. ------- the company has reduced costs, it has also managed to improve product quality.
(A) Meanwhile
(B) While
(C) Instead
(D) Because

18. Ms. Kang was unable to attend the shareholder meeting ------- her flight was delayed.
(A) owing to
(B) as
(C) where
(D) despite

19. The report confirmed ------- the new policy had a positive impact on employee productivity.
(A) what
(B) that
(C) if
(D) when

20. Please turn off your computer ------- leaving the building to save energy.
(A) nevertheless
(B) because
(C) before
(D) so that

21. We have a new device ------- can check the entire assembly line for problems.
(A) that
(B) what
(C) so
(D) near

22. The company is opening a new office ------- clients can meet with representatives in person.
(A) what
(B) whether
(C) where
(D) if

23. Please ensure that you complete all sections of the form; _____, your application may be delayed.
(A) otherwise
(B) therefore
(C) besides
(D) nonetheless

24. The CEO explained ------- the company decided to expand into international markets.
(A) which
(B) what
(C) whose
(D) why

25. The Sales team appreciated the fact ------- they were given additional time to complete the project.
(A) which
(B) how
(C) of
(D) that

26. The report has some figures that Carol ------- before the meeting.
(A) correct
(B) has been corrected
(C) to correct
(D) will correct

27. The report highlights ------- needs to be improved in the current system to enhance efficiency.
(A) that
(B) who
(C) what
(D) where

28. Part-time staff should check the schedule ------- was revised last night.
(A) which
(B) whose
(C) whom
(D) where

29. Please let Ms. Shim know ------- you are available to lead the project by Friday.
(A) than
(B) such
(C) whether
(D) whereas

30. There will be a brief period ------- the system is offline for maintenance next week.
(A) where
(B) when
(C) which
(D) what

UNIT 12 to부정사

to부정사는 동사가 변형되어 만들어진 형태이며 문장에서 명사, 형용사, 부사의 역할을 한다.

🧠 기본 개념 이해하기

1. to부정사의 형태와 특징

▶ to부정사는 『to + 동사원형』의 형태로 문장에서 명사, 형용사, 부사의 역할을 한다.

▶ to부정사는 문장에서 동사의 역할을 할 수는 없지만 동사의 성질은 남아있기 때문에 to 다음에 오는 동사에 따라 목적어나 보어, 수식어구를 취할 수 있다.

The committee has plans **to introduce** new regulations next month.
그 위원회는 다음 달에 새로운 규정을 도입할 계획이다.

It is crucial **to become** more efficient in our daily operations.
우리 일상 업무에서 더 효율적으로 되는 것이 중요하다.

To succeed, it is necessary **to work** diligently.
성공하기 위해서는 부지런히 일하는 것이 필요하다.

2. 명사 역할

▶ to부정사는 명사처럼 주어, 목적어, 보어 자리에 올 수 있다. 단, 전치사의 목적어로는 쓰지 않는다. 이때 to부정사는 '~하는 것, ~하기'라고 해석한다.

▶ to부정사가 주어로 쓰일 때는 단수 취급하므로 3인칭 단수 동사와 함께 쓰인다.

To finish this project on time **is** crucial for the company. 주어
이 프로젝트를 제시간에 끝내는 것은 회사에 매우 중요하다.

The boss wants **to improve** employee productivity. 목적어
그 사장은 직원의 생산성을 향상시키기를 원한다.

Our goal is **to improve** customer satisfaction. 주격 보어
우리 목표는 고객 만족도를 향상시키는 것이다.

The supervisor asked the team **to complete** the project by Friday. 목적격 보어
그 상사는 팀에게 금요일까지 프로젝트를 완료하라고 요청했다.

3. 형용사 역할

▶ 형용사처럼 명사를 뒤에서 꾸며줄 수 있으며 이때 to부정사는 '~하는, ~할'이라고 해석한다.

The team found a solution **to solve** the problem. 그 팀은 문제를 해결할 방법을 찾았다.

There is a lot of work **to finish** before the deadline. 마감 기한 전에 끝내야 할 일이 많다.

4. 부사 역할

▶ 부사처럼 동사, 형용사, 부사, 문장 전체를 수식하며 목적, 이유, 결과 등을 나타낼 수 있다. 이때 to부정사는 '~해서, ~하기 위해' 등으로 해석한다.

▶ to부정사가 '~하기 위해'로 해석될 때는 『in order to + 동사원형』, 『so as to + 동사원형』 형태로도 쓸 수 있다.

The company is eager **to expand** its market reach.
그 회사는 시장 범위를 확장하길 원한다.

To increase sales, the business implemented a new strategy.
= **In order to increase** sales, the business implemented a new strategy.
매출을 증가시키기 위해, 회사는 새로운 전략을 시행했다.

You need to register early **to secure** a spot in the workshop.
= You need to register early **in order to secure** a spot in the workshop.
워크숍에서 자리를 확보하기 위해서는 일찍 등록해야 한다.

✔ **문법 포인트** 토익 시험에서는 '목적'을 나타내는 부사 역할인 『(in order) to + 동사원형』 형태가 가장 많이 출제된다.

5. 가주어 it과 의미상의 주어

▶ to부정사가 주어로 쓰이면 주어가 너무 길어지므로 가짜 주어 it으로 대체할 수 있다. 이때 it은 뜻이 없다.

▶ to부정사의 행위자를 밝혀야 할 경우 to부정사의 바로 앞에 『for + 명사 / 목적격 대명사』의 형태로 의미상의 주어를 나타낼 수 있다.

To follow company policies is crucial for maintaining order.
= **It** is crucial **to follow** company policies for maintaining order.
It is crucial **for** all staff **to follow** company policies.
전 직원은 질서 유지를 위해 회사 정책을 따라야 한다.

6. to부정사의 태

▶ to부정사는 여전히 동사의 성질을 가지고 있어 동사와 마찬가지로 능동과 수동 형태가 있다. to부정사의 수동태는 『to + be + p.p.』의 형태이다.

▶ to부정사도 동사처럼 부사의 수식을 받는다.

The company wants **to improve** the workflow. 능동태
그 회사는 작업 흐름을 개선하고자 한다.

⋯ The Workflow needs **to be improved** by the company. 수동태
회사에서 작업 흐름은 개선될 필요가 있다.

The company wants **to significantly improve** the workflow. 능동태
회사는 작업 흐름을 크게 개선하고자 한다.

⋯ The workflow needs **to be significantly improved** by the company. 수동태
회사에서 작업 흐름은 크게 개선될 필요가 있다.

해설서 p.30

Q1 to부정사를 취하는 명사

The company's decision ------- a new marketing strategy has significantly improved its sales.

(A) implement   (B) implementing   (C) to implement   (D) implemented

>> **출제 포인트** **to부정사의 수식을 받는 명사 어휘를 알아둔다.**

● to부정사는 명사 뒤에서 '~할, ~하기 위한'의 의미로 명사를 수식하는 형용사 역할을 할 수 있다.

ability to 동사원형 ~하는 능력	plan to 동사원형 ~할 계획
effort to 동사원형 ~하기 위한 노력	decision to 동사원형 ~하겠다는 결정
chance to 동사원형 ~할 기회	intention to 동사원형 ~할 의도
opportunity to 동사원형 ~할 기회	right to 동사원형 ~할 권리
attempt to 동사원형 ~할 시도	time to 동사원형 ~할 시간
need to 동사원형 ~할 필요	way to 동사원형 ~할 방법

The company has **plans to expand** its operations to overseas markets next year.
그 회사는 내년에 해외 시장으로 사업을 확장할 계획이있다.

There is a **chance to win** a prize by participating in the survey.
설문조사에 참여하면 상을 받을 기회가 있다.

Q2 목적어 자리에 to부정사를 취하는 동사

The CEO agreed ------- the proposal during the meeting.

(A) review   (B) to review   (C) reviewing   (D) reviews

>> 출제 포인트 to부정사를 목적어로 취하는 동사를 알아둔다.

● to부정사를 목적어로 취하는 동사

「동사 + 목적어(to부정사)」		
희망	want to 동사원형 ~하기를 원하다 wish to 동사원형 ~하기를 바라다 need to 동사원형 ~하기를 필요로 하다	hope to 동사원형 ~하기를 희망하다 expect to 동사원형 ~하기를 기대하다 desire to 동사원형 ~하기를 바라다
계획 / 결정	plan to 동사원형 ~하기를 계획하다 intend to 동사원형 ~할 것을 의도하다 decide to 동사원형 ~하기를 결정하다	aim to 동사원형 ~할 것을 목표로 하다 promise to 동사원형 ~할 것을 약속하다
제안 / 거절	offer to 동사원형 ~할 것을 제안하다 refuse to 동사원형 ~할 것을 거절하다	ask to 동사원형 ~할 것을 요청하다
기타	manage to 동사원형 ~을 해내다 prefer to 동사원형 ~을 선호하다 hesitate to 동사원형 ~할 것을 주저하다	afford to 동사원형 ~할 여유가 있다 fail to 동사원형 ~을 실패하다 strive to 동사원형 ~을 분투하다

The company **plans to launch** a new product next month.
그 회사는 다음 달에 신제품을 출시할 계획이다.

Most employees **hesitate to take** on additional responsibilities.
대부분의 직원은 추가적인 책임을 맡는 것을 꺼린다.

✔ **문법 포인트** 토익 시험에서는 특정 동사 뒤에 to부정사를 넣는 문제가 주로 출제되나, 반대로 to부정사를 취하는 동사를 찾는 어휘 문제가 출제되기도 하니 『동사 + to부정사』 형태를 같이 기억하자.

Q3 목적격 보어 자리에 to부정사를 취하는 동사

To increase the company's market share, the new strategy requires all
employees ------- new sales techniques.

(A) learn   (B) to learn   (C) learning   (D) learned

>> **출제 포인트** to부정사를 목적격 보어로 취하는 동사를 알아둔다.

● **to부정사를 목적격 보어로 취하는 동사**

5형식 동사가 능동태로 쓰일 때 목적격 보어 자리에 to부정사를 취할 수 있으며 이때 '누가 ~하도록 …하다'라고 해석한다.

「5형식 동사 + 목적어 + 목적격 보어(to부정사)」		
희망	want 원하다 expect 예상하다	need 필요하다	
요청	ask / request / invite 요청하다	require 요구하다	
조언 / 권장	encourage 권장하다 advise 충고하다 convince 납득시키다 cause 야기하다	urge 촉구하다 persuade 설득시키다 remind 상기시키다	+ 목적어 + 목적격 보어(to부정사)
허가	allow / permit 허가하다	enable 가능하게 하다	

The company **needs** all employees to complete the safety training by the end of the week.
회사는 모든 직원들이 이번 주 말까지 안전 교육을 이수할 것을 요구한다.

The client **requested** us to submit the project proposal before the deadline.
고객은 우리에게 마감일 이전에 프로젝트 제안서를 제출해 달라고 요청했다.

✓ **문법 포인트** 토익 시험에서는 목적격 보어로 to부정사를 취하는 동사의 수동태 모양인 「목적어 + be p.p. + to부정사」가 주로
출제된다.

The new interns **were requested to** complete the training program within two weeks.
신입 인턴들은 2주 이내에 교육 프로그램을 완료하도록 요청받았다.

Q4 to부정사를 취하는 형용사

The committee is ------- to announce the results of the competition.

(A) ready　　　　(B) readiness　　　　(C) readily　　　　(D) readied

>> 출제 포인트 **to부정사를 취하는 형용사를 알아둔다.**

● to부정사를 취하는 형용사

「be동사 + 형용사 + to부정사」	
가능	be able to 동사원형 ~할 수 있다 be willing to 동사원형 기꺼이 ~하다 be eligible to 동사원형 ~할 자격이 있다 be about to 동사원형 막 ~하려고 하다	be likely to 동사원형 ~할 것 같다 be ready to 동사원형 ~할 준비가 되다 be sure to 동사원형 반드시 ~하다
감정	be pleased / delighted to 동사원형 ~하는 것이 기쁘다 be hesitant to 동사원형 ~하는 것을 주저하다 be eager to 동사원형 ~하는 것을 열망하다	be reluctant to 동사원형 ~하는 것을 꺼리다 be proud to 동사원형 ~하는 것이 자랑스럽다

The new software **is likely to improve** productivity across all departments.
새 소프트웨어는 모든 부서의 생산성을 향상시킬 것 같다.

☑ 문법 포인트 토익 시험에서는 형용사 뒤에 to부정사를 채우는 문제가 출제되거나, to부정사를 취하는 형용사를 찾는 어휘 문제
가 주로 출제된다.

1. The CEO of LMT Corporation ------- to provide college graduates with training programs this fall.

(A) promising
(B) being promised
(C) has promised
(D) promise

2. Due to the recent renovations, Glendale Suites are currently providing free breakfast vouchers ------- in guests.

(A) to bring
(B) brings
(C) bringing
(D) brought

3. The Administration Team requested staff members ------- suggestions to enhance office productivity.

(A) sharing
(B) shares
(C) shared
(D) to share

4. The organization is dedicated to ------- its local revenue.

(A) boost
(B) boosts
(C) boosted
(D) boosting

5. Because of the declining revenue, we decided ------- the production of the Redwood Laptop line.

(A) cease
(B) ceasing
(C) ceased
(D) to cease

6. It is crucial ------- our team to examine client feedback thoroughly.

(A) to
(B) for
(C) on
(D) with

7. The staff members are eager ------- methods to enhance client satisfaction.

(A) debating
(B) to debate
(C) debates
(D) debated

8. In order ------- about this position, visit the organization's website.

(A) to inquire
(B) inquiring
(C) inquired
(D) inquires

9. Nara International wants to employ candidates with a keen passion for ------- linguistics.

(A) studying
(B) to study
(C) studies
(D) study

10. The necessary ------- for the manager role is a business administration degree.

(A) qualification
(B) to qualify
(C) qualify
(D) qualifying

11. The cold spell is expected ------- until the end of the season.

(A) remain
(B) remained
(C) to remain
(D) remaining

12. The bistro is preparing a unique dish selection ------- its decade milestone.

(A) mark
(B) marks
(C) to mark
(D) marked

13. All goods ------- on the shelf must be checked in advance.

(A) to display
(B) to be displayed
(C) display
(D) is displaying

14. Mr. Tom Cheetham, the CEO of HydroTech Corp., is ------- to step down in April.

(A) scheduled
(B) interested
(C) offered
(D) considered

15. In order to ------- your membership, please complete the online questionnaire first.

(A) extend
(B) extension
(C) extends
(D) extending

16. The personnel department aims ------- more candidates with technical expertise.

(A) to recruit
(B) recruiting
(C) recruit
(D) recruited

17. The school board planned the community forum to be ------- on June 15.

(A) host
(B) hosts
(C) hostings
(D) hosted

18. The managers intend ------- the cafe to draw more patrons.

(A) renovate
(B) to renovate
(C) to be renovated
(D) renovating

19. To head to the Lavender Bistro, ------- the lift on the right side of the entrance hall.

(A) took
(B) taking
(C) take
(D) to take

20. The manager asked the team to ------- follow the new procedures.

(A) careful
(B) carefully
(C) carelessness
(D) carelessly

동명사

동명사는 동사를 명사화한 것으로 명사 역할을 하면서 동시에 동사 성질도 가지고 있다. 동명사와 명사의 자리는 같으므로 차이점을 구별해둔다.

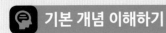 **기본 개념 이해하기**

1. 동명사의 형태와 특징

▶ 동명사는 「동사원형 + -ing」의 형태로 문장에서 명사와 같이 주어, 동사의 목적어, 전치사의 목적어, 보어 역할을 할 수 있다. 이때 동명사는 '~하는 것, ~하기'로 해석한다.

▶ 동명사가 주어로 시작하면 단수 취급하므로 3인칭 단수 동사로 수 일치를 시켜야 한다.

▶ 명사 역할을 할 수 있지만 동사의 성질이 남아있기 때문에 동사에 따라 목적어나 보어, 수식어구 등을 취할 수 있다.

Applying for a visa takes a lot of time and effort.
비자를 신청하는 것은 많은 시간과 노력이 든다.

The company postponed **launching** the new product until next quarter.
회사는 신제품 출시를 다음 분기까지 연기했다.

Remaining calm during a crisis is important.
위기 상황에서 침착함을 유지하는 것은 중요하다.

The most challenging part of the job is **dealing** with difficult customers.
이 일에서 가장 어려운 부분은 까다로운 고객을 상대하는 것이다.

2. 「전치사 + 동명사」

▶ to부정사와 명사적 쓰임이 같기 때문에 주어, 목적어, 보어 자리에는 to부정사로 바꿔 쓸 수 있다. 하지만 동명사만이 전치사의 목적어로 쓰일 수 있다는 점이 다르다.

Attending(= To attend) the workshop can enhance your skills. 주어
워크숍에 참석하는 것은 당신의 기술을 향상시킬 수 있다.

The manager began **revising(= to revise)** the report before the meeting. 동사의 목적어
매니저는 회의 전에 보고서를 수정하기 시작했다.

The main goal of the project is **reducing(= to reduce)** costs. 보어
그 프로젝트의 주요 목표는 비용을 줄이는 것이다.

The team is committed to **improving(= to improve ✕)** customer satisfaction. 전치사의 목적어
팀은 고객 만족도를 향상시키는 것에 전념하고 있다.

3. 동명사와 명사의 차이

▶ 동명사는 뒤에 목적어나 보어 등을 취할 수 있으며, 부사의 수식을 받는다.

▶ 명사는 목적어나 보어 등을 취할 수 없으며, 형용사의 수식을 받는다.

▶ 한정사 뒤에는 명사가 올 수 있지만, 동명사는 올 수 없다.

	목적어	수식어	한정사	수
동명사	O	부사	X	단수 취급
명사	X	형용사	O	단/복수 취급

The company is committed to **improving** customer satisfaction. 동명사 + 목적어
회사는 고객 만족도를 개선하는 데 전념하고 있다.

Quickly **responding** to emails is essential for effective communication. 부사 + 동명사
이메일에 빠르게 답장하는 것은 효과적인 소통에 필수적이다.

The quick **response** to the email was appreciated. 형용사 + 명사
그 이메일에 대한 빠른 응답은 감사히 여겨졌다.

The company's **improvement** in customer satisfaction is remarkable. 한정사 + 명사
회사의 고객 만족도 개선은 주목할 만하다.

4. 동명사의 관용 표현

be busy -ing ~하느라 바쁘다	spend 시간 / 돈 -ing 시간 / 돈을 ~하는 데 쓰다
keep (on) -ing 계속 ~하다	(up)on -ing ~하자마자
have difficulty (in) -ing ~하는 데 어려움을 겪다	be worth -ing ~할 가치가 있다
cannot help -ing ~하지 않을 수 없다	It is no use -ing ~해봐야 소용없다
go -ing ~하러 가다	feel like -ing ~하고 싶다

The team **spent hours discussing** the new project.
팀은 새로운 프로젝트에 대해 논의하는 데 몇 시간을 보냈다.

It is no use trying to convince him.
그를 설득하려고 해봐야 소용없다.

해설서 p.32

Q1 동명사의 자리

------- regularly helps improve work efficiency and reduce stress.

(A) Take breaks　　　(B) Took breaks　　　(C) Taking breaks　　　(D) Takes breaks

>> **출제 포인트** 동명사는 명사 자리에 들어갈 수 있다.

● 동명사는 문장 내에서 동사 역할이 아니라 명사 역할을 한다.

주어	**Implementing** new strategies can improve productivity. 새로운 전략을 실행하는 것은 생산성을 향상시킬 수 있다.
동사의 목적어	The company recommends **conducting** a market analysis before launching a new product. 회사는 신제품을 출시하기 전에 시장 분석을 수행할 것을 권장한다.
전치사의 목적어	The employees are interested in **learning** more about the company's policies. 직원들은 회사의 정책에 대해 더 배우는 것에 관심이 있다.
보어	One of the primary goals of the workshop is **enhancing** communication skills. 워크숍의 주요 목표 중 하나는 의사소통 능력을 향상시키는 것이다.

✓ **문법 포인트** 토익 시험에서는 동사의 목적어, 전치사의 목적어 자리에 동명사를 채우는 문제가 주로 출제된다. 특히, 전치사와 한정사가 붙은 명사 사이에는 동명사가 정답이다.

The manager emphasized the importance of **meeting** the deadlines.
매니저는 마감 기한을 지키는 것의 중요성을 강조했다.

Q2 동명사 vs. 명사

Although Jack was tired, he insisted on ------- the meeting.

(A) attend   (B) attending   (C) to attend   (D) attendance

>> **출제 포인트** 동명사는 동사의 성질이 남아있어 목적어 또는 보어를 가져올 수 있다.

● 동명사와 명사의 차이는 크게 3가지로 구분되어진다.

1. 목적어의 유무

명사	Thank you for your **assistance**. 도움 주셔서 감사합니다.
동명사 + 목적어	Thank you for **providing** feedback. 피드백 제공해 주셔서 감사합니다.

2. 수식어 차이

전치사 + 형용사 + 명사	With accurate **information**, the report will be finalized. 정확한 정보를 바탕으로 보고서가 작성될 것이다.
전치사 + 부사 + 동명사	With accurately **documenting** the process, errors can be minimized. 과정을 정확히 기록하면, 오류를 최소화할 수 있다.

3. 한정사 유무

한정사 + 명사	The **application** for the grant was submitted yesterday. 보조금 신청서가 어제 제출되었다.
한정사 + 동명사	The **inviting** new members is crucial for growth. 신규 회원 초대는 성장에 중요하다.

☑ **문법 포인트** 토익 시험에서는 전치사의 목적어 자리에 명사와 동명사를 구별하는 문제가 주로 출제된다. 특히, 한정사나 형용사의 수식을 받을 수 있는 '-ing 형태'의 명사들을 동명사로 착각하지 않도록 유의해야 한다.

accounting 회계	advertising 광고업	boarding 탑승	catering 출장 연회 서비스
cleaning 청소	dining 식사	funding 자금 지원	marketing 마케팅
opening 공석, 개막	processing 처리	planning 계획 수립	staffing 직원 채용
seating 좌석 배치	training 훈련	understanding 이해	widening 확장

Q3 목적어로 동명사를 취하는 동사

The committee postponed ------- the decision until next week.

(A) make   (B) making   (C) to make   (D) made

>> **출제 포인트** 동사의 목적어 자리에 to부정사와 동명사를 구분해서 선택해야 한다.

● 동사의 목적어로 to부정사가 아닌 동명사만 취하는 동사들이 있다.

「동사 + -ing」		
즐거움	enjoy -ing 즐기다	
제안	suggest -ing 제안하다	recommend -ing 추천하다 consider -ing 고려하다
중지 / 연기	finish -ing 끝내다 discontinue-ing 중단하다	quit -ing 그만두다 give up -ing 포기하다 postpone -ing 연기하다 delay -ing 연기하다
부정	avoid -ing 회피하다 deny -ing 부인하다	dislike -ing 싫어하다 mind -ing 꺼리다

The company **suggested implementing** a new training program to improve employee skills.
회사는 직원들의 능력을 향상시키기 위해 새로운 교육 프로그램을 시행할 것을 제안했다.

Most people **avoid traveling** during the peak holiday season to prevent overcrowding.
대부분의 사람들은 혼잡을 피하기 위해 성수기 동안 여행하는 것을 피한다.

✓ **문법 포인트** 토익 시험에서는 위의 동사들 뒤 목적어 자리에 to부정사와 동명사를 구별하여 선택하는 문제가 주로 출제된다.

Q4 「전치사 to + 동명사」

The company is committed to ------- the highest quality standards in its production processes.

(A) maintaining　　(B) to maintain　　(C) maintained　　(D) maintain

---

>> **출제 포인트** 전치사 to와 함께 쓰이는 동명사의 관용 표현을 묻는다.

● to부정사의 to 뒤에는 동사원형이 오는 반면에 전치사 to 뒤에는 동명사 또는 명사가 온다. 시험에서 이 두 가지를 혼동하지 않도록 「전치사 to + 동명사」의 형태를 숙어처럼 외워 두어야 한다.

대표적인 「전치사 to + 동명사」 표현	
be dedicated to -ing ∼하는 것에 헌신하다	be devoted to -ing ∼에 헌신하다
be committed to -ing ∼에 전념하다	contribute to -ing ∼에 공헌하다
look forward to -ing ∼하기를 고대하다	be used to -ing ∼에 익숙하다
object to -ing ∼에 반대하다	in addition to -ing ∼뿐만 아니라

The department **is committed to reducing** the carbon footprint.
그 부서는 탄소 발자국을 줄이는 것에 전념하고 있다.

The staff **is used to working** late hours to meet project deadlines.
직원들은 프로젝트 마감을 맞추기 위해 늦게까지 일하는 것에 익숙하다.

✓ **문법 포인트** 토익 시험에서는 전치사 to 뒤에 동사원형이 선택지에 같이 제시되니 동명사를 선택할 수 있어야 한다. 대표적인 「be + p.p. + to부정사」 구문과 정확하게 구별해서 기억해야 한다.

be + p.p. + to부정사	
be asked / requested to 동사원형 ∼하도록 요청되다	be required to 동사원형 ∼하도록 요구되다
be allowed / permitted to 동사원형 ∼하도록 허가되다	be encouraged to 동사원형 ∼하도록 권장되다
be urged to 동사원형 ∼하도록 촉구되다	be forced to 동사원형 ∼하도록 강요받다
be expected to 동사원형 ∼할 것으로 예상되다	be scheduled to 동사원형 ∼하도록 예정되다

1. Ordering a concert ticket via the app ------- less than five minutes.

   (A) is done
   (B) are done
   (C) be done
   (D) being done

2. ------- the workflow will result in increased output.

   (A) Revision
   (B) Revise
   (C) Revising
   (D) Revised

3. Learners are given additional materials for ------- enhancing the content in the course book.

   (A) effect
   (B) effects
   (C) effective
   (D) effectively

4. Clients will get complimentary dining vouchers for ------- in the questionnaire.

   (A) fill
   (B) filled
   (C) filling
   (D) to fill

5. This announcement is meant to notify motorists of ------- limitations on large vehicles in the underground parking lot.

   (A) specify
   (B) specific
   (C) specifics
   (D) specifically

6. TechNova, Inc., a global electronics -------, tries to fulfill the need for electric kettles.

   (A) provide
   (B) provider
   (C) providing
   (D) provision

7. Upon ------- examining the schedule, inform me of any necessary adjustments.

   (A) thoroughly
   (B) thoroughfare
   (C) thoroughness
   (D) thorough

8. Ms. Lee started seeking a partner following ------- a new position.

   (A) obtains
   (B) obtaining
   (C) obtained
   (D) to obtain

9. All the details regarding ------- hiring candidates are stored in the Personnel office.

   (A) current
   (B) currents
   (C) currently
   (D) currency

10. All laboratory workers are ------- to following safety protocols every day.

   (A) used
   (B) urged
   (C) expected
   (D) allowed

11. A reliable method of ------- clients is to offer a five-year warranty.

(A) engages
(B) engaging
(C) engaged
(D) engagement

12. The company has an ------- opening for a marketing manager.

(A) immediacy
(B) immediate
(C) immediately
(D) mediate

13. Next Thursday will be TechCorp's second anniversary of its -------.

(A) to launch
(B) launch
(C) launching
(D) launched

14. Event ------- will have the opportunity to sample traditional foods from various countries.

(A) participating
(B) participants
(C) participated
(D) participation

15. Glendale Industries ------- manufacturing consumer electronics due to declining sales.

(A) decided
(B) discontinued
(C) disappointed
(D) devoted

16. ------- additional technicians for the task will be our top concern.

(A) Recruiting
(B) Recruited
(C) Recruit
(D) Recruiter

17. The racks of the ChefMaster oven can be taken out for effortless -------.

(A) washed
(B) washing
(C) washer
(D) to wash

18. The concert organizer prohibited attendees from ------- the show.

(A) film
(B) filming
(C) filmed
(D) to film

19. Please be certain to acknowledge ------- of shipment #8921, expected to arrive this afternoon.

(A) receive
(B) received
(C) receipt
(D) receiving

20. The AquaPro diving device can be used underwater without losing -------.

(A) performance
(B) performed
(C) performing
(D) performative

분사

분사는 크게 현재분사와 과거분사로 나뉜다. 분사는 문장에서 형용사 역할을 하므로 명사를 수식하거나 주어와 목적어를 보충 설명해주는 보어 역할을 한다.

🗨 기본 개념 이해하기

1. 분사의 형태와 특징

▶ 현재분사: 『동사원형 + -ing』의 형태이며 능동 / 진행의 의미로 '∼하는, ∼하고 있는'이라고 해석한다.

▶ 과거분사: 『동사원형 + -ed』의 형태이며 수동 / 완료의 의미로 '∼된, ∼되는'이라고 해석한다.

▶ 분사는 문장에서 형용사 역할을 하며 명사를 앞 뒤에서 꾸며줄 수 있다.

	명사 앞 수식	명사 뒤 수식
현재분사	The **rising** cost 오르는 가격	the employees **working** at the office 사무실에서 일하고 있는 직원들
과거분사	The **updated** program 업데이트된 프로그램	The program **updated** last night 지난밤에 업데이트된 프로그램

2. 분사의 역할

▶ 분사는 형용사 역할을 하므로 명사를 수식할 뿐만 아니라 주어나 목적어를 보충 설명해주는 보어 자리에도 올 수 있다.

「2형식 동사 + 주격 보어(분사)」	The proposal seemed **promising** to the investors. 그 제안은 투자자들에게 유망해 보였다.
「5형식 동사 + 목적어 + 목적격 보어(분사)」	The presentation made the audience **amazed**. 그 발표는 청중을 놀라게 했다.

3. 형용사와 분사

▶ 형용사와 분사는 자리가 같지만, 만약 두개 중 하나를 선택해야 할 때는 의미상 차이가 없다면 형용사를 선택한다.

▶ 분사는 형용사와 마찬가지로 부사의 수식을 받는다.

The manager was [**hesitant** / hesitated] to approve the new budget proposal because it seemed too risky.
그 매니저는 새로운 예산 제안이 너무 위험해 보였기 때문에 승인을 망설였다.

The **newly** appointed CEO will meet with all employees next Monday. 부사 + 분사 + 명사
새로 임명된 최고 경영자는 다음 주 월요일에 전 직원들과 만날 예정입니다.

4. 자동사의 현재분사

▶ 자동사는 목적어가 없으므로 수동의 의미로 쓰일 수 없으며 과거분사의 형태가 없다. 즉, 반드시 현재분사 형태로만 쓰여야 한다.

현재분사로 자주 출제되는 대표적인 자동사			
work 일하다	rise 오르다	exist 존재하다	arrive 도착하다
happen 발생하다	occur 일어나다	miss 사라지다	emerge 나타나다
last 지속되다	live 살다	seem ~처럼 보이다	remain 남다

The employees **working** at the office are expected to complete the project by next Friday.
사무실에서 일하고 있는 직원들은 다음 주 금요일까지 프로젝트를 완료할 것으로 기대된다.

The **emerging** trends in technology are shaping the future of many industries.
기술에서 나타나고 있는 트렌드가 많은 산업의 미래를 형성하고 있다.

5. 분사구문

▶ 『접속사 + 주어 + 동사』의 부사절에서 『접속사 + 주어』를 생략한 후, 동사를 분사 형태로 전환하여 문장을 간결하게 만든 것을 분사구문이라고 한다. 이때 분사구문은 콤마(,)와 함께 주절의 앞 또는 뒤에 위치한다.

▶ 일반적으로 접속사를 생략하지만, 접속사의 의미를 강조하기 위해서 분사 앞에 남겨두기도 한다. 즉, 『접속사 + 분사』 형태로 쓰이기도 한다.

The report was completed, **highlighting** the key findings of the survey.
그 보고서는 작성되었으며, 설문조사의 주요 결과를 강조하고 있다.

(While) **taking** the train, passengers should ensure they have a valid ticket.
기차를 탈 때, 승객들은 유효한 티켓을 가지고 있는지 확인해야 한다.

Q1 명사를 앞에서 수식하는 분사

The ------- document was submitted to the board for review.

(A) preparing　　　(B) prepared　　　(C) prepare　　　(D) preparation

>> **출제 포인트** 분사가 명사를 앞에서 수식하는 경우는 해석을 통해 능동과 수동의 관계를 따진다.

❶ 분사가 수식하는 명사가 행동의 주체이면 능동(~중인), 그 행동을 당하는 대상이면 수동(~된) 관계가 된다. 즉, 능동으로 해석되면 현재분사를, 수동으로 해석되면 과거분사를 사용한다.

현재분사(~하는, ~중인)	the leading company 선도하는 회사
과거분사(~된, ~되는)	the limited time 제한된 시간

❷ 일반적으로 분사가 수식하는 명사와의 관계를 따져 현재분사인지 과거분사인지를 구별해야 하나, 현재분사와 과거분사를 구별할 필요없이 무조건 한 가지 형태로 굳어진 특정 분사들을 유의한다.

『현재분사 + 명사』	『과거분사 + 명사』
existing system 기존 시스템	preferred means 선호되는 수단
leading company 선두 기업	detailed information 자세한 정보
promising candidate 유망한 지원자	written permission 서면 허가
missing luggage 분실된 수화물	experienced worker 숙련된 직원
lasting impression 지속되는 인상	skilled worker 숙련된 직원
challenging task 어려운 업무	qualified applicant 자격 있는 지원자
demanding work 어려운 업무	accomplished musician 뛰어난 음악가
rewarding work 보람 있는 일	designated area 지정된 구역
remaining work 남은 업무	customized product 주문 제작된 상품
inviting offer 솔깃한 제안	reserved seats 예약된 자석
surrounding area 주변 지역	attached document 첨부된 서류

The **surrounding area** offers many recreational activities for visitors.
주변 지역은 방문객들에게 많은 레크리에이션 활동을 제공한다.

The **attached document** contains the terms and conditions of the agreement.
첨부된 서류에는 계약의 조건이 포함되어 있다.

Q2 명사를 뒤에서 수식하는 분사

The project ------- the new software will improve our productivity.

(A) developing　　　(B) developed　　　(C) development　　　(D) develop

>> **출제 포인트** 분사가 명사 뒤에서 수식하는 경우는 목적어 유무로 선택한다.

● 분사가 명사를 뒤에서 수식하는 경우는 해석이 아닌 목적어의 유무로 선택한다. 즉, 뒤에 목적어가 있으면 현재분사를, 목적어가 아닌 수식어구가 온다면 과거분사를 사용한다.

「현재분사 + 목적어」	The company received numerous applications **containing** detailed resumes. 회사는 상세한 이력서를 포함한 수많은 지원서를 받았다.
「과거분사 + 수식어구」	The documents **submitted** before the deadline will be reviewed first. 마감일 전에 제출된 문서들이 먼저 검토될 것이다.

✓ **문법 포인트** 단, 자동사의 경우는 전치 수식과 후치 수식의 여부와 상관없이 무조건 현재분사 형태로만 쓰이니 유의하자.

The students **participating** in the seminar will receive a certificate.
세미나에 참여하는 학생들은 인증서를 받을 것이다.

Q3 감정 관련 분사

The presentation was so ------- that it kept the audience engaged throughout.

(A) interesting   (B) interested   (C) interest   (D) interests

>> 출제 포인트 감정을 느끼는 대상을 찾아서 현재분사와 과거분사를 구별한다.

● 감정을 나타내는 분사는 감정을 유발하는 대상(주로 사물 명사)을 수식하면 현재분사를, 감정을 느끼게 되는 대상(주로 사람 명사)를 수식하면 과거분사를 쓴다. 즉, 사물을 수식하거나 보충 설명할 경우는 현재분사를, 사람을 수식하거나 보충 설명할 경우는 과거분사를 쓴다.

「사물 / 추상 명사 + 현재분사(-ing)」	「사람 명사 + 과거분사(p.p.)」
interesting 재미있는	interested 관심 있어 하는
exciting 신나는	excited 신이 난
pleasing 즐거운	pleased 기뻐하는
surprising 놀라운	surprised 놀란
satisfying 만족시키는	satisfied 만족한
depressing 우울하게 하는	depressed 우울한
disappointing 실망스러운	disappointed 실망한
confusing 혼란스러운	confused 혼란스러워하는
embarrassing 당황스러운	embarrassed 당황스러워하는
overwhelming 압도적인	overwhelmed 압도된
worrying 걱정스러운	worried 걱정하는
motivating 자극을 주는	motivated 자극받은
impressing 감동시키는	impressed 깊은 인상을 받은

The CEO delivered a **motivating** speech that inspired everyone.
최고 경영자는 모두에게 자극을 주는 연설을 했다.

The employees **surprised** by the unexpected bonus shared their excitement.
예상치 못한 보너스에 놀란 직원들은 기쁨을 함께 나눴다.

Q4 분사구문

------- the meeting, we decided to implement the new policy immediately.

(A) Complete   (B) Completed   (C) Completing   (D) Completes

>> 출제 포인트 **분사구문은 목적어의 유무로 푼다.**

● 분사구문의 경우, 주절의 주어와 분사구문이 능동 관계이면 현재분사를, 수동이면 과거분사를 쓴다. 이때 현재분사는 '~하면서', 과거분사는 '~되면서'로 해석하며 콤마(,)와 함께 주절의 앞이나 뒤에 위치한다.

As the company implemented the new regulations, the company managed to increase its revenue.
= (As) implementing the new regulations, the company managed to increase its revenue.
새로운 규정을 시행하면서, 회사는 수익을 증가시킬 수 있었다.

✔ 문법 포인트 일반적으로 분사를 선택할 때 주절의 주어와 능 / 수동 관계를 따지면서 풀어야 하지만, 목적어가 있으면 현재분사를 선택하고 없으면 과거분사를 고르면 되기 때문에 이 법칙만 이용하면 어렵지 않게 풀 수 있다.

When [**submitting** / submitted] the report, please ensure all sections are complete.
보고서를 제출할 때 모든 섹션이 완성되었는지 확인하세요.

When [inviting / **invited**] to the conference, prepare a presentation in advance.
회의에 초대되면 사전에 발표 자료를 준비하세요.

1. The plan ------- by the committee has received widespread support.

(A) revise
(B) revises
(C) revising
(D) revised

2. ------- restoration is required for the overpass above Maple Creek to be operational again.

(A) Substantiate
(B) Substantial
(C) Substantiated
(D) Substantiating

3. MediTech produces ------- surgical instruments for healthcare facilities in order to help reduce medical waste.

(A) reusable
(B) reuse
(C) reused
(D) reusing

4. The ------- completed report was submitted to the board just in time for the meeting.

(A) careful
(B) carefully
(C) caring
(D) carefulness

5. New employees must participate in the ------- orientation programs next Monday.

(A) designated
(B) designating
(C) designation
(D) designates

6. Numerous clients were ------- as the service failed to meet the promised standards.

(A) frustrated
(B) frustrating
(C) frustrate
(D) frustrates

7. The application ------- by H&K Solutions received an innovation prize in May.

(A) develop
(B) development
(C) developing
(D) developed

8. The tour guide made the tourists ------- with the historical explanations.

(A) satisfy
(B) satisfying
(C) satisfied
(D) satisfaction

9. As -------, our firm will arrange interviews for skilled developers next month.

(A) note
(B) notice
(C) noticing
(D) noted

10. "The Great Quest" is among the ------- films of this upcoming summer season.

(A) expect
(B) expectation
(C) expecting
(D) expected

11. Due to the ------- number of residents, construction companies are greatly needed.

(A) increase
(B) increases
(C) increasing
(D) to increase

12. The newly ------- review indicates that year-end sales have risen.

(A) publish
(B) publishing
(C) published
(D) be published

13. PSA, also ------- as the Photographic Services Association, conducts weekly workshops for enthusiasts.

(A) identified
(B) identifying
(C) identifies
(D) identify

14. Clients ------- products in large amounts may qualify for wholesale prices.

(A) acquire
(B) acquires
(C) acquiring
(D) acquired

15. Only ------- candidates will be considered for the managerial position.

(A) experience
(B) experiencing
(C) experienced
(D) experiences

16. Applicants ------- in the job should reach out to the Human Resources Department.

(A) attract
(B) attracting
(C) attracted
(D) attraction

17. The resort's ------- booking system enables guests to make reservations through the internet.

(A) renovated
(B) renovation
(C) renovate
(D) renovating

18. The new software package appears ------- and user-friendly, according to the reviews.

(A) relied
(B) relying
(C) reliable
(D) reliably

19. Any packages ------- in the storage room will be thrown away without any notice.

(A) stored
(B) storing
(C) stores
(D) store

20. The employees were ------- by the CEO's inspiring speech at the annual meeting.

(A) motivating
(B) motivated
(C) motivation
(D) motivates

비교

비교 구문은 둘 이상의 대상을 비교할 때 사용하며, 형용사와 부사의 모양을 변화시켜 원급, 비교급, 최상급 형태로 나타낸다.

 기본 개념 이해하기

1. 원급, 비교급, 최상급의 형태

▶ 비교급의 형태는 『형용사 / 부사 + -er』 또는 『more / less + 형용사 / 부사』로 표현한다.

▶ 최상급의 형태는 『형용사 / 부사 + -est』 또는 『most / least + 형용사 / 부사』로 표현한다

	원급	비교급	최상급
2음절 이하의 단어	high 높은	higher 더 높은	highest 가장 높은
2음절 이상의 단어	efficient 효율적인	more efficient 더 효율적인	most efficient 가장 효율적인

✓ **문법 포인트** 어떤 형용사와 부사는 위의 규칙을 따르지 않고 불규칙하게 형태가 변한다.

원급	비교급	최상급
good / well 좋은 / 잘	better 더 좋게	best 가장 좋은
bad / ill 좋지 않은	worse 더 좋지 않은	worst 가장 좋지 않은
many / much 많은	more 더 많은	most 가장 많은
little 적은	less 더 적은	least 가장 적은

2. 원급 비교

▶ 두 대상의 동등함을 나타내는 원급 비교는 『as + 형용사 / 부사 + as』 형태로 쓰며 이때 '~만큼 ~한'이라고 해석한다.

▶ 부정문은 『not as + 형용사 / 부사 + as』 형태로 쓰며, '~만큼 ~하지 않은'이라고 해석한다.

The new software is **as** user-friendly **as** the previous version.
새 소프트웨어는 이전 버전만큼 사용자 친화적이다.

The shipment arrived **as** quickly **as** expected.
배송은 예상만큼 빨리 도착했다.

The conference room is not **as** spacious **as** the main hall.
회의실은 대강당만큼 넓지 않다.

3. 비교급

▸ 비교급은 두 대상 중 하나가 우월하거나 열등함을 나타낼 때 비교급을 사용한다.

▸ 비교급의 형태는 『형용사 / 부사 + -er』 또는 『more / less + 형용사 / 부사』로 표현하며 '더 ~한 / 덜 ~한'이라고 해석한다.

▸ 일반적으로 비교 대상을 얘기할 때 than을 쓰지만, 비교 대상을 알 수 있는 경우는 than을 생략하기도 한다.

The budget for this year is **higher than** last year's.
올해 예산은 작년보다 더 높다.

The new printer is **more efficient than** the old one.
새 프린터는 예전 것보다 더 효율적이다.

Participants arrived **earlier than** scheduled.
참가자들은 예정된 시간보다 더 일찍 도착했다.

Employees need to work **more diligently** during peak season.
직원들은 성수기 동안 더 부지런히 일해야 한다.

The proposal was **less detailed than** anticipated.
그 제안서는 예상보다 덜 상세했다.

The updated software runs **more smoothly** on the computers (than the previous version).
업데이트된 소프트웨어는 컴퓨터에서 (이전 버전보다) 더 부드럽게 작동한다.

4. 최상급

▸ 최상급은 셋 이상의 대상들 중 최상을 나타낼 때 사용한다.

▸ 최상급의 형태는 『형용사 / 부사 + -est』 또는 『most / least + 형용사 / 부사』로 표현하며 '가장 ~한 / 가장 덜 ~한'이라고 해석한다.

▸ 최상급 앞에는 the나 소유격이 올 수 있다.

▸ 최상급 주위에는 비교 대상을 나타내는 『of + 복수 명사』, 『among + 복수 명사』, 『in + 장소』 등을 쓴다.

The latest software update is **the fastest** of all versions released this year.
최신 소프트웨어 업데이트는 올해 출시된 모든 버전 중에서 가장 빠르다.

The new product line is **the most successful** in the company's history.
새 제품 라인은 회사 역사상 가장 성공적이다.

This is **the least expensive** option among all available packages.
이것은 이용할 수 있는 모든 패키지 중에서 가장 저렴한 옵션이다.

Q1 원급 비교

The employee finished the task as ------- as possible.

(A) quick　　　　(B) quickly　　　　(C) quicker　　　　(D) quickest

>> **출제 포인트** **as ~ as 사이에는 형용사나 부사를 쓴다.**

❶ **as ~ as 비교급 사이의 형용사 / 부사 자리는 as ~ as를 지우고 구별한다.**

The report needs to be finished **as accurately as** possible.
보고서는 가능한 한 정확하게 완료되어야 한다

The equipment is **as reliable as** the latest model.
그 장비는 최신 모델만큼 신뢰할 수 있다.

❷ **여러 가지 원급 비교 표현**

as + many / much + 명사 + as	~만큼 많은
the same (+ 명사) + as	~와 같은 ~
as 형용사 / 부사 as possible	가능한 한 ~하게
not as 형용사 / 부사 as	~만큼 ~하지 않은

The company has **as many** projects **as** last year.
그 회사는 작년만큼 많은 프로젝트를 가지고 있다.

The new policy offers **the same** benefits **as** the old one.
새 정책은 이전 것과 같은 혜택을 제공한다.

Please complete the task **as efficiently as possible**.
작업을 가능한 한 효율적으로 완료해 주세요.

The product is **not as durable as** advertised.
그 제품은 광고만큼 내구성이 있지 않다.

Q2 비교급 비교

The new model is ------- than the old one in terms of energy efficiency.

(A) efficient　　　　(B) efficiently　　　　(C) more efficient　　　　(D) most efficient

>> **출제 포인트** **비교급은 형용사와 부사를 이용한다.**

❶ more ~ than 비교급 사이에 형용사 / 부사 자리는 more와 than을 지우고 구별한다.

Sales this year are **more** profitable **than** last year's due to the new marketing strategy.
올해의 매출은 새로운 마케팅 전략 덕분에 작년보다 수익성이 높다.

❷ 비교급을 강조하는 부사

비교급은 형용사와 부사로 이뤄지기 때문에 이를 꾸미는 부사가 비교급을 강조해줄 수 있다. -ly형태의 부사 외에도 아래 특정 부사들이 비교급을 강조해줄 수 있다.

even / much / still / far / a lot　　훨씬

The new design is **a lot** more appealing to customers.
새 디자인은 고객들에게 훨씬 더 매력적이다.

Our latest product is **far** more affordable than its competitors.
우리 최신 제품은 경쟁 제품들보다 훨씬 더 저렴하다.

✔ **문법 포인트** 원급만을 꾸미는 very, so, too, quite은 비교급을 강조해줄 수 없으니 비교급 앞에 선택하지 않는다.

The presentation was **so** impressive that it received a standing ovation.
프레젠테이션이 매우 인상적이어서 기립 박수를 받았다.

The workshop was **too** advanced for beginners.
워크숍은 초보자들에게는 너무 고급 수준이었다.

❸ -or형 비교급은 비교 대상 앞에 than 대신 to를 쓴다.

superior to	~보다 우수한
inferior to	~보다 열등한
prior to	~보다 이전에

The recently upgraded program is far **superior to** the old one.
최근에 업그레이드된 프로그램은 예전의 것보다 훨씬 더 우수하다.

Q3 **최상급 비교**

Among all the candidates, Jennifer is ------- qualified with her extensive experience in international marketing.

(A) more   (B) the most   (C) as   (D) less

>> **출제 포인트** **최상급은 형용사와 부사를 이용하며 비교 대상을 나타내는 범위가 있다.**

❶ **most 뒤의 형용사 / 부사 자리는 most를 지우고 구별한다.**

This product is **the most** popular among young consumers.
이 제품은 젊은 소비자들 사이에서 가장 인기가 많다.

❷ **최상급은 일반적으로 비교 대상을 나타내는 아래와 같은 범위 표현과 함께 쓰인다.**

in + 장소 명사	~안에서	among + 복수 명사	~사이에서
of + 복수 명사	~중에서	that + 주어 + have p.p.	~해왔던

This coffee shop offers the best service **in the neighborhood**.
이 커피숍은 동네에서 가장 좋은 서비스를 제공한다.

The book is the most interesting **of all the novels on the list**.
그 책은 목록에 있는 모든 소설 중에서 가장 흥미롭다.

This smartphone is the fastest **among the devices available**.
이 스마트폰은 사용 가능한 기기 중에서 가장 빠르다.

Malibu is the most beautiful beach **that I have visited so far**.
말리부는 내가 지금까지 방문한 해변 중 가장 아름다운 해변이다.

❸ **최상급을 강조하는 표현**

by far / even + 최상급	단연코
최상급 + possible	가능한 것 중에서
available	이용할 수 있는 것 중에서
ever / yet	여태껏 / 아직까지 모든 것 중에서

This solution is **by far** the most efficient we have ever used.
이 솔루션은 우리가 여태껏 사용한 것 중 단연코 가장 효율적이다.

This is the most comprehensive guide **possible** for new employees.
이것은 신입 직원들을 위한 가능한 것 중 가장 포괄적인 안내서이다.

Q4 비교 구문을 이용한 관용 표현

The old model is no ------- available for purchase.

(A) more   (B) longer   (C) later   (D) other

>> 출제 포인트 **비교급을 이용한 관용 표현들을 알아둔다.**

● 비교 구문을 이용한 관용 표현

no later than	늦어도 ~까지는	no longer	더 이상 ~않다
no sooner ~ than	~하자마자 ~하다	other than	~이외에
rather than	~보다	The 비교급 ~, the 비교급 …	~할수록 점점 더 ~하다

The report must be submitted **no later than** Friday.
보고서는 늦어도 금요일까지는 제출되어야 한다.

No sooner had the manager left the office **than** an important call came in.
매니저가 사무실을 떠나자마자 중요한 전화가 왔다.

We should focus on quality **rather than** quantity.
우리는 양보다는 질에 집중해야 한다.

The company **no longer** offers free shipping.
그 회사는 더 이상 무료 배송을 제공하지 않는다.

Other than the CEO, no one attended the meeting.
최고 경영자를 제외하고는, 아무도 회의에 참석하지 않았다.

The more you practice, **the better** you will become.
연습을 할수록 점점 더 나아질 것이다.

1. The trade organization is seeking a meeting location that is ------- bigger than NY Expo Hall.

(A) much
(B) rather
(C) slightly
(D) somewhat

2. Online advertisements are generally ------- than print ads due to lower posting costs.

(A) reason
(B) reasonably
(C) reasonable
(D) more reasonable

3. The project managers were reassured more ------- once they had reviewed the proposals.

(A) completely
(B) complete
(C) completion
(D) completing

4. Nobody at Johnson Enterprises has prepared the presentation ------- for the release of the new tablet than David Park.

(A) diligence
(B) diligently
(C) diligent
(D) more diligently

5. The new application allows staff members to assess client comments ------- than the previous method.

(A) precise
(B) more precise
(C) precisely
(D) more precisely

6. Mrs. Lee seems to be the most ------- of the other candidates.

(A) suit
(B) suits
(C) suitably
(D) suitable

7. Riverside Inn is the ------- of the region's many lodges.

(A) more charming
(B) most charming
(C) more charmingly
(D) most charmingly

8. Many client issues these days are addressed ------- quickly than in the past.

(A) as
(B) very
(C) more
(D) too

9. Glovatech acknowledges that its device is inferior ------- those created by rival firms.

(A) to
(B) than
(C) such
(D) very

10. The conference was rescheduled since the train was late by more ------- 60 minutes.

(A) for
(B) in
(C) than
(D) over

11. Mr. Kim prefers a backpack as ------- as the one he purchased last season.

(A) sturdy
(B) sturdiness
(C) more sturdy
(D) sturdily

12. Argotix's main item is cheaper ------- that of Fusion Tech.

(A) against
(B) over
(C) than
(D) by

13. Maple Shuttle's airport drop-off service is more ------- than any of its rivals'.

(A) efficiency
(B) efficiencies
(C) efficient
(D) efficiently

14. Dr. Lee's ------- report about Zenith Corp. is motivating to shareholders.

(A) late
(B) later
(C) latest
(D) lately

15. Zenon Inc. has become more ------- committed to producing smartphone parts over the last few years.

(A) tightly
(B) tight
(C) tightens
(D) tightening

16. It is crucial to select the ------- shipping materials available to prevent unintended harm.

(A) safe
(B) safer
(C) safety
(D) safest

17. Compared to last year's model, TechPro's new laptop is significantly more -------.

(A) light
(B) lighter
(C) lighting
(D) lightness

18. Zeta Electronics recently launched the ------- laptop in the market.

(A) compact
(B) more compact
(C) most compact
(D) compactly

19. Alpine Transport aims to establish the ------- system of train lines in the region.

(A) widen
(B) widespreadly
(C) more widespread
(D) most widespread

20. Sunset Airlines is renowned for providing the ------- flights from Los Angeles to San Francisco.

(A) afford
(B) most affordable
(C) most affordably
(D) affordability

REVIEW TEST 04

1. The company will make an attempt ------- its market share by launching a new product line.

(A) increase   (B) increasing
(C) increased   (D) to increase

2. The new software is ------- reliable than the older version, resulting in fewer errors.

(A) very   (B) much
(C) most   (D) more

3. Customers wishing ------- the botanical gardens may purchase tickets online or at the front gate.

(A) will explore   (B) explore
(C) exploring   (D) to explore

4. Employees are encouraged ------- in the upcoming training session to enhance their skills.

(A) participate   (B) participating
(C) to participate   (D) participation

5. Before ------- the new product, Xpando Corp did extensive research.

(A) develop   (B) developing
(C) developed   (D) to develop

6. The report ------- by the consultant contains recommendations for improving productivity.

(A) prepare   (B) prepared
(C) preparing   (D) preparation

7. The company's main plant is planning ------- production next month.

(A) to increase   (B) increasing
(C) increase   (D) increases

8. ------- to reserve the meeting room should be submitted to the receptionist.

(A) Request   (B) Requesting
(C) Requested   (D) Requests

9. The report about the ------- merger will be released tomorrow.

(A) proposed   (B) proposing
(C) propose   (D) proposal

10. LPS Machinery hopes its new product will be a ------- in the retail marketplace.

(A) succeed   (B) success
(C) successfully   (D) succeeding

11. The presenter made an ------- mistake during the speech, causing the audience to laugh.

(A) embarrassing   (B) embarrassed
(C) embarrasses   (D) embarrass

12. The manager asked the team to complete the project as ------- as possible to avoid any errors.

(A) accurate   (B) accurately
(C) more accurate   (D) more accurately

13. ------- all the data, the analyst prepared a detailed report for the management team.

(A) Collected   (B) Collection
(C) Collects   (D) Collecting

14. The oversupply of steel has made supplier prices very -------.

(A) attractive   (B) attraction
(C) attracted   (D) attracts

15. Proper safety precautions should make all workplace accidents -------.

(A) preventing   (B) preventable
(C) prevent   (D) prevention

16. All passengers are asked to ------- their airline ticket and passport to the boarding agent.

(A) presented   (B) presenting
(C) present   (D) presents

164 파고다 토익 기본 완성 RC

17. B.N. Enterprises is seeking ------- and motivated employees.

(A) to experience　(B) experienced
(C) experiences　(D) experience

18. All properties on Mulberry Lane have driveways that are capable of ------- two vehicles.

(A) parking　(B) parker
(C) parks　(D) park

19. The Vice President of the company was completely ------- with our presentation.

(A) satisfy　(B) satisfies
(C) satisfying　(D) satisfied

20. Genhardt Motors is currently considering ------- their supply tracking software.

(A) to change　(B) changing
(C) being changed　(D) changed

21. One of the ------- made by the committee will be implemented immediately.

(A) recommendations　(B) recommending
(C) recommenders　(D) recommendation

22. Our new office chairs provide the same level of comfort ------- the previous models.

(A) of　(B) for
(C) as　(D) in

23. Those interested in ------- professional development skills at the conference should sign up by October 10.

(A) to teach　(B) will teach
(C) teaching　(D) teaches

24. The antivirus software sends an alert when ------- to an external device.

(A) connecting　(B) connection
(C) connected　(D) connects

25. The latest smartphone model is ------- faster than the previous version, offering improved performance.

(A) most　(B) ever
(C) even　(D) very

26. Mr. Jones will be giving a speech to an ------- audience at the conference tomorrow.

(A) invite　(B) invitation
(C) inviting　(D) invited

27. The ------- corporate sponsors for the event are Indulsion, Inc. and M&K Enterprises.

(A) prominently　(B) more prominently
(C) most prominent　(D) prominence

28. The Marketing team is focused on ------- completing the project to meet the deadline.

(A) efficient　(B) efficiently
(C) efficiency　(D) efficiencies

29. The decline in profits made it ------- than ever to hire extra sales associates.

(A) harden　(B) hard
(C) harder　(D) hardly

30. The ------- the demand for a product, the more resources the company allocates to its production.

(A) high　(B) higher
(C) highest　(D) height

PAR

VOCA

▲

RT5

▼

단문 빈칸
채우기

UNIT 01 동사 어휘

🔍 어휘 유형 확인하기

1. 수동태 문장에서 주어로 접근하는 동사 어휘 문제

▶ 『주어 + be + p.p.』에서는 주어가 능동태에서 목적어였기 때문에 주어를 토대로 동사 어휘 문제를 푼다.

At next month's Trade Fair, Silky Cotton's new products will be [allowed / **introduced**].
다음 달 무역 박람회에서 실키 커튼의 신제품이 소개될 것이다.

The National Museum is conveniently [**located** / enclosed] near the subway.
국립 박물관은 지하철 근처에 편리하게 위치해 있다.

2. 목적어를 단서로 접근하는 동사 어휘 문제

▶ 타동사 어휘 문제는 뒤의 목적어와 문맥상 어울리는 동사를 찾는다.

The manager asked us to [**conduct** / operate] a survey before we develop products.
매니저는 우리가 제품을 개발하기 전에 설문 조사를 실시하라고 요청했다.

The company [examined / **implemented**] new policies for its hiring system.
회사는 채용 시스템을 위한 새로운 정책을 시행했다.

빈출 『타동사 + 목적어(명사)』

arrange an appointment	일정을 잡다	extend the deadline	마감일을 연장하다
address the issue	문제를 처리하다	implement the policy	정책을 실시하다
acknowledge the receipt of	~의 수령을 알리다	issue a parking permit	주차허가증을 발급하다
compile the document	문서를 편집하다	obtain a permit	허가증을 얻다
conduct a survey	설문조사 실시하다	meet the requirement	요건을 충족하다
consult the manual	매뉴얼을 참고하다	reserve the right	권리를 보유하다

3. 짝꿍 전치사를 이용한 자동사의 어휘 문제

▶ 자동사들 중에는 특정 전치사와 어울리는 『자동사 + 전치사』의 구조가 출제되기 때문에 덩어리째 기억해 두어야 한다.

The manager expects 100 people to [attend / **participate**] **in** the party.
매니저는 100명이 파티에 참여할 것으로 기대한다.

Please remember to [**register** / acquire] **for** the upcoming conference by Friday.
다가오는 회의에 금요일까지 등록하는 것을 잊지 마세요.

빈출 『자동사 + 전치사』

account for	~을 설명하다	proceed with / to	~을 / ~로 진행하다
adhere to	~을 고수하다	participate in	~에 참여하다
apply for / to	~에 지원 / 적용하다	qualify for	~할 자격을 갖추다
benefit from	~로부터 혜택을 얻다	respond / reply to	~에 반응하다 / 답변하다
collaborate with / on (사물)	~와 협력하다	refrain from	~을 삼가다
cooperate with	~와 협력하다	result from	~로부터 야기되다
compete with	~와 경쟁하다	refer to	~을 참고하다
comply with	~을 준수하다	register for (= enroll in)	~을 등록하다
contribute to	~에 기여하다	specialize in	~을 전문으로 하다
dispose of	~을 버리다 / 처분하다		

4. 빈칸 주변의 단어를 단서로 접근하는 동사 어휘 문제

▶ 해석을 하지 않아도 문장 구조를 활용하여 알맞은 동사를 선택한다.

Most companies do not [**allow** / approve] employees to smoke inside the building.
대부분의 회사는 건물 내부에서 직원들이 흡연하는 것을 허용하지 않는다.

The survey [**indicates** / intends] that more people prefer multiple jobs.
설문 조사는 더 많은 사람들이 여러 직업을 갖는 것을 선호한다는 것을 보여준다.

대표적인 『5형식 동사 + 목적어 + 목적격 보어(to부정사)』 어휘

ask + 목적어 + to부정사	요구하다	enable + 목적어 + to부정사	가능케 하다
request + 목적어 + to부정사	요구하다	encourage + 목적어 + to부정사	권장하다
require + 목적어 + to부정사	요구하다	urge + 목적어 + to부정사	강력히 권하다
remind + 목적어 + to부정사	상기시키다	expect + 목적어 + to부정사	예상하다
allow + 목적어 + to부정사	허가하다	advise + 목적어 + to부정사	조언하다
permit + 목적어 + to부정사	허가하다		

대표적인 『that절과 자주 출제되는 동사』 어휘

announce that	발표하다	ensure that	확실하게 하다
indicate that	보여주다	make sure that	확실하게 하다
confirm that	확인하다	suggest that	보여주다
complain that	불평하다	recommend that	추천하다
note that	주목 / 유의하다	anticipate that	예측하다

주의 announce와 같은 의미의 inform, notify가 어휘 문제로 제시된 경우에는 뒤에 대상(~에게)이 있는 경우만 정답이 될 수 있다.

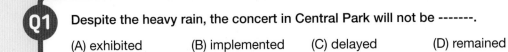

핵심 문제 유형

해설서 p.40

Q1 Despite the heavy rain, the concert in Central Park will not be -------.

(A) exhibited   (B) implemented   (C) delayed   (D) remained

Point ➤ 수동태 구조는 주어와 문맥상 어울리는 동사를 찾는다.

Q2 To ------- a library card, applicants must present a form and a valid photo ID.

(A) promote   (B) recommend   (C) complete   (D) obtain

Point ➤ 타동사 뒤 목적어와 문맥상 어울리는 동사를 찾는다.

Q3 The two firms agreed to ------- on the new project.

(A) cooperate   (B) locate   (C) invent   (D) manage

Point ➤ 빈칸 뒤 전치사와 짝을 이루는 동사를 찾아야 한다.

Q4 This voucher will ------- customers to buy clothes at half price.

(A) extend   (B) allow   (C) submit   (D) give

Point ➤ 빈칸 주변의 문장 구조를 활용하여 알맞은 동사를 찾는다.

Q5 The manager ------- employees of the new office policy.

(A) announced   (B) informed   (C) indicated   (D) conduct

Point ➤ 같은 의미의 동사가 나온다면 구조를 활용하여 구별해야 한다.

📖 필수 빈출 동사 어휘

1 **announce** 발표하다, 알리다
2 **administer** 관리 / 운영하다
3 **authorize** 승인하다
4 **approve** 승인하다
5 **appoint** 임명하다
6 **award** 수여하다
7 **address** (일 / 문제 등을) 처리하다, 연설하다
8 **benefit (from)** 혜택을 얻다
9 **accommodate** 수용하다
10 **commence** 시작하다
11 **acquire** 획득하다, 인수하다
12 **conduct** 수행하다
13 **assume** (직책 / 책임을) 떠맡다
14 **consult** 상담하다, 참고하다
15 **acknowledge** (수령을) 알리다, 인정하다
16 **compile** (문서 등을) 엮다, 편집하다
17 **allocate** 할당하다
18 **compensate** 보상하다, 배상하다
19 **arrange** 준비하다, 마련하다
20 **customize** 주문 제작하다
21 **confirm** 승인하다, 확인해주다
22 **feature** 특징으로 하다
23 **charge** 청구하다
24 **handle** (문제 등을) 다루다, 처리하다
25 **demonstrate** 보여주다, 입증하다
26 **intend (to부정사)** 의도하다
27 **display** 전시하다
28 **initiate** 시작하다
29 **designate** 지정하다
30 **implement** 시행하다

31 **extend** 연장하다
32 **issue** 발행하다, 발표하다
33 **endorse** 지지하다, 홍보하다
34 **indicate** 나타내다, 보여주다
35 **evaluate** 평가하다
36 **locate** 두다, 장소를 정하다
37 **ensure** 확실히 하다
38 **modify** 수정하다
39 **enclose** 동봉하다
40 **merge** 합병하다
41 **notify** 알리다, 통보하다
42 **represent** 나타내다, 대표하다
43 **obtain** 얻다, 구하다
44 **replace** 대체하다
45 **operate** 작동시키다
46 **release** 출시하다, 공개하다
47 **oversee** 감독하다
48 **reserve** 예약하다, (권한 등을) 보유하다
49 **propose** 제안하다, 의도하다
50 **secure** 확보하다
51 **present** 제시하다
52 **strive (to)** 노력하다
53 **proceed** 진행하다
54 **solicit** 요청하다, 간청하다
55 **qualify (for)** ~에 대한 자격을 갖추다
56 **undergo** (일 등을) 겪다, 경험하다
57 **register (for)** 등록하다
58 **verify** 확인하다, 입증하다
59 **retain** 유지하다, 보유하다
60 **waive** (요금을) 면제하다, 포기하다

VOCA UNIT 01

1. Please ------- the receipt of the shipment as soon as possible.

   (A) acknowledge
   (B) return
   (C) send
   (D) deliver

2. Before operating the new machinery, you should ------- the manual.

   (A) reject
   (B) consult
   (C) recognize
   (D) issue

3. The company plans to ------- the new dress code policy starting next quarter.

   (A) demonstrate
   (B) delay
   (C) implement
   (D) cancel

4. All candidates must ------- the requirement to be considered for the position.

   (A) indicate
   (B) meet
   (C) exceed
   (D) avoid

5. The concerns of the employees will be ------- at the monthly meeting.

   (A) relocated
   (B) addressed
   (C) dismissed
   (D) overlooked

6. Funds will be ------- to the departments based on their needs.

   (A) requested
   (B) arranged
   (C) allocated
   (D) inspected

7. Construction on the new office building is scheduled to ------- next month.

   (A) accommodate
   (B) commence
   (C) present
   (D) compensate

8. The team is working to ------- the data for the annual report.

   (A) compile
   (B) extend
   (C) register
   (D) appoint

9. The financial report will ------- for all the expenses incurred during the project.

   (A) adhere
   (B) account
   (C) comply
   (D) collaborate

10. Employees can ------- from the company's wellness program to improve their health.

    (A) refer
    (B) qualify
    (C) benefit
    (D) contribute

11. The trainer will ------- how to use the new software at the meeting.

(A) indicate
(B) demonstrate
(C) locate
(D) complicate

12. The celebrity agreed to ------- our new product in a series of advertisements.

(A) register
(B) endorse
(C) ensure
(D) refer

13. The company plans to ------- a new training program for all employees next quarter.

(A) initiate
(B) cooperate
(C) enclose
(D) merge

14. The employees were ------- to attend the training session by their manager.

(A) advised
(B) refused
(C) hesitated
(D) decided

15. The manager ------- his team to finish the project ahead of the deadline.

(A) secured
(B) strived
(C) suggested
(D) urged

16. The management ------- that the project would be completed ahead of schedule.

(A) proved
(B) committed
(C) anticipated
(D) included

17. To ------- a work visa, you must submit all the necessary documents.

(A) operate
(B) undergo
(C) obtain
(D) oversee

18. The company has ------- several key employees despite the restructuring.

(A) proceeded
(B) represented
(C) reserved
(D) retained

19. The marketing team plans to ------- a new product next month.

(A) replace
(B) notify
(C) release
(D) verify

20. The company ------- the shipping charge as part of the end-year sale.

(A) indicated
(B) waived
(C) secured
(D) enabled

명사 어휘

🔍 어휘 유형 확인하기

1. 명사 앞 단어를 단서로 접근하는 명사 어휘 문제

▶ 명사를 수식하는 형용사 및 복합 명사를 단서로 활용하여 명사를 선택한다.

The company plans to hire **qualified** [**applicants** / exhibitions] only.
회사는 자격을 갖춘 지원자만을 고용할 계획이다.

Employee [**productivity** / review] is closely related to the working environment.
직원 생산성은 근무 환경과 밀접한 관련이 있다.

빈출 『복합 명사』 어휘

budget estimate	예산 추정안	safety regulation / precaution	안전 규정 / 예방책
client satisfaction	고객 만족	sales figures	판매수치
job opening	일자리 공석	travel expenses	여행 경비
office supplies	사무용품	work shift	교대근무

2. 타동사를 단서로 접근하는 명사 어휘 문제

▶ 목적어 자리를 묻는 명사 어휘 문제는 빈칸 앞 동사와 문맥상 어울리는 단어를 찾는다.

Employees need to **follow** [**procedures** / permission] for safety.
직원들은 안전을 위해 절차를 따라야 한다.

Employees **need** [advancement / **permission**] to use parking.
직원들은 주차 공간을 사용하기 위해 허가가 필요하다.

3. 명사 뒤 전치사를 단서로 접근하는 어휘 문제

▶ 특정 전치사와 함께 『명사 + 전치사』의 구조로 쓰이는 표현들은 덩어리째 기억해 두어야 한다.

[**Admission** / participation] **to** the festival is free for residents.
축제 입장은 주민들에게 무료이다.

The company has a strong [**commitment** / presentation] **to** customer satisfaction.
회사는 고객 만족에 강한 헌신을 가지고 있다.

빈출 『명사 + 전치사』 어휘

access to	～에 대한 접근	decrease in	～에 감소
admission to	～에 입장	demand for	～에 대한 수요
alternative to	～의 대안	effect (= impact) on	～에 대한 영향
compliance with	～에 대한 준수	experience in	～에서의 경험
concern about	～에 대한 관심	emphasis on	～에 대한 강조
commitment to	～에 대한 전념 / 헌신	investment in	～에 대한 투자
contribution to	～에 공헌	increase in	～의 증가
confidence in	～에 대한 자신감	preference for	～에 대한 선호

4. 관용 표현을 이용한 명사 어휘 문제

▶ 빈칸 주변의 어구와 짝을 이루는 명사를 고르는 문제로 출제된다.

Mr. Chan received an [**opportunity** / approval] to visit the New York office this winter.
챈 씨는 올 겨울에 뉴욕 사무소를 방문할 기회를 얻었다.

We can upgrade your program online at no extra [effort / **charge**].
추가 비용 없이 온라인으로 귀하의 프로그램을 업그레이드할 수 있다.

빈출 『명사 + to부정사』 어휘

ability to부정사	～할 능력	intention to부정사	～할 의도
effort to부정사	～할 노력	opportunity to부정사	～할 기회
decision to부정사	～할 결정	obligation to부정사	～할 의무

빈출 『명사 관용어구』 표현

at no cost / charge	무료로	in advance	미리
a variety of	다양한	in transit	이동 중에
a series of	일련의	in writing	서면으로
at one's convenience	～가 편리한 때에	on call	상시 대기중인
in accordance with	～와 일치하여	until further notice	추후 통보가 있을 때까지

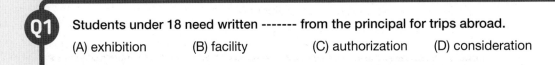

핵심 문제 유형

해설서 p.42

Q1 Students under 18 need written ------- from the principal for trips abroad.

(A) exhibition   (B) facility   (C) authorization   (D) consideration

Point 명사를 수식하는 형용사와 어울리는 명사 어휘를 찾는다.

Q2 Lab staff must observe safety ------- on the bulletin board.

(A) estimates   (B) contributions   (C) considerations   (D) regulations

Point 다른 명사와 함께 한 단어가 되는 『명사 + 명사』의 형태, 즉 '복합 명사'로도 출제된다.

Q3 The new proposal offers a viable ------- to the current system.

(A) decrease   (B) alternative   (C) maintenance   (D) initiative

Point 특정 전치사와 함께 『명사 + 전치사』의 구조로 쓰이는 명사 어휘를 찾는다.

Q4 Customer Service makes every ------- to answer questions quickly.

(A) review   (B) estimate   (C) explanation   (D) effort

Point to부정사의 수식을 받는 명사 어휘가 출제된다.

Q5 There are many things to take into ------- when planning an event.

(A) effort   (B) consideration   (C) equipment   (D) priority

Point 빈칸 주변의 어구와 같이 쓰이는 명사의 관용 표현이 출제된다.

필수 빈출 명사 어휘

1	**applicant** 지원자	
2	**compensation** 보상, 배상	
3	**approval** 승인	
4	**candidate** 지원자	
5	**authorization** 승인	
6	**construction** 건설, 공사	
7	**acquisition** 인수, 획득	
8	**division** 부서, 분할	
9	**authority** 권한, 권위자	
10	**department** 부서	
11	**alternative** 대안	
12	**demonstration** 입증, (시범) 설명	
13	**amenity** 편의시설	
14	**durability** 내구성	
15	**budget** 예산	
16	**demand** 수요, 요구	
17	**charge** 충전, 요금	
18	**entry** 입장, 출품작	
19	**compliance** 준수	
20	**evaluation** 평가	
21	**experience** 경험, 경력	
22	**issue** 문제, (정기 간행물의) 호	
23	**expertise** 전문 지식, 전문 기술	
24	**inquiry** 문의사항	
25	**expansion** 확장	
26	**initiative** 계획, 결단력	
27	**estimate** 견적, 추정, 견적서	
28	**maintenance** 유지, 보수	
29	**facility** 시설, 기관	
30	**notice** 공지	

31	**fee** 수수료, 요금	
32	**output** 생산량	
33	**inspection** 검사, 점검, 검열	
34	**opening** 공석, 개막식	
35	**identification** 신분증, 신원 확인	
36	**operating expense** 운영비, 경영비	
37	**innovation** 혁신, 획기적인 것	
38	**organization** 조직, 단체	
39	**invoice** 청구서, 송장	
40	**permission** 허가	
41	**policy** 정책	
42	**representative** 대표자, 담당 직원	
43	**productivity** 생산성	
44	**responsibility** 책임감, 책무	
45	**performance** 공연, 성과	
46	**replacement** 교체(품), 후임자	
47	**promotion** 홍보, 진급	
48	**requirement** 필요 조건	
49	**priority** 우선사항	
50	**reference** 추천, 참고	
51	**publication** 출판(물), 발행	
52	**renovation** 수리, 개조	
53	**precaution** 예방조치, 조심	
54	**reimbursement** 상환, 정산	
55	**proximity** 근접성	
56	**subscription** 구독	
57	**procedure** 절차	
58	**shift** 전환, 이동, 교대 근무 (시간)	
59	**qualification** 자격, 자질	
60	**testimonial** 추천 글	

VOCA UNIT 02

Practice

1. The company is looking to fill a job ------- in the marketing department.

(A) expense
(B) opening
(C) division
(D) description

2. Last quarter's sales ------- exceeded our expectations, showing significant growth.

(A) approval
(B) regulations
(C) figures
(D) capability

3. Employees must adjust to a new work ------- starting next month.

(A) durability
(B) satisfaction
(C) shift
(D) compliance

4. The project cannot proceed without the manager's -------.

(A) amenities
(B) compensation
(C) supplies
(D) approval

5. The company's recent ------- of a smaller firm will expand its market reach.

(A) acquisition
(B) refusal
(C) consent
(D) demand

6. If the first plan fails, we need a viable ------- to implement.

(A) demonstration
(B) authority
(C) alternative
(D) function

7. The winning ------- for the design competition will be announced next week.

(A) proof
(B) entry
(C) phase
(D) caution

8. Visitors must request ------- to the building after hours.

(A) experience
(B) issue
(C) access
(D) notice

9. The factory's operations are in strict ------- with safety regulations.

(A) compliance
(B) concern
(C) permission
(D) organization

10. The manager expressed ------- in the team's ability to meet the deadline.

(A) confidence
(B) inquiry
(C) innovation
(D) estimate

178 파고다 토익 기본 완성 RC

11. We require someone with technical ------- to lead the new project.

(A) fee
(B) identification
(C) expansion
(D) expertise

12. The annual ------- of the equipment is scheduled for next month.

(A) issue
(B) property
(C) inspection
(D) preference

13. All visitors must present valid ------- at the security desk.

(A) admission
(B) commitment
(C) innovation
(D) identification

14. The CEO announced a new ------- to improve workplace efficiency.

(A) impact
(B) initiative
(C) expansion
(D) sequence

15. The new employee demonstrated a strong ------- to handle multiple tasks efficiently.

(A) intention
(B) opportunity
(C) ability
(D) decision

16. All employees have an ------- to adhere to the company's code of conduct.

(A) obligation
(B) accordance
(C) reference
(D) appreciation

17. The office will remain closed until further ------- due to ongoing renovations.

(A) precautions
(B) notice
(C) details
(D) development

18. The company implemented a new ------- to improve workplace safety.

(A) productivity
(B) policy
(C) shift
(D) replacement

19. The ------- to the train station makes our office location very convenient.

(A) priority
(B) authority
(C) renovation
(D) proximity

20. Please provide a ------- from your previous employer to support your application.

(A) souvenir
(B) reference
(C) representative
(D) procedure

형용사 어휘

어휘 유형 확인하기

1. 주어를 단서로 접근하는 형용사 어휘

▶ be동사 뒤 보어 역할의 형용사로 쓰인 경우 주어를 보충 설명해주는 자리이므로 주어와 문맥상 어울리는 어휘를 찾아야 한다.

For guests' convenience, a manager is [**available** / operational] 24 hours a day.
손님의 편의를 위해 매니저가 24시간 대기한다.

Account information is protected and [**accessible** / effective] only to customers.
계정 정보는 보호되며 고객만 접근할 수 있다.

2. 형용사의 수식을 받는 명사를 단서로 접근하는 형용사 어휘

▶ 형용사는 명사를 수식하는 역할을 하기 때문에 수식을 받는 명사와 문맥상 어울리는 어휘를 찾아야 한다.

Ms. Smith showed [**exceptional** / acceptable] performance in her department.
스미스 씨는 그녀의 부서에서 뛰어난 성과를 보였다.

The smartphone made a [**significant** / useful] contribution to our lifestyle.
스마트폰은 우리의 생활 방식에 중요한 기여를 했다.

3. 짝꿍 전치사를 이용한 형용사 어휘 문제

▶ 특정 전치사와 함께 『be동사 + 형용사 + 전치사』의 구조로 쓰이는 표현들은 덩어리째 기억해 두어야 한다.

Our new software **is** [eligible / **capable**] **of** handling large data efficiently.
저희의 새 소프트웨어는 대용량 데이터를 효율적으로 처리할 수 있다.

Ms. Lee **is** [**familiar** / renowned] **with** the latest marketing strategies and trends.
이 씨는 최신 마케팅 전략과 트렌드에 익숙하다.

빈출 『be동사 + 형용사 + 전치사』

be aware of	~을 인식하다	be concerned about	~에 대해 걱정하다
be dedicated to	~에 헌신하다	be familiar with	~에 친숙하다
be devoted to	~에 헌신하다	be capable of	~을 할 수 있다
be committed to	~에 헌신하다	be famous for	~로 유명하다
be eligible for	~에 대한 자격이 있다	be known for	~로 유명하다
be consistent with	~와 일치하다	be renowned for	~로 유명하다
be enthusiastic about	~에 대해 열광하다	be compatible with	~와 호환되다
be responsible for	~에 대해 책임이 있다		

4. to부정사와 함께 쓰이는 형용사 어휘

▶ to부정사와 함께 『be동사 + 형용사 + to부정사』의 구조로 쓰이는 표현들은 덩어리째 기억해 두어야 한다.

We **are** not [**ready** / possible] **to launch** new products yet.
우리는 아직 신제품을 출시할 준비가 되지 않았다.

We **are** [**pleased** / available] **to announce** the promotion of Gilbert Noble.
길버트 노블의 승진을 발표하게 되어 기쁩니다.

빈출 『be동사 + 형용사 + to부정사』 표현

be able to do	~할 수 있다	be pleased to do	~하게 되어 기쁘다
be honored to do	~하게 되어 영광이다	be eager to do	~하는 것을 열망하다
be about to do	막 ~하려고 하다	be ready to do	~할 준비가 되다
be likely to do	~할 것 같다	be hesitant to do	~하는 것을 주저하다
be eligible to do	~할 자격이 있다	be sure to do	반드시 ~하다

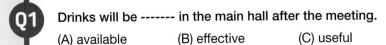

해설서 p.44

Q1 Drinks will be ------- in the main hall after the meeting.

(A) available   (B) effective   (C) useful   (D) operational

Point be동사 뒤 보어 자리의 형용사 어휘는 주어와 문맥상 어울리는 것을 찾는다.

Q2 The final stage removes ------- products from the line.

(A) vacant   (B) defective   (C) urgent   (D) responsible

Point 형용사가 수식해주는 명사와 문맥상 어울리는 어휘를 찾는다.

Q3 Companies should be ------- for their employees' safety.

(A) familiar   (B) responsible   (C) capable   (D) aware

Point 빈칸 뒤 특정 전치사와 짝을 이루는 형용사 어휘를 찾는다.

Q4 By surveying customers, the management were ------- to improve product quality.

(A) familiar   (B) able   (C) probable   (D) possible

Point 빈칸 뒤 to부정사와 짝을 이루는 형용사 어휘를 찾는다.

📖 필수 빈출 형용사 어휘

1	**available** 구할 수 있는		31	**effective** 효과적인
2	**confidential** 기밀의		32	**mandatory** 의무적인
3	**affordable** (가격이) 알맞은, 감당할 수 있는		33	**efficient** 효율적인
4	**complimentary** 무료의		34	**necessary** 필수적인, 불가피한
5	**appointed** 임명된, 지정된		35	**essential** 필수적인
6	**competitive** 경쟁력 있는		36	**ongoing** 진행 중인
7	**additional** 추가의, 부가적인		37	**frequent** 빈번한
8	**durable** 내구성이 있는		38	**operational** 운영의, 가동의
9	**accessible** 접근 가능한		39	**initial** 처음의, 초기의
10	**detailed** 상세한		40	**outstanding** 뛰어난, 미지불된
11	**accurate** 정확한		41	**promising** 유망한
12	**defective** 결함이 있는		42	**spacious** (공간이) 넓은
13	**beneficial** 유익한		43	**primary** 주요한
14	**dependent** 의존적인		44	**several** 몇몇의
15	**confident** 자신감 있는		45	**previous** 이전의
16	**dependable** 믿을 수 있는		46	**subsequent** 그 후의, 다음의
17	**competent** 유능한		47	**portable** 휴대할 수 있는
18	**distinct** 뚜렷한, 분명한		48	**thorough** 철저한, 꼼꼼한
19	**considerable** 상당한		49	**responsible** 책임감 있는
20	**diverse** 다양한		50	**temporary** 일시적인, 임시의
21	**extensive** 폭넓은		51	**reasonable** 합리적인, 타당한
22	**impressive** 인상적인		52	**tentative** 잠정적인
23	**exclusive** 독점적인		53	**renowned** 명성 있는
24	**imperative** 필수적인		54	**useful** 유용한, 도움이 되는
25	**experienced** 경력이 있는		55	**routine** 일상적인
26	**knowledgeable** 박학 다식한		56	**urgent** 긴급한
27	**exceptional** 뛰어난		57	**significant** 중요한, 상당한
28	**leading** 선도하는		58	**upcoming** 다가오는, 곧 있을
29	**eligible** 자격이 있는		59	**secure** 안전한, 확실한, 안심하는
30	**multiple** 다수의		60	**valid** (법적 / 공식적으로) 유효한

VOCA UNIT 03

1. The CEO is ------- about the future of the company.
   (A) economic
   (B) confidential
   (C) confident
   (D) valuable

2. The company offers ------- training sessions to all new employees.
   (A) accurate
   (B) defective
   (C) competent
   (D) additional

3. We need to find a ------- vendor to supply office materials regularly.
   (A) durable
   (B) dependent
   (C) dependable
   (D) distinct

4. The product received ------- attention at the trade show.
   (A) effective
   (B) competitive
   (C) considerable
   (D) considerate

5. Our company prides itself on offering ------- prices without compromising quality.
   (A) upcoming
   (B) affordable
   (C) available
   (D) ongoing

6. The new material is both lightweight and extremely -------.
   (A) comprehensive
   (B) eligible
   (C) durable
   (D) optimistic

7. The market for this product is highly -------, requiring constant innovation.
   (A) numerous
   (B) competitive
   (C) favorable
   (D) extensive

8. The new software update is ------- with most operating systems.
   (A) renowned
   (B) compatible
   (C) committed
   (D) compulsory

9. Employees are ------- to completing the project on time.
   (A) knowledgeable
   (B) exceptional
   (C) dedicated
   (D) familiar

10. Only those who meet the criteria will be ------- for the scholarship program.
    (A) eligible
    (B) frequent
    (C) capable
    (D) multiple

11. The director's performance in the recent project was truly -------.

(A) extended
(B) efficient
(C) imperative
(D) exceptional

12. Attending the training session is ------- for all new employees.

(A) aware
(B) responsible
(C) famous
(D) mandatory

13. The new employee was ------- to start working immediately.

(A) hesitant
(B) renowned
(C) responsible
(D) extensive

14. The project team is ------- to begin the next phase of the development.

(A) ready
(B) routine
(C) available
(D) competent

15. The price offered by the vendor was ------- and within our budget.

(A) significant
(B) reasonable
(C) tentative
(D) expensive

16. Ensure that all doors and windows are ------- before leaving the building.

(A) secure
(B) portable
(C) thorough
(D) tight

17. After the initial meeting, there were ------- discussions to finalize the deal.

(A) eager
(B) valid
(C) spacious
(D) subsequent

18. The sales position is ------- and will last for six months.

(A) primary
(B) competitive
(C) temporary
(D) numerous

19. The manager emphasized that this is an ------- matter requiring immediate attention.

(A) previous
(B) urgent
(C) ready
(D) renowned

20. Please ensure that your travel documents are ------- before departure.

(A) valid
(B) useful
(C) eligible
(D) ongoing

UNIT 04 부사 어휘

어휘 유형 확인하기

1. 동사로 접근하는 부사 어휘 문제

▶ 부사는 동사를 수식하는 역할을 하기 때문에 동사를 단서로 활용하여 부사를 선택한다.

Applicants must fill out the form [**completely** / somewhat].
지원자는 양식을 모두 작성해야 한다.

John Damon [**clearly** / exclusively] expressed his opinion at the conference.
존 데이몬은 회의에서 자신의 의견을 명확하게 표현했다.

빈출 『동사 + 부사』 표현

arrive punctually	정시에 도착하다	increase significantly	상당히 증가하다
begin promptly	즉시 시작하다	respond favorably	호의적으로 반응하다
decrease considerably	상당하게 감소하다	speak clearly	분명하게 말하다
expressly state	분명하게 명시하다	start immediately	즉시 시작하다
function properly	제대로 작동하다	work closely	긴밀하게 일하다

2. 형용사로 접근하는 부사 어휘 문제

▶ 부사는 형용사나 부사를 수식하는 역할을 하기 때문에 수식 받는 형용사 또는 부사와 어울리는 부사를 선택한다.

Wages are [equally / **consistently**] higher for night shift workers than day shift.
야간 근무 직원의 임금은 주간 근무 직원보다 일관되게 더 높다.

Online shopping is becoming [**increasingly** / efficiently] popular among consumers.
온라인 쇼핑은 소비자들 사이에서 점점 더 인기를 끌고 있다.

3. 특정 시제를 나타내는 부사 어휘 문제

▶ 시제를 나타내는 부사 어휘는 문장의 동사를 찾아 그 시제의 알맞은 부사 표현을 선택한다.

The company is [**currently** / previously] recovering from financial difficulties.
회사는 현재 재정적인 어려움에서 회복 중이다.

BC Appliances [recently / **periodically**] offers special discounts on their washing machines.
비씨 가전제품 회사는 그들의 세탁기에 한해서 정기적으로 특별 할인을 제공한다.

빈출 『특정 시제를 나타내는 부사』 표현

현재 시제	occasionally / sometimes 가끔	usually 보통	
	generally / typically 일반적으로	often 종종	periodically 주기적으로
현재 진행 시제	currently / now 현재		
과거 시제	previously / formerly 이전에	once 한때	
과거 / 현재 완료 시제	recently 최근에		
미래 시제	soon / shortly 곧		

4. 숫자를 수식하는 부사 어휘 문제

▶ 숫자의 품사는 형용사이기 때문에 숫자 앞에는 형용사를 수식하는 부사가 온다.

The fire drill at work is scheduled to begin at [**approximately** / closely] 10 A.M.
직장에서의 화재 훈련은 대략 오전 10시에 시작될 예정이다.

The construction is expected to take [completely / **nearly**] two years.
건설은 거의 2년이 걸릴 것으로 예상된다.

빈출 『숫자를 수식하는 부사』 표현

almost / nearly / approximately / about / around / roughly	거의, 대략
more than / over	~이상
less than / under	~이하
up to	최대 ~까지
at least	최소한
just / only	단지

🔖 핵심 문제 유형

Q1 You should dress ------- when you attend a job interview.

(A) previously   (B) thoroughly   (C) properly   (D) highly

Point 동사와 문맥상 어울리는 부사 어휘를 찾아야 한다.

Q2 The company seeks a ------- motivated sales director with 5 years' experience.

(A) increasingly   (B) equally   (C) nearly   (D) highly

Point 형용사와 문맥상 어울리는 부사 어휘를 찾는다

Q3 The company is ------- developing a new app for smartphone purchases.

(A) thoroughly   (B) previously   (C) currently   (D) properly

Point 특정 시제를 나타내는 부사 어휘는 동사를 찾아 일치시킨다.

Q4 Payday will be delayed ------- 10 days due to financial issues.

(A) generally   (B) thoroughly   (C) approximately   (D) recently

Point 수량 표현 앞에 쓰이는 부사 어휘를 찾아야 한다.

1	**approximately** 대략, 거의
2	**clearly** 분명하게
3	**automatically** 자동적으로
4	**currently** 지금, 현재
5	**anonymously** 익명으로
6	**closely** 밀접하게, 친밀하게
7	**accordingly** 그에 따라, 그에 맞춰
8	**considerably** 상당하게
9	**additionally** 추가적으로
10	**completely** 완전히
11	**annually** 일년에 한 번
12	**carefully** 조심스럽게
13	**at least** 적어도, 최소한
14	**dramatically** 극적으로
15	**briefly** 간단히
16	**directly** 곧장, 똑바로
17	**consistently** 지속적으로
18	**equally** 동일하게
19	**securely** 안전하게, 단단히
20	**efficiently** 능률적으로
21	**exclusively** 독점적으로
22	**greatly** 대단히, 크게
23	**eventually** 결국에
24	**highly** 매우, 대단히
25	**exactly** 정확하게
26	**hardly** 거의 ~않는
27	**exceptionally** 예외적으로, 유난히, 특별히
28	**immediately** 즉시
29	**extremely** 매우
30	**increasingly** 점점 더

31	**formerly** 이전에
32	**largely** 주로
33	**finally** 마침내, 최종적으로
34	**lately** 최근에
35	**frequently** 자주, 빈번히
36	**mainly** 주로
37	**generally** 일반적으로
38	**mutually** 상호적으로
39	**gradually** 점차, 서서히
40	**nearly** 대략, 거의
41	**overwhelmingly** 압도적으로
42	**significantly** 상당하게
43	**occasionally** 때때로, 가끔
44	**substantially** 상당하게
45	**previously** 이전에
46	**somewhat** 다소, 약간
47	**properly** 제대로, 적절히
48	**steadily** 꾸준하게
49	**promptly** 즉시, 신속하게
50	**shortly** 곧
51	**precisely** 정확하게
52	**thoroughly** 완전히, 철저히
53	**punctually** 시간을 엄수하여, 정각에
54	**typically** 일반적으로
55	**recently** 최근에
56	**temporarily** 임시로
57	**regularly** 정기적으로
58	**unanimously** 만장일치로
59	**rapidly** 빠르게
60	**unexpectedly** 예상외로, 뜻밖에

VOCA UNIT 04

1. The CEO ------- stated the company's new policy during the meeting.

   (A) equally
   (B) significantly
   (C) promptly
   (D) expressly

2. All employees are expected to arrive ------- for their shifts.

   (A) directly
   (B) randomly
   (C) punctually
   (D) carefully

3. The company's reputation increased ------- after the launch of the new product.

   (A) typically
   (B) considerably
   (C) shortly
   (D) closely

4. The team worked ------- to complete the project ahead of schedule.

   (A) approximately
   (B) favorably
   (C) closely
   (D) accordingly

5. The customer service representative responded ------- to the complaint.

   (A) punctually
   (B) nearly
   (C) efficiently
   (D) favorably

6. The manager ------- summarized the project's progress in the meeting.

   (A) briefly
   (B) comprehensively
   (C) accurately
   (D) directly

7. The new software update is ------- available to premium users.

   (A) eventually
   (B) once
   (C) exclusively
   (D) exactly

8. The company's CEO has been ------- mentioned in business magazines for his innovative strategies.

   (A) gradually
   (B) greatly
   (C) now
   (D) recently

9. The marketing campaign will launch ------- after the product release.

   (A) formerly
   (B) shortly
   (C) hardly
   (D) exceptionally

10. The two companies have ------- agreed on the terms of the merger.

   (A) mainly
   (B) mutually
   (C) previously
   (D) increasingly

11. The company's profits have increased
------- due to the new pricing strategy.

(A) immediately
(B) typically
(C) frequently
(D) largely

12. The building was ------- used as a
warehouse before being converted into
office space.

(A) formerly
(B) sometimes
(C) finally
(D) soon

13. The product launch was -------
successful, exceeding all sales
expectations.

(A) periodically
(B) extremely
(C) strictly
(D) separately

14. The report is ------- finished, with only a
few minor changes remaining.

(A) generally
(B) lately
(C) somewhat
(D) nearly

15. The meeting is expected to last -------
two hours.

(A) promptly
(B) roughly
(C) thoroughly
(D) steadily

16. You can apply for a loan of -------
$50,000.

(A) up to
(B) larger than
(C) shortly
(D) previously

17. The CEO ------- visits the overseas
branches to ensure everything is running
smoothly.

(A) promptly
(B) occasionally
(C) recently
(D) overwhelmingly

18. The manager expects the report to be
submitted ------- after the meeting.

(A) precisely
(B) almost
(C) promptly
(D) around

19. The new software update has made the
system ------- faster.

(A) properly
(B) almost
(C) regularly
(D) significantly

20. The office will be closed ------- for
renovations and will reopen next month.

(A) temporarily
(B) absolutely
(C) primarily
(D) evenly

REVIEW TEST

해설서 p.48

1. Before approving the budget, management requested an ------- for the total cost of the new office renovations.

(A) benefit (B) element
(C) incident (D) estimate

2. PT Beverages' marketing director ------- Ms. Kanakuro for the position.

(A) recommended (B) concluded
(C) deserved (D) recorded

3. The project timeline is ------- and may be adjusted based on the client's feedback.

(A) tentative (B) definite
(C) completed (D) immediate

4. The HR department will ------- new ID badges to all employees next week.

(A) issue (B) display
(C) remove (D) design

5. Ms. Johnson was ------- first prize for her painting in the national art contest.

(A) gotten (B) won
(C) obtained (D) awarded

6. The two departments have ------- roles within the company, with each focusing on different areas of expertise.

(A) distinct (B) common
(C) similar (D) vague

7. Riverton's Transportation Department ------- the city's bus and subway services.

(A) predicts (B) oversees
(C) views (D) commutes

8. The ------- for Ms. Nguyen's startup company was formed during her vacation in New Zealand.

(A) content (B) fact
(C) value (D) idea

9. The special discount from Heilen Groceries is available ------- until September 15.

(A) hardly (B) only
(C) barely (D) carefully

10. The new software is ------- of handling large amounts of data quickly and efficiently.

(A) aware (B) eligible
(C) familiar (D) capable

11. Many employees have expressed a ------- for flexible working hours to maintain a better work-life balance.

(A) demand (B) requirement
(C) preference (D) suggestion

12. The technician ensured that all equipment would ------- function before the event began.

(A) urgently (B) approximately
(C) properly (D) specifically

13. Customer satisfaction is a top ------- for the company, and all employees are trained to respond promptly to customer needs.

(A) priority (B) procedure
(C) obligation (D) opportunity

14. It is ------- that all employees attend the safety training to ensure a secure work environment.

(A) irrelevant (B) incomplete
(C) imperative (D) unnecessary

15. All lab technicians must adhere to official safety ------- when handling dangerous chemicals.

(A) matters (B) buildings
(C) procedures (D) installations

16. To get early notifications about ------- events, please provide your contact information.

(A) latest
(B) upcoming
(C) prepared
(D) advanced

17. The garden at Lascaux Plaza was ------- by popular outdoor artist Jean Dernier.

(A) concerned
(B) assumed
(C) planned
(D) affected

18. The new manager will ------- responsibility for overseeing the department starting next month.

(A) abandon
(B) transfer
(C) assume
(D) delegate

19. The manufacturer's decision on which model to produce is ------- on the study results.

(A) responsive
(B) dependent
(C) reliable
(D) subsequent

20. The package is currently in ------- and should arrive at the destination by tomorrow.

(A) delay
(B) shipment
(C) process
(D) transit

21. Designed last November, Fleet Footwear's new training shoes will ------- begin production next week.

(A) extremely
(B) precisely
(C) finally
(D) lately

22. A retirement reception for the Vice President will be ------ on Saturday, November 24, at the Morely Auditorium in Webster Center.

(A) opened
(B) secured
(C) invited
(D) held

23. Dr. Nasseri was ------- the department manager due to his impressive credentials.

(A) situated
(B) appointed
(C) provided
(D) decided

24. Starker Restaurant offers an ------- of menu items to appeal to diners of all ages.

(A) ingredient
(B) object
(C) array
(D) entity

25. ------- a month, Gatlin Construction Materials inspects the stock in all of its warehouses.

(A) Instantly
(B) Once
(C) Already
(D) every

26. The Wraith 1200 tablet PC ------- an improved, shatter-resistant screen.

(A) samples
(B) endures
(C) adjusts
(D) features

27. The tasks were divided ------- among all team members to ensure a fair workload.

(A) abundantly
(B) equally
(C) precisely
(D) rapidly

28. Although she studied chemical engineering, Ms. Phan ------- works in Marketing and Sales.

(A) now
(B) therefore
(C) fairly
(D) quite

29. The company continues to ------- to improve its customer service and exceed client expectations.

(A) strive
(B) reply
(C) plan
(D) achieve

30. The IT department updates the software ------- to ensure that the system remains secure and efficient.

(A) previously
(B) periodically
(C) instantly
(D) partially

PAR

RT6

장문 빈칸
채우기

PART 6

OVERVIEW

Part 6은 4문항의 문제가 있는 4개의 지문이 나와 총 16문항이 출제된다.
각각의 빈칸에 가장 적절한 단어나 구, 그리고 문장을 고르는 문제는
Part 5와 Part 7을 접목한 형태로 볼 수 있다.

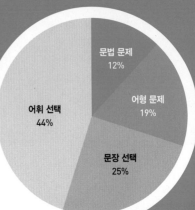

문법 문제
12%

어형 문제
19%

어휘 선택
44%

문장 선택
25%

문제 유형 분석

어형 문제 | 빈칸의 자리를 파악하여 선택지 중 알맞은 품사나 형태를 고르는 문제
어휘 선택 | 같은 품사의 네 개 어휘 중 정확한 용례를 파악하여 알맞은 단어를 고르는 문제
문법 문제 | 문장의 구조를 파악하여 구와 절을 구분하여 접속사나 전치사, 부사를 고르는 문제
문장 선택 | 앞뒤 문맥을 파악하여 네 개의 문장 중에 알맞은 문장을 고르는 문제

지문 유형

편지·이메일/기사/공지/지시문/광고/회람/설명서/발표문/정보문 등

최신 출제 경향

- 앞뒤 문맥을 통해 시제를 결정하는 문제의 출제 비중이 높다. 시제를 묻는 문제는 Part 5에서는 시간 부사구로 결정하지만, Part 6에서는 맥락으로 파악해야 한다.
- 두 문장을 자연스럽게 이어주는 접속부사를 선택하는 문제가 많이 출제된다.
- 맥락상으로 파악해야 하는 대명사의 인칭 일치 문제, 수 일치 문제가 출제된다.
- 어휘는 그 문장만 보고는 문제를 풀 수 없고 앞뒤 문맥을 파악하여 고르는 문제가 출제된다.

핵심 학습 전략

- Part 5처럼 단순히 문장 구조나 문법을 묻는 문제도 출제되지만, 전체적인 내용이나 앞뒤 문장 내용과 연결되는 어휘나 시제, 접속부사를 묻는 문제들이 주로 출제된다는 것에 유의한다.
- 문장 삽입 문제는 빈칸 앞뒤 문장의 대명사나 연결어 등을 확인하고 상관관계를 파악한다.
- 지문의 길이가 짧기 때문에 전체 내용을 파악하는 데 많은 시간이 걸리지 않으므로 정독해서 읽으면 오히려 더 쉽게 해결할 수 있다.

문제 풀이 전략

Questions 143-146 refer to the following article.

Jakarta, INDONESIA (5 June) — An Indonesian steelmaker, Irwan Steel Company, announced that it had named Maghfirah Baldraf its new Chief Operating Officer of the Java Division effective 1 September. His 30 years of experience in the ------- made him the obvious choice for the position.
143.
Baldraf majored in metal engineering at the National University of Indonesia. After graduation, he then ------- his career in the quality control department at Putirai Metal. 15 years ago, he joined
144.
Irwan Steel Company. -------. Baldraf will go to Java to oversee the daily operations of Irwan Steel
145.
Company ------- its inauguration on September 1.
146.

1. 어휘 선택

Part 5 어휘 문제와는 달리 그 한 문장만 봐서는 여러 개가 답이 될 수 있을 것 같은 선택지들이 나온다. 따라서 Part 6의 어휘 문제는 앞뒤 문맥을 정확히 파악하여 답을 골라야 한다.

143.	(A) license	(B) industry	(C) outset	(D) program

이 문제에서는 '그 산업 분야에서의 30년 경력 때문에 그가 그 자리에 확실한 선택이었다'라는 의미를 파악해서 (B)를 골라야 한다.

2. 어형 문제

한 단어의 네 가지 형태가 나오는 문제를 어형 문제 또는 자리 찾기 문제라고 한다. Part 5와 마찬가지 방법으로 풀면 되지만, 동사 시제 문제는 문맥을 파악하는 까다로운 문제로 출제된다.

144.	(A) started	(B) had started	(C) was starting	(D) will start

이 문제는 동사의 시제를 고르는 문제로 문맥상 이 사람이 처음으로 직장 생활을 시작한 것을 이야기하고 있으므로 과거 시제인 (A)가 답이 되며, then도 힌트가 될 수 있다.

3. 문장 선택

Part 6에서 가장 어려운 문제로 전체적인 문맥을 파악하고, 접속부사나, 시제 등을 종합적으로 봐야 답을 고를 수 있다.

145.	(A) The company also has a division in Singapore.
	(B) He has been interested in engineering since he was young.
	(C) Most recently, he has served as Vice President of Development of Irwan Steel Company.
	(D) As soon as Baldraf is appointed, the company will go through a major restructuring.

이 문제에서는 대학교 졸업 후부터 이 사람의 경력을 시간 순서로 나열하고 있으므로 (C)가 답이 된다.

4. 문법 문제

문법 문제는 보통 문장의 구조를 파악하여 구와 절을 구분하는 문제이다.

146.	(A) by the time	(B) as soon as	(C) when	(D) after

이 문제에서는 빈칸 뒤에 명사구가 있으므로 명사를 목적어로 취하는 전치사가 답이 되어야 하는데 보기 중에 전치사로 쓰일 수 있는 것은 (D)뿐이다.

 **시제**

Part 6의 시제 유형은 Part 5처럼 단순히 빈칸 바로 앞뒤에 있는 단서만으로 정답을 찾는 것이 아니라, 90%이상이 다른 문장 안에 단서가 있으므로 반드시 전체 지문의 흐름을 파악한 후 풀어야 한다. 따라서, 빈칸이 속한 문장 자체에서만 단서를 찾으려 한다면 함정에 빠지기 쉬우니 주의하자.

핵심 문제 유형

Question 1 refers to the following policy.

해설서 p.51

Returning goods

At Churchill Furnishing, we pride ourselves on providing great products at affordable prices. We are confident in the quality of the products we receive from our suppliers. If you are unsatisfied for any reason, call our customer service team at 384-555-1485 and you can receive a full refund. Our helpful team ------- you for your order number. When you send back your item, please include the
1.
order number. In any case where products must be shipped back to Churchill Furnishing, please note that we are not responsible for any shipping costs incurred.

---

1. (A) asking
(B) will ask
(C) asked
(D) to ask

>> 출제 포인트

1. Part 6에서 동사 선택지가 나와 있는 경우는 Part 5의 동사를 푸는 방식과 마찬가지로 『동사 자리 파악 → 가짜 동사 소거 → 수 일치 → 태 →시제』 순서로 접근한다. 시제는 전체 맥락을 파악한 후 풀어야 하기 때문에 가급적 마지막에 해결하는 것이 좋다.

2. 상단에 있는 글을 쓴 날짜나 지문 속에 있는 날짜를 통해 맥락을 파악할 수 있는 경우도 있으니 지문 속에 날짜가 나온 다면 확인해 두자.

해설서 p.51

Questions 1-4 refer to the following information.

ATTENTION LIBRARY GUESTS

The Littleton Library is preparing to revamp its online catalog system next weekend. The scheduled update ------- at 3 A.M. on Saturday, August 9. We predict that all work will be completed by 11 A.M. on Sunday, August 10. ------- this time, the library catalog system will not be available for use. -------. We thank you for your ------- and understanding.
1.   2.
3.   4.

---

1. (A) commenced
(B) had commenced
(C) to commence
(D) will commence

2. (A) On
(B) During
(C) Prior to
(D) About

3. (A) A staff member will provide assistance to you online.
(B) Some new initiatives have been proposed by the community.
(C) Some of our other services may also be affected.
(D) New library card holders will be ineligible to join.

4. (A) judgment
(B) contribution
(C) compromise
(D) patience

Questions 5-8 refer to the following job posting.

Hotel Front Desk Staff Wanted

Sumire Hill ------- for hotel front desk staff for its Hazelwood location. This role will involve
5.
booking guests in, checking guests in and out of rooms, and taking care of any requests
guests may have. Fulfilling these ------- will require you to have basic numeracy skills, excellent
6.
customer service skills, and strong attention to detail. The position requires a minimum of a high
school graduation certificate in basic office practices. ------- include knowledge of common
7.
computer software and e-mail and phone etiquette. -------.
8.

5. (A) looked
(B) had to look
(C) is looking
(D) have been looking

6. (A) qualifications
(B) guides
(C) managers
(D) duties

7. (A) These
(B) We
(C) Some
(D) Their

8. (A) Preference will be given to those with prior experience.
(B) Sumire Hill will be running a promotional event this summer.
(C) Please forward any complaints to our head office.
(D) The Hazelwood location is among our busiest.

Questions 9-12 refer to the following notice.

Attention, Palmdale Fitness Center members:

Our annual health fair is scheduled to take place on Saturday, January 3, from 1:30 P.M. to 4 P.M.

Fitness trainers, dieticians, and health educators will be attending to provide answers on any

questions you may have ------- your health goals, exercise plans, and your diet.
9.

-------. While no registration is necessary to attend, scheduling is recommended if you would like
10.

a personalized -------. We at Palmdale Fitness Center hope to see many of you in attendance
11.

and we ------- for a happy and prosperous new year.
12.

9. (A) onto
   (B) about
   (C) owing to
   (D) in place of

10. (A) The event will take place in the
       conference room on the second floor.
    (B) Any expenses should be reported to
       the finance team.
    (C) Suggestions to the current schedule
       are encouraged.
    (D) The promotion will run until the end of
       the month.

11. (A) forum
    (B) consultation
    (C) direction
    (D) reception

12. (A) wishing
    (B) wishes
    (C) wished
    (D) wish

Questions 13-16 refer to the following article.

Brothers Make a Difference

HAIG (11 October)—Over the past decade, Frank and Benny Horton have consistently been named the sharpest minds in the computing sector. -------. Their work has revolved around
13.
providing extensive software packages, which usually cost businesses thousands of dollars a year, at affordable prices to small businesses.

Both were high achievers at school, and some of the earliest accomplishments ------- turning
14.
PristineFlow Solutions into a household name. "Our parents ran their own store, and the prices they paid for basic software was ridiculous. Our mission was then to create solutions -------
15.
can benefit from," said Frank Horton. -------, Benny added that running a business should be
16.
something that is affordable.

---

13. (A) They were raised overseas.
(B) That has not changed this year.
(C) They were originally working as teachers.
(D) This award was well-deserved.

14. (A) are including
(B) will include
(C) can include
(D) include

15. (A) business owners
(B) students
(C) associations
(D) governments

16. (A) Although
(B) Likewise
(C) For instance
(D) Therefore

대명사

Part 6에서도 Part 5와 마찬가지로 빈칸에 알맞은 대명사를 선택하는 유형이 자주 등장한다. 대명사 뒤의 동사와 수 일치를 맞춰서 푸는 Part 5 대명사 문제 유형과는 다르게, Part 6는 문맥을 파악한 후 앞에 지칭하는 대상을 찾아 푸는 문제 유형이 출제된다. 즉, 수일치로 정답이 결정되는 경우는 드물다.

📖 핵심 문제 유형

Question 1 refers to the following announcement.

해설서 p.53

We invite you to Richmond Arts Center and enjoy a fun time learning how to craft neat ornaments and decorations for your home. The workshop will be open to all ages. We will teach you how to work with basic crafting tools and materials before moving onto a simple project that uses things you already have lying around your home. This is a terrific opportunity for you to refresh your house in time for summer. Best of all, this is a good way to upcycle and repurpose household items. Instead of ending up in landfills, you can give ------- new life.
1.

To register, visit www.richmondcenter.org.

1. (A) them
(B) we
(C) us
(D) their

PART 6   UNIT 02

>> 출제 포인트

1. Part 6의 지시어 문제는 바로 앞 문장에서 지칭하는 대상을 찾는 것이 중요하다. 따라서, 이전 문장을 읽으면서 대명사가 가리키는 대상이 무엇인지를 문맥상 파악해야 한다. 이때, 지칭하는 대상의 수(단수 / 복수), 인칭 등을 중점적으로 확인해야 한다.

가산 명사를 받는 부정대명사	단수: one, another, every, each 복수: many, both, few, a few, several
불가산 명사를 받는 부정대명사	much, little, a little
가산 / 불가산 명사를 받는 부정대명사	all, most, some, any

2. 대명사 this는 일반적으로 앞에 나온 특정 단어를 받아주는 대명사와는 다르게, 이전에 나온 문장 전체를 지칭할 때도 쓰일 수 있으니 기억해 두도록 하자.

The company has been recalling the X630 model. **This** is due to the faulty breaks.

이 회사는 X630 모델을 리콜하고 있다. 이는 결함 있는 브레이크 때문이다.

해설서 p.54

Questions 1-4 refer to the following letter.

May 14
Rhonda Harris
17 Lothian Woods
Leflore MI 38940

Dear Ms. Harris,

Thank you for expressing interest in securing a personal loan from Cularity Funds. Before we can consider your application, we will require you to provide ------- information.
                                                                                    1.

Please submit all of your bank statements and pay slips ------- the last three months. You may
                                                                     2.
send the documents to our corporate e-mail address at loans@cularityfunds.com. You can also deliver ------- in person to our loan officer Leonard Cole. -------. Once we have your documents,
         3.   **4.**
Mr. Cole will be in touch with you to let you know about your loan.

Sincerely,
Martin Quinn, Bank Manager
Cularity Funds

1.
(A) adding
(B) additional
(C) addition
(D) additive

2.
(A) from
(B) by
(C) when
(D) until

3.
(A) their
(B) them
(C) it
(D) its

4.
(A) Once you receive the contract, check for the interest rate.
(B) Personal loans can provide you with some financial flexibility.
(C) For security reasons, sending documents through the post is not an option.
(D) Our bank has seen growing customer numbers every year.

Questions 5-8 refer to the following e-mail.

To: shane@richardsonwebdesign.com
From: j_owen@powellcorp.com
Date: 7 November
Subject: website support

Hello Shane,

I would appreciate it if you could help me with my website as soon as possible. -------.
5.
Somehow, I erased a few paragraphs on the "About Us" page. They suddenly -------. I figured
6.
I could undo what I did myself, but after trying out a few things here and there, I decided that
I should stop before making the situation even -------. I really hope you can restore the lost
7.
content.

Also, do you think you would be able to show me how to make simple changes to the website?
I don't want to have to rely on ------- else whenever I need to make a basic update.
8.

Thank you.

Janelle Owen

5. (A) Working on this project has been rewarding.
(B) It's time for us to get a replacement.
(C) However, it's working much better now.
(D) I was trying to make some minor adjustments.

6. (A) disappeared
(B) closed
(C) dissolved
(D) expired

7. (A) worse
(B) worst
(C) worsen
(D) worsening

8. (A) who
(B) someone
(C) which
(D) anything

Questions 9-12 refer to the following e-mail.

From: Helpdesk <helpdesk@lilylakegym.org>
To: Doris Bowers <d.bowers@moserver.com>
Subject: Membership expiration
Date: August 14

Dear Ms. Bowers,

This email is to let you know that your membership at Lily Lake Gym will conclude one month from today. ------- must be renewed in order to continue using our facilities without disruptions to
          9.
your usual schedule. -------. To do so, you can speak to any of our staff members next time you
                     10.
are here.

------- you wish to terminate your membership, no further action is required. On the ------- date,
  11.   12.
your card will no longer grant you access to our facilities.

If you wish to talk about any parts of this notice, or you have any other questions, please respond directly to this email.

Sincerely,

Lily Lake Gym

9. (A) You
    (B) We
    (C) One
    (D) It

10. (A) A staff member will be here to review
        your membership options.
    (B) Our exercise routines can be
        downloaded onto any mobile device.
    (C) You may be eligible for a discount if
        you meet certain conditions.
    (D) Renewals take a few days to process,
        so we recommend doing it one week
        in advance.

11. (A) Should
    (B) However
    (C) Therefore
    (D) Due to

12. (A) specify
    (B) specifically
    (C) specificity
    (D) specified

Questions 13-16 refer to the following e-mail.

To: help@aspironsystems.com
From: sabrina@lucidworks.com
Date: 16 July
Subject: PZ9881 Speakers
Attachments: invoice; electrician's bill

To Whom It May Concern:

Last month, I made a purchase of eight PZ9881 speakers for some of my event halls. However,

we have found that at least half of them do not ------- as advertised. The sound was too low and
13.

came out distorted. I had a certified electrician look into the issue. He assured ------- that the
14.

root cause is to do with the products' components. -------.
15.

As a result of these issues, I would like to request a refund for all of the speakers and

reimbursement for the electrician's work. I have attached copies of the original invoice as well as

the electrician's bill. I am disappointed because I heard great things about Aspiron Systems from

my colleagues, so I hope the ------- is addressed quickly.
16.

Sincerely,
Sabrina Manning
Facility Manager, Lucid Works

---

13. (A) will be functioning
(B) have functioned
(C) functioning
(D) function

14. (A) me
(B) you
(C) it
(D) their

15. (A) I found the equipment to be well-designed.
(B) A fault is likely present in your manufacturing process.
(C) The electrician has 15 years of experience.
(D) Shipping costs may be too high.

16. (A) forecast
(B) problem
(C) strategy
(D) proposal

연결어

Part 6의 연결어 유형은 빈칸 바로 앞 문장과 뒤 문장의 관계를 파악하여 알맞은 접속부사를 선택하는 유형이다. Part 6에서 자주 출제되는 유형 중의 하나로 빈칸 앞 문장과 뒤 문장의 연결고리를 찾는 유형이기 때문에 전체 문맥보다는 빈칸 앞, 뒤에 정답의 단서가 있을 가능성이 높다.

📖 핵심 문제 유형

Question 1 refers to the following notice.   해설서 p.56

The Milford Woodworks Club is holding a furniture sale on Sunday, 11 August. The sale will run from 10:00 A.M. to 3 P.M. at the Milford Community Center at 59 Ryknield Road. There will be a variety of handmade furniture, from chairs to tables. Get here early because stocks won't last. -------, we have **1.** a wide selection of snacks and desserts for you to choose from. Stop by some of the workshops we'll be holding throughout the day and see how some of our members craft their goods. For more information, visit the Milford Woodworks Club at www.milfordwoodworks.co.nz/upcoming.

1.   (A) Therefore
    (B) Otherwise
    (C) Instead
    (D) In addition

≫ 출제 포인트

1. 빈칸 앞뒤 문장을 꼼꼼하게 해석한 후 두 문장 사이의 관계를 파악하여 적절한 접속부사를 선택한다.

2. 보기에 나온 단어의 품사를 구분하는 유형도 자주 등장하니 전치사, 접속사, 접속부사를 정확하게 알아둔다.

• 시험에 자주 출제되는 접속부사

인과	therefore / thus 그러므로	as a result 그 결과	accordingly 따라서	consequently 결과적으로
역접 / 대조	however 그러나 otherwise 그렇지 않으면 nevertheless / nonetheless 그럼에도 불구하고	in contrast 그에 반해서 even so 그렇다 하더라도	on the contrary 그와는 반대로 on the other hand 반면에	
추가	also 또한	in addition 게다가	additionally / moreover / furthermore / besides 게다가	
순서	previously 이전에 finally 마침내	formerly 이전에 until now 지금까지	afterwards 그 이후에 thereafter 그 후에	since then 그때 이후로
대안	instead 대신에	alternatively 대안으로		
예시	for instance / example 예를 들어			
기타	particularly 특히 above all 무엇보다도 rather 오히려	in particular 특히 if so 그렇다면 unfortunately 유감스럽게도	indeed 사실 in other words 다시 말해서 likewise 마찬가지로	in fact 사실 that is 즉 similarly 마찬가지로

Practice

해설서 p.56

Questions 1-4 refer to the following letter.

Dear Mr. Baker,

I am Sindhya Chand, the manager of SlipOne Media. --------1.--------. We specialize in creating a diverse range of advertising materials for small businesses such as yours. We understand that business owners are put off at the cost of --------2.-------- advertisements. --------3.--------, we can provide a premium service at a mere fraction of the cost. Our team will work tirelessly to ensure you are happy with the final product. If you are not happy with the final product, we --------4.-------- a full refund. We put our reputation on the line with every job we get.

If this sounds good to you, give us a call to receive a free consultation. We are also happy to discuss any questions you may have around scheduling and pricing.

1.
(A) Internet advertising has become more commonplace.
(B) Our office is located by the train station.
(C) Please bear in mind we do not work on weekends.
(D) I would like to tell you what we can offer.

2.
(A) presenting
(B) producing
(C) sharing
(D) acquiring

3.
(A) However
(B) Indeed
(C) In addition
(D) If not

4.
(A) will offer
(B) offered
(C) had offered
(D) can be offered

PART 6 UNIT 03

Questions 5-8 refer to the following letter.

September 8

Dear Ms. Moss,

I am writing to let you know of planned road maintenance on Regency Place. From 8 A.M. on September 16, we ------- closing off entry into Regency Place. -------. Due to the fact that your
       5.   **6.**

------- is located just off Regency Place, you should expect much higher traffic, particularly
7.

during rush hour, on this day. -------, you should consider letting your employees know that
                                    8.

parking spots may not be available due to the increased number of cars. The work is expected

to be completed by September 20, and we will inform you of any delays should they arise. Thank

you for your cooperation and understanding.

Sincerely,

Don Fox
Director of Transportation
Synergy

---

5. (A) will be
(B) have been
(C) can be
(D) should have

6. (A) The enclosed map shows the affected area.
(B) An alternative route would be to take Lavery Road.
(C) However, some city officials may be attending the event.
(D) We will be accepting votes until the end of this week.

7. (A) school
(B) business
(C) advertisement
(D) residence

8. (A) Rather
(B) Coincidentally
(C) Therefore
(D) Similarly

Questions 9-12 refer to the following advertisement.

Tropicool Water Works
93 Lorn Street, Spencer
Tennessee, United States

TropiCool Water Works was born out of a simple mission to provide clean water. When you partner with us, we will ensure you get ------- and clean drinking water every time. As part of our
9.
service, we will periodically test your water for mineral levels, inspect your pipes, and make any adjustments as needed. -------, if we feel that your pipes need replacing, we can do that at a
10.
cheaper rate than any other company.

Our team of highly trained and qualified technicians are always ready to share their knowledge with you. -------. Our reputation is ------- by our customer testimonials, which you can read at
11.   12.
www.tropicoolwater.com/reviews. Call us today at 926-555-2836 to receive a free consultation.

9.
(A) safe
(B) safest
(C) safely
(D) safety

10. (A) However
(B) Additionally
(C) Although
(D) Therefore

11. (A) Usually, the next available meeting will be early next month.
(B) We thank you for attending our workshop last month.
(C) The key to building a loyal customer base is through good advertising.
(D) Also, they are always staying up-to-date with new technologies and techniques.

12. (A) supports
(B) support
(C) supported
(D) supporting

Questions 13-16 refer to the following press release.

FOR IMMEDIATE RELEASE

BOWDON (March 13)—The Bowdon-based grocery chain Signet Brands made public its plans to open a new ------- in Sheffield in July. It will occupy the corner of Bonds Road in the same
                      13.
building that was once the Sheffield Post Office, which moved to a larger building last year.

Signet Brands CEO Wade Gilbert commented, "It is with great excitement that we can -------
                                                                                    14.
serve the Sheffield community. -------. The chance to open in such a prestigious location was too
                                15.
good to pass up."

Signet Brands is well known for investing heavily in the cities it operates, such as hiring from within the community. Approximately 70 percent of all employees it hires live within five kilometers of the store where they -------.
                                                          16.

---

13. (A) locate
(B) location
(C) to locate
(D) have located

14. (A) alternatively
(B) rather
(C) besides
(D) finally

15. (A) We were very interested in the area, but we wanted to wait for the right opportunity.
(B) The grand opening event will be covered by all of the major news publications throughout Sheffield.
(C) Our company has steadily raised our profits every year for the past five years.
(D) The Sheffield Post Office has been relocated close to the train station for easier access.

16. (A) employ
(B) reside
(C) plan
(D) work

어휘 선택

UNIT 04

Part 6의 어휘 유형은 Part 5처럼 빈칸이 속한 문장과 어울리는 어휘를 선택하는 유형이 아니라 전체 지문의 흐름에 맞는 알맞은 어휘를 선택하는 대표적인 문맥 유형이다. 각 지문당 1~2문항씩 출제된다. 즉, 지문의 다른 부분에서 정답의 단서를 찾아야 풀 수 있기 때문에 단서를 찾는 것이 다소 까다로울 수 있다.

📖 핵심 문제 유형

Question 1 refers to the following e-mail.

해설서 p.59

To: Roshi Madden
From: Beaumont Goods
Date: September 26
Subject: Order arrival

Dear Mr. Madden,

We are pleased to inform you that your special order of one high-power tower fan and one 80L oven have been delivered to our store. We are now ready to organize the delivery of these ------- to you.
1.
Please give us a call at 315-555-6795 and ask to speak to Zoey Lowery, who handles our deliveries. She can provide you with a form to fill out.

Customer Service, Beaumont Goods

1. (A) materials
(B) creations
(C) appliances
(D) furniture

>> 출제 포인트

1. 빈칸이 있는 문장 자체가 아니라 빈칸 주변으로 지문 전반에 정답의 단서가 되는 표현이나 어휘가 있기 때문에 빈칸 앞뒤 문장을 확인한다. 특히, 빈칸 주변에 있는 핵심 키워드와 유사한 어휘가 정답일 가능성이 높다.

2. 명사 어휘 문제인 경우 빈칸 앞에 있는 지시어(this / these), 정관사(the), 소유격이 있으면 지칭하는 대상이 앞 문장에 언급되어 있을 가능성이 높으므로 빈칸 바로 앞 문장에서 단서를 찾는 것이 중요하다.

Questions 1-4 refer to the following instructions.

Thank you for purchasing Morkad Shower Water Filter. With your new product, you will enjoy the benefits of the purest water every time you shower. To ensure you get the most out of our filter, it is ------- that you activate the filter before your first use. -------. Then simply attach the filter to
    1.   2.
your shower head by screwing it clockwise until it fits -------. If you notice that your shower has
                                                             3.
------- water flow, it may indicate that your filter will need replacing. Each filter should last around
  4.
three months.

1.   (A) suggested
      (B) anticipated
      (C) attempted
      (D) cautioned

2.   (A) Different cities may have different processes for filtering water.
      (B) Reducing water usage is an additional benefit.
      (C) There are three parts that are each sold separately.
      (D) To do this, soak the filter in some cold water for 20 minutes.

3.   (A) regularly
      (B) tightly
      (C) fairly
      (D) vastly

4.   (A) diminishes
      (B) diminished
      (C) diminishable
      (D) diminish

Questions 5-8 refer to the following e-mail.

To: All Staff
From: Joann Payne
Date: April 12
Subject: Bert Thornton

Good morning everyone,

We have some news to share about a ------- in the software development team. After helping
                                        5.
Capital Computers navigate an ever-changing environment, Bert Thornton will officially be retiring
from the position of director of software development.

In his place, Hannah Sandoval, who is our general manager of software development, will be
taking up the role. Mr. Thornton ------- Ms. Sandoval since she joined the company four years
                                    6.
ago.

Mr. Thornton's ------- day at Capital Computers will be April 25. We will be holding a retirement
                  7.
party in his honor at the Brooks Conference Hall at 3:00 P.M. -------.
                                                                8.

5. (A) switch
    (B) direction
    (C) procedure
    (D) intention

6. (A) has been mentoring
    (B) mentors
    (C) is mentoring
    (D) will mentor

7. (A) substantial
    (B) alternative
    (C) final
    (D) variable

8. (A) The position has been advertised.
    (B) Mr. Thornton was one of the founders
        of the company.
    (C) Capital Computers has been asked to
        release a statement.
    (D) More details will be posted soon.

I bought my new Nymous XL outdoor solar light a month ago. I had been quite dissatisfied with other solar lights I had bought in the past. They were always a bit dim, or they did not last very long. After getting some recommendations for the Nymous lights, I decided to order some, and it turned out to be a great decision. -------.
        9.

I would like to point out, however, that putting it together was not the easiest process. I felt that the instructions were confusing at times. Without the help of a friend who is quite skilled in this area, I am not sure I would have been able to ------- the product.
                10.

On a different note, I was pleasantly surprised at how ------- the stakes that come with the lights
                    11.
are. I was able to put them into the ground without having to ------- up the soil first.
                        12.

— E. Douglas

9. (A) Every suggestion was responded to.
   (B) That event was conducted with no big issues.
   (C) They exceeded my expectations.
   (D) The packaging was recently changed.

10. (A) organize
   (B) assemble
   (C) establish
   (D) detach

11. (A) sturdy
   (B) expensive
   (C) creative
   (D) crude

12. (A) loose
   (B) loosen
   (C) to loosen
   (D) loosest

Questions 13-16 refer to the following e-mail.

To: Samirah Ross <s.ross@rossdesigns.com>
From: Maisie Blaese <m.blaese@newtonboutique.com>
Subject: Great news!
Date: 24 February

Dear Samirah,

I recently received the shipment of 60 dresses and skirts from your latest line. They have been my top sellers for the past few weeks. Several of my ------- have praised the unique designs as
                                                     13.
well as the quality of the materials. -------.
                                      14.

As this shipment has been doing so well, I would like to increase the number of units in my next order. Would it be possible to ------- my order for the March shipment?
                                               15.

Finally, I was wondering whether you'd be interested in creating an exclusive line to sell in my stores. As I have stores throughout the country, I believe I can raise awareness of your brand and reach a wide audience quickly. In my opinion, this would benefit ------- both very well. If you are
                                                             16.
interested, please let me know.

Thank you.

Maisie Blaese
Newton Boutique

13. (A) members
    (B) editors
    (C) students
    (D) patrons

14. (A) The reasonable prices make your pieces that much more appealing.
    (B) An order of that size will likely not sell out fast enough.
    (C) Could you let me know of your availability for next week?
    (D) The invoice should have been settled already.

15. (A) feature
    (B) double
    (C) guarantee
    (D) halt

16. (A) you
    (B) we
    (C) us
    (D) them

문장 선택

Part 6 문장 선택 유형은 빈칸에 글의 흐름상 알맞은 문장을 넣어야 한다는 점에서 지문 전체의 문맥을 파악해서 풀어야 하는 독해 실력이 요구되는 유형이다. 하지만, 지문 전체를 단순히 무작정 해석해서 접근하기보다는 글의 기본적인 틀에 대한 이해와 연결어구나 지시어와 같은 단서를 토대로 푸는 전략을 익히는 것이 중요하다.

 핵심 문제 유형

Question 1 refers to the following article.

해설서 p.61

Supermarket Chain Announces Event

CRANMOOR (June 19)—Harmony Sale, the city's largest supermarket chain, is looking to recruit for a variety of positions in preparation for its new stores. To fill the vacancies, the company is hosting a recruiting event on June 30. The new positions will largely be for Harmony Sale's new stores opening next year. However, there will also be positions available at its current locations and its corporate headquarters. -------.
           1.

Those who are interested in attending should prepare copies of their résumé ahead of the event. It will take place at the Great Central Hall from 9 A.M. to 5 P.M.

---

1. (A) Previous events have been covered on the news.
    (B) These may include marketing and administration roles.
    (C) Many local supermarkets have reported difficulties in retaining staff members.
    (D) Harmony Sale has recently started expanding into new cities.

➤➤ 출제 포인트

1. 빈칸은 지문의 초반부, 중반부, 후반부에 모두 위치할 수 있으며 빈칸의 위치에 따라 글의 기본적인 틀은 정해져 있다.

   - 지문의 초반부 – 지문의 첫 시작 부분이기 때문에 인사말 또는 글의 주제나 목적을 나타내는 문장이 나온다.
   - 지문의 중반부 – 문장 선택 유형 중에서 문맥을 잡기에 가장 까다로운 위치이며 보통 빈칸 앞뒤 내용에 대한 부연 설명, 이유 등을 나타내는 문장이 나온다.
   - 지문의 후반부 – 글의 마지막 부분이기 때문에 맺음말 또는 마무리 멘트가 자주 등장한다. 또한 빈칸 앞의 내용에 대한 부연 설명이나 세부 사항을 나타내는 문장이 나온다.

2. 보기 또는 빈칸 앞뒤 문장에 나와 있는 정관사, 지시어, 대명사 등 단서를 활용하여 문제를 푼다. 선택지에 정관사, 지시어, 대명사 등이 있으면 빈칸 앞 문장에서 지칭하는 대상을 찾아 맥락을 파악하는 것이 중요하다. 특히, 선택지에 『the + 명사』가 있다면 빈칸 앞에 가리키는 대상이 있는지 꼭 살펴보아야 한다.

3. 보기 또는 빈칸 앞뒤에 제시된 연결어를 단서로 활용하여 문제를 푼다. 보기에 연결어인 접속부사가 포함된 선택지라면 빈칸 앞 문장과의 관계를 파악한다. 반대로, 빈칸 바로 뒤에 접속부사로 이어져 있다면 빈칸의 앞뒤 문장의 논리 관계를 파악한 후 알맞은 접속부사가 들어간 문장을 선택한다.

Questions 1-4 refer to the following letter.

Dear Carly,

Thank you so much for your ------- help in making the grand opening at Dontay Bay a success.
1.
We received some excellent reviews, and it was in large part thanks to your amazing work.

Our management team has been following your work for some time now, and they were happy

we could use your designs for our store. The interior of the store received a lot of ------- from
2.
our guests, and they have been posting a lot of pictures on social media. -------. If you recall
3.
from our last meeting, we briefly discussed our new location that will be opening in Clayville. A

meeting ------- the store will be organized soon, and we would love it if you could attend.
4.

Sincerely yours,

Marilyn Pena
Director, Malrine Boutique

1. (A) amazed
(B) amazing
(C) amazement
(D) amazingly

2. (A) suggestions
(B) interpretations
(C) compliments
(D) creations

3. (A) I was also wondering about your
availability in June.
(B) Dontay Bay has seen significant
investments recently.
(C) An increase in the budget has been
approved.
(D) You can refer to the information page
on our Web site.

4. (A) has planned
(B) will be planned
(C) plans
(D) to plan

Questions 5-8 refer to the following article.

WALBRIDGE (August 12)—The iconic Walbridge Museum will be undergoing its ------- renovation
5.
since its opening. The ownership group hopes that following the updates, the museum will be
able to play host to a greater variety of -------. Manager Denise Floyd explained that the priority is
6.
to appeal to younger demographics. To this end, the west wing will be turned into an interactive
space that will be used to run workshops for families to attend together. Although there were
initially concerns that noise from the workshops may disturb other guests, Ms. Floyd reassured
that the walls will be made from special materials designed ------- noise effectively. The museum
7.
will be open to the public early next year. -------.
8.

5. (A) more extensive
    (B) extensively
    (C) most extensive
    (D) extensive

6. (A) exhibitions
    (B) seasons
    (C) contexts
    (D) payments

7. (A) to block
    (B) blocking
    (C) have been blocked
    (D) block

8. (A) The management group is expected to
        undergo some changes.
    (B) Walbridge Museum is the largest
        museum in the state.
    (C) Donations are one way funds can be
        raised quickly.
    (D) The opening will be in time for the
        important tourist season.

Questions 9-12 refer to the following Web page information.

About Purer Packaging

Avanto Production has put in considerable ------- to combat the problem of plastic waste.
                                                    9.
The company has worked on designing alternatives to plastic packaging commonly seen in
supermarkets and retail stores. Last week, the company announced that it ------- a new material
                                                                              10.
derived from organic plant matter. Avanto Production mixes coconut fibers and tree bark to
create Purer Packaging. The fibers are usually disposed of ------- the bark is seen as a waste
                                                                11.
product. In producing Purer Packaging cheaper than plastic, Avanto Production aims to phase
plastic packaging out completely. -------.
                                       12.

9. (A) prices
    (B) efforts
    (C) information
    (D) results

10. (A) been developing
    (B) to develop
    (C) will develop
    (D) had developed

11. (A) although
    (B) while
    (C) therefore
    (D) instead

12. (A) Our sales team will get back to you as
        soon as possible.
    (B) A grant may be available for businesses
        focusing on green technologies.
    (C) Avanto Production is now hiring
        additional staff for a new project.
    (D) The first prototypes of the product will
        be released next year.

Questions 13-16 refer to the following memo.

To: All Employees
From: Andy Pittman, Cybersecurity Team
Date: September 23
Subject: Safety Training

It is time for this year's annual Internet safety training workshop. This year's workshop will focus on avoiding cyberattacks, such as those that steal your data or personal information. Rest assured, our cybersecurity team has installed security programs on company devices to protect us from attacks. -------, it is still imperative to understand what threats there are and what you
   13.
should do when you encounter one.

To accommodate -------, we will be conducting several workshops throughout the week. You will
   14.
be free to choose from any of the available ------- by logging onto our company's Web site. There
   15.
will be a link for "Cybersecurity Training."

-------. If you are unable to attend any of the sessions, please let your supervisor know and we
   16.
will work on a solution.

13. (A) Furthermore
(B) Likewise
(C) Alternatively
(D) However

14. (A) them
(B) everyone
(C) those
(D) itself

15. (A) conditions
(B) events
(C) options
(D) discussions

16. (A) The training is mandatory for all employees.
(B) An e-mail address can be found on the page.
(C) Last year's sessions were conducted online.
(D) Any suggestions should be sent to anyone from the cybersecurity team.

REVIEW TEST

해설서 p.64

Questions 1-4 refer to the following e-mail.

To: Andrew Connor <a.connor@expressline.com>
From: Maureen Sinfield <msinfield@creworse.com>
Date: 15 August
Subject: Follow-up
Attachment: Research supervisor description

Dear Mr. Connor,

We would like to thank you for coming in to interview for the product developer position last week. We were very impressed with your work experience and technical knowledge. ------- we **1.** are proceeding with a different candidate, we do have another position we think your skillset would be perfectly suited for. It is a role as a research supervisor at one of our offices.

-------. The attached document shows the full job description as well as the salary range. We **2.** have not advertised this ------- yet as we feel you are a great fit. If you are -------, please get **3.** **4.** back to me as soon as possible.

Sincerely,

Maureen Sinfield
Human Resources, Creworse Industries

1.
(A) Likewise
(B) Subsequently
(C) While
(D) Therefore

2.
(A) This role is in line with some of your previous positions.
(B) The manager will be in touch next week.
(C) Our company will be branching out into new industries this year.
(D) Your résumé has been received by our recruiting team.

3.
(A) operation
(B) measure
(C) endorsement
(D) opportunity

4.
(A) interest
(B) interested
(C) interesting
(D) interests

Questions 5-8 refer to the following notice.

Gamer's Paradise

Gamer's Paradise is the world's most trusted source for information on the latest ------- in the
5.
world of video games. What started as a hobby between a small group of friends ------- into
6.
one of the largest gaming content platforms in the world. We work around the clock to bring
you interviews from game developers, exclusive previews of upcoming releases, and special
discounts for our subscribers. We also update our terms of service per legal requirements.
Subscribers' ------- access to our platform requires the acceptance of our terms. Therefore,
7.
please take the time to review them at www.gamersparadise.com/terms. If you have any
questions, please contact our customer team at help@gamersparadise.com. -------.
8.

---

5. (A) variations
   (B) stories
   (C) episodes
   (D) directions

6. (A) has grown
   (B) will be growing
   (C) growing
   (D) growth

7. (A) continuation
   (B) continues
   (C) continue
   (D) continued

8. (A) The new law will come into effect early
       next year.
   (B) We have read user suggestions about
       our Web site and will be making
       improvements.
   (C) Our inbox is monitored 24 hours a day
       excluding holidays.
   (D) Exclusive benefits are available to
       those who subscribe for one year.

Questions 9-12 refer to the following review.

Home Cleaning Services: Air Conditioner Cleaning

Review by André Blatt

I've never written a review on this site before. -------, the service I received from Warden
9.
Cleaning Crew was so exceptional that I had to write one. First off, I want to mention how

professional ------- service was. As they were cleaning my air conditioner, I could see why I had
10.
been experiencing allergy symptoms recently. It was a real eyeopener. -------. It's been a week
11.
since I got my machine cleaned, and I can definitely report a noticeable ------- in my dust allergy
12.
symptoms. Thank you to the team at Warden Cleaning Crew!

9. (A) Therefore
(B) However
(C) To illustrate
(D) Moreover

10. (A) themselves
(B) they
(C) them
(D) their

11. (A) Some chemicals can be harmful if left
unattended.
(B) They even gave me some tips on how
to keep it clean.
(C) Many people have experienced noisy
air conditioners.
(D) It is important to schedule regular
sessions.

12. (A) reduction
(B) reduce
(C) reducing
(D) reducible

Questions 13-16 refer to the following e-mail.

To: Josh Dunn
From: Danielle Cross
Date: October 26
Subject: My thoughts
Attachment: Article

Dear Dr. Dunn,

I am sending this e-mail in response to a topic raised in yesterday's staff meeting. I enjoyed the discussion on how our clinic can better embrace our core values and mission. -------.
13.

At our clinic, many of our walls have been painted with a dull shade of gray and left undecorated. In my opinion, we ------- positivity and vibrancy wherever we can to show that we care about our
14.
patients. -------, our mission is to serve our communities to the best of our abilities.
15.

I have attached an article on medical centers that have brightened up their decors. The article details how patients responded positively to the changes. I hope you find it -------. Given how
16.
cost-effective this idea is, I think it's something worth considering.

Best regards,
Danielle Cross

13. (A) I had an idea on this topic that I would like to share.
(B) I would like to run another workshop in the future.
(C) I thought the meeting could have been conducted online instead.
(D) I wish we had organized the meeting sooner.

14. (A) have promoted
(B) should be promoting
(C) were promoting
(D) will promote

15. (A) Rather
(B) Otherwise
(C) After all
(D) However

16. (A) convenient
(B) helpful
(C) energetic
(D) peculiar

PAP

RT 7

독해

OVERVIEW

지문을 읽고 그에 해당하는 질문에 알맞은 답을 고르는 문제이다. 지문은 문자 메시지와 온라인 채팅과 같은 문자 대화문부터 신문 기사나 웹사이트 페이지까지 그 종류가 다양하며, 그 형태도 1개의 지문으로 된 단일 지문 문제, 2개의 지문으로 된 이중 지문 문제, 3개의 지문으로 이루어진 삼중 지문 문제로 구분할 수 있다. 단일 지문 29문항, 이중 지문 10문항, 삼중 지문 15문항씩 총 54문항이 출제된다.

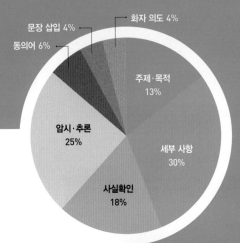

화자 의도 4%
문장 삽입 4%
동의어 6%
주제·목적 13%
세부 사항 30%
사실확인 18%
암시·추론 25%

문제 유형 분석

단일 지문(10개) | 이메일, 편지, 문자 메시지, 온라인 채팅, 광고, 기사, 양식, 회람, 공지, 웹페이지 등

이중 지문(2개) | 이메일−이메일, 기사−이메일, 웹페이지−이메일, 웹페이지(광고)−웹페이지(사용 후기) 등

삼중 지문(3개) | 다양한 세 지문들의 조합

최신 출제 경향

- 지문과 문제의 길이가 점점 길어지고 있다. 지문과 선택지를 일일이 대조할 필요가 있는 사실 확인 문제 유형의 비중을 늘려서 난이도를 조절하기도 한다.
- 암시·추론 문제의 비중이 증가하고 있다. 지문에 나와 있는 정보를 토대로 알 수 있는 사실 확인 및 암시·추론 문제가 많이 등장하고 있다.
- 동의어 문제가 매회 1~4문제의 출제 비율을 유지하고 있다.

핵심 학습 전략

- Part 7은 지문과 문항 수가 증가했고, 글의 흐름 파악이 중요해졌기 때문에 빠르고 정확한 독해력이 필요하다. 어휘력을 쌓고 문장의 구조를 파악하는 훈련을 통해 독해력을 뒷받침하는 기본기를 다져야 한다.
- 문자 메시지나 온라인 채팅은 난이도가 비교적 높지 않다. 그러나 구어체적 표현이 많이 나오고 문자 그대로의 사전적인 의미가 아닌 문맥상 그 안에 담겨 있는 숨은 뜻을 찾는 화자 의도 파악 문제가 꼭 출제되기 때문에 평소 구어체 표현을 숙지하고 대화의 흐름을 파악하는 연습을 한다.
- 질문의 키워드를 찾고 질문이 요구하는 핵심 정보를 본문에서 신속하게 찾아내는 연습이 필요하다.
- 본문에서 찾아낸 정답 정보는 선택지에서 다른 표현으로 제시되므로 같은 의미를 여러 가지 다른 표현들(paraphrased expressions)로 전달하는 패러프레이징 찾기 연습이 필요하다.

문제 풀이 전략

1. 지문 순서대로 풀지 말자.

Part 7은 처음부터 또는 마지막부터 순서대로 풀지 않아도 된다. 15개의 지문 중에서 당연히 가장 쉬운 것부터 먼저 풀고 어려운 문제는 시간이 남으면 푼다는 마음으로 풀어야 한다. 다음과 같은 순서로 문제를 풀어 보도록 한다.

첫 3개 지문 (147번~152번)

▼

광고, 온라인 채팅, 양식(청구서, 주문서, 초대장 등), 웹페이지

▼

이메일, 편지, 회람, 공지

▼

첫 번째 이중 지문, 첫 번째 삼중 지문

▼

기사, 두 번째 이중 지문, 나머지 삼중 지문

2. 패러프레이징(Paraphrasing)된 정답을 찾는 것이 핵심이다.

같은 표현은 절대 반복되지 않는다. 정답은 지문에 나온 표현을 다른 말로 바꿔 나온다.

> - **지문에서 나오는 표현** National Museum is located just minutes from Oxford Street Station in Richmont's shopping district. 국립 박물관은 리치몬트의 쇼핑가에 있는 옥스퍼드 가 역에서 단 몇 분 거리에 있다.
> - **문제** What is suggested about the National Museum? 국립 박물관에 관하여 암시되는 것은?
> - **정답** It is conveniently located. 편리한 곳에 위치해 있다.

3. 지문 내용에 기반하여 정답을 찾는다.

정답은 반드시 지문 내용에 기반하여 사실인 것만 고른다. 절대 '그럴 것 같다, 그렇겠지'라고 상상하여 답을 고르면 안된다. Part 7 문제 유형 중에는 추론해야 하는 문제들이 많이 나오기는 하지만 아무리 추론 문제이더라도 지문에 있는 근거 문장을 패러프레이징한 보기를 찾는 문제일 뿐이다. 추론 이상의 상상은 금물이다.

4. 문제를 먼저 읽고 키워드를 파악하자!

지문 유형 확인 ▶ **문제의 핵심어 확인** ▶ **지문 읽기** ▶ **문제 풀이**

- 주제나 목적, 대상을 묻는 문제는 대개 지문의 첫머리에 단서가 제시되므로 도입부 내용을 잘 확인하여 이 내용을 포괄할 수 있는 선택지를 고른다.
- 세부 사항, 사실 확인 문제의 경우 핵심 단어 및 표현에 집중하여 질문에서 키워드를 파악하고 관련 내용이 언급된 부분을 지문에서 찾아 문제를 해결한다.
- 동의어 문제에서는 해당 단어의 대표적인 의미를 무작정 선택하는 것이 아니라 반드시 문맥상 어떤 의미로 쓰였는지 확인하여 정답을 찾는다.

UNIT 01 주제·목적 문제

주제·목적 문제는 글의 주제나 목적을 정확하게 파악하고 있는지 묻는 질문 유형으로 평균 5~6문제 정도 출제된다. 보통 편지, 이메일, 공지, 기사 지문 유형에 등장하며 지문의 전체를 다 읽되 지문에서 말하고자 하는 핵심 내용을 기억하도록 노력해야 한다.

🔍 질문 유형 확인하기

▶ **글의 목적**

What is the **purpose** of the article?
기사의 목적은 무엇인가?

Why was the letter written?
이 편지는 왜 쓰였는가?

Why did Mr. Kim write the e-mil?
김 씨는 왜 이메일을 썼는가?

▶ **글의 주제**

What is the notice **mainly about**?
이 공지는 주로 무엇에 대한 것인가?

What is **mainly discussed** in the advertisement?
광고에서 주로 논의되는 것은 무엇인가?

What is the **subject / topic** of the article?
이 기사의 주제는 무엇인가?

독해 전략

1 글의 주제와 목적을 담은 문장은 주로 지문의 도입 부분에 나올 가능성이 높지만, 최근에는 전반적인 지문의 내용을 파악한 후에 풀 수 있는 문제의 출제 빈도수가 높아지고 있다.

2 전체적인 지문의 핵심 내용을 포괄할 수 있는 문장을 찾는 것이 중요하며 패러프레이징에 유의한다.

3 지문 속에 반전을 나타내는 표현(however, unfortunately, but, I am afraid that, by the way)이 나온다면, 그 뒤가 목적을 담고 있는 문장일 가능성이 높다.

▶ **주제·목적을 나타내는 정답 단서**
• Please 명령문 ~해주시기 바랍니다
• I am writing to ~ ~하기 위해 글을 씁니다
• This letter is to ~ / The purpose of this letter is to ~ 이 편지는 ~하기 위한 것입니다
• We would like to ~ 저희는 ~하고자 합니다
• Can / Could / Would you ~? ~ 해주시겠습니까?
• We announce / notify / inform / notify ~ 저희가 ~을 알려드립니다

Question 1 refers to the following memo.

To:	All employees
From:	Aileen Jang, Chief of Operations
Date:	April 9
Subject:	ID badges

❶ We will install a new security system next Monday, April 16. After activating this system, LV employees always have to carry identification badges. There are digital identification codes in the plastic cards. As a result, they enable you to have access to all buildings on the LV campus. You can pick up badges in the Marketing Department office on Friday, April 11.

Keep in mind that employees won't be able to enter any LV facilities after April 16 without their new ID badges. If you have any questions or concerns, please contact your manager.

• 수신인
발신인
날짜
제목

• 회람의 목적
새로운 보안 시스템
설치 안내

• 주의 사항
• 문의 사항이 있을 경우
연락할 사람

1. What is the purpose of the memo?

(A) To inform employees of the temporary closing of a building
(B) To introduce a company policy
(C) To notify employees that a department's location has moved
(D) To address a recent security problem

Questions 1-2 refer to the following notice.

Dear Customer,

The team at Hensong Foods is excited to tell you about the grand opening of our latest establishment. This location will feature an entirely new menu designed by our head chef, Melinda Lee. Melinda's menu includes elements of fusion dining, combined with a focus on organic ingredients. Customers can even design their own dishes from a combination of available ingredients through our mobile application.

Order a custom-made meal using our app today and receive 15 percent off your meal. Tables are limited, so book your place today!

1. What is the purpose of the notice?

(A) To announce a new restaurant
(B) To advertise a position
(C) To explain a recent trend
(D) To invite people to an event

2. According to the notice, how can customers receive a discount?

(A) By inviting a friend
(B) By ordering through an app
(C) By submitting a letter
(D) By entering a competition

Questions 3-4 refer to the following postcard.

Esther Poole
26 Parsons Street
Medina, Ohio 44256

18 June

Dear Ms. Poole,

It has been a year since you had your vehicle checked up. To maintain the safety of your vehicle and avoid costly repairs down the line, we recommend you make an appointment to get your car serviced by us. To do so, please call our office at 317-555-9618 or book an appointment online using our website (www.tekapomechanics. com). On our website, you can also find a range of products designed to keep your car running as smoothly as possible.

Sincerely,

Roy Diaz
Tekapo Mechanics
1395 Caxton Quay, Medina, Ohio 44256

3. Why did Mr. Diaz write to Ms. Poole?

(A) To inform her of a new policy
(B) To ask her to bring her car for a check-up
(C) To notify her of a cancelled appointment
(D) To remind her of a missed payment

4. What does Mr. Diaz mention about the website?

(A) It includes information on several products.
(B) It was launched on June 18.
(C) It features reviews from recent customers.
(D) It was recently revamped.

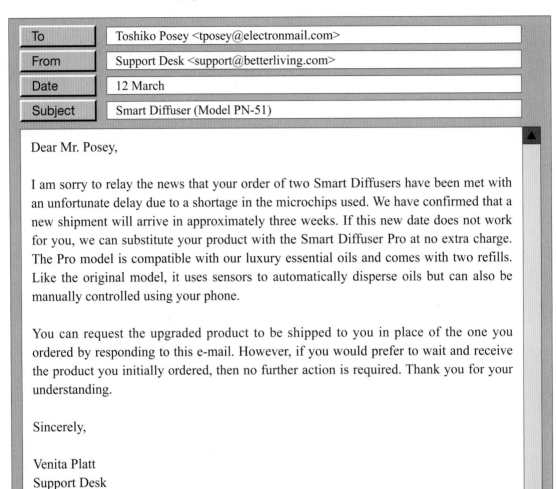

To	Toshiko Posey <tposey@electronmail.com>
From	Support Desk <support@betterliving.com>
Date	12 March
Subject	Smart Diffuser (Model PN-51)

Dear Mr. Posey,

I am sorry to relay the news that your order of two Smart Diffusers have been met with an unfortunate delay due to a shortage in the microchips used. We have confirmed that a new shipment will arrive in approximately three weeks. If this new date does not work for you, we can substitute your product with the Smart Diffuser Pro at no extra charge. The Pro model is compatible with our luxury essential oils and comes with two refills. Like the original model, it uses sensors to automatically disperse oils but can also be manually controlled using your phone.

You can request the upgraded product to be shipped to you in place of the one you ordered by responding to this e-mail. However, if you would prefer to wait and receive the product you initially ordered, then no further action is required. Thank you for your understanding.

Sincerely,

Venita Platt
Support Desk
Better Living

5. Why did Ms. Platt write the e-mail?

(A) To respond to a customer's complaint
(B) To share the benefits of a new product
(C) To inform about a revised policy
(D) To apologize for a delay

6. What is indicated about the Smart Diffuser Pro?

(A) It comes with additional oils.
(B) It is available in more colors than the original model.
(C) It has not been revealed to the public yet.
(D) It was reviewed favorably in a magazine.

Questions 7-9 refer to the following letter.

Thornton Civil Engineering Society
http://www.tces.org
3 March

Erin Hernandez
251 Marlborough Terrace
Ridgeland, WI 54763

Dear Ms. Erin,

— [1] —. On behalf of the Thornton Civil Engineering Society (TCES) and with special recognition of your work in designing public transportation-oriented cities throughout Thornton, we would like to invite you to deliver this year's keynote address at our conference in Dunn. — [2] —. This year's theme is designing for the future, and it is our view that future cities will borrow elements from your designs. Some of our other speakers can be found on our website. — [3] —. Just navigate to the Conference Schedule tab.

I hope our offer interests you, and you choose to speak at our conference. Please let me know if you have any questions. — [4] —. My phone number is (062) 555 0912.

Sincerely,

Clyde Jones
Event Organizer, TCES

7. What is the purpose of the letter?

(A) To offer a position at a firm
(B) To extend an invitation
(C) To respond to an inquiry
(D) To inform of a change in venue

8. What is indicated about Ms. Hernandez?

(A) She works in an office in Dunn.
(B) She has met Mr. Jones in person.
(C) She is a member of the TCES.
(D) She is thought of highly in her field.

9. In which of the positions marked [1], [2], [3] and [4] does the following sentence best belong?

"You may know some of them as they have worked with you on past projects."

(A) [1]
(B) [2]
(C) [3]
(D) [4]

세부사항 문제

Part 7에서 가장 많이 출제되는 문제 유형으로 육하원칙을 나타내는 '언제, 어디서, 어떻게, 누가'와 같은 의문사로 시작하는 질문 유형이다. 즉, 구체적인 정보를 찾는 문제 유형이며 지문의 일부만 보고도 비교적 빠르게 정답을 찾을 수 있으므로 난이도가 낮은 편이다.

🔍 질문 유형 확인하기

~는 누구인가? / 누가 ~하는가?	**Who** is (most likely) Mr. Lee? 이 씨는 (아마도) 누구인가? **Who** will be the representative of the company? 누가 회사의 대표가 될 건가?
무엇이 ~하는가?	**What** will new customers receive? 새로운 고객들은 무엇을 받을 것인가?
언제 ~하는가?	**When** did Mr. Kim attend the workshop? 언제 김 씨가 워크샵에 참석했는가?
어디서 ~하는가?	**Where** can Mr. Lee make a payment? 어디에서 이 씨가 지불을 할 수 있는가?
어떻게 ~하는가?	**How** did Mr. Kim learn about the Rainbow Hotel? 어떻게 김 씨가 레인보우 호텔에 대해 알았는가?
왜 ~하는가?	**Why** did Mr. Kim attend the meeting? 왜 김 씨가 미팅에 참석했는가?

 독해 전략

1. 질문에 쓰인 의문사와 키워드에 표시를 하고 질문을 정확하게 이해해야 한다.

2. 지문에서 해당 키워드가 그대로 언급되어 있는 부분이거나 패러프레이징이 되어 있는 부분을 빠르게 훑어가며 정답의 단서를 찾는다.

3. 지문에서 찾은 정답이 되는 단서가 똑같이 나와 있거나 패러프레이징한 보기를 선택한다.

▶ 정답 단서가 될 수 있는 키워드
- 숫자, 날짜, 수 표현과 기호
- 고유명사(사람 이름, 회사 이름, 상품명)
- 연락처(전화번호, 이메일 주소, 웹사이트 주소, 집 주소)

해설서 p.69

Question 1 refers to the following invitation.

❶ The BB Center Art Association
is going to host an exhibition.

Our Artists: Paintings and Drawings
by Chicago's Best Emerging Artists

Thursday, April 7, from 4:30 P.M. to 7:30 P.M.

Owen Performance Center
171 Grandriver Main Street
Chicago, IL 60007

Tickets to the event are $20 per person.

To make a reservation for your tickets,
please call or email by Friday, April 1.
TEL: 889-4000
E-mail: events@bbcenterarts.org

---• 예술 협회 전시회

---• 행사 세부 일정 안내
(참가자, 전시 작품, 시간, 장소, 비용)

---• 티켓 예약 방법

1. What type of event is being held?

(A) A concert
(B) An art show
(C) A business convention
(D) An auction

PART 7 UNIT 02

해설서 p.70

Questions 1-2 refer to the following sign.

Welcome to Dr. Bluth's Office

Before you take a seat, please fill out the sign-in sheet at the reception desk. Then have a seat in the waiting room. The receptionist will call your name and help take your paperwork as well as confirm the details of your appointment. If there are any payments to process, our receptionist will also assist with those.

Please note that if you are more than 15 minutes late for your appointment, the option to reschedule is at our discretion. Patients who fail to turn up will be charged $30.

---

1. According to the sign, what will the receptionist assist clients with?

(A) Submitting paperwork
(B) Entering the office
(C) Finding a seat
(D) Scheduling an appointment

2. What may happen to clients who arrive late?

(A) They may be directed to a different office.
(B) They may be charged an additional fee.
(C) They may be asked to write an e-mail.
(D) They may be scheduled at a different time.

Questions 3-4 refer to the following job posting.

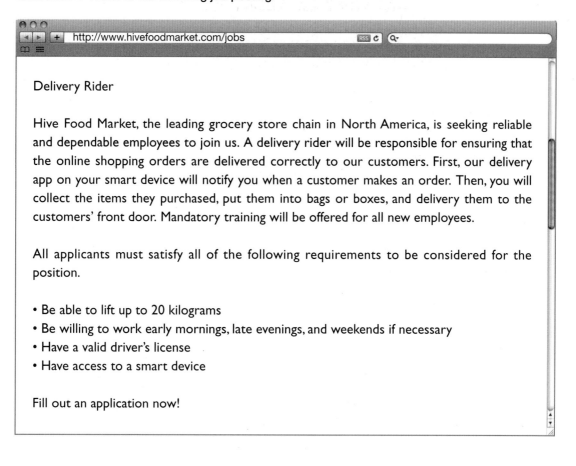

http://www.hivefoodmarket.com/jobs

Delivery Rider

Hive Food Market, the leading grocery store chain in North America, is seeking reliable and dependable employees to join us. A delivery rider will be responsible for ensuring that the online shopping orders are delivered correctly to our customers. First, our delivery app on your smart device will notify you when a customer makes an order. Then, you will collect the items they purchased, put them into bags or boxes, and delivery them to the customers' front door. Mandatory training will be offered for all new employees.

All applicants must satisfy all of the following requirements to be considered for the position.

• Be able to lift up to 20 kilograms
• Be willing to work early mornings, late evenings, and weekends if necessary
• Have a valid driver's license
• Have access to a smart device

Fill out an application now!

3. According to the job posting, what does the position provide?

(A) Company cars
(B) Shopping discount
(C) Growth opportunities
(D) Training sessions

4. What is NOT a requirement of the position?

(A) Knowledge of local geography
(B) Availability to work with a flexible schedule
(C) The ability to carry full bags of grocery
(D) A smart device with a message function

PART 7 UNIT 02

The uncharacteristically warm weather we've enjoyed this year has also led to a substantial increase in the amount of fruits and vegetables harvested. In fact, there are reports that growers have too much supply and not enough demand. Instead of letting your excess produce go to waste, consider donating to a good cause to feed the needy. Visit Whittaker Family Foundation (www.whittakerff. org) to find out where you can donate produce.

As a token of our appreciation, we have several mechanics who have kindly donated their time. In return for supporting our organization, our volunteers are offering to do simple fixes and tweaks on any machinery you have had problems with. Our website has more details about this service as well as helpful articles on composting and gardening.

5. For whom is the notice most likely intended?

(A) Car mechanics
(B) Restaurant managers
(C) Farmers
(D) Warehouse supervisors

6. What does the notice indicate about the weather?

(A) It was better than expected.
(B) It resulted in event cancellations.
(C) It caused delays in construction projects.
(D) It was predicted months in advance.

7. What service does the notice mention?

(A) Machinery repairs
(B) Composting workshops
(C) Transporting produce
(D) Packaging and preparing food

Questions 8-11 refer to the following e-mail.

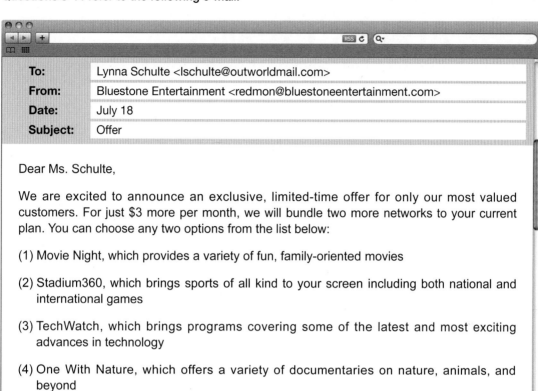

To: Lynna Schulte <lschulte@outworldmail.com>
From: Bluestone Entertainment <redmon@bluestoneentertainment.com>
Date: July 18
Subject: Offer

Dear Ms. Schulte,

We are excited to announce an exclusive, limited-time offer for only our most valued customers. For just $3 more per month, we will bundle two more networks to your current plan. You can choose any two options from the list below:

(1) Movie Night, which provides a variety of fun, family-oriented movies

(2) Stadium360, which brings sports of all kind to your screen including both national and international games

(3) TechWatch, which brings programs covering some of the latest and most exciting advances in technology

(4) One With Nature, which offers a variety of documentaries on nature, animals, and beyond

(5) Brain Games, which allows players to compete with one another in a wide range of games

To take advantage of this offer, simply respond to this e-mail with your two selections. This offer is only valid until August 5, so be quick!

Elvin Redmon, Entertainment Director
Bluestone Entertainment

PART 7 UNIT 02

8. What is suggested about Ms. Schulte?

   (A) She enjoys watching sports games.
   (B) She is a Bluestone Entertainment customer.
   (C) She is currently on a business trip.
   (D) She works in the television industry.

9. What is being offered?

   (A) A low-cost upgrade
   (B) A trial for a new service
   (C) A updated piece of hardware
   (D) An apology for a service disruption

10. The word "plan" in paragraph 1, line 3, is closest in meaning to

   (A) agenda
   (B) blueprint
   (C) preliminary schedule
   (D) payment program

11. What network is interactive?

   (A) Stadium360
   (B) One With Nature
   (C) Brain Games
   (D) TechWatch

사실확인 문제

TRUE 또는 NOT TRUE를 묻는 사실확인 문제는 Part 7에서 상세정보 질문 유형과 함께 자주 출제되는 빈출 유형이다. 지문의 내용과 각 보기의 선택지를 하나하나 꼼꼼하게 대조해 보면서 일치하거나 일치하지 않는 정보를 찾아서 풀어야 하므로 다소 시간이 소요되는 유형이다.

🔍 질문 유형 확인하기

▶ **키워드가 있는 경우**

What is **NOT mentioned** about the upcoming workshop?
다가오는 워크샵에 관해서 언급되지 않은 것은 무엇인가?

What is **true** about the new policy?
새로운 정책에 대해 사실인 것은 무엇인가?

What is **indicated / stated / mentioned** about the shipment?
배송에 관해서 언급된 것은 무엇인가?

▶ **키워드가 없는 경우**

What is **indicated** in the advertisement?
광고에 대해 언급된 것은 무엇인가?

What is **NOT mentioned** in the article?
기사에 언급되어 있지 않은 것은 무엇인가?

What is **true** about Mr. Lee?
이 씨에 관해서 사실인 것은 무엇인가?

독해 전략

1 키워드가 있는 질문의 경우, 질문에서 핵심 키워드를 먼저 확인한다. 지문에서 해당 키워드가 그대로 언급되어 있는 부분이나 패러프레이징한 부분에서 단서를 찾아 각 선택지와 하나씩 비교하며 오답을 소거한다.

2 키워드가 없는 질문의 경우, 지문 전반에 걸쳐 곳곳에서 정답의 단서가 언급될 수 있기 때문에 다른 질문 유형을 먼저 해결한 후 마지막에 푸는 것이 좋다. 지문을 어느 정도 읽은 후, 읽었던 지문 속 내용과 맞는 선택지가 있는지 하나씩 대조하면서 비교한다.

Questions 1-2 refer to the following advertisement.

Career Hope

회사명

Do you want an inexpensive way to attract new talent for your company? Post your openings in *Career Hope*, an employment-related newspaper. It offers many things job seekers need in addition to job postings. It contains information about career fairs, professional advice about writing a résumé, and tips on how to do well in interviews.

회사가 하는 일

Career Hope is distributed to many locations around East Saint Louis, and it is completely free of charge to job seekers. ❶ Using *Career Hope* is a great idea for hiring companies. Each posting costs $30 and lasts for one month.

회사 위치와 요금 안내

❷ Visit www.careerhopeprint.com/ad to make job postings. You can also view examples of effective job postings. Please upload the text you want to include in the posting, and then pay the final fee.

웹사이트에서 할 수 있는 것

Please note that your text will not be edited by *Career Hope*. If you want to hire an editor to write your advertisement, please contact us at 785-884-2370. There will be an additional fee for this service.

유의 사항

---

1. What is indicated about *Career Hope*?

(A) It has several offices in East Saint Louis.
(B) It hosts a job fair every year.
(C) It charges $30 for each job posting.
(D) It is published once a month.

2. What is NOT mentioned as something that can be done on the *Career Hope* website?

(A) Making a payment
(B) Seeing sample postings
(C) Applying for a position
(D) Submitting a document

PART 7 UNIT 03

Questions 1-2 refer to the following advertisement.

Jean's Pick-up Service

- Take you from the airport to your hotel for a flat fee
- Seat up to three other travelers
- Available 24 hours a day, 7 days a week
- Fully trained and vetted professional drivers
- No reservations needed. Call us at 195-555-1873 with your flight details, and we will schedule you in.

---

1. What is being advertised?

(A) A travel agency
(B) A hotel
(C) A transportation service
(D) A training program

2. What is indicated about Jean's Pick-up Service?

(A) It can cater to small groups.
(B) It requires a prior reservation.
(C) It is hiring additional employees.
(D) It operates in multiple cities.

Questions 3-5 refer to the following information.

Tips from Contact Electricity

This month's edition brings you some ways to keep your electronics safe while also minimizing your power bill.

1. Protect your devices: In bad weather, voltage spikes can occur. If not properly mitigated, these spikes can badly damage your equipment. Make this a non-issue by purchasing some surge protectors. They can be purchased from just about everywhere, and they can save you lots of money down the line.

2. Unplug when you're done: after you're finished using a device, unplug it from the wall. This will save you a bit of money in the long run.

3. Monitor your meter: A good habit to get into is to look at how much electricity your household uses. Sudden increases in electricity usage may indicate that something in your house is malfunctioning.

These tips are provided to Contact Electricity customers every month alongside your electricity bill. If you have any questions, speak to a Contact Technician at 315-555-4169.

---

3. For whom is the information intended?

(A) Contact Electricity employees
(B) Contact Electricity customers
(C) Real estate agents
(D) Construction workers

4. What is indicated about surge protectors?

(A) They are widely available.
(B) They must be properly installed.
(C) They are inexpensive to purchase.
(D) They are easy to use.

5. What is stated about the tips?

(A) They are available to the public.
(B) They are verified by an independent source.
(C) They are written for small businesses.
(D) They are sent out every month.

Questions 6-8 refer to the following notice.

Baked Beans Mandatory Recall Notice

November 8

In light of recent news, food production company Gown International is issuing a recall notice for its 14-ounce cans of baked beans. The recall is due to an error in the packing process, which may render the product unsafe for human consumption. While the extent of the issue is not known yet, we have pulled all affected cans from grocery store shelves.

Affected cans of Gown International baked beans will contain the product codes 603813 and 603815. Consumers should check their 14-ounce cans of Gown International baked beans to see if they contain one of the product codes. In the case that consumers possess a can with one of the product codes, they are urged to return it to the original place of purchase for a full refund. Alternatively, cans may be sent to us directly and a replacement will be sent back. The address can be found on our Web site at www.gowninternational.com/recall.

We would like to sincerely apologize for the inconvenience. Rest assured, Gown International will be investigating the processes in all of our canned meals, fruit, and soups to ensure this does not happen again.

Thank you for your loyalty.

Abel Thompson, CEO
Gown International

---

6. For whom is the notice intended?

   (A) Gown International customers
   (B) Gown International employees
   (C) Grocery store owners
   (D) Grocery store checkout operators

7. What is one action Mr. Thompson recommends?

   (A) Taking part in an online form
   (B) Joining a focus group
   (C) Speaking to a company representative
   (D) Receiving a refund for a product

8. What is mentioned about Gown International?

   (A) It has offices in three countries.
   (B) It sells canned fruit.
   (C) It imports its products.
   (D) It has a new website.

Questions 9-11 refer to the following e-mail.

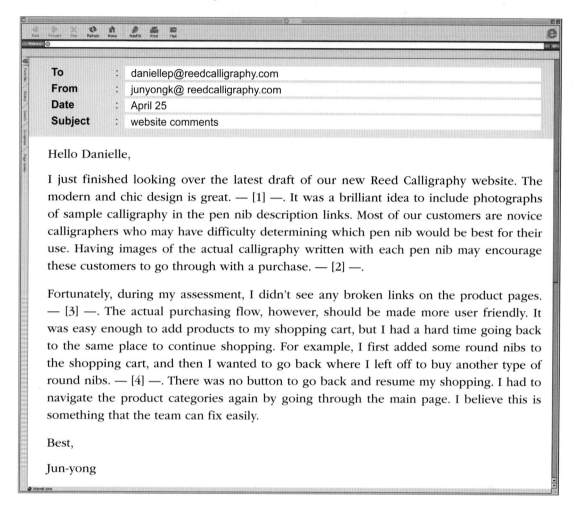

To : daniellep@reedcalligraphy.com
From : junyongk@ reedcalligraphy.com
Date : April 25
Subject : website comments

Hello Danielle,

I just finished looking over the latest draft of our new Reed Calligraphy website. The modern and chic design is great. — [1] —. It was a brilliant idea to include photographs of sample calligraphy in the pen nib description links. Most of our customers are novice calligraphers who may have difficulty determining which pen nib would be best for their use. Having images of the actual calligraphy written with each pen nib may encourage these customers to go through with a purchase. — [2] —.

Fortunately, during my assessment, I didn't see any broken links on the product pages. — [3] —. The actual purchasing flow, however, should be made more user friendly. It was easy enough to add products to my shopping cart, but I had a hard time going back to the same place to continue shopping. For example, I first added some round nibs to the shopping cart, and then I wanted to go back where I left off to buy another type of round nibs. — [4] —. There was no button to go back and resume my shopping. I had to navigate the product categories again by going through the main page. I believe this is something that the team can fix easily.

Best,

Jun-yong

---

9. What is mentioned about Reed Calligraphy customers?

(A) They take photographs of their calligraphy and send them to the company.
(B) They usually get their supplies from a stationery store.
(C) They prefer to buy a variety of pen nibs.
(D) They may be unfamiliar with different pen nibs.

10. What is suggested about the Web site?

(A) It takes a long time for each page to load.
(B) It is difficult to navigate while shopping.
(C) It is visually unappealing.
(D) Its links include some outdated pricing.

11. In which of the positions marked [1], [2], [3], and [4] does the following sentence best belong?

"As you asked, I thoroughly tested all of them, and they work well."

(A) [1]
(B) [2]
(C) [3]
(D) [4]

암시·추론 문제

암시·추론 문제는 지문의 내용을 근거로 지문에 나와 있지 않은 새로운 사항을 추론하는 문제 유형이다. 지문의 전체 흐름을 이해하고 난 후 풀 수 있는 경우가 대부분이기 때문에 Part 7에서 가장 까다로운 질문 유형으로 최근 들어 출제 비중이 점점 더 높아지고 있다.

🔍 질문 유형 확인하기

▶ 키워드가 있는 경우

Who will probably lead the conference?
누가 회의를 이끌 것 같은가?

What is suggested / implied about upcoming project?
다가오는 프로젝트에 관해서 암시 / 추론할 수 있는 것은 무엇인가?

What will most likely happen on March 8?
3월 8일에 무엇이 일어날 것 같은가?

▶ 키워드가 없는 경우

Where would this advertisement most likely be found?
이 광고는 어디서 볼 수 있을 것 같은가?

What can be inferred about this article?
이 기사에 관해 추론할 수 있는 것은 무엇인가?

For whom is this advertisement most likely intended?
이 광고는 누구를 대상으로 하는가?

 독해 전략

1. 키워드가 있는 질문의 경우, 질문의 핵심 키워드를 확인한 후 지문에 해당 키워드를 그대로 언급하거나 패러프레이징한 부분에서 정답의 단서를 찾는다. 다만, 암시·추론 문제의 정답은 항상 선택지에 해당 단어가 그대로 언급되어 있기보다는 패러프레이징되어 있는 점을 유의한다.

2. 키워드가 없는 질문의 경우, 대상이나 출처를 묻는 것과 같이 지문 전체를 읽고 이해해야만 풀 수 있는 문제가 대다수이므로 다른 세부사항을 묻는 문제를 먼저 해결한 후 푸는 것이 좋다. 또한, 정답을 찾을 때 본인이 아는 상식을 근거로 '그럴 것이다'라는 추측은 금물이며 반드시 지문을 바탕으로 추론할 수 있는 내용의 보기를 선택하는 것이 중요하다.

Question 1 refers to the following e-mail.

From: Aileen Park

To: Sue Kim

Date: May 1

Subject: New System

Dear Ms. Kim,

I would like to inform you that the company has decided to adopt the Tracker Time Reporting System (TTRS). The system is needed to record the staff hours. It is essential that all employees use the system. On April 20, I sent employees an e-mail explaining the system and described how to make an ID.

The system is going to be implemented on May 8, and all employees must have their IDs by May 5. Please click the TTRS icon on the company's homepage to make your ID. ❶ After creating your ID, it is possible to review your paycheck statements whenever you want to check them.

If you are faced with problems when you use the system, contact Mr. Kang, the help desk manager.

Thank you.

Aileen Park

Associate Director, Payroll Department

발신인
수신인
날짜
제목

새로운 시스템
도입 안내

전 직원들이 해야 할 일

문제가 있을 경우
연락 방법

발신인 정보
직책 및 부서

1. What is suggested about the new employee IDs?

(A) They require a fee to make.

(B) They are needed to access the Internet.

(C) They can be used to check salary statements.

(D) They are needed to enter a building.

PART 7 UNIT 04

해설서 p.76

Questions 1-2 refer to the following information.

PLEASE READ FIRST BEFORE USING

Thank you for being a Resensor customer.

Before unpacking, please refer to the list of components. As you unpack, we recommend checking off each item to ensure you have all of the necessary parts. If something is missing, contact us immediately, and we will send a replacement.

To assemble, find a flat surface with adequate lighting and follow the instructions. As electronic parts are delicate, never apply excess pressure when tightening screws. For your device to be eligible for warranty coverage, register your product on our website www.resensor.com.

1. Where is the information most likely found?

(A) In a box
(B) On a website
(C) On a brochure
(D) On an invoice

2. What kind of item is most likely discussed?

(A) A piece of office furniture
(B) A decorative ornament
(C) A desktop computer
(D) An item of clothing

Questions 3-4 refer to the following product review.

I have tried a lot of different headphones through my career, and in my opinion, the Dawnbreak SP2 noise-canceling headphones have offered the best experience. My work involves a lot of traveling as I scope out potential venues for upcoming shows and festivals. The Dawnbreak SP2 headphones allow me to sit back and relax on the plane or the bus with no distractions from other travelers. What makes the Dawnbreak SP2 headphones a cut above the competition is that they feel almost weightless. I sometimes forget that I am still wearing them!

— Ella Austin, 12 May

3. Who most likely is Ms. Austin?

(A) A commercial pilot
(B) A construction worker
(C) A sound engineer
(D) An event planner

4. Why does Ms. Austin prefer the Dawnbreak SP2 headphones to other products?

(A) They are lightweight.
(B) They are sturdier than other headphones.
(C) They come in a variety of designs.
(D) They can be used wirelessly.

Questions 5-6 refer to the following e-mail.

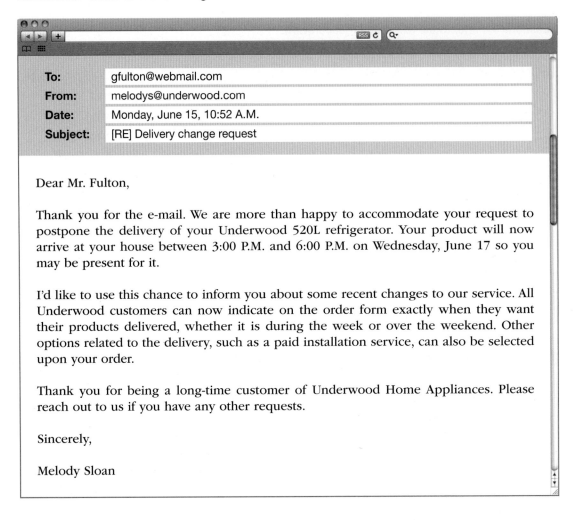

To: gfulton@webmail.com
From: melodys@underwood.com
Date: Monday, June 15, 10:52 A.M.
Subject: [RE] Delivery change request

Dear Mr. Fulton,

Thank you for the e-mail. We are more than happy to accommodate your request to postpone the delivery of your Underwood 520L refrigerator. Your product will now arrive at your house between 3:00 P.M. and 6:00 P.M. on Wednesday, June 17 so you may be present for it.

I'd like to use this chance to inform you about some recent changes to our service. All Underwood customers can now indicate on the order form exactly when they want their products delivered, whether it is during the week or over the weekend. Other options related to the delivery, such as a paid installation service, can also be selected upon your order.

Thank you for being a long-time customer of Underwood Home Appliances. Please reach out to us if you have any other requests.

Sincerely,

Melody Sloan

5. What does the e-mail suggest about Mr. Fulton?

(A) He requested for a paid installation service.
(B) He would like to cancel his order.
(C) He made an error in his order.
(D) He wanted to be home for a delivery.

6. What is a reason that Ms. Sloan wrote to Mr. Fulton?

(A) To promote a new shopping service for long-time customers
(B) To inform him that an additional fee must be paid in advance
(C) To describe updates to Underwood Home Appliances' order form
(D) To apologize for the late delivery of his Underwood 520L refrigerator

Questions 7-10 refer to the following online chat discussion.

Jared Lee (9:36 A.M.)
Vickie and Mindy. I just saw that neither of you will be attending tomorrow's quarterly meeting. Could you review the slide I will be presenting?

Vickie Bishop (9:37 A.M.)
Convenient timing. I received a copy of it, so I was reviewing it just then.

Jared Lee (9:38 A.M.)
Great. Can you take a close look at slides 3 and 4? They detail what our company has achieved this quarter and some of the challenges we faced, respectively. I want these to be clear to the management group.

Mindy Graves (9:40 A.M.)
Yes. I think it's particularly important to acknowledge the amazing work all of our departments have put in. The management group should know about their contributions despite all of the challenges.

Jared Lee (9:41 A.M.)
You got it.

Mindy Graves (9:42 A.M.)
I can review the slides after my afternoon meeting. Also, my morning client meeting got pushed back to next week, so I'll join you at the quarterly meeting.

Vickie Bishop (9:53 A.M.)
It's looking great. We should also include some of the new software we implemented in April. My Research Analyst Department has really benefited from this policy. Some of the new software we're using has completely changed the way we work.

[SEND]

7. What most likely is on slide 4?

(A) A list of new policies that have been implemented
(B) A list of attendees for the quarterly meeting
(C) A list of challenges the company has faced
(D) A list of the company's recent achievements

8. At 9:41 A.M., what does Mr. Lee most likely mean when he writes, "You got it"?

(A) He will express gratitude to employees for their work.
(B) He will remove a slide from his presentation.
(C) He will send a copy of his slide deck to the management group.
(D) He will invite others to present with him at the meeting.

9. What is indicated about Ms. Graves' morning meeting?

(A) It was scheduled to happen at the same time as another event.
(B) It was canceled upon Ms. Graves' request.
(C) It will be an online meeting.
(D) It will take place earlier in the morning.

10. What is suggested about Ms. Bishop?

(A) She will require more time to review a slide deck.
(B) She was recently promoted to a new position.
(C) She proposed a policy that was recently implemented.
(D) She is in charge of the Research Analyst employees.

UNIT 05 문장 삽입 문제

문장 삽입 문제는 지문의 흐름을 파악한 후 제시된 문장이 들어가기에 가장 적절한 위치를 고르는 유형으로 주어진 문장의 내용과 전체 지문의 맥락을 정확하게 파악해야 풀 수 있다. 단일 지문에서만 출제되며 매회 평균 2문제가 출제된다.

🔍 질문 유형 확인하기

In which of the positions marked [1], [2], [3], and [4] does the following sentence best belong?

"We are pleased to let you know that there is still space available."

[1], [2], [3], [4]로 표시된 곳 중에서 다음 문장이 들어가기에 가장 적절한 곳은 어디인가?

"우리는 당신에게 여전히 이용 가능한 공간이 있다는 것을 알려주게 되어 기쁩니다."

 독해 전략

1. 제시된 한 문장이 지문 내에 삽입될 곳을 찾는 유형인 만큼 전체적인 문맥 파악이 중요하다. 단일 지문의 마지막 문제로 출제되기 때문에 다른 문제를 먼저 풀면서 전체 문맥을 종합한 후에 푸는 것이 좋다.

2. 주어진 문장을 읽고 핵심 키워드를 확인한다. 이때, 대명사나 접속사와 같은 단서를 활용한다.

3. 주어진 문장 속의 핵심 키워드와 관련된 내용을 지문에서 찾아 빈칸이 있는 위치에 주어진 문장을 삽입해 본다. 지시어 (this, these, it)가 나와 있는 경우, 지시어가 지칭하는 대상을 찾는 것이 중요하다. 예를 들어, these는 복수 명사가 앞 문장에 있어야 한다. 또한, 접속부사(however, also, therefore)가 있다면 빈칸이 있는 위치의 앞뒤 맥락을 파악하여 삽입해 본다.

4. 마지막으로 주어진 문장을 지문의 위치에 대입해 봤을 때 논리적으로 자연스럽게 연결되는지 확인한다.

해설서 p.78

Question 1 refers to the following e-mail.

To: Eric Hopkins <erichopkins@vincent.com>

From: Wilma Mullins <wmullins@sche.org>

Date: August 27

Subject: Special Rates

Dear Mr. Hopkins,

The Society of Chemical Engineers (SCHE) is going to be holding its annual convention in London, England, this year from October 4–6. —[1]—. In case you have not yet made arrangements for accommodations, we would like to inform you of a special deal that has just been announced. ❶ Hillside Manor is offering SCHE members special rates during the convention. —[2]—. For only 120 pounds a night, you can get a double room, and for 205 pounds a night, you can reserve a suite. Both offers represent savings of more than 40 percent off the regular rates. —[3]—.

To take advantage of this special offer, use the special code SCHECONVENTION when making your reservation at www. hillsidemanor.com. —[4]—. But please hurry, as this offer is only valid until September 15.

We look forward to seeing you at this year's conference.

Sincerely,

Wilma Mullins
SCHE Convention Organizer

• 수신인
  발신인
  날짜
  제목

• 영국 런던에서 있을
  연례 회의 일정 안내

• 특별 할인 안내

• 할인 받는 방법

• 마무리 인사

• 발신인 정보
  직책

PART 7 UNIT 05

1. In which of the positions marked [1], [2], [3], and [4] does the following sentence best belong?

"It is conveniently located across the street from the convention center."

(A) [1]
(B) [2]
(C) [3]
(D) [4]

Questions 1-3 refer to the following notice.

Templeton Bridge Repairs Project

— [1] —. Templeton Bridge will be closed off to the public from February 1 to February 15 to undertake necessary repairs. The work will involve repairing a damaged suspender. — [2] —. During the process, work to re-paint the road markings will improve visibility for drivers.

Templeton Bridge is a traffic-heavy bridge that connects Templeton to Waterloo. During the closure, drivers are instead advised to take State Highway 17 to get to Waterloo. — [3] —. Buses have already updated their routes during this time, so please consult the latest timetables to understand how this might impact you.

For more information, please visit www.templetoncity.gov/bridgework. — [4] —.

---

1. What is the purpose of the notice?

(A) To revise a completion date
(B) To request feedback on a project
(C) To outline the importance of public transportation
(D) To announce a bridge closure

2. What is one project goal?

(A) A wider road
(B) Clearer road markings
(C) Creating a bike lane
(D) Installing new lights

3. In which of the positions marked [1], [2], [3], and [4] does the following sentence best belong?

"This is a result of the storm that occurred last month."

(A) [1]
(B) [2]
(C) [3]
(D) [4]

FOR IMMEDIATE RELEASE

Media Contact: Ed Brown <ebrown@porchaentertainment.co.nz>

AUCKLAND (13 February) — [1] —. Porcha Entertainment, one of the largest entertainment companies in New Zealand and the recipient of numerous industry awards for the hits *Void Space* and *Second Chances*, made an unexpected announcement on Thursday. — [2] —. Geraldine Abbott, president of Porcha Entertainment, disclosed that Michael Jennings would be stepping down from his position as creative director. Mr. Jennings, who has been with the company since its inception, hinted at an industry conference last year that he was considering retirement. However, the timing of the announcement has caught everyone off guard. — [3] —. Ms. Abbott shared that Mr. Jennings will stay on in a consultant capacity to assist with the company's expansion into the video game industry next month. "This marks a momentous occasion for our company, and I am excited for what the future holds," she noted. — [4] —.

4. What is the subject of the press release?

(A) A partnership
(B) A retirement
(C) An event
(D) An advertisement

5. According to the press release, what will Porcha Entertainment do in March?

(A) Open a new office
(B) Hire additional employees
(C) Host an awards event
(D) Expand into other areas

6. In which of the positions marked [1], [2], [3] and [4] does the following sentence best belong?

"It was expected to take place next year."

(A) [1]
(B) [2]
(C) [3]
(D) [4]

Questions 7-9 refer to the following Web page.

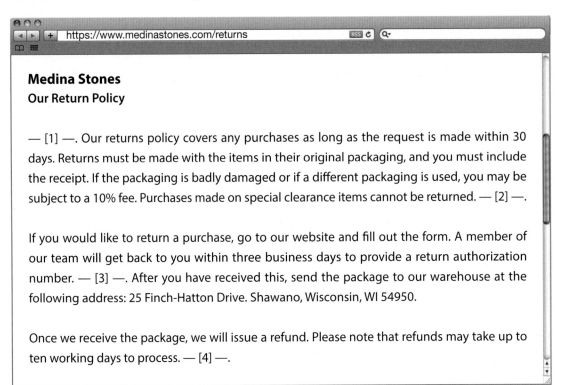

Medina Stones
Our Return Policy

— [1] —. Our returns policy covers any purchases as long as the request is made within 30 days. Returns must be made with the items in their original packaging, and you must include the receipt. If the packaging is badly damaged or if a different packaging is used, you may be subject to a 10% fee. Purchases made on special clearance items cannot be returned. — [2] —.

If you would like to return a purchase, go to our website and fill out the form. A member of our team will get back to you within three business days to provide a return authorization number. — [3] —. After you have received this, send the package to our warehouse at the following address: 25 Finch-Hatton Drive. Shawano, Wisconsin, WI 54950.

Once we receive the package, we will issue a refund. Please note that refunds may take up to ten working days to process. — [4] —.

7. According to the Web page, why does Medina Stones sometimes charge a fee for returns?

(A) Because the items are on sale.
(B) Because the packaging is in poor condition.
(C) Because the company pays for shipping costs.
(D) Because the receipt is not included.

8. What is indicated about Medina Stones' customers?

(A) They are expected to pay for expedited shipping.
(B) They can exchange returned items for store credit.
(C) They must provide proof of identification on Medina Stones' website.
(D) They will be contacted prior to returning items.

9. In which of the positions marked [1], [2], [3], and [4] does the following sentence best belong?

"If you are unhappy with your purchase, we offer full refunds."

(A) [1]
(B) [2]
(C) [3]
(D) [4]

Questions 10-13 refer to the following information.

The team at Vavaire Airlines encompasses more than 25,000 people from all around the world and from all walks of life. We are excited to announce that we are looking to fill some positions. — [1] —. We have openings in several departments, so we encourage everyone to apply. — [2] —. Some of the perks we offer all of our employees include discounted ticketing to let you travel the world at a fraction of the cost. — [3] —. Additionally, you can also enjoy flexible working hours, reimbursements on any learning and development courses you take, and free use of our health center and cafeteria. — [4] —. Our annual paid vacations let you focus on achieving what you want while working. If you need any more reason to work at Vavaire Airlines, just ask Team Builder Journal, who named us in their "Top 10 Employers to Work For" for the fifth consecutive year.

10. For whom is the information intended?

(A) Vavaire Airlines employees
(B) Vavaire Airlines customers
(C) Current job seekers
(D) Journal readers

11. In the information, what is NOT mentioned as being offered to employees?

(A) Free airline tickets
(B) Changeable working hours
(C) Payment for educational expenses
(D) Access to a gym

12. What is mentioned about Vavaire Airlines?

(A) It recently downsized its workforce.
(B) It has been mentioned in a trade publication.
(C) It has come under new management.
(D) It is planning on opening a new office.

13. In which of the positions marked [1], [2], [3], and [4] does the following sentence best belong?

"We understand that you may have personal goals you want to accomplish."

(A) [1]
(B) [2]
(C) [3]
(D) [4]

UNIT 06

동의어 문제

동의어 문제는 지문에 나오는 특정 단어와 같은 뜻을 지닌 단어를 보기 중에서 찾는 유형이다. 동의어 문제는 보통 한 가지 이상의 뜻을 가진 단어를 제시한 후, 사전적인 의미보다는 문맥상 가장 가까운 뜻을 지닌 단어를 보기에서 선택하는 문제이므로 지문을 읽으며 문맥상의 의미를 파악하는 것이 중요하다.

🔍 질문 유형 확인하기

▸ 단일 지문의 경우

The word "credit" in paragraph 3, line 1, is closest in meaning to
세 번째 단락, 첫 번째 줄의 단어 'credit'과 의미상 가장 가까운 것은

▸ 이중 / 삼중 지문의 경우

In the e-mail, the word "term" in paragraph 2, line 3, is closest in meaning to
이메일에서, 두 번째 단락, 세 번째 줄의 단어 'term'과 의미상 가장 가까운 것은

 독해 전략

① 질문에서 제시된 단어의 지문상에 위치를 확인한다.

② 지문에서 해당 문장을 해석하며 제시된 단어의 문맥상 의미를 파악한다. 해당 단어의 동의어이지만 문맥에서 쓰인 뜻과는 다른 단어가 제시될 수도 있다. 따라서, 너무 사전적인 의미만 생각하지 말고 문맥상 어떤 뜻으로 쓰였는지를 파악하는 것이 중요하다.

③ 토익에서 자주 출제되는 다의어 단어들을 중심으로 어휘력을 기르도록 한다.

▸ 빈출 동의어 리스트

cover	① 가리다	② 다루다	③ 취재하다	④ 대신하다	⑤ 보장하다
secure	① 획득하다	② 고정시키다	③ 보호하다	④ 안전한	
entry	① 입장	② 출품작	③ 참가 / 출전		
issue	① 발표하다	② 발급하다	③ 발행하다	④ 주제	⑤ 문제
balance	① 평형	② 균형	③ 잔고		
term	① 용어	② 학기	③ 기간 / 임기	④ 조건	

Question 1 refers to the following article.

(May 22) The city of Worcester has a cause to celebrate. It has managed to cut traffic jams in the downtown area by almost 25 percent compared to last year. According to transportation authorities, commutes were especially bad during the morning rush hour, but the conditions have improved significantly thanks to a smart initiative implemented last December to encourage citizens to commute by subway more often.

    ● 최근 시행된 교통 계획 안내

In order to attract more people to public transportation, subway fares were reduced, and the city decided to replace old subway trains with new ones and have them run more frequently. According to a survey of Worcester residents, these changes were important factors in their decision to use more public transportation. "The new schedules have made a huge impact," one resident said.

    ● 계획 시행 원인

❶ These measures appear to have had some positive effect in terms of financial viability of some subway operators. For example, the green subway line, which runs from Canal Street to Fergus Lane, rarely had any passengers, and operators once considered closing the line. However, this is no longer an issue since there are now enough passengers to maintain financial stability.

    ● 추가 지하철 운행의 긍정적인 측면

PART 7 UNIT 06

1. The word "measures" in paragraph 3, line 1, is closest in meaning to

(A) distances
(B) actions
(C) standards
(D) successes

Questions 1-3 refer to the following e-mail.

To	Mable Pittman <mablep@hmail.com>
From	Jim Lindstrom <jlindstrom@travelogymag.com>
Date	July 10
Subject	Subscription renewal

Dear Ms. Pittman,

Travelogy Magazine would like to express our gratitude for subscription over the last year. We at Travelogy aims to provide you with quality articles about destinations around the world from award-winning travel journalists.

Your subscription will run out at the end of this month. We deeply value your business and hope you will continue to remain with us.

If you extend your contract for another year, we will reduce 25 percent off your bill for the following three months (August, September, and October).

If you would like to take advantage of this offer, please reach out to us within the next two weeks. For additional information about your subscription and hot deals on vacation packages, please visit our Website, www.travelogy.com.

Sincerely,

Jim Lindstrom
Customer Relations Manager
Travelogy Magazine

1. When will Ms. Pittman's current subscription expire?

   (A) In July
   (B) In August
   (C) In September
   (D) In October

2. The word "value" in paragraph 2, line 1, is closest in meaning to

   (A) profit
   (B) expense
   (C) treasure
   (D) charge

3. What does Mr. Lindstrom offer Ms. Pittman?

   (A) A vacation package
   (B) A one-year contract
   (C) An international travel voucher
   (D) A discount on monthly payment

Questions 4-6 refer to the following e-mail.

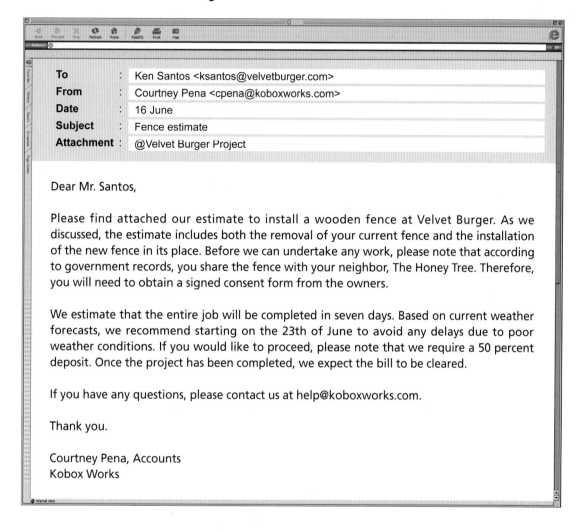

To : Ken Santos <ksantos@velvetburger.com>
From : Courtney Pena <cpena@koboxworks.com>
Date : 16 June
Subject : Fence estimate
Attachment : @Velvet Burger Project

Dear Mr. Santos,

Please find attached our estimate to install a wooden fence at Velvet Burger. As we discussed, the estimate includes both the removal of your current fence and the installation of the new fence in its place. Before we can undertake any work, please note that according to government records, you share the fence with your neighbor, The Honey Tree. Therefore, you will need to obtain a signed consent form from the owners.

We estimate that the entire job will be completed in seven days. Based on current weather forecasts, we recommend starting on the 23th of June to avoid any delays due to poor weather conditions. If you would like to proceed, please note that we require a 50 percent deposit. Once the project has been completed, we expect the bill to be cleared.

If you have any questions, please contact us at help@koboxworks.com.

Thank you.

Courtney Pena, Accounts
Kobox Works

---

4. What is indicated about the fence that will be installed?

(A) It will be paid for by two companies.
(B) It will require government consent.
(C) It will be made of metal.
(D) It will replace another fence.

5. What does Ms. Pena request that Mr. Santos do?

(A) Obtain permission to build
(B) Schedule an inspection date
(C) Purchase some materials
(D) Fill out a survey

6. The word "cleared" in paragraph 2, line 4, is closest in meaning to

(A) endorsed
(B) paid in full
(C) legitimate
(D) returned

Questions 7-9 refer to the following product review.

Excellent Washing Machine!

I've always used laundromats, so I've never looked for washing machines to own. After moving into my new house, I found myself requiring a washing machine as there were no laundromats in my area. I then came across a few advertisements for the Crysair 250. Although it was pricier and larger than other models, all of the reviews mentioned how long it has lasted them. That's important to me, so I decided to buy it. I've had mine for over a month now, and it has been simply amazing. My clothes come out clean and smelling fresh every time. Also, the machine is so quiet I sometimes forget that it is still running. Finally, I love how the machine can be controlled from my phone. As someone who spends a lot of time at work, my time is very valuable to me. I love how I can tell the machine to start the washing from anywhere. Overall, a fantastic purchase and highly recommended.

— Leon Welch

7. Why did Mr. Welch choose the Crysair 250 washing machine?

(A) It was available at a discount.
(B) It was the largest model available.
(C) It was designed by a reputable brand.
(D) It was mentioned as being durable.

8. The word "running" in paragraph 1, line 8, is closest in meaning to

(A) operating
(B) playing
(C) adapting
(D) shifting

9. What is indicated about Mr. Welch?

(A) He moved to a new company.
(B) He cares about saving time.
(C) He reviews home appliances professionally.
(D) He bought the washing machine a year ago.

Questions 10-13 refer to the following e-mail.

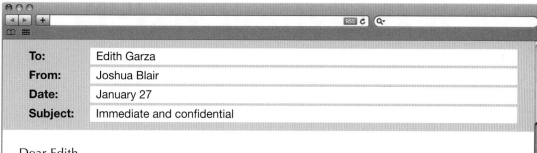

To: Edith Garza
From: Joshua Blair
Date: January 27
Subject: Immediate and confidential

Dear Edith,

Starting with the new fiscal year, a new option regarding retirement benefits can be exercised for all full-time employees at Prestige Partners. Instead of Prestige Partners matching contributions to an employee's retirement fund, there will now be an option to receive compensation in the form of company stock to deposit into your retirement portfolio.

This change has already been discussed with our retirement management firm Flagstaff Funds. Should one choose this new option, the firm will help make the transition and continue to provide customer support to Prestige Partners employees. The contact person for Flagstaff Funds is Eileen Castillo, and any inquiries related to this should be directed to her. Her contact details can be found on Flagstaff Funds' website.

Please work with Kirk Brady, head of human resources, to provide him with the necessary information he should include in his all staff communication regarding this change. Our CEO has stated that she would like to gather data on how many employees choose the stock option as soon as possible.

Thank you.

Joshua Blair, CFO
Prestige Partners

10. What is a purpose of the e-mail?

(A) To provide instructions
(B) To collect feedback
(C) To modify a proposal
(D) To report on a problem

11. The word "exercised" in paragraph 1, line 2, is closest in meaning to

(A) explored
(B) applied
(C) replaced
(D) worked

12. What is suggested about Flagstaff Funds?

(A) It offers its own retirement plan.
(B) It is located in the same office as Prestige Partners.
(C) It provides accounting services.
(D) It will help Prestige Partners employees with any issues.

13. Who is responsible for notifying all employees about the policy change?

(A) Ms. Garza
(B) Ms. Castillo
(C) Mr. Brady
(D) Mr. Blair

문자 대화문과 화자의도

대화문은 2인이 서로 대화를 주고받는 문자 메시지와 3인 이상이 대화를 주고받는 온라인 채팅으로 나뉜다. 주로 비즈니스 관련 대화나 일상생활에서 나누는 대화 등이 나오며 평균 2지문 정도 출제된다.

🔍 지문 유형 확인하기

회사 대 회사 대화문	· 회사 내 업무에 관한 내용 · 주문, 일정 계획, 간단한 문의에 관한 내용
회사 대 고객 대화문	· 고객 상담자와 고객 사이의 문제 해결에 관한 내용

🔍 질문 유형 확인하기

인물	What is suggested about Mr. Lee's team? 이 씨의 팀에 관해서 암시되는 것은 무엇인가?
주제 / 목적	Why did Ms. Paul contact Mr. Sato? 폴 씨는 왜 사토 씨에게 연락했는가?
상세 정보	What is Mr. Lee asked to do? 이 씨가 요청받은 것은 무엇인가?
의도	At 3:32 P.M., what does Mr. Kilday most likely mean when he writes, "that should be fine"? 3시 32분에 킬데이 씨가 "that should be fine"이라고 썼을 때, 그가 의도한 것은 무엇인가?
미래 상황	When will the dinner most likely be held? 언제 저녁 식사가 열리겠는가?

독해 전략

1 3인 이상의 온라인 채팅문에서는 많은 화자들이 나와 대화를 주고받는 형식의 지문이기 때문에 누가 어떤 이야기를 했는지 정확하게 구별해야 한다. 특히 사람 이름을 잘 파악하자.

2 채팅 지문 같은 경우는 간결하고 쉬운 말투로 대화가 진행되기 때문에 채팅상의 구어 표현을 익혀 두는 것도 좋다.

3 의도 파악 문제는 단순히 사전적인 의미를 묻기보다 대화의 흐름 속에 숨은 의미를 찾는 것이 중요하므로 인용 문장 앞뒤에 나오는 문장과 어떤 연관성이 있는지 파악하자.

 핵심 문제 유형

Question 1 refers to the following text message chain.

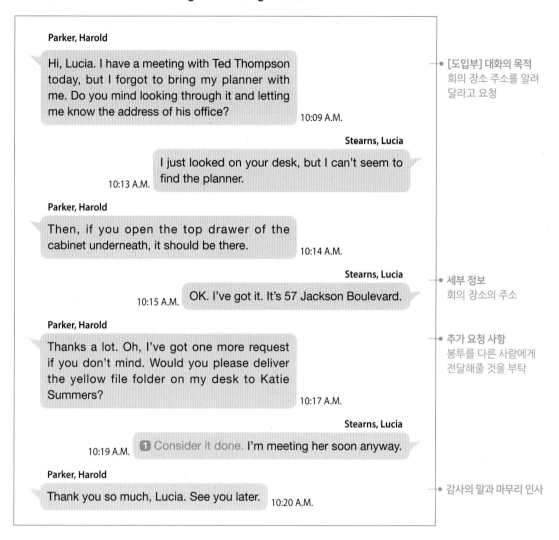

Parker, Harold

Hi, Lucia. I have a meeting with Ted Thompson today, but I forgot to bring my planner with me. Do you mind looking through it and letting me know the address of his office?
10:09 A.M.

Stearns, Lucia

10:13 A.M. I just looked on your desk, but I can't seem to find the planner.

Parker, Harold

Then, if you open the top drawer of the cabinet underneath, it should be there.
10:14 A.M.

Stearns, Lucia

10:15 A.M. OK. I've got it. It's 57 Jackson Boulevard.

Parker, Harold

Thanks a lot. Oh, I've got one more request if you don't mind. Would you please deliver the yellow file folder on my desk to Katie Summers?
10:17 A.M.

Stearns, Lucia

10:19 A.M. ❶ Consider it done. I'm meeting her soon anyway.

Parker, Harold

Thank you so much, Lucia. See you later. 10:20 A.M.

- [도입부] 대화의 목적
  회의 장소 주소를 알려 달라고 요청

- 세부 정보
  회의 장소의 주소

- 추가 요청 사항
  봉투를 다른 사람에게 전달해줄 것을 부탁

- 감사의 말과 마무리 인사

문맥상 화자 의도를 묻는 문제

1. At 10:19 A.M., what does Ms. Stearns mean when she writes, "Consider it done"?

(A) She will give a document to Ms. Summers.
(B) She will organize Mr. Parker's desk.
(C) She will lock a cabinet.
(D) She will contact Mr. Thompson.

PART 7 UNIT 07

Questions 1-2 refer to the following text message chain.

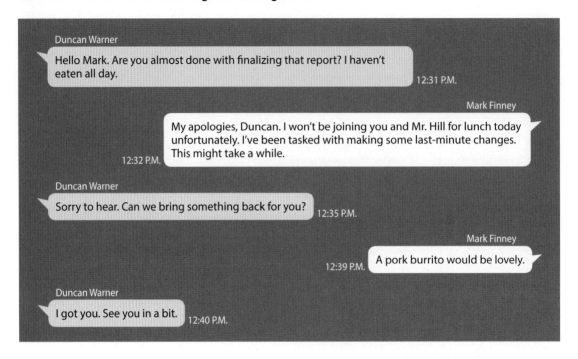

Duncan Warner

Hello Mark. Are you almost done with finalizing that report? I haven't eaten all day.

12:31 P.M.

Mark Finney

My apologies, Duncan. I won't be joining you and Mr. Hill for lunch today unfortunately. I've been tasked with making some last-minute changes. This might take a while.

12:32 P.M.

Duncan Warner

Sorry to hear. Can we bring something back for you?

12:35 P.M.

Mark Finney

12:39 P.M.   A pork burrito would be lovely.

Duncan Warner

I got you. See you in a bit.

12:40 P.M.

---

1. At 12:40 P.M., what does Mr. Warner most likely mean when he writes, "I got you"?

(A) Further changes may be necessary.
(B) Some assistance may be required.
(C) He has already fulfilled a request.
(D) He will bring lunch for Mr. Finney.

2. What will happen next?

(A) Mr. Warner and Mr. Hill will be out for a while.
(B) Mr. Warner will receive a copy of a presentation.
(C) Mr. Finney will make a phone call.
(D) Mr. Hill will revise a document.

Questions 3-4 refer to the following text message chain.

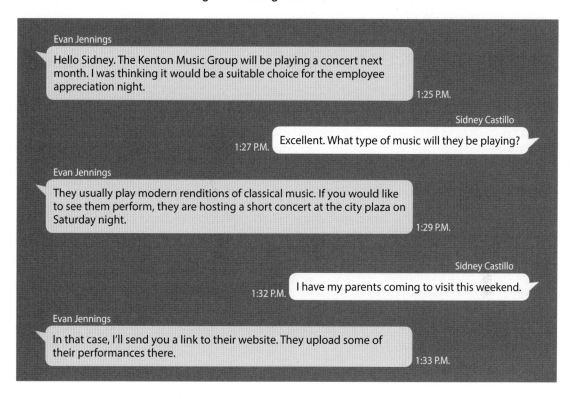

Evan Jennings

Hello Sidney. The Kenton Music Group will be playing a concert next month. I was thinking it would be a suitable choice for the employee appreciation night.

1:25 P.M.

Sidney Castillo

1:27 P.M. Excellent. What type of music will they be playing?

Evan Jennings

They usually play modern renditions of classical music. If you would like to see them perform, they are hosting a short concert at the city plaza on Saturday night.

1:29 P.M.

Sidney Castillo

1:32 P.M. I have my parents coming to visit this weekend.

Evan Jennings

In that case, I'll send you a link to their website. They upload some of their performances there.

1:33 P.M.

---

3. What is suggested about Mr. Jennings and Ms. Castillo?

(A) They are planning a company event.
(B) They live near the city plaza.
(C) They work in different offices.
(D) They will go on a business trip soon.

4. At 1:32 P.M., what does Ms. Castillo most likely mean when she writes, "I have my parents coming to visit this weekend"?

(A) She is frustrated that a plan was changed.
(B) She would like Mr. Jennings to confirm a detail.
(C) She cannot attend a musical performance.
(D) She will not be in the office next week.

Questions 5-8 refer to the following online chat discussion.

Chris Sandoval [2:11 P.M.] Hey, Isaac. I've invited Jean to this chatroom. As you know, she's also put in a lot of effort into this project.

Jean Ramsey [2:12 P.M.] Thank you, Chris. I heard that during the renovation, some workers found an old menu. Finding something from 200 or so years ago is fascinating.

Isaac Barret [2:13 P.M.] I agree. It's unbelievable.

Chris Sandoval [2:14 P.M.] So, Isaac and I decided to learn more about the building. We were aware that there was pharmacy on the property, but we had no idea about the bakery. We're hoping that maybe one day our bakers can recreate some of the items on the menu for our customers.

Isaac Barret [2:15 P.M.] They would be able to step into the past for a taste of history.

Jean Ramsey [2:16 P.M.] I've added the contractor into this chatroom so we can get the latest update. Hi, Laurie. Is everything on track?

Laurie Williams [2:17 P.M.] Hi, everyone. Most of the major construction work, including the wiring and plumbing, are completed. We're now putting in the finishing touches to the kitchen. I've spoken with the supplier, and the refrigerated display case should get here next Monday.

Jean Ramsey [2:18 P.M.] Does that mean we are on track for a February opening?

Laurie Williams [2:19 P.M.] We sure are.

SEND

---

5. Who most likely is Mr. Sandoval?

(A) A historical archeologist
(B) A building architect
(C) A future bakery owner
(D) An interior designer

6. At 2:13 P.M., what does Mr. Barret most likely mean when he writes, "It's unbelievable."?

(A) He was astounded by a recent discovery.
(B) He was unable to make a financial decision without more research.
(C) He had not expected to find items from the pharmacy on the construction site.
(D) He has reservations regarding a contractor's quotation.

7. What does Ms. Ramsey ask about?

(A) The exact location of a business
(B) The state of a remodeling project
(C) The agenda for a future meeting
(D) The building blueprints

8. What most likely will happen in February?

(A) A business will open.
(B) A new project will commence.
(C) A recruiting strategy will be reconsidered.
(D) Some equipment will be delivered.

Questions 9-12 refer to the following online chat discussion.

David Lowe [9:12 A.M.] Good morning everyone. The presentation containing our full product line-up should be going out to stores next week. They'll be interested to know what we've sold the most of as well as what reviews our new products have gotten.

Pete Holmes [9:13 A.M.] How is it looking?

David Lowe [9:15 A.M.] It's not finished yet. We're waiting on some information.

Nina Pierce [9:17 A.M.] We need the reviews for the new watch we are releasing. We just completed a test run, and we have some good user insights. The research and development office said we should receive it by Thursday at the latest.

Pete Holmes [9:20 A.M.] Absolutely, we can't discount that. If we haven't received the report by Wednesday, let's contact Krystal Moore and get her to send us a summary of the report.

David Lowe [9:22 A.M.] If we do receive the summary and we add the information into the slides, I think we should review the entire presentation together. Would Thursday or Friday work for both of you?

Pete Holmes [9:23 A.M.] I'm out of the office on Thursday, so is Friday afternoon possible?

Nina Pierce [9:25 A.M.] That's OK with me. I'll book the meeting room now.

---

9. What is indicated about a presentation?

(A) It will indicate the best-selling product.
(B) It will go out to the research and development team.
(C) It will be produced with help from several stores.
(D) It will be shown in person to attendees.

10. At 9:20 A.M., what does Mr. Holmes imply when he writes, "we can't discount that?"

(A) Further studies should be conducted.
(B) A file should be reviewed by more people.
(C) The price of a product has been set too high.
(D) Feedback from users is very important.

11. Who most likely is Ms. Moore?

(A) A sales supervisor
(B) A product researcher
(C) A store owner
(D) A marketing manager

12. When do the writers plan to meet to review a slide presentation?

(A) On Monday
(B) On Wednesday
(C) On Thursday
(D) On Friday

편지·이메일

편지와 이메일은 Part 7에서 가장 많이 출제되는 지문 유형으로 비즈니스 또는 일상생활과 관련된 다양한 주제로 출제된다. 일반적인 편지와 이메일의 논리 전개 방식에 따라(발신인 정보 → 수신인 정보 → 배경 및 주제, 목적 → 세부 내용 → 문의 및 제안 → 발신인 서명) 순서로 확인한다.

🔍 지문 유형 확인하기

회사 대 회사 편지	· 회사 내에서 행사 참여, 일정 취소 및 확정, 사업 제안 및 업무 내용
회사 대 고객 편지	· 상품 또는 서비스에 대한 항의, 불평, 불만 내용 · 환불 요청 및 배송 지연에 관한 내용 · 제품 또는 서비스에 대한 할인 혜택 제공 내용
구인 및 구직 편지	· 일자리 제안, 구직 지원, 구직자의 (불)합격 통보 내용

🔍 질문 유형 확인하기

주제 / 목적	What is the main purpose of this letter / e-mail? 이 편지 / 이메일의 주된 목적은 무엇인가? Why did Mr. Bryce write the letter / e-mail? 왜 브라이스 씨는 편지 / 이메일을 썼는가?
수 / 발신인	Who most likely is Mr. Paul? 폴 씨는 누구일 것 같은가? Who is this letter intended? 이 편지는 누구를 대상으로 하는가?
상세 정보	What is Mr. Kim asked / required / encouraged / recommended to do? 김 씨는 무엇을 하도록 요청 / 요구 / 권장 / 권고받았는가? Why should Ms. Yang visit the store at the end of next week? 양 씨는 왜 다음 주 말에 상점을 가야 하는가?
첨부 사항	What is enclosed / included / attached with this letter? 이 편지에 동봉 / 포함 / 첨부되어 있는 것은 무엇인가?
미래 행동	What should Mr. Brown do if he wants to respond to this letter? 브라운 씨는 이 편지에 답변하기를 원한다면 무엇을 해야 하는가?

독해 전략

① 반드시 수/발신자의 정보와 제목(subject)이나 Re(~에 관하여) 부분을 먼저 확인한다.

② 지문 속에 수/발신자에 관한 정보가 나올 경우 누구인지, 서로가 어떤 관계인지 정확하게 파악하는 것이 중요하다.

③ 요청 및 제안 사항과 첨부 사항은 주로 글의 중 후반 부분에 나온다.

④ 주제 및 목적, 요청 사항, 첨부된 것에 관한 관련 표현을 익혀 두면 정답의 단서를 쉽게 찾을 수 있다.

▶ 정답 근거가 되는 문장

주제 및 목적	I am writing to inform / announce / confirm ~ ~을 알려 / 발표 / 확인시켜 드리기 위해 글을 씁니다 I am very pleased / sorry to inform / tell you that ~ ~을 알려드리게 되어 기쁩니다 / 유감입니다 I would like to inform you that ~ ~을 알려드리고자 합니다 However / Unfortunately, ~ 하지만 / 유감스럽게도~
요청 사항 및 제안	Please + 동사원형 ~해주세요 Be sure to ~ 반드시 ~주세요 You should / must ~ 당신은~을 해야 합니다 Can / Could / Would you ~? ~해 주실 수 있을까요? I would appreciate it if you ~ ~해주시면 감사하겠습니다
첨부 사항	We have enclosed / included / attached ~ 우리는 ~을 동봉했다 You will find ~ 당신은 ~을 찾을 수 있을 거다

Questions 1-3 refer to the following letter.

Dear Ms. Park,

❶ We appreciate you writing a letter describing the exceptionally good service you received on February 3 from Ms. Angela Zhang. A copy of it has been placed in Ms. Zhang's personnel file.

It is rare that a customer takes the time to formally acknowledge the good service that an employee has provided, so we would like to do something for you in return. ❷ Please accept the enclosed voucher, which entitles you to a 15 percent discount on any item you wish to buy from any of our locations in the future.

Sincerely,

Brian Bae
❸ Brian Bae
Customer Service Manager
ENCLOSURE

• 수신인

• 편지의 목적
직원의 서비스를 칭찬하는 고객 편지에 대한 감사 표현

• 세부 정보:
동봉 · 첨부
감사의 표시로 15% 할인을 받을 수 있는 상품권 제공

• 발신인
발신인
관련 정보

편지의 목적

1. What is the purpose of the letter?

(A) To express gratitude
(B) To introduce an upcoming sale
(C) To respond to a complaint
(D) To announce a new location

세부사항: 편지와 동봉된 것

2. What is enclosed with the letter?

(A) A catalog
(B) A prepaid mailing label
(C) A product sample
(D) A coupon

세부사항: 인물의 정체 또는 직업

3. Who is Mr. Bae?

(A) A company executive
(B) A factory supervisor
(C) A customer service manager
(D) A news reporter

Practice

Questions 1-2 refer to the following e-mail.

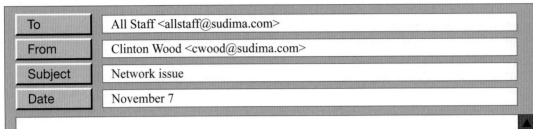

To	All Staff <allstaff@sudima.com>
From	Clinton Wood <cwood@sudima.com>
Subject	Network issue
Date	November 7

Dear Staff,

We experienced company-wide network failures earlier this morning. Many of you reported slow connections, intermittent connection issues, and experienced difficulties in sending or receiving e-mails. Our engineers have resolved the issue and verified that everything is running smoothly again. If you are continuing to experience issues, try restarting your computer before calling the Systems team for help.

Please note that if you sent e-mails between 9 and 10:30 A.M. this morning, there is a chance they did not go through. Fortunately, you can check whether they were delivered by going into your Send folder. All e-mails that were successfully delivered will show up there.

Thank you.

Clinton Wood
Systems Administrator, Sudima

1. Why did Mr. Wood send the e-mail?

   (A) To provide details on a technical problem
   (B) To warn staff against visiting unknown websites
   (C) To request feedback on the company's e-mail system
   (D) To inform staff about a recent update

2. What does Mr. Wood ask the staff to do?

   (A) Log into the company website
   (B) Check that some e-mails were correctly sent
   (C) Contact the Systems team
   (D) Attend an upcoming meeting on Internet security

Questions 3-4 refer to the following letter.

Alltria Bank
8291 Berry Drive
Sacramento, CA 92671
555-8993

December 8

Dear Ms. Huff,

Our records indicate that your checking account is overdrawn. On December 3, you wrote a check for $81.29 to the Federal Postal Service. However, your account balance at the time was $67.05. Unfortunately, your account does not have overdraft protection, so your account balance as of today is -$20.24. Please note that there is a $1-per-day fee when your checking account is overdrawn. Please contact me as soon as possible to take care of this matter.

Sincerely,

Jeanie Chitalli

Jeanie Chitalli
Manager, Sacramento Branch
Alltria Bank
555-8993

3. What is the main purpose of the letter?

(A) To inform a customer of an issue with an account
(B) To convey gratitude for a recent performance
(C) To seek some information about account benefits
(D) To promote a closer branch to a loyal customer

4. What is indicated about Alltria Bank?

(A) Many customers overdraw their accounts.
(B) It provides overdraft protection without request.
(C) It is willing to compromise with its customers.
(D) It charges a fee for overdrawn accounts.

Questions 5-7 refer to the following e-mail.

To	Video Project Group List
From	Josh Vega
Date	March 21
Subject	Information for video

Dear Video Project Group members,

Thank you for your co-operation in producing some 30-second videos to upload to our website. We hope to combine these videos into one that serves an important function. They will show to a wider audience your role and how it relates to our organization's vision. Our hope is that this will secure more funding by raising the visibility of our organization and attracting a wider range of investors.

Sometime this afternoon, you will all receive an e-mail with a finalized script. Please read through it carefully and do a few practice rounds of you reading it out. Tomorrow, we will travel together to a studio where a camera operator will walk you through what needs to be done. We will be leaving at 10:00 A.M. from our office, so please be here on time. It should also go without saying that you should look neat and presentable.

Sincerely,

Josh Vega
Vibetic Incorporated

5. What is the purpose of the video presentation?

(A) To attract potential investors
(B) To advertise the benefits of a product
(C) To explain the company's history
(D) To train new employees

6. What will members of the group receive?

(A) A video camera
(B) A map to a location
(C) A text to read aloud
(D) A schedule

7. What does Mr. Vega indicate about the video clips?

(A) They will be recorded at a studio.
(B) They will start recording at 10:00 A.M.
(C) They may exceed the time limit.
(D) They may be featured on television.

Questions 8-11 refer to the following letter.

Nuvallis Furniture

Aubree Thompson
General Manager, Stanner's Home Décor
1400 Terrace Road
Brisbane 4000, Australia

3 July

Dear Ms. Thompson,

This letter is to inform you that Nuvallis will be relocating soon. Effective Tuesday, 17 July, we will be closing down our store in Brisbane. Starting Tuesday, 2 August, we will be operating from 250 Flannigan Drive in Gold Coast. Our new location has much more space, which will allow us to stock a wider selection of furniture.

Please be aware that we will not be open from 17 July to 1 August while we carry out the move. On the day of our grand reopening, we will hold a celebration where we will introduce some of our newest products and hold a raffle for prizes. We also invite you to participate in the Know Your Furniture competition.

We regret to inform you that there will be a modest price increase in our products and delivery services as we have invested considerably in building our new facility. However, since your company has been our loyal customer for over 10 years, you will be excluded from the above-mentioned price increases for one year. In addition, we will take 15 percent off any products you purchase in the month of August.

Also, as of August 2, our new telephone number will be 07-843-9526. We appreciate your business and look forward to serving you again in the future.

Sincerely,

Lydia Perkins

Lydia Perkins
Director of Operations, Nuvallis Furniture

---

8. What is suggested about Nuvallis Furniture?

(A) It currently has two locations.
(B) It will expand its inventory.
(C) It has purchased another company.
(D) It will hire additional delivery drivers.

9. The phrase "carry out" in paragraph 2, line 1, is closest in meaning to

(A) remove
(B) reconsider
(C) accomplish
(D) lift

10. What can a Nuvallis Furniture customer do on August 2?

(A) Tour a factory in Brisbane
(B) Enter a contest
(C) Get a special discount
(D) Participate in a product survey

11. What is NOT indicated about Stanner's Home Décor?

(A) It has been operating for at least 10 years.
(B) It is located in Brisbane.
(C) It will receive a price cut on purchases made at Nuvallis Furniture next month.
(D) It plans to increase its orders from Nuvallis Furniture.

광고

광고는 편지 · 이메일 지문만큼 자주 출제되는 지문 유형으로 평균 2지문 정도 출제된다. 광고는 크게 구인 광고와 일반 상업 광고로 나누어진다.

🔍 지문 유형 확인하기

구인 광고 지문	· 인턴, 경력자, 관리자 공고 내용 · 신규 회원 모집 내용
상품 광고 지문	· 제품 광고 및 신규 서비스 광고 내용 · 회원 가입 혜택 안내, 지점 이전 안내, 여행사 및 호텔 패키지 안내 내용 · 새로운 건물 및 시설에 관한 광고 내용

🔍 질문 유형 확인하기

구인 광고 초반부	광고 대상	Who would be interested in this advertisement? 누가 이 광고에 관심을 갖겠는가? For whom is this advertisement intended? 이 광고는 누구를 대상으로 하는가?
	광고 목적	What is the purpose of this advertisement? 이 광고의 목적은 무엇인가?
	회사 정보	What kind of company is this? 어떤 종류의 회사인가?
구인 광고 중반부	자격 요건	What is NOT mentioned / indicated / stated as a requirement for the position? 그 직책의 자격 요건으로 언급되지 않은 것은 무엇인가? What is a requirement for the position? 그 직책의 한 가지 자격 요건은 무엇인가?
	직무 내용	What is NOT included in the manager's roles? 매니저의 역할로 포함되지 않은 것은 무엇인가?
	회사 혜택	What is NOT included in the benefits of joining the company? 회사에 입사하는 것의 혜택으로 포함되지 않은 것은 무엇인가?
구인 광고 후반부	지원 방법	How should the applicant apply for the position? 지원자들은 그 자리에 어떻게 지원할 수 있는가?
	연락 정보	How can the applicants find out more about the job? 지원자들은 그 직업에 관해 어떻게 더 많은 정보를 알 수 있는가?

제품 광고 초반부	광고 대상	For whom is this advertisement intended? 이 광고는 누구를 대상으로 하는가?
	광고 목적	What is the advertisement about? 무엇에 관한 광고인가?
	회사 정보	What does the company do? 그 회사는 무엇을 하는가?
제품 광고 중반부	제품 특징	Which of the following is NOT mentioned as a feature of the product? 다음 중 제품의 특징으로 언급되지 않은 것은 무엇인가?
	제품 혜택 / 장점	What is NOT indicated as an advantage of the product? 제품의 장점으로 언급되지 않은 것은 무엇인가?
	행사 정보	Where will the event take place? 행사는 어디서 개최되는가?
제품 광고 후반부	제품 구매 방법	What should customers do if they want to get the product? 고객이 상품을 받고 싶다면 무엇을 해야 하는가?
	환불 및 교환 방법	How can customers get a refund? 고객은 어떻게 환불을 받을 수 있는가?

 독해 전략

① 지문 도입 부분에서 광고 제목과 광고 목적 및 대상에 관한 기본적인 내용을 파악한다.

② 구인 광고인 경우, 일반적으로 직책 소개 → 업무 소개 → 지원 자격 → 복지 혜택 → 지원 방법 → 연락 방법의 논리 전개 방식을 따르므로 이를 활용하여 문제에 대한 단서를 지문에서 빠르게 찾는다.

③ 제품 및 서비스 광고인 경우, 특징 및 장점과 관련해서 일치하거나 일치하지 않는 것을 찾아내는 NOT/TRUE 질문 유형이 주로 출제되므로 선택지와 지문을 꼼꼼하게 대조하며 단서를 파악한다.

④ 구인 광고와 일반 상업 광고에 관한 관련 표현을 익혀 둔다면 정답의 단서를 쉽게 찾을 수 있다.

▶ 정답 근거가 되는 문장

구인 광고	담당 업무	The company is looking for / seeking ~ ~를 찾고 있는 중입니다 The primary responsibilities are ~ 주요 업무는 ~입니다 You will be responsible / in charge of ~ 당신은 ~을 담당하게 될 겁니다
	지원 자격	The applicant should / must ~ 지원자는 ~해야 합니다 ~ is required / needed ~이 요구됩니다 It is essential / necessary / mandatory that ~ ~은 필수입니다 ~ is preferred / helpful / advantageous / plus ~은 선호 / 도움 / 이익 / 플러스가 됩니다
	회사 혜택	We offer / provide / give ~ 우리는 ~을 제공합니다
	지원 방법	Please send a cover letter and letter of reference to ~ ~로 자기소개서와 추천서를 보내십시오
상품 광고	광고 목적	Are you interested in ~? ~에 관심이 있으십니까? Are you looking for ~? ~을 찾고 계신 가요?
	장점 및 혜택	We offer / provide / give ~ 우리는 ~을 제공합니다

Questions 1-3 refer to the following advertisement.

Job Opening: Mathematics Instructor

The Powell College of Technology is a leading private college offering degree and certification programs in the areas of technology, business, and health sciences. Instructors at the Powell College of Technology are responsible for the training and supervision of students as they prepare for their chosen career. Mathematics instructors are responsible for providing hands-on classroom instruction, preparing and utilizing approved lesson plans, and preparing student progress and grade reports.

❶ Applicants must have prior teaching experience. A master's degree in mathematics and excellent speaking and written communication skills are required. Candidates must have at least five years of teaching experience. We offer competitive salaries and generous benefits.

❷ ❸ Please send a copy of your résumé along with a cover letter and three letters of recommendation by August 23 to:

Ann Russo, Human Resources Director
Powell College of Technology
Columbia, South Carolina

• 구인 광고

• 회사 정보
기술 대학의
수학 강사 채용

• 업무 내용
교실 수업,
수업 계획안 준비,
학생의 학업
진척도와 성적 보고

• 채용 조건
교수 경력, 석사 학위,
의사소통 능력이 필수

• 지원 서류 및 지원 방법
이력서, 자기소개서,
추천서 제출

• 회사 위치

세부 사항: 채용 조건

1. What is NOT a requirement of the job?

(A) A degree
(B) Management skills
(C) Experience in teaching
(D) Outstanding speaking skills

세부 사항: 지원 서류

2. What must the applicant submit by August 23?

(A) Information about salary
(B) Letters of recommendation
(C) Contact information of previous employers
(D) An online application form

세부 사항: 지원 방법

3. How should the candidate apply for the job?

(A) By phone
(B) By e-mail
(C) By fax
(D) By mail

Questions 1-2 refer to the following advertisement.

A New Quillhouse Publications Title Is on Its Way!

The latest addition to Quillhouse Publication's marketing series, *Marketing Revolution: Using the Internet to Boost Your Sales*, will be available for purchase on May 27. It will be released in multiple formats at the affordable price of $12. Advance orders placed from now until May 25 will receive a 15 percent discount. Visit our website at www.quillhouse.com for more detail.

1. What is being advertised?

(A) A Web browser
(B) An Internet provider
(C) A computer
(D) A book

2. What is true about advance orders?

(A) They can only be placed in stores.
(B) They will be shipped on May 25.
(C) They cost $12.
(D) They will be sold at a discount.

Questions 3-4 refer to the following advertisement.

Massive Savings at Hijo This Week!

The weather is starting to take a cold turn, but Hijo's hot prices will warm you up. For the next week, Hijo is slashing prices on summer T-shirts, shoes, and beachwear. In addition, we've received new shipments on home exercise equipment and supplements. If working out more is one of your goals, come to one of our stores and talk to one of our fitness experts. We will also be releasing a monthly newsletter. Sign up today and receive an extra 10 percent off your next purchase.

Visit any of our stores nationwide. Alternatively, shop online at www.hijolook.com and take advantage of our free home deliveries.

---

3. What is the purpose of the advertisement?

(A) To advertise a new line of exercise equipment
(B) To promote an end-of-season sale of merchandise
(C) To introduce a new online delivery service
(D) To announce the results of a competition

4. What will customers receive when they sign up for Hijo's newsletter?

(A) An additional discount
(B) A complimentary item
(C) Free home deliveries
(D) Access to a wider selection

Questions 5-7 refer to the following advertisement.

Attention event planners and conference organizers!

The Thurmond Hall is now available for your next trade show, conference, or convention. Book now and take advantage of our brand-new premises to wow your attendees.

Our premises is located in the prestigious Wynyard Quarter and has only been available for the past month. Our 230,000 square metres of space can play host to thousands of attendees simultaneously, and state-of-the-art equipment will allow for seamless presentations and Internet streaming. The main hall can also be divided into ten smaller areas to better facilitate trade shows. Additionally, the upper floors include a plethora of private meeting rooms and access to the outdoor balconies.

The Thurmond Hall is situated next to several upscale hotels, convenient food options, and a bustling shopping district.

Ask about our availability today by e-mailing us at reservations@thurmandhall.com.

---

5. What type of building is the Thurmond Hall?

(A) A university dormitory
(B) A shopping mall
(C) A concert hall
(D) A convention center

6. According to the advertisement, how long has the Thurmond Hall been open?

(A) One month
(B) Four months
(C) One year
(D) Two years

7. What information is NOT given about the Thurmond Hall?

(A) Its location
(B) Its design
(C) Its cost
(D) Its size

Bagan Fitness and Recreation Center

Bagan Fitness and Recreation Center opened last month, bringing a spectacular new exercise facility to Belmont County. Located on top of a large hill, the 8,000 sq. ft. center offers a multitude of exercise options for everyone. From the olympic-size, ten-lane indoor swimming pool to its four indoor basketball courts, this place has it all!

In addition, Bagan Fitness and Recreation Center houses a daycare and play center. So, parents who visit for a workout can leave their young ones with our skillful and caring workers. And the kids will get plenty of exercise, too! The play center has a ball pool that kids just love. It also has a jungle gym, padded climbing walls, and an obstacle course.

For general information about Bagan Fitness and Recreation Center, feel free to visit our Web site at www.bagancenter.com. For information about pricing or to simply get directions, contact our front desk at 800-718-1000.

---

8. What is indicated about Bagan Fitness and Recreation Center?

(A) It will be opening soon.
(B) It offers swimming classes.
(C) It will host a sports competition.
(D) It is located in Belmont County.

9. What is available at Bagan Fitness and Recreation Center?

(A) Child care
(B) Basketball lessons
(C) Tennis courts
(D) Free parking

10. According to the advertisement, how can one get information about fees?

(A) By going to a website
(B) By emailing a director
(C) By calling a front desk
(D) By reading a pamphlet

공지·회람

공지는 회사 내 규정 변경이나 정책 방침을 전달하는 사내 공지와 앞으로 있을 행사나 시설 이용 안내에 관해 전달하는 일반 공지로 나뉜다. 반면에 회람은 회사 내에 일정 변경이나 업무와 관련된 공지 사항만을 알리는 글이다.

🔍 지문 유형 확인하기

공지 지문	· 사내 복장 규정 및 정책 변화 공지 · 사내 세미나 및 행사 관련 안내 공지 · 호텔이나 숙박 시설 이용 안내 공지 · 안전 수칙이나 공공시설의 이용 안내 공지
회람 지문	· 사내 세미나 및 행사 참석 안내 · 인사 발령 및 추가 근무에 관한 안내 · 회사 내 시설 보수 공사 안내

🔍 질문 유형 확인하기

주제 및 목적	What is the purpose of this announcement / memo? 이 공지 / 회람의 목적은 무엇인가? What is the memo mainly about? 이 회람은 무엇에 관한 것인가?
출처 및 대상	Where would be the notice most likely be found? 이 공지는 어디서 볼 수 있을 것 같은가? For whom is this notice most likely intended? 이 공지는 누구를 대상으로 하는가?
상세 정보	What are the staff required to do? 직원들은 무엇을 하도록 요청 받았는가? What must the manager do on March 8? 매니저는 3월 8일에 무엇을 해야 하는가?
미래 행동	What must the workers submit by May 30? 직원들은 5월 30일까지 무엇을 제출해야 하는가? What do interested workers plan to do next? 관심 있는 직원들은 다음에 무엇을 할 계획인가?

독해 전략

1 공지·회람 지문 유형은 세부 내용과 관련한 문제가 주로 출제되므로, 고유명사나 특정 요일과 날짜는 꼼꼼하게 확인한다.

2 공지인 경우, 일반적으로 수신인 정보 → 공지의 목적 및 주제 → 요청 / 변경 / 제안에 관한 세부 사항 → 발신인 정보의 논리 전개 방식을 따르므로 이를 활용하여 지문에서 정답의 단서를 빠르게 찾는다.

3 회람인 경우, 이메일과 비슷한 양식이기 때문에 수신자 / 발신자 정보와 제목(Subject, RE)을 확인한다. 일반적으로 수신인 정보 → 회람의 주제 및 목적 → 요청 사항 및 추후 일정 안내와 같은 세부 사항 → 발신인 정보의 논리 전개 방식을 따르므로 이를 활용하여 지문에서 정답의 단서를 빠르게 찾는다.

4 공지와 회람에 관한 관련 표현을 익혀 둔다면 정답의 단서를 쉽게 찾을 수 있다.

▶ 정답 근거가 되는 문장

주제 및 목적	We would like to announce / notify / inform / remind ~ 우리는 ~을 알립니다
제안 및 요청	We encourage our employees to ~ 우리는 직원들에게 ~을 권장합니다 You should / must / have to / need to ~ 당신은 ~을 해야 합니다 Please make sure / remember / note / keep in mind ~ 반드시 ~을 명심하세요 Don't forget to ~ ~을 잊지 마세요

Questions 1-2 refer to the following notice.

City Subway Service
Notice to All Passengers

❶ The Subway Workers' Union has announced a 48-hour strike on the city's subway network that will begin at 8 P.M. tonight, July 18 and end at 8 P.M. on July 20. ❷ Normal service will resume on July 21. The strike will cause significant disruption, and we do not expect any subway trains to be operational during this period. ❶ We therefore offer the following advice for passengers: Passengers arriving at City Airport will be able to travel downtown. The City Express (not part of the subway network) will be fully operational, and we plan to double the number of trains operating on this line during the strike period.

For passengers downtown, a large number of extra services will be provided to help you move around the city. Extra bus and river services, including free travel across the river from Buxley Bridge to Fenstatton Embankment, will be provided.

For further information, go to www.citytransportation.org.

회사 이름

공지 대상

공지의 목적
지하철 파업으로
인한 불편 공지

세부 정보
파업 기간 동안 이용
가능한 교통 수단

세부 정보
추가 교통편에 대한
더 자세한 교통 정보는
웹사이트에서 제공

공지의 목적

1. What is the main purpose of the notice?

(A) To notify riders of alternate services
(B) To encourage travelers to take a bus to the airport
(C) To explain the reasons for a strike
(D) To publicize a new director of the City Express

세부 사항:웹사이트

2. What will happen on July 21?

(A) Buxley Bridge will be closed.
(B) The city subway system will run normally.
(C) Bus fares will be reduced.
(D) The number of trains will double.

해설서 p.94

Questions 1-2 refer to the following notice.

City of Durham
Building Permit Office

Notice for individuals, companies, and contractors working in Durham

Effective starting Monday, September 1, the City of Durham's Building Permit Office, located at 918 Sunset Road, will no longer be open on Fridays and Saturdays. The hours for Monday to Thursday have not been changed. This means that applications for permits will not be accepted or processed on Friday to Sunday. The time to process a permit will remain at three business days. While this may be inconvenient, this is a necessary measure in order to reduce operating expenses while continuing to provide a necessary service for citizens of Durham.

---

1. What change is the Building Permit Office making?

(A) It is merging with another department.
(B) It is reducing the days it is open.
(C) It is simplifying the permit application process.
(D) It is moving to a new location.

2. According to the notice, why is the change being made?

(A) To improve on a service
(B) To respond to a suggestion
(C) To reduce costs
(D) To encourage more applications

Questions 3-4 refer to the following memo.

To: All employees
From: Marvin Greenwell, Director
Date: April 5
Subject: Road work

As most of you take the James Monroe Parkway to our facilities each day, it is important for you to know that the Maryland Department of Transportation will be doing some road work on the route and its exits. The project will get underway on April 12. At that time, one-mile sections of the road will be narrowed to one lane while the road gets resurfaced. Please plan ahead, as this is likely to cause considerable delays. Furthermore, on April 19, exit 4A, which is the exit to our facilities, will be closed. During this time, you will need to take exit 5A, and then, use Chantilly Boulevard to drive east three miles to our facilities. All work is expected to be completed by April 30. The Department of Transportation acknowledges that this project will cause traffic jams, but they ask you for patience while the work is being done.

3. What is being announced?

(A) A recent increase in traffic
(B) The opening of a new route
(C) Some repairs to a road
(D) A delay on a report

4. When will the employees have to take a detour?

(A) On April 5
(B) On April 12
(C) On April 19
(D) On April 30

Questions 5-7 refer to the following notice.

We are thrilled to have everyone here join us for today's show. — [1] —. Please take your time to read the guidelines below and make sure to adhere to them. This way, all attendees will be able to enjoy the performance.

When you are inside the venue, we ask that you turn all electronic devices off completely. — [2] —. The sounds and lights from devices can be incredibly distracting to everyone. Simply switching your devices to silent mode may still give off light that is highly visible in a dark room. Additionally, our terms and conditions state that recording any part of the performance without permission is strictly forbidden.

In the case of a fire, bags and other items in the aisles can hinder audience members from getting to the fire exits. — [3] —. If your bag is too big to fit under your seat, there are lockers available outside for $3. — [4] —. If you will need one, please let any of our attendants know.

Thank you.

---

5. Where most likely is the notice posted?

(A) At a lecture hall
(B) At an airport
(C) In a concert hall
(D) In a sports stadium

6. What is stated about large bags?

(A) They will be collected by the attendants.
(B) They can be put inside a secure box for a fee.
(C) They must be placed at the front of the venue.
(D) They should be clearly labelled to prevent theft.

7. In which of the positions marked [1], [2], [3] and [4] does the following sentence best belong?

"Please place all of your belongings under your seat."

(A) [1]
(B) [2]
(C) [3]
(D) [4]

Attention All Primavera Tech Employees:

As you may be aware, we will be migrating from Europa Central to the new WestGate data platform on July 1. On August 1, access to Europa Central will be disabled for all employees, and all Primavera-related work, such as company communications, file sharing and meeting room bookings will take place via WestGate.

To gain access to WestGate, employees must first register for an account at primavera.westgate.com. For security reasons, a verification step will then take place. You will first be asked to supply your employee identification number as well as your department code. After you enter these details, you will be directed to sign in using your company password. Once this is complete, you will be able to set up your account and begin using the WestGate platform. The entire process should only take around fifteen minutes. The file transfer process should be complete by the time you gain access to the platform, so we advise checking that you have all of your files. If you find that your files have not been transferred correctly, please let someone from the tech team know as soon as possible.

8. What is indicated about Primavera Tech?

(A) It is changing its data platform.
(B) It is moving to a new office.
(C) It is revising some of its work policies.
(D) It is preparing to launch a new product.

9. According to the notice, what is NOT needed from employees?

(A) An employee number
(B) An approval form
(C) A password
(D) A department code

10. What is stated about the process?

(A) It should not take much time.
(B) It involves receiving a code from WestGate.
(C) It will require help from the tech team.
(D) It must be completed before July 1.

11. The word "Once" in paragraph 2, line 5, is closest in meaning to

(A) until
(B) As soon as
(C) Finally
(D) In the case

UNIT 11

기사

경제, 기업, 사회 이슈와 관련하여 보도하는 형식인 기사 지문은 지문의 길이가 다소 길고 어휘 능력이 많이 요구되기 때문에 Part 7에서 어렵게 느껴지는 유형이다. 주제와 어휘가 딱딱한 반면 문제는 단순하게 출제되는 경향이 있으므로 평소에 기사문을 많이 읽으며 속독하는 연습을 해야 한다.

🔍 지문 유형 확인하기

기업 관련 기사	· 기업의 인수 합병, 구조 조정, 지점 설립 및 이전 기사
사회 및 경제 관련 기사	· 실업 문제, 국가 경제, 시장 상황, 산업 전망 기사
홍보성 기사	· 신제품 및 책 소개 기사 · 축제, 행사, 대회 개최 안내 기사 · 새로운 시설 및 건설 공사 안내 기사

🔍 질문 유형 확인하기

주제 및 목적	What does the article mainly discuss? 기사는 주로 무엇을 논의하고 있는가?
출처 및 대상	Where would this article most likely be found? 이 기사는 어디서 볼 수 있을 것 같은가? For whom is this article most likely intended? 이 기사는 누구를 대상으로 하는가?
상세 정보	What is NOT mentioned about the store in Portland? 포틀랜드에 있는 상점에 관해서 언급되지 않은 것은 무엇인가?
추론 및 암시	What is suggested about Yamato Electronics? 야마토 전자에 관해서 무엇이 암시되는가?
미래 상황 및 전망	What will Mr. Kim do after he retires? 김 씨는 은퇴한 후에 무엇을 할 것인가?

독해 전략

1. 기사 상단에 나오는 제목과 도입 부분에 나오는 주제 및 목적을 확인한다. 하지만 주제가 지문 끝부분에 나오기도 하므로 유의한다.

2. 지문 속에 고유명사(사람 이름, 회사 명칭)나 날짜 및 수치와 같은 표현은 질문의 키워드에 따라 체크해 둔다.

3. 미래에 대한 상황 및 전망에 관련된 질문의 정답 단서 표현(be expected / scheduled / planned to)은 주로 지문 후반부에 제시된다.

Questions 1-4 refer to the following article.

Century Communications and Oram International to Merge

Greenville, October 10 — ❶ ❷ Century Communications and Oram International have announced that they will soon be merging. ❸ The two companies, which were previously headquartered in Martinsburg, West Virginia, and Winston-Salem, North Carolina, will be forming the largest internet service provider in the region.

❸ The new company will be known as Century-Oram, and it is sure to do some great things. The two companies already have large customer bases. And after this merger, they will have little competition from their rivals. ❹ The new center of operations for Century-Oram will be in Roanoke, Virginia, at a newly constructed skyscraper named Century-Oram Tower.

Century-Oram will be looking to expand into Kentucky and southern Ohio by the end of next year. This move is likely to be a success as no other company has a strong presence in those markets.

기사 제목

기사의 주제
합병 안내

합병 이후 회사 이름과
회사 위치
두터운 고객층으로
인한 밝은 전망 및
회사 이전 위치 안내

시장 진출 계획
합병 이후 시장 진출
계획

기사의 주제

1. What is the purpose of this article?

(A) To announce a merger
(B) To explain a new service
(C) To report on sales figures
(D) To describe a market trend

세부 사항: 기사의 출처

2. In what section of the newspaper would the article most likely appear?

(A) Entertainment
(B) Travel
(C) Business
(D) Sports

세부 사항: 사업 분야

3. What kind of company will Century-Oram be?

(A) An internet service provider
(B) A computer retailer
(C) A phone manufacturer
(D) An advertising agency

세부 사항: 본사 위치

4. Where will Century-Oram's headquarters be located?

(A) In Greenville
(B) In Winston-Salem
(C) In Roanoke
(D) In Martinsburg

PART 7 UNIT 11

Questions 1-2 refer to the following article.

Located on Maritime Way near Anglers' Wharf, Neptune's Bounty opened 10 years ago and swiftly established itself as the premier seafood restaurant in Portland. Neptune's Bounty offers a large selection of dishes prepared with fresh seafood, much of which is caught locally. Because of this insistence on the freshest of ingredients, the menu changes with the types of seafood in season. The restaurant was closed for two months for renovations, but it reopened last week. The interior now looks like the inside of an old wooden sailing ship. It also features tanks of live lobsters, fish, and other sea creatures. As a part of their grand reopening, Neptune's Bounty will offer all diners a free appetizer.

1. What is the purpose of the article?

(A) To advertise a business
(B) To promote cooking classes
(C) To compare different restaurants
(D) To describe tourist attractions

2. What is NOT indicated about Neptune's Bounty?

(A) It reopened last week.
(B) Its interior was redesigned.
(C) Its menu varies throughout the year.
(D) It has moved to a new location.

Questions 3-5 refer to the following article.

Fresh and Fruity

WHITE PLAINS (17 June) — Leonard Martin opened his fruit salad store with small aspirations of becoming a treat among locals. Not once did he imagine that his fruit salads would be sweeping the nation. Owing to its unique combination of fresh fruits and flavorful dressings, customers have agreed that Leonard Martin's fruit salads are the perfect treat for any weather. Since its opening four years ago, Martin is now looking to open another location in Orestes.

Martin's business, TropiFruit, is known for blending fresh fruit from all over the world to create its famous fruit salads. While this may sound easy, Mr. Martin reminds us that it is anything but. "When it comes to fruit, it is all about finding the right supplier and retail partners," Mr. Martin explained. "We carefully vet our farmers to ensure high quality ingredients, and we choose local restaurants and stores to sell our fruit salads. We have to be selective as we want to remain a premium brand."

Mr. Martin used to run the White Plains location every day, but he has recently passed that duty onto Emily Cunningham, his business partner of three years. This will allow Mr. Martin to focus on creating more partnerships and opening the Orestes location. Its opening date has been set for 22 August.

---

3. What is the article mainly about?

(A) An emerging trend in an industry
(B) An application of a new advertising strategy
(C) The importance of healthy eating
(D) The expansion of a business

4. What is mentioned about TropiFruit?

(A) It received funding from the government.
(B) It sells its goods through local stores.
(C) It was featured on a television program.
(D) It only operates over the summer months.

5. What is suggested about Ms. Cunningham?

(A) She will sign a contract on August 22.
(B) She used to work as a farmer.
(C) She has worked at TropiFruit for three years.
(D) She will be moving to Orestes.

Questions 6-8 refer to the following article.

Celebrate the Life of Lorita Purdy

ENGLEWOOD (June 14) – All Englewood residents are invited to celebrate the achievements of local benefactor Lorita Purdy. — [1] —. A banquet to commemorate her retirement will be held at the Piute Hotel on June 22 from 6:00 P.M. to 9:30 P.M.

Lorita Purdy came into prominence through her own advertising firm, Purdy Creative. The firm achieved considerable success, and Ms. Purdy invested the profits back into the community. She was an integral part in the creation of after-school programs at Englewood High School teaching students about becoming entrepreneurs themselves. — [2] —. She also was a key sponsor for the renovation of the Monroe Community Hall and established the Vista Fund, which provides support to local entrepreneurs. — [3] —.

The event will start at 6:00 P.M. with dinner being served an hour later. The Englewood City Orchestra will provide music throughout the event. Tickets are currently on sale for $15, and they can be purchased at www.englewoodcity.org. — [4] —.

6. Where will the event take place?

(A) At Englewood High School
(B) At the Piute Hotel
(C) At the Monroe Community Hall
(D) At Purdy Creative headquarters

7. What is NOT indicated about Ms. Purdy?

(A) She assisted with an after-school program.
(B) She donated money for a renovation project.
(C) She moved to Englewood for her studies.
(D) She started her own business.

8. In which of the positions marked [1], [2], [3], and [4] does the following sentence best belong?

"The classes are taught by local businessowners."

(A) [1]
(B) [2]
(C) [3]
(D) [4]

Questions 9-12 refer to the following article.

Leicester Herald
Local News – 7 July

Peyton Fisher, the global food manufacturer, has announced its plans to open a research and development center in Leicester. The center, occupying the old Glenfield Shopping Plaza building, is set to open early October.

The redevelopment of the new center has been pushed back multiple times. Some access roads were closed temporarily due to the construction of the adjacent Anstey Medical Center. The Leicester City Council had to address a number of urban planning policy issues as well.

"The development took a lot of patience on our end," says Elvira Hayes, the company's chief marketing officer. "But it'll all have been worthwhile when we finally open for business in several months."

Peyton Fisher will be organizing a series of job fairs in the coming months throughout the region to recruit food scientists, flavor technologists, packaging developers, as well as administrative and maintenance staff for the new center.

---

9. What is the purpose of the article?

(A) To report on the remodeling of a facility
(B) To market a new food product
(C) To assess Leicester's business trends
(D) To announce the opening of a shopping plaza

10. The word "address" in paragraph 2, line 4, is closest in meaning to

(A) deal with
(B) take under
(C) make up
(D) root for

11. Who most likely is Ms. Hayes?

(A) A construction manager
(B) A medical center representative
(C) A Peyton Fisher executive
(D) A Leicester City Councilperson

12. According to the article, what does Peyton Fisher plan to do?

(A) Hire employees for various positions
(B) Request a deadline extension from the city council
(C) Renovate the center's lobby
(D) Make a formal complaint about a road closure

양식

일정표, 초대장, 청구서, 광고지와 같은 일상 생활 속에서 자주 쓰이는 양식들이 출제된다. 양식 지문은 다른 지문에 비해 짧고 간단하기 때문에 평소 토익에 자주 출제되는 양식의 구성을 정리해 두는 것이 문제 푸는 시간을 절약할 수 있다.

🔍 지문 유형 확인하기

일정표(schedule / itinerary)	· 행사 및 여행에 관련한 세부 일정
설문지(survey)	· 제품 및 서비스에 관한 고객 만족도 조사 · 호텔 및 식당 이용에 관한 고객 만족도 조사
송장(invoice)	· 제품 구매 내역
기타 양식	· 초대장(invitation), 계약서(contract), 보증서(warranty), 전단지(flyer), 신청서(application)

🔍 질문 유형 확인하기

주제 및 목적	What is the purpose of the event? 행사의 목적은 무엇인가?
출처 및 대상	Who will receive this order? 누가 이 주문을 받을 것인가?
상세 정보	When must the invoice be paid? 송장은 언제 지불되어야 하는가? What is NOT included in the cost of the event? 행사 비용으로 포함되지 않은 것은 무엇인가?

 독해 전략

1️⃣ 평소 토익에 자주 출제되는 양식 유형을 익혀두면 정답의 단서를 빠르게 파악할 수 있다.

2️⃣ 지문의 도입 부분에서 양식의 목적 또는 수/발신자에 관한 정보를 먼저 파악해 둔다.

3️⃣ 금액, 날짜, 수량, 일정 및 숫자에 관련된 질문은 질문을 먼저 읽고 지문 속에서 키워드를 빠르게 찾아간다.

4️⃣ 기호(*, −)가 들어간 문장이나 Note라고 적혀 있는 주의 사항이 자주 출제되므로 유의해서 읽어주도록 한다.

Questions 1-2 refer to the following invoice.

The Star Hotel
3815 Grandriver Ave.

Bill To: Sue Kim
      East Lansing, MI 48825

Date: April 20
Invoice number: 314

Invoice for one-day conference to be held on May 28.

Item	Rate	Total
❶ Standard Room Conference Space (300 guests)	$200.00/day	$200.00

Audiovisual equipment rental

❶ 2 wireless microphones	$40.00 / unit	$80.00
1 projector	$100.00 / unit	$100.00
1 projection screen	$70.00 / unit	$70.00
❶ Breakfast	$10.00 / person	$3000.00
❶ Lunch	$15.00 / person	$4500.00

Subtotal	$7750.00
Tax	$620.00
Total	$8370.00

❷ *Please send this amount by May 4 to reserve all services listed above.

업체명

청구서 정보
(청구인, 날짜, 청구서 번호)

세부 내역
(물품/가격)

요청 사항

사실 확인: 행사 비용에 포함되지 않은 것

1. What is NOT included in the cost of the event?

(A) Overnight hotel stay
(B) Microphones
(C) Meals for participants
(D) Conference room rental

세부 사항: 요청 사항

2. What is Ms. Kim asked to do?

(A) Confirm a reservation
(B) Return audiovisual equipment
(C) Make a payment
(D) Select items from a menu

해설서 p.100

Questions 1-2 refer to the following receipt.

```
Greville Gas Station
S15 Highway
17 Laystone Green
032-555-3286
17 September
------------------------------------------------------------
USB Phone Charger      $8.00
Black Cup Holder       $7.00
Air Freshener          $6.50
Tax                    $3.30

Total                  $24.80
------------------------------------------------------------
Sign up for Greville's Loyal Customer rewards card.
For your transaction today, you could have earned 24
Greville points.

You can use points to get discounts on food items
and petrol. You will also be eligible to enter member-
exclusive giveaways.
```

1. What was purchased on September 17?

(A) Snacks
(B) Petrol
(C) Car accessories
(D) Cleaning supplies

2. What does the receipt indicate about Greville Gas Station?

(A) It has a customer loyalty program.
(B) It holds contests every month.
(C) It offers price matching on petrol.
(D) It has several locations.

Questions 3-4 refer to the following invoice.

INVOICE

Date ordered: September 16

Delivered on: September 22

Place of origin:
Tremont Electronics Store
391 Coleridge Place
Grant, Minnesota 56531

Place of destination:
Eva Jennings
18 Mansfield Crescent, Apartment 302
Douglas, Wisconsin 54874

Item	Description	Quantity	Price
S6431	High-definition computer monitor, 27 inches	1	$205.00

Order Subtotal: $205.00
Tax: $10.00
Shipping: $6.50

TOTAL: $221.50

Promotion/sales event: -$22.15
Payment Due: $199.35

---

3. Where is the order being sent?

(A) To a home
(B) To a retail store
(C) To a warehouse
(D) To a government building

4. What does the invoice indicate?

(A) The product is eligible for a discount.
(B) The shipping is free.
(C) The item will arrive on September 16.
(D) The product comes with an extended warranty.

Questions 5-6 refer to the following chart.

ExaBuster Systems

Are you looking for a host for your website but want a plan that is right for you? We have a convenient chart that lets you quickly compare our available plans.

Features	Basic	Premium
Fully customizable site	✓	✓
Built-in credit and debit card processing	✓	✓
Monthly analytics reports	✓	✓
Password encryption for users	✓	✓
Unlimited data storage		✓
24/7 technical support		✓

---

5. What does the chart describe?

(A) Customer reviews
(B) Costs of features
(C) Development milestones
(D) Plan comparisons

6. What is NOT true about the basic option?

(A) It allows users to view data on its customers.
(B) It lets online purchases be made.
(C) It offers technical assistance at any time.
(D) It secures passwords for its users.

Questions 7-9 refer to the following flyer.

Have you just moved to London?

Attend a London Welcomes You Orientation Hosted by the London Resident Committee
25 May, 10:30 A.M. – 2:30 P.M.
London Times Square
Big Ben Center
Open to Everyone

Schedule of Presentations		
10:30 A.M.	How to Get Around: Available Public Transportation (Room 101)	
11:30 A.M.	Getting Housing in London (Room 103)	Waste Management Advice and Options (Room 104)
12:30 P.M.	Comprehending London's Local Banking System (Room 105)	Starting a Local Business in London (Room 104)
1:30 P.M.	What to do in London, Guide to Community Gatherings and Recreational Facilities (Room 101)	

Since two events may be held during the same time, attendees must choose which event best matches their interests. In addition, please be aware that due to high interests in the sessions on recreation and public transportation, you should plan on arriving early to secure a seat.

Although all presentations are in English, there are pamphlets available in Korean, Spanish, and French. Refreshments will be provided for purchase.

Following the last presentation, participants may join a one-hour guided tour throughout downtown London. This free tour will be provided by a long-time committee member and resident of London.

For further details regarding these events, please visit www.welcometolondon.co.uk.

---

7. Where will the most popular presentations occur?

(A) In Room 101
(B) In Room 103
(C) In Room 104
(D) In Room 105

8. What is indicated about the London Resident Committee?

(A) It provides materials in several languages.
(B) It will start to offer new services.
(C) It requires a membership fee.
(D) It holds monthly events.

9. According to the flyer, what can attendees do after the presentations?

(A) Enjoy free food and drinks
(B) Reserve seats for upcoming events
(C) Go on a tour of the city
(D) Sign up for a membership

UNIT 13

이중 지문

이중 지문은 서로 관련된 두 개의 지문이 한 세트를 이루며 각 세트당 5문항씩 출제된다. 단일 지문과 달리 두 개의 지문을 다 읽은 후 풀 수 있는 연계 질문이 1~2 문제 출제되므로 시간 관리에 신경을 써야 한다.

🔍 지문 유형 확인하기

편지 / 이메일 + 편지 / 이메일	· 제품 및 서비스에 관한 고객 만족도 · 주문 및 문의에 관한 회신 요청 및 답변 · 예약 및 일정 확인
광고 + 편지 / 이메일	· 구인 광고에 관한 구직 문의 · 상품 및 서비스에 관한 광고 및 질문 · 상품 및 서비스에 관한 불만 및 답변
기사 + 편지 / 이메일	· 지역 건설 계획 관련 기사에 관한 문의 내용 · 인물, 회사에 대한 기사에 관한 오류 정정 요구
양식[청구서 / 일정표 / 초대장] + 편지 / 이메일	· 잘못된 청구서에 관한 수정 요청 · 일정 및 숙박 예약에 관한 문의 · 초청장에 관한 참석 여부 및 감사 이메일

🔍 질문 유형 확인하기

주제 및 목적	What is the purpose of the letter? 편지의 목적은 무엇인가?
상세 정보	What does Mr. Barlow plan to do? 바로우 씨가 하려고 계획하는 것은 무엇인가?
동의어	In the e-mail, the word "credit" in paragraph 4, line 2, is closest in meaning to 4번째 단락에 2번째 줄의 단어 'credit'과 의미상 가장 가까운 것은 무엇인가?
추론 및 암시	What is suggested about the Mr. Kim? 김 씨에 관해서 암시되는 것은 무엇인가?

독해 전략

1 질문에 언급되어 있는 고유명사(사람 이름, 회사 명칭) 또는 the first e-mail과 같은 표현을 통해 어느 지문과 관련되어 있는지 순서를 정할 수 있다.

2 이중 지문의 문제 구성은 일반적으로 1~2번 문제는 첫 번째 지문, 3~4번 문제는 연계 질문, 5번 문제는 두 번째 지문과 관련된 경우가 많다. 따라서 1~2번 문제를 먼저 읽고 첫 번째 지문에서 정답을 찾은 뒤, 두 번째 지문을 읽은 후 나머지 문제 및 연계 문제를 해결하는 것이 좋다.

3 대체로 쉬운 주제 및 목적, 세부 사항, 어휘 문제를 먼저 풀고 많은 정보를 확인해야 하는 사실 확인 문제와 추론 및 암시 문제는 나중에 풀이한다. 특히, 선택지에 고유명사, 날짜, 숫자 등과 같은 단순 정보는 연계 문제일 가능성이 높으므로 유의한다.

PART 7 UNIT 13

 핵심 문제 유형

해설서 p.102

Questions 1-5 refer to the following e-mails.

To: Customer Service <customerservice@georgetownelectric.com>
From: Jeanie Syfu <j.syfu@speedmail.org>
Date: September 15
Subject: ❶ Billing Issue

To Whom It May Concern:

There seems to be a problem with my last electricity bill. Since the beginning of the new billing cycle, I have been paying a fixed rate of $50 a month for electricity. However, my bill for last month was for $73. ❷ I signed up for the fixed-rate service in order to save money on my electricity bills. ❸ However, this bill is $23 higher than what my contract states it should be. ❶ Please look into this matter right away, and let me know what happened.

Sincerely,

Jeanie Syfu

To: Jeanie Syfu <j.syfu@speedmail.org>
From: Customer Service <customerservice@georgetownelectric.com>
Date: September 16
Subject: Re: Billing Issue

Dear Ms. Syfu,

Thank you for contacting us regarding this matter. An investigation has revealed that a mistake was indeed made to your bill for last month. As you stated, you were overcharged by the amount indicated in your message. ❸ We have corrected this mistake, and the additional amount will appear as a credit on your bill for next month. Therefore, your bill for the month of September will be $27. We apologize for any inconvenience this problem may have caused. ❺ To compensate you further, we will take you 50 percent off of your power usage for the month of October.

To help us to ensure that our customers are receiving a high level of support, ❹ we kindly request that you complete a brief survey concerning the resolution of this issue. You can complete the survey form by visiting this link: www.georgetownelectric.com/customersurvey. Thank you for your being a loyal customer of Georgetown Electric, and we look forward to your continued business in the future.

Regards,

John Bates
Customer Service Representative
Georgetown Electric Company

이메일의 목적

1. What is the purpose of the first e-mail?

(A) To call attention to a problem
(B) To set up an appointment
(C) To announce a new payment option
(D) To describe a company policy

사실 확인

2. What is indicated about Ms. Syfu?

(A) She recommended Georgetown
Electric to one of her friends.
(B) She would like to create a separate
account.
(C) She expects to pay the same amount
for electricity each month.
(D) She has canceled her contract with
Georgetown Electric.

이중 지문 연계

3. How much money will be credited to
Ms. Syfu's account in September?

(A) $23
(B) $27
(C) $50
(D) $73

세부 사항

4. What does Mr. Bates encourage
Ms. Syfu to do?

(A) Contact the accounting office
(B) Call his supervisor
(C) Renew a subscription
(D) Fill out a questionnaire

세부 사항

5. What does Mr. Bates offer Ms. Syfu?

(A) A free month of service
(B) A discount
(C) A magazine
(D) A new phone

Practice

해설서 p.104

Questions 1-5 refer to the following e-mails.

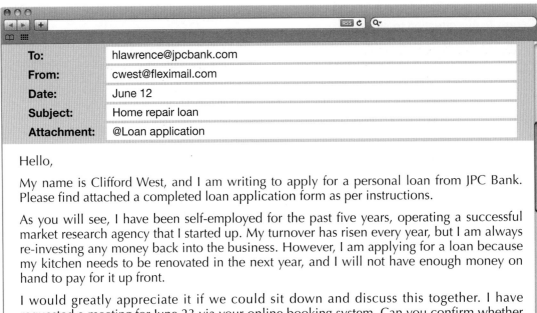

To: hlawrence@jpcbank.com
From: cwest@fleximail.com
Date: June 12
Subject: Home repair loan
Attachment: @Loan application

Hello,

My name is Clifford West, and I am writing to apply for a personal loan from JPC Bank. Please find attached a completed loan application form as per instructions.

As you will see, I have been self-employed for the past five years, operating a successful market research agency that I started up. My turnover has risen every year, but I am always re-investing any money back into the business. However, I am applying for a loan because my kitchen needs to be renovated in the next year, and I will not have enough money on hand to pay for it up front.

I would greatly appreciate it if we could sit down and discuss this together. I have requested a meeting for June 23 via your online booking system. Can you confirm whether this date is available?

Thank you.

Clifford West

To: cwest@fleximail.com
From: hlawrence@jpcbank.com
Date: June 25
Subject: Further action needed

Dear Mr. West,

Thank you for coming in to discuss your loan application. I would like to apologize once again for having you come in a day earlier than you requested. I hope that didn't cause many problems on your end.

I am happy to let you know that your loan is nearly finalized. However, as we discussed in our meeting, we will require you to send in the following items: 1) bank statements from the last three months, 2) your cashflow statements for your business for the past year, 3) a scan of your driver's license or passport, and 4) a signed copy of the amended loan application.

If we can receive these documents by June 29, that would be helpful. Following that, we can then approve your loan. The total amount requested will be transferred to you, and you will repay the loan in monthly installments at the agreed-upon interest rate.

Sincerely,

Hugh Lawrence
Loan Officer, JPC Bank

1. What is indicated about Mr. West?

   (A) He works as an investment banker.
   (B) He runs his own business.
   (C) He recently changed jobs.
   (D) He is employed at a bank.

2. Why does Mr. West ask for a bank loan?

   (A) To replace a roof
   (B) To construct a garage
   (C) To install heaters
   (D) To renovate a kitchen

3. When did Mr. West meet with Mr. Lawrence?

   (A) On June 12
   (B) On June 22
   (C) On June 23
   (D) On June 29

4. What does Mr. Lawrence indicate Mr. West should do?

   (A) Organize a meeting
   (B) Apply for a new card
   (C) Send some documents
   (D) Submit pictures of his house

5. In the second e-mail, what is suggested about Mr. West's loan?

   (A) It will have the interest rate that Mr. Lawrence discussed.
   (B) It will be transferred to Mr. West in multiple installments.
   (C) It will require another person to guarantee the loan.
   (D) It will be for a higher amount than Mr. West requested.

Questions 6-10 refer to the following e-mail and ticket.

To	gordon.burgess@whereitout.com
From	monica.kim@countent.com
Date	14 April
Subject	RE: Some suggestions

Dear Mr. Burgess,

Thank you very much for offering to come and pick up your order from our workshop. Although you even offered to pay any costs incurred from air or train transport, I would prefer to personally deliver your order in Garden Heights. It's really not a burden for myself as I happen to be heading that way to attend a trade show in Bay Pines. On my way there, I can stop by your house and drop off your order at your door.

Customer satisfaction is at the center of my business. As I am dealing with quite fragile items, the transportation process can be quite difficult. I've had too many experiences with unhappy customers receiving damaged items. From my experience, both ground or sea-based courier services come with their own problems, but neither seem sufficient. Therefore, I have taken it upon myself to deliver as many items myself.

I will arrive in Garden Heights on 27 April. I will send you another message closer to the day to let you know what time I will be getting in.

Sincerely,
Monica Kim
Countent

Pinellas Railway Services

Date of Issuance: 21 April
Passenger Name: Monica Kim

Platform Number: 17
Departing Park Falls: Friday, 27 April, 10:25 A.M.
Arriving at Garden Heights: Friday, 27 April, 2:05 P.M.

Baggage: 1 suitcase (medium), 1 sculpture (100 cm x 30 cm)

Total fare: $45

Thank you for choosing Pinellas Railway Services. We hope you enjoy your trip.

6. What is the purpose of the e-mail?

(A) To address a complaint
(B) To confirm a plan
(C) To accept a new order
(D) To change a delivery date

7. Why will Ms. Kim travel to Bay Pines?

(A) To attend an event
(B) To interview an applicant
(C) To visit a friend
(D) To deliver an item

8. What is indicated in the e-mail?

(A) Mr. Burgess has ordered from Countent before.
(B) Mr. Burgess operates a train company.
(C) Ms. Kim only takes online orders.
(D) Ms. Kim is not satisfied with any courier services.

9. What is most likely true about Mr. Burgess?

(A) He will meet Ms. Kim at a conference.
(B) He recently purchased a sculpture.
(C) He paid a fee to have his order delivered.
(D) He often travels for work.

10. How is Ms. Kim travelling to Garden Heights on April 27?

(A) By plane
(B) By car
(C) By boat
(D) By train

삼중 지문

삼중 지문은 서로 관련된 세 개의 지문이 한 세트를 이루며 각 세트당 5문항씩 출제된다. 이중 지문보다 지문이 한 개가 더 늘었다는 것과 연계 질문이 하나 더 나올 가능성이 있다는 것 외에는 이중 지문 문제 풀이 전략과 비슷하다. 지문 길이가 비교적 짧은 편이나 읽을거리가 많으므로 시간 관리에 유의한다.

🔍 지문 유형 확인하기

이메일 + 편지 + 양식	업무 요청 + 업무 요청에 관한 답변 + 그와 관련된 일정 및 양식
광고 + 청구서 + 이메일	제품 광고 + 제품 구매 영수증 / 청구서 + 제품에 관한 요청 및 수정
광고 + 이메일 + 이메일	구인 광고 + 구직자 자격요건 문의 + 인사 담당자 답변
이메일 + 양식 + 공지	행사 관련한 안내 + 행사 일정표 + 행사 관련한 변경 사항
기사 + 양식 + 이메일 / 편지	행사 및 시설에 관한 기사 + 신청 양식 + 행사 협조 요청

🔍 질문 유형 확인하기

주제 및 목적	What is being advertised? 광고되고 있는 것은 무엇인가?
상세 정보	How does Mr. Tom intend to pay for his classes? 톰 씨는 그의 수업료를 어떻게 지불하고자 하는가?
동의어	In the e-mail, the word "cutting-edge" in paragraph 3, line 2, is closest in meaning to 이메일에서, 3번째 단락, 2번째 줄의 단어 'cutting-edge'와 의미상 가장 가까운 것은 무엇인가?
추론 및 암시	What is most likely true about the Overland Hotel? 오버랜드 호텔에 관해서 무엇이 사실이겠는가?

독해 전략

1 이중 지문과 마찬가지로 질문에 제시되어 있는 고유명사(사람 이름, 회사 명칭)와 the first e-mail과 같은 표현을 통해 어느 지문과 관련되어 있는지 파악한다.

2 삼중 지문의 문제 구성은 일반적으로 1번 문제는 첫 번째 또는 두 번째 지문, 2번 문제는 두 번째 또는 세 번째 지문, 3~5번 문제는 연계 질문일 가능성이 높다. 따라서 1번 질문이 첫 번째 지문에서 해결이 안 된 경우 두 번째 지문을 읽은 후 1, 2번 문제를 해결한다. 마지막으로 세 번째 지문을 읽은 후 나머지 문제 및 연계 문제를 해결하는 것이 좋다.

3 대체로 쉬운 주제 및 목적, 세부 사항, 어휘 문제를 먼저 풀고 많은 정보를 확인해야 하는 사실 확인 문제와 추론 및 암시 문제는 나중에 풀이한다. 특히, 선택지에 고유명사, 날짜, 숫자 등과 같은 단순 정보는 연계 문제일 가능성이 높으므로 유의한다.

PART 7

UNIT 14

Questions 1-5 refer to the following advertisement, online form, and e-mail.

The Chandler School of Fine Arts

Do you enjoy sketching, painting, or creating other types of artwork in your free time? Maybe you have an ❶ aptitude for art that you should develop more. Or perhaps you just want to learn about art. If so, consider taking classes at the Chandler School of Fine Arts.

We are currently accepting applications for the fall semester. Each course lasts for three months and meets one to two times a week. ❷ To accommodate your busy schedule, classes are available in mornings, afternoons, and evenings from Monday through Saturday. The following are some of our most popular classes. For a complete listing, go to chandlerfa.com/fallschedule.

Class Name	Class Number	Instructor
Introduction to Oil Painting	53	Tim Haven
All About Sculpture	44	Lisa Watts
❸ Advanced Watercolor Painting	87	Maria Gomez
❺ How to Paint Like a Renaissance Artist	42	❺ Enrico Eco

The semester begins on September 2. ❸ All classes cost $250, but there are additional fees for materials for some classes.

The Chandler School of Fine Arts
Online Registration Form

Name: Fred Thomas
Address: 45 W. Thompson Street, Chandler, AZ 85214
Telephone Number: 393-2396
E-mail Address: fred_t@privatemail.com
Date: August 27

Class(es):

Class Name	Class Number	Cost
A History of Painting	31	$250
Advanced Watercolor Painting	87	❸ $315

How would you like to pay:
❹ cash [✓]   check [ ]   credit card [ ]

Thank you for registering with the Chandler School of Fine Arts. You will receive a confirmation e-mail within 24 hours.

광고 주체
미술 학교

광고 대상
미술에 관심이 있거나
소질이 있는 사람

광고 목적:
가을 학기 미술 수강생
모집

수강 시간표
강의명, 강의 번호,
강사명

개강일 및 수강료
9월 2일 개강, 전과목
동일 수강료: 250달러

서식 종류
온라인 등록 신청서

수강 신청자 개인 정보

날짜

수강 신청 과목 및 비용
회화의 역사와 고급
수채화

지불 방법 선택
현금

24시간 이내 등록 확인
이메일 발송 예정

To: Fred Thomas <fred_t@privatemail.com>
From: Tina Powell <tpowell@chandlerfa.com>
Date: August 28
Subject: Registration

Dear Mr. Thomas,

Thank you for registering for classes at the Chandler School of Fine Arts. We are always pleased to welcome new students to our institute.

I would like to inform you of one change in your schedule. You registered for class number 31, **5** A History of Painting. The instructor for that class has changed. Ms. Carmen Hooper will no longer teach it. Instead, **5** Mr. Enrico Eco will be the instructor. He is a talented instructor, and I am positive you will enjoy learning from him.

Please note that you must pay for the classes in full by the end of the first week of classes.

Sincerely,

Tina Powell
The Chandler School of Fine Arts

• 수신인
  발신인
  날짜
  제목

• 이메일 발송 목적
  수강 신청을 확인해
  주기 위함

• 수강 변경 사항 안내
  31번 강의의 강사가
  변경됨

• 수강료 지급 기한 안내
  개강 첫 주가 끝나기
  전에 수강료를 지불해
  야 함

• 발신인 정보

동의어

1. In the advertisement, the word "aptitude" in paragraph 1, line 2, is closest in meaning to

   (A) desire
   (B) talent
   (C) interest
   (D) mood

사실 확인

2. What is true about the classes at the Chandler School of Fine Arts?

   (A) They are held throughout the day.
   (B) They usually fill up fast.
   (C) They are taught by professional artists.
   (D) They are open only to skilled individuals.

이중 지문 연계

3. What is indicated about class number 87?

   (A) It is taught by a local artist.
   (B) Students must pay extra for supplies.
   (C) It is offered in the afternoon.
   (D) A limited number of people may take it.

세부 사항: 지불 방법

4. How does Mr. Thomas intend to pay for his classes?

   (A) By check
   (B) With cash
   (C) With a credit card
   (D) By wire transfer

이중 지문 연계

5. What is indicated about Mr. Eco?

   (A) He will retire next semester.
   (B) He has been teaching for many decades.
   (C) He will teach more than one course.
   (D) He is popular among students.

PART 7 UNIT 14

해설서 p.107

Questions 1-5 refer to the following signs and review.

Office Delight
----

129 Rue des Honnelles, Yvoir, Namur
0482 555 9302

Popular Services:
Photocopying and printing, scanning and laminating, business cards, data recovery, tech support

Hours of Operation

Monday	Closed
Tuesday	8 A.M. – 8 P.M.
Wednesday	7 A.M. – 9 P.M.
Thursday	8 A.M. – 8 P.M.
Friday	8 A.M. – 9 P.M.
Saturday	7 A.M. – 7 P.M.
Sunday	7 A.M. – 5 P.M.

100% Genuine Leather, Handmade, Artisan Wallets

Item	Model	Euros	Dollars
Mahanadi (Black)	2648 (square)	68.98	71.36
Meghna (Brown)	2535 (rectangle)	82.98	85.85
Tapti (Beige)	2722 (square)	106.98	110.68

Travel Review

By: Sylvester Dixon

Rating: ★★★★★
July 16

It was my first time visiting Belgium, and I was in Namur for a conference. Right when I got off the plane, I realized I had left my phone charger at home. I quickly rushed over to the closest office supply store I could find, which was Office Delight. Thankfully, they were still open on Thursday night, and I got in exactly at closing time. The staff there were very nice and friendly and showed me their range of phone chargers. On my way out, I happened to come across some handmade wallets that they were selling. They caught my eye because of their simple yet effective designs, and the quality looked amazing. I ended up going with the Tapti. As I was checking out, the owner told me that the designer of the wallets is an avid traveler, and he named his items after some rivers he visited. If you are ever in the area, I highly recommend visiting Office Delight and having a look for yourself!

1. What does the first sign indicate about Office Delight?

(A) It offers equipment rental services.
(B) It is located next to a hotel.
(C) It has several stores throughout Namur.
(D) It operates six days a week.

2. Why did Mr. Dixon visit Office Delight?

(A) To replace equipment he forgot to bring
(B) To send an e-mail to a co-worker
(C) To repair a defective item
(D) To scan some flyers for a conference

3. When did Mr. Dixon arrive at Office Delight?

(A) At 7:00 A.M.
(B) At 8:00 A.M.
(C) At 8:00 P.M.
(D) At 9:00 P.M.

4. What is indicated about the wallet that Mr. Dixon purchased?

(A) It is model number 2648.
(B) It is rectangle.
(C) It is beige.
(D) It is the store's least expensive item.

5. According to the review, what is each wallet named after?

(A) A river
(B) A city
(C) A forest
(D) A lake

Questions 6-10 refer to the following schedule, e-mail, and advertisement.

Iniosmart Photography schedule for _Home Additions_

Date and Venue	Project	Notes
Wednesday, March 9 Tabuki Works Studio	Painting walls	Photos of painting techniques
Friday, March 11 Home Additions Workshop	Measuring and cutting wood	Photos showing some tools and process of cutting wood
Tuesday, March 15 Kynn Hotel	Fixing holes in walls	Photos of Ms. Flowers fixing a hole at Kynn Hotel
Thursday, March 17 Home Additions Workshop	All about carpet	Photos of cleaning carpet stains
Monday, March 21 Delco Community Center	Tending to your garden	Photos of Ms. Flowers showing how to take care of plants
Thursday, March 24 Iniosmart Studio 3	Restoring furniture	Photos of some furniture before restoration and after

To	ethel_flowers@tinkermail.com
From	n.barber@iniosmart.com
Date	March 14
Subject	Final photography for _Home Additions_ book

Dear Ms. Flowers,

I'm very sorry to let you know that there has been a last minute adjustment to the photography schedule for _Home Additions_. We were scheduled to shoot your furniture shots on March 24 at our studio. However, we have been informed that the room will need to undergo some repairs to fix a persistent lighting issue. As work will only start in April, we will be unable to continue this shoot there. Since you will need all of your shots by March 24 in order to meet the launch date of November 29, I have asked Tabuki Works if we can use their studio on that date. It will not be a problem for us to set up all of our equipment there and shoot what we need.

When the owner of Tabuki Works gets back to me, I will update you with all of the necessary details.

Apologies once again for the inconvenience.

Norman Barber
Iniosmart Photography

Home Additions Book Launch Event

November 29 at 7:00 P.M.
Delco Room, Liberty Hall
39 Ecton Avenue, Edinboro

- Enjoy a Q&A session with author Ethel Flowers
- Purchase a copy of *Home Additions* and get it signed by Ms. Flowers
- Test a range of tools specially picked out by Ms. Flowers
- Refreshments and drinks will be available

For more information or to reserve a place at the event, contact Joey Santiago at 348-555-6483.

---

6. What project was photographed on March 15?

(A) Tending to your garden
(B) Fixing holes in walls
(C) Painting walls
(D) Restoring furniture

7. At what venue was a photography session canceled?

(A) Iniosmart Studio 3
(B) Tabuki Works
(C) Kynn Hotel
(D) Delco Community Center

8. In the e-mail, what problem did Mr. Barber mention?

(A) Some staff will be unavailable to assist.
(B) Some repairs will have to be conducted.
(C) A room was incorrectly booked.
(D) A piece of equipment has gone missing.

9. What can be concluded about Mr. Barber?

(A) He attended an event on November 29.
(B) He did some repairs at the Delco Room.
(C) He co-authored a book with Ms. Flowers.
(D) He was able to meet a project's deadline.

10. What will visitors to the event in Delco Room be able to do?

(A) Order some specialized tools
(B) Sign up for some classes
(C) Take part in a live demonstration
(D) Ask an author some questions

REVIEW TEST

해설서 p.110

Questions 1-2 refer to the following form.

Welcome to Nostimo Restaurant!

Due to high demand, we have transitioned to a reservation system. Please write down your name as well as the size of your party below. If you are not here when we call your name, we will be forced to remove your party from the list. During your wait, you may order drinks while looking through our menu. One is available on the front window of the restaurant. Please note that we can only accept payments in the form of cash. Thank you.

> 1. Mattie Holloway, party of 3
> 2. Pablo Coleman, party of 2
> 3. Miriam Gregory, party of 4
> 4. Jin-Ho Hong, party of 2
> 5. Cynthia Jensen, party of 1
> 6.
> 7.
> 8.
> 9.
> 10.

---

1. Where can customers find a menu?

(A) Printed on a sign by the entrance
(B) Posted on the front window
(C) On a chair near the form
(D) On the restaurant's Website

2. What is indicated about Nostimo Restaurant?

(A) It does not take online orders.
(B) It does not serve beverages.
(C) It does not accept credit cards.
(D) It does not operate during lunch hours.

Questions 3-4 refer to the following information.

https://www.monetatimes.com

Guidelines for Letters to the Editor

The purpose of the Letters to the Editor section is to give a voice to members of our community. We select between seven to ten letters to print in every edition of the paper, and we choose another an additional ten to post on our website.

While we would ideally print all of the letters we receive, the volume we receive makes this impossible. Here are some guidelines we use to select which ones are printed:

1. Be quick to the point. Ideally, your letter should be under 150 words.
2. Keep it current. Your letter should speak to an issue that was covered in the Moneta Times in the past week.
3. Opinions from those with expertise, qualifications, or work experience are welcome.

3. What does the information indicate about letters to the editor?

(A) They are available online.
(B) They should be signed using one's real name.
(C) They must be authored by an expert in the field.
(D) They are at least 150 words long.

4. What is the recommended time limit for commenting on an article?

(A) One day
(B) Four days
(C) Seven days
(D) Ten days

Questions 5-7 refer to the following advertisement.

Pascal Sales Systems

Let Pascal Sales Systems (PSS) simplify your payment system with its simple and intuitive point-of-sale devices. With PSS at your stores, you can forget about the burden of expensive sales devices and high transaction fees. With our devices and with help from our support team, you can focus solely on running your business and let us handle the payments.

Our system has been the recipient of several awards. Whether you conduct your sales in your store, through your website, or over the phone, PSS makes this a painless process while supporting you with 24-7 technical expertise. Our devices are equipped to accommodate a variety of payment types, from chip readers for credit cards, a built-in scanner for checks, and a mobile app for Web payment services. This ensures that you never miss a potential sale.

Sign up for PSS by heading to our website and filling out the form. Once you submit the form, our team will contact you to gather more details about your business. As a welcoming gift, once we approve your business, you can try out PSS for thirty days at no cost. Go to www.pascalsolutions.com today to take advantage of this offer!

5. The word "supporting" in paragraph 2, line 3, is closest in meaning to

(A) confirming
(B) backing
(C) advancing
(D) subjecting

6. What payment method is NOT mentioned in the advertisement?

(A) Check
(B) Mobile app
(C) Cash
(D) Credit card

7. What is PSS offering as a sales promotion?

(A) A thirty-day free trial
(B) A new laptop
(C) A free training session
(D) A discount on devices

Questions 8-9 refer to the following text-message chain.

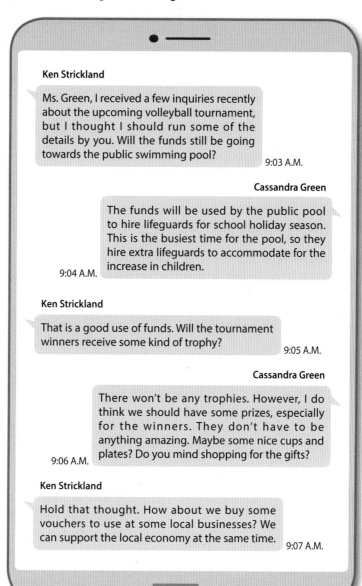

Ken Strickland

Ms. Green, I received a few inquiries recently about the upcoming volleyball tournament, but I thought I should run some of the details by you. Will the funds still be going towards the public swimming pool?

9:03 A.M.

Cassandra Green

The funds will be used by the public pool to hire lifeguards for school holiday season. This is the busiest time for the pool, so they hire extra lifeguards to accommodate for the increase in children.

9:04 A.M.

Ken Strickland

That is a good use of funds. Will the tournament winners receive some kind of trophy?

9:05 A.M.

Cassandra Green

There won't be any trophies. However, I do think we should have some prizes, especially for the winners. They don't have to be anything amazing. Maybe some nice cups and plates? Do you mind shopping for the gifts?

9:06 A.M.

Ken Strickland

Hold that thought. How about we buy some vouchers to use at some local businesses? We can support the local economy at the same time.

9:07 A.M.

8. What is suggested about the volleyball tournament?

(A) It is a reward for staff at the swimming pool.
(B) It is being held for children.
(C) It is raising money for a public facility.
(D) It is an annual event among locals.

9. At 9:07 A.M., what does Mr. Strickland most likely mean when he writes, "Hold that thought."?

(A) He believes he has a better alternative to Ms. Green's suggestion.
(B) He is too busy to fulfill a request.
(C) He prefers last year's gift ideas.
(D) He thinks a date should be reconsidered.

Questions 10-11 refer to the following e-mail.

From	Flora Elliott <felliott@advancenow.com>
To	Nelson Salazar <nsalazar@urushine.com>
Date	May 18
Subject	Training workshop

Hello Mr. Salazar,

This email is to confirm that our AdvanceNow training team will be hosting the Urushine Support Team at our office on May 25 to deliver a training workshop. The training will begin with a presentation to teach your team how to best diagnose and fix common issues with electric vehicles. Additionally, there will be a focus on how to advise customers on taking proper care of their vehicles to avoid receiving expensive repair bills.

The presentation will be followed by a hands-on activity in our workshop of some of the issues covered. We will divide you into groups, and each group will get to look at a different vehicle. Group members will then work together to correctly diagnose and fix the issue.

Please let me know if you have any questions.

Sincerely,

Flora Elliott
President, AdvanceNow

10. What is a feature of the training workshop described?

(A) A video conference
(B) A tour of a factory
(C) A meeting with a client
(D) A group activity

11. What is most likely true of Urushine?

(A) It manufactures electronic devices.
(B) It provides automotive repair services.
(C) It helps customers with home repairs.
(D) It sells office furniture.

Questions 12-15 refer to the following checklist.

New-Hire Checklist

Supervisors should refer to this list to ensure new hires are appropriately onboarded.

☐ **Workstation / laptop setup**
When a new employee is hired, supervisors should put in a request for a new workstation and laptop at www.yalyn.com/itrequest. It is expected that new employees are provided laptops and introduced to their workstations on their start date.

☐ **Yalyn credentials**
New employees will be sent a username and a temporary password. They should log in and create a new password.

☐ **Entry card**
Entry cards are required to gain access to Yalyn's buildings. They can be picked up from Human Resources on the fourth floor. Entry cards are differentiated based on one's department, so ensure that the correct card is received. This will determine which facilities the employee will gain access to.

☐ **Office telephone setup**
All workstations should come equipped with a phone. Make sure that the employee sets up a voice mail box and sets an out-of-office message. Place directions on how to do this next to the phone for convenience.

☐ **Yalyn Messenger Service**
New employees should be added to the company-wide chat room as well as their respective team chat room. Human Resources can add employees to the company-wide chat room while team leaders of each team can add employees to team chat rooms.

---

12. Who most likely will use the checklist?

(A) A Yalyn job applicant
(B) A Yalyn client
(C) A new employee's supervisor
(D) A Human Resources team member

13. What do employees receive on their first day at Yalyn?

(A) A contract
(B) A congratulatory message
(C) A survey
(D) A computer

14. What is NOT indicated about Yalyn ID cards?

(A) They provide access to certain areas.
(B) They vary depending on the department.
(C) They feature Yalyn's logo on them.
(D) They can be obtained from the fourth floor.

15. According to the checklist, where should some helpful instructions be put?

(A) In a mailbox
(B) By a telephone
(C) Inside a desk drawer
(D) On a Web site

Questions 16-18 refer to the following letter.

17 October

Cooper Pearson, Facility Manager
Insurra Solutions
81 Merton Bank
McCulloch, Texas 76836

Dear Mr. Cooper,

We are pleased to announce that you have been nominated for McCulloch Business Association's Excellence in Business Practices award. — [1] —. This is in recognition of the work you did in helping local businesses improve their work practices and processes. This has been instrumental in helping these companies get off the ground. — [2] —.

The ceremony will take place on 7 December, and we will announce the winner of the award after a brief commencement speech. — [3] —. As you are a nominee, you may bring up to two guests with you. At your earliest convenience, please let us know if you will be attending the event and with how many guests.

If you are the winner of the award, you will be awarded with a $5,000 cash prize. — [4] —. As there will be some reporters at the event, they may also interview you for an article.

Congratulations on this terrific achievement.

Yours sincerely,

Evelyn Osborne
President, McCulloch Business Association

16. Why was Mr. Cooper nominated for the award?

(A) For assisting some businesses
(B) For organizing a conference
(C) For creating a training program
(D) For providing some work equipment

17. What does Ms. Osborne request from Mr. Cooper?

(A) An updated résumé
(B) A prepared speech
(C) A response to an invitation
(D) A schedule for an event

18. In which of the positions marked [1], [2], [3], and [4] does the following sentence best belong?

"This will be followed by a catered dinner."

(A) [1]
(B) [2]
(C) [3]
(D) [4]

Questions 19-21 refer to the following article.

Amelia's Opens in Emerson

(December 22) — The commercial district in the city of Emerson has seen significant redevelopment in the past few years. Consequentially, many new businesses sprung up in the area, including The Play Castle, a children's toy retailer; Tom Garza, a musical instrument dealer, and Crescendo, a fashion boutique selling both casual and formal looks for women.

Amelia's is the newest business to enter the thriving Emerson commercial district. The business, named after its owner, Amelia Warren, offers handcrafted, one-of-a-kind gifts such as scented soaps, soy wax candles, fragrance oils, as well as resin art pieces.

When asked why she chose Emerson to build her business, Ms. Warren responded, "For most of my life, I've lived in Oak Brook, which was quite low key. I've always wanted to live in a bustling city where I could fulfill my life-long dream of owning my own gift shop."

"Early last year, I happened to see a news report about the redevelopment of Emerson's commercial district, and I knew right away that the city would be the ideal place for me to live and launch my shop," Ms. Warren continued. "That's why I'm here now."

Ms. Warren ended her explanation by saying, "Since Emerson has a great railway system with frequent connections to Oak Brook and other distant cities and towns, I can visit my friends and family as much as I'd like. All in all, I'm excited that I've chosen Emerson as my new home."

---

19. Where most likely could a shopper purchase a drum set?

(A) At The Play Castle
(B) At Tom Garza
(C) At Crescendo
(D) At Amelia's

20. What is a purpose of the article?

(A) To compare the cost of living in two different cities
(B) To update the readers about a status of a project
(C) To report on the difficulties faced by small business owners
(D) To provide an explanation for a decision

21. What is NOT indicated about the city of Emerson?

(A) It is a fast-paced city.
(B) It is an hour away from Oak Brook.
(C) Its commercial district is expanding.
(D) It can be accessed by train.

Questions 22-25 refer to the following e-mail.

To:	jfields@reverber.com
From:	khopkins@southernlife.com
Date:	August 12
Subject:	Order Number 219636

Mr. Fields,

Thank you for getting in touch with us regarding order number 219636. — [1] —. We have just started operations at our new warehouse, so our team has been working around the clock to integrate it into our delivery system. As a result, there were some delays shipping out our orders. We would like to sincerely apologize for any inconvenience caused. According to our records, your order was shipped last week, so you should be receiving your order on Monday. — [2] —.

We understand that this may have caused considerable frustration. If the delay is unacceptable and you would like to request a refund, we will be happy to arrange that for you. Simply let us know, and we will process a refund right away. — [3] —.

We would once again like to apologize. We understand how important the customer experience is, and we work tirelessly to ensure our customers are happy. As a token of our appreciation for your ongoing support, please use the code "VALUED" to use with your next order to receive a reusable bag made of recycled materials bearing our logo. — [4] —.

Sincerly,

Kate Hopkins
Customer Support, Southern Life

22. Why does Ms. Hopkins contact Mr. Fields?

(A) To respond to an inquiry
(B) To fulfill a refund request
(C) To request some feedback
(D) To promote a new product

23. What is indicated about Southern Life?

(A) It is hiring additional employees.
(B) It recently opened a warehouse.
(C) It does not ship internationally.
(D) It is reducing its prices.

24. What is suggested about a shopping bag?

(A) It will ship in seven days.
(B) It is not sold separately.
(C) It is made of plastic.
(D) It has a company's logo on it.

25. In which of the positions marked [1], [2], [3], and [4] does the following sentence best belong?

"If there is a further delay, please let us know immediately."

(A) [1]
(B) [2]
(C) [3]
(D) [4]

Questions 26-29 refer to the following online chat discussion.

Cheryl Johnston [11:21 A.M.]
Hello, Ian and Claire. I'm so glad the university's carpooling program is finally launching. I've been waiting for this for a long time. I think I'll be able to save around $350 on just fuel costs this year alone.

Ian Lowe [11:23 A.M.]
Me too. And I was just reminded that we will be allowed to use the carpool lanes on the way into campus. That should cut down on our travel times.

Cheryl Johnston [11:24 A.M.]
My car is at the shop, and it will only be ready in two weeks. I'm afraid somebody else will have to do the driving next week. Would you be able to drive us, Claire?

Claire Zhang [11:27 A.M.]
I'm so sorry, but I don't think I can do Monday anymore. My husband will be using the car that day as he has an out-of-town trip.

Cheryl Johnston [11:29 A.M.]
Ian, you're our last hope!

Ian Lowe [11:30 A.M.]
Not a problem. I can drive us next week. I've been itching to drive more these days anyway. However, I'll be attending a three-day conference on Wednesday.

Claire Zhang [11:32 A.M.]
Yes, I remember you telling us. It's that one on digital privacy. Except for Monday, I'll be able to drive us into campus, so that's OK. Oh, and Susie from the geology department asked if she could join the three of us.

Cheryl Johnston [11:34 A.M.]
Of course she is welcome. In that case, we should write down all of our addresses somewhere so that we can figure out the optimal order to pick us up. I'll send a document around for us to fill out.

Claire Zhang [11:36 A.M.]
Excellent. I'll also stop by the campus security office today to pick up a parking pass for carpoolers. According to the notice, we'll be allowed to use the central carpark if there's at least three of us.

SEND

---

26. What is suggested about the writers?

(A) They are employed at a university.
(B) They live next to one another.
(C) They are attending a conference together.
(D) They are all new to the city.

27. What is NOT mentioned as a benefit of the employee programs?

(A) It reduces car-related expenses.
(B) It allows access to a carpark.
(C) It improves the air quality.
(D) It reduces travel time to work.

28. At 11:29 A.M. what does Ms. Johnston most likely mean when she writes, "Ian, you're our last hope"?

(A) Mr. Lowe should cancel a work event.
(B) Mr. Lowe must fill out a form.
(C) Mr. Lowe needs to invite a colleague.
(D) Mr. Lowe is the only employee available to drive.

29. How many people will most likely go to work together on Monday?

(A) One
(B) Two
(C) Three
(D) Four

Questions 30-34 refer to the following brochure and e-mail.

Nodaway Community Center Space for Rent

The recently completed Nodaway Community Center (NCC) is now available for citizens to hire out rooms for business meetings and private functions. The details are as below:

Rooms	Cost per Hour	Capacity (seated/standing)
Lower Meeting Room	$75	15/30
Upper Meeting Room	$100	71/131
Dining Room	$130	52/98
Conference Hall	$200	103/207

* We offer discounted rates for schools and charitable organizations.
* Rooms are equipped with a screen, a projector, microphones, tables, and chairs.
* A $50 deposit must be paid upon reservation. If a booking is canceled at least 30 days in advance, 50% of the deposit will be refunded. Cancellations made less than 30 days before the booked date will result in a forfeiture of the deposit.

For any inquiries, please send an e-mail to bookings@nodawaycommunitycenter.org.

To:	bookings@nodawaycommunitycenter.org
From:	w.martin@bastropcitymission.com
Date:	August 16
Subject:	Notice of cancellation

To Whom It My Concern,

Due to a difficult financial year, I would like to inform NCC that Bastrop City Mission (BCM) will be unable to host our annual volunteer appreciation dinner as planned. Therefore, we would like to put in our notice of cancellation made for September 8.

Our charity has always had strong support from local businesses for the past six years. However, the recession has hit businesses stronger than expected. As such, we will be looking into a smaller scale event this year until conditions improve. We hope that by next year, we will hold an event at the NCC for our annual celebration.

Sincerely,

Wayne Martin
BCM President

30. What does the brochure suggest about the NCC?

(A) It charges an additional fee for parking.
(B) It is located next to a public transportation station.
(C) It has a maximum capacity of 150 people.
(D) It was recently constructed.

31. What is included in the cost of renting space at the NCC?

(A) Audiovisual equipment
(B) Food catering
(C) Valet parking
(D) Cleaning services

32. What is suggested about the BCM?

(A) It receives support from businesses worldwide.
(B) It primarily works with local schools.
(C) It was eligible for a discount at the NCC.
(D) It was started five years ago.

33. According to the e-mail, why must the BCM cancel its reservation?

(A) It is postponing its event.
(B) It requires specialized equipment.
(C) It did not receive sufficient funding.
(D) It prefers a larger venue.

34. How much will the BCM have to pay as a cancellation fee?

(A) $25
(B) $50
(C) $75
(D) $100

Questions 35-39 refer to the following e-mails.

To	service@eminencehotel.com
From	wgarcia@snoopmail.com
Date	March 19
Subject	Hotel stay

To Whom It May Concern,

It was an absolute pleasure being a guest at the Eminence Hotel—Pataskala earlier this month. While I have been to other Eminence Hotels, my stay at the Pataskala location made a strong impression.

From the moment we arrived at the hotel, we felt like valued guests. A staff member was communicating with us on the day of our check-in to make sure we could get to the hotel on time. Once we had arrived, we were provided with exceptional service. Our receptionist, Candace Rodgers, showed us all of the good tourist spots and helped us arrange transportation to and from our excursions. We were traveling with my parents, Mr. and Mrs. Freeman, and they have traveled all around the world. Even they thought that the experience at Eminence Hotel is unrivaled, which is why they are frequent guests of other hotels in your chain.

We were also highly impressed with your hotel's restaurant on the top floor. We traveled to Pataskala because it is known for great food. Your restaurant was no exception, which is why we ended up dining there twice.

All the best,

Wendy Garcia

To	wgarcia@snoopmail.com
From	cdouglas@eminencehotel.com
Date	March 21
Subject	Thank you!

Thank you for the very kind words. I have passed on your comments to our receptionist.

We would also like to publish your comments on our Web site as we were so touched by your words. If that is OK, could you reply to this e-mail to give us your permission to do so?

Thank you.

Craig Douglas, Manager
Guest Services

35. What is the purpose of the first e-mail?

(A) To request details on a reservation
(B) To promote a new service
(C) To provide feedback on a recent stay
(D) To suggest that an offering be changed

36. In the first e-mail, the word "chain" in paragraph 2, line 8, is closest in meaning to

(A) franchise
(B) order
(C) team
(D) link

37. What does Ms. Garcia indicate about Pataskala's cuisine?

(A) Her parents were the ones to recommend it.
(B) Good examples of it were available at the hotel.
(C) It incorporates locally grown ingredients.
(D) It is featured in travel documentaries.

38. Who did Mr. Douglas forward Ms. Garcia's e-mail to?

(A) Ms. Garcia
(B) Eminence Hotels' kitchen staff
(C) Ms. Rodgers
(D) Mr and Mrs. Freeman

39. What does Mr. Douglas ask Ms. Garcia to do?

(A) Give permission to publish a review
(B) Book a new date for a visit
(C) Send photos of her stay
(D) Claim an unused voucher

Questions 40-44 refer to the following survey response, e-mail, and job advertisement.

CUSTOMER SATISFACTION SURVEY

Overall, how satisfied were you with your most recent service experience at Shining Motors of Albany?
(1 = Completely Dissatisfied, 5 = Completely Satisfied)

1	2	3	4	5
○	○	○	●	○

Please comment on your rating:
The service I received was great. The mechanic was very friendly, knowledgeable, and I appreciated that he took the time to explain all of the repairs that he had done. However, I did notice that when I received my car back, it had not been cleaned. While I am accustomed to this lack of attention from local mechanics, I would have hoped that Shining Motors, who receive high ratings because of its excellent service, would include washing and vacuuming the interior of the car.

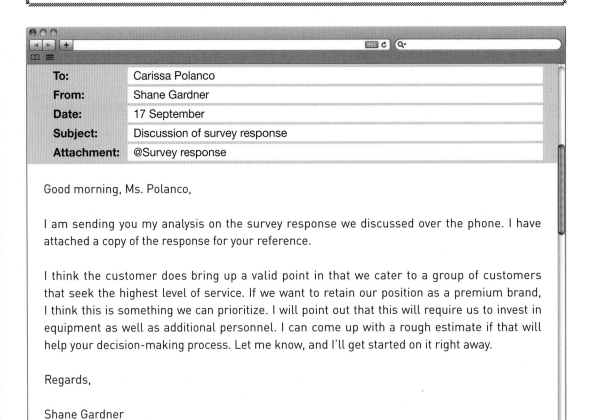

To:	Carissa Polanco
From:	Shane Gardner
Date:	17 September
Subject:	Discussion of survey response
Attachment:	@Survey response

Good morning, Ms. Polanco,

I am sending you my analysis on the survey response we discussed over the phone. I have attached a copy of the response for your reference.

I think the customer does bring up a valid point in that we cater to a group of customers that seek the highest level of service. If we want to retain our position as a premium brand, I think this is something we can prioritize. I will point out that this will require us to invest in equipment as well as additional personnel. I can come up with a rough estimate if that will help your decision-making process. Let me know, and I'll get started on it right away.

Regards,

Shane Gardner
Customer Experience Team, Shining Motors of Albany

Shining Motors of Albany are seeking entry-level car wash attendants for all of our locations. No prior experience is necessary as all training is provided. Your responsibilities will include:

- Driving vehicles from the workshop and through the automated car wash
- Cleaning off interior surfaces of vehicles
- Vacuuming floor mats and seats to remove any dirt and debris
- Delivering cleaned vehicles to the front for customer pickup

Apply online at jobs@shiningmotors.com or come to a store and ask for an application form.

40. What does the survey response indicate about the service department at Shining Motors?

(A) Its prices are unusually high.
(B) Its reservation process is too cumbersome.
(C) Its attention to detail should be improved.
(D) Its mechanics waste too much time.

41. What is one purpose of Mr. Gardner's e-mail?

(A) To notify Ms. Polanco of an upcoming inspection
(B) To offer to estimate the cost of a proposed change
(C) To suggest running a promotional event
(D) To order additional parts for a project

42. What most likely is the service that Mr. Gardner references in the e-mail?

(A) Providing temporary vehicles
(B) Filling up petrol tanks
(C) Cleaning customers' vehicles
(D) Offering refreshments in the waiting area

43. What is most likely true about Ms. Polanco?

(A) She approved an expense.
(B) She is the owner of Shining Motors of Albany.
(C) She has worked as a mechanic.
(D) She conducted a customer survey.

44. What most likely is a requirement for the advertised job at Shining Motors?

(A) Experience working with customers
(B) The ability to work on weekends
(C) A technical certificate
(D) A driver's license

Questions 45-49 refer to the following announcement, form, and e-mail.

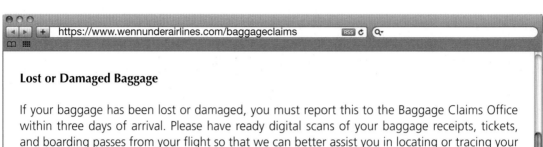

https://www.wennunderairlines.com/baggageclaims

Lost or Damaged Baggage

If your baggage has been lost or damaged, you must report this to the Baggage Claims Office within three days of arrival. Please have ready digital scans of your baggage receipts, tickets, and boarding passes from your flight so that we can better assist you in locating or tracing your baggage as quickly as possible.

We understand that this process sometimes takes time, and you may need necessities that were in your baggage. Our policy is to reimburse the cost of necessities such as toiletries and clothing. Please note that our policy does not extend to electric devices.

If we have lost or damaged your luggage, go to www.wennunderairlines.com/baggageclaims/ claim_form and fill out your details. Before you submit the form to us, ensure that you have included digital scans of any receipts. If you are unable to complete the form online, you should print out the form, fill it out, and send the form along with your original receipts by mail to:

Wennunder Airlines Baggage Services
2195 Colonial Lane
Hickory, North Carolina (NC), 28601

---

www.wennunderairlines.com/baggageclaims/claim_form

Wennunder Airlines Baggage Claim

Baggage receipt number	0736532
Reported date of loss	February 11, 4:30 P.M.
Total bags checked	1
Total bags lost or damaged	1
Attached receipts	jhammes_receipts
Flight number	WU320
Departure location	El Paso, Texas
Connection information	Nonstop
Arrival location	San Jose, California
Arrival date and time	February 11, 8:15 P.M.
Passenger name	Julia Hammes
Passenger address	906 Hummingbird Drive, San Jose, California 95125
Passenger e-mail	jhammes@qwikmail.com
Passenger phone	310-555-9725

To	Wennunder Airlines Baggage Services <baggageservice@wennunderairlines.com>
From	Julia Hammes <jhammes@qwikmail.com>
Date	February 20
Subject	Claim for Baggage Receipt Number 0736532

Hello,

I filed a claim for my missing baggage to your office shortly after I landed on February 11. A few days later, my suitcase was found and sent to my hotel room on February 13. However, I had to buy some items during the two days I was without my suitcase. I submitted the receipts for all of my expenses I incurred on February 14, but I noticed that I did not receive the full reimbursement I should be entitled to. Below is a list of items I submitted a claim for. Please let me know if there was a problem with any of the items.

Item Purchased	Price
1. Toothbrush and toothpaste	$6.00
2. Shampoo	$4.00
3. Socks	$5.00
4. Hairdryer	$29.00
5. Towel	$10.00
6. Jacket	$40.00
Total:	$94.00

Sincerely,

Julia Hammes

45. According to the Web page, what must customers do when filling a claim?

(A) Visit the Baggage Claims Office
(B) Speak to a representative
(C) Include copies of all receipts
(D) Pay a refundable deposit

46. What is suggested about Ms. Hammes?

(A) She fulfilled the airline's requirements for filing for lost baggage.
(B) She has traveled with Wennunder Airlines in the past.
(C) She missed a connecting flight due to losing her suitcase.
(D) She traveled to Texas for a family event.

47. According to the e-mail, when did Ms. Hammes receive her baggage?

(A) On February 11
(B) On February 13
(C) On February 14
(D) On February 20

48. What item on Hammes' list is ineligible for reimbursement?

(A) Item 1
(B) Item 2
(C) Item 3
(D) Item 4

49. What does Ms. Hammes indicate in the e-mail?

(A) She bought all her items on the same day.
(B) She purchased some toiletries.
(C) She visited a department store.
(D) She refunded the jacket she bought.

Questions 50-54 refer to the following Web page and e-mails.

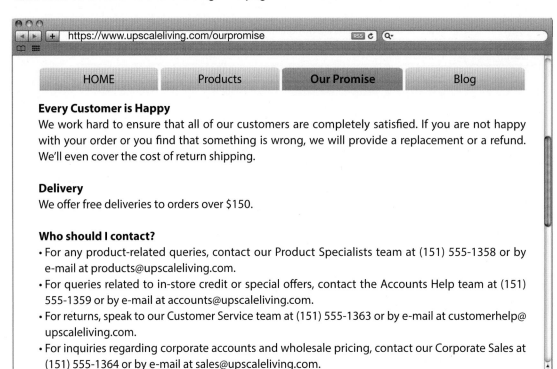

HOME	Products	**Our Promise**	Blog

Every Customer is Happy
We work hard to ensure that all of our customers are completely satisfied. If you are not happy with your order or you find that something is wrong, we will provide a replacement or a refund. We'll even cover the cost of return shipping.

Delivery
We offer free deliveries to orders over $150.

Who should I contact?
• For any product-related queries, contact our Product Specialists team at (151) 555-1358 or by e-mail at products@upscaleliving.com.
• For queries related to in-store credit or special offers, contact the Accounts Help team at (151) 555-1359 or by e-mail at accounts@upscaleliving.com.
• For returns, speak to our Customer Service team at (151) 555-1363 or by e-mail at customerhelp@upscaleliving.com.
• For inquiries regarding corporate accounts and wholesale pricing, contact our Corporate Sales at (151) 555-1364 or by e-mail at sales@upscaleliving.com.

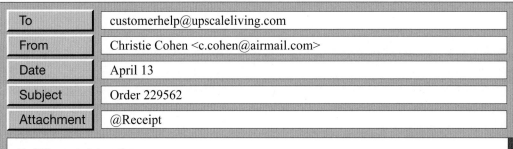

To	customerhelp@upscaleliving.com
From	Christie Cohen <c.cohen@airmail.com>
Date	April 13
Subject	Order 229562
Attachment	@Receipt

To Whom it May Concern:

I reported an issue with the ergonomic office chair I bought on February 14 of this year. I received the chair on February 16, but I immediately noticed that the chair constantly squeaked, which made it difficult to concentrate on work. I have tried all possible ways to mitigate this issue. However, I believe it is a defect with the chair itself. It is disappointing because I have been satisfied with all of my other products from Upscale Living.

I requested a refund in early March by calling the number for returns listed on your Web site. The team informed me that I would receive a shipping label by April 2. However, I have not yet received anything. Would it be possible to receive a return label so that I can proceed with my refund? I have attached my receipt to this e-mail for your convenience.

Thank you.

Christie Cohen

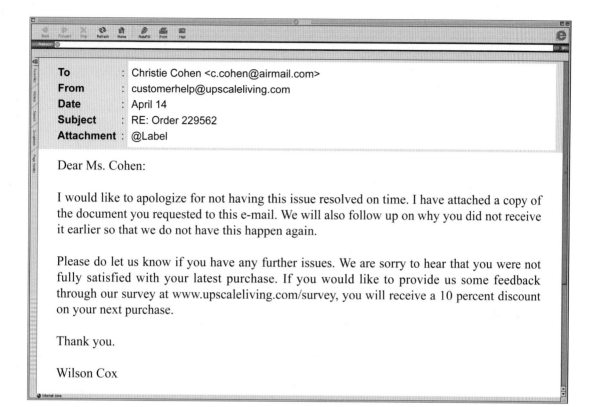

To : Christie Cohen <c.cohen@airmail.com>
From : customerhelp@upscaleliving.com
Date : April 14
Subject : RE: Order 229562
Attachment : @Label

Dear Ms. Cohen:

I would like to apologize for not having this issue resolved on time. I have attached a copy of the document you requested to this e-mail. We will also follow up on why you did not receive it earlier so that we do not have this happen again.

Please do let us know if you have any further issues. We are sorry to hear that you were not fully satisfied with your latest purchase. If you would like to provide us some feedback through our survey at www.upscaleliving.com/survey, you will receive a 10 percent discount on your next purchase.

Thank you.

Wilson Cox

---

50. According to the Web page, what does Upscale Living offer?

(A) Expedited shipping on large orders
(B) Free returns on any purchases
(C) Discounts on bulk orders
(D) Seasonal promotions on certain products

51. What is suggested about the chair that Ms. Cohen purchased?

(A) It can be folded up to save space.
(B) It was purchased at a discount.
(C) It was designed to be used for work purposes.
(D) It is no longer available for purchase.

52. When did Ms. Cohen place her order?

(A) On February 14
(B) On February 16
(C) On April 2
(D) On April 13

53. What office did Ms. Cohen call at Upscale Living?

(A) The Accounts Help team
(B) The Product Specialists team
(C) The Corporate Sales team
(D) The Customer Service team

54. What did Mr. Cox most likely send to Ms. Cohen?

(A) A set of assembly instructions
(B) A list of approved logistics companies
(C) A map with Upscale Living office locations
(D) A copy of a shipping label

MEMO

MEMO

MEMO

파고다 토익 RC

4th Edition

RC

기본 완성

PAGODA Books

4th Edition

파고다 토익 RC 해설서

파고다교육그룹 언어교육연구소, 김나래 I 저

기본 완성

PAGODA Books

PART 5

UNIT 01. 문장의 구조와 수 일치

핵심 문제 유형
본서 p.26

1. (B) **2.** (A) **3.** (B) **4.** (B) **5.** (B) **6.** (B)

Q1. 그 조직은 직원들의 기술을 개발하기 위해 정기적인 교육 프로그램을 실시하고 있다.

해설 빈칸은 관사 뒤에 쓰여 명사 자리이고 문맥상 정기적인 교육 프로그램을 실시하는 주어는 '조직'이 적절하므로 (B) organization이 정답이다.

어휘 organization 조직, 단체 I conduct 수행하다, 실행하다 I regular 정기적인 I develop 개발하다 I skill 기술, 능력

Q2. 우리는 각 주제를 꼼꼼히 다루기 위해 발표를 세 부분으로 나누었다.

해설 빈칸은 주격 대명사 뒤에 위치하는 동사 자리이므로 (A) broke가 정답이다.

어휘 presentation 발표, 제시 I section 부분, 구역 I cover 다루다 I thoroughly 철저히, 완전히

Q3. 존슨 화장품은 새로운 친환경 포장 라인을 출시할 계획이다.

해설 이 문장에는 동사가 없으므로 빈칸이 동사 자리라는 것을 알 수 있고 Johnson Cosmetics는 회사명으로 고유명사에 해당하여 단수로 취급하므로 단수 동사인 (B) is launching이 정답이다.

어휘 launch 출시하다, 시작하다 I eco-friendly 친환경적인 I packaging 포장, 패키징

Q4. 여러 엔지니어들에 의해 설립된 그 회사는 혁신적인 소프트웨어를 개발했다.

해설 이 문장에는 동사가 없으므로 빈칸이 동사 자리라는 것을 알 수 있고 주어가 several engineers (복수)가 아닌, the company (단수)이므로 단수 동사인 (B) has developed가 정답이다.

어휘 found 설립하다 I innovative 혁신적인, 독창적인

Q5. 모든 관리자는 직원의 생산성을 평가하기 위해 성과 평가를 수행한다.

해설 빈칸에는 단수 명사 앞에 쓰일 수 있는 부정형용사 (B) Every가 와야 한다.

어휘 performance 수행, 성과 I evaluation 평가 I assess 평가하다, 분석하다 I productivity 생산성

Q6. 직원들 모두가 이번 달에 성과 평가를 받을 예정이다.

해설 이 문장에는 동사가 없으므로 빈칸이 동사 자리라는 것을 알 수 있고 부정대명사 All이 주어로 사용된 경우 수 일치의 기준은 전치사 뒤에 있는 복수 명사이므로 복수 동사인 (B) are가 정답이다.

어휘 undergo 겪다, 경험하다

Practice
본서 p.32

1. (B) **2.** (C) **3.** (A) **4.** (D) **5.** (C)
6. (A) **7.** (B) **8.** (D) **9.** (A) **10.** (A)
11. (A) **12.** (C) **13.** (A) **14.** (D) **15.** (A)
16. (D) **17.** (B) **18.** (A) **19.** (C) **20.** (C)

1. 교육 분야의 퍼스트 컨텐츠는 혁신적인 학습 솔루션을 개발했다.

해설 수식어구 in the education field를 걷어내면 문장의 주어가 First Contents임을 알 수 있고, 고유명사는 -s로 끝나더라도 항상 단수 취급하므로 단수 동사인 (B) has developed가 정답이다.

어휘 field 분야 I innovative 혁신적인 I learning solution 학습 솔루션

2. 백스터 사는 이번 분기에 영업팀을 15퍼센트 증원했다.

해설 빈칸은 동사 자리로, 동사 자리에 들어갈 수 없는 to부정사 (A)와 -ing 형태의 (B), 그리고 명사인 (D)를 탈락시키면 정답은 (C) expanded 이다.

어휘 expand 확대하다, 확장하다 I sales team 영업팀 I quarter 사분기

3. 귀하는 온라인으로 고멧 클럽 뉴스레터 등록을 취소할 수 있습니다.

해설 빈칸은 동사 cancel의 목적어 자리이므로 명사형인 (A) enrollments 가 정답이다.

어휘 cancel 취소하다 I enrollment 등록

4. 우리의 시장 범위를 확장하는 계획들이 승인되었다.

해설 주어 plans를 수식하는 to expand our market reach를 걷어 내면, 빈칸은 동사를 완성하는 조동사 have의 알맞은 형태를 골라야 하는데, -ing 형태의 (A)와 to부정사 (C)는 동사 형태가 아니므로 답에서 제외시킨다. 단수형인 (B)와 복수형인 (D) 중 주어(plans)가 복수이므로 (D) have가 정답이다.

5. 주간 직원 설문조사에서 받은 피드백은 대체로 긍정적이다.

해설 be동사 is는 2형식 동사로, 주격 보어가 이미 favorable로 나와 있으므로 빈칸은 문장의 필수 요소가 아닌 수식어구 자리이며, 형용사 앞에 들어갈 수 있는 품사는 부사이다. 따라서 정답은 (C) generally이다.

어휘 weekly 주간의, 매주의 I favorable 호의적인

6. 각 제안서가 어제 검토되었다.

해설 보기 모두 부정대명사로 쓰여 뒤에 of the를 이끌 경우 복수 명사를 취하지만, 동사가 단수(was reviewed)이므로 (A) Each가 정답이다.

어휘 proposal 제안(서) I review 검토하다

7. 이번 주말에, 서점은 모든 고객들에게 20퍼센트 할인을 제공할 것이다.

해설 빈칸은 명사 customer를 수식하는 자리로, 의미로 접근했을 때 보기 모두 답으로 보이지만, customer가 단수로 쓰였고, 단수 명사를 수식하는 부정형용사는 (B) every 뿐이다.

어휘 bookstore 서점 | customer 고객 | discount 할인

8. 이 프로젝트의 완료는 5월 중순까지 예상된다.

해설 빈칸은 주어 자리로 명사가 필요하므로 (D) Finalization이 정답이다. 동명사 (B) Finalizing도 주어 역할을 할 수 있지만, 빈칸 뒤에 동명사의 목적어가 없으므로 답이 될 수 없다.

어휘 finalization 완료, 마무리 | anticipate 예상하다

9. 주방에서 일하는 요리사들은 레스토랑의 일일 메뉴를 준비한다.

해설 주어는 The chefs이고, 현재분사구인 working in the kitchen은 chefs를 뒤에서 수식하는 수식어구이다. 빈칸은 동사 자리로 주어가 복수인 chefs이므로 복수 동사 (A) prepare가 정답이다.

어휘 chef 요리사, 주방장 | daily 매일의

10. 레이크사이드로 가는 버스는 내일 오전 9시에 정확히 출발할 것이다.

해설 '떠나다, 출발하다'란 의미로 쓰인 동사 leave가 1형식 동사로 사용되어 이미 완전한 문장이다. 따라서, 빈칸은 뒤의 전치사구(at 9 A.M.)를 수식하는 부사 자리이므로 (A) promptly가 정답이다.

어휘 leave 출발하다 | promptly 즉시, 정확히

11. 가게 관리자 박 씨는 자주 신제품을 디자인한다.

해설 빈칸은 동사 자리이고 주어인 Ms. Park는 단수이므로 단수형인 (A) designs가 정답이다.

어휘 design 설계하다 | supervisor 관리자 | frequently 자주

12. 버젯 숍 포털에서 요청된 사항들은 일반적으로 완료하는 데 3일이 걸린다.

해설 made ~ portal까지는 주어 Requests의 수식어구이므로 빈칸은 동사 자리이다. 부사 generally는 동사를 수식한다. -ing 형태와 to부정사는 동사가 될 수 없으므로 답에서 제외시키면 단수 동사 (A)와 복수 동사 (C)가 남는데, 주어가 복수로 쓰였으므로 (C) require가 정답이다.

어휘 require 필요로 하다 | portal 포털 사이트 | complete 완료하다

13. 새로운 애플리케이션을 설정하기 전에 안내서를 철저히 검토하세요.

해설 명령문 문장으로 빈칸은 동사가 들어갈 자리인데. 명령문은 항상 동사원형으로 시작하므로 (A) examine이 정답이다.

어휘 examine 검토하다, 조사하다 | guide 안내서 | thoroughly 철저히

14. 에코 패션 사는 지속 가능하고 스타일리시한 의류를 매장에 공급해오고 있다.

해설 빈칸은 동사 자리이므로 -ing 형태인 (A)는 동사가 될 수 없다. 주어 Eco Fashion Ltd.는 고유명사로, 단수 취급하므로 (D) has been supplying이 정답이다.

어휘 supply 공급하다 | sustainable 지속 가능한 | apparel 의류

15. 모든 직원들은 다음 주까지 보안 교육을 이수해야 한다.

해설 빈칸은 조동사 should에 이어지는 동사원형 자리이다. 따라서 (A) finish가 정답이다.

어휘 finish 끝내다, 완료하다 | security course 보안 교육

16. 오늘 공항 라운지에는 여러 개의 짐이 있었다.

해설 「There + be동사 + 주어」 구조의 문장으로, 빈칸은 be동사가 들어갈 자리이며, be동사의 수는 뒤에 오는 명사에 일치시켜야 하는데, 명사가 복수이므로(several luggage pieces) 복수 동사 (D) were가 정답이다.

어휘 luggage 짐, 수하물

17. 이번 시즌의 테크 엑스포에 참석한 각 참석자는 새로운 제품 출시에 대해 기대하고 있다.

해설 수식어 at this season's Tech Expo를 걷어내면, 주어는 Each of the attendees이고, 빈칸은 동사 자리이므로 동사 자리에 들어갈 수 없는 (D) being은 답에서 제외시킨다. Each of the attendees의 주명사는 Each로 단수 취급하므로 단수 동사 (B) is가 정답이다.

어휘 attendee 참석자 | product launch 제품 출시

18. 여행객들은 블루 메트로 라인을 이용하여 도심 지역에 쉽게 접근할 수 있다.

해설 부사 effortlessly는 수식어이므로 걷어내면, 빈칸은 조동사 뒤 동사원형이 와야 할 자리이다. 따라서 (B) access가 정답이다.

어휘 effortlessly 쉽게 | downtown area 도심 지역 | access 접근하다, 이용하다

19. 지원자 중 한 명이 그의 지원서에 일부 부정확한 자료를 입력했다.

해설 「one of the + 복수 명사」는 주어가 one이므로, 복수 동사인 (B) insert는 답이 될 수 없고 -ing와 to부정사 역시 동사 자리에 올 수 없다. 따라서, (C) inserted가 정답이다.

어휘 insert 삽입하다 | applicant 지원자

20. 손상된 물품 중 일부는 중앙 창고로 보내질 예정이었다.

해설 빈칸은 동사 자리이므로 -ing 형태는 답이 될 수 없고 「Some of the + 명사」가 주어로 사용된 경우, 전치사 of 뒤에 있는 명사가 수 일치의 기준이므로 복수 동사 (C) were이 정답이다.

어휘 damaged 손상된, 파손된 | item 물품 | schedule 일정을 잡다 | central depot 중앙 창고

UNIT 02. 시제

핵심 문제 유형
본서 p.36

1. (B) 2. (D) 3. (B) 4. (C)

Q1. 영업팀은 프로젝트 업데이트를 논의하기 위해 정기적으로 만난다.

해설 이 문장에는 동사가 없으므로 빈칸이 동사 자리라는 것을 알 수 있고

the team은 단수 주어에 해당하므로 단수 동사가 쓰여야 하며 문맥 상 업데이트를 정기적으로 한다는 것을 보아 반복적으로 만난다는 것을 알 수 있으므로 현재 시제인 (B) meets가 정답이다.

어휘   **sales** 판매 | **team** 팀 | **regularly** 정기적으로 | **discuss** 논의하다

Q2.   그 소프트웨어 회사는 지난 10년 동안 크게 성장해 왔다.

해설   이 문장에는 동사가 없으므로 빈칸이 동사 자리라는 것을 알 수 있고 the software company는 단수 주어이므로 단수 동사가 쓰여야 하며, over the past decade는 현재 완료 시제와 어울려 쓰이는 시간 부사구이므로 (D) has grown이 정답이다.

어휘   **grow** 성장하다 | **significantly** 상당히 | **past** 지난 | **decade** 10년

Q3.   배송이 제시간에 도착하면, 우리는 기한을 맞출 수 있을 것이다.

해설   빈칸은 부사절 접속사 if가 이끄는 종속절의 동사 자리이고 the shipment는 단수 주어이므로 단수 동사가 쓰여야 하며, 주절의 동사가 미래 시제인 것으로 보아 조건을 나타내는 부사절에서는 현재 시제가 미래 시제를 대신하므로 (B) arrives가 정답이다.

어휘   **shipment** 발송 | **on time** 제시간에 | **be able to** 할 수 있다 | **meet deadline** 마감 기한을 맞추다

Q4.   책임자는 팀이 이달 말까지 프로젝트를 완료해달라고 요청했다.

해설   빈칸은 명사절 접속사 that이 이끄는 종속절의 동사 자리로, that절을 목적어로 취하는 동사가 '요청'을 의미하므로 that절의 동사는 should 동사원형 또는 should가 생략된 동사원형을 써야 한다. 따라서 (C) complete가 정답이다.

어휘   **director** 감독 | **request** 요청하다 | **complete** 완료하다 | **by the end of** ~말까지

Practice

본서 p.40

1. (A)	2. (A)	3. (B)	4. (C)	5. (A)
6. (C)	7. (D)	8. (C)	9. (A)	10. (C)
11. (C)	12. (A)	13. (D)	14. (A)	15. (A)
16. (C)	17. (B)	18. (D)	19. (A)	20. (B)

1.   김 씨는 지난주에 발표를 마무리했다.

해설   빈칸은 동사 자리이다. -ing 형태와 to부정사는 답이 될 수 없고 last week는 과거 시제에 어울리는 시간 부사구이므로 정답은 (A) finalized이다.

어휘   **finalize** 마무리 짓다 | **presentation** 발표

2.   이 씨는 그 회사가 새 소프트웨어를 즉시 도입할 것을 권했다.

해설   「recommend that + S + (should) + 동사원형」이다. 당위성을 나타 내는 조동사 should가 생략된 문장이므로 주절의 동사로 제안, 요청, 의무 동사가 와야 하므로 (A)가 정답이다. 참고로, (B), (C), (D)는 모두 사람을 목적어로 취하므로 답이 될 수 없다.

어휘   **introduce** 도입하다 | **immediately** 즉시

3.   존슨 씨는 팀장으로 승진한 이후로 프로젝트 일정을 감독하고 있다.

해설   since 뒤에 주어가 나왔으니 빈칸에는 동사가 와야 하므로 (A) is와 (B) was 중 하나가 답이 된다. 또한, 주절의 시제가 현재 완료 진행이 므로 since 뒤에는 '존슨 씨가 팀장으로 승진한 이후로'라는 의미가 되어야 하므로 과거 시제가 쓰여야 한다. 따라서, 정답은 (B) was이다.

어휘   **oversee** 감독하다 | **project timelines** 프로젝트 일정 | **promote** 승진시키다

4.   경제학 권위자인 존슨 박사는 최근에 학과장으로 임명되었다.

해설   was appointed는 과거 시제의 수동태로 이미 완벽한 문장이므로 be p.p. 사이에서 동사를 수식하면서 과거 시제와 함께 쓰일 수 있는 부사인 (C) recently가 정답이다.

어휘   **authority** 권위자 | **economics** 경제학 | **recently** 최근에 | **appoint** 임명하다 | **department head** 학과장

5.   많은 카페들이 작년부터 고객들에게 멤버십 카드를 제공해왔다.

해설   빈칸은 동사 자리로 to부정사 형태는 동사가 될 수 없으므로 (D)는 탈 락이다. 주어(Many cafes)가 복수이므로 단수 동사 (C) has offered 도 탈락이다. '~이후로'를 뜻하는 「since + 과거 시점」 표현인 since last year는 현재 완료 시제에 어울리는 시간 부사구이므로 정답은 (A) have offered이다.

어휘   **offer** 제공하다 | **loyalty card** 고객 (포인트 적립)카드

6.   공원을 개발하는 의회의 프로젝트는 곧 완료될 것이다.

해설   빈칸은 동사 자리로, '곧'이라는 뜻의 부사 soon은 미래 시제와 함께 쓰이므로 정답은 (C) will be completed이다.

어휘   **complete** 완료하다 | **develop** 개발하다

7.   뤼기즈 비스트로는 훌륭한 분위기와 맛있는 음식 때문에 손님들이 자 주 찾는다.

해설   빈칸은 동사 자리이다. 빈도 부사 generally는 '일반적으로'라는 의미 로 현재 시제와 함께 쓰이므로 정답은 (C)와 (D)가 가능하다. 주어가 복수이므로 수 일치를 위해 정답은 (D) come back이다.

어휘   **ambiance** 분위기

8.   우리는 늘 그렇듯이 서비스 기준을 향상시키기 위한 귀하의 노력을 인 정합니다.

해설   빈칸은 동사 자리로, typically '일반적으로, 늘 그렇듯이'는 현재 시제 와 어울려 쓰이는 빈도 부사이므로 정답은 (C) acknowledge이다.

어휘   **acknowledge** 인정하다 | **effort** 노력 | **enhance** 향상시키다 | **standard** 기준, 표준

9.   존 씨가 회사에 입사한 이후로 수익이 거의 25% 증가했다.

해설   「since + 과거 시제」가 나오면, '과거 이래로 현재까지 그래왔다'는 뜻 이므로 정답은 현재 완료 시제인 (A)와 (C)에서 골라야 한다. 주어가 복수이므로 수 일치를 위해 정답은 (A) have improved이다.

어휘   **improve** 증가시키다 | **revenue** 수익

10. 스미스 엠포리움은 20년 이상 운영되고 있으며, 여전히 훌륭한 서비스를 제공하고 있다.

해설 「for + 기간」은 '~동안'이라는 뜻으로 현재완료와 함께 쓰이므로, 정답은 (C)와 (D)가 될 수 있다. 주어가 단수이므로 단수 동사 (C) has been이 정답이다.

어휘 operational 운영할 준비가 된 | decade 10년

11. 지난 세 달 동안, 이 박사의 세미나 참석자 수가 크게 증가했다.

해설 「over + 기간」은 현재 완료와 함께 쓰이고, 문맥상 '~동안'이라는 의미가 되어야 적절하므로 정답은 (C) Over이다.

어휘 rise 증가하다 | significantly 크게, 상당히

12. 이 씨가 서울 사무소로 이동하기 전에, 톰슨 프로젝트를 감독할 것이다.

해설 빈칸은 동사 자리이며, 주어 Ms. Lee는 단수이므로 복수 동사인 (B)는 탈락이다. 주절이 미래 시제이므로 의미상 서울 지사로 이전할 것이라는 미래 시제가 적절해 보이지만, 종속절을 이끄는 시간 접속사 before는 미래를 나타낼 때 미래 시제 대신 현재 시제를 취하므로 정답은 (A) moves이다.

어휘 move 이동하다 | oversee 감독하다

13. 브라운 씨는 미리 예약했기 때문에 뮤지컬 티켓을 얻을 수 있었다.

해설 빈칸은 동사 자리이다. 예약한 것이 티켓을 얻은 것보다 먼저 일어난 사건이므로 과거보다 더 이전인 과거 완료 시제를 써야 한다. 따라서 정답은 (D) had reserved이다.

어휘 manage to ~을 해내다 | ahead of time 사전에, 미리

14. 클락 씨는 다음 해 3월에 새 공장이 가동되면 운영을 담당하게 될 것이다.

해설 빈칸은 동사 자리이다. 뒤 문장의 when 시간 부사절에서 next March이면 미래 시제가 나와야 하는데, 시간, 조건 부사절에서는 미래 시제를 현재 시제로 바꾸므로 현재 시제(starts)가 쓰였다. 앞 문장의 주절은 시제를 바꾸지 않고 그대로 쓰기 때문에 해석상 미래 시제가 와야 하므로 정답은 (A) will supervise이다.

어휘 management 관리, 경영 | supervise 감독하다

15. HR 부서는 이달 말까지 새로운 교육 프로그램 신청서를 받을 것이다.

해설 빈칸은 동사 자리이다. until the end of this month(이번 달 말까지)라고 했으므로 미래 시제가 알맞다. 따라서 정답은 (A) will accept이다.

어휘 application 신청서

16. 톰슨 씨는 지난 세 달 동안 새로운 물품 목록 시스템을 만들고 있다.

해설 빈칸은 동사 자리이며, 「over the last + 기간」은 현재완료 시제와 어울리는 시간 부사구이므로 정답은 (C) has been creating이다.

어휘 create 만들다 | inventory 물품 목록

17. 다음 주 화요일부터 루미나 몰은 폐점 시간을 오후 11시로 변경할 것이다.

해설 빈칸은 동사 자리이다. Beginning next Tuesday가 미래 시제를 나타내고 있으므로 정답은 (B) will change이다.

어휘 beginning ~부터

18. 오후 7시 이후 고객 지원 라인에 접수된 문의는 다음 영업일에 처리될 것이다.

해설 주어 Inquiries가 복수이므로 (B)는 수 일치에 어긋나며, the next business day '다음 영업일'이라고 했으므로 미래 시제가 알맞다. 따라서 정답은 (D) will be addressed이다.

어휘 inquiry 문의 | address 처리하다

19. 넥슨 사는 달라스에서 생산 능력을 곧 확장할 것이다.

해설 shortly는 '곧'이라는 뜻으로 미래 시제와 함께 쓰이므로 정답은 (A) shortly이다. (B)와 (D)는 빈도를 나타내는 부사로 주로 현재 시제와 쓰이고 (C) lately는 현재 완료 또는 과거 시제와 쓰인다.

어휘 expand 확장하다 | production capability 생산 능력

20. 김 씨와 박 씨는 거의 10년 동안 제니스 사에서 근무하고 있다.

해설 for는 '~동안'이라는 뜻으로 '기간'을 나타내며 현재 완료와 함께 쓰이므로 정답은 (B) have been employed이다.

어휘 employ 고용하다 | decade 10년

PART 5 UNIT 03

UNIT 03. 능동태와 수동태

핵심 문제 유형
본서 p.44

1. (A)   **2.** (B)   **3.** (C)   **4.** (A)

Q1. 마케팅 팀은 새로운 캠페인을 성공적으로 시작했다.

해설 이 문장에는 동사가 없으므로 빈칸이 동사 자리라는 것을 알 수 있고 빈칸 뒤에 목적어(the new campaign)가 있으므로 능동태 동사인 (A) launched가 정답이다.

어휘 launch 출시하다, 시작하다 | successfully 성공적으로

Q2. 직원들은 매니저로부터 새로운 업무를 받았다.

해설 이 문장에는 동사가 없으므로 빈칸이 동사 자리라는 것을 알 수 있고, 빈칸 뒤에 목적어로 명사구가(new assignments)가 있어, 능동태를 고르기 쉽지만, give는 목적어가 2개인 4형식 동사이므로 뒤에 목적어가 있더라도 문맥상 능동인지, 수동인지를 가릴 필요가 있다. 직원들이 매니저에게서 업무를 받았다고 해야 자연스러우므로 수동태인 (B) were given가 정답이다.

어휘 assignment 과제, 할당

Q3. 그 보고서는 위원회에 의해 정확하다고 판명되었다.

해설 이 문장에는 동사가 없으므로 빈칸이 동사 자리라는 것을 알 수 있고, 빈칸 뒤에 목적어가 없으므로 수동태라는 것을 알 수 있다. 보기 중 능동태인 (A), (B)를 제외하고 (C)와 (D) 중 단수 주어와 수 일치를 이루

PART 5 GRAMMAR   **5**

는 단수 동사 (C) was found가 정답이다. 참고로, 빈칸 뒤에는 형용사(accurate)가 있는데, 5형식 동사의 수동태 뒤에는 형용사가 목적격 보어로 남는다는 점을 기억하자.

어휘   report 보고서 | accurate 정확한 | committee 위원회

Q4. 그 행사는 매년 타운 홀에서 열린다.

해설   이 문장에는 동사가 없으므로 빈칸이 동사 자리라는 것을 알 수 있고 the ceremony는 단수 주어이므로 단수 동사가 쓰여야 하며 자동사는 수동태로 사용할 수 없기 때문에 (A) takes place가 정답이다.

어휘   ceremony 의식, 행사 | take place 열리다, 개최되다

Practice

본서 p.48

1. (D)	**2.** (A)	**3.** (A)	**4.** (D)	**5.** (C)
6. (C)	**7.** (A)	**8.** (A)	**9.** (A)	**10.** (D)
11. (B)	**12.** (D)	**13.** (D)	**14.** (A)	**15.** (A)
16. (A)	**17.** (D)	**18.** (A)	**19.** (D)	**20.** (A)

1.   안내 책자의 모든 사진은 ABC Foundation에서 친절하게 제공되었다.

해설   were provided는 수동태로 이미 완벽한 문장이다. 따라서 be p.p. 사이에서 동사를 수식하는 부사 (D) kindly가 정답이다.

어휘   provide 제공하다

2.   엔지니어링 팀은 제시간에 작업을 완료한다.

해설   빈칸은 동사 자리이다. (B)의 -ing, (C)의 to부정사 형태는 동사가 될 수 없다. complete는 3형식 동사인데 빈칸 뒤에 목적어인 명사 the task가 나왔으므로 능동태 (A) completes가 정답이다.

어휘   task 작업 | on time 제시간에

3.   월간 프로젝트 회의는 보통 오후에 열린다.

해설   동사 is가 있으므로 (B)는 탈락이다. 단수 명사인 (D)는 앞에 관사가 있어야 하므로 정답이 될 수 없다. (A)를 넣으면 is held로 현재 시제 수동태가 되고, (C)를 넣으면 현재 진행 능동태가 된다. hold의 목적어(명사)가 빈칸 뒤에 없고, 전치사구(수식어구)만 있으므로 정답은 수동태인 (A) held이다.

어휘   monthly 매달의

4.   센트럴 파크 근처에 대형 사무실 건물이 건설될 것이다.

해설   빈칸은 동사 자리이다. (B)는 명사이므로 탈락이다. construct는 3형식 동사인데 빈칸 뒤에 전치사구, 즉 수식어구가 나와 있고 목적어가 될 수 있는 명사가 없으므로 수동태인 (D) will be constructed가 정답이다.

어휘   construct 건설하다

5.   배송 시간 조정은 물류 담당자와 직접 논의되어야 한다.

해설   discuss는 '~을 논의하다'라는 의미의 3형식 동사로서 빈칸 뒤

에 목적어 없이 전치사구가 연결되어 있으므로 수동태가 들어가야 할 자리이다. 보기 중 수동태는 (C)와 (D) 둘 뿐인데, 주어가 복수(Adjustments)이므로 단수형인 (D)는 답이 될 수 없다. 따라서 정답은 (C) should be discussed이다.

어휘   adjustment 조정 | logistics coordinator 물류 담당자

6.   아키라 엔터프라이즈는 몇 달 동안 경제 문제를 겪고 있다.

해설   빈칸은 동사 자리이다. encounter는 3형식 동사로 목적어(명사)를 동반하는데, 빈칸 뒤에 목적어가 있으므로 능동태 (A), (B), (C)가 정답이 될 수 있다. for many monthes라는 기간은 현재 완료 시제와 함께 쓸 수 있으므로 (B)와 (C)가 가능하지만 주어가 단수이므로 정답은 (C) has encountered이다.

어휘   economic issue 경제 문제

7.   최고 실적자는 지난달 최고 경영자에 의해 발표되었다.

해설   빈칸은 동사 자리이다. announce는 3형식 동사인데 빈칸 뒤에 목적어(명사)가 없으므로 수동태를 찾아야 한다. 따라서 정답은 (A) was announced이다.

어휘   Top Performer 최고 실적자 | announce 발표하다

8.   등산객들은 등산로 지도를 받기 위해 공원 안내소에 전화하도록 권장된다.

해설   advise는 '목적어 + 목적격 보어'를 이끄는 5형식 동사이며, 목적격 보어로 to부정사를 취하는데, 문제에서 목적어가 주어 자리로 빠지는 수동태(are advised)로 쓰였으므로 to부정사가 바로 연결되어야 한다. 따라서 정답은 (A) to call이다.

어휘   advise 권장하다 | trail map 등산로 지도

9.   이 처방은 충분한 수분과 함께 섭취되어야 한다.

해설   조동사 뒤에는 동사원형이 와야 하므로 (C)와 (D)는 탈락이다. comsume은 3형식 동사인데 빈칸 뒤에 전치사구(수식어구)만 있고 목적어(명사)가 없으므로 수동태임을 알 수 있다. 따라서 정답은 (A) be consumed이다.

어휘   prescription 처방 | plenty of 충분한 | fluid 수분 | consume 섭취하다

10.   고객으로부터 수집된 모든 민감한 데이터는 엄격한 개인정보 보호 정책에 따라 기밀로 유지될 것이다.

해설   keep은 형용사를 목적격 보어로 취하는 5형식 동사이다. 그런데 문장이 수동태이므로 목적어는 빠지고, 목적격 보어만 남는다. 따라서 빈칸에는 목적격 보어 자리에 올 수 있는 형용사가 와야 한다. 따라서 정답은 (D) confidential이다.

어휘   sensitive 민감한 | privacy policy 개인정보 보호 정책 | confidential 기밀의

11.   모든 신입 사원은 8월 마지막 날까지 멘토를 제공받아야 한다.

해설   should 뒤에는 동사원형이 와야 한다. (A)와 (D)는 동사원형이 아니다. offer는 '제공하다'라는 의미인데 여기서는 신입 사원들이 멘토를 제공받는 대상으로 해석되므로 수동태임을 알 수 있고, offer는 4형식

동사로 쓰이므로 수동태이지만 목적어가 뒤에 하나 남을 수 있음에 유의하자. 따라서 정답은 (B) be offered이다.

어휘 **recruit** 신입 사원

12. 그린우드 타워즈의 냉각 시스템은 지금 유지 보수 팀에 의해 점검받고 있다.

해설 빈칸은 동사 자리이다. check는 3형식 동사로 빈칸 뒤에 목적어(명사)가 나와야 한다. 전치사구(수식어구)밖에 없으므로 현재 진행 수동태인 (D) is being checked가 정답이다.

어휘 **cooling system** 냉각 시스템 ㅣ **maintenance** 유지 보수

13. 전 직원은 회사에서 12개월 동안 근무한 후에 급여 인상을 요청할 수 있다.

해설 빈칸은 동사 자리로 -ing형태인 (C) being은 답이 될 수 없다. for twelve months는 현재 완료가 와야 한다는 힌트이므로 정답은 (A) have been이다.

어휘 **request** 요청하다 ㅣ **raise** 급여 인상

14. 그 식당의 모든 식사는 유명 셰프 로버트 스미스에 의해 준비되었다.

해설 were라는 동사가 있으므로 빈칸에 동사 (B)는 올 수 없다. (D) cookery는 '요리법'을 의미하는 명사로 문맥상 자연스럽지 않다. cook은 3형식 동사로 빈칸 뒤에 목적어(명사)가 있어야 하는데, 전치사구(수식어구)만 있으므로 수동태를 찾으라는 의미이다. were cooked는 과거 시제의 수동태이다. 따라서 정답은 (A) cooked이다.

어휘 **meal** 식사 ㅣ **bistro** 식당

15. 이 씨가 없는 동안 김 박사가 모든 회의 준비를 할 것이다.

해설 조동사 will 뒤에 동사원형이 와야 하므로 (A)와 (B)가 정답이 될 수 있다. organize는 3형식 동사이고 빈칸 다음에 목적어 all meeting arrangements가 있으므로 능동태 (A) organize가 정답이다.

어휘 **arrangement** 준비 ㅣ **absence** 부재

16. 직원들은 일주일에 이틀을 원격으로 일하는 것이 허용될 것이다.

해설 보기 중 목적격 보어 자리에 to부정사를 취하는 5형식 동사는 permit뿐이다. 빈칸 뒤에 목적어(명사) employees가 주어로 사용되었으므로 수동태 (A) permitted가 정답이다.

어휘 **remotely** 원격으로

17. 열차 지연의 주요 원인은 기술적인 문제 때문이었다.

해설 전치사 by를 쓰지 않는 수동태 표현 be attributed to를 외우도록 하자. 정답은 (D) to이다.

어휘 **primary** 주요한 ㅣ **reason** 이유 ㅣ **attribute** ~의 탓으로 돌리다

18. 휴가 신청서는 최소 10일 전에 관리자에게 제출되어야 한다.

해설 be동사가 있으므로 동사 (C)와 (D)는 답이 될 수 없다. send는 타동사로 빈칸 뒤에 목적어(명사)가 있어야 하는데, 없으므로 수동태인 (A) sent가 정답이다.

어휘 **application** 신청서 ㅣ **leave** 휴가

19. 임상 시험 결과는 그 절차가 효과적임을 보여준다.

해설 빈칸은 동사 자리이다. show의 목적어가 that절이므로 능동태인 (C)와 (D)가 가능한데, 주어가 복수이므로 복수 동사 (D) show가 정답이다.

어휘 **clinical trial** 임상 시험 ㅣ **outcome** 결과 ㅣ **effective** 효과적인

20. 행사 진행자들은 손님들을 위해 숙소를 예약했다.

해설 빈칸은 동사 자리이다. book은 3형식 동사이고 빈칸 뒤에 목적어(명사)가 있으므로 능동태 (A), (C), (D)가 가능하지만, 주어가 복수이므로 (A) have booked가 정답이다.

어휘 **coordinator** 진행자 ㅣ **accommodation** 숙소

REVIEW TEST 01
본서 p.50

1. (C)	2. (B)	3. (D)	4. (A)	5. (C)
6. (C)	7. (B)	8. (B)	9. (A)	10. (B)
11. (B)	12. (B)	13. (D)	14. (A)	15. (D)
16. (A)	17. (A)	18. (A)	19. (B)	20. (B)
21. (C)	22. (A)	23. (C)	24. (A)	25. (D)
26. (C)	27. (B)	28. (C)	29. (D)	30. (D)

1. 지원자는 해당 직책에 고려되기 위해 마감 기한 전에 모든 필요한 서류를 제출했다.

해설 빈칸은 문장의 주어가 들어갈 자리로 명사 (B) Application과 (C) Applicant 중에서 답을 골라야 하는데, 서류를 제출한 주체는 사람이므로 '지원자'를 뜻하는 (C) Applicant가 정답이다.

어휘 **submit** 제출하다 ㅣ **required** 요구되는, 필요한 ㅣ **document** 서류 ㅣ **deadline** 기한, 마감일 ㅣ **position** 자리, 직책

2. 프로젝트가 시작되면 마케팅 팀은 매주 모여 진행 상황을 논의할 것이다.

해설 접속사 when이 이끄는 시간 부사절의 시제가 미래를 대신하는 현재 시제(starts)로 쓰였으므로, 주절은 미래 시제인 (B) will meet이 정답이다. 참고로, 시간 부사절이 현재 시제일 때, 주절은 현재 시제와 미래 시제가 모두 가능하지만, 주절의 주어가 단수(team)이므로 동사의 복수형인 (A) meet은 수 일치에 어긋난다.

어휘 **weekly** 매주 ㅣ **discuss** 논의하다 ㅣ **progress** 진행 상황

3. 각 팀원은 마감일 전에 완료할 과제를 할당받았다.

해설 빈칸 뒤에 목적어로서 명사(tasks)가 있다고 해서 능동태 동사인 (B) assigned나 (C) has assigned 중에서 답을 고민해선 안 된다. assign은 '맡기다, 할당하다'란 뜻의 4형식 동사로서 두 개의 목적어를 동반하기 때문에 수동태 문장에서도 동사 뒤에 목적어가 뒤따를 수 있다. 이 문제에서도 문맥상 각 팀원들이 과제를 할당받은 대상이므로 수동태 동사인 (D) was assigned가 정답이다.

어휘 **task** 과제, 임무 ㅣ **complete** 완료하다, 완성시키다 ㅣ **deadline** 마감일, 기한

4. 홍 씨의 책 2판이 7월 1일에 출간되었다.

해설 빈칸은 동사 자리이다. (B)의 -ing 형태는 동사가 될 수 없고, (C)의 동사원형은 조동사가 없으므로 나올 수 없다. 주어가 단수이므로 정답은 (A) was이다.

어휘 edition (출간된 책의 형태로 본) 판, 호 | publish 출판하다

5. 새 경영진의 계획은 직장 내 효율성과 직원 만족도를 향상시키는 것을 목표로 한다.

해설 빈칸은 문장의 주어가 들어갈 자리로 (B)와 (C)의 initiative는 '계획'을, (D)의 initiation은 '시작, 개시'를 뜻하는데, 경영진에 의한 '계획'이 ~의 향상을 목표로 한다는 의미가 적절하므로 (B)와 (C) 중에서 답을 골라야 하며, 동사가 단수(aims)이므로 단수 명사인 (C) initiative가 정답이다.

어휘 management 경영(진) | aim to do ~하는 것을 목표로 하다 | improve 개선하다 | workplace 직장, 업무현장 | efficiency 효율(성) | satisfaction 만족

6. 제이몬 테크 솔루션즈의 모든 관리자들은 이달의 영업 워크숍에 참석해야 한다.

해설 should는 조동사이므로 빈칸에는 동사원형이 와야 한다. 따라서 정답은 (C) attend이다.

어휘 sales 영업 | attend 참석하다

7. 온라인으로 쇼핑하는 고객들의 수가 지난 10년 사이 급격하게 증가했다.

해설 주어가 The number로 단수이다. 단수 동사 (B)와 (C) 중에 over the past decade는 현재완료 시제와 함께 쓰이는 표현이므로 정답은 (B) has이다.

어휘 the number of ~의 수 | rapidly 빨리, 급속히, 순식간에

8. 컴퓨터의 기능 사양이 사용자 설명서에 상세히 적혀 있다.

해설 빈칸은 동사 자리이므로 동사 자리에 들어갈 수 없는 (C)는 오답이며, detail은 '~을 상세히 기록하다'라는 뜻의 3형식 동사로 빈칸 뒤에 목적어 없이 수식어구가 바로 연결되어 있어 수동태가 들어갈 자리이므로 정답은 (B) are detailed이다.

어휘 technical 기술적인 | specification 사양; 명세 | user manual 사용자 설명서 | detail 상세히 기록하다, 세부 사항

9. 창문 수리의 총 비용은 원래의 견적을 초과할 것으로 예상된다.

해설 동사 is가 있으므로 (C)와 (D)는 답이 될 수 없다. expect는 5형식 동사로 목적격 보어 자리에 to부정사를 취한다. 목적격 보어는 있지만 목적어(명사)는 빠져 있는 형태이므로 수동태가 정답이다. be동사는 이미 나와 있으므로 (A) expected가 정답이다.

어휘 cost 비용 | repair 수리, 수선 | exceed 초과하다, 넘다 | estimate 견적(서), 추정치

10. 경쟁력을 유지하기 위해서, HI 전자는 제품의 가격을 가끔 낮춘다.

해설 이 문장은 lowers라는 현재 시제 동사가 나온 문장이다. (A) previously, (C) recently는 보통 과거 시제와 함께 쓰이고, (D) soon은 미래 시제와 함께 쓰이므로 답이 될 수 없다. occasionally는 현재

시제와 어울려 쓰이므로 정답은 (B) occasionally이다.

어휘 competitive 경쟁력 있는 | lower 내리다, 낮추다 | occasionally 가끔씩

11. 탬 씨의 이력서를 검토했던 위원회 회원들은 그의 폭넓은 업무 경력에 매우 깊은 인상을 받았다.

해설 were이라는 be동사 뒤에는 형용사 보어가 나와야 하므로 정답은 형용사인 (B) impressed이다.

어휘 review 재검토하다 검토 | résumé 이력서 | impressed 감명[감동]을 받은, 인상 깊은

12. 부장은 모든 직원들에게 주말까지 프로젝트 업데이트를 제출할 것을 요청했다.

해설 주절에 요청 동사인 requested가 쓰였으므로 그 뒤의 that절의 동사는 should가 생략된 동사원형을 쓴다. 따라서 (B) submit이 정답이다.

어휘 request 요청하다

13. 그 회사는 작년부터 세 개의 새로운 나라들로 사업을 확장해 왔다.

해설 문장 끝의 since last year(작년부터)는 현재완료 시제와 함께 쓰이는 시간부사 표현이므로 (C)와 (D) 중에서 답을 골라야 하는데, 빈칸 뒤에 목적어(its operations)가 있으므로 능동형인 (C) has expanded가 정답이다.

어휘 operation 사업, 영업 | since ~이후로

14. 지난해, 토푸오 화학사는 매일 약 14톤의 실리콘을 생산했다.

해설 빈칸은 동사 자리이다. (D) -ing나 (C) to부정사 형태는 동사가 될 수 없다. 주어가 고유명사여서 단수 취급해야 하므로 복수 동사인 (B)는 탈락이다. 따라서 정답은 (A) produced이다.

어휘 about 약 | produce 생산하다

15. 온라인 쇼핑몰은 다른 제품들과의 가격 비교를 더 쉽게 해준다.

해설 빈칸은 동사 자리이다. (A) -ing와 (D) to부정사 형태는 동사가 될 수 없다. make는 5형식 동사로 it가 목적어(명사)이고 easier는 목적격 보어(형용사)이다. 목적어가 있으므로 정답은 능동태인 (B) make이다.

어휘 compare 비교하다 | price 가격

16. 퍼스트롬 사는 30여 년간 전자 제품을 제조해왔다.

해설 빈칸은 동사 자리이다. 「for + 기간」은 '~동안'이라는 뜻으로 현재완료와 함께 쓰이는 표현이므로 (A)와 (D)가 답이 될 수 있다. manufacture의 목적어(명사)가 빈칸 뒤에 있으므로 정답은 능동태 (A) has manufactured이다.

어휘 manufacture 제조하다, 만들어 내다

17. 휴가 기간 동안 증가하는 수요를 맞추기 위해 임시 직원들이 고용될 것이다.

해설 빈칸은 동사 자리이다. 빈칸 뒤에 hire의 목적어(명사)가 없으므로 수동태 (A) will be hired가 정답이다.

어휘 temporary 임시의, 일시적인 | meet 충족시키다 | demand 요구, 수요 | hire 고용하다

18. 최근 사업 확장 이후에, 챈토라 사는 여러 명의 추가 직원들을 고용했다.

해설 빈칸에는 3형식 동사 hire의 목적어가 와야 하므로 명사 자리이다. several, additional은 명사를 꾸미는 형용사이다. 해석상 '고용'이 아니라 '직원'을 고용했다라는 것이 적절하고, several 뒤에는 복수 명사가 와야 하므로 (A) employees가 정답이다.

어휘 hire 고용하다 | several 몇몇의 | additional 추가적인

19. 관리자의 상세한 발표에도 불구하고 오리엔테이션 중 제공된 정보 중 일부가 불분명했다.

해설 빈칸은 문장의 주어가 들어갈 자리로, (A) Many, (C) One, (D) Either가 부정대명사로 쓰여, [부정대명사 + of the 명사]의 구조로 쓰일 때 이 명사 자리에는 가산 복수 명사가 와야 하는데, 빈칸 뒤의 명사 information은 불가산 명사이므로 불가산 명사와 가산 복수 명사를 모두 취할 수 있는 (B) Some이 정답이다.

어휘 information 정보 | provided 제공된 | unclear 명확하지 않은 | despite ~에도 불구하고 | detailed presentation 상세한 발표

20. 그 재활용 정책은 그 회사가 운영비를 줄일 수 있도록 도와줄 것이다.

해설 help는 5형식 동사로 company는 목적어이고, 빈칸은 목적격 보어 자리이다. help는 목적격 보어 자리에 to부정사가 오는데 여기서 to는 생략 가능하다. 따라서 정답은 (B) reduce이다.

어휘 recycling policy 재활용 정책 | operating cost 운영비 | reduce 감소시키다

21. 소프트웨어 업데이트 중 기술적 문제가 발생하여 프로젝트 일정에 지연이 생겼다.

해설 빈칸은 문장의 동사 자리이므로 동사 자리에 들어갈 수 없는 (B) occurring은 답에서 먼저 제외시킨다. 주어가 단수(issue)이므로 동사의 복수형인 (A) occur 또한 수 일치에 어긋나므로 답이 될 수 없다. 빈칸 뒤에 목적어 없이 전명구(during the software update)가 연결되어 있어 수동태로 생각하고 (D) was occurred를 고르기 쉬운데, '일어나다, 발생하다'란 뜻의 occur는 목적어를 동반하지 않는 1형식 자동사이기 때문에 수동태 문장을 만들 수 없다. 따라서 (C) occurred가 정답이다.

22. 마케팅 부서 소속 15명 이상의 직원들이 성공적으로 영업 교육을 이수했다.

해설 from ~ department는 주어를 수식하고 있고, 주어는 '15명 이상의 직원들'로 복수이다. 빈칸은 동사 자리인데, -ing와 to부정사 형태는 동사가 될 수 없다. 따라서 복수 동사 (A) have가 정답이다.

어휘 successfully 성공적으로, 잘 | complete 완료하다

23. 워크숍에 등록했던 직원들은 월간 사보를 받을 것이다.

해설 who ~ workshop은 주어인 Employees를 꾸미고 있는 수식어구이다. 빈칸 앞에 조동사 will이 나왔고, 빈칸 뒤에는 목적어(명사)가 있으므로 빈칸에는 동사원형이 와야 된다. 따라서 정답은 (C) receive이다.

어휘 register 등록하다

24. 모든 직원은 다음 주 금요일에 예정된 안전 교육 세션에 참석해야 한다.

해설 빈칸은 명사 주어를 수식하는 형용사 자리이며, '직원'을 의미하는 employee는 가산 명사이고, 문장에서 복수(employees)로 쓰였으므로 가산 단수 명사를 수식하는 (B) Each와 (C) Every와 불가산 명사를 수식하는 (D) Much는 오답이다. 따라서, 가산 복수 명사 또는 불가산 명사를 모두 수식할 수 있는 (A) All이 정답이다.

어휘 attend 참석하다 | scheduled for ~로 예정된

25. 모든 공장 근로자들은 이 안전 규정을 따라야 하는 것이 필수이다.

해설 「It is essential that + S + (should) 동사원형」이므로 빈칸 앞에는 조동사 should가 생략되어 있다. 따라서 정답은 동사원형인 (D) follow이다.

어휘 essential 필수적인 | safety regulation 안전 규정

26. 새 소프트웨어가 설치되면 직원들은 업데이트된 기능을 사용하기 시작할 수 있다.

해설 주절의 동사 can begin은 미래 시제에 상응하므로 시간 접속사 once (일단 ~하면)가 이끄는 부사절의 동사도 미래를 나타내야 하는데, 이때 현재 시제가 미래 시제를 대신하므로 (A)와 (C) 중에서 답을 골라야 하며, 소프트웨어는 설치되는 대상이므로 현재 시제 수동태인 (C) is installed가 정답이다.

어휘 updated 업데이트된, 최신의 | feature 기능

27. 내일 회의가 끝날 무렵에 충분한 시간이 있다면, 가르손 씨가 벤쿠버 미술 축제에 대해 잠깐 이야기할 것이다.

해설 '내일 회의에서'라는 말이 있기 때문에 미래 시제를 써야 하지만, if가 조건 부사절이므로 미래 시제 대신 현재 시제를 써야 한다. 따라서 정답은 (A)와 (C)가 될 수 있는데, there로 시작하는 문장은 주어와 동사가 도치된 것으로 주어가 불가산 명사 (enough time)이므로 단수 동사 (A) is가 정답이다.

어휘 enough 충분한 | briefly 짧게, 간단히

28. 오엘렛 씨가 새 지점의 관리자로 고용되었으며, 다음 달부터 전체의 사업 운영을 감독할 것이다.

해설 빈칸이 주어 she와 목적어 all business operations 사이에 있으므로 동사 자리인데, 문장 맨 끝에 starting next month가 있으므로 미래 시제인 (C) will oversee가 정답이다.

어휘 hire 고용하다 | location 장소, 위치 | business operation 사업 운영

29. 우수한 성과를 보여준 직원들은 보상으로 추가 휴가를 부여받을 수 있다.

해설 빈칸 앞에 조동사(may)가 있으므로 빈칸은 동사원형이 들어갈 자리이므로 (A) grant와 (D) be granted 중에서 답을 골라야 하는데, 빈칸 뒤에 목적어로서 명사구(additional vacations days)가 와있다고 해서 능동태 동사인 (A)를 선택하면 안 된다. grant는 '주다, 부여하다'란 뜻의 4형식 동사이므로 수동태 문장에서도 동사 뒤에 목적어가 올 수

있는 점에 주의한다. 이 문제에서도 문맥상 성과를 보인 직원들은 추가 휴가를 받을 수 있는 대상이므로 수동태 동사인 (D) be granted가 정답이다.

어휘 demonstrate 보이다, 입증하다 | exceptional 예외적인, 탁월한 | performance 성과 | additional 추가의 | reward 보상

30. 직원 만족도 조사의 결과가 경영진에 의해 긍정적으로 여겨졌다.

해설 be동사 were가 있으므로 동사 (B)는 답이 될 수 없다. be동사 뒤에 명사 (C)가 오면 주격 보어 자리에 명사가 온 것이므로 주어와의 관계가 동격이어야 한다. '직원 만족도 조사 결과≠고려'이므로 탈락이다. consider는 5형식 동사로 목적어(명사)가 와야 하는데, 빈칸 뒤에 목적격 보어인 형용사 positive는 있지만 목적어(명사)는 없으므로 수동태가 정답이다. 이미 be동사는 나와 있으므로 (D) considered가 정답이다.

어휘 satisfaction 만족 | positive 긍정적인 | management 경영진

UNIT 04. 명사

핵심 문제 유형
본서 p.54

1. (A) **2.** (B) **3.** (B) **4.** (D)

Q1. 그 발표가 대강당에서 진행되었다.

해설 빈칸은 관사 뒤에 위치하여 명사 자리이고 단수 동사 앞에 있으므로 단수 주어인 (A) presentation이 정답이다.

어휘 presentation 발표 | hold 열다 | auditorium 강당

Q2. 성공적인 계획 수립은 우리의 사업 목표를 달성하는 데 매우 중요하다.

해설 빈칸은 형용사 뒤에 위치하여 명사 자리이고 동사가 단수이므로 단수 주어가 와야 하는데, (A), (B) 중 '계획'을 뜻하는 plan은 가산 명사여서 한정사 없이는 단독으로 쓰일 수 없으므로 답이 될 수 없다. 따라서 '계획 수립'을 의미하는 불가산 명사 (B) planning이 정답이다.

어휘 successful 성공적인 | crucial 중대한 | achieve 달성하다

Q3. 그 업무는 제시간에 완료되기 위해 신중한 위임이 필요하다.

해설 빈칸은 앞의 형용사의 수식을 받는 명사 자리이므로 (A), (B) 중에서 답을 골라야 하는데, (A) delegate는 '대표자'라는 뜻의 사람 명사로 가산 명사이므로 한정사 없이 단독으로 쓰일 수 없다. 따라서 '위임'이라는 뜻의 추상명사인 (B) delegation이 정답이다.

어휘 careful 신중한 | delegation 위임 | finish 완료하다 | on time 제시간에

Q4. 직원들은 생산성 향상에 관한 기조 연설에 참석하도록 권장된다.

해설 빈칸은 관사 뒤에 위치하여 명사 자리이고 문맥상 생산성 향상에 관한 기조 연설에 참석하도록 권장된다는 것이 자연스러우므로 (D)

speech가 정답이다.

어휘 encourage 격려하다 | attend 참석하다 | keynote 기조연설 | productivity 생산성 | improvement 향상

본서 p.58
Practice

1. (A)	**2.** (B)	**3.** (B)	**4.** (B)	**5.** (D)
6. (A)	**7.** (A)	**8.** (A)	**9.** (A)	**10.** (D)
11. (A)	**12.** (C)	**13.** (B)	**14.** (A)	**15.** (A)
16. (B)	**17.** (C)	**18.** (A)	**19.** (A)	**20.** (A)

1. 톰슨 박사가 환자들과 소통하는 능력은 놀랍다.

해설 소유격 뒤에는 명사가 들어가야 한다. 또한 빈칸은 주어 자리, 즉 명사 자리이기도 하다. 따라서 정답은 (A) skill이다.

어휘 skill 능력 | interact 소통하다 | remarkable 놀라운

2. 그린웨이 슈퍼마켓은 세일 기간 동안 구매한 모든 에코 뷰티 제품에 대해 할인을 제공할 것이다.

해설 빈칸에는 offer의 목적어가 와야 하므로 명사 자리이다. 정답은 (A)와 (B)가 될 수 있는데, discount는 가산 명사이므로 a discount 또는 discounts로 써야 한다. 따라서 정답은 (B) discounts이다.

3. 그 최신 스마트폰은 시장의 선두 주자가 될 것으로 예상된다.

해설 관사 a 뒤에는 가산 단수 명사가 나와야 한다. 또한, market leader '시장 주도 상품'은 하나의 복합 명사로 기억하자. 정답은 (B) leader이다.

어휘 anticipate 예상하다 | lead 이끌다

4. 디자인 팀은 시의회로부터 건설 계획에 대한 제안들을 받았다.

해설 빈칸은 received의 목적어 자리이므로 명사가 와야 한다. 따라서 정답은 (B) proposals이다.

어휘 proposal 제안 | construction plan 건설 계획 | city council 시의회

5. 우리는 현 소프트웨어 시스템의 대안을 탐구하고 있다.

해설 빈칸은 문장의 목적어 자리로 명사가 필요하여 일반 명사 형태인 (C) alternation을 답으로 고르기 쉽지만, (D) alternative 역시 -tive로 끝나는 주의해야 할 명사로서 현 소프트웨어 시스템의 '교대(alternation)'를 탐구하는 것이 아닌, '대안(alternative)'을 탐구한다는 의미가 적절하므로 (D)가 정답이다.

어휘 explore 탐험하다, 탐구하다 | current 현재의

6. 저명한 예술가들의 전시품이 행사에서 많은 사람들을 끌어모았다.

해설 빈칸은 주어 자리이므로 명사가 와야 한다. 빈칸 앞에 관사가 없으므로 복수 명사인 (A) Exhibits가 정답이다.

어휘 exhibit 전시품 | renowned 저명한 | crowd 군중

7. 계속되는 가뭄으로 인해 농업용 물 소비가 증가할 것이다.

해설 가뭄 때문에 '물이 증가할 것이다'가 아니고, '물 소비(복합 명사)가 증가할 것이다'가 문맥상 적합하다. 따라서 빈칸은 주어로 '소비'라는 명사가 나와야 하므로 정답은 (A) consumption이다.

어휘 dry spell 가뭄 | farming 농업 | rise 증가하다

8. 새로운 안전 조치에 관한 논의가 연기되었다.

해설 빈칸은 정관사 뒤에 위치하면서 주어 자리이므로 명사가 와야 한다. 동명사 (C)는 관사와 함께 쓰일 수 없으므로 정답이 될 수 없고, 동사가 단수이므로(has been postponed) 복수 주어인 (D)는 수 일치에 어긋난다. 따라서 정답은 (A) discussion이다.

어휘 discussion 논의 | safety measures 안전 조치 | postpone 연기하다

9. 업무를 신속히 끝내기 위해 우리는 전문가를 고용할 것이다.

해설 빈칸이 부정관사 an 다음에 있으므로 단수 명사가 쓰여야 한다. 또한 employ의 목적어 자리로도 볼 수 있다. 목적어 자리 역시 명사 자리이다. 명사 (A), (B), (D) 중에 '전문적 지식을 고용하는 것'이 아니고, '전문가를 고용하는 것'이므로 정답은 (A) expert이다.

어휘 finish 마무리 짓다 | assignment 과제 | promptly 신속히 | employ 고용하다 | expert 전문가

10. 그 워크숍은 기업들이 부품 조립을 개선하는 방법을 다룰 것이다.

해설 소유격 뒤에는 명사가 쓰여야 한다. 동명사 (C)는 빈칸 뒤에 목적어 없이 전치사구가 있으므로 정답이 될 수 없다. (B)와 (D)가 명사이지만 해석상 '부품 조립을 개선하는 방법'이 자연스러우므로 (D) assembly가 정답이다.

어휘 assemble 조립하다 | assembly 조립 | assembler 조립 기술자 | component 부품

11. 고객들은 월말 전에 구독을 갱신하는 것이 좋다.

해설 빈칸은 주어 자리로 명사가 와야 한다. 명사는 (A)와 (C)가 있는데, 해석상 (C) customs '세관'이 갱신하는 것이 아니라 고객들이 구독을 갱신하는 것이므로 정답은 (A) customers이다.

어휘 advise 조언하다 | update 갱신하다 | subscription 구독

12. 저희는 신제품 광고를 위해 별도의 예산을 배정했습니다.

해설 빈칸은 전치사 뒤 명사 자리로 보기 중 (B) advertisement '광고'와 (C) advertising '광고 행위, 광고업' 중에서 답을 골라야 하는데, advertisement는 가산 명사이므로 단수로 쓰일 때는 반드시 앞에 관사나 소유격 등의 한정사가 필요하다는 점에서 불가산 명사인 (C) advertising이 정답이다.

어휘 allocate 배정하다, 할당하다 | budget 예산 | specifically 특별히

13. 우리는 더 나은 가격을 확보하기 위해 주요 공급업체와 새로운 조건을 협상하고 있다.

해설 빈칸은 소유격(our) 뒤 명사 자리로, 사물/추상 명사인 (A) supplies와 사람 명사인 (B) suppliers 중에서 고르면 되는데, 새로운 조건을 재협상하는 대상은 사람이므로 (B) suppliers가 정답이다.

어휘 negotiate 협상하다 | terms 조건, 비용 | ensure 보장하다, 확보하다 | pricing 가격 책정

14. 그 부지에서 건설 공사를 시작하기 전에 허가증을 받아야 한다.

해설 빈칸은 부정관사(a) 뒤 명사 자리로 '허가증'을 의미하는 (A) permit과 '허가'를 의미하는 (D) permission 중에서 답을 고르면 되는데, permission은 불가산 명사이므로 앞에 부정관사를 취할 수 없다. 따라서 가산 명사인 (A) permit이 정답이다.

어휘 obtain 얻다, 획득하다 | construction work 건설 공사 | property 부지

15. 쉘던 사의 가장 최근 브림스톤 사와의 합병은 시장 점유율을 높였다.

해설 latest는 명사를 꾸미는 형용사이고, Chalden Corporation's라는 소유격 뒤에는 명사가 와야 하므로 정답은 (A) merger이다.

어휘 merger 합병 | market share 시장 점유율

16. 저희 뉴욕 사무소에서 마케팅 매니저 직책에 대한 채용 공고가 있습니다.

해설 빈칸은 목적어 자리로 앞의 명사 job과 복합 명사를 이루는 명사가 필요한 자리이다. 마케팅 매니저 자리에 대한 '채용 공고'가 있다는 의미가 적절하므로 '빈 자리, 공석'을 뜻하는 (B) opening이 정답이다.

17. 브릿지스톤 계획의 시행은 회사의 수익을 증가시킬 것으로 예상된다.

해설 빈칸은 주어 자리로 명사가 와야 한다. 따라서, 정답은 (C) Implementation이다.

어휘 implementation 시행 | initiative 계획 | anticipate 예상하다 | boost 신장시키다 | revenue 수익

18. 연례 관광 세미나 참가자들은 입구에서 통행증을 제시해야 한다.

해설 빈칸은 주어 자리로 명사가 와야 한다. 보기에서 명사는 (A)와 (D)이다. 문맥상 '참가'가 아닌 '참가자들'이 적절하므로 정답은 (A) Participants이다.

어휘 participant 참가자 | present 보여주다 | pass 통행증 | entrance 입구

19. 풋웨이 풋웨어 아울렛은 신규 구매자들에게 특별 할인 쿠폰을 제공한다.

해설 전치사 to 뒤에는 명사가 와야 한다. new는 형용사이다. 따라서 빈칸은 명사 자리이므로 (A), (B), (D)가 될 수 있다. 그런데 구매자는 사람으로 가산 명사이므로 a shopper 또는 shoppers로 써야 하는데, 관사가 없으므로 정답은 (A) shoppers이다.

어휘 provide 제공하다 | voucher 쿠폰

20. 새 은행에서 계좌를 개설하기 위해 필요한 모든 서류를 제출해야 한다.

해설 빈칸은 to부정사(to open)의 목적어로서 명사가 들어갈 자리이다. 빈칸 앞에 부정관사(an)가 있으므로 복수형인 (B) accounts와 불가산 명사인 (C) accounting은 답에서 제외시킨다. 해석을 했을 때 '계좌를 개설하기 위한 서류들'이란 의미가 적절하므로 '계좌'를 의미하는 (A) account가 정답이다.

어휘 provide 제공하다 | necessary 필요한 | document 서류

UNIT 05. 대명사

핵심 문제 유형

1. (B)　　**2.** (D)　　**3.** (C)　　**4.** (D)

Q1. 금요일까지 신청서를 제출하세요.

해설　빈칸은 명사 앞에 있으므로 소유격 대명사인 (B) your가 정답이다.

어휘　submit 제출하다 | application 신청서

Q2. 최고 경영자가 직접 새로운 전략을 발표했다.

해설　빈칸이 없어도 주어, 동사, 목적어를 모두 갖춘 완전한 문장이므로 빈칸은 수식어가 들어갈 자리이며, 최고 경영자가 직접 새 전략을 발표했다는 의미로 '직접, 스스로'를 뜻하여 주어를 강조하는 재귀대명사 (D) herself가 정답이다.

어휘　present 보여주다 | strategy 전략

Q3. 새 회사에서 제안한 급여가 이전 회사에서 제안한 급여보다 더 높다.

해설　새 회사에서 제안한 급여가 이전 회사에서 제안한 것보다 더 높다는 의미로 빈칸은 앞의 명사를 대신할 지시대명사가 들어갈 자리이다. 의미상 가리키는 명사가 salary이며 단수로 쓰였으므로 (C) that이 정답이다.

어휘　salary 급여 | offer 제안하다

Q4. 네 개의 제안서 중 하나는 승인되었고, 나머지는 거절되었다.

해설　빈칸은 주어 자리로 보기의 구성으로 미루어 부정대명사가 들어가야 하는데, 빈칸 뒤의 동사가 복수(were rejected)이므로 단수형인 (A) another와 (C) the other는 답에서 제외시킨다. 4개의 제안서 중 하나(one)는 수락되었고, 나머지 세 개가 다 거절되었다는 의미로 대상이 4개로 정해져 있으므로, 정해진 수 중에서 나머지 전부를 의미하는 (D) the others가 정답이다.

어휘　proposal 제안 | accept 받아들이다 | reject 거절하다

Practice

1. (B)　　**2.** (B)　　**3.** (D)　　**4.** (B)　　**5.** (A)
6. (C)　　**7.** (D)　　**8.** (C)　　**9.** (B)　　**10.** (D)
11. (D)　　**12.** (D)　　**13.** (B)　　**14.** (B)　　**15.** (B)
16. (D)　　**17.** (D)　　**18.** (B)　　**19.** (A)　　**20.** (D)

1. 존슨 씨가 자리를 비운 동안, 그의 개인 비서에게 연락해 주세요.

해설　명사 앞에 빈칸이 있다. 명사 앞에는 소유격이 들어가므로 정답은 (B) his이다.

어휘　personal assistant 개인 비서 | away 자리를 비운

2. 이 씨는 모든 직원들에게 새로운 판매 전략에 대해 자신과 직접 조율하도록 요구한다.

해설　전치사 다음은 전치사의 목적어 자리이고 대명사의 목적격이 와야 하므로 정답은 (B) her이다. (C) hers (그녀의 것)도 전치사 뒤에 쓰일 수 있지만, 문맥상 조율을 함께하는 대상은 사물이 될 수 없다. (D) herself (그녀 자신)은 Lee 씨가 자기 자신과 조율한다는 의미가 되므로 어색하다.

어휘　coordinate 조율하다 | regarding ~에 관하여

3. 휴가가 남아 있는 직원은 12월 31일 전에 사용해야 한다.

해설　빈칸은 utilize의 목적어 자리이므로 대명사의 목적격이 들어가야 한다. 문맥상 '남아있는 휴가들을 사용해야 한다'는 의미이므로 정답은 (D) them이다. 목적어 자리에 (C) themselves가 들어가려면 주어와 목적어가 같아야 하므로 정답이 아니다.

어휘　remaining 남아 있는 | leave day 휴가 | utilize 사용하다

4. 제니스 사는 다음 분기에 자사의 주요 경쟁사인 맥슨 사를 인수할 계획이다.

해설　빈칸 뒤에는 명사가 나와 있다. 명사 앞에는 소유격이 와야 하므로 정답은 (B) its이다.

어휘　take over 인수하다 | chief rival 주요 경쟁사

5. 직원들은 그들의 최종 보고서를 경영진에 제출했다.

해설　빈칸에는 명사 report를 수식하는 대명사가 들어가야 하므로 정답은 소유격 (A) their가 된다.

어휘　present 제시하다, 제출하다 | final 최종의 | management 경영(진)

6. 최근 배송된 XR30 태블릿 중 많은 것이 운송 중에 파손되었다.

해설　(A) These는 뒤에 of 이하의 수식어구를 취할 수 없다. (B) Every는 형용사로 주어 자리에 들어갈 수 없다. (D) One은 형용사와 대명사 모두 가능하므로 주어 자리에 올 수 있지만, 단수 취급이므로 동사 were와 맞지 않다. (C) Many는 형용사와 대명사 모두 가능하므로 주어 자리에 올 수 있고 복수 취급하여 동사 were와도 수 일치 되므로 정답은 (C) Many이다.

어휘　ship 배송하다 | break 깨다, 부수다 | in transit 운송 중에

7. 보고서가 여러 이사들에 의해 평가된 후, 최종적으로 승인되었다.

해설　빈칸은 be동사 was 앞이므로 주어 자리이다. was는 단수 동사이므로 복수 대명사인 they는 수 일치에 어긋난다. 따라서 주격 대명사 (D) it가 정답이다.

어휘　evaluate 평가하다 | ultimately 최종적으로 | approve 승인하다

8. 우리 팀원들이 사용하는 대부분의 기기는 그들의 것이 아니라 회사에서 제공한 것이다.

해설　빈칸은 be동사 뒤 보어 자리이며, '팀원들이 사용하는 장비들 대부분이 그들의 것이 아니다'라는 의미로 「소유격 + 명사 (their + devices)」 형태인 소유대명사가 들어가야 적절하므로 정답은 (C) theirs이다.

어휘　device 기기 | organization 기관, 조직

12　파고다 토익 기본 완성 RC

9. 박 씨는 마케팅 팀에 헌신적이고 중요한 인재임을 보여주었다.

해설 빈칸은 목적어 자리로 박 씨가 스스로를 헌신적이고 중요한 사람임을 보여주었다는 의미인데, 이처럼 주어와 목적어가 같은 대상일 때는 재귀대 명사를 써야 하므로 정답은 (B) herself이다.

어휘 dedicated 헌신적인 | valuable 소중한 | asset 자산

10. 기술자는 부품이 품절되었기 때문에 프린터를 수리할 수 없었다.

해설 '부품'이라는 명사 앞에 빈칸이 있으므로 소유격이 정답이다. 보 기 모두 소유격이지만, 빈칸이 지칭하는 명사는 사물이고 단수 명사 (printer)이므로 정답은 (D) its이다.

어휘 technician 기술자 | component 부품 | out of stock 품절된

11. 프로젝트에 대해 질문이 있는 사람은 누구든지 관리자에게 직접 연락 해야 한다.

해설 빈칸은 주어 자리이다. (B) Every는 명사를 수식하는 한정사이기 때문 에 단독으로 주어 자리에 올 수 없고, (C) They는 뒤에 수식어구를 취 할 수 없으므로 답에서 제외시킨다. (A) Those와 (D) Anyone 둘 다 Those who '~하는 사람들' Anyone who '~하는 사람은 누구나' 와 같이 who 이하의 수식어구를 이끌 수 있는데, Those는 복수 취급, Anyone은 단수 취급한다는 점에서 관계절의 동사가 단수(who has questions ~)이므로 (D)이므로 (D)가 정답이다.

어휘 contact 연락하다 | directly 직접

12. 럭셔 스킨케어와 퓨어글로우 코스메틱스가 올해 손실을 입었지만, 둘 다 내년에 더 높은 매출을 예상한다.

해설 (A), (B), (C)는 대명사로 쓰이지만, 단수 취급하므로 단수 동사 predicts가 와야 한다. (D) both는 대명사로 주어 자리에 쓰인 것이 고, 럭셔 스킨케어와 퓨어글로우 코스메틱스 둘 다를 가리키므로 정답 은 (D) both이다.

어휘 suffer ~을 입다 | loss 손실 | predict 예상하다 | sales 매출(액)

13. 존슨 씨는 그녀의 발표를 끝냈지만, 스미스 씨는 아직 자신의 발표를 준비하고 있다.

해설 빈칸이 전치사 뒤에 위치하여 전치사의 목적어로서 목적격 대명사 (C) him이나 재귀대명사 (D) himself를 답으로 생각하기 쉽지만, 소유격 형태인 (B) his는 「소유격 대명사 + 명사」의 결합 형태인 소유대명사로 도 쓰인다는 점을 알고 있어야 한다. 존슨 씨는 그녀의 발표를 끝냈지 만, 스미스 씨는 그의 발표를 아직 준비 중이라는 의미이므로 문맥상 앞의 명사 presentation을 받아 his presentation을 대신하는 소유 대명사 (B) his가 정답이다.

어휘 complete 완료하다, 끝내다 | presentation 발표

14. 회사의 수익은 전년도에 비해 크게 개선되었다.

해설 빈칸은 profits를 받는 자리이다. 앞에 언급한 명사를 다시 받을 때, that이나 those를 쓰는데 복수 명사(the profits)를 받았으므로 정답 은 (B) those이다.

어휘 profit 수익 | improve 개선시키다 | compared to ~와 비교하여

15. 어려운 작업이었지만, 김 씨는 혼자서 복잡한 가구를 조립할 수 있었다.

해설 by himself는 '그 스스로, 홀로'라는 의미의 재귀대명사 관용 표현이 므로 정답은 (B) himself이다.

어휘 assemble 조립하다 | complicated 복잡한

16. 팀원들은 프로젝트 내내 잘 협력하고 서로를 도왔다.

해설 팀원들이 잘 협력하고 서로 도왔다는 의미로 셋 이상 간의 '서로'를 의 미하는 부정대명사 (D) one another가 정답이다. (A) other는 부정 형용사이므로 목적어 자리인 빈칸에 들어갈 수 없으며, '(나머지) 하나' 를 의미하는 (B) the other나, '또 다른 하나'라는 의미의 (C) another 는 문맥상 어색하다.

어휘 collaborate 협력하다 | support 돕다, 지원하다 | throughout 내내, ~동안 쭉

17. 레빈슨 대학 졸업생들은 정규직 취업을 시작하기 전에 인턴십을 한다.

해설 빈칸 뒤에 명사 employment가 왔다. 명사 앞에는 소유격을 쓰므로 정답은 (D) their이다.

어휘 graduate 졸업생 | take on 맡다 | initial 초기의 | full-time employment 정규직 취업

18. 첸 씨에게 도쿄 지사로의 저희 출장 일정이 연기되었다고 알려 주세요.

해설 that절 내의 has been postponed가 동사이므로 trip은 동사가 아 니라 명사로 쓰인 것이다. 명사 앞에는 소유격을 쓰므로 정답은 (B) our이다.

어휘 postpone 연기하다 | trip 출장 | branch 지사

19. 문서를 검토하시고 다른 정보가 필요하시면 알려주세요.

해설 빈칸은 불가산 명사 information을 수식하는 형용사 자리이므로 대 명사인 (C) each other, (D) one another는 답에서 제외시킨다. (A) other와 (B) another가 우리말로 해석하면 구분하기 어려운데, other는 불가산 명사를 수식할 수 있고, another는 가산 단수 명사를 수식한다는 점에서 (A)가 정답이다.

어휘 review 검토하다 | document 문서

20. 비가 오는 와중에도 대부분의 참가자들이 야외 콘서트에 참여했다.

해설 (A) Another는 복수 명사 앞에 쓰일 수 없다. (B) Others와 (C) The others는 대명사 역할을 하므로 명사 participants 앞에 쓰 일 수 없다. Most는 형용사와 대명사 역할이 모두 가능하며, 명사 participants를 수식하는 형용사 자리이므로 정답은 (D) Most이다.

어휘 outdoor 야외의 | participant 참가자

PART 5 UNIT 05

PART 5 GRAMMAR   **13**

UNIT 06. 형용사

핵심 문제 유형

본서 p.74

1. (C)   **2.** (A)   **3.** (B)   **4.** (C)

Q1. 우리는 사무실에 프린터를 더 구매해야 한다.

해설 빈칸은 명사 printer 앞에 위치하여 이를 수식하는 형용사 자리이므로 (C) additional이 정답이다.

어휘 additional 추가적인

Q2. 매니저는 그 보고서가 정확하다고 생각했다.

해설 빈칸은 5형식 동사 found의 목적격 보어 자리이고 문맥상 매니저는 그 보고서가 정확하다고 생각했다는 것이 자연스러우므로 (A) accurate이 정답이다.

어휘 find 알다 ㅣ accurate 정확한

Q3. 회사는 그 일자리 공고에 대해 많은 지원서를 받았다.

해설 빈칸은 복수 명사 앞에 위치하므로 (B) many가 정답이다.

어휘 receive 받다 ㅣ application 신청서 ㅣ job opening 구인 공고

Q4. 매니저는 직원들을 기쁘게 하는 배려 깊은 결정을 내렸다.

해설 빈칸은 명사 앞에 위치하여 형용사 자리이고, 문맥상 직원들을 기쁘게 하는 사려 깊은 결정을 내렸다는 것이 자연스러우므로 (C) considerate가 정답이다.

어휘 make a decision 결정하다 ㅣ considerate 사려 깊은 ㅣ please 기쁘게 하다

Practice

본서 p.78

1. (A)   **2.** (C)   **3.** (C)   **4.** (D)   **5.** (C)

6. (A)   **7.** (A)   **8.** (C)   **9.** (B)   **10.** (A)

11. (A)   **12.** (A)   **13.** (A)   **14.** (D)   **15.** (D)

16. (A)   **17.** (B)   **18.** (B)   **19.** (A)   **20.** (C)

1. 크리스탈 코브는 저렴한 숙박비 때문에 가격을 중시하는 관광객들이 좋아하는 휴양지이다.

해설 빈칸이 소유격 its와 명사 lodging 사이에 위치해 있으므로 명사 수식 형용사 (A) economical이 정답이다.

어휘 economical 저렴한, 경제적인 ㅣ budget-conscious 가격을 중시하는 ㅣ tourist 관광객

2. 이 교수는 이 혁신적인 접근법에 대한 학생들의 피드백을 간절히 받고 싶어 한다.

해설 빈칸이 지시형용사 this와 명사 approach 사이에 위치해 있으므로 명사 수식 형용사 (C) innovative가 정답이다.

어휘 eager 간절히 바라는 ㅣ feedback 피드백, 반응 ㅣ innovative 혁신적인

3. 요즘, 많은 사람들이 너무 게을러서 자신의 영양에 신경 쓰지 않는다.

해설 are는 be동사로 2형식 동사이다. 빈칸에는 주격 보어가 와야 하며, 상태를 설명하는 형용사 자리이므로 정답은 (C) lazy이다. 「too ~ to ~」는 '너무 ~해서 ~할 수 없다'라는 뜻이다.

어휘 nutrition 영양 ㅣ laziness 게으름 ㅣ lazy 게으른

4. 오랜 논의 끝에, 양측은 파트너십 조건에 만족하는 듯 보였다.

해설 seem은 2형식 동사이다. 따라서 빈칸은 주격 보어 자리로서 형용사가 들어가야 하므로 정답은 (D) acceptable이다.

어휘 extend 연장하다 ㅣ discussion 토론, 논의 ㅣ seem ~처럼 보이다 ㅣ acceptable 받아들일 수 있는 ㅣ condition 조건

5. 스미스 씨는 마케팅 부서의 여러 직원들을 위해 워크숍을 열 작정이다.

해설 every, each는 단수 가산 명사와 함께 쓰이므로 employees가 올 수 없다. (D)는 불가산 명사와 함께 쓰이므로 탈락이다. several이 복수 가산 명사와 함께 쓰이므로 정답은 (C) several이다.

어휘 intend (~하려고) 생각하다 ㅣ hold 열다, 개최하다 ㅣ department 부서

6. 그 뜨거운 논쟁은 신속한 방식으로 해결되었다.

해설 빈칸이 관사 a와 명사 fashion 사이에 위치해 있으므로 정답은 명사를 수식하는 형용사 (A) prompt이다.

어휘 debate 논쟁 ㅣ settle 해결하다 ㅣ prompt 신속한

7. 모든 고객의 피드백을 철저히 분석하는 것은 우리의 서비스 품질을 향상시킬 것이다.

해설 (B) several은 셀 수 있는 복수 명사와 써야 하므로 clients가 와야 한다. most와 all은 셀 수 있을 때 복수로 쓰고, 셀 수 없을 때 단수로 쓰는데 이 경우 고객은 셀 수 있으므로 clients가 와야 한다. every는 단수 취급하므로 client와 쓸 수 있다. 따라서 정답은 (A) every이다.

어휘 thoroughly 철저히 ㅣ analyze 분석하다 ㅣ enhance 향상시키다

8. 공장이 완전히 가동되면, 더 많은 직원이 필요할 것이다.

해설 부사 completely는 문장을 완성하는 데 없어도 되는 수식어구이고, 빈칸이 2형식 동사 become 뒤의 주격 보어 자리에 위치해 있으므로 상태 설명 형용사가 와야 한다. 따라서 정답은 (C) functional이다.

어휘 plant 공장 ㅣ functional 가동되는 ㅣ require 필요로 하다

9. 고퍼스트 트래블즈는 존슨 씨를 폭넓은 서비스 업계 지식 때문에 고용했다.

해설 빈칸이 소유격 대명사 her와 명사 knowledge 사이에 위치해 있으므로 명사를 수식하는 형용사 (B) broad가 정답이다.

어휘 broad 폭넓은 ㅣ hospitality industry 서비스 (호텔 등) 업계

10. 피드백에 따르면, 상당수의 고객들은 잰드로의 최신 신발 컬렉션이 매우 매력적이라고 생각했다.

해설 consider는 5형식 동사로 빈칸은 목적격 보어 자리이다. 신발의 상태

가 매력적이라는 의미가 되는 것이 자연스러우므로 목적격 보어 자리에는 형용사가 와야 한다. 정답은 (A) appealing이다.

어휘　majority 대다수 | extremely 극도로, 대단히 | appealing 매력적인

11. 애코캐리에서 생산한 배낭은 튼튼하고 유행을 따른다.

해설　2형식 동사 are 다음에는 주격 보어 자리이므로 상태 설명 형용사가 와야 한다. 「both A and B」는 'A, B 둘 다'라는 뜻으로 A와 B 자리에 형용사 두 개를 대등하게 연결했으므로 정답은 (A) sturdy이다. (D) sturdist도 형용사이지만 최상급은 주로 정관사 the와 쓰인다.

어휘　produce 생산하다 | sturdy 튼튼한 | fashionable 유행을 따르는

12. 트리니티 컨설팅 사는 다양한 비즈니스 해법을 제공한다.

해설　부정관사 a와 명사 range 사이에 빈칸이 있으므로 빈칸은 형용사 자리이다. 따라서 정답은 (A) diverse이다.

어휘　diverse 다양한 | range 범위 | solution 해법, 해결책

13. 노스리지 철도 노선 중 몇몇은 꼼꼼한 유지보수가 필요하다.

해설　빈칸이 명사 앞에 있으므로 형용사 자리이다. (D) thoroughest도 형용사이지만 최상급은 보통 정관사 the와 쓰이므로 정답은 (A) thorough이다.

어휘　thorough 철저한 | maintenance 유지보수

14. 우리는 생산 기한을 맞추기 위해 신뢰할 수 있는 공급자가 필요하다.

해설　빈칸은 명사 supplier를 수식하는 형용사 자리로, 보기 중 (C) reliant와 (D) reliable에서 고를 수 있어야 한다. reliant는 '의존하는'을 의미하고, reliable은 '신뢰할 수 있는'을 뜻하여 형태는 비슷하지만 의미가 달라 주의해야 한다. '신뢰할 수 있는 업체가 필요하다'는 의미가 적절하므로 (D) reliable이 정답이다.

어휘　supplier 공급업체 | meet 충족하다 | production deadline 생산 기한

15. 회의 전에 파일들을 질서 정연하게 정리해야 한다.

해설　빈칸은 명사 manner를 수식하는 형용사 자리로 파일이 질서 있는 방식으로 정리되어야 한다는 문맥이므로 '질서 있는, 정돈된'을 뜻하는 -ly형 형용사 (D) orderly가 정답이다. in an orderly manner는 '질서 정연하게'라는 의미이다.

어휘　organize 정리하다 | manner 방식

16. 회의에 참석한 모든 직원들은 보안이 가장 중요한 측면 중 하나라는 것을 인식했다.

해설　빈칸이 정관사 the와 명사 aspects 사이에 위치해 있으므로 빈칸은 명사 수식 형용사 자리이다. 따라서 정답은 (A) significant이다.

어휘　recognize 인식하다 | security 보안 | significant 중요한

17. 그 마케팅 전략은 조직의 수익을 증대하는 데 효과적이었다.

해설　빈칸이 2형식 동사인 be동사 뒤에 위치해 있으므로 빈칸은 주격 보어 자리이고 상태 설명 형용사나 주어와 동격을 이루는 명사가 와야 하는데, 마케팅 전략은 '효과'와 동격 관계를 이루지 못하므로 형용사 (B) effective가 정답이다.

어휘　effective 효과적인 | boost 증가시키다

18. 그 가게는 여러 취향을 만족시키기 위해 다양한 제품을 취급한다.

해설　빈칸 앞에 위치한 a variety of는 '다양한'이란 의미의 수량형용사로서 뒤에는 가산 복수 명사를 취하므로 (B) products가 정답이다.

어휘　carry 취급하다 | cater to ~을 충족시키다 | different 다른, 다양한 | taste 기호, 취향

19. 그린테크 솔루션즈는 20년 이상 지속 가능성 프로젝트를 지원하는 데 중요한 역할을 해왔다.

해설　빈칸은 be동사의 현재완료 시제 형태 뒤 주격 보어 자리이며, 그린테크 솔루션즈가 '중요한 역할을 해왔다'는 의미로, 주어를 서술해 주는 형용사가 들어가야 적절하므로 정답은 (A) instrumental이다.

어휘　instrumental 중요한 역할을 하는 | support 지원하다 | sustainability 지속 가능성 | decade 10년

20. 전략적 계획 수립과 운전자 교육을 통해 많은 교통 충돌을 피할 수 있다.

해설　빈칸이 2형식 동사 are 뒤의 주격 보어 자리에 위치해 있으므로 상태를 설명하는 형용사가 와야 한다. 따라서 정답은 (A) avoidable이다

어휘　avoidable 피할 수 있는 | collision 충돌 | strategic 전략적인 | planning 계획 수립

UNIT 07. 부사

핵심 문제 유형

본서 p.84

1. (B)　　2. (B)　　3. (A)　　4. (A)

Q1. 회사는 지난달 완전히 새로운 제품 라인을 도입했다.

해설　빈칸은 형용사를 수식하는 부사 자리이고, 문맥상 완전히 새로운 제품 라인을 도입했다는 것이 자연스러우므로 (B) completely가 정답이다.

어휘　introduce 소개하다 | completely 완전히

Q2. 회사는 신중하게 고객 서비스를 향상시키는 데 전념하고 있다.

해설　빈칸은 동명사를 수식하는 부사 자리이고, 문맥상 신중하게 고객 서비스를 향상시키는 것이 자연스러우므로 (B) carefully가 정답이다.

어휘　dedicate 헌신하다 | carefully 신중히 | enhance 향상시키다

Q3. 그 프로젝트는 완료하는 데 대략 6개월이 걸릴 것이다.

해설　빈칸은 숫자를 수식하는 부사 자리이고, 문맥상 대략적으로 6개월이 걸린다는 것이 자연스러우므로 (A) approximately가 정답이다.

어휘　approximately 대략 | complete 완료하다

Q4. 팀은 그 문제에 대해 매우 혁신적인 해결책을 개발했다.

해설　빈칸은 형용사를 수식하는 부사 자리이고, 문맥상 매우 혁신적인 해결

책을 개발했다는 것이 자연스러우므로 (A) highly가 정답이다.

어휘 develop 개발하다 | highly 매우 | solution 해결책

Practice

본서 p.88

1. (B)	**2.** (B)	**3.** (B)	**4.** (C)	**5.** (D)
6. (C)	**7.** (B)	**8.** (A)	**9.** (C)	**10.** (A)
11. (C)	**12.** (C)	**13.** (A)	**14.** (D)	**15.** (C)
16. (A)	**17.** (B)	**18.** (B)	**19.** (A)	**20.** (A)

1. 약 150명의 직원이 입문 교육을 효과적으로 마쳤다.

해설 have와 과거분사 사이에는 부사가 들어가므로 정답은 (B) effectively 이다.

어휘 nearly 거의 | effectively 효과적으로 | introductory training 입문 교육

2. 메인 가의 다운타운 카페는 특별 프로모션 주간을 정기적으로 연다.

해설 이미 3형식의 완벽한 문장이므로 빈칸에는 없어도 되는 부사가 들어가야 된다. 동사 앞에서 동사를 수식하는 부사 (B) regularly가 정답이다.

어휘 hold 개최하다 | regularly 정기적으로

3. 테크웨이브의 암호화 프로토콜 개발은 이 씨에 의해 전적으로 지원되었다.

해설 '전적으로 지원되었다'는 의미로 수동태인 been assisted 사이에 들어갈 수 있는 품사는 부사이므로 정답은 (B) completely이다.

어휘 completely 완전히 | encryption 암호화

4. 가장 높이 호평 받는 클래식 음악 축제 중 하나가 비엔나에서 열린다.

해설 형용사 acclaimed 앞에 빈칸이 있으므로 부사 자리이다. (A)와 (C) 모두 부사지만 '물리적 높이나 수준'을 나타내는 high '높이'는 문맥상 부자연스럽다. 따라서 정답은 (C) highly이다.

어휘 highly 매우 | acclaimed 호평 받는

5. 직원 수를 줄임으로써, 브라이튼 테크놀로지의 생산량이 상당히 감소했다.

해설 1형식 동사인 decreased로 문장이 끝났다. 빈칸은 부사 자리인데, 문맥상 (D) considerably '상당히'가 동사 '감소하다'를 가장 적절하게 수식한다. (A) somehow '어떻게든', (B) quietly '조용히', (C) randomly '무작위로'는 직원 수를 줄인 것과 생산량이 감소한 것 간의 인과관계를 논리적으로 표현하지 못한다. 따라서, 정답은 (D) considerably이다.

어휘 reduce 줄이다 | output 산출량 | considerably 상당히

6. 대이븐포트 사는 노바테크를 약 1,500만 달러에 인수했다.

해설 빈칸은 수 형용사를 수식하는 부사 자리이다. 보기 중 숫자를 수식할 수 있는 부사는 nearly뿐이므로 정답은 (C) nearly이다.

어휘 nearly 거의 | acquire 인수하다

7. 향상된 의료 스캐너는 진단 오류를 상당히 줄이는 것을 목표로 한다.

해설 to부정사를 수식하는 부사는 to와 동사원형 사이에 위치한다. 따라서 정답은 (B) considerably가 정답이다.

어휘 advanced 발전된 | considerably 상당히 | reduce 줄이다 | diagnostic errors 진단 오류

8. 조립 라인 작업자는 안전상의 이유로 해당 장비를 사용할 수 없다.

해설 문장이 끝났다고 생각해서 부사 (D) reasonably를 고르게 되면 '합리적으로 안전을 위해 해당 장비를 사용할 수 없다'라고 해석되어 의미가 맞지 않다. 이런 경우는 앞의 safety와 함께 복합명사가 되는 명사 reasons를 골라야 한다. '안전상의 이유로 해당 장비를 사용할 수 없다'가 의미상 맞으므로 정답은 명사 (A) reasons이다.

어휘 assembly 조립 | prohibit 금지하다 | equipment 장비

9. 업데이트된 제품 포장에 대한 고객 반응은 일관되게 긍정적이다.

해설 형용사 favorable 앞에 빈칸이 있으므로 부사 (C) uniformly가 정답이다.

어휘 wrapping 포장 | remain 여전히 ~이다 | uniformly 일관되게 | favorable 긍정적인

10. 노바 프로모션즈가 만든 홍보 전략은 귀하의 서비스를 고객에게 더 매력적으로 만들 것이다.

해설 빈칸에 부사를 고르면 make를 수식하게 되어 의미상 맞지 않고, make는 형용사를 목적격 보어로 취하는 5형식 동사로 시험에 출제된다는 점을 명심하고 make가 나오면 목적어 뒤에 형용사 보어를 고른다. 정답은 형용사 (A) desirable이다.

어휘 strategy 전략 | desirable 탐나는, 매력적인 | client 고객

11. 이사회 구성원들은 업데이트된 마케팅 전략에 완전히 만족하지 못했다.

해설 빈칸은 형용사 happy를 수식하는 부사 자리이다. 따라서 (C) fully가 정답이다.

어휘 fully 완전히 | marketing strategy 마케팅 전략

12. 고객 서비스 담당직에 지원하는 지원자는 정보를 명확하게 전달해야 한다.

해설 '정보를 정확히 전달하다'라는 의미로 빈칸은 동사 convey를 수식하는 자리이며, 동사를 수식하는 품사는 부사이므로 정답은 (C) clearly 이다.

어휘 applicant 지원자 | convey 전달하다 | clearly 명확하게

13. 깨지기 쉬운 물건은 배송 중 손상을 방지하기 위해 개별적으로 포장해야 한다.

해설 빈칸에 들어갈 단어가 빠지더라도 이미 완벽한 문장이므로 빈칸은 동사 be packed를 수식하는 부사 자리이다. 따라서 정답은 (A) individually이다.

어휘 breakable 깨지기 쉬운 | object 물건 | pack 포장하다 | individually 개별적으로 | prevent 방지하다

14. 팀원들은 일정을 맞춰서 작업을 마무리하기 위해 효과적으로 협업해야 한다.

해설　work는 '일하다'라는 의미로 쓰일 때 목적어나 보어를 취하지 않는 1형식 자동사이므로 빈칸에는 동사를 수식하는 부사가 들어가야 한다. 따라서 정답은 (D) effectively이다.

어휘　require 요구하다 | on schedule 일정대로

15. 테크 이노베이터즈는 고객과 지속적으로 관계를 맺으면서 수익을 증대시키고자 한다.

해설　'고객들과 지속적으로 관계를 맺으면서'라는 의미로 전치사(by)와 동명사(engaging) 사이에 위치하여 동명사를 수식하는 품사는 부사이므로 정답은 (C) continually이다.

어휘　seek ~하려고 시도하다 | boost revenue 수익을 증대시키다 | continually 계속해서 | engage with ~와 관계를 맺다

16. 참가자들은 토론이 끝난 후 조용히 회의장을 떠나도록 요청받는다.

해설　빈칸 앞의 leave the conference hall으로 「동사 + 목적어」의 3형식 구조가 완성되었으므로 빈칸에는 부사가 들어가야 한다. 따라서 (A) calmly가 정답이다.

어휘　participant 참가자 | request 요청하다 | leave 떠나다 | calmly 침착하게 | discussion 토론 | conclude 끝나다

17. 500명 이상의 사람들이 최신 테크 트렌즈 뉴스레터에 등록했다.

해설　빈칸은 수 형용사 500을 수식하는 부사 자리이다. 보기 중 more than은 500명 넘게 등록했다는 의미를 완성하므로 정답은 (B) More than이다.

어휘　more than ~이상 | sign up for ~에 등록하다

18. 예기치 않은 문제가 발견된 후에 회의가 곧 종료되었다.

해설　빈칸이 없어도 완전한 수동태 문장이므로 빈칸은 부사가 들어갈 자리이다. 빈칸 뒤의 after와 shortly가 함께 쓰여 예상치 못한 문제가 발생한 '직후에' 회의가 끝났다는 의미가 되어야 하므로 (B) shortly가 정답이다. 참고로, (A) short도 '(예상보다) 짧게'라는 의미의 부사로 쓰일 수 있지만, shortly와 달리 after / before와는 함께 쓰이지 않음에 주의한다.

어휘　end 끝나다, 종료하다 | due to ~때문에 | unexpected 예상치 못한 | issue 사안, 문제

19. 최근에, 김 씨는 보고서를 제시간에 마치기 위해 늦게까지 남아서 일해오고 있다.

해설　완벽한 문장이고 문장 맨 앞에 빈칸이 있으므로 부사가 들어가야 하는 자리임을 알 수 있다. 정답은 (A) Recently이다.

어휘　stay 머물다 | on time 제시간에

20. 대중교통 수단을 늘리는 것이 도시 대기 오염을 줄이는 데 유익한 것으로 나타났다.

해설　'유익한 것으로 드러났다'라는 의미로 해석상으로는 부사가 들어갈 자리로 보이지만, be동사는 주격 보어를 취하는 2형식 동사이므로 정답은 형용사인 (A) beneficial이다.

어휘　public transport 대중교통 | beneficial 유익한

UNIT 08. 전치사

핵심 문제 유형　　　　　　　본서 p.96

1. (C)　　**2.** (B)　　**3.** (A)　　**4.** (D)

Q1. 회의는 5시에 시작할 것이다.

해설　빈칸은 명사 앞에 있으므로 전치사 자리이고, 특정 시간을 나타낼 때 사용하는 전치사인 (C) at가 정답이다.

어휘　meeting 회의

Q2. 연구원은 도서관 선반에 있는 수십 권의 책들 사이에서 열쇠를 찾았다.

해설　빈칸은 명사 앞에 있으므로 전치사 자리이고, 복수 명사 앞에 쓰여 문맥상 많은 책들 사이에서 열쇠를 찾았다는 것이 자연스러우므로 (B) among이 정답이다.

어휘　researcher 연구자 | find 발견하다 | dozens of 많은, 수십의 | library 도서관 | shelf 선반

Q3. 회의 전에 결정을 내릴 것이다.

해설　빈칸은 전치사 to와 함께 쓰이는 하나의 구 전치사 자리이므로 (A) prior가 정답이다.

어휘　make a decision 결정하다

Q4. 새 사무실 건물은 현재 공사 중이다.

해설　under construction은 '공사 중'이라는 의미의 숙어 표현으로 사용되므로 (D) under가 정답이다.

어휘　currently 현재 | under construction 공사 중인

Practice　　　　　　　본서 p.100

1. (B)	**2.** (C)	**3.** (D)	**4.** (B)	**5.** (B)
6. (B)	**7.** (D)	**8.** (A)	**9.** (B)	**10.** (D)
11. (D)	**12.** (C)	**13.** (C)	**14.** (C)	**15.** (B)
16. (D)	**17.** (B)	**18.** (D)	**19.** (A)	**20.** (B)

1. 선셋 디너는 특별한 행사로 인해 8월 15일 수요일에 문을 닫는다.

해설　빈칸은 '문을 닫는' 이유를 나타내는 전치사가 들어갈 자리이다. 빈칸 뒤에 절이 없으므로 접속사 (C) because는 정답이 될 수 없다. 따라서, 정답은 (B) due to이다.

어휘　due to ~ 때문에 | occasion (특별한) 행사

2. 블레이즈 제약은 추가 예산 지원을 통해 새로운 연구 장비를 마련했다.

해설 '추가 예산 지원으로 새 연구 장비를 마련했다'는 의미로 '~을 통해'라는 뜻의 수단의 전치사인 (C) through가 정답이다. (A) by도 수단의 전치사이지만 교통수단이나 도구와 같은 직접적인 방법을 나타낸다.

어휘 acquire 획득하다 | additional 추가적인 | budget 예산

3. 운전자들은 대중교통을 이용함으로써 교통 혼잡을 줄이는 데 도움을 줄 수 있다.

해설 「by -ing」는 '~함으로써'라는 의미이므로 정답은 (D) by이다.

어휘 traffic congestion 교통 체증 | mass transit 대중교통

4. 미란다 테크니컬 인스티튜트의 등록은 한 달 내내 언제든지 가능하다.

해설 throughout the month는 '한 달 내내'라는 의미로 기간을 나타내는 명사(the month)를 취할 수 있는 (B) throughout가 정답이다. 접속사 (A) while도 '동안에'라는 의미로 문맥에는 적합하지만 빈칸 뒤에는 주어와 동사가 없으므로 정답이 될 수 없다.

어휘 enrollment 등록 | admit 받아들이다, 허락하다

5. 하모니 호텔은 인기 있는 명소에서 차로 이동할 수 있는 거리에 이상적으로 위치해 있다.

해설 문맥상 차로 갈 수 있는 거리나 범위를 나타내는 전치사가 적절하므로 정답은 (B) within이다.

어휘 ideally 이상적으로, 최적으로 | situate 위치시키다 | landmark 주요 지형지물

6. 추운 날씨와 폭설로 인해 학기가 3월 말까지 연장될 것이다.

해설 해석상 until과 by가 가장 잘 어울리지만, until은 계속적 의미일 때 쓰고 by는 완료의 의미일 때 쓰인다. 이 문장에서는 extend가 '연장될 것이다'라는 계속적 의미로 쓰였으므로 정답은 (B) until이다.

7. 제안서가 예산 보고서와 함께 제출되었다.

해설 제안서가 예산 보고서와 함께 제출되었다는 의미이므로 '~와 함께'라는 뜻의 구전치사 (D) along with가 정답이다. (A) according to '~에 따르면', (B) based on '~을 기반으로 (C) such as '~와 같은' 모두 문맥상 적합하지 않다.

어휘 proposal 제안(서) | submit 제출하다 | budget report 예산 보고서

8. 회의실은 시설의 정문 옆에 위치해 있다.

해설 해석상 next와 close가 가장 자연스럽지만, 둘 다 전치사 to와 함께 쓰일 때 명사를 동반할 수 있으므로 탈락이다. 참고로 next는 형용사로 close는 형용사 또는 부사로 쓰인다. 따라서 전치사인 (A) beside가 정답이다.

어휘 situate 위치시키다 | main door 정문 | facility 시설

9. 고객이 계약서를 받은 직후에 확인 이메일을 보냈다.

해설 '계약서를 받은 후에 바로 확인 이메일을 보냈다'는 의미가 적절하므로 '~후에'를 의미하는 전치사 (B) after가 정답이다. right after는 '~직후에', right before는 '~직전에'로 한 단어처럼 기억해두자.

어휘 client 고객 | confirmation 확인, 확정 | shortly 이내, 곧 | contract 계약(서)

10. 김 씨는 10년 넘게 테크 사에서 근무해 왔다.

해설 문맥상 for가 '~동안'이란 의미로 가장 적합하다. 같은 의미의 (B) while은 절을 이끄는 접속사인데, 빈칸 뒤에 주어와 동사가 없으므로 답이 될 수 없다. for는 현재완료(has p.p.)와 함께 쓰이므로 정답은 (D) for이다. (A) since도 현재완료와 쓰일 수 있지만, 과거 시점을 나타내는 명사 앞에 쓰인다. over a decade '10년 이상'은 기간에 해당한다.

어휘 employ 고용하다 | decade 10년

11. 우리는 다가오는 프로젝트 마감일에 관한 이메일을 받았다.

해설 문맥상 '다가오는 프로젝트 마감일에 관한 이메일'이 자연스러우므로 정답은 (D) regarding이다.

어휘 upcoming 다가오는, 곧 있을 | deadline 마감일, 기한

12. 사무실 리모델링에 대한 견적서는 영업일 기준 3일 이내에 전달될 것이다.

해설 빈칸 다음에 '영업일 기준 3일'이라는 기간이 나왔다. 특정 시점을 이끄는 전치사 (A)와 (B)는 탈락이고, '영업일 기준 3일 이내에 전달될 것이다'가 의미상 적절하므로 정답은 (C) within이다. (D) throughout도 기간 전치사이지만 '3일 내내 전달 될 것이다'라는 의미는 어색하다.

어휘 quotation 견적서 | refurbishment 개조, 보수 | business day 영업일

13. 디자인 팀은 고객의 사전 동의 없이 레이아웃을 변경하지 않을 것이다.

해설 빈칸 뒤에 명사 agreement가 있으므로 빈칸은 전치사 자리로 (A) though는 접속사이므로 불가하다. 해석상 without '~없이'라는 의미가 문맥상 가장 적합하므로 정답은 (C) without이다. (D) except for '~제외하고'는 문맥상 어색하다.

어휘 alter 변경하다 | layout 배치 | prior agreement 사전 동의

14. 여행 일정은 참가자 수에 따라 책자에 나와 있는 일정과 달라질 수 있다.

해설 문맥상 변화의 원인을 나타내는 '~에 따라'라는 의미가 적절하므로 정답은 (C) based on이다. (A) according to는 according to the report '보고서에 따르면'처럼 출처나 정보의 근거를 나타낼 때 사용된다.

어휘 itinerary 여행 일정표 | booklet 소책자

15. 서울로 이사하기 전에, 잭 씨는 지점장으로 근무했었다.

해설 보기에 모두 전치사가 나왔다. as '~로서'가 문맥상 가장 적합하므로 정답은 (B) as이다.

어휘 employ 고용하다 | branch manager 지점장

16. 오전 9시 전에 보낸 메시지는 오후에 검토될 것임을 유의하십시오.

해설 빈칸은 뒤에는 9시라는 시점을 나타내는 명사가 있으므로 시간 전치사 자리이다. (A) prior는 형용사로 (D) before와 같은 의미이지만 전치사로 사용되려면 to가 필요하다. (B) under '~아래', (C) through

'~통해서'는 시간 전치사가 아니다. 따라서 (D) before가 정답이다.

어휘　aware ~을 알고 있는 ǀ review 검토하다

17. 회의실 유지 관리를 담당하는 직원은 하루에 두 번 공간을 점검해야 한다.

해설　be charge of는 '~할 책임이 있다'는 의미의 관용 표현이므로 (D) of 가 정답이다.

어휘　maintain 유지관리하다 ǀ inspect 점검하다

18. 문서를 컴퓨터에 백업한 후 반드시 저장하세요.

해설　'문서를 백업한 후에 저장하라'는 의미가 적절하므로 '~후에'라는 의미의 전치사 (D) following이 정답이다.

어휘　make sure to do 반드시 ~하다 ǀ save 저장하다 ǀ back ~ up (파일, 프로그램 등을) 백업하다

19. 지난 몇 주 동안 매이플우드 대학의 등록이 급격히 증가했다.

해설　보기에 모두 전치사가 나왔다. 보기 중 (C)를 제외하고 모두 시간 전치사인데, 기간 표현(the last few weeks)을 취할 때 '~동안'을 의미하는 (A) Over가 답으로 적절하다. (B) following '~후에'와 (D) at '~에'는 시점 전치사이다.

어휘　enrollment 등록 ǀ rise 증가하다 ǀ sharply 급격히

20. 정전으로 인해, 그린 비스트로는 추가 통지가 있을 때까지 영업을 중단할 것이다.

해설　영업을 중단하게 된 원인이 정전이므로 '~때문에'가 가장 적절하다. 구전치사 표현인 (B) Due to가 정답이다. (C)와 (D)도 같은 의미이지만 접속사이므로 답이 될 수 없다.

어휘　power outage 정전 ǀ remain 여전히 ~이다

REVIEW TEST 02

본서 p.102

1. (A)	2. (D)	3. (D)	4. (C)	5. (B)
6. (B)	7. (A)	8. (D)	9. (D)	10. (D)
11. (C)	12. (B)	13. (C)	14. (D)	15. (C)
16. (B)	17. (B)	18. (B)	19. (B)	20. (D)
21. (A)	22. (A)	23. (A)	24. (D)	25. (A)
26. (A)	27. (B)	28. (D)	29. (A)	30. (B)

1. 조컴 광고사는 조직 관리 기술을 보유한 판매 사원들을 고용하고자 한다.

해설　전치사와 명사 사이에 빈칸이 있으므로 형용사인 (A) organizational 이 정답이다.

어휘　hire 고용하다 ǀ organizational 조직(상)의

2. 이 씨는 팀의 도움 없이 혼자서 전체 프로젝트를 완료했다.

해설　빈칸은 전치사 by의 목적어 자리이며, 문맥상 이 씨가 혼자서 전체 프로젝트를 완료했다는 의미이므로 '혼자서'라는 뜻의 재귀대명사 관용 표현, by oneself를 완성하는 (D) himself가 정답이다.

어휘　entire 전체의 ǀ without ~없이 ǀ assistance 지원, 도움

3. 드림 버드 가구는 모든 고객들에게 모든 구매에 대해서 환불 보장을 제공한다.

해설　문맥상 빈칸에는 '구매자'가 아닌 '구매'가 들어가야 하므로 (B), (C)는 탈락이다. purchase는 '구매한 물건이나 개별적인 구매 건'을 의미할 때는 가산 명사이고 '구매 행위'를 뜻할 때는 불가산 명사이다. 환불의 대상은 '구매 행위' 자체가 아니라 '구매한 물건 또는 개별적인 구매 건'이므로 가산 명사가 사용되었는데, all은 복수 가산 명사와 불가산 명사와 같이 쓰이므로 복수 가산 명사인 (D) purchases가 정답이다.

어휘　money-back guarantee 환불 보장

4. 모든 직원의 안전을 위해 건물 전체에 보안 카메라가 설치되었다.

해설　보안 카메라가 건물 전역에 설치되었다는 의미가 적절하므로 장소 명사를 동반하여 '~도처에'를 의미하는 (C) throughout이 정답이다.

어휘　security 보안 ǀ install 설치하다 ǀ ensure 보장하다 ǀ safety 안전

5. 인사 관리자는 직원들에게 작성 완료된 서식을 회의에 가져오도록 상기시켰다.

해설　빈칸이 전치사 뒤에 위치해 있으므로 전치사의 목적어 자리에 올 수 있는 목적격대명사 (B) them과 소유대명사 (D) theirs 중에서 답을 골라야 하는데, 「bring + something + with」구조로, 작성된 서식은 직원들이 가져오는 것이므로 (B) them이 정답이다.

어휘　remind 상기시키다 ǀ completed 작성된 ǀ form 서식, 양식

6. IT 매니저는 팀의 필요를 잘 배려하며 항상 지원적인 업무 환경을 조성하는 것으로 유명하다.

해설　빈칸은 be동사 뒤 형용사가 들어갈 자리로 빈칸 뒤 전치사 of를 동반하여 '~을 배려하는, ~에 사려 깊은'을 의미하는 (B) considerate이 정답이다. (A) considerable은 '양이 많은, 상당한', (C) considered는 '고려되는, 깊이 생각한 후의'란 의미로 문맥상 어울리지 않는다.

어휘　be known for ~으로 유명하다 ǀ need 요구, 필요 ǀ ensure 보장하다 ǀ supportive 지원하는 ǀ work environment 업무 환경

7. 추가 교육 세션과 함께 새로운 정책 변경 사항이 다음 달에 시행될 예정이다.

해설　'~와 함께'라는 의미의 구 전치사 along with를 완성하는 (A) along 이 정답이다.

어휘　policy 정책, 방침 ǀ additional 추가의 ǀ implement 시행하다, 이행하다

8. 올해 회사의 판매 실적이 주요 경쟁사의 실적을 초과하여 강력한 시장 성장을 보여주고 있다.

해설　회사의 매출액이 경쟁사의 매출액을 초과했다는 의미로 빈칸은 전치사 구 [of its main competitor]의 후치 수식을 받는 지시대명사 자리로 (A)와 (B)는 불가하다. (C)와 (D) 중 복합명사 sales figures는 복수 명사이므로 (D) those가 정답이다.

어휘　sales figure 매출액, 판매량 ǀ exceed 초과하다 ǀ main 주된, 주요한 ǀ competitor 경쟁사

9. 재썸 사는 새로운 제품에 관한 당신의 제안을 환영한다.

해설 소유격 다음에 빈칸이 있으며, welcome의 목적어 자리이기도 하므로 명사가 와야 한다. 따라서 정답은 (D) suggestions이다.

어휘 welcome 환영하다 | concerning ~에 관한 | suggestion 제안

10. 회사는 고객 만족도를 높이고 가능한 모든 불만을 완전히 피하는 데 전념하고 있다.

해설 '~에 헌신하다'를 뜻하는 be dedicated to의 to는 전치사로서 동명사 improving과 avoiding이 이끄는 명사구가 연결된 형태이다. 따라서 빈칸은 전치사와 동명사 사이에 들어갈 수 있는 품사 자리인데, 동명사를 수식하는 품사는 부사이므로 (D) completely가 정답이다.

어휘 improve 개선하다 | customer satisfaction 고객 만족 | avoid 피하다 | potential 잠재적인 | complaint 불만, 불평

11. 에어컨은 구매일로부터 6개월 이내에 무상으로 반품할 수 있다.

해설 빈칸 뒤에 6 months라는 '시점'이 아닌 '기간'이 나왔다. 시점을 써야 하는 (A), (B), (D)는 모두 탈락이다. within 다음에는 기간이 와야 하고, 문맥상 적합하므로 정답은 (C) within이다.

어휘 air conditioner 에어컨 | purchase 구매 | free of charge 무료로

12. 그 회사의 새로운 웹사이트는 제품 정보를 고객들에게 더 쉽게 접근할 수 있도록 만들 것이다.

해설 make의 목적어인 product information이 나와 있고, 목적격 보어 자리에 상태 설명 형용사 accessible이 나와 있다. 따라서 빈칸은 문법적으로 필수적인 요소가 아닌 형용사를 수식하는 형용사 앞이므로 부사 (B) readily가 정답이다.

어휘 accessible 접근 가능한 | readily 손쉽게, 순조롭게

13. 품질관리팀은 모든 제품이 회사의 기준을 충족하도록 생산을 면밀히 모니터링한다.

해설 빈칸은 동사 monitors를 수식하는 부사이므로 (A) close와 (C) closely 중에서 의미상 어울리는 부사를 골라야 한다. (A) close는 형용사와 부사의 의미가 동일하여 각각 '가까운', '가까이에'를 의미하며, (C) closely는 '주의 깊게, 면밀하게'를 의미하는데, 문맥상 생산을 면밀히 모니터링한다는 의미가 적절하므로 (C) closely가 정답이다.

어휘 quality control 품질관리 | monitor 추적 관찰하다, 모니터링하다 | ensure 보장하다 | meet 충족시키다 | standard 기준

14. 증가하는 생산성의 결과로, 그 회사는 직원들에게 인센티브를 제공하고 있다.

해설 빈칸은 형용사 increasing 뒤에 있으므로 명사 (A)와 (D)가 가능하다. 문맥상 '증가하는 생산자'가 아니고, '증가하는 생산성'이므로 정답은 (D) productivity이다.

어휘 productivity 생산성 | offer 제공하다

15. 수요가 많아서 다가오는 워크숍에 이용 가능한 좌석이 몇 개 남지 않았다.

해설 형용사 available은 명사 앞과 뒤에서 모두 수식이 가능한데, 빈칸 뒤에 전치사 구(for the upcoming workshop)가 명사 seats를 뒤에서 함께 수식하고 있으므로 (C) available이 정답이다.

어휘 demand 수요 | upcoming 다가오는, 곧 있을

16. CEO는 협력적인 업무 환경을 조성하기 위해 팀원들 간의 원활한 소통을 장려했다.

해설 팀원들 간의 소통을 장려했다는 의미이므로 '(셋 이상) 사이에'를 의미하는 (B) among이 정답이다. (A) between은 '(둘) 사이에'를 의미한다.

어휘 encourage 장려하다 | foster 조성하다 | collaborative 협력적인

17. 라이언은 어제 보고서를 제출했고, 수잔은 오늘 중으로 자신의 것을 제출할 것이다.

해설 문맥상 빈칸 앞의 do는 submit을 뜻하는 대동사이고, 빈칸은 동사 뒤 목적어 자리이므로 주격대명사인 (D) she는 답에서 먼저 제외시킨다. 라이언이 그의 보고서를 어제 제출했고, 수잔이 그녀의 보고서를 오늘 중으로 제출할 거라는 의미이므로 목적어에 들어갈 대명사는 her report 즉, [소유격 + 명사]를 충족하는 소유대명사가 필요하다. 따라서 (B) hers가 정답이다.

어휘 submit 제출하다 | report 보고서

18. 재무 부서는 몇몇 계좌가 제대로 업데이트되지 않아 즉각적인 주의가 필요하다고 보고했다.

해설 빈칸은 that절의 주어 자리이며, 빈칸 앞에 가산 복수 명사를 수식하는 수량형용사 a few가 위치해 있으므로 가산 단수 명사인 (A) account나 불가산 명사인 (C) accounting은 답에서 먼저 제외시킨다. 문맥상 몇몇 계좌가 업데이트되지 않았다는 의미가 적절하므로 (B) accounts가 정답이다.

어휘 finance 재무, 재정 | properly 적절하게 | immediate 즉각적인 | attention 주의

19. 공장 노동자들은 청력 보호 장치를 착용해야 한다.

해설 '보호 장치'로 복합 명사이다. 따라서 정답은 (B) protection이다.

어휘 wear 입다, 쓰다, 착용하다 | hearing 청력, 청각 | device 장치 | protection 보호

20. 이 씨는 마케팅 부서 자리의 최종 후보자들을 직접 인터뷰할 예정이다.

해설 빈칸 앞은 3형식의 완벽한 문장이므로 빈칸은 필요 없는 자리이다. 빈칸은 주어 자리가 아니므로 주어 자리에 올 수 있는 주격 대명사 (A) she는 올 수 없다. 빈칸 뒤에 명사가 없으므로 명사 앞에 오는 소유격 (B) her도 올 수 없다. (B) her를 목적격이라고 봐도 빈칸은 목적어 자리가 아니므로 답이 될 수 없다. 소유대명사인 (C) hers 역시 올 수 없다. 필요 없는 자리에 재귀대명사를 넣으면 강조 역할이 되므로 정답은 (D) herself이다.

어휘 candidate 후보자

21. 세미나에 참석하기를 원하는 사람들은 창 씨에게 연락해야 한다.

해설 빈칸은 주어 자리이다. (C) Other는 형용사로 쓰이므로 주어 자리에 올 수 없다. 재귀대명사인 (D) Themselves도 주어 자리에 올 수 없다. (A) Those는 people과 같은 의미로 복수이고 (B) Anyone은 단수이다. who 다음에 want라는 복수 동사가 온 것을 보면 빈칸에는 복수 명사가 와야 함을 알 수 있다. 따라서 정답은 (A) Those이다.

어휘 attend 참석하다 | contact 연락하다

22. 스마이드 씨는 팀에 디자이너가 단 두 명뿐이었고, 그 중 한 명이 휴가 중이었기 때문에 초과 근무를 해야 했다.

해설 두 명 중 한 명을 먼저 언급하고 나머지 한 명을 뒤에 언급할 때는 the other를 쓰므로 정답은 (A) the other이다. (B)와 (C)는 대명사이므로 뒤에 designer라는 명사가 올 수 없다. (D) other는 형용사로 명사 designer 앞에 올 수 있지만, 가산 명사일 땐 복수 명사와, 불가산 명사일 땐 단수 명사와 함께 쓰인다. 이 문장에서 (D)가 정답이 되려면, designer는 가산 명사이므로 designers가 와야 한다.

어휘 work overtime 야근하다

23. 많은 동료들은 회사를 그만둔 후에도 꾸준히 서로 연락한다.

해설 전치사 with 다음에는 명사 또는 대명사가 와야 한다. (C) other는 형용사이므로 올 수 없다. (B) another는 형용사와 대명사 모두로 쓰이지만, 문맥상 동료들이 또 다른 사람과 연락하는 것이 아니고 동료들끼리 서로 연락하는 것이므로 답이 될 수 없다. (D) each도 '각각'이라는 의미로 맞지않다. (A) one another는 '서로'라는 뜻의 대명사이므로 전치사 뒤에 쓸 수 있고, 문맥도 맞으므로 정답은 (A) one another이다.

어휘 colleague 동료 | stay in touch 연락을 유지하다

24. 많은 학생들이 쿠마르 교수의 역사 강의에 참석할 것으로 기대된다.

해설 Another와 Every는 단수 가산 명사와 쓰이는데, students는 복수 명사이므로 (A), (C)는 탈락이다. much는 셀 수 없는 명사와 쓰이는데, students는 셀 수 있는 명사이므로 탈락이다. Many는 복수 가산 명사와 쓰이므로 students와 쓸 수 있다. 따라서 정답은 (D) Many이다.

어휘 expect 기대하다, 예상하다 | attend 참석하다 | lecture 강의

25. 몇몇 직원들은 도로 공사의 소음이 그들의 근무에 방해가 된다고 생각했다.

해설 5형식 동사 found를 사용한 문장이며 빈칸은 목적격 보어 자리이므로 형용사 (A) disruptive가 정답이다.

어휘 disruptive 지장을 주는

26. 대변인은 그 사건이 단순한 실수였으며 심각한 문제가 아니라고 밝혔다.

해설 빈칸 앞에 부사가 있다고 해서 부사의 수식을 받을 수 있는 형용사를 고르면 안 된다. 부사 simply는 명사구 수식이 가능한 부사이며, 그 사건이 단순히 실수였다는 의미이므로 주어와 동격을 이루는 명사 (A) mistake가 정답이다.

어휘 spokesperson 대변인 | clarify 분명히 말하다 | incident 일, 사건 | simply 단순히 | serious 심각한, 중요한 | concern 일, 문제

27. 보안 요원들은 건물의 안전을 위해 항상 근무 상태를 유지해야 한다.

해설 보안 요원들이 항상 근무 상태를 유지해야 한다는 의미로, 빈칸 앞의 전치사 on과 함께 '근무 중인'이라는 의미를 뜻하는 (B) duty가 정답이다.

어휘 security guard 보안 요원 | remain 계속 ~이다 | at all times 언제나, 항상 | ensure 보장하다 | safety 안전 | premise 부지, 구내

28. 모든 사무실 컴퓨터들은 현재 업데이트된 소프트웨어로 바르게 작동하고 있다.

해설 work가 1형식 동사이므로 빈칸은 부사 자리이다. 따라서 정답은 (D) correctly이다.

어휘 work 작동하다

29. 모든 직원들이 경력 수준에 상관없이 교육 세션에 참석할 것으로 예상된다.

해설 경력 수준에 상관 없이 교육에 참석할 거라는 의미가 적절하므로 (A) regardless of가 정답이다.

어휘 attend 참석하다 | level 수준 | experience 경험, 경력, 경험하다

30. 게리슨 법률 센터는 20년이 넘는 기간 동안 지역 사회에 서비스를 제공해왔다.

해설 빈칸 앞의 for가 이미 전치사이므로 between, from, during과 같은 전치사를 또 넣을 수 없다. over는 전치사로도 쓸 수 있지만, 숫자 앞에서는 '~이상'이라는 의미의 부사로도 쓰이므로 정답은 (B) over이다.

어휘 serve (서비스를) 제공하다 | local community 지역 사회

UNIT 09. 접속사

핵심 문제 유형
본서 p.108

1. (A)   2. (C)   3. (C)   4. (B)

Q1. 새로운 정책은 직원 만족도를 높일 뿐만 아니라 이직률도 줄일 것이다.

해설 빈칸은 상관접속사 not only와 짝을 이루면서 빈칸 앞과 뒤의 구와 구를 연결해 주는 등위접속사 (A) but also가 정답이다.

어휘 policy 정책 | improve 개선하다 | satisfaction 만족 | reduce 줄이다 | turnover rate 이직률

Q2. 최고 경영자가 자리에 없었기 때문에 회의가 연기되었다.

해설 빈칸은 주절과 종속절 사이의 부사절 접속사 자리이고 회의가 연기된 이유를 나타내고 있으므로 (C) since가 정답이다.

어휘 postpone 연기하다 | unavailable 부재 중인, 시간이 없는

Q3. 류바 씨는 피곤했음에도, 늦은 밤까지 프로젝트를 계속했다.

해설   빈칸은 주어와 동사를 이끄는 부사절 접속사 자리이므로 (C) Although가 정답이다.

어휘   **although** 비록 ~일지라도 | **continue** 계속하다

Q4. 교통이 혼잡했지만, 참가자들은 회의에 늦지 않게 도착했다.

해설   빈칸의 앞뒤로 각각 독립된 문장을 갖추고 있으며, 세미콜론(;) 뒤에는 접속부사 자리이므로 (D) However가 정답이다.

어휘   **traffic** 교통 | **heavy** 혼잡한 | **participant** 참가자 | **arrive** 도착하다 | **on time** 제시간에

Practice   본서 p.112

1. (B)	2. (B)	3. (D)	4. (C)	5. (B)
6. (D)	7. (A)	8. (D)	9. (B)	10. (A)
11. (B)	12. (B)	13. (A)	14. (B)	15. (C)
16. (B)	17. (A)	18. (A)	19. (B)	20. (B)

1.   무료 배송을 제공하는 것 외에도, 대량 주문 시 추가 10퍼센트 할인을 고객에게 제공한다.

해설   빈칸 뒤에 동명사가 있으므로 빈칸에는 전치사가 와야 한다. (A)와 (B) 중 문맥상 (B) Besides가 정답이다. (C)는 등위접속사, (D)는 접속부사로 둘 다 문장 맨 앞에 쓰일 수 없다. 참고로, beside '~옆에'와 in addition to '~이외에'는 전치사라는 점을 유의한다.

어휘   **provide** 제공하다 | **free shipping** 무료 배송 | **large order** 대량 주문

2.   우리 팀의 일원이 되기 전에, 존슨 씨는 경쟁 회사 직원이었다.

해설   빈칸 뒤에 동명사가 있으므로 빈칸에는 전치사가 와야 한다. 문맥상 '이전에, 앞서'라는 의미의 (B) Before가 정답이다.

어휘   **become** ~이 되다 | **employ** 고용하다 | **rival company** 경쟁 회사

3.   브룩사이드는 유명한 휴양지이며 관광을 활성화하고 있는 곳이다.

해설   빈칸은 두 개의 절을 연결하는 접속사 자리인데, promotes의 주어가 is의 주어 Brookside와 중복되어 생략되었으므로 등위접속사 자리인 것을 알 수 있다. (B)와 (C)는 주어를 생략할 수 없다. (A)는 대조를 나타내므로 이 문맥에 적합하지 않다. (D) and는 두 문장을 자연스럽게 연결하므로 정답은 (D) and이다.

어휘   **famous** 유명한 | **holiday spot** 휴양지 | **promote** 촉진하다 | **tourism** 관광

4.   등록 절차를 완료하지 않으면 온라인 강좌를 들을 수 없다.

해설   빈칸은 수식어 자리이므로 빈칸 뒤에 완전한 절을 이끄는 부사절 접속사가 필요하다. unless는 '~하지 않으면'이라는 부정적인 조건을 나타내는 접속사로, 문맥상 가장 적합하다. 따라서, 정답은 (C) unless이다.

어휘   **access** 접근하다, 이용하다 | **course** 교육과정 | **complete** 완료하다 | **registration process** 등록 과정

5.   직원들은 미리 등록하면 교육에 참여할 수 있다.

해설   구조상 네 개의 보기가 모두 빈칸에 들어갈 수 있지만 문맥상 '~하면'이라는 의미의 (B) if가 정답이다.

어휘   **participate in** 참여하다 | **training session** 교육(과정) | **register** 등록하다 | **beforehand** 미리

6.   직원들이 5시까지 퇴근해야 했지만, 몇몇은 자주 초과 근무를 했다.

해설   (A)와 (B)는 전치사이기 때문에 「주어 + 동사」 앞에 사용할 수 없다. 문맥상 '~에도 불구하고'라는 의미의 (D) Although가 정답이다.

어휘   **leave** 퇴근하다 | **frequently** 자주 | **work overtime** 초과 근무하다

7.   최근에 개업한 레스토랑은 매우 성공적이어서 직원을 추가로 채용해야 했다.

해설   「so + 형용사/부사 + that + 주어 + 동사」는 '매우 (너무) ~해서 …하다'라는 의미로 정답은 (A) that이다.

어휘   **recently** 최근에 | **successful** 성공적인 | **recruit** 채용하다 | **employee** 직원

8.   도서관은 리모델링 중에 이용할 수 없을 것이다.

해설   빈칸 뒤에 「주어 + 동사」의 구조가 있으므로 접속사 자리이다. (C)와 (D) 중 문맥상 '동안에'라는 의미의 (D) while이 정답이다.

어휘   **library** 도서관 | **inaccessible** 접근할 수 없는

9.   직원들이 데이터를 더 효율적으로 찾을 수 있도록 고객 관리 소프트웨어가 향상되었다.

해설   빈칸 앞뒤로 주어, 동사를 갖춘 절이 연결되어 있으므로, 빈칸에는 두 절을 이어줄 수 있는 부사절 접속사 자리이다. '직원들이 데이터를 더 효율적으로 찾을 수 있도록 하기 위해 소프트웨어가 향상되었다'는 의미가 적절하므로 목적을 나타내는 접속사 (B) so that이 정답이다.

어휘   **enhance** 향상시키다 | **staff** 직원 | **locate** 찾다 | **efficiently** 효율적으로

10.   새로운 에너지 절약 계획은 비용 절감이 입증되면 시행될 것이다.

해설   빈칸은 두 개의 절을 연결할 수 있는 접속사 자리이다. (D)는 전치사이고 접속사인 (A), (B), (C)가 가능한데, 문맥상 '일단 ~하면'이라는 조건의 의미가 적합하므로 정답은 (A) once이다.

어휘   **initiative** 계획 | **implement** 시행하다 | **prove** 입증하다 | **reduce** 줄이다 | **cost** 비용

11.   고객의 동의가 없다면 데이터를 공유할 수 없다.

해설   빈칸 다음에 명사가 나왔으므로 빈칸은 전치사 자리이다. 보기 중 '데이터를 공유할 수 없다'는 부정문과 연결하여 '~이 없다면'이라는 조건을 나타내는 전치사 (B) without이 정답이다.

어휘   **share** 공유하다 | **client** 고객 | **approval** 동의

12.   직원들은 성과 목표를 달성하거나 초과하면 보상을 받을 자격이 있다.

해설   빈칸은 두 개의 절을 연결할 수 있는 접속사 자리이다. (A), (D)는 접속부사, (C)는 to부정사이다. 따라서, 보기 중 유일한 접속사인 (B)

providing that이 정답이다.

어휘   qualify for ~할 자격이 있다 | reward 보상 | achieve 달성하다 | surpass 초과하다 | performance target 성과 목표

13. 에어컨 시스템은 성능이 저하되었기 때문에 교체될 것이다.

해설   빈칸 다음에 명사가 있으므로 전치사 자리이다. (B)는 접속부사, (C)는 동사원형이 빈칸 뒤에 없으므로 답이 될 수 없다. (D)는 접속사인데, 빈칸 뒤에 주어와 동사가 없으므로 불가하다. 따라서, 정답은 (A) because of이다.

어휘   replace 교체하다 | ineffective 비효율적인 | performance 성능

14. 대회에서 우승하는 참가자들은 상품권과 상금을 모두 받을 것이다.

해설   빈칸은 receive의 목적어 자리로 뒤에 「A (a gift voucher) and B (money)」 구조가 연결되어 있으므로 상관접속사 「both A and B」 'A, B 둘 다'를 떠올릴 수 있어야 한다. 따라서 정답은 (B) both이다.

어휘   participant 참가자 | win 우승하다 | competition 대회 | receive 받다 | gift voucher 상품권

15. 교육 프로그램을 이수한 후, 존은 마케팅 분야의 여러 직책에 지원했다.

해설   빈칸 다음에 동명사가 나왔으므로 빈칸은 전치사 자리이다. (A)와 (B)는 접속사이다. (C)와 (D)는 접속사와 전치사에 모두 해당하지만, (D) since는 주절의 동사 시제가 현재완료이어야 한다. 따라서, (C) After가 정답이다.

어휘   complete 완료하다 | apply for ~에 지원하다 | field 분야

16. 8시까지 반납한다면, 회사 차량을 빌릴 수 있다.

해설   빈칸 뒤에는 완전한 절을 이끄는 접속사가 필요하다. (D)는 전치사이므로 탈락한다. (A)와 (C)는 접속사에 해당하지만, 문맥상 '~한다면'이라는 의미인 긍정문을 이끄는 조건 접속사 (B) as long as가 정답이다.

어휘   borrow 빌리다 | company car 회사 차량 | return 돌려주다, 반환하다

17. 프로젝트 예산이 추가 장비 비용을 충당하기 위해 조정되었다.

해설   빈칸 다음에 동사원형이 왔다. (B)는 전치사이므로 뒤에 명사가 와야 하고, (D)는 접속부사이다. (C) in order that은 접속사이므로 뒤에 완전한 절이 이어져야 한다. 「so as to + 동사원형」은 '~하기 위해서'라는 의미로 문맥상 적합하다. 따라서, 정답은 (A) so as to이다. 참고로, in order는 전치사 구이고 in order to는 '하기 위해서'라는 의미의 to 부정사라는 점에 유의한다.

어휘   budget 예산 | adjust 조정하다 | cover (비용을) 부담하다 | cost 비용 | equipment 장비

18. 전 직원은 작년에 참석했더라도 곧 있을 워크숍에 참석해야 한다.

해설   빈칸 앞뒤로 주어, 동사를 갖춘 절이 연결되어 있어, 빈칸에는 두 절을 이어줄 수 있는 부사절 접속사가 들어가야 할 자리이므로 전치사 (B), (D)를 해석 없이 소거시킬 수 있다. (A)와 (C) 중 문맥상 '~에도 불구하고'라는 의미의 (A) although가 정답이다.

어휘   upcoming 다가오는 | attend 참석하다 | previous 이전의

19. 유지보수 예상 비용이 정확하지 않아서, 수정된 청구서를 첨부했다.

해설   빈칸은 두 개의 절을 연결할 수 있는 접속사 자리이다. (D)를 제외하고는 모두 등위접속사이다. 접속부사 therefore는 단독으로 절과 절을 연결할 수 없지만, and와 함께 쓰이면 예외적으로 가능하다. 따라서 정답은 (B) and이다.

어휘   cost 비용 | estimate 추정하다 | maintenance 유지보수 | incorrect 정확하지 않은 | include 포함하다 | revise 수정하다 | bill 청구서

20. 밀텍 사가 샌프란시스코에서 큰 성공을 거두었기 때문에, 도쿄에 새로운 사무실을 설립할 계획이다.

해설   빈칸은 두 개의 절을 연결할 수 있는 접속사 자리이다. (C)는 접속부사로 문장과 문장 사이에 위치하고, 접속사 (D)는 절과 절 사이에서 연결하므로 둘 다 문장 맨 앞에 쓰일 수 없다. (A)는 절과 절을 연결할 수 없다. 따라서, 정답은 (B) Because이다.

어휘   achieve 달성하다 | success 성공 | establish 설립하다

UNIT 10. 명사절 접속사

핵심 문제 유형   본서 p.116

1. (C)   **2.** (A)   **3.** (B)   **4.** (B)

Q1. 매니저는 프로젝트 마감일이 일주일 연장되었다고 알렸다.

해설   빈칸은 동사의 목적어 자리에 쓰인 명사절 자리이고, 빈칸 뒤에는 완전한 절이 이어지므로 (C) that이 정답이다.

어휘   announce 발표하다 | extend 연장하다

Q2. 그 연구는 회사가 다음 분기에 출시할 계획이 무엇인지 보여준다.

해설   빈칸은 동사의 목적어 자리에 쓰인 명사절 접속사 자리이고 빈칸 뒤에는 launch의 목적어가 없는 불완전한 절이 이어지므로 (A) what이 정답이다.

어휘   study 연구하다 | launch 출시하다 | quarter 분기

Q3. 이해관계자들이 새 프로젝트에 투자할지 여부는 내일 결정될 예정이다.

해설   빈칸은 전치사의 목적어 자리로 명사절 접속사 자리이며, 문맥상 투자 여부가 불확실하고, if는 전치사의 목적어로 사용할 수 없으므로 (B) whether가 정답이다.

어휘   decision 결정 | stakeholder 이해관계자 | invest 투자하다

Q4. 매니저는 내일 회의에 누가 참석 가능한지 알지 못했다.

해설   빈칸은 동사의 목적어 자리로 주어가 없는 불완전한 절을 이끄는 명사절 접속사 자리에 해당하고 참석할 사람이 누구인지를 몰랐다는 문맥으로 (B) who가 정답이다.

어휘   available 이용할 수 있는, 시간이 있는

Practice

본서 p.120

1. (B)	2. (C)	3. (A)	4. (B)	5. (C)
6. (C)	7. (A)	8. (A)	9. (A)	10. (C)
11. (D)	12. (D)	13. (B)	14. (D)	15. (D)
16. (A)	17. (D)	18. (B)	19. (A)	20. (A)

1. 회사가 투자했던 것은 효율성을 개선하기 위한 혁신적인 기술이었다.

해설 빈칸은 주절의 동사 was의 주어 자리이므로 명사 역할을 할 수 있는 접속사가 필요하다. (C)와 (D)는 부사절 접속사로 제외한다. 동사 invested in의 목적어가 없는 불완전한 절이므로 불완전한 절을 이끄는 명사절 접속사 (B) what이 정답이다.

어휘 invest in ~에 투자하다 | innovative 혁신적인 | improve 개선하다 | efficiency 효율성

2. 이사회는 그 조직과 협력할지 여부를 결정할 것이다.

해설 (C)를 제외한 나머지는 모두 접속사로 두 개의 절을 연결한다. 빈칸 뒤에는 주어와 동사가 없으므로 탈락이다. whether는 뒤에 나오는 명사절의 「주어 + 동사(the board will collaborate)」를 to부정사 형태로 축약할 수 있지만, (D) if는 불가하다. 따라서 whether to ~ organization이 determine의 목적어 역할을 하므로 정답은 (C) whether이다.

어휘 board 이사회 | determine 결정하다 | collaborate 협력하다 | organization 조직

3. 최신 조사에 따르면 많은 관광객이 앱으로 숙소를 예약하는 것을 선호한다고 나타났다.

해설 빈칸에는 완전한 절을 이끄는 명사절 접속사 that을 목적어로 취하는 동사가 필요하다. (A)를 제외한 나머지는 모두 사람을 목적어로 취하므로 답이 될 수 없다. 따라서 정답은 (A) indicated이다.

어휘 latest 최신의 | research 연구, 조사 | indicate 나타내다 | tourist 관광객 | prefer 선호하다 | reserve 예약하다 | accommodation 숙소

4. 위원회는 연례 회의 준비를 담당할 사람을 결정해야 한다.

해설 빈칸은 determine의 목적어 자리로 명사절이 쓰여야 한다. 빈칸 뒤에는 will be의 주어가 없는 불완전한 절이 이어지므로 (C)와 (D)는 답이 될 수 없다. 의문사 who는 명사절을 이끄는 접속사로 사용될 수 있다. 문맥상 '연례 회의를 조직하는 책임을 질 사람'을 결정해야 한다는 의미로 (B) who가 정답이다.

어휘 determine 결정하다 | be responsible for ~을 책임지다 | organize 조직(준비)하다 | annual 연례의

5. 그 제안의 결과는 팀원들이 어떻게 서로 협력할 수 있는지에 달려 있다.

해설 이 문장은 두 개의 절로 구성되어 있어 접속사가 아닌 전치사 (D)는 제외한다. 빈칸은 전치사 뒤에 위치하고 있으므로 명사 자리이고 빈칸 뒤에 완전한 절이 이어지고 있으므로 불완전한 절을 이끄는 (B) what은 답이 될 수 없다. (A) that은 완전한 절을 이끌 수는 있지만, 전치사

뒤에 올 수 없고 문맥상 '그 제안의 결과는 팀원들이 어떻게 서로 협력할 수 있는지에 달려 있다'고 했으므로 방법을 나타내는 접속사가 적절하다. 따라서 의문부사인 (C) how가 정답이다.

어휘 outcome 결과 | proposal 제안 | depend on ~에 달려 있다 | collaborate 협력하다 | one another 서로

6. 그 직원들은 지정된 날짜에 경영진과의 인터뷰를 부담스러워하고 있다.

해설 that절을 이끄는 관용적인 형용사 표현 중 하나인 「be afraid that + 완전한 문장」의 형태로 정답은 (C) that이다.

어휘 management 경영진 | certain date 특정 날짜

7. 글리밍 잼은 고객이 다섯 개 이상의 상품을 구매할 때 총 금액의 30퍼센트를 할인해 준다.

해설 이미 4형식 완전한 절이 나와 있으므로 빈칸에는 두 개의 절을 연결하는 부사절 접속사를 찾아야 한다. when은 '~할 때'라는 의미의 부사절 접속사로 정답은 (A) when이다.

어휘 offer 제공하다 | customer 고객 | total bill 총 금액 | purchase 구매하다

8. 회의의 목적은 새 정책이 다음 분기에 시행될지 여부를 결정하는 것이다.

해설 보기 모두 접속사에 해당하지만, 빈칸은 determine의 목적어 역할을 할 수 없는 부사절인 (D) because는 답이 될 수 없다. whether는 주로 '(~할지 말지를) 결정하다' 의미를 가진 동사들과 함께 사용된다. 따라서, (A) whether가 정답이다.

어휘 purpose 목적 | determine 결정하다 | policy 정책 | implement 시행하다 | quarter 분기

9. 그녀의 뛰어난 성과를 고려할 때, 레베카 씨가 부서장으로 임명된 것은 놀랄 일이 아니다.

해설 「It ~ that ~」 구문으로 It은 가주어이고 that이 진주어이다. 따라서, 정답은 (A) it이다.

어휘 considering ~을 고려하면 | outstanding 뛰어난 | performance 실적, 성과 | appoint 임명하다 | head of department 부서장

10. 창고로 배송하기 전에, 모든 태그가 패키지에 올바르게 부착되었는지 확인하십시오.

해설 빈칸은 절과 절을 이어주는 접속사 자리이다. 빈칸 뒤에는 완전한 절이 이어지고 있고 선택지 네 개 모두 명사절 접속사이지만, make sure는 목적어로 명사절 접속사 that과 함께 사용된다. 따라서, 정답은 (C) that이다.

어휘 make sure 확인하다 | attach 부착하다 | deliver 배송하다 | storage 창고

11. 정책은 기기에 문제가 있을 경우 교환을 보장한다.

해설 빈칸에는 ensure의 목적어 역할을 할 수 있고 뒤에 있는 절을 이끌 수 있는 명사절 접속사가 필요하다. (C)를 제외한 나머지는 모두 완전한 절을 이끄는 접속사이다. 문맥상 '교환될 것을 보장한다'는 의미이므로 정답은 (D) that이다.

어휘 policy 정책 | ensure 보장하다 | device 기기 | exchange 교환하다 | issue 문제

12. 매니저는 공사가 예기치 않은 상황으로 인해 연기되었다고 발표했다.

해설 빈칸은 announced의 목적어 자리이므로 부사절 (B)와 (C)는 답이 될 수 없고 빈칸 뒤에는 완전한 절이 이어지고 있으므로 명사절 접속사 (D) that이 정답이다.

어휘 announce 발표하다 | construction 건설 | postpone 연기하다 | due to ~때문에 | unforeseen circumstance 예기치 않은 상황

13. 마케팅 팀은 현재 시장에서 캠페인이 성공할지 안 할지 여부를 논의하고 있다.

해설 빈칸에는 discussing의 목적어 역할을 할 수 있는 명사절 접속사가 필요하다. or not과 함께 쓰일 수 있는 접속사는 whether '~인지 아닌지' 뿐이므로 (B) whether가 정답이다.

어휘 discuss 논의하다 | succeed 성공하다 | current 현재의

14. 그 팀은 매니저가 이번 주말까지 허가하면 프로젝트를 시작할 것이다.

해설 빈칸은 콤마 앞에 위치하여 수식어 자리이므로 부사절 접속사가 쓰여야 한다. 따라서, (A) What과 (C) That은 답이 될 수 없다. (B) Whether '~인지 아닌지'도 부사절로 쓰일 수는 있지만, 문맥상 조건절이 적절하므로 (D) If가 정답이다.

어휘 permission 허가 | by ~까지

15. 프레넥스 사가 새로운 공장을 설립할지 여부는 향후 수요에 따라 달라질 수 있다.

해설 빈칸은 주절의 동사 could change의 주어 자리이다. 부사절 접속사 (A)와 (C)를 빈칸에 넣으면 could change의 주어가 없으므로 정답이 될 수 없다. 빈칸 뒤에 완전한 절 (Frenex Corp. establishes a new plant)이 이어지므로 불완전한 절을 이끄는 (B) What은 쓰일 수 없다. Whether는 완전한 절 앞에 쓰일 수 있으므로 (D) Whether가 정답이다. (A) If는 Whether를 타동사 뒤 목적어 자리에서만 대체할 수 있다.

어휘 establish 설립하다 | new plant 새로운 공장 | depending on ~에 따라 | future demand 향후 수요

16. 회사가 변경된 주소를 받지 못했음에도, 소포는 제시간에 배달되었다.

해설 콤마 앞 수식어에 해당하므로 명사절 (C)와 (D)는 답이 될 수 없다. 또한, 빈칸 뒤에는 주어와 동사가 있으므로 전치사 (B)도 불가하다. 따라서, 정답은 (A) Even though이다.

어휘 receive 받다 | updated address 변경된 주소 | package 소포 | deliver 배달하다 | on time 제시간에

17. 나탈리야 씨는 회의 때문에 일주일 동안 자리를 비울 것이라고 우리에게 말했다.

해설 빈칸에 부사 (B) there이나 부사절 접속사 (D) while이 쓰이면 told의 직접목적어가 없으므로 정답이 될 수 없다. (C) what과 (D) that 중에서 빈칸 뒤에 완전한 절이 나와 있으므로 정답은 (D) that이다.

어휘 be away 자리를 비우다 | conference 회의

18. 관리자는 팀원들에게 프로젝트 마감 기한이 일주일 연장되었다는 것을 알릴 것이다.

해설 빈칸은 「간접목적어(사람) + 직접목적어(that절)」 형태를 취하는 4형식 동사 자리이다. 따라서, 정답은 (B) inform이다.

어휘 inform (~에게 …을) 알리다 | deadline 마감시한 | extend 연장하다

19. 엔지니어는 무엇이 시스템을 멈추게 했는지 정확히 알아낼 것이다.

해설 본동사 find out 뒤에 주어가 빠진 불완전한 절이 연결되어 있으며, '무엇이 시스템을 멈추게 했는지 정확히 알아낼 것이다'라는 의미가 자연스러우므로 의문대명사로 쓰인 명사절 접속사 (A) what이 정답이다.

어휘 find out 찾아내다 | precisely 정확하게 | lead to ~로 이어지다

20. 위원회는 회사의 정책에 여러 조정이 적용되어야 한다고 제안했다.

해설 빈칸은 명사절 that을 목적어로 취하는 동사 자리이다. 구조상 보기 네 개 모두 들어갈 수 있지만, that절에는 be동사가 원형으로 되어있는데, 이것은 당위성을 나타내는 조동사 should가 생략되었다는 것을 의미한다. 따라서 제안의 의미를 나타내는 (A) suggested가 정답이다.

어휘 committee 위원회 | suggest 제안하다 | multiple 많은, 다수의 | adjustment 조정 | apply 적용하다 | firm 회사 | policy 정책

UNIT 11. 형용사절 접속사

핵심 문제 유형

본서 p.124

1. (A) **2.** (A) **3.** (B) **4.** (A)

Q1. 가장 높은 점수를 받은 지원자가 그 직책을 제안받을 것이다.

해설 빈칸은 동사 received의 주어 자리로 선행사 사람을 수식하는 주격 관계대명사인 (A) who가 정답이다.

어휘 applicant 지원자 | receive 받다 | score 점수 | offer 제공하다

Q2. 경영진에 의해 시행된 새로운 정책은 직원 만족도를 향상시키는 것을 목표로 한다.

해설 빈칸은 선행사를 수식하는 주격 관계대명사절의 동사 자리이고 단수 주어에 일치하는 단수 동사 (A) was implemented가 정답이다.

어휘 policy 정책 | implement 실행하다 | management 경영진 | aim ~을 목표로 하다 | improve 개선하다 | satisfaction 만족

Q3. 이것이 바로 제가 문제를 해결하는 데 필요한 것이었다.

해설 빈칸은 주격 보어 자리로 목적어가 없는 불완전한 절을 이끌고 있고 선행사가 필요하지 않는 (B) what이 정답이다.

어휘 exactly 정확히 | solve 해결하다 | problem 문제

Q4. 우리가 어제 회의를 열었던 회의실은 3층에 위치해 있다.

해설 빈칸은 선행사를 수식하면서 완전한 절을 이끄는 관계부사 자리이고
회의실은 장소에 해당하므로 (A) where가 정답이다.

어휘 conference 회의 | hold 열다 | locate 위치하다 | floor 층

Practice
본서 p.128

1. (A)	2. (A)	3. (B)	4. (D)	5. (D)
6. (B)	7. (A)	8. (A)	9. (A)	10. (B)
11. (D)	12. (A)	13. (B)	14. (D)	15. (A)
16. (A)	17. (B)	18. (A)	19. (A)	20. (A)

1. 시스템을 운영하는 기술자 명단이 게시판에 게시된다.

해설 빈칸은 주격 관계대명사 뒤에 위치하므로 동사 자리이다. '시스템을 운
영하다'의 주어는 '명단(list)'이 아니라 '기술자(technicians)'이므로
단수 동사 (B)와 (C)는 답이 될 수 없다. 또한, 빈칸 뒤에 목적어가 있
으므로 수동태인 (D)는 불가하다. 따라서, 복수 동사 (A) operate가
정답이다.

어휘 operate 운영하다 | post 게시하다 | notice board 게시판

2. 우리가 검토한 문서는 경영진에게 제시될 것이다.

해설 빈칸은 주어 The document와 동사 will be presented가 사이에
있으므로 수식어의 역할을 하는 형용사절 접속사 자리이다. 소유격 관
계대명사 (C) whose는 불완전한 절 앞에는 쓰일 수 없다. 빈칸 뒤에
examined의 목적어가 없으므로 목적격 관계대명사가 쓰여야 하며
선행사는 사물(document)이므로 정답은 which를 대신해서 쓰일 수
있는 (A) that이다.

어휘 document 문서 | examine 검토하다 | present 제시하다 |
management team 경영진

3. 새로운 판매 전략을 요약한 보고서는 이번 주말까지 당신에게 발송될
것이다.

해설 빈칸은 The report를 선행사로 하는 주격 관계대명사 that 뒤에 있으
므로 동사 자리이다. (C) to부정사와 (D) -ing 형태는 준동사이므로 정
답이 될 수 없다. 선행사기 단수 명사이므로 복수 동사 (A) outline도
불가하다. 따라서, 정답은 (B) outlines이다.

어휘 report 보고서 | sales strategy 판매 전략 | end of this week
이번 주말

4. 그 일자리에 지원했던 많은 지원자들은 매우 유능했다.

해설 빈칸은 주어 A number of the candidates와 동사 were 사이에 있
으므로 수식어의 역할을 하는 형용사절 접속사 자리이다. 목적격 관계
대명사 whom, 소유격 관계대명사는 whose는 주어 자리에 쓰일 수
없다. (C) what 앞에는 선행사가 없으므로 탈락이다. (D) who는 빈칸
뒤에 주어가 없으므로 주격 관계대명사가 정답이 될 수 있다. 따라서
정답은 (D) who이다.

어휘 candidate 후보자 | apply for 지원하다 | competent 유능한

5. 인터넷에서 자주 광고를 내는 블루웨이브 사는 새로운 서비스를 도입

하고 있다.

해설 빈칸 뒤에는 3형식 동사의 수동태로 완전한 절이 이어지므로 (A), (B),
(C)는 모두 불가하다. 또한, commercial과 Bulewave Ltd.의 관계
는 소유격 관계이므로, 정답은 (D) whose이다.

어휘 commercial 광고 | introduce 도입하다

6. 그 창고는 모든 제품이 배송 전에 보관되는 곳입니다.

해설 빈칸 뒤 문장이 완전한 형식을 갖추고 있으므로 불완전한 절을 이끄
는 (A)와 (D)는 불가하다. 또한, 선행사(the place)가 있으므로 명사
절 접속사 (C) what도 답이 될 수 없다. 따라서, 장소의 관계부사 (B)
where이 정답이다.

어휘 warehouse 창고 | store 보관하다 | shipping 배송

7. 새로운 기계를 운영할 직원들을 위한 오리엔테이션이 10월 7일에 계
획되어 있다.

해설 이 문장의 주어는 An orientation이고 동사는 is planned이므로 그
사이는 수식어 자리이다. 빈칸 다음에 주어가 없기 때문에 주격 관계
대명사가 쓰여야 하며, 선행사가 사람(staff members)이므로 정답은
who를 대신할 수 있는 (A) that이다.

어휘 operate 운영하다

8. 재사용 가능한 포장 재료를 생산하는 그린우드 공장은 노스우드로 이
전했다.

해설 빈칸 다음에 주어가 없기 때문에 완전한 절을 이끄는 관계부사 (C)
는 답이 될 수 없다. 선행사가 있기 때문에 (B) what도 불가하다. 빈
칸에는 주격 관계대명사가 와야 하며, 선행사가 사물인 Greenwood
Factory이므로 정답은 (A)와 (D)가 될 수 있지만, that은 콤마와 함께
쓸 수 없으므로 정답은 (A) which이다.

어휘 reusable 재사용 가능한 | packaging material 포장 재료 |
move 이전하다

9. 구독을 취소하고 싶은 분들은 7월 20일까지 지원팀에 연락해야 한다.

해설 주격 관계대명사 who 앞에 쓰일 수 있는 지시대명사는 보기 중 (A)
Those '사람들'뿐이다. 따라서 (A) Those가 정답이다.

어휘 unsubscribe 구독을 취소하다 | contact 연락하다 | support
team 지원팀

10. 그 설문조사는 사회학 분야에서 인정을 받은 한 회사에 의해 수행되
었다.

해설 빈칸 다음에 주어가 없으므로 완전한 절을 이끄는 소유격 관계대명사
(A) whose와 목적격 관계대명사 (C) whom도 올 수 없다. (D) what
앞에는 선행사가 올 수 없으므로 정답이 될 수 없다. 따라서, 빈칸에는
주격 관계대명사가 와야 하며, 정답은 선행사 사람과 사물을 모두 대
신할 수 있는 (B) that이다.

어휘 survey 설문조사 | conduct 수행하다 | earn recognition 인정
을 받다 | field 분야 | sociology 사회학

11. 라벨에 주소가 누락된 사람을 택배 회사가 찾지 못해 배송이 지연되
었다.

해설 빈칸은 the person을 선행사로 하는 형용사절 접속사 자리이다. 빈칸 뒤에 완전한 절이 이어지고 있으므로 정답은 (D) whose이다.

어휘 shipment 배송(물) | courier 택배 회사, 배달원

12. 브라운 씨는 니콜 씨가 과제를 늦게 제출한 날짜를 알고 싶어한다.

해설 빈칸에는 뒤에 연결된 완전한 절이 이어지므로 관계대명사 (B)와 (D)를 답에서 제외한다. (C)는 선행사가 the date이므로 역시 정답이 될 수 없다. the date는 시간을 나타내므로 관계부사 (A) when이 정답이다.

어휘 curious 궁금한 | submit 제출하다 | assignment 과제 | late 늦게

13. 계정이 이번 달에 만료되는 VIP 클럽 회원들은 30일 전에 갱신해야 한다.

해설 이 문장의 주어는 members이고 동사는 are asked to renew이다. 따라서 빈칸에는 앞에 있는 명사 members를 수식하는 형용사절 접속사 즉, 관계대명사가 필요하며, 빈칸 다음은 1형식의 완벽한 문장이므로 소유격 관계대명사가 들어가야 한다. 따라서 정답은 (B) whose이다.

어휘 account 계정 | expire 만료되다 | renew 갱신하다

14. 회사가 채용한 모든 신입 직원들은 뛰어난 성과를 보이고 있다.

해설 이 문장은 recruited 뒤에 목적어가 없는 것을 고려하여 employees 뒤에 목적격 관계대명사 whom이 생략되었다는 것을 파악해야 한다. 따라서, 이 문장의 주어는 All of the new employees이고 빈칸이 동사 자리이다. 주어가 복수이므로 복수 동사 (D) are이 정답이다.

어휘 recruit 채용하다 | outstanding performance 뛰어난 성과

15. 현재 에딘버그에서 JH 주식회사의 시설을 감독하고 있는 카샌드라 씨는 다음 분기에 운영 관리자로 임명받을 것이다.

해설 이 문장은 동사 oversees의 주어가 없는 불완전한 절로 구성되어 있다. 따라서, 완전한 절을 이끄는 소유격 관계대명사 (B)와 관계부사 (D)는 정답이 될 수 없다. 빈칸은 주격 관계대명사 자리이며 선행사가 사람이므로 (C) which도 불가하므로 (A) who가 정답이다.

어휘 currently 현재 | oversee 감독(관리)하다 | facility 시설 | appoint 임명하다

16. 전기 요금이 몇 주 동안 서서히 올랐으며, 그 대부분은 10월에 감소할 것으로 예상된다.

해설 are predicted to decrease의 주어는 the costs이므로 사람을 선행사로 하는 (B) who와 (C) whom은 정답이 될 수 없다. 또한, 이 문장은 두 개의 절로 구성되어 있어 접속사가 필요하므로 대명사인 (D) them은 제외한다. 따라서, 정답은 (A) which이다.

어휘 cost 비용 | electricity 전기 | rise 오르다 | gradually 서서히 | predict 예측하다 | decrease 감소하다

17. 7일 이내에 찾아가지 않는 모든 소지품은 폐기될 것이다.

해설 that은 주격 관계대명사이고 선행사는 belongings이다. 따라서, 복수 동사가 와야 하므로 정답은 (B) are이다.

어휘 belonging 소지품 | retrieve 회수하다 | within ~이내에 | throw away 폐기하다, 버리다

18. 테라노바 건설은 이글 하이츠 프로젝트의 계획이 거의 완료되었다고 보고했다.

해설 빈칸에는 reported의 목적어 역할을 할 수 있고 뒤에 있는 절을 이끌 수 있는 명사절 접속사가 필요하다. 빈칸 뒤에 완전한 절이 나와 있으므로 정답은 (A) that이다.

어휘 report 보고하다 | planning 계획 | almost 거의 | finish 완료하다

19. 대규모 참석자를 수용할 수 있는 개조된 LX 이벤트 센터는 11월에 개장할 예정이다.

해설 이 문장에 동사가 두 개(can hold, is scheduled)인 점을 고려하면 두 개의 절이 필요하므로 빈칸은 접속사 자리이다. 따라서, 대명사 (D)는 소거한다. 콤마와 콤마 사이에는 수식어구가 자리인데, 빈칸 다음에 주어가 없으므로 완전한 절을 이끄는 (C) where는 쓰일 수 없고 주격 관계대명사가 쓰여야 한다. 선행사가 사물(LX Event Center)이므로 정답은 (A)와 (B)가 될 수 있다. 단, that 앞에는 콤마를 사용할 수 없으므로 정답은 (A) which이다.

어휘 renovate 개조하다 | hold 수용하다 | attendee 참석자

20. 그 기관은 최근 성과가 뛰어난 직원을 고용했다.

해설 빈칸 뒤에는 완전한 절이 이어지고 있으므로 소유격 관계대명사 (B), (C), (D) 모두 불가하다. 또한, 선행사 an employee와 빈칸 뒤의 명사 performance는 소유격 관계이므로 정답은 (A) whose이다.

어휘 organization 기관, 조직 | hire 고용하다 | outstanding 뛰어난, 눈에 띄는

REVIEW TEST 03 본서 p.130

1. (B)	2. (B)	3. (B)	4. (B)	5. (D)
6. (B)	7. (C)	8. (A)	9. (C)	10. (D)
11. (A)	12. (A)	13. (B)	14. (B)	15. (B)
16. (C)	17. (B)	18. (B)	19. (B)	20. (C)
21. (A)	22. (B)	23. (A)	24. (B)	25. (D)
26. (D)	27. (B)	28. (A)	29. (C)	30. (B)

1. 새 소프트웨어는 사용하기 쉽지만 원활하게 작동하려면 더 높은 시스템 요건이 필요하다.

해설 문맥상 알맞은 등위접속사를 고르는 문제이다. 빈칸 앞으로 주어, 동사를 갖춘 절이 연결되어 있는데, 새 소프트웨어가 사용하기는 쉽지만 더 높은 시스템 요건을 필요로 한다는 의미로 두 절이 대조를 이루고 있으므로 역접의 의미를 갖는 등위접속사 (B) but이 정답이다.

어휘 requirement 요구사항, 요건 | run 작동하다 | smoothly 원활하게, 순조롭게

2. 매출 신장을 위한 다양한 노력에도 불구하고, 회사의 수입은 증가하지 않았다.

해설 빈칸 뒤에 명사가 왔다. 따라서 빈칸은 전치사 자리이므로 부사인 (A) 와 접속사인 (C)와 (D)는 소거한다. 전치사는 (B)가 문맥상 '~에도 불구하고'가 적합하므로 정답은 (B) Despite이다.

어휘 boost 신장시키다 ㅣ revenue 이윤, 수입

3. 곧 은퇴할 윌슨 씨는 우수 직원상을 수여 받을 것이다.

해설 빈칸은 주어 자리이므로 소유격 또는 목적격 대명사 (C)는 불가하다. 주격 대명사 (A)를 넣으면, 빈칸 앞에 이미 주어 Ms. Wilson이 있어 주어가 중복되므로 답이 될 수 없다. 콤마와 콤마 사이는 수식어 자리인데, 빈칸 뒤에 주어가 없고 동사만 있으므로 주격 관계대명사 자리인 것을 알 수 있다. 선행사는 사람이므로 (D)는 제외한다. 따라서, 정답은 (B) who이다.

어휘 retire 은퇴하다 ㅣ present 수여하다

4. 재키 식당의 스테이크 요리는 밥이나 고구마 중 하나의 사이드 메뉴와 함께 제공된다.

해설 either 뒤에 rice와 sweet potatoes가 연결되어 있는 구조이므로 상관접속사 either A or B (A, B 둘 중 하나)를 떠올릴 수 있어야 한다. 따라서 정답은 (B) or이다.

어휘 dish 요리 ㅣ come with ~이 딸려 있다

5. 주로 젊은 근로자들에게 많이 의존하는 매장들은 적합한 지원자를 찾는 데 애를 먹고 있다.

해설 주격 관계대명사 that 다음에는 동사가 꼭 필요하므로 빈칸에는 동사가 와야 한다. 선행사는 복수(stores)이므로 정답은 복수 동사 (D) rely 이다.

어휘 heavily 심하게, 아주 많이, 무겁게 ㅣ rely 의지하다

6. 새 마케팅 전략은 브랜드 인지도를 높이는 데 성공했으며, 더욱이 매출도 크게 증가시켰다.

해설 빈칸 앞에 세미콜론(;)이 있으므로 절이 아닌 독립된 문장이 있다는 것을 알 수 있다. 따라서, 빈칸에는 접속사가 아닌 접속부사가 쓰여야 하므로 (A)는 제외시킨다. 문맥상 마케팅 전략이 브랜드 인지도를 높이고 매출도 증대시켰다는 동일한 맥락의 문장이 연결되어 있으므로 '첨가'의 의미를 갖는 (B) moreover이 정답이다.

어휘 strategy 전략 ㅣ successful 성공적인 ㅣ brand awareness 브랜드 인지도 ㅣ boost 신장시키다, 북돋우다 ㅣ sales 매출액, 판매량 ㅣ significantly 상당히, 크게

7. 세무 사무소의 결론은 그 회사가 예산 책정을 개선할 필요가 있다는 것이었다.

해설 (A)와 (D)는 빈칸 앞에 선행사가 없으므로 답이 될 수 없다. (B) what 다음에는 불완전한 문장이 와야 하는데 완전한 문장이 왔으므로 답이 될 수 없다. (C)는 빈칸 앞에 선행사가 없으므로 관계대명사가 아닌 명사절로 봐야 한다. 명사절을 이끄는 접속사 that 다음에 완전한 문장이 올 수 있고, that절이 명사로 이 문장에서 주격 보어 역할을 하므로 정답은 (C) that이다.

어휘 conclusion 결론 ㅣ tax consulting firm 세무 사무소 ㅣ budgeting 예산 편성

8. 그 임대차 계약서는 세입자와 임대주가 사인하기만 하면 공인될 것이다.

해설 빈칸 앞뒤로 주어, 동사를 갖춘 절이 연결되어 있으므로 두 절을 이어줄 수 있는 부사절 접속사가 필요한 자리이며, 계약서에 사인하는 대로 공인될 거라는 의미가 적절하므로 '~하기만 하면; ~하자마자'라는 뜻의 (A) once가 정답이다.

어휘 lease agreement 임대차 계약(서) ㅣ official 공인된, 공식적인 ㅣ tenant 세입자 ㅣ landlord 임대주

9. 고 에이드는 아시아 전역의 생활 환경을 개선하는 것을 목표로 하는 단체이다.

해설 what은 앞에 선행사가 올 수 없으므로 답이 될 수 없다. 빈칸 다음에 2형식의 완전한 문장이 왔으므로 빈칸에는 소유격 관계대명사가 와야 하므로 (C)가 정답이다.

어휘 living condition 생활 환경

10. FG 광고는 저렴한 요금을 제공하는 반면 DTO 광고는 평판이 더 좋다.

해설 빈칸에는 두 개의 문장을 연결하는 접속사가 와야 한다. 등위접속사 (B)는 문두에 올 수 없고, 접속부사 (C)는 부사이므로 문장을 연결할 수 없다. (A)와 (D) 중에서 문맥상 '반면에'가 적합하므로 정답은 (D) While이다.

어휘 advertising 광고, 광고업 ㅣ reasonable 가격이 저렴한

11. 제 10회 조경 콘퍼런스에서 페탈 씨는 그녀가 지난달에 디자인한 정원 설계도를 발표할 것이다.

해설 이 문장에는 동사가 두 개인데 접속사가 없다. 따라서 선행사 plan 뒤에 목적격 관계대명사 which가 생략되었음을 파악하면 빈칸은 designed의 주어 자리라는 것을 알 수 있으므로 정답은 (A) she이다.

어휘 present 발표하다 ㅣ gardening plan 정원 설계도

12. 구매 부서는 아달렛 사에서 새 복사기를 구매할지를 결정할 것이다.

해설 빈칸에는 decide의 목적어 역할을 할 수 있고 뒤에 있는 절을 이끌 수 있는 명사절 접속사가 필요하다. 명사절 접속사가 아닌 (B) neither와 (D) even if는 답이 될 수 없고 뒤에 주어, 동사가 있는 완전한 절이 아니라 to부정사가 나와 있으므로 정답은 (A) whether이다.

어휘 purchase 구매하다 ㅣ photocopier 복사기

13. 국제 무역을 규제하는 법이 개정되었다.

해설 주격 관계대명사 which 뒤에는 동사가 와야 한다. 빈칸 다음에 international trade가 있으므로 능동태를 찾아야 하고, 선행사가 단수(the law)이므로 단수 동사를 찾아야 한다. 따라서 정답은 (B) regulates이다.

어휘 regulate 규제하다, 조절하다 ㅣ international trade 국제 무역

14. 우리는 그 부품들이 즉시 교체되어야 한다고 요청했지만, 수리 예약을 잡는 데는 며칠이 걸렸다.

해설 빈칸에는 두 개의 문장을 연결하는 접속사가 필요하다. (A)와 (C)는 접속부사로 문장을 연결할 수 없고, (D)는 등위접속사로 문두에 올 수 없다. 따라서 정답은 양보의 부사절 접속사 (B) Although이다.

어휘 request 요청하다 ㅣ immediate 즉각적인 ㅣ replacement 교체

15. 매니저는 프로젝트의 가장 비용 효율이 높은 옵션이 무엇인지 결정할 필요가 있다.

해설 타동사 determine의 목적어로 불완전한 절이 연결되어 있으므로 불완전한 절을 이끄는 의문대명사 (B) what이 정답이다. 명사절 접속사 (A) that이나, 의문부사 (C) where, (D) how는 모두 완전한 절을 이끈다.

어휘 determine 결정하다 | cost-effective 비용 효율이 높은

16. 강 씨와 이 씨 둘 다 기획위원회에 임명되지 않았다.

해설 빈칸 뒤에 'A (Ms. Kang) nor B (Ms. Lee)' 구조가 연결되어 있으므로 상관접속사 「neither A nor B: A, B 둘 다 아닌」를 떠올릴 수 있어야 한다. 따라서 정답은 (C) Neither이다.

어휘 appoint 임명하다 | planning committee 기획위원회

17. 회사는 비용을 절감하면서 제품 품질도 향상시키려고 애썼다.

해설 문장이 「------ + 주어 + 동사, 주어 + 동사」 구조이므로 빈칸은 두 개의 절을 연결해주는 부사절 접속사가 필요한 자리이므로 부사 (C) Instead는 제외한다. 문맥상 회사가 비용을 줄이면서 제품 품질도 향상시켰다는 의미이므로 '~하면서, ~하는 동안'을 뜻하는 (B) While이 정답이다. (A) Meanwhile도 비슷한 의미 이기는 하지만 접속사가 아닌, 역시 부사이기 때문에 접속사 없이 문장 맨 앞에 올 수 없다는 점을 기억해두자.

어휘 reduce 줄이다. 감소시키다 | manage to do 용케 ~하다 | improve 개선하다. 향상시키다

18. 비행기가 지연되었기 때문에, 강씨는 주주총회에 참석할 수 없었다.

해설 빈칸에는 두 개의 문장을 연결할 수 있는 접속사가 필요하다. (A)와 (D)는 전치사이고 (C)는 관계부사이다. 문맥상 '~때문에'라는 의미의 접속사가 들어가는 것이 적합하므로 정답은 (B) as이다.

어휘 delay 미루다. 연기하다 | shareholder 주주

19. 그 보고서는 새로운 정책이 직원 생산성에 긍정적인 영향을 미쳤음을 확인했다.

해설 빈칸 뒤에 동사 confirmed의 목적어로서 주어, 동사, 목적어를 모두 갖춘 완전한 절이 연결되어 있으므로 불완전한 절을 이끄는 (A) what은 제외한다. 문맥상 새로운 정책이 직원 생산성에 긍정적인 영향을 미쳤다는 것을 보고서를 통해 확인했다는 의미가 되어야 하므로 (C) if와 (D) when은 문맥상 부적절하다. 따라서, (B) that이 정답이다.

어휘 confirm 확인하다. 확정하다 | policy 정책, 방침 | have an impact on ~에 영향을 주다 | employee productivity 직원 생산성

20. 에너지를 절약하기 위해 건물에서 나가기 전에 컴퓨터를 꺼 주세요.

해설 빈칸 다음에 -ing 형태의 동명사가 있다. (B)와 (D)는 접속사이므로 뒤에 주어와 동사가 와야 하고, (A)는 접속부사이다. (C)는 접속사와 전치사의 역할 모두 가능하지만, 빈칸 다음에 동명사가 왔으므로 정답은 전치사로 쓰인 (C) before이다.

어휘 turn off 끄다 | leave 떠나다

21. 우리는 공장의 전체 조립 라인 문제를 점검할 수 있는 새 장치를 가지고 있다.

해설 (D) near는 전치사로 다음에 동사가 올 수 없다. 빈칸 다음에 주어가 없으므로 that이 빈칸에 오면 주격 관계대명사로 선행사 device를 꾸미게 되므로 정답은 주격 관계대명사 (A) that이다.

어휘 check 점검하다 | entire 전체의 | assembly 조립

22. 회사는 고객들이 대면으로 담당자와 만날 수 있는 새로운 사무실을 개설할 예정이다.

해설 빈칸은 앞에 선행사를 취하면서 뒤에 완전한 절을 이끄는 관계부사 자리이고 사무실(office)은 장소에 해당하므로 (C) where이 정답이다.

어휘 client 고객 | representative 담당자 | in person 대면으로, 직접

23. 모든 양식 항목을 작성해 주세요. 그렇지 않으면 귀하의 신청이 지연될 수 있습니다.

해설 빈칸 앞뒤로 주어, 동사를 갖춘 절이 연결되어 있고, 「세미콜론(;) + ------ + 콤마(,)」의 형태로 보아 접속부사가 들어갈 자리이다. 보기가 모두 접속부사이므로 해석이 필요한데, 양식의 모든 항목을 작성하지 않으면 신청서가 지연될 수 있다는 의미가 자연스러우므로 '그렇지 않으면'이란 뜻의 (A) otherwise가 정답이다.

어휘 ensure 반드시 ~하게 하다 | complete 작성하다 | form 양식. 서식 | application 신청(서) | delay 지연시키다

24. 최고 경영자는 회사가 국제 시장으로 확장하기로 결정한 이유를 설명했다.

해설 빈칸 뒤에 타동사 explained의 목적어로서 완전한 절이 연결되어 있으므로 빈칸은 완전한 절을 이끌어 문장의 목적어 역할을 할 수 있는 명사절 접속사가 와야 하는데, that이나 whether 이외에 의문사가 그 역할을 할 수 있다. 이때 (A) which나 (B) what은 의문대명사로서 뒤에 불완전한 절을 이끌고, 의문형용사로 쓰일 때는 뒤에 바로 명사를 취해야 한다. (C) whose 역시 의문사형용사로서 바로 명사가 이어져야 한다는 점에서 (A), (B), (C)는 답이 될 수 없다. when, where, how, why는 의문부사로서 뒤에 완전한 절을 취하므로 (D) why가 정답이다.

어휘 expand 확장하다 | international market 국제 시장

25. 영업팀은 프로젝트를 완료할 추가 시간이 주어졌다는 사실을 감사하게 생각했다.

해설 명사 fact, news, confirmation 등은 뒤에 「that + 완전한 절」 이끌어 명사와 동격을 이룬다. (그들이 추가 시간을 받았다는 사실) 따라서 명사절 접속사 (D) that이 정답이다.

어휘 appreciate 감사하게 생각하다 | additional 추가의 | complete 완료하다

26. 그 보고서는 회의 전에 캐롤이 수정해야 하는 수치들을 포함하고 있다.

해설 that은 목적격 관계대명사로 선행사 figures를 수식한다. 빈칸에는 동사가 와야 하는데, (C)는 동사가 아니라서 탈락이고 (A)는 주어가 단수이므로 단수 동사인 corrects가 와야 하므로 탈락이다. 빈칸 다음에 목적어가 없는 이유는 that이 목적격 관계대명사이기 때문이다. 그러

므로 목적어가 없는 것이 아니라 앞에 있는 것이므로 수동태 (B) has been corrected는 답이 될 수 없다. 따라서 정답은 (D) will correct 이다.

어휘　figure 수치 | correct 수정하다

27. 그 보고서는 효율성을 높이기 위해 현재 시스템에서 개선이 필요한 것을 강조하고 있다.

해설　빈칸 뒤에 주어 없이 동사가 연결된 불완전한 절이 와 있으므로 관계 대명사가 필요하며, 앞에 선행사가 없으므로 선행사를 포함한 관계대명사 (C) what이 정답이다.

어휘　highlight 강조하다 | improve 개선하다 | current 현재의 | enhance 향상시키다 | efficiency 효율성

28. 파트타임 직원들은 어젯밤 수정된 일정표를 확인해야 한다.

해설　빈칸 앞에 선행사 the schedule이 있고 빈칸 뒤에 동사 was revised가 있으므로 빈칸에 들어가야 하는 정답은 주격 관계대명사 (A) which이다.

어휘　part-time 파트타임인 | revise 수정하다

29. 심 씨에게 당신이 프로젝트 매니저를 맡아줄 수 있는지 금요일까지 알려 주세요.

해설　빈칸 뒤의 절이 빈칸 앞 동사 know의 목적어가 되도록 명사절 접속사를 선택해야 한다. 보기 중 명사절 접속사는 whether밖에 없으므로 (C) whether가 정답이다.

어휘　available 시간이 있는 | lead 이끌다

30. 다음 주에 시스템이 유지 관리를 위해 오프라인 상태가 되는 짧은 기간이 있을 예정이다.

해설　빈칸은 앞에 선행사를 취하면서 뒤에 완전한 절을 이끄는 관계부사 자리이고 기간(period)은 시간에 해당하므로 (B) when이 정답이다.

어휘　brief 짧은 | period 기간 | offline 오프라인 상태의, 인터넷으로 바로 하는 것이 아닌 | maintenance 유지보수

UNIT 12. to부정사

핵심 문제 유형

1. (C)　2. (B)　3. (B)　4. (A)

Q1. 회사의 새로운 마케팅 전략을 추진하기로 한 결정은 매출을 크게 향상 시켰다.

해설　이 문장에 동사가 있으므로 빈칸은 준동사 자리이고 to부정사의 수식을 받는 명사 뒤에 있으므로 (C) to implement가 정답이다.

어휘　decision 결정 | strategy 전략 | significantly 상당히 | improve 향상시키다 | sales 매출

Q2. 최고 경영자는 회의 중에 그 제안을 검토하기로 동의했다.

해설　빈칸 앞의 agreed는 목적어로 to부정사를 취하는 동사이므로 (B) to review가 정답이다.

어휘　agree 동의하다 | proposal 제안

Q3. 회사의 시장 점유율을 늘리기 위해, 새로운 전략은 모든 직원들이 새로운 영업 기술을 배우도록 요구한다.

해설　동사 require는 to부정사를 목적격 보어로 취하므로 (B) to learn이 정답이다.

어휘　increase 증가 시키다 | market share 시장 점유율 | require 요구하다 | learn 배우다

Q4. 그 위원회는 대회의 결과를 발표할 준비가 되어 있다.

해설　빈칸은 주격 보어 자리로 to부정사를 취하는 형용사인 (A) ready가 정답이다.

어휘　committee 위원회 | announce 발표하다 | result 결과 | competition 경쟁

Practice

1. (C)　2. (A)　3. (D)　4. (D)　5. (D)
6. (B)　7. (B)　8. (A)　9. (A)　10. (A)
11. (C)　12. (C)　13. (B)　14. (A)　15. (A)
16. (A)　17. (D)　18. (B)　19. (C)　20. (B)

1. LMT 사의 최고 경영자는 이번 가을에 대학 졸업생들에게 교육 프로그램을 제공하겠다고 했다.

해설　빈칸은 to부정사를 목적어로 취하는 동사 자리이다. (A)와 (B)는 동명사로 동사가 될 수 없다. (D)는 주어와 수 일치가 맞지 않는다. 따라서, 정답은 (C) has promised이다.

어휘　promise 약속하다 | provide 제공하다 | college 대학교 | graduate 졸업생

2. 최근 리모델링으로 인해 글렌데일 스위츠는 현재 투숙객을 유치하기 위해 무료 조식 쿠폰을 제공하고 있다.

해설　주절에는 이미 3형식의 완전한 문장이 왔으므로, 빈칸은 필요 없는 수식어구이다. 문장 맨 마지막에 오는 수식어구는 보통 부사이다. to부정사는 '~하기 위해서'라는 의미로 부사 기능을 하므로 정답은 (A) to bring이다.

어휘　renovation 보수(개조) 공사 | currently 현재 | voucher 상품권, 쿠폰

3. 경영지원팀은 직원들에게 업무 생산성을 높이기 위한 제안을 공유하도록 요청했다.

해설　request는 5형식 동사로 목적격 보어 자리에 to부정사가 들어간다. 목적어는 staff members이고 빈칸이 목적격 보어 자리이므로 정답은 (D) to share이다.

30　파고다 토익 기본 완성 RC

어휘 request 요청하다 | suggestion 제안 | enhance 향상시키다 | office productivity 업무 생산성

4. 그 조직은 지역 수익을 증대시키는 데 전념하고 있다.

해설 「be dedicated to」에서 to는 to부정사가 아닌 전치사 to이다. 따라서 to 다음에는 동사원형이 아니라, 명사나 동명사가 나와야 한다. 이 문장에서는 빈칸 뒤에 명사가 나오므로 빈칸에는 동명사가 와야 한다. 빈칸 뒤에 나오는 명사는 동명사의 목적어이다. 따라서 정답은 (D) boosting이다.

어휘 organization 조직 | local 지역의, 현지의 | revenue 수익

5. 매출 감소로 인해, 우리는 레드우드 노트북 라인의 생산을 중단하기로 했다.

해설 decide는 to부정사를 목적어로 취하는 동사이다. 따라서 (D) to cease가 정답이다.

어휘 decline 감소하다 | revenue 매출 | production 생산 | cease 중단시키다

6. 우리 팀이 고객 피드백을 철저히 검토하는 것이 중요하다.

해설 「It(가주어) ~ for (의미상 주어) ~ to부정사(진주어)」 구문으로 정답은 (B) for이다.

어휘 crucial 중요한 | examine 검토하다 | thoroughly 철저히

7. 직원들은 고객 만족도를 높이기 위한 방법을 논의하고 싶어 한다.

해설 eager는 to부정사의 수식을 받는 형용사이다. 정답은 (B) to debate 이다.

어휘 eager 간절히 바라는 | method 방법 | satisfaction 만족

8. 이 포지션에 대해 문의하려면, 회사의 웹사이트를 방문하십시오.

해설 「------- + 전치사구, 명령문」 구조이므로 빈칸은 수식어 자리이다. In order 뒤에는 '~를 하기 위해'라는 의미로 부사적으로 쓰일 수 있는 to부정사 (A) to inquire가 정답이다.

어휘 inquire 문의하다 | position 직책

9. 나라 인터네셔널은 언어학 연구에 강한 열정을 가진 후보자를 고용하고자 한다.

해설 빈칸은 전치사 다음에 있다. 전치사 다음에는 명사나 동명사가 올 수 있고, to부정사는 올 수 없다. 따라서 (B)는 탈락이고, 동사인 (C)와 (D)도 탈락이다. 따라서 정답은 (A) studying이다.

어휘 employ 고용하다 | candidate 후보자 | keen 열정적인 | linguistics 언어학

10. 관리자 직무를 위한 필수 자격 요건은 경영학 학위이다.

해설 빈칸은 관사 the와 형용사 necessary 뒤에 위치하고 있으므로 명사 자리이다. to부정사 (B) to qualify와 동명사 (D) qualifying도 명사 역할을 할 수 있지만, 동사의 성질을 가지기 때문에 목적어가 따라와야 하므로 정답은 (A) qualification이다.

어휘 necessary 필수적인 | business administration 경영학 | degree 학위

11. 추위는 이번 겨울이 끝날 때까지 지속될 것으로 예상된다.

해설 「be expected + to부정사」이므로 정답은 (C) to remain이다.

어휘 cold spell 추위 | expect 예상하다 | remain 계속 ~이다

12. 그 식당은 10주년을 기념하기 위해 특별한 요리를 준비하고 있다.

해설 이미 3형식의 완전한 문장이므로 빈칸부터는 수식어구가 나와야 한다. 동사 (A)와 (B)는 올 수 없고 과거분사 (D) marked는 빈칸 뒤에 목적어 its decade milestone이 있기 때문에 사용할 수 없다. (C)의 to부정사는 수식어구 기능을 할 수 있으므로 정답은 (C) to mark이다. 여기서 to부정사는 '~하기 위해서'라는 의미의 부사 역할로 쓰였다

어휘 bistro 식당 | prepare 준비하다 | unique 독특한 | decade 10년 | milestone 중요한 사건이나 단계

13. 판매대에 진열될 모든 상품은 미리 확인받아야 한다.

해설 주어 All goods와 동사 must be checked 사이에 수식어구가 필요한 자리이다. 주어와 동사 사이에 오는 수식어구는 보통 주어(명사)를 수식하므로 형용사 기능을 하는 것이 와야 한다. (C)는 동사 또는 명사, (D)는 동사이므로 탈락이고, to부정사는 형용사 기능을 하므로 가능하다. 이 문장에서 display의 목적어가 없으므로 to부정사를 수동태 형태로 써야 하기 때문에 정답은 (B) to be displayed이다.

어휘 goods 상품 | shelf 선반 | in advance 미리

14. 하이드로 테크 사의 최고 경영자인 톰 치탬 씨는 4월에 사임할 예정이다.

해설 be supposed to는 '~하기로 예정되어 있다'는 의미로 to부정사와 함께 쓰이는 표현이다. 정답은 (A) supposed이다.

어휘 announce 발표하다 | step down 사임하다

15. 회원권을 연장하려면 먼저 온라인 설문지를 작성하십시오.

해설 빈칸은 콤마 앞에 위치하므로 수식어 자리이다. 문장의 맨 앞에서 부사구를 이끌 수 있는 품사는 to부정사이므로 (A) extend가 정답이다.

어휘 extend 연장하다 | complete 작성하다 | questionnaire 설문지

16. 인사과는 기술 전문 지식을 가진 더 많은 지원자를 모집하는 것을 목표로 한다.

해설 aim은 to부정사를 목적어로 취하는 동사이므로 (A) to recruit이 정답이다.

어휘 personnel department 인사과 | aim ~을 목표로 하다 | candidate 후보자 | expertise 전문적 지식

17. 학교 이사회는 6월 15일에 커뮤니티 포럼을 개최하기로 계획했다.

해설 host는 타동사이다. 빈칸 뒤에 목적어가 없으므로 수동태를 써야 한다. be동사는 이미 있으므로 (D) hosted가 정답이다.

어휘 board 위원회, 이사회 | forum 토론회

18. 매니저들은 더 많은 고객을 끌어들이기 위해 카페를 리모델링할 계획이다.

해설 빈칸에는 동사 intend의 목적어가 필요한데, 동명사를 목적어로 취하지 않기 때문에 (D)는 정답이 될 수 없고, intend는 to부정사를 목적어로 사용하는데, 빈칸 뒤에 목적어가 있기 때문에 능동태인 (B) to renovate가 정답이다.

어휘 intend ~하려고 하다 | draw 끌어들이다 | patron 고객

19. 라벤더 식당에 가려면 입구의 오른쪽에 있는 엘리베이터를 타십시오.

해설 콤마 앞은 수식어구이고, 빈칸부터 문장이 시작되는데 동사가 없다. 따라서 빈칸에는 동사가 와야 하며, 동사부터 시작하는 문장은 명령문이다. 명령문은 동사원형으로 시작하므로 정답은 (C) take이다.

어휘 lift 엘리베이터 | entrance 입구

20. 관리자는 팀에게 새로운 절차를 철저하게 지켜달라고 요청했다.

해설 빈칸은 to부정사 사이에 위치하고 있으므로 동사를 수식하는 부사가 쓰여야 한다. 보기 중 (B)와 (D)가 부사인데, 문맥상 '새로운 절차를 철저하게 지켜달라고 요청했다'가 자연스러우므로 (B) carefully가 정답이다.

어휘 carefully 꼼꼼히, 철저하게 | carelessly 부주의하게 | procedure 절차

UNIT 13. 동명사

핵심 문제 유형
본서 p.142

1. (C)   **2.** (B)   **3.** (B)   **4.** (A)

Q1. 규칙적으로 휴식을 취하는 것은 업무 효율성을 높이고 스트레스를 줄이는 데 도움이 된다.

해설 빈칸은 주어 자리이고 동명사는 단수 동사와 수를 일치시키므로 (C) Taking breaks가 정답이다.

어휘 take a break 휴식을 취하다 | regularly 정기적으로 | improve 개선하다 | efficiency 효율성 | reduce 줄이다

Q2. 잭은 피곤했지만, 회의에 참석하겠다고 고집했다.

해설 빈칸은 전치사 목적어 자리이다. 목적어 자리에 올수 있는 것은 (B), (C), (D)가 있는데, to부정사는 전치사 뒤에 쓰일 수 없다. (B)와 (D) 중 빈칸 뒤에 목적어의 역할을 하는 명사(the meeting)가 있으므로 동명사 (B) attending이 정답이다.

어휘 although 비록 ~일지라도 | tired 피곤한 | insist on 고집하다 | attend 참석하다

Q3. 위원회는 결정하는 것을 다음 주까지 미루었다.

해설 빈칸은 동사의 목적어 자리이고 postpone은 동명사를 목적어로 취하는 동사이므로 (B) making이 정답이다.

어휘 committee 위원회 | postpone 연기하다 | make a decision 결정하다

Q4. 회사는 생산 과정에서 최고 품질 기준을 유지하는 데 전념한다.

해설 빈칸은 전치사 to와 함께 쓰이는 관용 표현으로 (A) maintaining이 정답이다.

어휘 be committed to 전념하다 | maintain 유지하다 | quality 품질 | standard 기준 | production 생산 | process 과정

Practice
본서 p.146

1. (A)   **2.** (C)   **3.** (D)   **4.** (C)   **5.** (B)
6. (B)   **7.** (A)   **8.** (B)   **9.** (C)   **10.** (A)
11. (B)   **12.** (B)   **13.** (C)   **14.** (B)   **15.** (B)
16. (A)   **17.** (B)   **18.** (B)   **19.** (C)   **20.** (A)

1. 앱을 통해 콘서트 티켓을 주문하는 데는 5분도 채 걸리지 않는다.

해설 빈칸은 동사 자리이다. 주어가 동명사(Ordering a concert ticket)로 단수 취급하므로 정답은 (A) is done이다.

어휘 order 주문하다 | via ~을 통해서

2. 작업 흐름을 수정하면 출력이 증가할 것이다.

해설 동사 will result가 있는 것으로 보아 빈칸은 주어 자리로 동사 (B)는 탈락이다. 과거분사 (D)는 형용사로 쓰일 경우 관사 the 앞에 쓰일 수 없다. 명사 (A)는 빈칸 뒤에 목적어 the workflow가 있으므로 불가하고, 동명사 (C) Revising이 정답이다.

어휘 workflow 작업 흐름 | result in (결과적으로) ~낳다

3. 학습자들은 교재 내용을 효과적으로 향상시킬 수 있는 보충 자료를 받는다.

해설 빈칸에는 전치사 뒤에 동명사를 수식할 부사가 필요하다. 정답은 (D) effectively이다.

어휘 additional material 보충자료 | enhance 향상시키다 | content 내용 | course book 교재

4. 고객은 설문지를 작성하면 무료 식사 쿠폰을 받는다.

해설 전치사 for 다음에는 명사나 동명사가 나와야 한다. 또한 fill in은 구동사로 동명사의 목적어는 the questionnaire이다. 따라서, 동명사 (C) filling이 정답이다.

어휘 complimentary 무료의 | dining voucher 식사 쿠폰 | fill in 작성하다 | questionnaire 설문지

5. 이 공지는 지하 주차장의 대형 차량에 대한 구체적인 제한 사항을 운전자에게 알리기 위한 것이다.

해설 전치사 뒤에 있는 명사는 형용사가 수식한다. 정답은 (B) specific이다. (C) specifics가 '세부 사항'이라는 뜻의 명사라는 점에 유의한다.

어휘 announcement 공지, 발표 | motorist 운전자 | vehicle 차량 | underground parking lot 지하 주차장

6. 글로벌 전자제품 공급업체인 데크노바 사는 전기 주전자의 필요성을 충족시키기 위해 최선을 다한다.

해설 부정관사 a 뒤에는 단수 명사가 와야 한다. global은 형용사이므로 빈칸은 명사 자리이다. 명사 역할을 할 수 있는 보기는 (B), (C), (D)인데, (D) provision '공급'은 콤마 앞의 회사명 TechNova와 동격이 아니다. 동명사 (C)는 동사의 성질 때문에 동명사의 목적어를 수반하여야 한다. 빈칸 뒤에는 목적어가 없으므로 정답은 (B) provider이다.

어휘 electronics 전자기기 | fulfill 충족시키다 | kettle 주전자

7. 일정을 철저히 검토한 후 필요한 조정 사항을 알려주세요.

해설 전치사 Upon 다음에 동명사 -ing가 오고, 동명사의 목적어(the schedule)도 나왔다. 따라서, 동명사 앞에서 수식할 수 있는 부사 (A) thoroughly가 정답이다.

어휘 examine 검토하다 | inform 알리다 | adjustment 조정

8. 이 씨는 새로운 직책을 얻은 후 파트너를 찾기 시작했다.

해설 전치사 following 다음에는 명사나 동명사가 와야 한다. 그런데 빈칸 뒤에 명사가 나왔고 이는 동명사의 목적어로 볼 수 있기 때문에 정답은 동명사 (B) obtaining이다.

어휘 seek 찾다 | following ~후에 | position 지위, 자리

9. 현재 지원자를 고용하는 것과 관련된 모든 세부 정보는 인사팀에 보관된다.

해설 전치사 regarding 뒤에 동명사 -ing가 나왔으므로 빈칸에는 동명사를 수식하는 부사가 필요하다. 정답은 (C) currently이다.

어휘 detail 세부 사항 | regarding ~에 관해 | store 저장하다 | personnel 인사과

10. 모든 실험실 직원들은 매일 안전 수칙을 따르는 것에 익숙하다.

해설 to 뒤에 동사원형이 아닌 -ing형 동명사가 있으므로 빈칸 뒤의 to는 to부정사가 아니라 전치사라는 것을 알 수 있다. (A)를 제외하면 모두 to부정사와 쓰일 수 있으므로 정답은 (A) used이다. 참고로 「used to부정사」는 '~하는데 사용되어지다'라는 의미이므로 혼동하지 않도록 유의한다.

어휘 laboratory 실험실 | safety protocol 안전 수칙

11. 고객을 끌어들이는 확실한 방법은 5년 보장을 제공하는 것이다.

해설 전치사 of 뒤에는 명사나 동명사가 와야 한다. 또한 빈칸 뒤에 명사가 있다는 것은 동명사의 목적어가 나왔다는 의미이므로 정답은 동명사 (B) engaging이다.

어휘 reliable 신뢰할 수 있는 | engage (관심, 주목)을 끌다 | offer 제공하다

12. 그 회사는 마케팅 매니저를 즉시 채용할 있는 자리가 있다.

해설 관사 뒤에 위치한 opening은 동명사가 아니라 명사이므로 형용사가 수식을 해야 한다. 정답은 (B) immediate이다. (D) mediate '중재하다'는 형용사가 아니라 동사라는 점에 유의한다.

어휘 opening 공석 | immediate 즉각적인

13. 다음 주 목요일은 테크코프 사가 창립한 지 2주년이다.

해설 its는 소유격이므로 빈칸에는 명사가 나와야 한다. (A) to부정사는 소

유격 뒤에 쓰일 수 없으므로 탈락이다. 명사는 (B)와 (C)인데, (B)는 '발사 장치'를 뜻하므로 문맥상 적합하지 않다. 따라서, '창립'이라는 뜻의 ing 형태의 명사인 (C) launching이 정답이다.

어휘 anniversary 기념일

14. 행사 참가자들은 다양한 나라의 전통 음식을 맛볼 기회를 얻게 될 것이다.

해설 빈칸은 주어 자리로 구조상 (C)를 제외하고 모두 명사에 해당한다. participate는 자동사로 동명사 (A)는 동명사의 목적어 없이 사용 될 수 있지만, 문맥상, '축제의 참가가 음식을 맛볼 기회를 얻게 될 것'이 아니고 '축제의 참가자들이 음식을 맛볼 기회를 얻게 될 것'이므로 정답은 (B) participants이다.

어휘 opportunity 기회 | sample 맛보다 | traditional 전통적인 | various 다양한

15. 글렌데일 산업은 매출 감소로 가전제품 생산을 중단했다.

해설 빈칸 뒤에 consumer electronics는 동명사의 목적어이므로 빈칸에는 동명사를 목적어로 취하는 동사가 필요하다. 따라서, 정답은 (B) discontinued이다. 또한, 빈칸 뒤 consumer electronics는 동명사의 목적어이다.

어휘 discontinue 중단하다 | manufacture 제조, 제조하다 | consumer electronics 가전제품 | decline 감소하다 | sales 매출

16. 그 작업을 위한 기술자 추가 채용이 가장 중요한 관심사가 될 것이다.

해설 동사 will be가 있으므로 (C) Recruit이 동사일 경우는 탈락이고 명사 (D)는 빈칸 뒤에 목적어 additional technicians가 있으므로 답이 될 수 없다. (B)는 과거 동사일 경우에는 탈락이고, 과거분사 형용사가 되는 경우에는 주어는 technicians로 복수이다. 그러면 보어가 단수 명사 our top concern이므로 탈락이다. 따라서, 동명사 (A)가 주어가 되는 것이 적절하므로 (A) Recruiting이 정답이다.

어휘 recruit 모집하다 | technician 기술자 | task 작업, 일 | concern 관심사

17. 셰프마스터 오븐 선반은 손쉬운 세척이 가능하도록 분리할 수 있다.

해설 빈칸은 형용사 effortless의 수식을 받는 명사 자리이며, 손쉬운 세척을 위해 선반을 분리할 수 있다는 의미가 적절하므로 '세척'을 뜻하는 -ing형 명사인 (B) washing이 정답이다. (C) washer '세탁기, 세탁하는 사람'도 명사이지만 의미상 맞지 않다.

어휘 rack 선반 | take out 꺼내다 | effortless 손쉬운

18. 콘서트 주최자는 관객이 공연을 촬영하는 것을 금지했다.

해설 「prohibit A from -ing」는 'A가 ~하지 못하게 하다'이므로 정답은 (B) filming이다.

어휘 organizer 주최자 | attendee 참석자 | film 촬영하다

19. 오늘 오후에 도착할 예정인 #8921 배송 수령을 반드시 확인해 주세요.

해설 빈칸은 acknowledge의 목적어 자리, 즉 명사 자리이다. 명사 역할을 할 수 있는 보기는 (C)와 (D)인데, 동명사는 동사의 성질 때문에 동명

사의 목적어가 또 나와야 한다. 그런데 빈칸 뒤에는 명사가 없으므로
정답은 (C) receipt이다.

어휘   certain 확실한 ∣ acknowledge 받았음을 알리다 ∣ expect 예상
하다 ∣ arrive 도착하다

20. 아쿠아프로 다이빙 장치는 성능 감소 없이 물속에서 사용할 수 있다.

해설   전치사 without 뒤에 동명사 losing이 연결되어 있으므로 그 뒤에
는 동명사의 목적어 역할을 하는 명사가 와야 한다. 따라서 정답은 (A)
performance이다.

어휘   underwater 물속에서 ∣ performance 성능

UNIT 14. 분사

핵심 문제 유형

본서 p.150

1. (B)   **2.** (A)   **3.** (A)   **4.** (C)

Q1. 작성된 문서는 검토를 위해 이사회에 제출되었다.

해설   빈칸은 명사를 수식하는 형용사 자리로 문맥상 문서는 작성되어 있는
수동 관계이므로 (B) prepared가 정답이다.

어휘   prepare 준비하다 ∣ document 문서 ∣ submit 제출하다 ∣
board 이사회 ∣ review 검토하다

Q2. 새 소프트웨어를 개발하는 프로젝트는 생산성을 향상시킬 것이다.

해설   빈칸은 명사를 후치 수식하는 형용사 자리이며 빈칸 뒤에는 목적어가
있으므로 (A) developing이 정답이다.

어휘   develop 개발하다 ∣ improve 개선하다 ∣ productivity 생산성

Q3. 프레젠테이션은 너무 흥미로워서 청중을 계속 참여시켰다.

해설   빈칸은 주격 보어 자리이고 주어가 사물이므로 감정을 유발하고 있으
므로 (A) interesting이 정답이다.

어휘   presentation 발표 ∣ interesting 흥미로운 ∣ audience 청중 ∣
engage 몰입시키다 ∣ throughout 내내

Q4. 회의를 마치면서 우리는 새로운 정책을 즉시 시행하기로 결정했다.

해설   빈칸은 부사절에서 접속사가 생략된 수식어 자리로 빈칸 뒤에 목적어
가 있으므로 주어와 능동과의 관계인 (C) Completing이 정답이다.

어휘   complete 완료하다 ∣ decide 결정하다 ∣ implement 시행하다 ∣
policy 정책 ∣ immediately 즉시

Practice

본서 p.154

1. (D)   **2.** (B)   **3.** (A)   **4.** (B)   **5.** (A)
6. (A)   **7.** (D)   **8.** (C)   **9.** (D)   **10.** (D)
11. (C)   **12.** (C)   **13.** (A)   **14.** (C)   **15.** (C)
16. (C)   **17.** (A)   **18.** (C)   **19.** (A)   **20.** (B)

1. 위원회에 의해 수정된 계획이 광범위한 지지를 받았다.

해설   빈칸 앞의 명사를 수식하는 형용사가 들어가야 한다. 분사 형용사 (C)
와 (D) 중에 '수정하는 계획'이 아니고 '수정된 계획'이므로 정답은 과
거분사 (D) revised이다.

어휘   revise 수정하다 ∣ committee 위원회 ∣ receive 받다 ∣
widespread 광범위한

2. 매이플 크릭 위의 육교가 다시 운영되려면 상당한 복구가 필요하다.

해설   명사 restoration 앞에 빈칸이 있으므로 형용사 자리이다. 문맥
상 상당히 많은 복구가 필요하다는 의미이므로 일반 형용사 (B)
Substantial이 정답이다. 분사 형용사는 동사의 의미를 그대로 가져
와서 능동의 의미를 갖는 현재분사 형용사와 수동의 의미를 갖는 과거
분사 형용사로 구별된다는 점에서 (C) Substantiated '입증된'이나,
(D) Substantiating '입증시키는'은 문맥상 어색하다.

어휘   substantial 상당한 ∣ restoration 복구 ∣ overpass 육교 ∣
operational 운영할 준비가 된

3. 메디테크는 의료 폐기물을 줄이기 위해 의료 시설에서 재사용 가능한
외과 기구를 생산한다.

해설   복합명사 surgical instruments 앞에 빈칸이 있으므로 형용사가 와
야 한다. (A) reusable은 일반 형용사이고, (C) reused '재사용 되는'
과 (D) reusing '재사용하는'은 분사 형용사이다. 문맥상 재사용할 수
있는 기구의 의미가 적절하므로 일반 형용사 (A)가 정답이다.

어휘   reusable 재사용 가능한 ∣ surgical instrument 외과 기구 ∣
healthcare facility 의료 시설 ∣ reduce 줄이다 ∣ medical
waste 의료 폐기물

4. 꼼꼼히 작성된 보고서는 회의에 맞춰 이사회에 제출되었다.

해설   정관사 The와 명사 report 사이의 completed는 과거분사 형용사이
다. 형용사는 부사의 수식을 받으므로 (B) carefully가 정답이다.

어휘   complete 작성하다 ∣ submit 제출하다 ∣ board 위원회

5. 신입 직원은 다음 주 월요일에 지정된 오리엔테이션 프로그램에 참여
해야 한다.

해설   관사 the와 명사 orientation programs 사이에 빈칸이 있으므로 형
용사가 정답이다. 분사 형용사 (A)와 (B) 중에 '지정하는 프로그램'이
아닌, '지정된 프로그램'이 적절하므로 수동의 의미를 갖는 과거분사
(A) designated가 정답이다.

어휘   designate 지정하다 ∣ new employee 신입 직원 ∣ participate
in ~에 참여하다

6. 서비스가 약속된 기준을 충족하지 못해서 많은 고객들이 불만을 토로했다.

해설   2형식 동사 were 다음에 빈칸이 있으므로 주격 보어 자리, 즉 상태 설명 형용사가 와야 한다. 보기 중 형용사는 (A)와 (B)인데, 주격 보어이므로 주어와의 관계를 본다. '고객들이 불만스럽게 만든 것'이 아니라, '고객들이 불만을 느낀 것'으로 주어가 사람(clients)이므로 과거분사 (A) frustrated가 정답이다.

7. H&K 솔루션즈에 의해 개발된 애플리케이션이 5월에 혁신상을 받았다.

해설   이미 3형식의 완벽한 문장으로 빈칸에는 수식어구가 들어가야 한다. (C)와 (D)가 분사 형용사로 명사 The application을 수식할 수 있는데, '개발하는 애플리케이션'이 아니라 '개발된 애플리케이션'이므로 정답은 (D) developed이다.

어휘   receive 받다 ｜ innovation 혁신 ｜ prize 상

8. 그 관광 가이드는 역사 설명으로 관광객들을 만족시켰다.

해설   빈칸은 5형식 동사 make의 목적격 보어 자리로 형용사가 들어가야 한다. (B)와 (C) 중 감정을 나타내는 분사 형용사는 수식받는 대상인 목적어가 사람이면 과거분사 형태로 쓰므로 (C) satisfied가 정답이다.

어휘   satisfy 만족시키다 ｜ historical explanation 역사 설명

9. 언급한 대로, 당사는 다음 달에 숙련된 개발자들을 위한 인터뷰를 준비할 것이다.

해설   as noted는 '언급된 대로'라는 과거분사 관용 표현으로 한 단어처럼 기억해두자. 따라서, 정답은 (D) noted이다.

어휘   firm 회사 ｜ arrange 준비하다 ｜ skilled 숙련된 ｜ developer 개발자

10. "더 그레잇 퀘스트"는 다가오는 여름 시즌에 기대되는 영화 중 하나이다.

해설   명사 films 앞에 빈칸이 있으므로 형용사가 들어가야 한다. 분사 형용사 (C)와 (D) 중에 의미상 '기대하는 영화'가 아니고 '기대되는 영화'이므로 정답은 (D) expected이다.

어휘   expect 기대하다 ｜ among ~중에 ｜ upcoming 다가오는

11. 거주자의 수가 증가함에 따라, 건설 회사들이 많이 필요하다.

해설   정관사 the와 명사 number 사이에 빈칸이 있으므로 형용사가 와야 한다. increase가 '증가하다' 의미로 사용될 때는 1형식 자동사이므로 현재분사가 목적어 없이 명사 앞에서 수식이 가능하다. 따라서, (C) increasing이 정답이다.

어휘   increase 증가하다 ｜ resident 거주자 ｜ construction 건설

12. 새롭게 발행된 보고서는 연말 판매량이 증가했음을 나타낸다.

해설   빈칸 뒤의 명사 review를 수식할 형용사가 필요하다. 형용사는 (B)와 (C)가 가능한데, '발행하는' 보고서가 아니고 '발행된' 보고서이므로 정답은 (C) published이다.

어휘   indicate 나타내다 ｜ year-end sales 연말 판매량

13. 포토그래픽 서비스 협회로 알려진 PSA는 애호가들을 위해 매주 워크숍을 개최한다.

해설   문장에 이미 동사 conducts가 있고 쉼표 사이의 삽입 구문이므로 빈칸에는 동사가 들어갈 수 없다. 분사인 (A)와 (B) 중 선택해야 하는데, 빈칸 뒤에 목적어가 없으므로 과거분사 (A) identified가 정답이다.

어휘   identify 식별하다 ｜ conduct 수행(실시)하다 ｜ weekly 매주의 ｜ enthusiast 애호가

14. 대량으로 제품을 구매하는 고객들은 도매 가격을 적용받을 수 있다.

해설   문장의 동사 may qualify가 이미 있기 때문에 빈칸에 동사인 (A)와 (B)는 들어갈 수 없고, 분사인 (C)와 (D)가 가능한데, '구매되는' 고객이 이니고 '구매하는' 고객이므로 정답은 (C)이다. 또한 분사가 안의 명사를 뒤에서 수식할 때 보통 목적어를 동반하면 현재분사이고, 목적어를 동반하지 않으면 과거분사라고 기억하면 좋다. 이 문장에서는 목적어 products가 있으므로 정답은 (C) acquiring이다.

어휘   amount 양 ｜ qualify for ~의 자격을 얻다 ｜ wholesale price 도매가격

15. 경험이 많은 후보자들만이 관리직에 고려될 것이다.

해설   빈칸은 명사 앞에서 수식하는 형용사 자리이다. 분사 형용사 (B)와 (C) 중에 '경험이 많은'이라는 의미는 과거분사 형태로만 쓰이므로 (C) experienced가 정답이다.

어휘   candidate 후보자 ｜ consider 고려하다 ｜ managerial position 관리직

16. 그 일자리에 관심 있는 지원자들은 인사부에 연락해야 한다.

해설   attract는 '~의 마음을 끌다'는 의미의 감정 동사로, 감정 동사가 사람을 수식할 때는 과거분사를, 사물을 수식하거나 서술할 때는 현재분사를 쓰는 데 수식을 받는 명사가 사람(Applicants)이므로 정답은 과거분사 형태의 형용사 (C) attracted이다.

어휘   applicant 지원자 ｜ reach out 연락하다 ｜ Human Resources Department 인사부

17. 리조트의 개선된 예약 시스템은 고객들이 인터넷을 통해 예약할 수 있게 한다.

해설   소유격 's와 명사 booking system 사이에 빈칸이 있으므로, 빈칸에는 형용사가 들어가야 한다. 형용사는 (A)와 (D)가 가능한데, '개선하는' 예약 시스템이 아니라 '개선된' 예약 시스템이므로 정답은 (A) renovated이다.

어휘   renovate 개조(보수)하다 ｜ enable 가능하게 하다 ｜ reservation 예약

18. 후기에 따르면, 새로운 소프트웨어 패키지는 신뢰할 수 있고 사용하기 편리해 보인다.

해설   빈칸은 2형식 동사 appears의 주격 보어 자리로 형용사가 들어가야 한다. 동사 rely '의존하다'의 분사 형용사 (A)와 (B)는 보통 전치사 on(upon)과 함께 동사구로 쓰인다. 문맥상 새로운 소프트웨어가 신뢰할 수 있는 것처럼 보인다는 의미가 적절하므로 (C) reliable이 정답이다.

어휘 reliable 신뢰할 수 있는 | according to ~에 따르면

19. 창고에 보관된 모든 패키지는 사전 통보 없이 폐기될 것이다.

해설 문장에 이미 will be thrown away라는 동사가 있기 때문에 동사인 (C)와 (D)는 정답이 될 수 없고, 분사인 (A)와 (B) 중 선택해야 한다. 상자가 '보관되는' 것이며, 빈칸 뒤에 목적어도 없으므로 과거분사인 (A) stored가 정답이다.

어휘 storage room 창고 | throw away 폐기하다 | notice 통보

20. 직원들은 연례 회의에서 최고 경영자의 감동적인 연설에 동기부여를 받았다.

해설 빈칸은 2형식 동사 be동사 뒤 보어 자리이므로 형용사가 들어가야 한다. 감정을 나타내는 분사 형용사는 주어가 사람일 때는 과거분사 형태로 쓰인다. 따라서, 정답은 (B) motivated이다.

어휘 inspiring 감동적인

UNIT 15. 비교

핵심 문제 유형

본서 p.158

1. (B)　　**2.** (C)　　**3.** (B)　　**4.** (B)

Q1. 그 직원은 가능한 한 빨리 업무를 끝냈다.

해설 빈칸은 목적어 뒤에서 동사를 수식하는 부사 자리이고 as ~ as 사이에는 원급만 쓰일 수 있으므로 (B) quickly가 정답이다.

어휘 task 업무 | as quickly as possible 가능한 한 빨리

Q2. 새 모델은 에너지 효율성 면에서 이전 모델보다 더 효율적이다.

해설 빈칸은 보어 자리이고 비교 대상인 than the old one이 있으므로 비교급인 (C) more efficient가 정답이다.

어휘 model 모델 | efficient 효율적인 | in terms of ~의 관점에서 | efficiency 효율

Q3. 모든 후보자 중에서 제니퍼가 국제 마케팅에서의 폭넓은 경험을 가지고 있어서 가장 자격이 있다.

해설 전치사 among 뒤에는 셋 이상의 후보자가 있으므로 최상급 비교인 (B) the most가 정답이다.

어휘 candidate 후보 | qualified 자격을 갖춘 | extensive 폭넓은 | experience 경험 | international 국제적인

Q4. 구형 모델은 더 이상 구매할 수 없다.

해설 이미 완전한 문장이므로 빈칸은 부사 자리이다. 문맥상 관용 표현 no longer '더 이상 ~하지 않는다'를 완성하는 (B) longer가 정답이다.

어휘 available 이용할 수 있는 | purchase 구매하다

Practice

본서 p.162

1. (A)	**2.** (D)	**3.** (A)	**4.** (D)	**5.** (D)
6. (D)	**7.** (B)	**8.** (C)	**9.** (A)	**10.** (C)
11. (A)	**12.** (C)	**13.** (C)	**14.** (C)	**15.** (A)
16. (D)	**17.** (B)	**18.** (C)	**19.** (D)	**20.** (B)

1. 그 무역 기구는 NY 엑스포 홀보다 훨씬 더 큰 회의 장소를 찾고 있다.

해설 비교급 앞에 빈칸이므로 비교급 강조 표현을 써야 한다. 비교급은 much, still, a lot, far, even으로 강조할 수 있으므로 정답은 (A) much이다.

어휘 trade organization 무역 기구 | meeting location 회의 장소

2. 온라인 광고는 게시 비용이 낮기 때문에 일반적으로 인쇄 광고보다 더 저렴하다.

해설 2형식 동사 are이 있으므로, 빈칸은 주격 보어 자리로 상태 설명 형용사가 와야 한다. 형용사는 (C)와 (D)인데, 뒤에 than이 있으므로 비교급을 찾으라는 말이다. 따라서 정답은 (D) more reasonable이다.

어휘 generally 일반적으로 | reasonable 저렴한 | cost 비용

3. 프로젝트 매니저들은 제안서를 검토한 후 더 확실하게 안심했다.

해설 이미 수동태의 완벽한 문장이므로 빈칸은 부사 자리이다. 따라서 정답은 (A) completely이다.

어휘 reassure 안심시키다 | review 검토하다 | proposal 제안서

4. 존슨 엔터프라이즈에서는 누구도 데이비드 박보다 더 성실하게 새 태블릿 출시를 위한 발표를 준비하지 않았다.

해설 빈칸 뒤에 than이 있으므로 비교급을 써야 하며, 이미 3형식 문장이 나와 있으므로 정답은 부사인 (D) more diligently이다.

어휘 prepare 준비하다 | presentation 발표 | release 출시 | diligently 부지런히

5. 새로운 애플리케이션은 직원들이 이전 방법에 비해 더 정확하게 고객의 의견을 평가할 수 있게 해준다.

해설 빈칸은 동사 assess를 수식하는 부사 자리이며, 빈칸 뒤에 than이 있으므로 비교급 부사인 (D) more precisely가 정답이다.

어휘 assess 평가하다 | comment 의견 | method 방법

6. 이 씨는 다른 후보자들 중에서 가장 적합한 것 같다.

해설 to be는 to부정사이지만, 동사의 성질 때문에 상태 설명이 필요하다. be동사는 2형식 동사이므로 빈칸은 보어 자리이므로 형용사 (D) suitable이 정답이다.

어휘 seem ~인 것 같다 | candidate 후보자 | suitable 적합한

7. 리버사이드 여관은 이 지역의 많은 숙소 중 가장 매력적인 곳이다.

해설 2형식 동사 is 뒤에 빈칸이 있으므로 주격 보어 자리, 즉 상태 설명 형용사가 적합한 자리이다. 보기 중 형용사는 (A)와 (B)인데, the 뒤에는

최상급을 써야 하고, of라는 전치사는 '~사이에서 가장'이라는 최상급의 의미를 찾으라는 힌트이다. 따라서 정답은 (B) most charming이다.

어휘 region 지역 ㅣ lodge 여관 ㅣ **charming** 매력적인

8. 요즘 많은 고객 이슈가 과거보다 더 빨리 해결되고 있다.

해설 빈칸 뒤에 비교 구문인 than이 와 있으므로 부사 quickly의 비교급을 완성하는 (C) more가 정답이다.

어휘 client 고객 ㅣ issue 문제 ㅣ **these days** 요즘 ㅣ address 해결하다 ㅣ quickly 빨리

9. 글로바테크는 자사 기기가 경쟁사에서 만든 것들보다 열등하다는 것을 인정한다.

해설 비교의 뜻이지만 than이 아닌 to를 사용하는 관용 표현 inferior to '~보다 열등한'을 기억해 두자. 따라서, 정답은 (A) to이다.

어휘 acknowledge 인정하다 ㅣ device 장치

10. 기차가 60분 이상 지연되었기 때문에 회의 일정이 재조정되었다.

해설 「more than」은 '~이상'이라는 뜻으로 정답은 (C) than이다.

어휘 conference 회의 ㅣ reschedule 일정을 재조정하다 ㅣ late 늦은

11. 김 씨는 지난 시즌에 구입한 것만큼 튼튼한 배낭을 선호한다.

해설 as와 as 사이에 빈칸이 있으므로 원급이 필요한데, 형용사인 (A)와 부사인 (D)가 있다. a backpack 뒤에 '주격 관계대명사 + be동사'인 which is가 생략되어 있다는 것을 간파하고 be동사 뒤 보어 자리에 형용사인 (A) sturdy를 정답으로 선택해야 한다.

어휘 prefer 선호하다 ㅣ backpack 배낭 ㅣ sturdy 튼튼한 ㅣ purchase 구매하다

12. 아르고틱스의 주요 품목은 퓨전 테크의 것보다 더 저렴하다.

해설 빈칸 앞에 형용사 cheap의 비교급인 cheaper가 있으므로 '~보다'라는 뜻의 비교 구문을 완성하는 (C) than이 정답이다.

어휘 item 품목

13. 메이플 셔틀의 공항 데려다 주기 서비스는 경쟁사들보다 더 효율적이다.

해설 비교 구문 more ~ than은 문장 성분에 영향을 주지 않으므로 걸어내면, 빈칸은 be동사 뒤 보어 자리이며, 주어(airport drop-off service)를 설명해주는 형용사가 들어가야 하므로 (C) efficient가 정답이다.

어휘 **drop-off** (어떤 장소에) ~을 내려주는 것 ㅣ efficient 효율적인 ㅣ rival 경쟁 상대

14. 제니스 사에 대한 이 박사의 최신 보고서는 주주들에게 동기를 부여하고 있다.

해설 소유격 's 뒤에 명사 report가 있으므로 그 사이에는 형용사가 와야 하며, 'Zenith 사에 관한 최신 보고서'란 의미가 적절하므로 (C) latest가 정답이다.

어휘 report 보고서 ㅣ motivate 동기를 부여하다 ㅣ shareholder 주주

15. 제논 사는 지난 몇 년 동안 스마트폰 부품 생산에 더 단단히 전념하게 되었다.

해설 more는 문장 성분에 영향을 주지 않으므로 걸어내면, 빈칸은 형용사 committed를 수식하는 부사 자리이므로 (A) tightly가 정답이다.

어휘 become 되다 ㅣ committed 전념하는 ㅣ produce 생산하다

16. 의도치 않은 손상을 방지하기 위해 사용할 수 있는 가장 안전한 배송 자재를 선택하는 것이 중요하다.

해설 정관사 the와 명사 shipping materials 사이에 빈칸이 있으므로 빈칸에는 형용사 자리인데, 최상급을 강조하는 available이 명사 shipping materials를 뒤에서 수식하고 있으므로 (D) safest가 정답이다.

어휘 crucial 중요한 ㅣ select 선택하다 ㅣ **shipping material** 배송자재 ㅣ available 사용 가능한 ㅣ unintended 의도치 않은 ㅣ harm 손상

17. 작년 모델에 비해, 테크프로의 새로운 노트북은 훨씬 더 가볍다.

해설 2형식 동사 is가 나왔으므로 빈칸은 주격 보어 자리로 상태 설명 형용사가 와야 된다. significantly는 비교급을 강조 부사이고, 비교 구문의 more가 와 있으므로 비교급 형용사 (B) lighter가 정답이다.

어휘 **compared to** ~와 비교하여 ㅣ **significantly** 상당히 ㅣ light 가벼운

18. 제타 전자는 최근 시장에서 가장 소형의 노트북을 출시했다.

해설 빈칸이 정관사 the와 명사 laptop 사이에 있으므로 형용사가 필요한데, '시장에서(in the market)'라는 범위를 한정하는 표현으로 미루어 최상급을 찾으라는 의미임을 알 수 있다. 따라서, 정답은 (C) most compact이다.

어휘 recently 최근에 ㅣ launch 출시하다 ㅣ compact 소형의

19. 알파인 트랜스포트는 이 지역에서 가장 광범위한 철도 시스템을 구축하는 것을 목표로 한다.

해설 정관사 the와 명사 system 사이에 빈칸이 있으므로 빈칸은 형용사 자리이다. 형용사는 (C)와 (D)이다. 빈칸 앞에 the가 있으므로 비교급이 아닌 최상급이 정답이다. 따라서 정답은 (D) most widespread이다.

어휘 aim 목표로 하다 ㅣ establish 구축하다 ㅣ region 지역

20. 선셋 에어라인은 로스앤젤레스에서 샌프란시스코까지 가장 저렴한 항공편을 제공하는 것으로 유명하다.

해설 정관사 the와 명사 flights 사이에 빈칸이 있으므로 빈칸에는 형용사가 와야 한다. 형용사는 (B)뿐이고, 빈칸 앞에 the가 있으므로 최상급으로 쓰였음을 알 수 있다. 따라서 정답은 (B) most affordable이다.

어휘 **renowned** 유명한 ㅣ **provide** 제공하다 ㅣ **flight** 항공편 ㅣ **affordable** 저렴한

REVIEW TEST 04

본서 p.164

1. (D)	2. (D)	3. (D)	4. (C)	5. (B)
6. (B)	7. (A)	8. (D)	9. (A)	10. (B)
11. (A)	12. (B)	13. (D)	14. (A)	15. (B)
16. (C)	17. (B)	18. (A)	19. (D)	20. (B)
21. (A)	22. (C)	23. (C)	24. (C)	25. (C)
26. (D)	27. (C)	28. (B)	29. (C)	30. (B)

1. 회사는 신제품 라인을 출시하여 시장 점유율을 높이려는 시도를 할 것이다.

해설 빈칸은 명사구(its market share)를 목적어로 취하는 준동사 자리이고, 빈칸 앞의 attempt는 to부정사의 수식을 받는 명사이므로 (D) to increase가 정답이다.

어휘 make an attempt to do ~하는 것을 시도하다 | market share 시장 점유율 | launch 출시하다

2. 새 소프트웨어는 이전 버전보다 더 신뢰할 수 있어 오류가 적게 발생한다.

해설 빈칸 뒤에 than이 와 있으므로 비교급을 완성하는 부사 (D) more가 정답이다

어휘 reliable 믿을 수 있는, 신뢰할 수 있는 | result in ~을 야기하다, ~ 결과를 낳다

3. 식물원을 둘러보고자 하시는 고객들께서는 온라인이나 정문에서 티켓을 구매하실 수 있습니다.

해설 wish는 to부정사를 목적어로 취하는 동사이므로 정답은 (D) to explore이다.

어휘 botanical garden 식물원 | explore 답사하다, 탐구하다

4. 직원들은 자신의 기술을 향상시키기 위해 다가오는 교육 세션에 참여하도록 권장된다.

해설 동사 encourage는 「encourage + 목적어 + to부정사」의 형태로 목적격 보어 자리에 to부정사를 취하므로 수동태로 쓰일 때 「be encouraged to부정사」의 구조를 갖는다. 따라서 (C) to participate가 정답이다.

어휘 encourage 권장하다, 장려하다 | upcoming 다가오는, 곧 있을 | enhance 향상시키다 | skill 기술, 기량

5. 신제품을 개발하기 전에, X판도 사는 광범위한 조사를 했다.

해설 전치사 Before 다음에는 명사나 동명사가 와야 한다. to부정사는 전치사 뒤에 올 수 없으므로 (D)는 탈락이다. 빈칸 뒤에 명사가 또 있다는 것은 동명사의 목적어라는 의미이므로 정답은 동명사 (B) developing이다.

어휘 extensive 광범위한, 폭넓은 | develop 개발하다, 발달시키다

6. 컨설턴트에 의해 작성된 보고서는 생산성 향상을 위한 권장 사항을 포함하고 있다.

해설 빈칸은 문장의 주어인 report를 뒤에서 수식하는 자리로 보기 중 과거분사 (B) prepared와 현재분사 (C) preparing이 가능한데, 의미상 보고서는 준비되는 대상이며, 빈칸 뒤에 목적어 없이 전명구(by the consultant)가 연결되어 있다는 점에서 수동의 의미를 갖는 과거분사 (B) prepared가 정답이다.

어휘 contain 포함하다 | recommendation 권고(사항) | improve 개선하다 | productivity 생산성

7. 그 회사의 주 공장은 다음 달에 생산량을 증가시키는 것을 계획하고 있다.

해설 빈칸은 타동사 plan의 목적어 자리이다. 빈칸 뒤에는 increase의 목적어가 있으므로 명사 (C), (D)는 정답이 될 수 없다. 또한, 동사 plan은 동명사와는 쓰이지 않기 때문에 (B)도 답이 될 수 없다. 따라서, to부정사 (A) to increase가 정답이다.

어휘 plant 공장

8. 회의실을 예약하기 위한 요청서는 접수 담당자에게 제출되어야 한다.

해설 빈칸은 주어 자리로 명사가 온다. 명사는 (A), (B), (D)이다. 동명사는 뒤에 목적어(명사)가 나와야 하는데, 빈칸 뒤에 명사가 없으므로 (B)는 탈락이다. 또한 request는 가산 명사이므로 a request 또는 requests를 써야 하므로 정답은 (D) Requests이다.

어휘 reserve 예약하다 | submit 제출하다 | receptionist 접수 담당자 | request 요청, 신청서, 요청하다

9. 제안된 합병에 대한 보고서가 내일 발표될 것이다.

해설 정관사 the와 명사 merger 사이에 빈칸이 있으므로 빈칸에는 형용사가 온다. 형용사는 (A)와 (B)가 가능한데, '제안하는 합병'이 아니고 '제안된 합병'이므로 정답은 (A) proposed이다.

어휘 merger 합병 | release 발표하다 | propose 제안하다 | proposal 제안(서)

10. LPS 중공업은 신제품이 소매 시장에서 성공을 거두기를 바란다.

해설 부정관사 a 다음에는 명사가 와야 하므로 빈칸은 명사 자리이다. 명사는 (B)와 (D)인데, 동명사는 부정관사와 함께 쓸 수 없으므로 정답은 (B) success이다.

어휘 retail 소매, 소매하다 | marketplace 시장 | succeed 성공하다 | success 성공 | successfully 성공적으로

11. 발표자는 연설 중 당황스러운 실수를 저질러 청중을 웃게 만들었다.

해설 빈칸은 명사 mistake를 수식하는 형용사 자리로, 보기 중 형용사 자리에 들어갈 수 있는 (A) embarrassing과 (B) embarrassed가 정답 후보인데, embarrass는 '~을 당황시키다'라는 의미의 감정동사로서 감정동사는 주로 사물을 수식/서술하면 현재분사를, 사람을 수식/서술하면 과거분사를 쓴다. 따라서 현재분사 (A) embarrassing이 정답이다.

어휘 presenter 발표자 | make a mistake 실수하다 | speech 연설 | cause 야기시키다 | audience 청중

12. 매니저는 오류를 피하기 위해 팀에게 가능한 한 정확하게 프로젝트를 완료해 달라고 요청했다.

해설 '~만큼 …한'을 의미하는 as …as는 원급 비교 구문으로 as ~ as 사이에는 원급 형용사/부사가 들어가는데, 수식/서술의 대상을 파악하여 원급 형용사를 고를지, 원급 부사를 고를지 결정해야 한다. 문맥상 수식하는 대상이 동사 complete이고, 동사를 수식하는 품사는 부사이므로 (B) accurately가 정답이다.

어휘 complete 완료하다 | avoid 피하다 | error 오류, 실수

13. 모든 데이터를 수집한 후, 분석가는 경영 팀을 위한 상세한 보고서를 작성했다.

해설 문장 맨 앞에 접속사 없이 빈칸이 와 있고, 콤마 뒤의 주절과 연결되어야 할 때 접속사와 주어가 생략되고 주절과 연결될 수 있도록 동사가 현재분사 또는 과거분사로 바뀌는 분사구문을 떠올릴 수 있어야 한다. 이때 주로 빈칸 뒤에 목적어가 있으면 능동의 현재분사를, 목적어가 없으면 수동의 과거분사를 선택하면 되는데, 빈칸 뒤에 목적어로서 명사구(all the data)가 와 있으므로 현재분사 (D) Collecting이 정답이다.

어휘 analyst 분석가 | detailed 상세한, 세부적인 | management 경영, 관리

14. 철강의 공급 과잉이 공급 가격을 매우 매력적으로 만들어 주었다.

해설 make는 5형식 동사로 목적어로 supplier prices가 왔다. 빈칸은 목적격 보어 자리로 상태 설명 형용사가 와야 한다. 형용사인 (A)와 (C) 중에서 목적어와의 관계를 봤을 때, '공급 가격들이 매료된 것'은 문맥상 적합하지 않으므로 정답은 (A) attractive이다.

어휘 oversupply 공급 과잉 | steel 철강 | supplier price 공급 가격 | attractive 매력적인

15. 적절한 안전 예방 조치는 작업장의 모든 사고를 예방 가능하게 해 줄 것이다.

해설 동사 make는 5형식 동사이며 빈칸은 목적격 보어 자리이므로 형용사 (B) preventable이 정답이다.

어휘 proper 적절한, 제대로 | safety precaution 안전 예방 조치 | preventable 막을 수 있는, 예방할 수 있는

16. 모든 승객들은 탑승 요원에게 그들의 탑승권과 여권을 보여줄 것을 요구받는다.

해설 ask는 5형식 동사로 목적격 보어 자리에 to부정사를 취한다. ask를 수동태로 썼으므로 목적어는 빠지고 바로 목적격 보어 to부정사가 왔다. 따라서 정답은 (C) present이다.

어휘 boarding agent 탑승 요원 | present 제시하다

17. B.N. 사는 경험 있고 동기 부여된 직원들을 찾고 있다.

해설 명사인 employees 앞에서 형용사 두 개가 and로 대등하게 연결된 형태이므로 정답은 (B) experienced이다.

어휘 seek 찾다 | motivated 동기 부여된, 자극 받은 | experienced 경험 있는, 능숙한

18. 멀베리 로의 모든 건물들은 두 대의 차량을 주차할 수 있는 진입로를 갖추고 있다.

해설 전치사(of)와 명사구(two vehicles) 사이는 전치사의 목적어로서 명사

의 기능과 명사구를 목적어로 취하는 동사의 기능을 동시에 할 수 있는 동명사 자리이므로 (A) parking이 정답이다.

어휘 property 건물; 부동산 | driveway 진입로 | capable of ~을 할 수 있는

19. 그 회사의 부사장은 우리 발표에 완전히 만족했다.

해설 was 뒤에 형용사 보어 자리이다. 동사 (A)와 (B)는 탈락이고 분사형 중에서 '사람이 만족하다'라는 의미로 수동의 의미가 있으므로 정답은 (D) satisfied이다.

어휘 completely 완전히

20. 젠하르트 자동차는 현재 공급 추적 소프트웨어의 교체를 고려하고 있다.

해설 빈칸은 consider의 목적어 자리로 to부정사와는 함께 쓰이지 않기 때문에, 명사의 역할을 할 수 있는 동명사 (B)와 (C)가 정답이 될 수 있다. 그런데 change의 목적어 their supply tracking software가 있으므로 능동 형태인 (B) changing이 정답이다.

어휘 currently 현재 | supply tracking software 공급 추적 소프트웨어

21. 위원회의 추천 사항 중 하나가 즉시 시행될 것이다.

해설 정관사 the 뒤에는 명사가 와야 하는데, 동명사는 관사와 함께 쓸 수 없으므로 (B)는 정답이 될 수 없다. 「one of the + 복수 명사」 형태로 (A)와 (C)가 가능한데, 위원회에 의해서 만들어진 '추천자'가 아니고, '추천 사항'이므로 정답은 (A) recommendations이다.

어휘 implement 시행하다 | recommendation 추천, 추천서

22. 우리의 새 사무실 의자는 이전 모델과 같은 수준의 편안함을 제공한다.

해설 빈칸 앞의 the same을 보고 원급 비교 표현인 「the same + 명사 + as」를 떠올릴 수 있어야 한다. 따라서 (C) as가 정답이다.

어휘 comfort 편안함, 안락함 | previous 이전의

23. 학회에서 전문성 개발 방법을 가르치는 것에 관심이 있는 사람들은 10월 10일까지 등록해야 한다.

해설 전치사 뒤에는 명사나 동명사가 와야 하고, to부정사는 올 수 없으므로 (A)는 탈락이다. 따라서 정답은 (C) teaching이다.

어휘 professional development 전문성 개발

24. 안티바이러스 소프트웨어는 외부 장치에 연결되면 알림을 보낸다.

해설 접속사 뒤에 주어 없이 동사의 알맞은 형태를 묻는다면 주절의 주어(antivirus software)와 동일하여 생략하고, 동사를 현재분사나 과거분사로 바꾸는 분사구문을 떠올릴 수 있어야 한다. 이때 주로 빈칸 뒤에 목적어가 있으면 능동의 현재분사를, 목적어가 없으면 수동의 과거분사를 선택하면 되는데, 빈칸 뒤에 목적어 없이 전명구(to an external device)가 와 있으므로 과거분사 (C) connected가 정답이다.

어휘 alert 경보, 알림 | external 외부의 | device 장치

25. 최신 스마트폰 모델은 이전 버전보다 훨씬 더 빠르며, 향상된 성능을 제공한다.

PART 5 ▶ REVIEW TEST 04

해설　빈칸 뒤에 비교급 faster than이 쓰인 것으로 미루어 빈칸은 비교급 수식 부사 자리임을 알 수 있고, '훨씬'의 의미로 쓰이는 비교급 강조 부사로는 even, much, still, far, a lot이 있으므로 (C) even이 정답이다.

어휘　latest 최신의 | previous 이전의 | improved 개선된, 향상된 | performance 성능

26. 존스 씨는 내일 회의에서 초대받은 청중들에게 연설할 것이다.

해설　명사 audience 앞에 빈칸이 있으므로 형용사가 들어가야 한다. 형용사는 (C)와 (D)인데, '초대하는 청중들'이 아니고 '초대된 청중들'이므로 정답은 (D) invited이다.

어휘　give a speech 연설하다 | audience 청중

27. 행사의 가장 중요한 후원 업체들은 인델전 사와 M&K 사이다.

해설　정관사 The 뒤에 명사가 있으므로 빈칸은 형용사 자리이다. 따라서 정답은 (C) most prominent이다.

어휘　sponsor 후원업체, 후원자 | prominent 중요한, 현저한

28. 마케팅 팀은 기한을 맞추기 위해 프로젝트를 효율적으로 완료하는 데 집중하고 있다.

해설　빈칸은 전치사와 동명사 사이에 위치해 있으며 생략해도 문장 성분에 영향을 주지 않는 부사 자리이다. 동명사를 수식하는 품사 역시 부사이므로 (B) efficiently가 정답이다.

어휘　meet the deadline 기한을 맞추다

29. 수익 감소는 추가로 영업 사원을 고용하는 것을 어느 때보다 더 어렵게 만들었다.

해설　make는 5형식 동사로 가목적어는 it이고 진목적어는 to부정사 이하이다. 빈칸은 목적격 보어 자리로 상태 설명 형용사가 들어가야 한다. 형용사는 (A)와 (C)가 가능하지만 than이 있으므로 정답은 (C) harder이다.

어휘　decline 감소 | sales associate 영업 사원 | hard 어려운

30. 제품에 대한 수요가 높을수록 회사는 그 제품의 생산에 더 많은 자원을 할당한다.

해설　「the+최상급」을 생각하고, (C) highest를 고르면 안 된다. 「The+비교급 ~, the+비교급」은 '~할수록 점점 더 …하다'란 의미의 비교급 관용 표현이므로 (B) higher가 정답이다.

어휘　demand 수요 | resource 자원 | allocate 할당하다 | production 생산

VOCA

UNIT 01. 동사 어휘

핵심 문제 유형

본서 p.170

1. (C)　　**2.** (D)　　**3.** (A)　　**4.** (B)　　**5.** (B)

1. 폭우에도 불구하고, 센트럴 파크의 콘서트는 연기되지 않을 것이다.

해설　빈칸은 수동태 『be + p.p.』구조를 묻는 문제이다. 수동태 구조의 주어는 능동태 문장의 목적어였기 때문에 주어와 문맥상 어울리는 동사 어휘를 찾아야 한다. 앞에 수식어구(Despite ~) 내용과 주어 the concert를 고려했을 때 '폭우에도 불구하고 콘서트가 연기되지 않을 것이다'란 해석이 자연스럽기 때문에 (C) delayed가 정답이 된다.

어휘　despite ~에도 불구하고 | heavy rain 폭우 | delay 연기 시키다

2. 도서관 카드를 받으려면, 신청자는 양식과 사진이 있는 유효한 신분증을 제출해야 한다.

해설　빈칸은 to부정사에 속한 동사를 찾는 문제이며 빈칸 뒤에 목적어인 a library card는 빈칸에 들어갈 동사의 목적어이므로 목적어와 가장 어울리는 동사 어휘를 찾는 게 핵심인데, 도서관 카드를 (A) 홍보하거나 승진하는 것도, (B) 추천하는 것도, (C) 완료하는 것도 어울리지 않는다. 즉, obtain a library card '도서관 카드를 얻다'라는 표현을 완성하는 (D) obtain이 정답이다.

어휘　obtain 얻다 | applicant 지원자 | present 보여주다 | form 양식 | valid 유효한

3. 두 회사는 새 프로젝트에서 협력하기로 합의했다.

해설　이 문제의 경우 문맥으로 답을 선택할 수도 있지만, 문법적으로 접근했을 때 빈칸 뒤에 전치사가 있으므로 on과 짝을 이루는 자동사 어휘 문제이다. 따라서 cooperate on '~에 대해 협력하다'라는 표현을 완성하는 (A) cooperate가 정답이다. 나머지 선택지들은 동사 뒤의 전치사 없이 목적어가 바로 오는 타동사들이므로 정답이 될 수 없다.

어휘　firm 회사 | agree 동의하다 | cooperate 협력하다

4. 이 쿠폰으로 고객은 옷을 반값에 구매할 수 있다.

해설　모든 동사 어휘를 해석을 하지 않아도 문장 구조가 「동사 + 목적어 + to부정사」이므로 목적격 보어 자리에 to부정사를 취하는 「allow + 목적어 + to do」 '~가 ~하는 것을 가능하게 하다'라는 표현을 완성하는 (B) allow가 정답이다.

어휘　voucher 쿠폰 | allow 허용하다 | customer 고객 | clothes 옷 | half price 반값

5. 관리자는 직원들에게 새로운 사무실 정책을 알렸다.

해설　문맥상 (A) 발표하다와 (B) 알리다가 비슷해 보이지만 이 문제의 핵심은 동사 뒤의 목적어 자리에 사람(~에게)을 취할 수 있는 동사를 찾는 문제이다. 따라서 「inform + 사람 + of 명사」 '~에게 ~을 알려주다'의 표현을 완성하는 (B) informed가 정답이다. 같은 의미의 (A)는 동사 바로 뒤 목적어 자리에 사람 명사를 취할 수 없으므로 정답이 될 수 없다.

어휘   manager 관리자 ǀ inform 알리다 ǀ employee 직원 ǀ office policy 사무실 정책

Practice

1. (A)	2. (B)	3. (C)	4. (B)	5. (B)
6. (C)	7. (B)	8. (A)	9. (B)	10. (C)
11. (B)	12. (B)	13. (A)	14. (A)	15. (D)
16. (C)	17. (C)	18. (D)	19. (C)	20. (B)

1. 되도록 빨리 배송품을 수령했음을 알려주세요.

해설   배송품을 수령했음을 되도록 빨리 알려달라는 의미가 적절하므로, '받았음을 알리다'라는 뜻의 (A) acknowledge가 정답이다. acknowledge the receipt of '~의 수령을 알리다'를 덩어리째 기억해두자.

어휘   receipt 수령 ǀ shipment 배송 ǀ as soon as possible 되도록 빨리 ǀ acknowledge (편지, 소포 등을) 받았음을 알리다 ǀ return 반품시키다, 반납하다 ǀ send 보내다 ǀ deliver 배달하다

2. 새 기계를 작동하기 전에 매뉴얼을 참조해야 한다.

해설   기계를 작동하기 전에 매뉴얼을 참고하라는 의미가 적절하므로 '참고하다'라는 뜻의 (B) consult가 정답이다. consult the manual '매뉴얼을 참고하다'를 덩어리째 기억해두자.

어휘   operate 작동하다, 조작하다 ǀ machinery 기계(류) ǀ manual 설명서, 매뉴얼 ǀ reject 거절하다 ǀ consult 찾아보다, 참고하다 ǀ recognize 알아보다, 인정하다 ǀ issue 발행하다

3. 회사는 다음 분기부터 새 복장 규정 정책을 시행할 계획이다.

해설   다음 분기부터 새 복장 규정 정책을 시행한다는 의미가 적절하므로 '시행하다'라는 뜻의 (C) implement가 정답이다. implement the policy '정책을 시행하다'를 덩어리째 암기해두자.

어휘   plan to do ~할 계획이다 ǀ dress code 복장 규정 ǀ policy 정책, 방침 ǀ quarter 사분기 ǀ demonstrate 입증하다 ǀ delay 지연시키다 ǀ implement 시행하다, 실시하다 ǀ cancel 취소하다

4. 모든 후보자는 해당 직위에 고려되기 위해 요건을 충족해야 한다.

해설   특정 직책에 고려되기 위해 요건을 충족해야 한다는 의미가 적절하므로 '충족시키다'라는 뜻의 (B) meet가 정답이다. meet the requirement '요건을 충족하다'를 덩어리째 기억해두자.

어휘   candidate (일자리의) 후보자 ǀ requirement 필요조건, 요건 ǀ consider 고려하다 ǀ position 직책 ǀ indicate 가리키다, 나타내다 ǀ meet 충족시키다 ǀ exceed 초과하다 ǀ avoid 피하다

5. 직원들의 우려 사항은 월례 회의에서 다루어질 것이다.

해설   우려 사항들이 회의에서 다루어질 거라는 의미가 적절하므로 '(일, 문제 등을) 다루다, 처리하다'라는 의미의 (B) addressed가 정답이다.

어휘   concern 걱정, 우려 ǀ monthly 한 달에 한 번의, 월례의 ǀ relocate 이전하다 ǀ address (일, 문제 등을) 다루다, 처리하다 ǀ dismiss 해고하다 ǀ overlook 간과하다; 내려다보다

6. 자금은 부서의 요구에 따라 배정될 것이다.

해설   자금은 부서의 요구에 따라 배정될 것이라는 의미가 적절하므로 '할당하다'라는 뜻의 (C) allocated가 정답이다.

어휘   fund 자금 ǀ department 부서 ǀ needs 요구 ǀ request 요청하다 ǀ arrange 마련하다. (일을) 처리하다, 정리(배열)하다 ǀ allocate 할당하다 ǀ inspect 조사하다

7. 새 사무실 건물의 공사가 다음 달에 시작될 예정이다.

해설   건물 공사가 다음 달에 시작될 거라는 의미가 적절하므로 '시작하다'라는 뜻이 (B) commence가 정답이다.

어휘   construction 건설, 공사 ǀ be scheduled to do ~하기로 예정되어 있다 ǀ accommodate 수용하다 ǀ commence 시작하다 ǀ present 보여주다 ǀ compensate 보상하다

8. 팀은 연례 보고서를 위한 데이터를 편집하고 있다.

해설   연례 보고서를 위한 데이터를 편집한다는 의미가 적절하므로 '(문서 등을) 엮다, 편집하다'라는 뜻의 (A) compile이 정답이다.

어휘   annual 연례의 ǀ report 보고서 ǀ compile 엮다, 편집하다 ǀ extend 연장하다 ǀ register 등록하다 ǀ appoint 임명하다

9. 재무 보고서는 프로젝트 중 발생한 모든 비용을 반영할 것이다.

해설   프로젝트 중에 발생된 모든 비용을 재무보고서에서 설명할 거란 의미로, 빈칸 뒤 전치사 for의 짝꿍 동사는 보기 중 (B) account뿐이다. account for '~을 설명하다'를 덩어리째 기억해두자.

어휘   financial report 재무 보고서 ǀ expense 비용 ǀ incur 초래하다 ǀ adhere to ~을 고수하다 ǀ account for ~을 설명하다 ǀ comply with ~을 준수하다 ǀ collaborate with ~와 협력하다

10. 직원들은 건강을 개선하기 위해 회사의 웰니스 프로그램에서 혜택을 받을 수 있다.

해설   직원들이 회사의 건강 프로그램으로부터 혜택을 받을 수 있다는 의미로, 빈칸 뒤 전치사 from의 짝꿍 동사는 보기 중 (C) benefit뿐이다. benefit from '~로부터 혜택을 받다'를 덩어리째 기억해두자.

어휘   wellness 건강 ǀ improve 개선하다 ǀ refer to ~을 참고하다 ǀ qualify for ~할 자격을 갖추다 ǀ benefit from ~로부터 혜택을 얻다 ǀ contribute to ~에 기여하다

11. 트레이너가 회의에서 새 소프트웨어 사용법을 시연할 것이다.

해설   회의 때 트레이너가 새 소프트웨어 사용법을 시연할 거라는 의미가 적절하므로 '보여주다, 시연하다'라는 뜻의 (B) demonstrate가 정답이다.

어휘   trainer 교육시키는 사람, 트레이너 ǀ indicate 나타내다 ǀ demonstrate 보여주다, 입증하다 ǀ locate (특정 위치에) 두다 ǀ complicate 복잡하게 만들다

12. 그 연예인은 일련의 광고들에서 자사의 신제품을 홍보하는 데 동의했다.

해설   그 연예인이 자사의 신제품을 홍보하기로 했다는 의미가 적절하므로, '홍보하다'라는 뜻의 (B) endorse가 정답이다.

PART 5 VOCA   **41**

어휘 celebrity 유명 인사, 연예인 | agree 동의하다 | a series of 일련의 | register for ~을 등록하다 | endorse 지지하다, 홍보하다 | ensure 확실히 하다, 보장하다 | refer to ~을 참고하다

13. 회사는 다음 분기에 전 직원을 대상으로 새로운 교육 프로그램을 시작할 계획이다.

해설 문맥상 '새로운 교육 프로그램을 시작하다'라는 의미가 적절하므로 (A) initiate가 정답이다.

어휘 plan to do ~할 계획이다 | quarter 사분기 | initiate 시작하다 | cooperate with ~와 협력하다 | cooperate on ~에 대해 협력하다 | enclose 동봉하다 | merge 합병하다

14. 직원들은 매니저에 의해 교육 세션에 참석하도록 권장되었다.

해설 빈칸 뒤에 to부정사가 연결되어 있는 걸 보고, to부정사를 목적어로 취할 수 있는 (B), (C), (D)를 답으로 고려하기 쉽지만, 수동태 문장(were ------- to attend)이므로 「동사 + 목적어 + to do → be p.p. to do」와 같이 목적격 보어로 to부정사를 취하는 동사를 골라야 한다. (A)가 목적격 보어로 to부정사를 취하는 대표적인 동사이며, 직원들이 참석하도록 권장되었다는 의미를 완성하므로 (A) advised가 정답이다.

어휘 attend 참석하다 | training session 연수회 | advise 권고하다, 조언하다 | refuse 거절하다 | hesitate 주저하다 | decide 결정하다

15. 매니저는 그의 팀에 마감일 전에 프로젝트를 완료하도록 촉구했다.

해설 문장 구조가 「------- + 목적어 + to do」이므로 목적격 보어 자리에 to부정사를 취할 수 있는 (D) urged가 정답이다.

어휘 finish 끝내다, 마무리짓다 | ahead of ~보다 빨리 | deadline 마감일, 기한 | secure 확보하다 | strive 분투하다 | suggest 제안하다 | urge 촉구하다

16. 경영진은 프로젝트가 일정보다 앞서 완료될 것으로 예상했다.

해설 빈칸 뒤에 목적어로 that절이 연결되어 있으므로 that절을 목적어로 취할 수 있는 (A), (C) 중에서 답을 골라야 하며, 프로젝트가 일정보다 빨리 완료될 것으로 예상했다는 의미가 적절하므로 (C) anticipated가 정답이다.

어휘 management 경영진 | complete 완료하다 | ahead of schedule 일정보다 앞서 | prove 증명하다, 입증하다 | committed 헌신적인 | anticipate 예상하다 | include 포함하다

17. 취업 비자를 얻으려면 필요한 모든 서류를 제출해야 한다.

해설 취업 비자를 얻기 위해 서류를 제출해야 한다는 의미가 적절하므로 (C) obtain이 정답이다.

어휘 work visa 근로 비자 | submit 제출하다 | necessary 필요한 | operate 운영하다 | undergo 겪다 | obtain 얻다 | oversee 감독하다

18. 회사는 구조조정에도 불구하고 여러 핵심 직원들을 유지했다.

해설 구조조정에도 불구하고 핵심 직원들을 유지했다는 의미가 적절하므로 (D) retained가 정답이다.

어휘 key 가장 중요한, 핵심적인 | despite ~에도 불구하고 | restructuring 구조조정 | proceed (계속) 진행하다 | represent 대표하다 | reserve 예약하다; 보류하다 | retain 유지하다, 보유하다

19. 마케팅 팀은 다음 달에 신제품을 출시할 계획이다.

해설 신제품을 출시할 계획이라는 의미가 적절하므로 (C) release가 정답이다. (A)는 「replace A with B」 'A를 B로 교체하다'의 패턴을 취하며, (B)는 뒤에 사람 목적어가 온다. 「notify + 사람 + of / that절」 형태도 기억해두자.

어휘 plan to do ~할 계획이다 | replace 교체하다 | notify 알려주다, 통보하다 | release 출시하다; 공개하다 | verify 확인하다, 입증하다

20. 회사는 연말 세일의 일환으로 신제품에 대한 배송비를 면제했다.

해설 문맥상 '연말 세일의 일환으로'와 '배송비를 면제했다'가 연결되므로 (B) waived가 정답이다.

어휘 shipping charge 배송료 | end-year sale 연말 세일 | indicate 나타내다, 보여주다 | waive 면제하다, 포기하다 | secure 확보하다; 고정시키다 | enable ~을 가능하게 하다

UNIT 02. 명사 어휘

핵심 문제 유형

본서 p.176

1. (C) **2.** (D) **3.** (B) **4.** (D) **5.** (B)

1. 18세 미만의 학생들은 해외 여행을 위해 교장의 서면 허가가 필요하다.

해설 빈칸 앞 단어인 written과 함께 교장으로부터 받는 '인증' 또는 '허가'라는 의미의 명사가 필요하다. 따라서 written authorization '서면 허가'라는 표현을 완성하는 (C) authorization이 정답이 된다.

어휘 written authorization 서면 허가 | principal 교장 | trip 여행 | abroad 해외로

2. 실험실 직원은 게시판에 있는 안전 규정을 준수해야 한다.

해설 빈칸 앞 단어 safety와 함께 쓰이는 복합 명사의 의미를 갖는 명사가 빈칸에 필요하다. 따라서, safety regulations '안전 규정'의 복합 명사 표현을 완성하는 (D) regulations가 정답이다.

어휘 lab 실험실 | staff 직원 | observe 준수하다 | safety regulations 안전 규정 | bulletin board 게시판

3. 새로운 제안은 현재 시스템에 대한 실행 가능한 대안을 제공한다.

해설 이 문제의 경우 문맥상으로 답을 선택할 수도 있지만, 문법적으로 접근했을 때 빈칸 뒤의 전치사가 있으므로 to와 짝을 이루는 명사 어휘 문제이다. 따라서 alternative to '~의 대안'라는 표현을 완성하는 (B) alternative가 정답이다.

어휘 proposal 제안 | offer 제공하다 | viable 실행 가능한 | alternative 대안 | current system 현재 시스템

4. 고객 서비스 부서는 질문에 신속히 답변하기 위해 모든 노력을 기울인다.

해설 빈칸 뒤에 to부정사가 나왔으므로 to부정사의 수식을 받는 명사 어휘를 선택해야 한다. 따라서 make every effort to '~하는 데 최선의 노력을 하다' 표현을 완성하는 (D) effort가 정답이다.

어휘 customer service 고객 서비스 | make an effort 노력하다 | quickly 빠르게

5. 행사를 계획할 때 고려해야 할 사항이 많다.

해설 빈칸은 앞에 take into와 함께 쓰이는 명사 어휘를 묻는 문제이다. 따라서 take into consideration '~을 고려하다' 표현을 완성하는 (B) consideration이 정답이다.

어휘 take into consideration 고려하다 | plan 계획하다

본서 p.178

Practice

1. (B)	**2.** (C)	**3.** (C)	**4.** (D)	**5.** (A)
6. (C)	**7.** (B)	**8.** (C)	**9.** (A)	**10.** (A)
11. (D)	**12.** (C)	**13.** (D)	**14.** (B)	**15.** (C)
16. (A)	**17.** (B)	**18.** (B)	**19.** (D)	**20.** (B)

1. 회사는 마케팅 부서의 공석을 채우는 것을 고려하고 있다.

해설 동사 fill의 목적어로서 빈칸 앞의 job과 복합 명사를 이루는 명사를 고르는 문제이다. 마케팅 부서의 공석을 채운다는 의미가 적절하므로 (B) opening이 정답이다. '공석'을 뜻하는 복합 명사 job opening을 한 단어처럼 기억해두자.

어휘 look to do ~하는 것을 고려하다 | fill 채우다 | expense 비용, 경비 | opening 빈자리, 공석 | division (조직의) 부, 분과 | description 서술, 기술

2. 지난 분기의 매출액은 상당한 성장을 보여주며, 우리의 기대를 넘어섰다.

해설 빈칸 앞의 sales와 복합 명사를 이루는 명사를 고르는 문제로, 지난 분기의 판매 수치가 기대치를 넘어섰다는 의미이므로 (C) figures가 정답이다. '판매 수치'를 뜻하는 복합 명사 sales figures를 한 단어처럼 기억해두자.

어휘 quarter 사분기 | sales 판매량, 매출액 | exceed 넘어서다, 초과하다 | expectation 기대, 예상 | show 보여주다 | significant 중요한, 의미 있는 | growth 성장 | approval 승인 | regulation 규정 | figure 수치 | capability 능력, 성능

3. 직원들은 다음 달부터 새로운 교대 근무에 적응해야 한다.

해설 빈칸 앞의 명사 work와 복합 명사를 이루는 명사를 고르는 문제로, 직원들이 새로운 교대 근무에 적응해야 한다는 의미가 적절하므로 (C) shift가 정답이다. '교대 근무'를 뜻하는 work shift를 한 단어처럼 기억해두자.

어휘 adjust to ~에 적응하다 | satisfaction 만족 | shift 교대 근무 (시간); 교대조 | compliance 준수

4. 프로젝트는 매니저의 승인이 없으면 진행될 수 없다.

해설 매니저의 승인 없이는 프로젝트가 진행될 수 없다는 의미이므로 소유격(manager's)의 수식을 받기에 적절한 명사는 (D) approval이다.

어휘 proceed 진행하다[되다] | amenities 편의 시설 | compensation 보상(금) | supplies 용품, 저장품 | approval 승인

5. 회사가 소규모 회사를 최근 인수함에 따라 시장 범위가 확대될 것이다.

해설 규모가 작은 회사의 최근 인수로 시장을 늘릴 거란 의미이므로 of a smaller firm의 수식을 받기에 적절한 명사는 (A) acquisition이다.

어휘 recent 최근의 | firm 회사 | expand 확대하다 | market reach 시장 범위 | acquisition (기업) 인수 | refusal 거절, 거부 | consent 동의, 합의 | demand 수요

6. 첫 번째 계획이 실패할 경우, 우리는 실행할 수 있는 대안을 필요로 한다.

해설 첫 번째 계획이 실패할 경우, 실행 가능한 대안이 필요하다는 의미이므로 형용사 viable의 수식을 받기에 적절한 명사는 (C) alternative 이다.

어휘 fail 실패하다 | viable 실행 가능한 | implement 시행하다 | demonstration 시연, (시범) 설명 | authority 권한; 권위자 | alternative 대안 | function 기능; 행사

7. 디자인 경연대회의 당선작은 다음 주에 발표될 예정이다.

해설 형용사 winning의 수식을 받기에 적절한 명사를 고르는 문제로, 경연대회의 당선작이 발표될 거라는 의미이므로 (B) entry가 정답이다. '당선작'을 뜻하는 winning entry를 한 단어처럼 기억해두자.

어휘 winning 이긴, 승리한 | competition (경연) 대회 | announce 발표하다 | proof 증거 | entry 출품작 | phase 단계, 국면 | caution 주의, 경계

8. 방문객들은 근무 시간 이후에 건물에 접근 요청을 해야 한다.

해설 빈칸 뒤 전치사 to와 어울리는 명사는 access to '~에 대한 접근' 즉, 건물 접근 요청을 해야 한다는 의미이므로 (C) access가 정답이다. (A)는 전치사 in과 어울려 쓰인다.

어휘 visitor 방문객 | request 요청(서) | after hours 근무시간 후에, 폐점 후에 | experience 경험, 경력 | issue 사안, 문제 | access 접근; 접속 | notice 알림, 통지

9. 공장의 운영은 안전 규정을 엄격히 준수한다.

해설 빈칸 뒤 전치사 with와 어울리는 명사는 compliance with '~에 대한 준수' 즉, 안전 규정을 준수한다는 의미이므로 (A) compliance가 정답이다. (B)는 전치사 about과 어울려 쓰인다.

어휘 operation 운영 | strict 엄격한 | safety regulation 안전 규정 | compliance 준수, 따름 | concern 관심, 우려 | permission 허가 | organization 조직, 단체

10. 매니저는 팀이 마감일을 맞출 수 있을 것이라는 자신감을 표했다.

해설 빈칸 뒤 전치사 in과 어울리는 명사는 confidence in '~에 대한 자신감' 즉, 마감일을 맞추기 위한 팀 능력에 대한 자신감을 보였다는 의미이므로 (A) confidence가 정답이다. (B)는 전치사 about과 어울려

쓰인다.

어휘 express 표현하다 | ability to do ~할 능력 | meet 맞추다, 충족시키다 | deadline 마감일, 기한 | confidence 자신감 | inquiry 질문, 문의 | innovation 혁신 | estimate 추정(치); 견적서

11. 우리는 새 프로젝트를 이끌 기술 전문 지식이 있는 사람이 필요하다.

해설 프로젝트를 이끌기 위해 기술 부문의 전문 지식을 가진 사람이 필요하다는 의미이므로 (D) expertise가 정답이다.

어휘 require 요구하다, 필요로 하다 | technical 기술적인 | lead 이끌다 | fee 수수료 | revenue 수입, 소득 | expansion 확대, 확장 | expertise 전문 지식

12. 장비의 연례 점검이 다음 달에 예정되어 있다.

해설 장비의 연례 점검이 다음 달에 예정되어 있다는 의미이므로, of the equipment의 수식을 받기에 적절한 명사는 (C) inspection이다.

어휘 annual 연례의 | equipment 장비 | be scheduled for ~로 예정되어 있다 | issue 사안, 문제 | property 부동산, 건물 | inspection 점검, 검사 | preference 선호

13. 모든 방문자들은 경비실에 유효한 신분증을 보여줘야 한다.

해설 경비실에 유효한 신분증을 보여줘야 한다는 의미이므로 형용사 valid의 수식을 받기에 적절한 명사는 (D) identification이다.

어휘 visitor 방문객 | present 보여주다; 제시하다 | valid 유효한 | security desk 경비실 | admission 입장(료) | commitment 헌신 | innovation 혁신 | identification 신원 확인; 신분증

14. 최고 경영자는 직장 효율성을 개선하기 위해 새로운 계획을 발표했다.

해설 직장 효율성 개선을 위한 새로운 계획을 발표했다는 의미이므로 (B) initiative가 정답이다.

어휘 announce 발표하다 | improve 개선하다 | workplace 직장, 업무현장 | efficiency 효율성 | impact 영향 | initiative 계획, 결단력 | expansion 확대, 확장 | sequence 순서, 연속

15. 새 직원은 여러 작업을 효율적으로 처리할 수 있는 강한 능력을 보여주었다.

해설 빈칸 뒤에 to부정사가 연결되어 있어, 먼저 to부정사를 취하는 명사를 고려해야 하는데, 보기 모두 to부정사를 동반할 수 있으므로 해석을 해봐야 한다. 다양한 업무를 효율적으로 다루는 능력을 보여줬다는 의미가 적절하므로 (C) ability가 정답이다.

어휘 employee 직원 | demonstrate 입증하다, 보여주다 | handle 다루다 | multiple 다수의, 다양한 | task 일, 과제 | efficiently 효율적으로 | intention 의도; 의사 | opportunity 기회 | ability 능력 decision 결정

16. 전 직원은 회사의 행동 규칙을 준수할 의무가 있다.

해설 빈칸 뒤에 to부정사를 동반할 수 있는 명사는 obligation to do '~할 의무' 즉, 행동 규칙을 준수할 의무가 있다는 의미이므로 (A) obligation이 정답이다

어휘 adhere to ~을 따르다[고수하다] | code 규칙, 규정 | conduct

행동; 수행 | obligation 의무 | accordance 일치, 조화 | reference 참고, 추천 | appreciation 감사

17. 사무실은 진행 중인 보수 공사로 인해 추후 공지가 있을 때까지 폐쇄된다.

해설 빈칸 앞의 until further만 보고도 (B)를 고를 수 있어야 하는 문제이다. 추후 공지가 있을 때까지 폐쇄될 거라는 의미로, 관용 표현 until further notice '추후 공지가 있을 때까지'를 완성하는 (B) notice가 정답이다.

어휘 remain 계속 ~이다 | closed 폐쇄된 | until further notice 추후 공지가 있을 때까지 | due to ~때문에 | ongoing 진행 중인 | renovation 수리, 보수 | precautions 예방조치 | notice 통지, 통보 | details 세부 사항 | development 개발

18. 회사는 작업장 안전을 개선하기 위해 새로운 정책을 시행했다.

해설 작업장 안전을 개선하기 위해 새로운 정책을 시행했다는 의미가 적절하므로 (B) policy가 정답이다.

어휘 implement 시행하다 | improve 개선하다 | workplace 작업장, 업무 현장 | safety 안전 | productivity 생산성 | policy 정책, 방침 | shift 교대 근무 (시간), 교대조 | replacement 교체(품); 후임자

19. 기차역과의 근접함은 우리의 사무실 위치를 매우 편리하게 해준다.

해설 빈칸 뒤에 전치사 to와 어울리는 명사가 보기 중 (D)이고, 기차역과 가까운 것이 사무실 위치를 편리하게 해준다는 의미이므로 (D) proximity가 정답이다.

어휘 location 위치 | convenient 편리한 | priority 우선사항, 우선권 | authority 권한; 권위자; 당국 | renovation 수리, 보수 | proximity 근접, 가까움

20. 귀하의 지원서를 뒷받침하기 위해 이전 고용주로부터 받은 추천서를 제출해 주십시오.

해설 이전 고용주의 추천서를 제출하라는 의미가 적절하므로 (B) reference가 정답이다.

어휘 provide 제공하다, 주다 | previous 이전의 | employer 고용주 | support 지지하다, 뒷받침하다 | application 지원(서) | souvenir 기념품 | reference 추천서 | representative 대표(자) | procedure 절차

UNIT 03. 형용사 어휘

핵심 문제 유형   본서 p.182

1. (A)   **2.** (B)   **3.** (B)   **4.** (B)

1. 음료는 회의 후 본관 홀에서 이용할 수 있다.

해설 빈칸은 be동사 뒤 주격 보어인 형용사의 자리이다. 주격 보어는 주어

를 보충해주는 자리이므로 문맥상 '음료가 메인홀에서 이용 가능하다'라는 해석이 어울리므로 (A) available이 정답이다.

어휘   drink 음료 | available 이용 가능한 | main hall 본관 홀 | meeting 회의

2. 최종 단계에서 결함이 있는 제품을 라인에서 제거한다.

해설   빈칸은 remove의 목적어인 명사 products를 수식하는 형용사의 자리이다. 형용사 뒤에 수식을 받는 명사가 있다면 명사와 문맥상 어울리는 어휘를 먼저 찾는 것이 중요하다. 즉, 뒤에 '제품'이란 단어와 어울리면서 앞에 remove '제거하다'라는 동사가 나와있으므로 문맥상 어울리는 (B) defective '결함이 있는'이 정답이다.

어휘   final stage 마지막 단계 | remove 제거하다 | defective 불량의 | product 제품

3. 회사는 직원들의 안전에 대해 책임을 져야 한다.

해설   빈칸은 be동사 뒤 보어인 형용사의 자리이다. 해석상 어울리는 것을 찾아도 되지만 빈칸 뒤 전치사가 있다면 특정 전치사와 짝을 이루는 형용사 어휘 문제일 가능성이 높다. 빈칸 뒤에 for가 있으므로 be responsible for '~에 대해 책임이 있다'라는 표현을 완성하는 (B) responsible이 정답이다.

어휘   company 회사 | be responsible for ~에 책임 있다 | employee 직원 | safety 안전

4. 고객 설문 조사를 통해 경영진은 제품 품질을 개선할 수 있었다.

해설   빈칸은 be동사 뒤 보어로 쓰이면서 to부정사를 취하는 형용사를 선택하는 문제라는 점을 파악해야 한다. 따라서 be able to '~할 수 있다'라는 표현을 완성하는 (B) able이 정답이다.

어휘   survey 조사하다 | management 경영진 | able 할 수 있는 | improve 개선하다 | product quality 제품 품질

Practice

1. (C)	**2.** (D)	**3.** (C)	**4.** (C)	**5.** (B)
6. (C)	**7.** (B)	**8.** (B)	**9.** (C)	**10.** (A)
11. (D)	**12.** (D)	**13.** (A)	**14.** (A)	**15.** (B)
16. (A)	**17.** (D)	**18.** (C)	**19.** (B)	**20.** (A)

1. 최고 경영자는 회사의 미래에 대해 자신감을 보인다.

해설   최고 경영자가 회사의 미래에 자신 있어 한다는 의미가 적절하므로 (C) confident가 정답이다. 생김새가 비슷한 confidential '기밀의'를 혼동하지 않도록 주의하자.

어휘   CEO (=Chief Executive Officer) 최고 경영자 | economic 경제적인 | confidential 기밀의, 은밀한 | confident 자신감 있는, 확신하는 | valuable 가치 있는, 소중한

2. 회사는 모든 신입 직원들에게 추가 교육 세션을 제공한다.

해설   신입 직원들에게 추가적인 교육 세션을 제공한다는 의미가 적절하므로 (D) additional이 정답이다.

어휘   offer 제공하다 | employee 직원 | accurate 정확한 | defective 결함이 있는 | competent 유능한 | additional 추가적인

3. 우리는 정기적으로 사무용품을 공급할 신뢰할 수 있는 공급업체를 찾아야 한다.

해설   믿을 수 있는 업체를 찾아야 한다는 의미가 적절하므로 (C) dependable이 정답이다. 생김새가 비슷한 dependent '의존적인'과 혼동하지 않도록 주의하자.

어휘   vendor 판매 회사 | supply 공급하다 | office materials 사무용품 | regularly 정기적으로 | durable 내구성이 있는, 오래가는 | dependent 의존적인 | dependable 믿을 수 있는 | distinct 뚜렷한, 분명한

4. 이 제품은 무역 박람회에서 상당한 관심을 받았다.

해설   문맥상 상당한 정도의 관심을 받았다는 의미이므로 (C) considerable이 정답이다. 생김새가 비슷한 (D) considerate '사려 깊은'과 혼동하지 않도록 주의하자.

어휘   receive 받다 | attention 관심 | trade show 무역 박람회 | effective 효과적인 | competitive 경쟁력 있는 | considerable 상당한 | considerate 사려 깊은

5. 우리 회사는 품질을 타협하지 않고 저렴한 가격을 제공하는 것을 자랑스럽게 생각한다.

해설   보기 중 가격의 특성을 설명하는 형용사는 affordable '저렴한' 밖에 없으므로 정답은 (B) affordable이다.

어휘   pride oneself on ~을 자랑으로 여기다 | compromise 타협하다 | quality 품질 | upcoming 다가오는 | affordable 합리적인, 저렴한 | available 이용 가능한 | ongoing 진행 중인

6. 새로운 재료는 가볍고 매우 내구성이 있다.

해설   빈칸은 재료의 물리적인 특성을 나타내는 형용사가 필요하므로 (C) durable '내구성이 있는'이 정답이다.

어휘   material 소재 | lightweight 가벼운 | extremely 매우 | comprehensive 포괄적인 | eligible 자격이 있는 | durable 내구성이 있는 | optimistic 낙관적인

7. 이 제품의 시장은 매우 경쟁이 치열하여 지속적인 혁신이 필요하다.

해설   '지속적인 혁신이 필요하다'라는 문맥상 경쟁이 '치열하다'는 의미가 적절하므로 (B) competitive가 정답이다.

어휘   highly 매우 | require 필요로 하다 | innovation 혁신 | numerous 많은 | competitive 경쟁이 치열한 | favorable 우호적인 | extensive 광범위한

8. 새 소프트웨어 업데이트는 대부분의 운영 체제와 호환된다.

해설   업데이트를 해야 한다는 문맥이 아니라 업데이트가 운영 체제와 어떻게 작용하는지를 나타내는 문맥이어서 '호환된다'는 의미가 적절하므로 (B) compatible이 정답이다. 또한, (C) committed는 주로 전치사 to와 함께 쓰인다.

VOCA   UNIT 03

PART 5 VOCA   **45**

어휘 operating system 운영 체제 | renowned 유명한 | compatible 호환되는 | committed 헌신적인 | compulsory 의무적인

9. 직원들은 기한 내 프로젝트를 완료하기 위해 전념하고 있다.

해설 빈칸 뒤의 to는 to부정사가 아닌 동명사 앞에 쓰인 전치사이다. 따라서 be dedicated to '~에 헌신하다'라는 표현을 완성하는 (C) dedicated가 정답이다.

어휘 complete 완료하다 | on time 제시간에 | knowledgeable 지식이 있는 | exceptional 뛰어난 | dedicated 헌신적인 | familiar 익숙한

10. 기준을 충족하는 사람들만 장학금 프로그램에 자격이 주어진다.

해설 be eligible for '~에 대한 자격이 있다' 표현을 완성하는 (A) eligible 이 정답이다. (C) capable은 전치사 of와 쓰인다는 점을 기억하자.

어휘 criteria 기준 | scholarship program 장학금 프로그램 | eligible 자격이 있는 | frequent 빈번한 | capable 능력이 있는 | multiple 다수의

11. 감독자의 최근 프로젝트에서의 성과는 정말 뛰어났다.

해설 문맥상 '감독의 프로젝트에서의 성과가 뛰어났다'는 의미로 (D) exceptional이 정답이다.

어휘 director 감독 | performance 성과 | recent 최근의 | extended 확장된 | efficient 효율적인 | imperative 필수적인 | exceptional 뛰어난

12. 교육 세션에 참석하는 것은 모든 신입 직원에게 필수적이다.

해설 문맥상 모든 신입 사원들이 교육에 참석해야 한다는 의미로 '의무적인'이라는 (D) mandatory가 정답이다. (A) aware는 전치사 of와 (B) responsible과 (C) famous는 전치사 for과 짝을 이룬다.

어휘 training session 교육 세션 | aware 알고 있는 | responsible 책임 있는 | famous 유명한 | mandatory 의무적인

13. 새 직원이 바로 업무를 시작하는 것을 주저했다.

해설 보기 중 to부정사와 함께 사용되는 형용사 (A) hesitant가 정답이다. (B) renowned와 (C) responsible은 전치사 for와 쓰인다.

어휘 immediately 즉시 | hesitant 주저하는 | renowned 유명한 | responsible 책임이 있는 | extensive 광범위한

14. 프로젝트 팀은 다음 개발 단계를 시작할 준비가 되어 있다.

해설 「be동사 + 형용사 + to부정사」 표현을 완성하는 선택지는 (A)와 (C)가 있는데, 문맥상 프로젝트 팀이 '이용 가능한 상태'가 아니라 '준비가 된 상태'이므로 (A) ready가 정답이다.

어휘 phase 단계 | development 개발 | ready 준비된 | routine 정기적인 | available 이용할 수 있는 | competent 능숙한

15. 공급업체가 제시한 가격은 합리적이고 우리의 예산 내에 있었다.

해설 문맥상 '예산 내에 있었다'라는 부분과 연결하여 '합리적인'이라는 뜻의 (B) reasonable이 정답이다.

어휘 price 가격 | vendor 공급업체 | budget 예산 | significant

상당한 | reasonable 합리적인 | tentative 잠정적인 | expensive 비싼

16. 건물을 나오기 전에 모든 문과 창문이 확실히 고정되었는지 확인하십시오.

해설 문과 창문이 건물을 나오기 전에 어떤 상태에 있어야 하는지를 설명하는 형용사 자리로 문맥상 '안전한'이라는 뜻의 (A) secure가 정답이다.

어휘 ensure 확인하다, 보장하다 | leave 떠나다 | secure 안전한, 단단히 잠긴 | portable 휴대 가능한 | thorough 철저한 | tight 꽉 조여진

17. 첫 번째 회의 후, 거래를 최종 결정하기 위해 후속 논의가 있었다.

해설 문맥상 '첫 회의 후 최종 결정을 위한' 후속 논의가 있었다는 의미로 (D) subsequent가 정답이다.

어휘 initial 초기의 | finalize 마무리하다 | deal 거래 | eager 열렬한 | valid 유효한 | spacious 널찍한 | subsequent 후속의, 그 다음의

18. 영업직은 임시직이며 6개월 동안 지속될 것이다.

해설 문맥상 '6개월 동안 지속될 것'이라는 표현과 어울리는 '임시의'라는 뜻의 (C) temporary가 정답이다.

어휘 sales position 영업직 | last 지속되다 | primary 주요한 | competitive 경쟁적인 | temporary 임시의 | numerous 많은

19. 매니저는 이것이 즉각적인 주의가 필요한 긴급한 문제라고 강조했다.

해설 문맥상 '즉각적인 주의가 필요한'이라는 표현과 어울리는 '긴급한'이라는 뜻의 (B) urgent가 정답이다.

어휘 emphasize 강조하다 | immediate 즉각적인 | attention 주의, 관심 | previous 이전의 | urgent 긴급한 | ready 준비된 | renowned 유명한

20. 출발 전에 여행 서류가 유효한지 확인하십시오.

해설 문맥상 '출발 전에 여행 서류를 확인하십시오'와 어울리는 '유효한'이라는 뜻의 (A) valid가 정답이다. (C) eligible은 사람을 수식하지 않으며, 보통 전치사 for이 함께 쓰인다.

어휘 ensure 확인하다, 보장하다 | travel document 여행 서류 | departure 출발 | valid 유효한 | useful 유용한 | eligible 자격이 있는 | ongoing 진행 중인

UNIT 04. 부사 어휘

핵심 문제 유형

본서 p.188

1. (C) **2.** (D) **3.** (C) **4.** (C)

1. 당신은 채용 면접에 참석할 때 적절하게 갖춰 입어야 한다.

해설 빈칸은 동사인 dress를 수식해주는 부사의 자리이다. 따라서 해석상 '제대로 갖춰 입어라'가 어울리기 때문에 (C) properly가 정답이다. 나

머지 선택지는 해석상 어울리지 않을 뿐만 아니라 (A) previously '이전에'는 과거 시제를, (B) thoroughly '철저하게'는 검사를 의미하는 동사와, (D) highly '매우'는 형용사와 부사만을 수식하는 부사인 점도 같이 숙지해 둔다면 쉽게 정답을 가려낼 수 있다.

어휘 dress 입다 | properly 적절히 | attend 참석하다 | job interview 면접

2. 회사는 최소 5년 경력의 동기 부여가 높은 영업 이사를 찾고 있다.

해설 빈칸 뒤 형용사 motivated '동기 부여된'을 적절하게 수식하는 부사를 선택하는 문제이다. 따라서 해석상 '매우 동기 부여된'이란 표현을 완성하는 (D) highly가 정답이다.

어휘 seek 찾다 | highly 매우 | motivated 동기 부여가 높은 | sales director 영업 이사 | experience 경력

3. 회사는 현재 새 스마트폰 구매용 앱을 개발 중이다.

해설 빈칸은 언뜻 보기에 일반적인 부사 어휘 문제 같지만, 현재 진행 시제 동사 사이에 들어가는 부사 어휘 문제라는 점을 파악해야 한다. 따라서, 현재 진행 시제와 어울리는 (C) currently '현재'가 정답이다.

어휘 company 회사 | currently 현재 | develop 개발하다 | purchase 구매

4. 급여일이 재정 문제로 약 10일 연기될 것이다.

해설 주로 숫자 앞에 잘 쓰이는 부사는 '대략' 또는 '거의'라는 의미를 가진 부사이므로 정답은 (C) approximately '대략'이다. 나머지 선택지로 (A) generally '일반적으로'는 현재 시제를, (B) thoroughly '철저하게'는 검토를 의미하는 동사와, (D) recently '최근에'는 과거 시제, 현재 완료 시제를 나타내는 부사라는 점을 숙지해 둔다면 쉽게 정답을 가릴 수 있다.

어휘 payday 급여일 | delay 연기 시키다 | approximately 대략 | financial issue 재정 문제

Practice

1. (D)	2. (C)	3. (B)	4. (C)	5. (D)
6. (A)	7. (C)	8. (D)	9. (B)	10. (B)
11. (D)	12. (A)	13. (B)	14. (D)	15. (B)
16. (A)	17. (B)	18. (C)	19. (D)	20. (A)

1. 최고 경영자는 회의 중에 회사의 새로운 정책을 명확히 언급했다.

해설 동사 state와 짝을 이루는 부사는 '명확히'라는 의미의 (D) expressly가 정답이다.

어휘 state 발표하다, 명시하다 | policy 정책 | equally 동등하게 | significantly 상당히 | promptly 신속하게 | expressly 명확히, 분명히

2. 모든 직원은 교대 근무 시간에 정시에 도착해야 한다.

해설 동사 arrive '도착하다'와 짝을 이루는 부사는 '정시에'라는 뜻의 (C) punctually가 정답이다.

어휘 arrive 도착하다 | shift 교대 근무 | directly 직접적으로 | randomly 무작위로 | punctually 정시에 | carefully 신중하게

3. 새 제품 출시 후 회사의 명성이 상당히 증가했다.

해설 회사의 명성이 증가한 정도를 설명하는 부사로 문맥상 '상당히'라는 뜻의 (B) considerably가 정답이다.

어휘 reputation 명성 | increase 증가하다 | typically 전형적으로 | considerably 상당히 | shortly 곧 | closely 면밀히, 밀접하게

4. 팀은 일정을 앞당겨 프로젝트를 완료하기 위해 긴밀히 협력했다.

해설 동사 work와 짝을 이루는 부사로 '긴밀히'라는 의미의 (C) closely가 정답이다.

어휘 work 일하다 | complete 완료하다 | ahead of schedule 일정보다 앞서 | approximately 대략적으로 | favorably 호의적으로 | closely 긴밀히 | rapidly 신속히

5. 고객 서비스 직원은 불만에 대해 긍정적으로 응답했다.

해설 동사 respond와 짝을 이루는 부사로 '호의적으로'라는 의미의 (D) favorably가 정답이다.

어휘 representative 직원 | respond 응답하다 | complaint 불만 | punctually 정시에 | nearly 거의 | efficiently 효율적으로 | favorably 호의적으로, 긍정적으로

6. 매니저는 회의에서 프로젝트 진행 상황을 간략히 요약했다.

해설 매니저가 프로젝트 진행 상황을 요약한 방식을 설명하는 부사로 문맥상 '간략히'라는 뜻의 (A) briefly가 정답이다.

어휘 summarize 요약하다 | progress 진행 상황 | briefly 간략히 | comprehensively 종합적으로 | accurately 정확하게 | directly 직접적으로

7. 새 소프트웨어 업데이트는 프리미엄 사용자에게만 독점적으로 이용 가능하다.

해설 문맥상 '프리미엄 사용자들에게'와 어울리는 '독점적으로'라는 뜻의 (C) exclusively가 정답이다.

어휘 available 이용 가능한 | eventually 결국 | once 한 번 | exclusively 독점적으로 | exactly 정확히

8. 회사의 최고 경영자는 그의 혁신적인 전략으로 비즈니스 잡지에 최근 언급되었다.

해설 현재 완료 시제를 나타내는 부사로 '최근에'라는 (D) recently가 정답이다. (C) now는 현재 진행 시제에 쓰인다.

어휘 mention 언급하다 | innovative 혁신적인 | gradually 점차적으로 | greatly 크게 | now 지금 | recently 최근에

9. 마케팅 캠페인은 제품 출시 직후 시작될 것이다.

해설 미래 시제를 나타내는 부사로 '곧'이라는 의미의 (B) shortly가 정답이다.

어휘 launch 시작하다 | product release 제품 출시 | formerly 이전에 | shortly 곧 | hardly 거의 ~하지 않다 | exceptionally 예외적으로

VOCA

UNIT 04

PART 5 VOCA **47**

10. 두 회사는 합병 조건에 상호 동의했다.

해설 두 회사가 동의한 방식을 설명하는 부사로 문맥상 '상호 간에'라는 뜻의 (B) mutually가 정답이다.

어휘 company 회사 | agree 동의하다 | terms 조건 | merger 합병 | mainly 주로 | mutually 상호 간에 | previously 이전에 | increasingly 점차적으로

11. 회사의 수익은 주로 새로운 가격 전략 덕분에 증가했다.

해설 회사의 수익이 증가한 원인을 설명하는 부사로 문맥상 '주로'라는 뜻의 (D) largely가 정답이다. (A) immediately는 '즉시'라는 의미로 증가가 일어난 시간이나 속도를 나타내는 부사이기 때문에 문맥상 적합하지 않다.

어휘 profit 수익 | increase 증가하다 | pricing strategy 가격 전략 | immediately 즉시 | typically 전형적으로 | frequently 자주 | largely 주로

12. 건물은 사무실 공간으로 전환되기 이전에 창고로 사용되었다.

해설 과거 시제를 나타내는 부사로 '이전에'라는 뜻의 (A) formerly가 정답이다.

어휘 warehouse 창고 | convert 전환하다 | formerly 이전에 | sometimes 때때로 | finally 마침내 | soon 곧

13. 제품 출시는 매우 성공적이었고 모든 판매 기대치를 초과했다.

해설 제품 출시가 얼마나 성공적이었는지 형용사를 수식하는 부사로 '매우'라는 뜻의 (B) extremely가 정답이다.

어휘 launch 출시 | successful 성공적인 | exceed 초과하다 | sales expectation 판매 기대치 | periodically 주기적으로 | extremely 매우 | strictly 엄격하게 | separately 따로

14. 보고서는 거의 완료되었으며 몇 가지 사소한 변경만 남아 있다.

해설 보고서가 완료된 정도를 설명하는 부사로 문맥상 '거의'라는 뜻의 (D) nearly가 정답이다.

어휘 report 보고서 | finish 완료하다 | minor 사소한 | remain 남다 | generally 일반적으로 | lately 최근에 | somewhat 다소 | nearly 거의

15. 회의는 대략 두 시간 동안 지속될 것으로 예상된다.

해설 숫자를 수식하는 부사로 '대략'이라는 뜻의 (B) roughly가 정답이다.

어휘 expect 예상하다 | last 지속되다 | promptly 신속하게 | roughly 대략 | thoroughly 철저히 | steadily 꾸준히

16. 최대 5만 달러까지 대출을 신청할 수 있다.

해설 숫자를 수식하는 부사로 '최대 ~까지'라는 뜻의 (A) up to가 정답이다.

어휘 apply for ~을 신청하다 | loan 대출 | up to 최대 ~까지 | larger than ~보다 큰 | shortly 곧 | previously 이전에

17. 최고 경영자는 모든 것이 원활하게 운영되고 있는지 확인하기 위해 가끔 해외 지사를 방문한다.

해설 현재 시제를 나타내는 빈도부사로 문맥상 '가끔'이라는 뜻의 (B) occasionally가 정답이다.

어휘 overseas 해외의 | branch 지사 | ensure 보장하다 | run 운영되다 | smoothly 원활하게 | promptly 신속하게 | occasionally 가끔 | recently 최근에 | overwhelmingly 압도적으로

18. 매니저는 회의 후 즉시 보고서를 제출할 것을 기대한다.

해설 전치사 after와 연결하여 '직후'를 나타내는 (C) promptly가 정답이다.

어휘 expect 기대하다 | submit 제출하다 | report 보고서 | precisely 정확히 | almost 거의 | promptly 신속하게 | around 대략

19. 새 소프트웨어 업데이트는 시스템을 상당히 빠르게 만들었다.

해설 시스템 속도 변화 정도를 설명하는 부사로 문맥상 새 소프트웨어 업데이트로 속도가 상당히 빨라졌다는 것을 나타내는 (D) significantly가 정답이다.

어휘 properly 적절히 | almost 거의 | regularly 정기적으로 | significantly 상당히

20. 사무실은 보수 공사로 인해 일시적으로 폐쇄되며 다음 달에 다시 열릴 것이다.

해설 보수 공사로 인해 폐쇄되고 다음 달에 다시 열릴 것이라고 했으므로 문맥상 '일시적으로'라는 뜻의 (A) temporarily가 정답이다.

어휘 renovation 보수 공사 | temporarily 일시적으로 | absolutely 절대적으로 | primarily 주로 | evenly 고르게

REVIEW TEST

본서 p.192

1. (D)	2. (A)	3. (A)	4. (A)	5. (D)
6. (A)	7. (B)	8. (D)	9. (B)	10. (D)
11. (C)	12. (C)	13. (A)	14. (C)	15. (C)
16. (B)	17. (C)	18. (C)	19. (D)	20. (D)
21. (C)	22. (D)	23. (B)	24. (C)	25. (B)
26. (D)	27. (B)	28. (A)	29. (A)	30. (B)

1. 예산을 승인하기 전에, 경영진은 새로운 사무실 수리에 대한 총 비용 견적을 요청했다.

해설 예산을 승인하기 전에 총 비용에 대한 견적을 요청했다는 의미가 자연스러우므로 '견적(서)'라는 뜻의 (D) estimate가 정답이다.

어휘 approve 승인하다 | budget 예산 | management 경영(진) | request 요청하다 | renovation 수리 | benefit 혜택 | element 요소 | incident 일, 사건

2. PT 음료 회사의 마케팅 이사는 그 직위에 가나쿠로 씨를 추천했다.

해설 빈칸은 가나쿠로 씨를 목적어로 취하는 동사 자리로 '그 자리에 가나쿠로 씨를 적극 추천했다'는 의미가 자연스러우므로 '추천하다'라는 뜻의 (A) recommended가 정답이다.

어휘 beverage 음료 | director 이사 | position 직위, 일자리

conclude 결론을 내리다 | deserve ~할 만하다 | record 녹음하다

3. 프로젝트 일정은 임시적이며, 고객의 피드백에 따라 조정될 수 있다.

해설 프로젝트의 일정이 임시적이어서, 고객 피드백에 따라 조정될 수 있다는 의미가 자연스러우므로 '임시의, 잠정적인'이란 뜻의 (A) tentative가 정답이다.

어휘 timeline 일정, 시간표 | adjust 조정하다 | based on ~에 근거하여 | client 고객 | feedback 피드백 | tentative 임시의 | definite 확실한, 분명한 | completed 완료된, 완성된 | immediate 즉시의, 즉각적인

4. 인사부는 다음 주에 모든 직원에게 새 신분증을 발급할 것이다.

해설 인사부가 전 직원들에게 새 신분증을 발급할 거란 의미가 자연스러우므로 '발급하다, 발행하다'라는 뜻의 (A) issue가 정답이다.

어휘 HR 인사부(= Human Resources) | ID badge 신분증 | display 진열하다, 전시하다 | remove 제거하다 | design 디자인하다, 설계하다

5. 존슨 씨는 전국 미술 경연대회에서 그녀의 그림으로 대상을 수상했다.

해설 빈칸은 문장의 동사 자리로 '존슨 씨가 그녀의 그림으로 대상을 수상했다'는 의미가 자연스러우므로 '수여하다'라는 뜻의 (D) awarded가 정답이다. 참고로 award는 두 개의 목적어를 취하여 '~에게 ...을 주다'라는 기본 의미를 갖는 4형식 동사이므로 문제에서처럼 수동태 문장에서도 명사구를 목적어로 취할 수 있음에 유의한다.

어휘 national 전국의 | contest 경연대회 | win 이기다, 승리하다 | obtain 얻다, 획득하다

6. 그 두 부서는 회사 내에서 각기 다른 역할을 가지고 있으며, 각각 다른 전문 분야에 중점을 둔다.

해설 두 부서가 서로 다른 전문 분야에 중점을 둔다는 내용으로 미루어 회사 내에서 구별되는 역할을 가지고 있다는 의미가 자연스러우므로 '구별되는, 별개의'라는 뜻의 (A) distinct가 정답이다.

어휘 role 역할 | within ~이내에 | focus on ~에 중점을 두다 | area 분야 | expertise 전문 지식[기술] | common 공통의 | similar 비슷한 | vague 모호한

7. 리버튼 교통부는 도시의 버스와 지하철 서비스를 감독한다.

해설 빈칸은 문장의 동사 자리로 '교통부가 시의 버스와 지하철 서비스를 감독한다'는 의미가 자연스러우므로 '감독하다'라는 뜻의 (B) oversees가 정답이다.

어휘 transportation department 교통부 | predict 예상하다 | oversee 감독하다 | view 보다; 여기다 | commute 통근하다

8. 누옌 씨의 스타트업 회사를 위한 아이디어는 뉴질랜드에서 휴가를 보내는 동안 형성되었다.

해설 빈칸은 문장의 주어 자리로 '스타트업 회사를 위한 아이디어가 휴가 기간 동안 형성되었다'는 의미가 자연스러우므로 '아이디어'라는 뜻의 (D) idea가 정답이다. 참고로 명사 idea는 전치사 for나 of를 동반한다는 점에서 빈칸 뒤의 전치사 for가 문제를 푸는 단서가 된다는 점을

알아두자.

어휘 startup company 스타트업 기업, 신생기업 | form 형성시키다, 만들어 내다 | vacation 휴가 | content 내용물; 목차 | fact 사실 | value 가치

9. 헤일렌 식료품점의 특별 할인은 9월 15일까지만 가능하다.

해설 빈칸은 앞의 형용사 available을 수식하는 부사 자리로 '특별 할인이 9월 15일까지만 이용 가능하다'는 의미가 자연스러우므로 '오직 ~만'이라는 뜻의 (B) only가 정답이다.

어휘 special discount 특별 할인 | available 이용 가능한 | hardly 거의 ~하지 않는 | only 오로지, 단지 | barely 겨우, 간신히 | carefully 주의 깊게

10. 새 소프트웨어는 많은 양의 데이터를 신속하고 효율적으로 처리할 수 있다.

해설 새 소프트웨어가 많은 양의 데이터를 처리할 수 있다는 의미로 빈칸 뒤 전치사 of를 동반하여 '~할 수 있는'을 뜻하는 형용사 (D) capable이 정답이다. (A) aware도 전치사 of를 동반하지만 의미가 어울리지 않고, (B) eligible은 to부정사나 전치사 for를, (C) familiar는 전치사 with를 동반한다.

어휘 handle 처리하다 | quickly 신속하게 | efficiently 효율적으로 | aware 알고 있는 | eligible ~을 할 수 있는, 자격이 있는 | familiar ~에 익숙한, 잘 아는

11. 많은 직원들이 더 나은 일과 생활의 균형을 유지하기 위해 유연한 근무 시간을 선호한다고 밝혔다.

해설 많은 직원들이 유연한 근무 시간을 선호한다고 밝혔다는 의미로 빈칸 뒤 전치사 for를 동반하여 '~에 대한 선호(도)'를 뜻하는 명사 (C) preference가 정답이다.

어휘 express 밝히다, 표현하다 | flexible 유연한 | working hours 근무시간 | maintain 유지하다 | work-life balance 일과 생활의 균형 | demand 요구(사항) | requirement 요건, 필요조건 | suggestion 제안

12. 그 기술자는 행사 시작 전에 모든 장비가 제대로 작동하도록 확인했다.

해설 장비가 제대로 작동할 것이라는 의미가 자연스러우므로 '제대로, 적절히'라는 뜻의 (C) properly가 정답이다.

어휘 technician 기술자 | ensure 보장하다, 확인하다 | equipment 장비 | function 작동하다 | urgently 긴급하게 | approximately 약, 대략 | specifically 분명히, 명확하게

13. 고객 만족은 회사의 최우선 사항이며, 모든 직원은 고객의 요구에 신속히 대응하도록 교육을 받는다.

해설 고객 만족이 회사의 최우선 사항이라는 의미가 자연스러우므로 '우선 순위'를 뜻하는 (A) priority가 정답이다.

어휘 customer satisfaction 고객 만족 | train 교육하다 | respond 응답하다 | promptly 즉시, 신속하게 | need 요구 | procedure 절차 | obligation 의무 | opportunity 기회

14. 안전한 근무 환경을 보장하기 위해 모든 직원이 안전 교육에 참석하는 것이 필수적이다.

해설 안전한 근무 환경을 위해 전 직원이 안전 교육에 반드시 참석해야 한다는 의미가 자연스러우므로 '반드시 해야 하는, 필수의'라는 뜻의 (C) imperative가 정답이다.

어휘 attend 참석하다 | ensure 보장하다 | secure 안전한 | work environment 근무 환경 | irrelevant 무관한, 상관 없는 | incomplete 불완전한 | unnecessary 불필요한

15. 모든 연구실 기술자들은 위험한 화학 물질을 다룰 때면 공식 안전 절차들을 준수해야 한다.

해설 빈칸 앞 safety와 복합 명사를 이루기에 적절한 명사 자리로 '안전 절차들을 준수해야 한다'라는 의미가 자연스러우므로 '절차, 규정'을 뜻하는 (C) procedures가 정답이다.

어휘 technician 기술자 | adhere to ~을 고수하다 | official 공식적인 | safety 안전 | handle 다루다 | chemical 화학 물질 | matter 문제, 사안 | installation 설치

16. 곧 있을 행사에 대해 일찍 공지를 받으시려면, 귀하의 연락처를 제공해주시기 바랍니다.

해설 빈칸은 명사 events를 수식하는 형용사 자리로 '곧 있을 행사에 관한 공지를 일찍 받으려면, 연락처를 제공하라'는 의미가 자연스러우므로 '곧 있을, 다가오는'이라는 뜻의 (B) upcoming이 정답이다.

어휘 notification 알림, 통지 | contact information 연락처 | latest 최신의 | prepared 준비된 | advanced 진보된; 고급의

17. 라스코 플라자의 정원은 유명 야외 예술가인 장 테르니에에 의해 계획되었다.

해설 빈칸은 문장의 동사 자리로 '라스코 플라자 정원이 유명 예술가에 의해 기획되었다'는 의미가 자연스러우므로 '계획하다'라는 뜻의 (C) planned가 정답이다.

어휘 popular 인기가 많은 | outdoor 옥외의, 야외의 | artist 예술가 | concern 우려하다 | assume 가정하다 | affect 영향을 끼치다

18. 새 매니저는 다음 달부터 부서를 감독하는 책임을 맡게 될 것이다.

해설 새 매니저가 부서를 감독하는 책임을 맡게 될 거라는 의미가 자연스러우므로 '책임을 맡다'라는 의미의 (C) assume이 정답이다.

어휘 responsibility 책임 | oversee 감독하다 | abandon 포기하다 | transfer 옮기다, 이동하다 | delegate (권한을) 위임하다

19. 어떤 모델을 제작할지에 대한 제조사의 결정은 연구 결과에 달려 있다.

해설 빈칸은 be동사 뒤 보어 자리로 '어느 모델을 제작할지에 대한 제조사의 결정이 연구 결과에 달려 있다'라는 의미가 자연스러우므로 '~에 달려 있는, ~에 좌우되는'이라는 뜻의 (B) dependent가 정답이다. 참고로 형용사 dependent는 전치사 on이나 upon을 동반한다는 점에서 빈칸 뒤 on이 문제 해결의 단서가 될 수 있으니 참고해두자.

어휘 manufacturer 제조사 | decision 결정 | result 결과 | responsive ~에 반응하는(to) | reliable 믿을 수 있는 | subsequent 그 다음의, 차후의

20. 소포는 현재 운송 중이며 내일 도착할 예정이다.

해설 소포가 현재 운송 중이라는 의미로 빈칸 앞의 전치사 in과 함께 쓰여 '수송 중인, 운송 중인'이라는 뜻을 완성하는 명사 (D) transit가 정답이다.

어휘 package 소포 | currently 현재 | destination 목적지, 도착지 | delay 지연 | shipment 수송(품) | process 과정

21. 작년 11월에 디자인된 플리트 풋웨어의 새 운동화가 마침내 다음 주에 생산을 시작할 것이다.

해설 빈칸은 동사 begin을 수식하는 부사 자리로 '작년 11월에 디자인된 운동화가 마침내 생산을 시작할 것이다'라는 의미가 자연스러우므로 '마침내, 결국'이라는 뜻의 (C) finally가 정답이다.

어휘 design 디자인하다, 설계하다 | training shoes 운동화 | production 생산 | extremely 극도로, 극히 | precisely 정확히 | lately 최근에

22. 부사장을 위한 은퇴식이 11월 24일 토요일 웹스터 센터의 모얼리 강당에서 개최될 것이다.

해설 문장의 주어는 A retirement reception으로 은퇴식이 개최될 것이라는 의미가 자연스러우므로 '(행사를) 개최하다'는 의미를 갖는 (D) held가 정답이다. 해석상 opened도 가능해 보이지만, opened는 문이나 뚜껑 등 닫혀 있는 것을 또는 점포 등을 '열었다'라는 의미이므로 retirement reception을 주어로 받기에 어색하다.

어휘 retirement reception 은퇴 연회 | vice president 부사장 | auditorium 강당

23. 나세리 박사는 인상적인 자격증 때문에 부서의 관리자로 임명되었다.

해설 빈칸은 문장의 동사 자리로 '인상적인 자격증 때문에 부서장으로 임명되었다'는 의미가 자연스러우므로 '임명하다'라는 뜻의 (B) appointed가 정답이다. 참고로 appoint는 목적어와 목적격 보어를 취하는 5형식 동사로 수동태 문장에서도 명사 보어가 연결될 수 있다는 점에 유의한다.

어휘 department 부서 | impressive 인상적인 | credential 자격증

24. 스타커 식당은 모든 연령대의 손님들의 관심을 끌만한 다양한 메뉴를 제공한다.

해설 빈칸은 문장의 목적어 자리로 '스타커 식당이 다양한 메뉴를 제공한다'는 의미가 자연스러우므로 '다수, 다량'이라는 뜻의 (C) array가 정답이다. 참고로 an array of는 '다양한'이라는 의미의 관용 표현이므로 덩어리째 암기해두자.

어휘 appeal to ~의 관심을 끌다 | diner 식사하는 사람 | ingredient 재료 | object 물건 | entity 독립체

25. 개틀린 건설 자재는 한 달에 한 번씩 모든 창고의 재고를 조사한다.

해설 빈칸은 부사구에 들어갈 부사 자리로 '한 달에 한 번'이라는 의미를 완성하는 (B) Once가 정답이다.

어휘 inspect 조사하다 | stock 재고, 재고품 | warehouse 창고 | instantly 즉각, 즉시 | once 한 번 | already 이미, 벌써

26. 레이드 1200 태블릿 PC는 향상된 비산 방지 화면을 특징으로 하고 있다.

해설 빈칸은 문장의 동사 자리로, '향상된 비산 방지 화면을 특징으로 한다'는 의미가 자연스러우므로 '~을 특징으로 삼다'라는 뜻의 (D) features가 정답이다.

어휘 improved 향상된, 개선된 | shatter-resistant 비산 방지의(유리가 깨졌을 때 유리조각이 흩어지는 것을 방지하는 기술) | sample 시도해보다 | endure 견디다 | adjust 조정하다

27. 공정한 업무량을 보장하기 위해 모든 팀원들 간에 업무가 공평하게 분배되었다.

해설 팀원들 간의 업무가 공평하게 분배되었다는 의미가 자연스러우므로 '공평하게, 똑같이'라는 뜻의 (B) equally가 정답이다. '정확하게'라는 뜻의 (C) precisely는 수치상의 정확성을 내포하기 때문에 문맥상 어색하다.

어휘 task 업무 | divide 나누다, 분배하다 | ensure 보장하다 | fair 공정한 | workload 업무량, 작업량 | abundantly 풍부하게 | rapidly 빠르게

28. 판 씨는 화학 공학을 전공했음에도 불구하고 현재 마케팅 영업부에서 근무한다.

해설 빈칸은 동사 works를 수식하는 부사 자리로 '판 씨가 화학 공학을 전공했지만, 지금은 영업 마케팅 부서에서 근무한다'는 의미가 자연스러우므로 '지금'이라는 뜻의 (A) now가 정답이다.

어휘 chemical engineering 화학 공학 | therefore 그러므로, 그러니 | fairly 상당히, 꽤 | quite 상당히, 꽤

29. 회사는 고객 서비스를 개선하고 고객 기대치를 넘어서기 위해 계속 분투하고 있다.

해설 빈칸 뒤에 to부정사가 와 있으므로 to부정사를 목적어로 취할 수 있는 동사여야 하며, 회사가 고객 서비스와 기대치를 위해 계속 분투하고 있다는 의미가 자연스러우므로 '분투하다'라는 뜻의 동사 (A) strive가 정답이다.

어휘 improve 개선하다, 향상시키다 | exceed 초과하다 | client expectation 고객 기대치 | reply to ~에 답하다 | plan to do ~할 계획이다 | achieve 달성하다, 성취하다

30. IT 부서는 시스템이 안전하고 효율적으로 유지되도록 주기적으로 소프트웨어를 업데이트한다.

해설 소프트웨어를 주기적으로 업데이트한다는 의미가 자연스러우므로 '주기적으로'라는 뜻의 (B) periodically가 정답이다.

어휘 ensure 보장하다 | remain 계속 ~이다 | secure 안전한 | efficient 효율적인 | previously 이전에 | instantly 즉각, 즉시 | partially 부분적으로

PART 6

UNIT 01. 시제

핵심 문제 유형

1. (B)

[1] 다음 정책에 관한 문제입니다.

> **제품 반품**
>
> 처칠 가구에서는 훌륭한 제품을 저렴한 가격에 제공하는 것에 자부심을 가지고 있습니다. 저희는 공급 업체들로부터 받는 제품의 품질에 자신 있습니다. 어떠한 이유로든 불만족하신 경우, 저희 고객 서비스 팀 384-555-1485로 전화 주시면 전액 환불 받으실 수 있습니다. 기꺼이 돕는 저희 팀에서 귀하께 주문 번호를 **1** 물어볼 것입니다. 제품을 반송하실 때는 주문 번호를 포함해 주세요. 제품을 처칠 가구로 반송해야 하는 경우 발생하는 배송비는 저희가 책임지지 않으니 유의해 주시기 바랍니다.

어휘 return 반품하다 | goods 상품 | furnishing 가구 | pride oneself on ~에 자부심이 있다 | provide 제공하다 | affordable 저렴한 | confident 자신 있는 | supplier 공급업체 | unsatisfied 불만족한 | reason 이유 | refund 환불 | helpful 기꺼이 돕는, 도움이 되는 | ship 운송하다 | note 주의하다 | shipping 배송 | cost 비용 | incur (비용을) 발생시키다

해설 빈칸은 주어 Our helpful team과 목적어 you 사이 문장의 동사 자리이다. 빈칸 앞 문장에서 '불만족한 경우, 고객 서비스 팀으로 전화하면 전액 환불 받을 수 있다'며 가정된 상황에 대해 이야기하고 있음을 고려할 때, '(전화를 하면) 팀에서 주문 번호를 물어볼 것'이라는 미래 시제의 내용으로 이어져야 문맥상 연결이 자연스러우므로 (B) will ask가 정답이다.

Practice

1. (D)	**2.** (B)	**3.** (C)	**4.** (D)	**5.** (C)
6. (D)	**7.** (A)	**8.** (A)	**9.** (B)	**10.** (A)
11. (B)	**12.** (D)	**13.** (B)	**14.** (D)	**15.** (A)
16. (B)				

[1-4] 다음 정보에 관한 문제입니다.

> 도서관 이용객에게 알려 드립니다.
>
> 리틀턴 도서관에서 다음 주 주말에 온라인 도서 목록 시스템 개편을 준비하고 있습니다. 예정된 업데이트는 8월 9일 토요일 오전 3시에 **1** 시작할 예정입니다. 모든 작업은 8월 10일 일요일 오전 11시에 완료될 것으로 예상합니다. 이 시간 **2** 동안, 도서관 도서 목록 시

PART 6 UNIT 01

스템은 이용할 수 없습니다. **3** 다른 일부 서비스도 영향을 받을 수 있습니다. 여러분의 **4** 인내 및 이해에 감사드립니다.

어휘 attention 알립니다, 주목하세요 | prepare 준비하다 | revamp 개편하다, 개조하다 | catalog 도서 목록, 카탈로그 | scheduled 예정된 | predict 예상하다 | complete 완료 하다 | available 이용 가능한 | understanding 이해

1. **해설** 빈칸은 문장의 주어 The scheduled update에 대한 동사 자 리이다. 빈칸 앞 문장의 '다음 주 주말에 도서 목록 시스템 개편을 준 비 중'이라는 내용을 고려할 때, 미래 시제 문장이 되어야 문맥상 연결 이 자연스러우므로 (D) will commence가 정답이다.

2. **해설** 빈칸은 this time을 목적어로 취하는 전치사 자리이다. 빈칸 뒤 이어지는 '도서관 시스템을 이용할 수 없다'는 내용을 고려할 때, '이 (업데이트) 시간 동안'이라는 내용이 들어가야 문맥상 자연스러우므로 기간 전치사 (B) During이 정답이다.

3. (A) 직원이 온라인으로 도움을 드릴 예정입니다.
(B) 커뮤니티에서 몇 가지 새로운 계획이 제안 되었습니다.
(C) 다른 일부 서비스도 영향을 받을 수 있습니다.
(D) 새로 등록한 도서관 회원은 가입이 불가합니다.

해설 빈칸 앞 문장의 '이 시간 동안, 도서관 도서 목록 시스템은 이용 할 수 없다'는 내용을 고려할 때, 도서관 서비스 이용과 관련된 내용으 로 이어져야 문맥상 연결이 자연스러우므로 (C) Some of our other services may also be affected.가 정답이다.

4. **해설** 빈칸은 전치사 for의 목적어 자리이다. 빈칸 앞 문장들의 '이 시간 동안 도서관 카탈로그 시스템을 이용할 수 없으며 다른 서비 스도 영향을 받을 수 있다'는 내용을 고려할 때, '인내 및 이해에 감 사드린다'는 내용으로 이어져야 문맥상 연결이 자연스러우므로 (D) patience가 정답이다.

[5-8] 다음 구인 공고에 관한 문제입니다.

호텔 프런트 직원 구인

수미르 힐에서 해이즐우드 지점의 호텔 안내 데스크 직원을 **5** 찾고 있습니다. 이 역할에는 투숙객 예약 받기, 투숙객 객실 체크인 및 체 크아웃하기, 투숙객의 요청 사항 처리하기가 포함됩니다. 이 **6** 직 무를 이행하려면 기본 계산 능력, 우수한 고객 서비스 능력, 꼼꼼함 이 필요합니다. 이 직무는 최소한의 기본적인 사무 실무에 고등학교 졸업장이 필요합니다. **7** 여기에는 일반 컴퓨터 소프트웨어 및 이메 일과 전화 예절에 관한 지식이 포함됩니다. **8** 경력이 있는 사람에 게 우선권이 주어집니다.

어휘 location 지점 | role 역할 | book in (호텔을) 예약하다 | guest 손님, 투숙객 | check in (호텔에서) 체크인하다 | check out (호텔에서) 체크아웃하다 | take care of 처리 하다 | request 요청 | fulfill 수행하다 | require 요구하다 | basic 기본적인 | numeracy 산술 능력 | skill 기술, 능력 |

customer service 고객 서비스 | attention to detail 꼼꼼함 | position 일자리 | a minimum of 최소한의 | graduation certificate 졸업장, 졸업 증명서 | office practice 사무 업무 | include 포함하다 | knowledge 지식 | common 흔한, 보통의 | etiquette 에티켓, 예의

5. **해설** 빈칸은 문장의 동사 자리이다. 빈칸 뒤에 for가 있으므로 look for '~를 찾다'를 완성하는 자리이며, 직원을 구하는 구인 공고라는 지 문의 성격을 고려할 때, '호텔 안내 데스크 직원을 찾고 있다'는 의미가 되어야 문맥상 자연스러우므로 현재진행 시제 (C) is looking이 정답이 다.

6. **해설** 빈칸은 문장의 주어인 동명사구에서 동명사 fulfilling의 목적 어인 명사 자리이다. 빈칸을 수식하는 지시 대명사 these가 가리키는 빈칸 앞 문장의 내용을 고려할 때, '투숙객 예약 및 체크인과 체크아웃 업무, 투숙객 요청 사항 처리라는 이러한 업무를 수행하는 것'이라는 내용이 되어야 문맥상 연결이 자연스러우므로 (D) duties가 정답이다.

7. **해설** 빈칸은 문장의 주어 자리이다. 빈칸 앞 문장에서 '직무 최소 요 건으로 기본 사무 업무 수행 능력을 인증하는 고등학교 졸업장이 필요 하다'라고 했으며 빈칸 뒷부분에서 '일반 컴퓨터 소프트웨어 및 이메일 과 전화 예절이 포함된다'고 했으므로, 바로 앞 문장에서 언급한 명사 구를 지칭하는 지시 대명사 (A) These가 정답이다.

8. **(A) 경력이 있는 사람에게 우선권이 주어집니다.**
(B) 스미레 힐에서 이번 여름에 프로모션 행사를 진행할 예정입니다.
(C) 불만 사항은 본사로 전달해 주시기 바랍니다.
(D) 헤이즐우드 지점은 가장 바쁜 지점 중 하나입니다.

해설 앞선 문장들에서 모집하는 직무에 관한 업무의 세부 요건을 설명하고 있음을 고려할 때, 모집 직무 관련 내용으로 이어져야 문맥 상 연결이 자연스러우므로 (A) Preference will be given to those with prior experience.가 정답이다.

[9-12] 다음 공지에 관한 문제입니다.

팸대일 피트니스 센터 회원 여러분, 안내 말씀 드립니다:

연례 건강 박람회가 1월 3일 토요일 오후 1시 30분부터 오후 4시까 지 개최될 예정입니다. 헬스 트레이너, 영양사, 건강 교육자가 참석 해 여러분의 건강 목표, 운동 계획, 식습관 **9** 에 관해 궁금해하실 만한 질문에 답변해 드릴 예정입니다.

10 행사는 2층 회의실에서 열립니다. 참석하는 데 등록할 필요는 없 지만, 개인 **11** 상담을 원한다면 예약하시기를 권장 드립니다. 팸대 일 피트니스 센터에서는 많은 분이 참석하시기를 바라며, 새해에는 행복하고 번창하시길 **12** 기원합니다.

어휘 annual 연례의 | fair 박람회 | schedule 예정하다 | take place 열리다, 개최되다 | fitness trainer 헬스 트레이너 | dietician 영양사 | educator 교육자 | diet 식사, 식습관 | registration 등록 | attend 참석하다 | schedule 일정을

잡다 | recommend 권장하다 | personalize 개인의 필요에 맞추다 | in attendance 참석한 | prosperous 번영한, 번창한

9. 해설 빈칸은 뒤에 나열된 명사구를 목적어로 취하는 전치사 자리이다. 전치사구가 수식하는 명사가 questions임을 고려할 때, '여러분의 건강 목표, 운동 계획, 식습관에 관한 질문'이라는 의미가 되어야 문맥상 연결이 자연스러우므로 (B) about이 정답이다.

10. (A) 행사는 2층 회의실에서 열립니다.
(B) 모든 비용은 재무팀에 보고해야 합니다.
(C) 현재 일정에 대한 제안은 환영합니다.
(D) 프로모션은 이달 말까지 진행됩니다.

해설 빈칸 뒤 문장의 '참석하는 데 등록할 필요는 없다'는 내용을 고려할 때, 행사에 관해 안내하는 내용이 앞에 들어가야 문맥상 연결이 자연스러우므로 (A) The event will take place in the conference room on the second floor.가 정답이다.

11. 해설 빈칸은 a personalized의 수식을 받는 명사 자리이다. 접속사 while로 연결된 종속절의 내용을 고려할 때, '참석 등록은 필요 없지만, 개인 상담을 원할 경우 예약이 권장된다'는 내용이 되어야 문맥상 연결이 자연스러우므로 (B) consultation이 정답이다.

12. 해설 빈칸은 주어 we에 대한 동사 자리이다. '행복하고 번창하는 새해가 되기를 바란다'는 의미가 되어야 문맥상 자연스러우므로 현재 시제 (D) wish가 정답이다.

[13-16] 다음 기사에 관한 문제입니다.

형제가 변화를 만들어내다

헤이그 (10월 11일)—지난 10년 동안 프랭크와 베니 호튼은 꾸준히 컴퓨터 사용 부문에서 최고의 지성인으로 선정되었다. **13** 그것은 올해도 변함없었다. 그들의 작업은 사업체에 보통 연간 수천 달러의 비용이 드는 광범위한 소프트웨어 패키지를 합리적인 가격으로 중소기업에 제공하는 일을 중심에 뒀다.

둘 다 학교에서 우등생이었는데, 초기에 이룬 업적은 프리스틴플로우 솔루션즈를 대중 브랜드로 바꿔 놓은 것을 **14** 포함한다. "저희 부모님은 가게를 운영하셨는데, 그분들이 기본 소프트웨어에 지불하는 가격이 터무니없었어요. 당시 저희 임무는 **15** 사업주들이 도움을 받을 수 있는 해결책을 만드는 것이었습니다."라고 프랭크 호튼이 말했다. **16** 마찬가지로, 베니는 사업을 운영하는 것은 합리적인 비용이 드는 일이어야 한다고 덧붙였다.

어휘 decade 10년 | consistently 지속적으로, 꾸준히 | name 명명하다, 이름 붙이다 | sharp 영리한 | mind (지적 능력의 소유자로서의) 사람 | computing 컴퓨터 사용 | sector 부문, 분야 | revolve around ~를 중심으로 다루다 | extensive 광범위한 | cost (비용이) 들다 | business 사업체 | affordable (가격이) 적당한, 알맞은 | achiever (사회적으로) 크게 성공한

사람 | accomplishment 업적 | household name 누구나 아는 이름 | run 운영하다 | ridiculous 터무니없는 | mission 임무 | solution 해결책 | benefit from 혜택을 입다

13. (A) 그들은 해외에서 자랐다.
(B) 그것은 올해도 변함없었다.
(C) 그들은 원래 교사로 일하고 있었다.
(D) 이 상을 충분히 받을 자격이 있다.

해설 빈칸 앞 문장의 '지난 10년 동안 프랭크와 베니 호튼은 꾸준히 컴퓨터 사용 부문에서 최고의 지성인으로 선정되었다'는 내용을 고려할 때, '그 상황은 올해에도 바뀌지 않았다'는 내용으로 이어져야 문맥상 연결이 자연스러우므로 (B) That has not changed this year.가 정답이다.

14. 해설 빈칸은 주어와 목적어 사이의 동사 자리이다. and로 연결된 두 문장의 관계를 고려할 때, 앞 문장의 '학창 시절 높은 성취를 이뤘다(우등생이었다)'는 내용에 이어, 초기 업적에 해당하는 일화를 하나의 현재적 사실로서 소개하고 있으므로 현재 시제 (D) include가 정답이다.

15. 해설 빈칸은 solutions를 선행사로 하는 관계절 내 주어 자리이다. '가게를 운영하셨던 부모님이 기본 소프트웨어에 지불하는 금액이 터무니없었다'는 빈칸 앞 문장의 내용을 고려할 때, '(부모님 같은) 사업주들이 도움을 받을 수 있는 해결책을 만드는 것이 자신들의 임무였다'는 내용으로 이어져야 문맥상 연결이 자연스러우므로 (A) business owners가 정답이다.

16. 해설 빈칸은 문두에서 두 문장을 연결하는 접속부사 자리이다. 빈칸 앞 문장의 '저희 임무는 사업주들이 도움을 받을 수 있는 해결책을 만드는 것'이라는 내용과 빈칸 뒷부분의 '사업을 운영하는 것은 합리적인 비용이 드는 일이어야 한다고 덧붙였다'는 내용을 고려할 때, 비슷한 맥락에서 이야기를 추가하고 있으므로 (B) Likewise가 정답이다.

UNIT 02. 대명사

핵심 문제 유형

본서 p.203

1. (A)

[1] 다음 공지에 관한 문제입니다.

리치몬드 아트 센터에 여러분을 초대하오니 집에 놓을 아기자기한 소품 및 장식품 만드는 법을 배우며 즐거운 시간을 보내시기 바랍니다. 공방은 모든 연령에게 열려 있습니다. 집 여기저기에 널려있는 이미 가지고 있는 것들을 사용하는 간단한 프로젝트로 넘어가기 전

에 기본 공예 도구 및 재료로 작업하는 방법을 가르쳐 드립니다. 이는 여름을 맞이하여 집을 새롭게 할 아주 좋은 기회입니다. 무엇보다도, 가정용품을 업사이클하고 용도를 변경하는 좋은 방법이 됩니다. 쓰레기 매립지로 보내는 대신, **1** 그것들에 새 생명을 줄 수 있습니다.

등록하시려면 www.richmondcenter.org를 방문해 주세요.

어휘 invite 초대하다 | enjoy 즐기다 | learn 배우다 | craft 공예품을 만들다 | neat 아기자기한, 단정한 | ornament 장식품 | decoration 장식(품) | workshop 공방 | teach 가르치다 | basic 기본적인 | tool 도구 | move onto ~로 이동하다 | simple 단순한 | use 사용하다 | lie 있다, 놓여 있다 | terrific 아주 좋은 | opportunity 기회 | refresh 새롭게 하다 | in time for ~하는 시간에 맞춰 | upcycle (재활용품을) 더 나은 것으로 만들다 | repurpose 다른 용도로 변경하다 | household item 가정용품 | instead of ~대신에 | end up in 결국 ~로 끝나다 | landfill 쓰레기 매립지 | register 등록하다

해설 빈칸은 동사 give의 목적어 자리로 빈칸 앞 문장을 통해 '새 생명을 줄 수 있는 대상'이 household items임을 알 수 있으므로 이를 지칭하는 목적격 인칭 대명사 (A) them이 정답이다.

Practice

1. (B)	2. (A)	3. (B)	4. (C)	5. (D)
6. (A)	7. (A)	8. (B)	9. (D)	10. (D)
11. (A)	12. (D)	13. (D)	14. (A)	15. (B)
16. (B)				

[1-4] 다음 편지에 관한 문제입니다.

5월 14일

론다 해리스
로디언 우즈 17번지
레플로어 MI 38940

해리스 씨께,

컬레러티 펀즈에서 개인 대출을 진행하는 데 관심을 보여주셔서 감사합니다. 귀하의 신청을 고려하기 전, 귀하께 **1** 추가 정보를 제공해 주실 것을 요청 드립니다.

지난 세 달 **2** 간 발생한 은행 입출금 내역서와 급여 명세서를 제출해 주시기 바랍니다. 저희 기업 이메일 주소인 loans@cularityfunds.com로 문서를 보내주시면 됩니다. 대출 담당자 레오나르도 콜 씨에게 **3** 그것들을 직접 가져다주셔도 됩니다. **4** 보안상의 이유로, 서류를 우편으로 보내실 수는 없습니다. 서류를 받는 대로, 콜 씨가 연락드려 귀하의 대출에 관해 알려드릴 것입니다.

진심으로,

마틴 퀸, 은행 지점장
컬레러티 펀즈

어휘 express 표현하다 | interest 관심 | secure (담보를 잡혀) 지불 보증하다 | loan 대출 | consider 고려하다 | application 신청(서) | submit 제출하다 | bank statement 은행 입출금 내역서 | pay slip 급여 명세서 | corporate 기업의 | deliver 배달하다

1. 해설 빈칸은 information을 수식하는 자리로 '추가적인 정보를 요청한다'는 의미가 되어야 문맥상 자연스러우므로 형용사 (B) additional이 정답이다.

2. 해설 빈칸은 the last three months를 목적어로 취하는 전치사 자리로 '지난 세 달간 발생한 급여 명세서'라는 의미가 되어야 하므로 (A) from이 정답이다.

3. 해설 빈칸은 동사 deliver의 목적어 자리이다. '문서를 기업 이메일 주소로 보내달라'는 빈칸 앞 문장의 내용을 고려할 때, 빈칸에는 documents를 지칭하는 표현이 들어가야 문맥상 자연스러우므로 (B) them이 정답이다.

4. (A) 계약서를 받으면 이자율을 확인하세요.
(B) 개인 대출은 약간의 재정적 유연성을 제공할 수 있습니다.
(C) 보안상의 이유로, 서류를 우편으로 보내실 수는 없습니다.
(D) 저희 은행은 매년 고객 수가 증가하고 있습니다.

해설 빈칸 앞부분의 '서류를 기업 이메일 주소로 보내거나 대출 담당자에게 직접 가져다줘도 된다'는 내용을 고려할 때, 서류 제출 방법에 관한 안내와 연관된 내용으로 이어지는 것이 문맥상 자연스러우므로 (C) For security reasons, sending documents through the post is not an option.이 정답이다.

[5-8] 다음 이메일에 관한 문제입니다.

수신: shane@richardsonwebdesign.com
발신: j_owen@powellcorp.com
날짜: 11월 7일
제목: 웹 사이트 지원

셰인, 안녕하세요.

제 웹 사이트 문제를 최대한 빨리 도와주시면 감사하겠습니다. **5** 제가 몇 군데 소소하게 수정을 시도했어요. 어찌 된 일인지 제가 '소개' 페이지에서 몇 단락을 삭제했어요. 그것들이 갑자기 **6** 사라져버렸어요. 제가 한 일을 직접 되돌릴 수 있을 줄 알았는데, 여기저기 몇 가지 시도를 해보고 상황이 더 **7** 심각해지기 전에 멈춰야 한다고 생각했어요. 사라진 콘텐츠를 복구해 주시길 간절히 바랍니다.

그리고, 웹 사이트에 간단히 수정하는 방법을 알려주실 수 있을까요? 기본적인 업데이트를 해야 할 때마다 다른 **8** 누군가에게 의지하고 싶지 않아요.

54 파고다 토익 기본 완성 RC

감사합니다.

자넬 오원

어휘 appreciate 고마워하다 | somehow 왠지, 어쩐지 | erase 지우다, 삭제하다 | paragraph 단락 | suddenly 갑자기 | figure 판단하다, 생각하다 | undo 원상태로 돌리다 | try out 시험 삼아 해보다 | situation 상황 | restore 복구하다, 되찾게 하다 | lost 잃어버린 | show 보여주다 | rely on ~에 의지하다 | basic 기본적인 | update 업데이트

5. (A) 이 프로젝트를 진행하는 것은 보람 있었어요.
(B) 이제 교체할 때가 되었어요.
(C) 그러나 지금은 훨씬 더 잘 작동하고 있어요.
(D) 제가 몇 군데 소소하게 수정을 시도했어요.

해설 빈칸 앞 문장의 '제 웹 사이트 문제를 최대한 빨리 도와달라'는 내용과 뒤에 이어지는 '소개 페이지에 몇 단락을 삭제했다'는 내용을 고려할 때, '수정을 하려고 시도했었다'는 내용이 들어가야 문맥상 연결이 자연스러우므로 (D) I was trying to make some minor adjustments.가 정답이다.

6. 해설 빈칸은 문장의 동사 자리이다. 빈칸 앞 문장의 '제가 몇 단락을 삭제했다'는 내용을 고려할 때, They는 a few paragraphs를 가리키므로 '그것들이 사라져 버렸다'는 내용으로 이어져야 문맥상 연결이 자연스러우므로 (A) disappeared가 정답이다.

7. 해설 빈칸은 동사 make에 대한 목적격 보어 자리로 빈칸 앞 비교급 강조 부사 even이 있으므로 비교급 형용사 (A) worse가 정답이다. 동사 make는 5형식 문장에서 「make + 목적어 + 목적격 보어」 '~을 ~한 상태로 만들다'의 구조를 취한다.

8. 해설 빈칸은 rely on의 목적어 자리이다. 빈칸 앞 문장의 '웹 사이트에 간단히 수정하는 방법을 알려달라'는 내용을 고려할 때, '기본적인 업데이트를 해야 할 때마다 다른 누군가에게 의지하고 싶지 않다'는 내용으로 이어져야 문맥상 연결이 자연스러우므로 (B) someone이 정답이다.

[9-12] 다음 이메일에 관한 문제입니다.

발신: 안내데스크 〈helpdesk@lilylakegym.org〉
수신: 도리스 보우어즈 〈d.bowers@moserver.com〉
제목: 회원권 만료
날짜: 8월 14일

보우어즈 씨께,

이 이메일은 귀하의 릴리 레이크 체육관 회원권이 오늘부터 한 달 후 종료됨을 알려 드리기 위함입니다. 귀하의 평소 일정에 지장을 받지 않고 계속해서 저희 시설을 이용하시려면 **9** 그것은 반드시 갱신되어야 합니다. **10** 갱신이 처리되는 데는 며칠 소요되니, 일주일 전에 미리 하시기를 권장 드립니다. 그렇게 하시려면, 다음에 오실

때 저희 직원에게 말씀해 주시면 됩니다.

회원권 종료를 원하실 **11** 경우, 추가 조치는 필요하지 않습니다. **12** 지정된 날짜에 귀하의 카드가 더 이상 저희 시설에의 입장을 허용하지 않게 됩니다.

이 안내의 내용에 관해 말씀하고 싶은 내용이 있으시거나, 그밖에 다른 질문이 있으시면, 이 이메일에 바로 회신해 주시기 바랍니다.

진심으로,

릴리 레이크 체육관

어휘 expiration 만료, 만기 | gym 체육관 | conclude 끝나다 | renew 갱신하다 | continue 계속하다 | facility 시설 | disruption 지장, 방해 | usual 평소의 | schedule 일정 | staff member 직원 | terminate 종료하다 | further 추가의 | action 조치, 행동 | require 필요로 하다 | no longer 더 이상 ~않다 | grant 승인하다 | access 입장 | respond 답장을 보내다 | directly 직접

9. 해설 빈칸은 문장의 주어 자리이다. 빈칸 뒤 동사를 고려할 때 문장의 주어 자리에는 갱신되어야 하는 대상이 와야 하며, 빈칸 앞 문장에서 '회원권이 오늘부터 한 달 후 종료된다'고 했으므로, 갱신 대상이 회원권임을 알 수 있으므로 회원권을 지칭하는 (D) It이 정답이다.

10. (A) 직원이 회원님의 멤버십 옵션을 검토해 드릴 것입니다.
(B) 운동 루틴은 모든 모바일 기기에 다운로드할 수 있습니다.
(C) 특정 조건을 충족하면 할인 혜택을 받을 수 있습니다.
(D) 갱신이 처리되는 데는 며칠 소요되니, 일주일 전에 미리 하시기를 권장 드립니다.

해설 빈칸 앞 문장의 '지장 없이 계속해서 시설을 이용하시려면 반드시 갱신되어야 한다'는 내용과 빈칸 뒤 문장의 '그렇게 하시려면 다음에 오실 때 저희 직원에게 말씀해 주시면 됩니다'라는 내용을 고려할 때, 갱신과 관련된 내용이 들어가야 문맥상 연결이 자연스러우므로 (D) Renewals take a few days to process, so we recommend doing it one week in advance.가 정답이다.

11. 해설 빈칸은 두 개의 문장을 연결하는 부사절 접속사 자리이다. '회원권 종료를 원할 경우, 추가 조치는 필요하지 않다'는 의미가 되어야 문맥상 자연스러우므로 조건절의 의미를 전달하는 (A) Should가 정답이다. 참고로, 희박한 가능성에 대한 추측의 의미를 담은 조건절 표현인 「If + 주어 + should + 동사원형」 '혹시 ~한다면'은 접속사 if를 생략하고 주어와 동사를 도치한 형태인 「Should + 주어 + 동사원형」으로도 사용된다.

12. 해설 빈칸은 명사 date를 수식하는 자리로 회원권이 종료되는 지정된 날짜로서의 의미를 담고 있어야 문맥상 자연스러우므로 (D) specified가 정답이다.

[13-16] 다음 이메일에 관한 문제입니다.

수신: help@aspironsystems.com
발신: sabrina@lucidworks.com
날짜: 7월 16일
제목: PZ9881 스피커
첨부: 송장; 전기 기사 청구서

관계자분께:

지난달 저는 제 행사장에 놓을 PZ9881 스피커 8개를 구입했습니다. 하지만 최소한 그중 절반이 광고처럼 **13** 작동하지 않는 것을 발견했습니다. 소리가 너무 낮고 왜곡돼서 나왔습니다. 저는 공인 전기 기사에게 그 문제를 살펴보게 했습니다. 그는 **14** 저에게 근본적인 문제는 제품의 부품과 관련이 있다고 확실히 말해줬습니다. **15** 귀사의 제조 공정에 결함이 있는 것 같습니다.

이러한 문제의 결과 저는 전체 스피커에 대한 환불 및 전기 기사의 작업비 배상을 요청하는 바입니다. 전기 기사 청구서 및 원래 영수증 사본을 첨부해 드립니다. 동료들에게 아스피론 시스템즈에 대해 아주 좋은 이야기를 들었던 터라 실망스럽기에 **16** 문제가 조속히 해결되기를 바랍니다.

진심으로,

사브리나 매닝
시설 관리자, 루시드 웍스

어휘 attachment 첨부 | invoice 송장, 청구서 | electrician 전기 기사 | bill 청구서 | purchase 구매 | speaker 스피커 | at least 최소한 | advertise 광고하다 | sound 소리 | low 낮은 | distort 일그러뜨리다, 비틀다 | certified 공인된 | look into 조사하다, 살펴보다 | assure 장담하다 | root cause 근본 원인 | root 근원, 뿌리 | product 제품 | component 부품, 구성요소 | as a result of ~의 결과로 | request 요청하다 | refund 환불 | reimbursement 변상, 배상 | attach 첨부하다 | copy 사본 | original 원래의 | disappointed 실망한 | colleague 동료 | address 처리하다 | quickly 빠르게 | facility 시설

13. 해설 빈칸은 that 명사절 내 주어 half of them에 대한 동사 자리이다. 빈칸 앞에 동사의 부정형을 만들어주는 do not이 있음을 고려할 때, 빈칸은 동사원형 자리이므로 (D) function이 정답이다.

14. 해설 빈칸은 동사 assure의 목적어 자리이다. 빈칸 앞 문장의 '저는 공인 전기 기사에게 그 문제를 살펴보게 했습니다'라는 내용을 고려할 때, 전기 기사가 나에게 확실히 말해줬다는 의미가 되어야 문맥상 자연스러우므로 (A) me가 정답이다.

15. (A) 장비가 잘 설계되었다고 생각했습니다.
(B) **귀사의 제조 공정에 결함이 있는 것 같습니다.**
(C) 그 전기 기술자는 15년의 경력을 보유하고 있습니다.
(D) 배송비가 너무 비쌀 수 있습니다.

해설 빈칸 앞부분의 스피커 소리에 문제가 있어 전기 기사에게 그 문제를 살펴보게 한 결과 전기 기사는 부품 문제라고 확신했다는 내용

을 고려할 때, 스피커 문제와 관련된 내용으로 이어져야 문맥상 자연스러우므로 (B) A fault is likely present in your manufacturing process.가 정답이다.

16. 해설 빈칸은 동사 hope의 목적어인 명사절 내 주어 자리이다. 빈칸 앞부분에서 스피커 문제로 인한 전체 환불 및 전기 기사 출장비 배상을 요청하며 실망한 상태임을 표현하고 있음을 고려할 때, '해당 문제가 빠르게 처리되기를 바란다'는 내용으로 이어져야 문맥상 자연스러우므로 (B) problem이 정답이다.

UNIT 03. 연결어

핵심 문제 유형
본서 p.208

1. (D)

[1] 다음 공지에 관한 문제입니다.

밀포드 우드웍스 클럽에서 8월 11일 일요일에 가구 세일을 개최합니다. 세일은 오전 10시부터 오후 3시까지 리크닐드 가 59번지에 있는 밀포드 커뮤니티 센터에서 진행됩니다. 의자부터 탁자까지 다양한 수제 가구가 있을 예정입니다. 재고가 오래 가지 않으니 일찍 오세요. **1** 또한 고르실 수 있는 다양한 종류의 간식과 디저트도 있습니다. 저희가 그날 내내 진행할 예정인 작업장에 들러서 저희 회원들이 어떻게 상품을 만드는지 알아 보세요. 더 많은 정보를 알아보시려면 www.milfordwoodworks.co.nz/upcoming로 밀포드 우드웍스 클럽을 방문해 주세요.

어휘 furniture 가구 | sale 할인 판매, 세일 | run 진행되다 | a variety of 다양한 | handmade 수제의 | stock 재고 | a wide selection of 다양한 | snack 간식 | dessert 디저트 | choose 선택하다 | stop by 들르다 | workshop 작업장 | hold 주최[개최]하다 | craft 만들다 | goods 상품

해설 빈칸 앞쪽의 '다양한 수제 가구가 있을 예정입니다'라는 내용과 빈칸 뒷 부분의 '다양한 종류의 간식과 디저트도 있습니다'라는 내용을 고려할 때, 가구뿐만 아니라 먹거리도 있을 것이라는 내용으로 연결되어야 문맥상 자연스러우므로 부가의 의미를 갖는 부사 (D) In addition이 정답이다.

Practice
본서 p.209

1. (D)	**2.** (B)	**3.** (A)	**4.** (A)	**5.** (A)
6. (A)	**7.** (B)	**8.** (C)	**9.** (A)	**10.** (B)
11. (D)	**12.** (C)	**13.** (B)	**14.** (D)	**15.** (A)
16. (D)				

[1-4] 다음 편지에 관한 문제입니다.

베이커 씨께,

저는 슬립원 미디어의 매니저인 신디아 챈드입니다. **1** 저희가 제공해드릴 수 있는 것을 말씀드리고자 합니다. 저희는 귀사처럼 소규모 사업체를 대상으로 광범위한 종류의 광고물을 제작하는 일을 전문으로 합니다. 저희는 사업주들이 광고 **2** 제작 비용 때문에 단념하게 되는 것을 잘 알고 있습니다. **3** 하지만, 저희는 그 비용에서 극히 일부만으로 고급 서비스를 제공해 드릴 수 있습니다. 저희 팀은 최종 결과물에 대한 만족을 보장해 드리기 위해 쉬지 않고 작업해 드립니다. 최종 결과물에 만족하지 않으시는 경우, 전액 환불을 **4** 제공해 드리겠습니다. 저희는 맡은 모든 작업에 저희의 명성을 걸고 임합니다.

이것이 마음에 드신다면, 저희에게 전화 주셔서 무료 상담을 받아 보세요. 일정 조정 및 가격 책정 관련하여 궁금해하실 만한 모든 질문에 얼마든지 답변해 드리겠습니다.

어휘　specialize in ~를 전문으로 하다 | create 만들어내다 | a range of 다양한 | diverse 다양한 | advertising 광고 | material 자료 | business 사업체 | owner 주인 | put ~ off ~의 의욕을 꺾다, 단념하게 하다 | cost 비용 | advertisement 광고 | provide 제공하다 | premium 고급의 | mere 겨우, 단지 | fraction 부분, 일부 | tirelessly 지칠 줄 모르고 | ensure 보장하다 | final 최종의 | product 제품, 결과물 | full 완전한, 모든 | refund 환불 | put ~ on the line ~를 걸다 | reputation 명성 | sound ~처럼 들리다 | free 무료의 | consultation 상담 | scheduling 일정 관리 | pricing 가격 책정

1.　(A) 인터넷 광고가 더 보편화되었습니다.
　　(B) 저희 사무실은 기차역 근처에 위치해 있습니다.
　　(C) 주말에는 근무하지 않는다는 점을 유의해 주세요.
　　(D) 저희가 제공해드릴 수 있는 것을 말씀드리고자 합니다.

　　해설　빈칸 앞 문장에서 '저는 슬립원 미디어의 매니저인 신디아 챈드'라며 자신을 소개하고 빈칸 뒤 문장에서 '귀사처럼 소규모 사업체를 대상으로 광범위한 종류의 광고물을 제작하는 일을 전문으로 한다'며 회사에서 제공하는 서비스를 소개하고 있음을 고려할 때, 서비스 소개를 시작하는 성격의 문장이 들어가야 문맥상 연결이 자연스러우므로 (D) I would like to tell you what we can offer.가 정답이다.

2.　해설　빈칸은 명사 advertisements를 목적어로 취하는 전치사 of의 목적어인 동명사 자리이다. 빈칸 앞 문장의 '광고물 제작을 전문으로 한다'는 내용과 빈칸 뒷 문장의 '극히 일부 비용으로 고급 서비스를 제공한다'는 내용을 고려할 때, '사업주들이 광고 제작 비용 때문에 단념하게 되는 것을 잘 알고 있다'는 내용이 들어가야 문맥상 연결이 자연스러우므로 (B) producing이 정답이다.

3.　해설　빈칸은 두 문장을 연결하는 접속부사 자리이다. 빈칸 앞 문장의 '사업주들이 광고 제작 비용 때문에 단념하게 되는 것을 잘 알고 있다'는 내용과 빈칸 뒷 부분의 '그 비용에서 극히 일부만으로 고급 서비스를 제공해 드릴 수 있다'는 내용을 고려할 때, 두 문장의 내용이 서로

반대되는 의미를 전달하고 있으므로 (A) However가 정답이다.

4.　해설　빈칸은 주어와 목적어 사이 동사 자리이다. 빈칸 뒤 목적어가 있으므로 능동태 동사이며, 빈칸 뒤 문장의 '맡은 모든 작업에 저희의 명성을 걸고 임한다'는 내용을 고려할 때, '최종 결과물에 만족하지 않는 경우 전액 환불을 제공하겠다'는 내용으로 이어져야 문맥상 자연스러우므로 정답은 (A) will offer이다.

[5-8] 다음 편지에 관한 문제입니다.

9월 8일

모스 씨께,

리젠시 플레이스에 예정된 도로 정비에 대해 알려 드리고자 편지를 드립니다. 9월 16일 오전 8시부터 리젠시 플레이스로의 출입을 차단할 **5** 예정입니다. **6** 동봉된 지도에 영향을 받는 지역이 나와 있습니다. 귀하의 **7** 사업체가 리젠시 플레이스에서 가까이 위치해 있다는 점으로 인해 이날에는 특히 출퇴근 시간 동안 훨씬 더 많은 교통량을 예상하셔야 합니다. **8** 따라서, 늘어난 차량 수로 인해 주차 자리가 없을 수도 있음을 직원들에게 알려주는 것을 고려하셔야 합니다. 작업은 9월 20일까지 완료될 예정이며, 혹시 지연이 발생하게 된다면 지연에 대해서는 귀하께 알려드릴 것입니다. 협조 및 이해해 주셔서 감사합니다.

진심으로,

돈 폭스
교통국장
시너지

어휘　planned 계획된 | road 도로 | maintenance 유지 보수, 정비 | close off 차단시키다 | entry 출입, 들어감 | due to ~로 인해 | fact 사실 | locate (특정 위치에) 두다 | expect 예상하다, 기대하다 | traffic 교통(량) | particularly 특히 | rush hour 출퇴근 혼잡 시간 | consider 고려하다 | parking 주차 | spot 자리 | increased 늘어난 | number 수 | complete 완료하다, 마무리하다 | inform 알리다 | delay 지연 | arise 발생하다, 생기다 | cooperation 협조, 협력 | understanding 이해 | transportation 운송, 교통 (기관)

5.　해설　빈칸은 현재분사 closing과 함께 주어 we에 대한 동사 구문을 완성하는 자리이다. 빈칸 앞 문장의 '예정된 도로 정비에 대해 알려 드린다'는 내용을 고려할 때, 미래 진행 시제로 이어져야 문맥상 연결이 자연스러우므로 (A) will be가 정답이다.

6.　**(A) 동봉된 지도에 영향을 받는 지역이 나와 있습니다.**
　　(B) 대체 경로로는 레이버리 로드를 이용하실 수 있습니다.
　　(C) 그러나 일부 시 공무원들이 행사에 참석할 수도 있습니다.
　　(D) 이번 주말까지 투표를 접수할 예정입니다.

　　해설　빈칸 앞 문장의 '리젠시 플레이스로의 출입을 차단할 예정'이라는 내용을 고려할 때, 출입 차단 지역과 관련된 내용으로 이어져야 문맥상 연결이 자연스러우므로 (A) The enclosed map shows the affected area.가 정답이다.

---

7. **해설** 빈칸은 that 명사절 내 주어 자리이다. 빈칸 뒷 부분의 '주차 자리가 없을 수도 있음을 직원들에게 알려주는 것을 고려해야 한다'는 내용을 고려할 때, 귀하의 사업체가 리젠시 플레이스 가까이 위치해 있다는 점'이라는 내용이 되어야 문맥상 흐름이 자연스러우므로 (B) business가 정답이다.

---

8. **해설** 빈칸은 문두에서 앞 문장과의 연결을 매끄럽게 하는 접속부사 자리이다. 빈칸 앞 문장의 '특히 출퇴근 시간 동안 훨씬 더 많은 교통량을 예상해야 한다'는 내용과 빈칸 뒷 부분의 '주차 자리가 없을 수도 있음을 직원들에게 알려주는 것을 고려해야 한다'의 내용을 고려할 때, 두 문장이 인과 관계로 이어져야 문맥상 연결이 자연스러우므로 (C) Therefore가 정답이다.

[9-12] 다음 광고에 관한 문제입니다.

트로피쿨 워터 웍스
93 론 가, 스펜서
테네시 주, 미국

트로피쿨 워터 웍스는 깨끗한 물을 공급하겠다는 단순한 사명에서 탄생했습니다. 저희와 제휴를 맺으면, 매번 **9** 안전하고 깨끗한 식수 제공을 보장해 드립니다. 서비스의 일환으로 저희는 정기적으로 귀하의 식수의 미네랄 수준을 검사해 드리고, 배관을 점검해 드리며, 필요시 고쳐드립니다. **10** 또한, 파이프에 교체가 필요하다고 판단하면 타사보다 저렴한 가격에 해드릴 수 있습니다.

고도의 훈련을 받았으며 자격을 갖춘 기술자들로 이루어진 저희 팀은 언제나 여러분과 지식을 공유할 준비가 되어 있습니다. **11** 게다가 언제나 신규 기술 및 기법에 관한 최신 동향을 파악하고 있습니다. 저희의 평판은 고객 추천 후기로 **12** 확인되며, www.tropicoolwater.com/reviews에서 읽어보실 수 있습니다. 무료 상담을 받으시려면 오늘 926-555-2836으로 전화 주세요.

어휘 mission 임무 | provide 제공하다, 공급하다 | clean 깨끗한 | partner with ~와 제휴하다 | ensure 보장하다 | drinking water 식수 | periodically 정기적으로 | test 시험하다 | mineral 무기물, 미네랄 | inspect 점검하다 | pipe (배)관 | adjustment 수정 | replace 교체하다 | cheaper 더 저렴한 | rate 가격 | highly 고도로 | trained 훈련을 받은 | qualified 자격을 갖춘 | technician 기술자 | ready 준비가 된 | share 공유하다 | knowledge 지식 | reputation 명성, 평판 | customer 고객 | testimonial 추천의 글 | consultation 상담

---

9. **해설** 빈칸은 형용사 clean과 함께 명사구 drinking water를 수식하는 형용사 자리이므로 (A) safe가 정답이다.

---

10. **해설** 빈칸은 두 문장을 연결하는 접속부사 자리이다. 빈칸 앞 문장에서 제공하는 서비스를 나열하고 있으며, 빈칸 뒷 부분에서도 마찬가지로 제공 가능한 서비스를 언급하고 있음을 고려할 때, 부가의 의미를 전달하는 접속부사가 들어가야 문맥상 연결이 자연스러우므로 (B)

Additionally가 정답이다.

---

11. (A) 보통 다음 회의는 다음 달 초에 열릴 것입니다.
(B) 지난달 워크숍에 참석해 주셔서 감사합니다.
(C) 충성도 높은 고객 기반을 구축하는 비결은 좋은 광고에 있습니다.
(D) 게다가 언제나 신규 기술 및 기법에 관한 최신 동향을 파악하고 있습니다.

해설 빈칸 앞 문장의 '고도의 훈련을 받았으며 자격을 갖춘 기술자들로 이루어진 저희 팀은 언제나 지식을 공유할 준비가 되어 있다'는 내용을 고려할 때, 팀원의 자질 또는 능력과 관련된 내용으로 이어져야 문맥상 연결이 자연스러우므로 (D) Also, they are always staying up-to-date with new technologies and techniques.가 정답이다.

---

12. **해설** 빈칸 앞뒤로 be동사와 by가 있음을 고려할 때, 수동태 동사 구문을 완성하는 과거분사 자리임을 알 수 있으므로 (C) supported가 정답이다.

[13-16] 다음 보도 자료에 관한 문제입니다.

즉시 배포용

보던 (3월 13일) — 보던에 본사를 둔 식료품 체인점 시그닛 브랜즈에서 7월에 셰필드에 신규 **13** 지점을 개장할 계획을 공표했다. 작년에 더 규모가 큰 건물로 이전한, 한때 셰필드 우체국이 있었던 건물에서 본즈 가의 모퉁이를 차지하게 된다.

시그닛 브랜즈의 최고 경영자인 웨이드 길버트가 말하길, "저희가 **14** 마침내 셰필드 지역 사회에 기여할 수 있어 대단히 기쁩니다. **15** 저희는 그 지역에 아주 관심이 많았지만 적당한 기회를 기다려야 했습니다. 그렇게 명망 있는 위치에 개장하는 기회는 너무 좋아서 놓칠 수 없었습니다."

시그닛 브랜즈는 지역 사회 내 고용처럼 운영하는 도시 내에 많은 투자를 하는 것으로 유명하다. 고용하는 전체 직원의 약 70퍼센트는 자신들이 **16** 근무하는 매장에서 5킬로미터 반경에 거주한다.

어휘 immediate 즉각적인 | release 공개, 발표 | based ~에 본사를 둔 | grocery 식료품점 | chain 체인점 | make public (대중 매체를 통해) 일반에 알리다 | occupy 차지하다 | post office 우체국 | move 이동하다, 이사하다 | comment 견해를 밝히다 | excitement 흥분, 신남 | serve 기여하다, 도움이 되다 | community 지역 사회 | chance 기회 | prestigious 명망 있는, 유명한 | location 위치, 지점 | pass up 거절하다, (기회를) 놓치다 | be known for ~로 알려져 있다 | invest 투자하다 | heavily 많이, 심하게 | operate 영업하다, 운영하다 | such as ~같이, 처럼 | hire 고용하다 | approximately 대략 | employee 직원

---

13. **해설** 빈칸은 a new의 수식을 받는 명사 자리이므로 (B) location이 정답이다.

---

14. **해설** 빈칸은 동사를 수식하는 부사 자리이다. '식료품 체인점 시그닛

---

58 파고다 토익 기본 완성 RC

브랜즈에서 셰필드에 신규 지점을 개장할 계획을 공표했다'는 앞 단락의 내용을 고려할 때, '마침내 셰필드 지역 사회에 기여할 수 있어 기쁘다'는 내용으로 이어져야 문맥상 연결이 자연스러우므로 (D) finally가 정답이다.

15. (A) 저희는 그 지역에 아주 관심이 많았지만 적당한 기회를 기다려야 했습니다.
(B) 개업 행사는 셰필드의 전역의 모든 주요 뉴스 매체에서 모두 다룰 예정입니다.
(C) 저희 회사는 지난 5년 동안 매년 꾸준히 수익을 증가시켰습니다.
(D) 셰필드 우체국은 접근성을 높이기 위해 기차역 근처로 이전되었습니다.

해설 빈칸 뒤 문장의 '그렇게 명망 있는 위치에 개장하는 기회는 너무 좋아서 놓칠 수 없었다'는 내용을 고려할 때, '그 지역에 아주 관심이 많았지만 적당한 기회를 기다려야 했다'는 내용이 앞에 들어가야 문맥상 연결이 자연스러우므로 (A) We were very interested in the area, but we wanted to wait for the right opportunity.가 정답이다.

16. 해설 빈칸은 주어 they에 대한 동사 자리이다. 빈칸 앞 문장의 '지역 사회 내 고용처럼 운영하는 도시 내에 많은 투자를 하는 것으로 유명하다'는 내용 및 문맥상 they가 지칭하는 대상이 employees임을 고려할 때, '고용하는 전체 직원의 약 70퍼센트는 자신들이 근무하는 매장에서 5킬로미터 반경에 거주한다'는 내용이 되어야 문맥상 자연스러우므로 (D) work가 정답이다.

UNIT 04. 어휘 선택

핵심 문제 유형

본서 p.213

1. (C)

[1] 다음 이메일에 관한 문제입니다.

수신: 로시 매든
발신: 보몬트 상품
날짜: 9월 26일
제목: 주문품 도착

매든 씨께,

귀하의 특별 주문품인 고성능 타워 팬 1개와 80리터 오븐 1개가 저희 매장에 배송되었음을 알려드리게 되어 기쁩니다. 이제 귀하께 이 **1** 가전제품들을 배송해 드릴 준비가 되었습니다. 315-555-6795로 전화하셔서 배송을 담당하는 조이 로우리와 통화하겠다고 요청해 주세요. 그녀가 작성하실 양식을 제공해 드릴 수 있습니다.

고객 서비스, 보몬트 상품

어휘 order 주문 | arrival 도착 | pleased 기쁜 | inform 알리다 | high-power 강력한, 고성능의 | tower fan 타워팬, 수직형 선풍기, 환풍기 | oven 오븐 | deliver 배송하다 | ready 준비가 된 | delivery 배송

해설 빈칸은 these의 수식을 받는 명사 자리이다. 빈칸 앞 문장의 '고성능 타워 팬 1개와 80리터 오븐 1개가 매장에 배송되었다'는 내용을 고려할 때, '이 가전제품들을 배송할 준비가 됐다'는 내용으로 이어져야 문맥상 연결이 자연스러우므로 (C) appliances가 정답이다.

Practice

본서 p.214

1. (A)	**2.** (D)	**3.** (B)	**4.** (B)	**5.** (A)
6. (A)	**7.** (C)	**8.** (D)	**9.** (C)	**10.** (B)
11. (A)	**12.** (B)	**13.** (D)	**14.** (A)	**15.** (B)
16. (C)				

[1-4] 다음 설명서에 관한 문제입니다.

모카드 샤워 워터 필터를 구매해 주셔서 감사합니다. 새 제품으로 샤워하실 때마다 가장 깨끗한 물의 혜택을 누리게 되실 겁니다. 필터를 최대한으로 활용하려면 첫 사용 전에 필터를 활성화하는 것이 **1** 권장됩니다. **2** 이를 위해서는 필터를 20분간 찬물에 담가 주세요. 그런 다음 **3** 꽉 맞을 때까지 시계 방향으로 돌려 조이는 방법으로 필터를 샤워기 헤드에 부착하기만 하면 됩니다. 샤워기의 물줄기가 **4** 약해졌다고 느껴지면, 필터 교체가 필요하다는 표시일 수도 있습니다. 각 필터는 세 달 정도 지속됩니다.

어휘 purchase 구매하다 | shower 샤워기, 샤워하다 | filter 필터 | enjoy 즐기다, 누리다 | benefit 혜택, 이득 | purest 가장 순수한 | ensure 반드시 ~하다, 보장하다 | get the most out of ~를 최대한으로 활용하다 | activate 작동시키다, 활성화시키다 | simply 단순히 | attach 붙이다 | shower head 샤워기 헤드 | screw 돌려서 조이다 | clockwise 시계 방향으로 | fit 맞다 | notice 알아채다, 의식하다 | water flow 유수량 | indicate 나타내다, 보여주다 | replace 교체하다 | last 지속되다

1. 해설 빈칸은 be동사 뒤 수동태 동사 구문을 완성하는 과거분사 자리이다. 가주어 it, 진주어 that절로 이루어진 문장으로, 빈칸 앞쪽의 '모카드 샤워 워터 필터를 구매해 주셔서 감사하다'는 내용과 '필터를 최대한으로 활용하려면'이라는 내용을 고려할 때, '첫 사용 전에 필터를 활성화하는 것이 권장된다'는 내용으로 이어져야 문맥상 자연스러우므로 (A) suggested가 정답이다.

2. (A) 도시마다 물을 정화하는 과정이 다를 수 있습니다.
(B) 물 사용량을 줄이는 것은 추가적인 이점입니다.
(C) 각각 따로 판매되는 세 가지 부품이 있습니다.
(D) 이를 위해서는 필터를 20분간 찬물에 담가 주세요.

해설　빈칸 앞 문장의 '첫 사용 전에 필터를 활성화하라'는 내용을 고려할 때, 필터 활성화 방법을 안내하는 내용으로 이어져야 문맥상 자연스러우므로 (D) To do this, soak the filter in some cold water for 20 minutes.가 정답이다.

3.　해설　빈칸은 동사 fit을 수식하는 부사 자리이다. 주절과 until 종속절과의 관계를 고려할 때, '꽉 맞을 때까지 시계 방향으로 돌려 필터를 샤워기 헤드에 부착하라'는 내용이 되어야 문맥상 자연스러우므로 (B) tightly가 정답이다.

4.　해설　빈칸은 명사 water flow를 수식하는 형용사 자리이다. 빈칸 앞에 has 동사가 있고, 그 뒤에 water flow는 diminished의 수식을 받는 명사구이다. 따라서 '샤워기의 유수량이 줄었다면'이라는 의미가 되어야 하므로 형용사 (B) diminished가 정답이다. (D) diminishable도 형용사이나 '줄일 수 있는'이란 의미로 해석상 어울리지 않는다.

[5-8] 다음 이메일에 관한 문제입니다.

수신: 전 직원
발신: 조안 페인
날짜: 4월 12일
제목: 버트 손턴

여러분, 안녕하세요.

소프트웨어 개발팀 내 **5** 변동에 관해 알려 드릴 소식이 있습니다. 캐피털 컴퓨터스가 시시각각 변화하는 환경에서 헤쳐 나가도록 도와주셨던 버트 손턴께서 소프트웨어 개발 이사직에서 공식적으로 물러나실 예정입니다.

그를 대신하여 소프트웨어 개발 실장인 한나 샌도발이 그 역할을 맡게 됩니다. 손턴 씨께서는 샌도발 씨가 4년 전 회사에 합류했을 때부터 **6** 멘토 역할을 해주셨습니다.

손턴 씨의 캐피털 컴퓨터스에서의 **7** 마지막 날은 4월 25일이 될 것입니다. 저희는 그에게 경의를 표하여 오후 3시에 브룩스 회의실에서 퇴임 기념 파티를 열 예정입니다. **8** 조만간 자세한 내용이 게시될 예정입니다.

어휘　share 공유하다 | development 개발 | navigate 길을 찾다, 항해하다 | ever-changing 변화무쌍한 | environment 환경 | officially 공식적으로 | retire 은퇴하다 | position 직책 | director 이사 | place 자리 | take up (누군가가 하던 일을) 이어서 계속 하다 | role 역할 | hold 주최[개최]하다 | retirement 은퇴 | in one's honor ~에게 경의를 표하며, ~를 축하하여

5.　해설　빈칸은 전치사 about의 목적어인 명사 자리이다. 빈칸을 후치 수식하는 in 전치사구와 빈칸 뒤 문장의 '버트 손턴 씨께서 소프트웨어 개발 이사직에서 공식적으로 물러날 예정'이라는 내용을 고려할 때, 소프트웨어 개발팀 내 인력 교체 소식임을 알 수 있으므로 (A) switch가 정답이다.

6.　해설　빈칸은 주어와 목적어 사이 동사 자리이다. 문장 뒷 부분에

since 부사절이 있음을 고려할 때, 현재 완료 진행 시제 문장을 완성하는 (A) has been mentoring이 정답이다. 전치사 겸 접속사 since는 과거 시점을 나타내는 표현과 함께 현재 완료 시제의 문장에서 사용된다.

7.　해설　빈칸은 뒤 Mr. Thornton's와 함께 문장의 주어인 day를 수식하는 형용사 자리이다. 빈칸 뒤 문장의 '오후 3시에 퇴임 기념 파티를 열 예정'이라는 내용을 고려할 때, '손턴 씨의 (출근) 마지막 날'이라는 의미가 되어야 문맥상 자연스러우므로 (C) final이 정답이다.

8.　(A) 해당 직책이 공고되었습니다.
(B) 손턴씨는 회사의 설립자 중 한 명이었습니다.
(C) 캐피털 컴퓨터스는 성명 발표를 요청 받았습니다.
(D) 조만간 자세한 내용이 게시될 예정입니다.

해설　빈칸 앞 문장들에서 마지막 날과 퇴임 기념 파티에 관해 언급하고 있음을 고려할 때, 해당 행사와 관련된 내용으로 이어져야 문맥상 연결이 자연스러우므로 (D) More details will be posted soon.이 정답이다.

[9-12] 다음 고객 후기에 관한 문제입니다.

저는 한 달 전에 나이무스 XL 야외 태양광 조명을 새로 구입했습니다. 과거에 구입했던 다른 태양광 조명이 상당히 불만족스러웠습니다. 모두 다소 어두침침하거나 오래 가지 않았습니다. 나이무스 조명에 대한 추천을 받은 후 몇 개 주문하기로 결정했는데, 아주 훌륭한 결정이었습니다. **9** 기대 이상이었어요.

하지만 제가 지적하고 싶은 부분은 조립하는 것이 쉬운 과정이 아니었다는 것입니다. 설명서에 헷갈리는 부분이 있다고 느꼈습니다. 이 분야에 상당히 숙련된 친구의 도움이 없었더라면, 제가 제품을 **10** 조립해 낼 수 있었을지 모르겠네요.

다른 부분으로는 조명에 딸려 오는 말뚝이 정말 **11** 튼튼해서 기분 좋게 놀랐습니다. 흙을 먼저 **12** 부드럽게 풀어줄 필요 없이 땅속에 넣을 수 있었습니다.

— E. 더글라스

어휘　outdoor 실외의 | solar 태양광의 | dissatisfied 불만족스러운 | past 과거 | a bit 다소, 조금 | dim 어둑한, 흐릿한 | last 지속되다 | recommendation 추천 | turn out (결과가 특정 방식으로) 되다 | decision 결정 | point out 지적하다 | put ~ together 조립하다 | process 과정 | instructions 설명서 | confusing 헷갈리는 | at times 가끔씩, 때로는 | skilled 숙련된, 전문적인 | area 분야 | pleasantly 기분 좋게 | surprised 놀란 | stake 말뚝, 막대 | sturdy 튼튼한 | loosen up 풀어주다

9.　(A) 모든 제안에 답변했습니다.
(B) 그 행사는 큰 문제 없이 진행되었습니다.
(C) 기대 이상이었어요.
(D) 포장이 최근에 변경되었습니다.

해설　빈칸 앞 문장의 '추천을 받은 후 주문하기로 한 결정이 아주 훌

륭한 결정이었다'는 내용을 고려할 때, '기대 이상이었다'는 내용으로 이어져야 문맥상 연결이 자연스러우므로 (C) They exceeded my expectations.가 정답이다.

10. 해설 빈칸은 would have been able to와 함께 동사구를 완성하는 동사 자리이다. '조립 과정이 쉽지 않았으며 설명서가 헷갈렸다'는 빈칸 앞부분의 내용을 고려할 때, '숙련된 친구의 도움이 없었더라면 제품을 조립해 내지 못했을 것 같다'는 내용으로 이어져야 문맥상 연결이 자연스러우므로 (B) assemble이 정답이다.

11. 해설 빈칸은 how 명사절 내에서 how의 수식을 받는 형용사 자리이다. '조명에 딸려 오는 막대가 아주 튼튼해서 기분 좋게 놀랐다'라는 의미가 되어야 문맥상 자연스러우므로 (A) sturdy가 정답이다.

12. 해설 빈칸은 조동사 have to 뒤 동사원형 자리이다. 빈칸 뒤 up이 있으며, '(단단한 땅의) 흙을 부드럽게 풀어줄 필요 없이도 말뚝을 땅속에 넣을 수 있었다'는 의미가 되어야 문맥상 자연스러우므로, loosen up '단단한 부분을 풀어주다'라는 의미를 완성하는 동사 (B) loosen이 정답이다.

[13-16] 다음 이메일에 관한 문제입니다.

수신: 사미라 로스 〈s.ross@rossdesigns.com〉
발신: 메이지 블레이즈 〈m.blaese@newtonboutique.com〉
제목: 아주 좋은 소식!
날짜: 2월 24일

사미라 씨께,

저는 최근 당신의 최신 라인에서 원피스와 스커트 60벌을 배송 받았습니다. 그것들은 지난 몇 주간 가장 잘 팔린 제품들이었습니다. 제 **13** 고객들 중 몇 명은 재질뿐만 아니라 독특한 디자인을 칭찬했습니다. **14** 합리적인 가격은 당신의 작품을 그만큼 훨씬 더 매력적으로 만들어 줍니다.

이번 배송품이 너무 잘 나가고 있기에, 다음 주문에서는 단위 수량을 늘리고 싶습니다. 3월 배송분에는 제 주문을 **15** 두 배로 늘리는 게 가능할까요?

마지막으로, 저희 매장에 전용 판매 라인을 만드는 것에 관심이 있으신지 궁금합니다. 저는 전국에 매장을 가지고 있어서, 당신의 브랜드에 대한 인지도를 높이고 폭넓은 사람들에게 빠르게 다가갈 수 있을 거라 생각합니다. 제 생각에는 **16** 저희 둘 다에게 매우 이익이 될 것 같습니다. 관심 있으시면 알려 주세요.

감사합니다.

메이지 블레이즈
뉴턴 부티크

어휘 recently 최근 | shipment 발송, 배송 | latest 최신의 | top seller 가장 잘 팔리는 상품 | several 몇 개 | praise 칭찬하다 | unique 독특한, 특별한 | quality 질 | material 재료 | increase 늘리다 | number 수 | unit 단위 | next 다음의 | order 주문 | possible 가능한 | finally 마지막으로 |

wonder 궁금해하다 | interested 관심 있는 | create 창조하다 | exclusive 독점적인, 전용의 | sell 팔다 | throughout 도처에 | raise 높이다 | awareness 인지, 의식, 관심 | brand 브랜드 | reach 이르다, 닿다 | wide 넓은 | audience 청중, 지지자 | quickly 빠르게 | opinion 의견 | benefit 이익이 되다 | boutique 양품점, 부티크

13. 해설 빈칸은 문장의 주어이자 my의 수식을 받는 명사 자리이다. 빈칸 앞 문장들에서 자신이 주문한 원피스와 스커트가 가장 잘 팔린 제품들이었다고 했음을 고려할 때, '제 고객들 몇몇은 고유한 디자인을 칭찬했다'는 내용으로 이어져야 문맥상 연결이 자연스러우므로 (D) patrons가 정답이다.

14. (A) 합리적인 가격은 당신의 작품을 그만큼 훨씬 더 매력적으로 만들어 줍니다.
(B) 해당 사이즈의 주문은 빠르게 소진되지 않을 가능성이 높습니다.
(C) 다음 주 가능한 시간을 알려주시겠습니까?
(D) 송장은 이미 정산되었어야 했습니다.

해설 빈칸 앞 문장의 '고객들이 제품의 재질과 디자인을 칭찬했다'는 내용을 고려할 때, 제품에 대한 칭찬의 말로 이어져야 문맥상 연결이 자연스러우므로 (A) The reasonable prices make your pieces that much more appealing.이 정답이다.

15. 해설 빈칸은 to부정사 구를 완성하는 동사 자리이다. 빈칸 앞 문장에서 '다음 주문의 수량을 늘리고 싶다'고 했으므로, '주문 수량을 두 배 늘리는 것이 가능한지' 묻는 내용으로 이어져야 문맥상 연결이 자연스러우므로 (B) double이 정답이다.

16. 해설 빈칸은 문장의 목적어 자리이다. 빈칸 앞 문장의 '제 매장에 (당신의 의류) 전용 판매 라인을 만드는 것에 관심이 있으신지 궁금하다'는 내용과 빈칸 뒤 both가 있음을 고려할 때, '이것은 우리 둘 다에게 이득이 될 것'이라는 내용이 되어야 문맥상 연결이 자연스러우므로 (C) us가 정답이다.

UNIT 05. 문장 선택

핵심 문제 유형
본서 p.218

1. (B)

[1] 다음 기사에 관한 문제입니다.

슈퍼마켓 체인점에서 행사를 발표하다

크랜무어 (6월 19일) — 도시의 최대 슈퍼마켓 체인점인 하모니 세일

에서 신규 매장에 대한 준비로 다양한 직무를 채용할 예정이다. 공석을 채우기 위해 회사에서는 6월 30일에 채용 행사를 개최할 예정이다. 새 일자리는 내년에 개장하는 하모니 세일의 신규 점포를 위한 것이다. 하지만 현 지점들 및 기업 본점에도 일자리가 있을 것이다. **1** 여기에는 마케팅 및 행정직이 포함될 수 있다.

참석에 관심 있는 사람들은 행사 전에 이력서 사본을 준비해야 한다. 오전 9시부터 오후 5시까지 그레이트 센트럴홀에서 열릴 것이다.

어휘 supermarket 슈퍼마켓 | chain 체인점 | announce 발표하다, 알리다 | a variety of 다양한 | position 직무, 일자리 | in preparation for ~의 준비로 | fill 채우다 | largely 대체로, 주로 | available 이용 가능한 | current 현재의 | location 지점 | corporate 기업의 | headquarters 본사 | attend 참석하다 | prepare 준비하다 | copy 한 부, 복사본 | résumé 이력서 | ahead of ~에 앞서 | take place 개최되다, 열리다

(A) 이전 행사들은 뉴스에서 보도된 적이 있다.
(B) 여기에는 마케팅 및 행정직이 포함될 수 있다.
(C) 많은 지역 슈퍼마켓들이 직원 유지에 어려움을 겪고 있다고 보고했다.
(D) 하모니 세일은 최근 새로운 도시로 확장하기 시작했습니다.

해설 빈칸 앞 문장의 '현 지점들 및 기업 본점에도 일자리가 있을 것'이라는 내용을 고려할 때, 해당 일자리와 관련된 내용으로 이어져야 문맥상 연결이 자연스러우므로 (B) These may include marketing and administration roles.가 정답이다.

Practice

1. (B)	**2.** (C)	**3.** (A)	**4.** (D)	**5.** (C)
6. (A)	**7.** (A)	**8.** (D)	**9.** (B)	**10.** (D)
11. (B)	**12.** (D)	**13.** (D)	**14.** (B)	**15.** (C)
16. (A)				

[1-4] 다음 편지에 관한 문제입니다.

컬리 씨께,

돈테이 베이 개점을 성공적으로 만드는 데 **1** 엄청난 도움을 주셔서 정말 감사합니다. 저희는 훌륭한 평가를 받았는데, 상당 부분은 당신의 대단한 작업 덕분이었습니다. 저희 운영 팀에서 지금까지 한동안 당신이 한 작업을 지켜보고 있었는데, 저희 매장에 당신의 디자인을 사용할 수 있음에 기뻐했습니다. 매장 내부는 손님께 많은 **2** 칭찬을 받은 데다, 손님들께서 소셜 미디어에 사진을 많이 올려주고 계세요. **3** 저는 당신이 6월에 시간이 되시는지도 궁금합니다. 지난번 회의 내용을 기억하신다면, 저희가 클레이빌에 개장할 신규 지점에 대해 짧게 이야기 나눴었는데요. 조만간 그 매장 **4** 계획을 세우는 회의가 마련될 예정인데, 참석해 주신다면 정말 좋겠습니다.

진심으로,

마릴린 페나
책임자, 마릴린 양품점

어휘 grand opening 개장, 개점 | success 성공 | review 후기 | part 부분 | thanks to ~덕분에 | management 관리, 경영 | follow 따르다, 따라잡다 | design 설계, 디자인 | interior 내부 | guest 손님 | post 게시하다 | recall 기억해 내다 | briefly 간단히 | location 장소 | organize 준비하다 | attend 참석하다

1. 해설 빈칸은 소유격 대명사와 명사 사이 명사 help를 수식하는 자리이다. '엄청난 도움'이라는 의미가 되어야 문맥상 자연스러우므로 형용사 (B) amazing이 정답이다.

2. 해설 빈칸은 동사 received의 목적어인 명사 자리이다. and로 이어진 뒤 문장의 '손님들이 소셜 미디어에 사진을 많이 올린다'는 내용을 고려할 때, '손님들의 칭찬을 많이 받았다'는 의미가 되어야 문맥상 자연스러우므로 (C) compliments가 정답이다.

3. **(A) 저는 당신이 6월에 시간이 되시는지도 궁금합니다.**
(B) 돈테이 베이는 최근 상당한 투자를 받았습니다.
(C) 예산 증액이 승인되었습니다.
(D) 저희 웹사이트의 정보 페이지를 참조하시면 됩니다.

해설 빈칸 뒤 문장들에서 '지난 회의 때 신규 지점 개장 관련 이야기를 나눴으며, 회의에 참석해 주면 좋겠다'라고 했으므로, 이와 관련하여 운을 떼는 이야기가 들어가야 문맥상 연결이 자연스러우므로 (A) I was also wondering about your availability in June.이 정답이다.

4. 해설 빈칸은 두 명사를 연결하는 자리이다. 해당 문장에 시제가 들어간 동사가 이미 존재하므로 빈칸은 준동사 자리이며, '매장을 계획하는 회의가 조만간 마련될 것'이라는 의미가 되어야 문맥상 자연스러우므로 주어인 a meeting을 수식하는 to부정사 구를 완성하는 (D) to plan이 정답이다.

[5-8] 다음 기사에 관한 문제입니다.

월브릿지 (8월 12일) — 상징적인 월브릿지 박물관이 개관 이래 **5** 가장 광범위한 보수 작업에 들어갈 예정이다. 오너 그룹에서는 업데이트를 거친 후 박물관에서 훨씬 더 다양한 **6** 전시를 개최할 수 있게 되기를 희망한다. 책임자인 데니스 플로이드는 젊은 층의 관심을 끄는 데 우선순위가 있다고 설명했다. 이러한 목적을 위해 서관은 가족이 함께 참여하는 워크숍 운영에 사용될 쌍방향 공간으로 변신할 것이다. 초반에는 워크숍에서 발생하는 소음이 다른 손님들에게 방해가 될 수 있다는 우려가 있었지만, 효과적으로 소음을 **7** 차단하도록 고안된 특수 자재로 벽이 만들어질 것이라고 플로이드 씨가 안심시켰다. 박물관은 내년 초 대중에 개방될 예정이다. **8** 개장은 중요한 관광 시즌에 맞춰 이루어질 것이다.

어휘 iconic ~의 상징이 되는 | undergo (변화 등을) 겪다, 받다 |

62   파고다 토익 기본 완성 RC

5. 해설 빈칸은 소유격 대명사 its와 함께 문장의 목적어인 명사 renovation을 수식하는 형용사 자리이다. 문장 뒷 부분의 since its opening이라는 표현이 있음을 고려할 때, '개장 이래 가장 광범위한 보수 작업'이라는 내용으로 이어져야 자연스러우므로 최상급 표현 (C) most extensive가 정답이다.

6. 해설 빈칸은 a greater variety of의 수식을 받는 명사 자리이다. '박물관에서 훨씬 더 다양한 전시를 개최할 수 있게 되기를 희망한다'는 의미가 되어야 자연스러우므로 (A) exhibitions가 정답이다.

7. 해설 빈칸은 명사구 special materials를 후치 수식하는 분사 designed와 명사 noise 사이의 자리이다. 문장 내 본동사 will be made가 이미 존재하여 준동사 자리임을 알 수 있으며, '효과적으로 소음을 차단하도록 고안된 특수 자재'라는 목적의 의미를 담고 있어야 문맥상 자연스러우므로 부사적 용법의 to부정사 구를 완성하는 (A) to block이 정답이다.

8. (A) 경영 그룹에 일부 변화가 있을 것으로 예상된다.
(B) 월브리지 박물관은 주에서 가장 큰 박물관이다.
(C) 기부는 자금을 빠르게 모을 수 있는 한 가지 방법이다.
(D) 개장은 중요한 관광 시즌에 맞춰 이루어질 것이다.

해설 빈칸 앞 문장의 '박물관은 내년 초 대중에 개방될 예정'이라는 내용을 고려할 때, 박물관 개장 시기와 관련된 내용으로 이어져야 문맥상 연결이 자연스러우므로 (D) The opening will be in time for the important tourist season.이 정답이다.

[9-12] 다음 웹 페이지 정보에 관한 문제입니다.

순수 포장재 소개

아반토 프러덕션에서는 플라스틱 쓰레기 문제와 싸우기 위해 상당한 **9** 노력을 들였습니다. 회사는 슈퍼마켓과 소매점에서 흔히 보이는 플라스틱 포장재의 대체재를 만드는 일에 몰두해 왔습니다. 지난주, 회사는 유기농 식물 성분에서 얻은 새로운 물질을 **10** 개발했다고 발표했습니다. 아반토 프러덕션에서는 코코넛 섬유질과 나무껍질을 혼합해 순수 포장재를 제작합니다. 껍질은 폐기물로 인식되는 **11** 반면 섬유질은 보통 처리됩니다. 순수 포장재에서는 플라스틱보다 저렴한 순수 포장재를 생산하면서 플라스틱 포장재를 단계적으로 완전히 없애는 것을 목표로 합니다. **12** 첫 시제품은 내년에 출시됩니다.

9. 해설 빈칸은 considerable의 수식을 받는 명사 자리이다. '상당한 노력을 들였다'는 의미가 되어야 문맥상 자연스러우므로 (B) efforts가 정답이다.

10. 해설 빈칸은 주어 it에 대한 동사 자리이다. 빈칸 앞 문장의 '플라스틱 포장재의 대체안을 만드는 일에 몰두해 왔다'는 내용을 고려할 때, '회사에서 새로운 물질을 개발했다고 발표했다'는 내용으로 이어져야 문맥상 연결이 자연스러우므로 (D) had developed가 정답이다.

11. 해설 빈칸은 두 개의 문장을 연결하는 부사절 접속사 자리이다. 두 가지 물질의 특성을 대조하고 있으므로 (B) while이 정답이다.

12. (A) 저희 영업팀이 가능한 한 빨리 연락 드리겠습니다.
(B) 친환경 기술에 중점을 둔 기업들은 보조금을 받을 수 있을지도 모릅니다.
(C) 아반토 프러덕션은 새로운 프로젝트를 위해 추가 직원을 채용하고 있습니다.
(D) 첫 시제품은 내년에 출시됩니다.

해설 빈칸 앞 문장들에서 '플라스틱 포장재의 대체안으로 새롭게 개발한 순수 포장재'에 대해 설명하고 있음을 고려할 때, 포장재와 관련된 내용으로 이어져야 문맥상 연결이 자연스러우므로 (D) The first prototypes of the product will be released next year.가 정답이다.

[13-16] 다음 회람에 관한 문제입니다.

수신: 전 직원
발신: 앤디 피트만, 사이버 보안 팀
날짜: 9월 23일
제목: 안전 교육

올해 연례 인터넷 안전 교육 워크숍의 시기가 왔습니다. 올해 워크숍에서는 자료나 개인 정보 도난 같은 사이버 공격을 피하는 것을 중점적으로 다룰 예정입니다. 저희 사이버 보안 팀에서 공격으로부터 보호하기 위해 회사 기기들에 보안 프로그램을 설치했으니 안심하세요. **13** 하지만, 어떤 위험이 존재하고 이를 맞닥뜨렸을 때 무엇을 해야 하는지 이해하는 것은 여전히 필요합니다.

⓮ 모든 분을 수용하기 위해 저희는 일주일 동안 여러 번의 워크숍을 실시할 예정입니다. 회사 웹 사이트에 접속하셔서 이용 가능한 ⓯ 보기들 중에서 자유롭게 선택하시면 됩니다. '사이버 보안 교육'이라는 링크가 있을 겁니다.

⓰ 교육은 모든 직원에게 필수입니다. 세션에 참석하실 수 없는 경우, 상사에게 알려 주시면 저희가 해결 방안을 마련해 드리겠습니다.

어휘 cybersecurity 사이버 보안 | safety 안전 | training 교육 | annual 연례의 | focus on ~에 중점을 두다 | avoid 피하다 | cyberattack 사이버 공격 | steal 훔치다 | personal 개인적인 | information 정보 | rest assured ~라고 확신하다 | install 설치하다 | still 여전히 | imperative 반드시 해야 하는 | understand 이해하다 | threat 위협 | accommodate 수용하다 | conduct 실시하다 | be free to 자유롭게 ~하다 | choose 선택하다 | available 이용 가능한 | log onto ~에 접속하다 | link 링크 | unable 할 수 없는 | attend 참석하다 | session 세션 | supervisor 상사 | solution 해결책

13. **해설** 빈칸은 두 문장의 연결을 매끄럽게 만드는 접속부사 자리이다. 빈칸 앞 문장의 '사이버 보안 팀에서 공격으로부터 지키기 위해 회사 기기들에 보안 프로그램을 설치했으니 안심하세요'라는 내용과 빈칸 뒷 부분의 '어떤 위협이 존재하고 이를 맞닥뜨렸을 때 무엇을 해야 하는지 이해하는 것은 여전히 필요하다'는 내용이 상반됨을 알 수 있으므로 역접의 접속 부사 (D) However가 정답이다.

14. **해설** 빈칸은 to부정사 To accommodate의 목적어 자리이다. 빈칸 앞 단락의 '연례 안전 교육 워크숍의 시기가 왔다. 어떤 위협이 존재하고 이를 맞닥뜨렸을 때 무엇을 해야 하는지 알고 있어야 한다'는 내용과 빈칸 뒷 부분의 '일주일 동안 여러 번의 워크숍을 실시할 예정'이라는 내용을 고려할 때, '(회사의) 모든 사람을 수용하기 위해'라는 내용이 되어야 문맥상 자연스러우므로 (B) everyone이 정답이다.

15. **해설** 빈칸은 the available의 수식을 받는 명사 자리이다. 빈칸 앞 문장의 '일주일 동안 여러 번의 워크숍을 실시할 예정'이라는 내용을 고려할 때, '웹 사이트에 접속해서 이용 가능한 (워크숍) 보기들 중 자유롭게 선택하면 된다'는 내용이 되어야 문맥상 자연스러우므로 (C) options가 정답이다.

16. (A) 교육은 모든 직원에게 필수입니다.
(B) 이메일 주소는 해당 페이지에서 찾을 수 있습니다.
(C) 지난해 세션은 온라인으로 진행되었습니다.
(D) 모든 제안 사항은 사이버 보안 팀의 직원에게 보내야 합니다.

해설 빈칸 뒤 문장의 '세션에 참석하실 수 없는 경우 상사에게 알리면 해결 방안을 마련하겠다'는 내용을 고려할 때, 교육 참석과 관련된 내용이 앞에 들어가야 문맥상 연결이 자연스러우므로 (A) The training is mandatory for all employees.가 정답이다.

REVIEW TEST
본서 p.224

1. (C)	2. (A)	3. (D)	4. (B)	5. (B)
6. (A)	7. (D)	8. (C)	9. (B)	10. (D)
11. (B)	12. (A)	13. (A)	14. (B)	15. (C)
16. (B)				

[1-4] 다음 이메일에 관한 문제입니다.

수신: 앤드류 코너 〈a.connor@expressline.com〉
발신: 모린 신필드 〈msinfield@creworse.com〉
날짜: 8월 15일
제목: 후속 조치
첨부: 연구 감독관 직무 기술서

코너 씨께,

지난주 제품 개발자 직무 면접에 와 주신 것에 감사드립니다. 저희는 귀하의 경력 및 기술 지식에 매우 깊은 인상을 받았습니다. 저희는 다른 지원자와 진행할 예정 ❶ 이지만, 저희가 판단하기에 귀하의 능력이 완벽하게 들어맞을 것으로 보이는 다른 직무가 있습니다. 저희 지점에서의 연구 감독관 직무입니다.

❷ 이 직무는 귀하의 이전 직무들과 일부 일치합니다. 첨부된 문서에 급여 범위 및 전체 직무 내용이 나와 있습니다. 저희는 귀하가 아주 적합한 대상자라고 판단하기에 이 ❸ 기회를 아직 광고하지 않았습니다. ❹ 관심 있으시면 최대한 빨리 저에게 회신 부탁드립니다.

진심으로,

모린 신필드
인사부, 크레워스 산업

어휘 follow-up 후속 조치 | research 연구, 조사 | supervisor 감독관, 관리자 | description 서술, 기술 | interview 면접, 인터뷰 | product 제품 | developer 개발자 | position 직무, 일자리 | proceed 진행하다, 계속해서 ~하다 | candidate 지원자 | skillset 다양한 능력 | perfectly 완벽하게 | suit 맞다, 어울리다 | attach 첨부하다 | document 문서 | show 보여주다, 나타내다 | full 전체의 | job description 직무 내용 | salary 급여 | range 범위 | advertise 광고하다 | fit 적합한 사람[것] | get back to ~에게 회신 연락을 하다 | as soon as possible 최대한 빨리

1. **해설** 빈칸은 두 개의 완전한 문장을 연결하는 부사절 접속사 자리이므로 (C) While이 정답이다. 「------ 문장 1, 문장 2」의 구조에서 빈칸은 부사절 접속사 자리다.

2. (A) 이 직무는 귀하의 이전 직무들과 일부 일치합니다.
(B) 매니저가 다음 주에 연락을 드릴 것입니다.
(C) 저희 회사는 올해 새로운 산업으로 확장할 예정입니다.
(D) 귀하의 이력서는 저희 채용 팀에 접수되었습니다.

해설 빈칸 앞 단락에서 연구 감독관이라는 새로운 직무를 제안했고, 빈칸 뒤 문장에서 해당 직무에 대한 상세 정보를 제공하고 있음을 고

려할 때, 해당 직무와 관련된 내용으로 이어져야 문맥상 연결이 자연스러우므로 (A) This role is in line with some of your previous positions.이 정답이다.

3. 해설 빈칸은 this의 수식을 받는 문장의 목적어 자리이다. 빈칸 앞 문장들에서 연구 감독관 직무에 관한 정보를 제공하고 있음을 고려할 때, '이 일자리에 관한 구인 공고를 아직 올리지 않았다'는 내용으로 이어져야 문맥상 연결이 자연스러우므로 해당 일자리를 지칭하는 표현 (D) opportunity가 정답이다.

4. 해설 빈칸은 if 종속절 내 주격 보어 자리이다. 주어 자리에 사람 명사 you가 있으며 '관심 있으면 최대한 빨리 회신해 달라'는 내용이 되어야 문맥상 자연스러우므로 과거분사 (B) interested가 정답이다. 과거분사 interested는 '흥미를 느끼는' 상태를 현재분사 interesting은 '흥미를 유발시키는' 상태를 나타낸다.

[5-8] 다음 공지에 관한 문제입니다.

게이머 파라다이스

게이머 파라다이스는 비디오 게임 세상 속 최신 **5** 소식에 관한 정보를 제공하는 세계에서 가장 신뢰받는 정보 제공처입니다. 친구들 몇 명이서 취미로 시작한 일이 세계 최대 규모의 게임 콘텐츠 플랫폼으로 **6** 성장했습니다. 당사는 밤낮없이 일하며 게임 개발자 인터뷰, 출시 예정작 독점 시사회, 구독자 대상 특별 할인을 알려드립니다. 또한 당사는 법적 요건에 따라 서비스 약관을 업데이트합니다. 구독자의 **7** 지속적인 당사 플랫폼 접속에는 약관 수락이 필요합니다. 따라서 시간 내시어 www.gamersparadise.com/terms에서 살펴봐 주시기 바랍니다. 궁금한 점이 있으시면 당사 고객팀 help@gamersparadise.com으로 연락 주시기 바랍니다. **8** 당사 수신함은 휴일을 제외하고 24시간 내내 관리됩니다.

어휘 gamer 게임광, 게이머 | paradise 낙원 | trusted 신뢰할 수 있는 | source 출처 | information 정보 | latest 최신의 | hobby 취미 | large (규모가) 큰 | gaming 게임을 하는 것 | content 내용물, 콘텐츠 | platform 플랫폼 | work around the clock 밤낮없이 일하다 | bring 가져다 주다 | developer 개발자 | exclusive 독점적인 | preview 미리보기, 시사회 | upcoming 다가오는, 곧 있을 | release 출시, 공개 | subscriber 구독자 | term 조건 | per ~에 대하여 | legal 법률과 관련된 | requirement 요건 | access 접속 | require 필요로 하다, 요구하다 | acceptance 수락 | review 검토하다

5. 해설 빈칸은 the latest의 수식을 받는 명사 자리이다. '비디오 게임 세상 속 최신 소식에 관한 정보'라는 의미가 되어야 문맥상 자연스러우므로 (B) stories가 정답이다.

6. 해설 빈칸은 What 명사절 주어에 대한 동사 자리이다. 빈칸 앞 문장의 '게이머 파라다이스는 세계에서 가장 신뢰받는 정보 제공처'라는 내용을 고려할 때, '취미로 시작한 일이 세계 최대 규모의 게임 콘텐츠 플랫폼으로 성장했다'는 내용으로 이어져야 문맥상 연결이 자연스러우

므로 현재완료 시제 (A) has grown이 정답이다.

7. 해설 빈칸은 명사 access를 수식하는 자리이므로 형용사 역할을 하는 과거분사 (D) continued가 정답이다.

8. (A) 새로운 법은 내년 초에 발효될 예정입니다.
(B) 저희는 웹사이트에 대한 사용자 제안을 검토하였으며 개선을 진행할 예정입니다.
(C) 당사 수신함은 휴일을 제외하고 24시간 내내 관리됩니다.
(D) 1년 구독하시는 분들께 독점 혜택이 제공됩니다.

해설 빈칸 앞 문장의 '궁금한 점이 있으시면 당사 고객팀으로 연락'하라는 내용을 고려할 때, 연락과 관련된 내용으로 이어져야 문맥상 연결이 자연스러우므로 (C) Our inbox is monitored 24 hours a day excluding holidays.가 정답이다.

[9-12] 다음 후기에 관한 문제입니다.

홈 클리닝 서비스: 에어컨 청소

앙드레 블랫 작성 후기

저는 이 사이트에 후기를 써본 적이 한 번도 없습니다. **9** 하지만 제가 워드 클리닝 크루에서 받은 서비스가 너무 뛰어나서 하나 작성해야만 했습니다. 우선, **10** 그들의 서비스가 얼마나 전문적이었는지에 대해 언급하고 싶습니다. 그들이 제 에어컨을 청소할 때 저는 왜 제가 최근에 알레르기 증상을 겪었었는지 알 수 있었습니다. 정말로 놀라운 경험이었습니다. **11** 그들은 심지어 청결하게 유지하는 법에 관해 팁도 알려줬습니다. 제 에어컨을 청소한 지 일주일이 지났는데, 확실히 먼지 알레르기 증상에서 현저한 **12** 감소를 알릴 수 있습니다. 워드 클리닝 크루 팀에 감사드려요!

어휘 review 후기 | cleaning 청소 | air conditioner 에어컨 | site 사이트 | exceptional 뛰어난, 이례적일 정도로 우수한 | first off 우선, 먼저 | mention 언급하다 | professional 전문적인 | experience 겪다 | allergy 알레르기 | symptom 증상 | recently 최근 | real 진짜의 | eyeopener 눈을 뜨게 해주는 놀라운 경험 | machine 기계 | definitely 확실히 | report 알리다 | noticeable 뚜렷한, 현저한 | dust 먼지

9. 해설 빈칸은 앞 문장과의 흐름을 매끄럽게 만들어주는 접속부사 자리이다. 빈칸 앞 문장의 '이 사이트에 후기를 써본 적이 한 번도 없다'는 내용과 빈칸 뒷 부분의 '서비스가 너무 뛰어나서 (후기를) 하나 작성해야만 했다'의 내용을 고려할 때, 서로 상반되는 내용을 이어주는 연결어가 들어가야 문맥상 자연스러우므로 (B) However가 정답이다.

10. 해설 빈칸은 명사 service를 수식하는 자리이므로 소유격 인칭 대명사 (D) their가 정답이다.

11. (A) 일부 화학물질은 방치되면 해로울 수 있습니다.
(B) 그들은 심지어 청결하게 유지하는 법에 관해 팁도 알려줬습니다.
(C) 많은 사람들이 시끄러운 에어컨을 경험했습니다.

(D) 정기적인 세션을 예약하는 것이 중요합니다.

해설　빈칸 앞부분의 '그들이 에어컨을 청소할 때 왜 제가 최근에 알레르기 증상을 겪었었는지 알 수 있었다'는 내용을 고려할 때, 에어컨 청소 및 관리와 관련된 내용으로 이어져야 문맥상 연결이 자연스러우므로 (B) They even gave me some tips on how to keep it clean.이 정답이다.

---

12. 해설　빈칸은 a noticeable의 수식을 받는 문장의 목적어인 명사 자리이므로 (A) reduction이 정답이다. 동명사는 관사의 수식을 받을 수 없으며, 타동사의 동명사는 목적어를 필요로 한다는 점을 기억 해두자.

[13-16] 다음 이메일에 관한 문제입니다.

수신: 조쉬 던
발신: 대니엘 크로스
날짜: 10월 26일
제목: 제 생각
첨부: 기사

던 씨께,

어제 있었던 직원 회의 때 제기된 주제와 관련해서 이메일을 드립니다. 우리 병원에서 핵심 가치 및 사명을 보다 잘 수용할 만한 방법에 관한 토론은 정말 좋았습니다. **13** 이 주제에 대해 제가 공유하고 싶은 아이디어가 떠올랐어요.

우리 클리닉에 있는 벽의 상당 부분이 칙칙한 회색으로 칠해진 데다 장식도 안 되어 있는 상태입니다. 제 생각에는 우리가 환자들에게 관심을 갖고 있다는 것을 보여주기 위해 할 수 있는 모든 곳에 긍정과 활기를 **14** 불어넣어야 할 거예요. **15** 결국, 우리 임무는 가진 능력을 다해 지역 사회에 기여하는 겁니다.

장식을 화사하게 했던 병원에 대한 내용을 다룬 기사를 첨부해 드립니다. 기사에서는 환자들이 변화에 어떻게 긍정적으로 반응을 보였는지에 관해 자세히 다루고 있어요. 그게 **16** 도움이 되기를 바랍니다. 이 아이디어가 얼마나 비용 효율적인지를 감안하면 제 생각에는 고려할 만한 가치가 있는 것 같습니다.

친애하는,

대니엘 크로스

어휘　thought 생각 | article 기사 | in response to ~에 답하여, 응하여 | topic 주제 | raise 제기하다 | discussion 논의, 토론 | clinic 병원, 클리닉 | embrace 포용하다, 아우르다 | core 핵심의 | value 가치 | mission 사명 | wall 벽 | paint 페인트칠하다 | dull 칙칙한 | shade 색조, 음영 | gray 회색 | leave ~한 상태로 그대로 두다 | undecorated 장식하지 않은 | positivity 긍정성, 적극성 | vibrancy 활기 | care about ~에 관심을 가지다, 마음을 쓰다 | patient 환자 | serve 도움이 되다, 기여하다 | community 지역 사회 | to the best of ~이 미치는 한 | ability 능력 | attach 첨부하다 | brighten up 밝히다 | décor 장식 | detail 상세히 알리다 | respond 반응하다 | positively 긍정적으로 | given ~를 고려하면 | cost-effective 비용 효율적인 | worth ~할 가치가 있는 | consider 고려하다

13. **(A) 이 주제에 대해 제가 공유하고 싶은 아이디어가 떠올랐어요.**
(B) 앞으로 다른 워크숍을 진행하고 싶습니다.
(C) 회의를 대신 온라인으로 진행할 수도 있었을 것 같다고 생각했습니다.
(D) 우리가 회의를 더 일찍 준비했더라면 좋았을 텐데요.

해설　빈칸 앞 문장의 '어제 회의 때 제기된 주제와 관련해 이메일을 보낸다'는 내용과 빈칸 다음 단락에서 '우리 병원의 벽 색상이 칙칙하고 장식도 없다'며 자신의 의견을 제시하고 있음을 고려할 때, 자신에게 회의 주제에 관한 아이디어가 있다는 내용이 들어가야 문맥상 연결이 자연스러우므로 (A) I had an idea on this topic that I would like to share.이 정답이다.

---

14. 해설　빈칸은 주어와 목적어 사이 동사 자리이다. 빈칸 앞 문장에서 병원의 벽 색상과 장식에 대한 이야기를 꺼낸 후 해당 문장에서는 병원에서 추후 취할 만한 조치에 대한 자신의 의견을 제시하고 있음을 고려할 때, '할 수 있는 모든 곳에 긍정과 활기를 불어넣어야 할 것이다'라는 내용으로 이어져야 문맥상 자연스러우므로 (B) should be promoting이 정답이다.

---

15. 해설　빈칸은 문두에 들어가 앞 문장과의 연결을 매끄럽게 만들어 주는 접속부사 자리이다. 빈칸 앞 문장의 '우리가 환자들에게 관심을 갖고 있다는 것을 보여주기 위해 할 수 있는 모든 곳에 긍정과 활기를 불어넣어야 한다'는 내용과 빈칸 뒷 부분의 '우리 임무는 가진 능력을 다해 지역 사회에 기여하는 것'이라는 내용을 고려할 때, 뒤에 이어지는 내용이 앞선 발언을 하게 된 이유로서의 논리적인 설명의 역할을 해야 문맥상 연결이 자연스러우므로 (C) After all이 정답이다.

---

16. 해설　빈칸은 동사 find의 목적격 보어 자리이다. it이 가리키는 대상이 the article이므로 '기사가 도움이 되기를 바란다'는 의미가 되어야 문맥상 자연스러우므로 (B) helpful이 정답이다.

PART 7

UNIT 01. 주제·목적 문제

핵심 문제 유형

본서 p.233

1. (B)

---

[1] 다음 회람에 관한 문제입니다.

수신인: 모든 지원들
발신인: 애일린 장, 운영 실장
날짜: 4월 9일
제목: ID 명찰

1 우리는 다음 주 월요일 4월 16일에 새로운 보안 시스템을 설치할 것입니다. 이 시스템을 작동시킨 후에, LV 직원들은 신분 확인 명찰을 항상 소지해야 합니다. 이 플라스틱 카드 안에는 디지털 식별 코드가 있습니다. 그 결과, 그것은 여러분이 LV 캠퍼스 내에 있는 모든 건물에 접근할 수 있도록 해줍니다. 여러분은 4월 11일 금요일에 마케팅 부서에서 명찰을 가져갈 수 있습니다.

4월 16일 이후에는 직원들이 그들의 새 명찰 없이는 그 어떠한 LV 시설물에도 들어갈 수 없을 것이라는 사실을 명심하세요. 만약 어떤 질문이나 염려되는 것이 있다면, 여러분의 매니저에게 연락하시기 바랍니다.

어휘 install 설치하다 I security 보안 I activate 작동시키다 I carry 지니고 다니다, 운반하다 I identification 신분 확인 I identification code 식별 코드 I enable 가능하게 하다 I have access to ~에 접근하다 I facility 시설 I without ~없이 I temporary 일시적인, 임시의

---

1. 이 회람의 목적은 무엇인가?
(A) 직원들에게 건물의 임시 폐쇄를 알리기 위해
(B) 회사 정책을 소개하기 위해
(C) 직원들에게 부서의 위치가 이동되었다라는 것을 통보하기 위해
(D) 최근의 보안 문제를 해결하기 위해

해설 질문의 purpose를 보고 글의 주제나 목적을 찾는 문제인지 확인한 후, 글의 앞부분 또는 마지막 부분에서 단서를 찾는다. 지문의 전반부에서 새로운 보안 시스템 설치를 알리기 위한 글임을 알 수 있다. 지문의 내용을 다른 단어로 바꾸어 표현(paraphrasing)한 선택지에 유의하여 정답을 고른다. 새 보안 시스템 설치로 인해 앞으로 직원들이 명찰을 지니고 다녀야 시설물 입장이 가능하다는 것을 알리는 것으로 회사 보안 시스템, 즉 회사 보안 정책이 변경된 것을 알리기 위한 글이다. 따라서 정답은 (B) To introduce a company policy이다.

Practice

본서 p.234

1. (A)　　2. (B)　　3. (B)　　4. (A)　　5. (D)
6. (A)　　7. (B)　　8. (D)　　9. (C)

[1-2] 다음 공지에 관한 문제입니다.

고객 여러분께,

1 핸송 푸즈의 팀에서는 기쁜 마음으로 저희의 최신 시설의 개장 소식을 전해드립니다. 이 지점에서는 저희 수석 요리사인 멜린다 리가 고안한 완전히 새로운 메뉴를 선보입니다. 멜린다의 메뉴는 퓨전 요리의 요소를 포함하며, 유기농 재료에 초점을 맞추고 있습니다. 고객은 모바일 앱을 통해 이용 가능한 재료를 조합해 직접 자신의 요리를 디자인할 수 있습니다.

2 오늘 앱으로 주문 제작 식사를 주문하시고 15퍼센트 할인을 받아보세요. 테이블이 한정되어 있으니, 오늘 자리를 예약하세요!

어휘 latest 최신의 I establishment 시설, 기관 I location 지점 I feature ~를 특징으로 하다 I head 수석의, 우두머리의 I include 포함하다 I element 요소 I fusion 퓨전 I dining 식사 I combined with ~와 결합된 I focus 초점, 주목 I organic 유기농의 I ingredient 재료 I own 자신의 I dish 요리 I combination 조합, 결합 I available 이용 가능한 I mobile application 모바일 앱 I custom-made 주문 제작한 I meal 식사 I limited 한정된, 제한된 I book 예약하다 I place 자리

---

1. 공지의 목적은 무엇인가?
(A) 신규 레스토랑을 알리는 것
(B) 일자리를 광고하는 것
(C) 최신 트렌드를 설명하는 것
(D) 행사에 사람들을 초대하는 것

해설 첫 번째 단락에서 핸송 푸즈 팀에서는 기쁜 마음으로 최신 시설의 개장 소식을 전해드린다고 했으므로 (A) To announce a new restaurant가 정답이다.

---

2. 공지에 따르면, 고객은 어떻게 할인을 받을 수 있는가?
(A) 친구를 초대해서
(B) 앱으로 주문해서
(C) 편지를 제출해서
(D) 대회에 참가해서

해설 두 번째 단락에서 오늘 앱으로 주문 제작 식사를 주문하시고 15퍼센트 할인을 받아 보라고 했으므로 (B) By ordering through an app이 정답이다.

[3-4] 다음 엽서에 관한 문제입니다.

에스더 풀
26 파손스 가
메디나, 오하이오 44256

6월 18일

풀 씨께,

3 차량 점검을 받으신 지 1년이 되었습니다. 귀하의 차량 안전을 유지하고, 고가의 수리를 완전히 피하시려면, 저희에게 차량을 점검받는

예약을 잡으실 것을 권해 드립니다. 그렇게 하시려면, 저희 사무실 317-555-9618로 전화주시거나 웹 사이트(www.tekapomechanics. com)를 이용해 온라인으로 예약해 주시기 바랍니다. **4** 저희 웹 사이트에서는 차량을 최대한 원활하게 운행하도록 고안된 다양한 제품도 살펴보실 수 있습니다.

진심으로,

로이 디아즈
테카포 매키닉스
1395 캑스톤 큐에이, 메디나, 오하이오 44256

어휘 vehicle 자동차 | maintain 유지하다 | safety 안전 | avoid 피하다 | costly 많은 돈이 드는 | repair 수리 | down the line 완전히, 철저히 | recommend 권하다 | make an appointment 일정을 잡다 | service (차량을) 점검하다 | book 예약하다 | design 설계하다 | run 작동하다, 달리다 | smoothly 부드럽게, 원활하게 | as ~ as possible 최대한 ~하게 | mechanic 정비공 | revamp 개편하다

3. 디아즈 씨는 왜 풀 씨에게 편지를 썼는가?
   (A) 새로운 규정을 알려주려고
   (B) 점검을 위해 차를 가져오도록 요청하려고
   (C) 취소된 예약에 대해 알려주려고
   (D) 누락한 지불에 대해 상기시켜 주려고

해설 차량 점검을 받은 지 1년이 되었고 차량 안전을 유지하고 고가의 수리를 완전히 피하기 위해 차량을 점검받는 예약을 잡으실 것을 권해 드린다고 했으므로 (B) To ask her to bring her car for a check-up 이 정답이다.

4. 디아즈 씨가 웹 사이트에 관하여 언급한 것은?
   (A) 여러 제품에 대한 정보를 포함한다.
   (B) 6월 18일에 출시됐다.
   (C) 최근 고객들의 후기를 담고 있다.
   (D) 최근 개편되었다.

해설 웹 사이트에서는 차량을 최대한 원활하게 운행하도록 고안된 다양한 제품도 살펴보실 수 있다고 했으므로 (A) It includes information on several products.가 정답이다.

[5-6] 다음 이메일에 관한 문제입니다.

수신: 토시코 포세이 〈tposey@electronmail.com〉
발신: 지원 데스크 〈support@betterliving.com〉
날짜: 3월 12일
제목: 스마트 디퓨저 (모델명 PN-51)

포세이 씨께,

5 죄송하게도 귀하께서 주문하신 스마트 디퓨저 상품 두 개에 사용되는 마이크로칩의 물량 부족으로 인해 안타깝게도 지연되었다는 소식을 전해 드립니다. 새로운 배송이 약 3주 후에 도착할 것으로 확인되었습니다. 만약 이러한 새로운 날짜가 귀하의 일정과 맞지 않으시다면, 추가 요금 없이 귀하의 상품을 스마트 디퓨저 프로로 변경해

드릴 수 있습니다. **6** 프로 모델은 저희 고급 에센셜 오일과 호환되며 리필 2개를 포함합니다. 오리지널 모델과 마찬가지로, 센서를 이용해 자동으로 오일을 분사하지만, 핸드폰을 이용해 수동으로도 조절할 수 있습니다.

이 이메일에 회신하는 방법으로 주문하신 물건을 대신해 업그레이드 제품이 배송되기를 요청하실 수 있습니다. 하지만 기다리셨다가 처음에 주문하신 제품을 받아보길 원하실 경우, 아무런 조치를 취하지 않으셔도 됩니다. 이해해 주셔서 감사합니다.

진심으로,

베니타 플랫
지원 데스크
베터 리빙

어휘 relay (정보, 뉴스 등을) 전달하다 | diffuser 디퓨저 | unfortunate 유감스러운 | delay 지연 | shortage 부족 | microchip 마이크로칩 | confirm 확인하다 | shipment 배송 | approximately 대략 | date 날짜 | substitute 대체하다 | product 제품 | charge 요금 | compatible with ~와 호환되는 | luxury 고급의 | essential oil 에센셜 오일 | refill 리필 제품 | sensor 센서 | automatically 자동으로 | disperse 분사시키다 | manually 수동으로 | control 조절하다, 제어하다 | request 요청하다 | ship 배송하다 | in place of ~를 대신해서 | respond to ~에 답하다 | prefer 선호하다 | initially 처음에 | further 추가의 | require 요구하다

5. 플랫 씨는 왜 이메일을 작성했는가?
   (A) 고객의 불만에 답변하려고
   (B) 신제품의 이점을 알려주려고
   (C) 개정된 정책에 대해 알려주려고
   (D) 지연에 사과하려고

해설 첫 번째 단락에서 귀하께서 주문하신 스마트 디퓨저 상품 두 개에 사용되는 마이크로칩의 물량 부족으로 인해 안타깝게도 지연되었다는 소식을 전해 드린다고 했으므로 (D) To apologize for a delay가 정답이다.

6. 스마트 디퓨저 프로에 관하여 언급된 것은?
   (A) 추가 오일이 딸려 온다.
   (B) 오리지널 모델보다 색상이 더 다양하다.
   (C) 아직 대중에 공개되지 않았다.
   (D) 잡지에서 호평을 받았다.

해설 첫 번째 단락에서 프로 모델은 고급 에센셜 오일과 호환되며 리필 2개를 포함한다고 했으므로 (A) It comes with additional oils.가 정답이다.

쏜톤 토목 공학 협회
http://www.tces.org
3월 3일

8 에린 헤르난데즈
251 말보로 테라스
리질랜드, WI 54763

에린 씨께,

— [1] —. **8** 쏜톤 토목 공학 협회(TCES)를 대표하여 쏜톤 전역에 대중교통 중심 도시들을 설계하신 귀하의 업적에 대한 특별 공로의 의미로, **7** 올해 듄에서 열리는 저희 학회에서 기조 연설을 맡아 주시기를 요청 드립니다. — [2] —. **8** 올해의 주제는 미래를 설계하는 것이며, 귀하의 설계에서 미래 도시적 요소를 차용하게 된다는 것이 저희의 관점입니다. **9** 저희 웹 사이트에서 일부 다른 연사분들을 확인하실 수 있습니다. — [3] —. 학회 일정 탭으로 이동하시면 됩니다.

저희의 제안이 귀하의 관심을 끌어 저희 학회에서 연설하시는 방향으로 선택해 주셨으면 합니다. 궁금한 점이 있으시면 저에게 알려 주세요. — [4] —. 제 전화번호는 (062) 555 0912입니다.

진심으로,
클라이드 존스
행사 기획자, TCES

어휘 civil engineering 토목 공학 | society 협회 | on behalf of ~를 대신하여, 대표하여 | recognition 인정, 표창 | design 설계하다 | public transportation 대중 교통 | oriented ~를 지향하는, ~중심의 | city 도시 | throughout ~도처에 | invite 초대하다, (정식으로) 요청하다 | deliver (연설 등을) 하다 | keynote address 기조 연설 | theme 주제 | future 미래 | view 관점, 견해 | borrow 빌리다 | element 요소 | navigate 길을 찾다, 탐색하다 | tab (컴퓨터) 탭 | offer 제안 | interest ~의 관심을 끌다 | choose 선택하다

7. 편지의 목적은 무엇인가?
(A) 회사에 일자리를 제공하려고
(B) 초대하려고
(C) 문의에 답하려고
(D) 행사장소 변경을 알리려고

해설 첫 번째 단락에서 올해 듄에서 열리는 학회에서 기조 연설을 맡아 주시기를 요청 드린다고 했으므로 (B) To extend an invitation이 정답이다.

8. 헤르난데즈 씨에 관하여 언급된 것은?
(A) 듄에 있는 사무실에서 근무한다.
(B) 존스 씨를 직접 만난 적이 있다.
(C) TCES의 회원이다.
(D) 자신의 분야에서 존경받는다.

해설 에린 헤르난데즈에게 보낸 편지의 첫 번째 단락에서 쏜톤 토목 공학 협회(TCES)를 대표하여 쏜톤 전역에 대중교통 중심 도시들을 설계

하신 귀하의 업적에 대한 특별 공로의 의미라고 했으므로 (D) She is thought of highly in her field.가 정답이다.

9. [1], [2], [3], [4]로 표시된 곳 중, 다음 문장이 들어갈 위치로 가장 적절한 것은?

"몇몇 분들은 과거 프로젝트에서 함께 작업한 적이 있으셔서 아실 수도 있습니다."

(A) [1]
(B) [2]
(C) [3]
(D) [4]

해설 첫 번째 단락에서 저희 웹 사이트에서 일부 다른 연사분들을 확인하실 수 있다고 하여, 주어진 문장이 뒤에 이어져야 자연스러우므로 (C) [3]가 정답이다.

UNIT 02. 세부사항 문제

핵심 문제 유형 본서 p.239

1. (B)

[1] 다음 초대에 관한 문제입니다.

1 BB 센터 예술 협회는 전시회를 개최할 예정입니다.

우리의 예술가들: 시카고 최고 신인 예술가들의 회화와 소묘

4월 7일 목요일, 오후 4시 30분에서 오후 7시 30분까지

시카고, IL 60007의
그랜드리버 매인 가 171번지에
있는 오웬 공연 센터에서 진행됩니다.

행사 티켓은 인당 20달러입니다.

티켓을 예매하려면,
4월 1일 금요일까지 전화하거나 이메일을 보내세요.
전화: 889-4000
이메일: events@bbcenterarts.org

어휘 association 협회 | host 개최하다 | exhibition 전시회 | emerging 떠오르는, 부상하는 | per ~당 | person 사람 | reservation 예약, 예매

1. 어떤 종류의 행사가 개최되는가?
(A) 콘서트
(B) 미술 전시회
(C) 비즈니스 컨벤션
(D) 경매

해설 어떤(What) 종류의 행사가 열리고 있는지를 묻는 세부 사항 문제
이다. 질문의 키워드를 파악한 후, 지문에서 언급된 부분을 찾는
다. 지문의 첫 번째 줄에서 예술 협회가 주최하는 전시회이므로 다
른 종류를 언급한 (A), (C), (D)는 소거한다. 지문의 첫 번째 줄 Art
Association(예술 협회)란 단어가 보이고, 다음 줄에는 예술가들
(Artists)에 의한 '회화와 소묘(Paintings and Drawings)'라고 나와
있다. 따라서 정답은 (B) An art show이다.

Practice

본서 p.240

1. (A)	2. (D)	3. (D)	4. (A)	5. (C)
6. (A)	7. (A)	8. (B)	9. (A)	10. (D)
11. (C)				

[1-2] 다음 안내판에 관한 문제입니다.

블러스 박사 사무실에 오신 것을 환영합니다.

자리에 앉기 전에 접수처에서 신청서를 작성해 주십시오. 그런 다음
대기실에 있는 자리에 앉아 주세요. **1** 접수 담당자가 이름을 불러
예약 세부 사항 확인 및 서류 접수를 도와드립니다. 처리해야 할 결
제가 있는 경우, 마찬가지로 접수 담당자가 도와드릴 것입니다.

2 예약 시간보다 15분 이상 늦는 경우, 일정을 다시 잡는 것은 저희
재량에 달려 있다는 점을 유의해 주시기 바랍니다. 오지 않은 환자
에게는 30달러의 요금이 부과됩니다.

어휘 **take a seat** 자리에 앉다 | **fill out** 작성하다 | **sign-
in sheet** 신청서 | **reception desk** 접수처 | **waiting
room** 대기실 | **receptionist** 접수 담당자 | **call** 부르다 |
paperwork 서류(작업) | **confirm** 확인하다 | **detail**
세부사항 | **appointment** 예약 | **payment** 결제, 지불 |
process 처리하다 | **assist with** ~를 돕다 | **note** 유의하
다 | **reschedule** 일정을 다시 잡다 | **at one's discretion**
~의 재량에 따라 | **patient** 환자 | **fail** ~하지 않다, 실패하다 |
turn up 나타나다 | **charge** 청구하다

1. 안내판에 따르면, 접수 담당자는 고객에게 무엇을 도와줄 것인가?
   (A) 서류 제출하는 것
   (B) 사무실에 들어가는 것
   (C) 자리를 찾는 것
   (D) 예약 일정을 잡는 것

해설 첫 번째 단락에서 접수 담당자가 이름을 불러 예약 세부 사항 확인 및
서류 접수를 도와드린다고 했으므로 (A) Submitting paperwork가
정답이다.

2. 늦게 도착한 고객에게 무슨 일이 생길 수 있는가?
   (A) 다른 사무실로 보내질 수 있다.
   (B) 추가 요금이 부과될 수 있다.
   (C) 이메일을 작성하라는 요청을 받을 수 있다.
   (D) 다른 시간으로 일정이 잡힐 수 있다.

해설 두 번째 단락에서 예약 시간보다 15분 이상 늦는 경우, 일정을 다시 잡
는 것은 저희 재량에 달려 있다는 점을 유의해 달라고 했으므로 (D)
They may be scheduled at a different time.이 정답이다.

[3-4] 다음 구인 공고에 관한 문제입니다.

http://www.hivefoodmarket.com/jobs

배송 기사

북미의 선두 식료품 체인점 하이브 푸드 마켓에서 저희와 함께 할,
믿고 신뢰할 수 있는 직원을 구합니다. 배송 기사는 온라인 쇼핑 주
문이 고객에게 제대로 배송되도록 책임집니다. 먼저, 고객이 주문을
하면, 자신의 스마트 기기에 있는 자사 배달 앱으로 알림이 갑니다.
그러면, 고객이 주문한 상품을 모아서 봉지나 상자에 담아 고객의
현관까지 배송합니다. **3** 모든 신입 직원에게는 필수 교육이 제공됩
니다.

직무에 고려되려면 모든 지원자는 다음 요건을 모두 충족해야 합니다.

▶ **4C** 20킬로그램 무게까지 들어 올릴 수 있는 능력
▶ **4B** 필요시 이른 아침, 늦은 저녁, 주말 근무 가능
▶ 유효한 운전 면허증 보유
▶ **4D** 스마트 기기 이용 가능

지금 지원서를 작성하세요!

어휘 **delivery** 배송 | **rider** 기사, 라이더 | **leading** 선두적인 |
grocery store 식료품점 | **chain** 체인점 | **seek** 구하다,
찾다 | **reliable** 신뢰할 수 있는 | **dependable** 믿을 수
있는 | **employee** 직원 | **be responsible for** ~에 책
임지다 | **ensure** 보장하다 | **deliver** 배송하다 | **correctly**
제대로 | **notify** 알리다 | **collect** 모으다, 수집하다 | **item**
상품 | **purchase** 구입하다 | **mandatory** 필수의 |
applicant 지원자 | **satisfy** 충족시키다 | **following** 다음의 |
requirement 요건 | **consider** 고려하다 | **be able to V**
~할 수 있다 | **lift** 들어올리다 | **up to** ~까지 | **be willing to**
기꺼이 ~하다 | **valid** 유효한 | **driver's license** 운전 면허증 |
fill out (서식을) 작성하다 | **application** 지원서

3. 구인 공고에 따르면, 직무에서 무엇을 제공하는가?
   (A) 회사 차량
   (B) 쇼핑 할인
   (C) 성장 기회
   (D) 교육 과정

해설 첫 번째 단락에서 모든 신입 직원에게는 필수 교육이 제공된다고 했으
므로 (D) Training sessions가 정답이다.

4. 직무 요건에 해당하지 않는 것은?
   (A) 지역 지리에 대한 지식
   (B) 유연한 일정으로 근무 가능
   (C) 가득 찬 식료품 봉지를 옮기는 능력
   (D) 메시지 기능이 있는 스마트 기기

해설 지문의 단서와 보기를 매칭시키면, 두 번째 단락에서 '20킬로그램 무
게까지 들어 올릴 수 있는 능력'이 (C)로 '필요시 이른 아침, 늦은 저녁,

주말 근무 가능'이 (B)로, '스마트 기기 이용 가능'이 (D)와 일치하지만, 지역 지리에 대한 내용은 언급된 바 없으므로 (A) Knowledge of local geography가 정답이다.

[5-7] 다음 공지에 관한 문제입니다.

5 **6** 올해 누렸던 평소답지 않은 따뜻한 날씨로 수확한 과일과 야채의 양 또한 상당히 증가했습니다. **5** 실제 재배 농가에 공급이 너무 많고 수요는 부족하다는 보도가 있습니다. 남아도는 농산물을 폐기 처리하는 대신, 어려운 사람들을 먹일 수 있는 좋은 뜻에 기부하는 것을 고려해 주세요. Whittaker 가족 재단(www.whittakerff.org)을 방문하시면 농산물을 어디에 기부할 수 있는지 알아보실 수 있습니다.

감사의 표시로, 저희에게는 자신의 시간을 기꺼이 기부해 주시는 몇 분의 정비사분들이 계십니다. **7** 저희 단체를 지원해 주신 것에 대한 답례로, 저희 자원봉사자들이 문제를 겪고 계신 기계에 간단한 수리 및 변경 작업을 제공해 드리고 있습니다. 저희 웹 사이트에 퇴비화 및 원예에 관한 유용한 글뿐만 아니라 이 서비스에 관한 보다 자세한 내용이 담겨 있습니다.

어휘 uncharacteristically 평소답지 않게 | warm 따뜻한 | weather 날씨 | lead to ~로 이어지다 | substantial 상당한 | increase 증가 | amount 양 | vegetable 야채 | harvest 수확하다 | grower 재배자 | supply 공급 | demand 수요 | excess 여분의, 초과한 | produce 농산물 | go to waste 낭비되다, 버려지다 | consider 고려하다 | donate 기부하다 | good cause 대의명분 | feed 먹을 것을 주다 | needy (경제적으로) 어려운, 궁핍한 | as a token of ~의 표시로 | appreciation 감사 | several 몇몇의 | mechanic 정비사 | kindly 호의적으로, 쾌히, 기꺼이 | in return for ~의 답례로 | support 지원하다 | organization 단체, 기관 | volunteer 자원봉사자 | fix 수리 | tweak 수정, 변경 | machinery 기계류 | article 글, 기사 | compost 퇴비를 주다[만들다] | garden 정원을 가꾸다

5. 공지는 누구를 대상으로 하는가?
(A) 자동차 정비사
(B) 레스토랑 매니저
(C) 농부
(D) 창고 감독관

해설 첫 번째 단락에서 올해 누렸던 평소답지 않은 따뜻한 날씨로 수확한 과일과 야채의 양 또한 상당히 증가하였고, 실제 재배 농가에 공급이 너무 많고 수요는 부족하다는 보도가 있으며, 남아도는 농산물을 폐기 처리하는 대신, 어려운 사람들을 먹일 수 있는 좋은 뜻에 기부하는 것을 고려해 달라고 했으므로 (C) Farmers가 정답이다.

6. 공지에서 날씨에 관하여 언급한 것은?
(A) 예상보다 좋았다.
(B) 행사 취소를 야기했다.
(C) 건설 프로젝트의 지연 원인이 됐다.
(D) 몇 달 전에 미리 예측되었다.

해설 첫 번째 단락에서 올해 누렸던 평소답지 않은 따뜻한 날씨로 수확

한 과일과 야채의 양 또한 상당히 증가했다고 했으므로 (A) It was better than expected.가 정답이다.

7. 공지에서 어떤 서비스를 언급하는가?
(A) 기계 수리
(B) 퇴비화 워크숍
(C) 농산물 수송
(D) 식품 포장 및 준비

해설 두 번째 단락에서 단체를 지원해 주신 것에 대한 답례로, 자원봉사자들이 문제를 겪고 계신 기계에 간단한 수리 및 변경 작업을 제공해 드린다고 했으므로 (A) Machinery repairs가 정답이다.

[8-11] 다음 이메일에 관한 문제입니다.

8 수신: 리나 셜트 〈lschulte@outworldmail.com〉
발신: 블루스톤 엔터테인먼트
〈redmon@bluestoneentertainment.com〉
날짜: 7월 18일
제목: 할인

셜트 씨께,

8 저희의 가장 소중한 고객만을 위한 기간 한정 독점 할인을 알려드리게 되어 기쁩니다. **9** **10** 매달 3달러만 더 내시면, 현재 요금제에 방송망을 두 개 더 결합해 드립니다. 아래 목록에서 두 가지를 선택하실 수 있습니다.

(1) 무비 나이트, 재미있는 가족 영화를 다양하게 제공합니다.

(2) 스테디움 360, 국내 및 국제 경기를 포함한 모든 종류의 스포츠를 당신의 화면으로 가져다줍니다.

(3) 테크워치, 최신 기술의 가장 흥미진진한 발전을 다루는 프로그램을 보여줍니다.

(4) 원 위드 네이처, 자연, 동물, 그 이상을 다루는 다양한 다큐멘터리를 제공합니다.

(5) **11** 브레인 게임즈, 다양한 게임에 참가해 서로 경쟁할 수 있습니다.

이 혜택을 이용하시려면, 두 가지를 선택하셔서 이 이메일에 답장을 보내주시기만 하면 됩니다. 할인은 8월 5일까지만 유효하니, 서두르세요!

엘빈 레드몬, 엔터테인먼트 책임자
블루스톤 엔터테인먼트

어휘 announce 알리다 | exclusive 독점적인 | limited-time 시간이 한정된 | offer 제안, 할인 제공하다 | valued 소중한 | customer 고객 | bundle 묶다 | current 현재의 | choose 선택하다 | provide 제공하다 | a variety of 다양한 | bring 가져오다 | national 전국의, 국가의 | international 국제적인 | cover 포함시키다, 다루다 | advance 진전, 발전 | documentary 다큐멘터리 | nature 자연 | beyond 그 이후에 | allow 허용하다 | player 참가자, 선수 | compete with ~과 겨루다 | take advantage of ~를 이용하다 | respond 답장을 보내다 | selection 선택(된 것) | valid 유효한

8. 셜트 씨에 관하여 알 수 있는 것은?

(A) 스포츠 경기 관람을 즐긴다.

(B) 블루스톤 엔터테인먼트의 고객이다.

(C) 현재 출장 중이다.

(D) 텔레비전 산업에 종사한다.

해설 블루스톤 엔터테인먼트에서 리나 셜트에게 보낸 이메일의 첫 번째 단락에서 가장 소중한 고객만을 위한 기간 한정 독점 할인을 알려드리게 되어 기쁘다고 했으므로 (B) She is a Bluestone Entertainment customer.가 정답이다.

---

9. 무엇이 제공되고 있는가?

(A) 저렴한 비용의 업그레이드

(B) 신규 서비스 시험 사용

(C) 개선된 장비 부품

(D) 서비스 중단에 대한 사과

해설 첫 번째 단락에서 매달 3달러만 더 내면, 현재 요금제에 방송망을 두 개 더 결합해 준다고 했으므로 (A) A low-cost upgrade가 정답이다.

---

10. 첫 번째 단락, 세 번째 줄의 단어, 'plan'과 의미상 가장 가까운 것은?

(A) 안건 목록

(B) 설계도

(C) 예비 일정

(D) 지불제

해설 첫 번째 단락의 '매달 3달러만 더 내시면, 현재 요금제에 방송망을 두 개 더 결합해 드립니다'에서 plan은 '요금제'라는 의미로 쓰였으므로 같은 의미를 전달하는 (D) payment program이 정답이다.

---

11. 어떤 방송망이 양방향인가?

(A) 스테디움 360

(B) 원 위드 네이처

(C) 브래인 게임즈

(D) 테크워치

해설 항목 (5)에서 브래인 게임즈, 다양한 게임에 참가해 서로 경쟁할 수 있다고 했으므로 (C) Brain Games가 정답이다.

UNIT 03. 사실확인 문제

핵심 문제 유형

1. (C) 2. (C)

[1-2] 다음 광고에 관한 문제입니다.

당신의 회사를 위한 새로운 인재를 끌어들일 저렴한 방법을 원하십

니까? 고용 관련 신문 〈커리어 호프〉에 구인 공고를 올리세요. 신문은 일자리 외에도 구직자가 필요로 하는 많은 것들을 포함하고 있습니다. 취업 박람회에 관한 정보와 이력서 쓰는 것에 대한 전문가들의 조언, 그리고 어떻게 하면 면접을 잘 볼 수 있는지에 대한 팁도 포함하고 있습니다.

〈커리어 호프〉는 이스트 세인트 루이스 주변의 많은 지역에 배포되고, 구직자들에게는 전액 무료입니다. ■① 〈커리어 호프〉를 이용하는 것은 구인 회사를 위해 아주 좋은 생각입니다. 각 공고는 30달러이며, 한 달 동안 유지됩니다.

■② 구인 광고를 내기 위해 careerhopeprint.com/ad를 방문하세요. 당신은 또한 효과적인 구인 광고 예시들을 볼 수도 있습니다. 당신이 구인 광고에 포함시키고 싶은 문구를 업로드하고 나서 최종 요금을 지불하세요.

당신의 글은 〈커리어 호프〉에 의해서 편집되지 않을 것이라는 것을 알아두세요. 만약 당신의 광고 글을 작성할 편집자를 고용하고 싶으면, 우리에게 785-884-2370으로 연락주세요. 이 서비스에 대한 추가 요금이 있을 것입니다.

어휘 inexpensive 비싸지 않은 | talent 인재 | employment-related 고용과 관련된 | job seeker 구직자 | contain 포함하다 | career fair 취업박람회 | résumé 이력서 | distribute 배포하다, 보급하다 | last 지속하다 | effective 효과적인 | text 본문, 글, 문서 | edit 편집하다 | advertisement 광고 | additional 추가적인

---

1. 〈커리어 호프〉에 관하여 언급된 것은 무엇인가?

(A) 이스트 세인트 루이스에 몇 개의 사무실을 두고 있다.

(B) 매년 취업 박람회를 개최할 것이다.

(C) 각 구인 광고당 30달러를 부과한다.

(D) 한 달에 한 번 발행된다.

해설 〈커리어 호프〉에 대해서 무엇이 언급되는지를 묻는 문제이므로 〈커리어 호프〉를 키워드로 삼아 지문에 언급된 부분을 찾는다. 첫 번째 단락에 〈커리어 호프〉가 취업 박람회에 관한 정보를 포함하고 있다는 이야기는 있었고, 두 번째 단락에 이스트 세인트 루이스 주변 지역에 〈커리어 호프〉가 배포된다는 말은 있었다. 그러나 취업 박람회를 개최하거나 이스트 세인트 루이스에 몇 개의 사무실이 있다든가, 한 달에 한 번 발행된다는 말은 지문에서 언급된 적이 없다. 두 번째 단락에서 광고를 게시하는 건당 비용이 30달러라고 한 지문 내용을 언급했으므로 정답은 (C) It charges $30 for each job posting.이다.

---

2. 〈커리어 호프〉 웹사이트에서 행해질 수 있는 것으로 언급되지 않은 것은 무엇인가?

(A) 요금을 지불하는 것

(B) 샘플 공고를 보는 것

(C) 일자리에 지원하는 것

(D) 서류를 제출하는 것

해설 질문에서 웹사이트를 키워드로 삼아 지문에서 〈커리어 호프〉 웹사이트가 언급된 부분을 찾는다. 지문 세 번째 단락에서 효과적인 구인 광고의 예시들이 있을 것이니, 당신이 구인 광고에 포함시키고 싶은 글을 게시한 후 최종 요금을 지불하라는 언급이 있으므로 (A), (B), (D)는 소

거한다. 보기에서 언급되지 않은 것은 일자리 지원에 관한 내용이므로 정답은 (C) Applying for a position이다.

Practice
본서 p.246

1. (C)	**2.** (A)	**3.** (B)	**4.** (A)	**5.** (D)
6. (A)	**7.** (D)	**8.** (B)	**9.** (D)	**10.** (B)
11. (C)				

[1-2] 다음 광고에 관한 문제입니다.

진 픽업 서비스

- **1** 정액 요금으로 공항에서 호텔까지 모셔다드립니다
- **2** 여행객 최대 3명까지 수용
- 일주일 내내 하루 24시간 이용 가능
- 숙련 및 검증된 전문 운전기사
- 예약이 필요 없습니다. 195-555-1873으로 전화하셔서 탑승 정보를 알려주시면 일정을 잡아 드립니다.

어휘 pick-up service 공항으로 손님을 마중 나가는 서비스 | airport 공항 | flat fee 정액 요금 | seat 앉히다, 수용하다 | up to 최대 ~까지 | traveler 여행객 | available 이용 가능한 | fully trained 숙련된 | vetted 검증된 | professional 전문적인 | reservation 예약 | flight 항공편 | detail 세부 정보 | schedule 일정을 잡다

1. 무엇이 광고되고 있는가?
   (A) 여행사
   (B) 호텔
   (C) 수송 서비스
   (D) 교육 프로그램

해설 정액 요금으로 공항에서 호텔까지 모셔다드린다고 했으므로 (C) A transportation service가 정답이다.

2. 진 픽업 서비스에 관하여 언급된 것은?
   (A) 소규모 그룹에 서비스를 제공한다.
   (B) 사전 예약이 필요하다.
   (C) 직원을 추가로 채용 중이다.
   (D) 여러 도시에서 운영한다.

해설 여행객 최대 3명까지 수용이라고 했으므로 (A) It can cater to small groups.가 정답이다.

[3-5] 다음 안내에 관한 문제입니다.

컨택 일렉트릭시티에서 드리는 팁

이번 달 호에서는 전자 제품을 안전하게 지키면서 전기세를 최소화하는 방법 몇 가지를 소개해 드립니다.

1. 당신의 기기를 보호하세요: 굥은 날씨에는 전압 스파이크가 발생

할 수 있습니다. 제대로 관리하지 않으면 이러한 스파이크가 당신의 장비에 심각한 손상을 입힐 수 있습니다. 전류 급증 보호 장치를 구입하셔서 이 문제를 예방하세요. **4** 어디서나 구입하실 수 있으며, 앞으로 많은 돈을 절약하게 만들어줍니다.

2. 사용 완료하면 플러그를 뽑아주세요: 기기 사용을 완료한 후 벽에서 전원 플러그를 뽑으세요. 장기적으로는 돈을 어느 정도 절약하게 됩니다.

3. 계량기를 추적 관찰하세요: 들이면 좋은 습관은 당신의 가정에서 얼마나 많은 전기를 사용하는지 살펴보는 것입니다. 전기 사용량의 갑작스러운 증가는 가정 내 무언가가 제대로 작동하지 않고 있음을 나타내는 지표가 될 수도 있습니다.

3 **5** 이러한 팁은 컨택 일렉트릭시티 고객에게 매달 전기세 고지서와 함께 제공됩니다. 궁금하신 사항은 315-555-4169로 전화 주셔서 컨택 기사에게 말씀해 주세요.

어휘 electricity 전기, 전력 | edition (간행물의) 호 | bring 가져다 주다 | electronics 전자 제품 | safe 안전한 | minimize 최소화하다 | power bill 전기세 | protect 보호하다 | device 기기 | weather 날씨 | voltage spike 전압 스파이크 | occur 일어나다, 발생하다 | properly 제대로 | mitigate 완화시키다 | badly 심하게 | damage 손상을 주다 | equipment 장비 | non-issue (주제가) 하찮은 것 | surge 전류 급등 | protector 보호 장치 | down the line 앞으로 | unplug 플러그를 뽑다 | in the long run (장기적으로 보면) 결국에는 | monitor 추적 관찰하다 | meter 계량기 | household 가정 | sudden 갑작스러운 | increase 증가 | usage 사용(량) | indicate 나타내다, 보여주다 | malfunction 제대로 작동하지 않다 | alongside ~와 함께 | technician 기술자 | verify 검증하다

3. 안내는 누구를 대상으로 하는가?
   (A) 컨택 일렉트릭시티 직원
   (B) 컨택 일렉트릭시티 고객
   (C) 부동산 중개인
   (D) 건설 인부

해설 다섯 번째 단락에서 이러한 팁은 컨택 일렉트릭시티 고객에게 매달 전기세 고지서와 함께 제공된다고 했으므로 (B) Contact Electricity customers가 정답이다.

4. 전류 급증 보호 장치에 관하여 언급된 것은?
   (A) 많은 곳에서 구할 수 있다.
   (B) 제대로 설치되어야 한다.
   (C) 구입하기에 저렴하다.
   (D) 사용하기 쉽다.

해설 두 번째 단락에서 어디서나 구입하실 수 있으며, 앞으로 많은 돈을 절약하게 만들어준다고 했으므로 (A) They are widely available.이 정답이다.

5. 팁에 관하여 언급된 것은?

(A) 대중이 이용할 수 있다.

(B) 독자적인 정보원의 검증을 받는다.

(C) 중소기업을 위해 작성된다.

(D) 매달 발송된다.

해설 다섯 번째 단락에서 이러한 팁은 컨택 일렉트릭시티 고객에게 매달 전기세 고지서와 함께 제공된다고 했으므로 (D) They are sent out every month.가 정답이다.

[6-8] 다음 공지에 관한 문제입니다.

베이크드 빈 의무 회수 공지

11월 8일

최근의 뉴스를 고려해, 식품 생산 기업 고원 인터네셔널에서는 14온스 베이크드 빈 통조림 상품에 대해 회수 공지를 발표합니다. 회수는 포장 과정상의 문제로 인한 조치로, 사람이 먹기에 안전하지 않은 상태로 변질될 수 있습니다. 문제의 정도가 아직 파악되지 않았기에, 관련 상품 전체를 식료품점 매대에서 철수했습니다.

6 해당 고원 인터네셔널 베이크드 빈 통조림에는 제품 코드 603813과 603815가 포함되어 있을 것입니다. 소비자는 가지고 계신 14온스 통조림을 확인해 해당 제품 코드가 있는지 살펴봐야 합니다. **7** 소비자가 해당 제품 코드가 포함된 통조림을 가지고 있는 경우, 최초 구입 장소에서 반품 후 전액 환불 처리 바랍니다. 그렇지 않으면, 자사로 직접 통조림을 보낼 수 있고 교환품으로 돌려받게 될 것입니다. 주소는 자사 웹 사이트 www.gowninternational.com/recall에서 확인할 수 있습니다.

불편을 끼쳐 드려 진심으로 사과 드립니다. **8** 고원 인터네셔널에서는 다시는 이런 일이 일어나지 않도록 통조림 식사, 과일, 수프 전 제품의 과정에 조사를 실시할 예정이니 안심하셔도 됩니다.

계속 이용해 주셔서 감사드립니다.

아벨 탐슨, 최고 경영자
고원 인터네셔널

어휘 mandatory 의무적인 | recall 회수, 리콜 | in light of ~를 고려하여 | issue 발표하다 | ounce 온스 | can 통조림, 캔 | baked bean 토마토소스에 넣어 삶은 콩 | error 문제 | pack 포장하다 | process 과정, 절차 | render (어떤 상태가 되게) 만들다 | unsafe 안전하지 않은 | consumption 소비 | extent 크기, 규모 | pull (없애기 위해) 빼다, 잡아당기다 | affect 영향을 미치다 | grocery store 식료품점 | shelf 선반, 매대 | contain 들어있다, 포함되어 있다 | consumer 소비자 | in the case ~하는 경우에 | possess 소유하다 | urge 강력히 권고하다 | return 반품하다 | original 원래의 | place 장소 | purchase 구입 | refund 환불 | alternatively 그렇지 않으면, 대신에 | directly 직접 | replacement 교체(품) | address 주소 | sincerely 진심으로 | apologize 사과하다 | inconvenience 불편 | rest assured 안심하세요 | investigate 조사하다 | process 과정 | canned 통조림으로 된 | meal 식사 | ensure 보장하다 | loyalty 충성, 의리

6. 공지는 누구를 대상으로 하는가?

(A) 고원 인터네셔널 고객

(B) 고원 인터네셔널 직원

(C) 식료품점 주인

(D) 식료품점 계산대 직원

해설 두 번째 단락에서 해당 고원 인터네셔널 베이크드 빈 통조림에는 제품 코드 603813과 603815가 포함되어 있으며 소비자는 가지고 계신 14온스 통조림을 확인해 해당 제품 코드가 있는지 살펴봐야 한다고 했으므로 (A) Gown International customers가 정답이다.

7. 탐슨 씨가 권장하는 조치에 해당하는 것은?

(A) 온라인 양식에 참여하기

(B) 포커스 그룹에 합류하기

(C) 회사 담당 직원에게 이야기하기

(D) 제품 환불 받기

해설 두 번째 단락에서 소비자가 해당 제품 코드가 포함된 통조림을 가지고 있는 경우, 최초 구입 장소에서 반품 후 전액 환불 처리 바란다고 했으므로 (D) Receiving a refund for a product가 정답이다.

8. 고원 인터네셔널에 관하여 언급된 것은?

(A) 세 나라에 사무실이 있다.

(B) 과일 통조림을 판매한다.

(C) 제품을 수입한다.

(D) 신규 웹 사이트가 있다.

해설 세 번째 단락에서 고원 인터네셔널에서는 다시는 이런 일이 일어나지 않도록 통조림 식사, 과일, 수프 전 제품의 과정에 조사를 실시할 예정이니 안심하셔도 된다고 했으므로 (B) It sells canned fruit.가 정답이다.

[9-11] 다음 이메일에 관한 문제입니다.

수신: daniellep@reedcalligraphy.com
발신: junyongk@ reedcalligraphy.com
날짜: 4월 25일
제목: 웹 사이트에 대한 의견

다니엘, 안녕하세요.

리드 캘리그래피의 신규 웹 사이트 초안 최신 본 검토를 방금 마쳤어요. 현대적이고 세련된 디자인이 아주 좋습니다. — [1] —. 펜촉 설명 링크에 캘리그라피 샘플 사진을 넣은 아이디어가 훌륭했어요. **9** 우리 고객들 대부분은 어떤 펜촉을 사용하는 것이 가장 좋을지 결정하는 것을 어려워할 수 있는 초보 서예가예요. 각 펜촉으로 적은 실제 서예 이미지가 있으면 이들 고객이 구매까지 갈 수 있도록 권장할 수도 있어요. — [2] —.

11 다행히도 제가 살펴보는 동안에는 제품 페이지 링크가 깨진 건 보이지 않았어요. — [3] —. **10** 하지만 실제 구매 흐름이 보다 사용자 친화적이어야 해요. 장바구니에 제품을 추가하는 것은 쉬웠지만, 쇼핑을 계속하기 위해서 같은 장소로 돌아가는 데 애를 먹었어요. 이를테면, 저는 처음에 둥근 펜촉을 장바구니에 넣은 후 제가 중단한 곳으로 다시 돌아가 다른 종류의 둥근 펜촉을 사고 싶었어요. — [4] —. 돌아가서 쇼핑을 다시 시작하는 버튼이 없었어요. 메인 화

면을 통하는 방법으로 제품 카테고리에서 다시 탐색해야 했어요. 제 생각에 이건 팀에서 쉽게 손볼 수 있는 부분일 것 같습니다.

안부를 드리며,

준용

어휘 calligraphy 서예 | finish 끝내다 | look over 살펴보다 | latest 최신의 | draft 초안 | modern 현대적인 | chic 멋진, 세련된 | brilliant 멋진, 뛰어난 | photograph 사진 | nib 펜촉 | description link 링크 | novice 초보자 | calligrapher 서예가 | encourage 권장하다, 부추기다 | go through with ~를 거치다 | purchase 구매 | fortunately 다행히 | assessment 평가 | broken 깨진 | actual 실제의 | flow 흐름 | user friendly 사용자 친화적인 | leave off 중단하다, 멈추다 | resume 다시 시작하다 | navigate 길을 찾다 | go through ~를 거치다 | fix 고치다 | easily 쉽게

9. 리드 캘리그래피 고객에 관하여 언급된 것은?
(A) 자신의 서예 사진을 찍어서 회사로 보내준다.
(B) 보통 문구점에서 물품을 구입한다.
(C) 다양한 종류의 펜촉을 구입하는 것을 선호한다.
(D) 여러 가지 펜촉에 익숙하지 않을 수 있다.

해설 첫 번째 단락에서 우리 고객들 대부분은 어떤 펜촉을 사용하는 것이 가장 좋을지 결정하는 것을 어려워할 수 있는 초보 서예가라고 했으므로 (D) They may be unfamiliar with different pen nibs.가 정답이다.

10. 웹 사이트에 관하여 알 수 있는 것은?
(A) 각 페이지를 로딩하는 데 시간이 오래 걸린다.
(B) 쇼핑 중 탐색하기가 어렵다.
(C) 시각적으로 끌리지 않는다.
(D) 링크에 있는 가격이 최신 정보가 아니다.

해설 두 번째 단락에서 실제 구매 흐름이 보다 사용자 친화적이어야 한다며 장바구니에 제품을 추가하는 것은 쉬웠지만, 쇼핑을 계속하기 위해서 같은 장소로 돌아가는 데 애를 먹었다고 했으므로 (B) It is difficult to navigate while shopping.가 정답이다.

11. [1], [2], [3], [4]로 표시된 곳 중, 다음 문장이 들어갈 위치로 가장 적절한 것은?

"요청하신 대로 모두 철저히 테스트해 봤는데, 잘 작동합니다."

(A) [1]
(B) [2]
(C) [3]
(D) [4]

해설 두 번째 단락에서 다행히도 제가 살펴보는 동안에는 제품 페이지 링크가 깨진 건 보이지 않았다고 하여 주어진 문장이 뒤에 이어지기에 자연스러우므로 (C) [3]가 정답이다.

UNIT 04. 암시·추론 문제

핵심 문제 유형
본서 p.251

1. (C)

[1] 다음 이메일에 관한 문제입니다.

발신: 에일린 박
수신: 수 김
날짜: 5월 1일
제목: 새로운 시스템

김 씨에게,

저는 당신에게 우리 회사가 트랙커 타임 보고 시스템(TTRS)을 채택하기로 결정했다는 것을 알려드립니다. 그 시스템은 직원 근무 시간을 기록하기 위해서 필요합니다. 모든 직원들이 그 시스템을 이용해야 합니다. 4월 20일에 저는 직원들에게 그 시스템을 설명하는 이메일을 보냈고, 그들의 ID를 만드는 방법을 설명하였습니다.

시스템은 5월 8일에 시행될 것이고, 모든 직원들은 5월 5일까지 그들의 ID를 가지고 있어야 합니다. 당신의 ID를 만들기 위해서 회사 홈페이지에 있는 TTRS 아이콘을 클릭하세요. **1** 당신의 ID를 만든 후, 당신의 급여 명세서를 확인하고 싶을 때마다 다시 보는 것이 가능합니다.

만약 당신이 시스템을 사용하는 데에 문제가 있다면, 업무 지원 센터 매니저 강 씨에게 연락해 주세요.

감사합니다.

에일린 박
경리부 차장

어휘 adopt 채택하다 | record 기록하다 | essential 필수적인, 극히 중요한 | explain 설명하다 | implement 시행하다 | statement 내역서, 명세서, 진술서 | face 직면하다 | payroll 급여 대상자 명단

1. 새로운 직원 ID에 관해 암시된 것은 무엇인가?
(A) 만들려면 요금을 내야 한다.
(B) 인터넷 접속을 위해 필요하다.
(C) 급여 명세서를 확인하는 데 사용될 수 있다.
(D) 건물에 입장하기 위해 필요하다.

해설 지문에 suggested '암시된'이 나왔으므로 추론 문제이다. 새로운 직원 ID에 관하여 암시된 것을 묻고 있으므로 employees' new ID를 키워드로 잡아 지문에서 ID 키워드 부분을 표시해 둔다. 요금을 내야 한다는 말은 지문에서 언급된 적이 없으므로 (A)를, 지문에서 인터넷 접속에 대한 언급 자체가 없으므로 (B)를, 건물 출입을 위해 필요하다는 말은 지문에 언급된 적이 없으므로 (D)를 각각 소거한다. 직원 신규 ID를 만들면 급여(paycheck)에 관한 정보를 확인 가능하다는 지문의 단서 문장을 바탕으로 직원 신규 ID가 직원들의 급여 정보를 확인하는 데 필요한 것임을 유추 가능하므로 정답은 (C) They can be used to check salary statements.이다.

Practice

본서 p.252

1. (A)   **2.** (C)   **3.** (D)   **4.** (A)   **5.** (D)
6. (C)   **7.** (C)   **8.** (A)   **9.** (A)   **10.** (D)

[1-2] 다음 안내문에 관한 문제입니다.

사용하시기 전에 먼저 읽어 주세요

레젠서의 고객이 되어 주셔서 감사합니다.

포장을 풀기 전에 부품 목록을 참고해 주시기 바랍니다. **1** 포장을 풀 때는 모든 필수 부품이 있는지 확실히 하기 위해 각 부품을 확인하시기를 권장 드립니다. 빠진 것이 있는 경우, 바로 저희에게 연락 주시면 교체품을 보내드리겠습니다.

조립하시려면, 적절한 조명이 있는 평평한 표면을 찾으신 후 설명서를 따라 주세요. **2** 전자 부품은 부서지기 쉬우니, 나사를 조일 때는 절대 과도한 압력을 가하지 마십시오. 귀하의 기기에 품질 보증 적용을 받으시려면, 저희 웹 사이트 www.resensor.com에서 제품을 등록해 주십시오.

어휘 customer 고객 | unpack 풀다, 꺼내다 | refer to ~를 참고하다 | list 목록 | component 부품 | recommend 권장하다 | check off ~에 체크 표시를 하다 | item 품목, 물품 | ensure 보장하다, 반드시 ~하다 | necessary 필요한 | part 부분, 부품 | missing 없어진 | immediately 즉시 | replacement 교체(품) | assemble 조립하다 | flat 평평한 | surface 표면 | adequate 적절한 | lighting 조명 | follow 따르다 | instructions 사용 설명서 | electronic 전자의 | delicate 부서지기 쉬운 | apply 가하다, 적용하다 | excess 과도한 | pressure 압력 | tighten 조이다 | screw 나사 | device 기기 | be eligible for ~의 대상이 되다, 자격이 있다 | warranty 품질 보증 | coverage 적용 범위 | register 등록하다

1. 안내문은 어디서 발견되겠는가?
   (A) 상자 안에서
   (B) 웹 사이트에서
   (C) 안내 책자에서
   (D) 송장에서

해설 첫 번째 단락에서 포장을 풀 때는 모든 필수 부품이 있는지 확실히 하기 위해 각 부품을 체크하며 확인하시기를 권장드린다고 했으므로 (A) In a box가 정답이다.

2. 어떤 종류의 제품에 관해 이야기되겠는가?
   (A) 사무용 가구
   (B) 장식용 소품
   (C) 탁상용 컴퓨터
   (D) 의류

해설 두 번째 단락에서 전자 부품은 부서지기 쉬우니, 나사를 조일 때는 절대 과도한 압력을 가하지 말라고 했으므로 (C) A desktop computer가 정답이다.

[3-4] 다음 제품 후기에 관한 문제입니다.

제가 직장 생활을 하면서 수많은 헤드폰을 사용해 봤는데, 제 생각에는 던브레이크 SP2 소음 차단 헤드폰이 최고의 경험을 선사해줬습니다. **3** 다가오는 쇼와 축제를 위한 후보 장소들을 살펴봐야 하기에 저는 업무상 이동이 잦습니다. 던브레이크 SP2 헤드폰 덕분에 저는 다음 여행자의 방해를 받지 않고 비행기나 버스에서 편히 앉아 휴식을 취할 수 있습니다. **4** 던브레이크 SP2 헤드폰이 경쟁사 대비 우수한 점은 무게가 거의 느껴지지 않는다는 것입니다. 가끔씩은 제가 이어폰을 끼고 있다는 사실을 잊을 때도 있습니다!

— 엘라 오스턴, 5월 12일

어휘 headphone 헤드폰 | career 직장[사회] 생활 | opinion 의견 | noise-canceling 소음 차단의 | offer 제공하다 | experience 경험 | involve 수반하다, 포함하다 | scope out ~을 자세히 살피다 | potential 잠재적인 | venue 장소 | upcoming 다가오는, 곧 있을 | festival 축제 | allow 가능하게 하다 | distraction 방해, 주의산만 | traveler 여행자 | cut above ~보다 한 수 위 | competition 경쟁 상대 | weightless 무게가 없는 | forget 잊다 | wear 입다, 끼다

3. 오스턴 씨는 누구겠는가?
   (A) 민간 항공기 조종사
   (B) 공사장 인부
   (C) 음향 기사
   (D) 행사 기획자

해설 다가오는 쇼와 축제를 위한 후보 장소들을 살펴봐야 하기에 저는 업무상 이동이 잦다고 했으므로 (D) An event planner가 정답이다.

4. 오스턴 씨는 왜 던브레이크 SP2 헤드폰을 다른 제품보다 선호하는가?
   (A) 가볍다.
   (B) 다른 헤드폰보다 견고하다.
   (C) 다양한 디자인으로 나온다.
   (D) 무선으로 사용 가능하다.

해설 던브레이크 SP2 헤드폰이 경쟁사 대비 우수한 점은 무게가 거의 느껴지지 않는다고 했으므로 (A) They are lightweight.가 정답이다.

[5-6] 다음 이메일에 관한 문제입니다.

수신: gfulton@webmail.com
발신: melodys@underwood.com
날짜: 6월 15일 월요일 오전 10시 52분
제목: [회신] 배송 변경 요청

펄튼 씨께,

이메일 주셔서 감사합니다. 귀하의 언더우드 520L 냉장고 배송 연기 요청을 수용해 드리게 되어 기쁩니다. **5** 귀가가 배송을 위해 자리하실 수 있도록 이제 귀하의 제품은 6월 17일 수요일 오후 3시에서 오후 6시 사이에 귀하의 자택에 도착하게 됩니다.

이 기회를 빌어 귀하께 당사 서비스상 최근 변경 사항에 대해 알려 드리고자 합니다. **6** 모든 언더우드 고객은 이제 주중이든 주말이든 제품이 배송되기를 원하는 시점을 정확히 주문서에 표시할 수 있습니다. 유료 설치 서비스처럼 배송 관련 기타 옵션 또한 주문 시 선택 가능합니다.

언더우드 가전의 오랜 고객이 되어 주셔서 감사드립니다. 그밖에 다른 요청사항이 있으시면 저희에게 연락해 주시기 바랍니다.

진심으로,

멜로디 슬로언

어휘 accommodate 수용하다 | request 요청 | postpone 연기하다 | delivery 배송 | refrigerator 냉장고 | product 제품 | arrive 도착하다 | present 있는, 출석한 | chance 기회 | inform 알리다 | indicate 나타내다 | exactly 정확히 | deliver 배송하다 | related to ~에 관련된 | paid 유료의 | installation 설치 | select 선택하다 | long-time 오랜 | home appliance 가전 제품 | reach out to ~에 연락을 취하다

5. 이메일에서 펄튼 씨에 관해 무엇을 암시하는가?
(A) 유료 설치 서비스를 요청했다.
(B) 주문을 취소하고 싶어한다.
(C) 주문하면서 실수를 했다.
(D) 배송 때 집에 있기를 원했다.

해설 첫 번째 단락에서 이제 귀하의 제품은 6월 17일 수요일 오후 3시에서 오후 6시 사이에 귀하의 자택에 도착하므로 그 자리에 계실 수 있다라고 했으므로 (D) He wanted to be home for a delivery.가 정답이다.

6. 슬로언 씨가 펄튼 씨에게 편지를 보낸 이유는 무엇인가?
(A) 오랜 고객을 위한 신규 쇼핑 서비스를 홍보하려고
(B) 추가 요금이 미리 지불되어야 한다고 알려주려고
(C) 언더우드 가전의 주문서의 변경 사항을 설명하려고
(D) 그의 언더우드 520L 냉장고의 늦은 배송에 대해 사과하려고

해설 두 번째 단락에서 모든 언더우드 고객은 이제 주중이든 주말이든 제품이 배송되기를 원하는 시점을 정확히 주문서에 표시할 수 있다고 했으므로 (C) To describe updates to Underwood Home Appliances' order form.가 정답이다.

[7-10] 다음 온라인 채팅 대화문에 관한 문제입니다.

재러드 리 (오전 9시 36분)
비키, 민디. 두분 모두 내일 분기 회의에 참석하시지 않는 걸 방금 알았어요. 제가 발표할 슬라이드를 검토해 주실 수 있으세요?

비키 비숍 (오전 9시 37분)
타이밍 좋네요. 사본을 받아서 막 검토하던 중이었어요.

재러드 리 (오전 9시 38분)
잘됐네요. 슬라이드 3과 4를 자세히 살펴봐 주실래요? **7** 이번 분

기에 우리 회사에서 달성한 성과와 직면했던 난제를 각각 열거하고 있어요. 저는 이 부분을 경영진에 명확하게 전달하고 싶어요.

민디 그레이브즈 (오전 9시 40분)
네. 모든 부서에서 쏟아부은 엄청난 노력을 인정해 주는 것이 특히 중요할 것 같아요. **8** 모든 난제에도 불구하고 그들이 기여한 바에 관해 경영진에서 알아야 해요.

재러드 리 (오전 9시 41분)
8 알았어요.

민디 그레이브즈 (오전 9시 42분)
전 오늘 오후 회의 끝난 후에 슬라이드를 살펴볼 수 있어요. **9** 그리고 제 오전 고객 회의가 다음 주로 연기됐으니 분기 회의에 참석할게요.

비키 비숍 (오전 9시 53분)
아주 좋아 보여요. 우리가 4월에 실시한 신규 소프트웨어도 포함해야해요. **10** 제 연구 분석 부서에서는 이 규정으로 혜택을 많이 봤어요. 저희가 지금 사용하는 신규 소프트웨어로 업무 방식이 완전히 바뀌었어요.

어휘 attend 참석하다 | quarterly 분기의 | review 검토하다 | slide 슬라이드 | present 발표하다 | convenient 편리한 | timing 타이밍 | detail 열거하다, 상세히 알리다 | achieve 성취하다 | quarter 분기 | challenge 도전, 난제 | face 직면하다 | respectively 각각 | clear 명확한 | management 경영진 | particularly 특히 | acknowledge 인정하다 | put in 투입하다 | contribution 기여 | despite ~에도 불구하고 | push back 미루다 | implement 시행하다 | benefit from ~로부터 이익[혜택]을 얻다 | policy 규정 | completely 완전히

7. 슬라이드 4에는 무엇이 있겠는가?
(A) 시행된 새 규정 목록
(B) 분기 회의 참석자 목록
(C) 회사가 직면한 난제 목록
(D) 회사의 최근 성과 목록

해설 이번 분기에 우리 회사에서 달성한 성과와 직면했던 난제를 각각 열거하고 있다고 한 말을 보아 (C) A list of challenges the company has faced가 정답이다.

8. 오전 9시 41분에, 이 씨가 "알았어요"라고 할 때 무엇을 의미하겠는가?
(A) 직원들의 작업에 대해 감사를 표하겠다.
(B) 자신의 프레젠테이션에서 슬라이드 하나를 없애겠다.
(C) 자신의 슬라이드 자료 사본을 경영진에게 보내겠다.
(D) 다른 사람들에게 회의에서 자신과 함께 발표하자고 청하겠다.

해설 오전 9시 40분 ~ 9시 41분 대화에서 민디 그레이브즈가 모든 난제에도 불구하고 그들이 기여한 바에 관해 경영진에서 알아야 한다고 한 말에 재러드 리가 알았다고 말한 것이므로 (A) He will express gratitude to employees for their work.가 정답이다.

9. 그레이브즈 씨의 오전 회의에 관하여 언급된 것은?

(A) 같은 시간에 다른 행사로 열릴 예정이었다.

(B) 그레이브즈 씨의 요청으로 취소되었다.

(C) 온라인 회의가 될 것이다.

(D) 오전 일찍 일어날 것이다.

해설 오전 9시 42분에 민디 그레이브즈가 오전 고객 회의가 다음주로 연기됐으니 분기 회의에 참석한다고 했으므로 (A) It was scheduled to happen at the same time as another event.가 정답이다.

---

10. 비숍 씨에 관하여 알 수 있는 것은?

(A) 슬라이드 덱을 살펴볼 시간이 더 필요할 것이다.

(B) 최근 새 직책으로 승진했다.

(C) 최근 실시된 규정을 제안했다.

(D) 연구 분석 직원들의 책임자다.

해설 오전 9시 53분에 비키 비숍이 '제 연구 분석 부서에서는 이 규정으로 혜택을 많이 봤다'고 했으므로 (D) She is in charge of the Research Analyst employees.가 정답이다.

UNIT 05. 문장 삽입 문제

핵심 문제 유형

본서 p.257

1. (B)

[1] 다음 이메일에 관한 문제입니다.

수신: 에릭 홉킨스 〈erichopkins@vincent.com〉
발신: 윌마 뮬린즈 〈wmullins@sche.org〉
날짜: 8월 27일
제목: 특별가

홉킨스 씨에게,

화학 공학자 협회(SCHE)는 올해 10월 4일에서 6일까지 영국 런던에서 연례 회의를 열 것입니다. — [1] —. 당신이 숙박을 아직 마련하지 못한 경우에 대비해서, 우리는 방금 공지된 특별 요금을 당신께 알려드리고 싶습니다. **1** 힐사이드 매너는 SCHE 회원들에게 회의 기간 동안에 특별 요금을 제공 중입니다. — [2] — 하룻밤에 오직 120파운드로 당신은 더블룸에서 지낼 수 있고, 205파운드로 당신은 스위트룸을 예약할 수 있습니다. 두 가지 모두 평상시 가격보다 40퍼센트 이상을 절약할 수 있습니다. — [3] —.

이 특별 제안을 이용하려면, 당신이 www.hillsidemanor.com에서 예약을 할 때, 특별코드 SCHECONVENTION을 사용하세요. — [4] —. 하지만 이러한 혜택은 9월 15일까지만 유효하니 서두르세요.

우리는 당신을 올해 회의에서 뵙기를 고대합니다.

진심으로,

윌마 뮬린즈
SCHE 회의 조직자

어휘 hold 개최하다 | convention 협회, 회의, 대회 | arrangement 마련, 준비, 배열 | accommodations 숙소, 거처 | announce 발표하다 | rate 요금 | represent 대표하다 | savings 절약, 저축한 돈 | regular rate 정가 | take advantage of ~을 이용하다 | valid 유효한 | look forward to -ing ~하기를 고대하다

1. [1], [2], [3], 그리고 [4]로 표시되어 있는 자리 중 다음 문장이 들어갈 가장 적절한 곳은 어디인가?

"그것은 컨벤션 센터 길 건너에 편리하게 위치해 있습니다."

(A) [1]

(B) [2]

(C) [3]

(D) [4]

해설 주어진 문장을 먼저 읽고, 접속사나 대명사 등의 단서를 파악해야 하는데, 이 문장에서는 it이라는 대명사에서 단서를 찾는다. 지문에 표시된 위치의 앞뒤 문장을 읽고, 주어진 문장과 흐름상 연결되는지 확인한다. 여기서 대명사 it은 힐사이드 매너를 가리키고 있음을 파악한다. 바로 앞문장에서 힐사이드 매너가 SCHE 회원들에게 회의 기간 동안에 특별가를 제공 중이라는 것을 알리고 이어서 힐사이드 매너는 컨벤션 센터 길 건너에 위치해 있다는 위치를 소개하는 것이 문맥상 가장 자연스러우므로 정답은 (B) [2]이다.

Practice

본서 p.258

1. (D)	**2.** (B)	**3.** (B)	**4.** (B)	**5.** (D)
6. (C)	**7.** (B)	**8.** (D)	**9.** (A)	**10.** (C)
11. (A)	**12.** (B)	**13.** (D)		

[1-3] 다음 공지에 관한 문제입니다.

템플레톤교 보수 프로젝트

— [1] —. **1** 템플레톤교가 2월 1일부터 2월 15일까지 필요한 수리 작업을 위해 일반에 폐쇄됩니다. **3** 작업에는 손상된 서스펜더 보수가 포함됩니다. — [2] —. **2** 그 과정 중에 도로 표식을 다시 칠하는 작업으로 운전자 가시성을 개선합니다.

템플레톤교는 템플레톤과 워터루를 잇는 교통이 혼잡한 다리입니다. 폐쇄 기간 동안 운전자는 워터루까지 17번 주도를 대신 이용해 주시기 바랍니다. — [3] —. 이 기간 동안 버스 노선이 이미 업데이트되어 있으니, 이로 인해 받게 될 영향을 알아보시려면 최신 시간표를 참조해 주시기 바랍니다.

더 많은 정보를 원하시면, www.templetoncity.gov/bridgework를 방문해 주시기 바랍니다. — [4] —.

어휘 repair 수리, 수리하다 | close off 폐쇄시키다 | public 일반인, 대중 | undertake (일을) 맡다, 착수하다 | necessary 필요한 | involve 포함하다, 수반하다 | damaged 손상된 | suspender 다리를 지탱하기 위해 매는 재료, 서스펜더 | process 과정 | re-paint 다시 칠하다 | road marking 도로 표식 | improve 향상시키다, 개선하다 | visibility 가시성 | driver 운전자 | traffic-heavy 교통이 혼잡한 | connect 연결하다, 잇다 | closure 폐쇄 | state highway 주립 고속도로 | instead 대신에 | be advised to ~하도록 권고되다 | route 노선, 경로 | consult 참고하다 | timetable 시간표 | impact 영향을 주다

---

1. 공지의 목적은 무엇인가?
(A) 완료 일자를 정정하는 것
(B) 프로젝트에 대한 피드백을 요청하는 것
(C) 대중교통의 중요성을 설명하는 것
(D) 다리 폐쇄를 알리는 것

해설 첫 번째 단락에서 템플레톤교가 2월 1일부터 2월 15일까지 필요한 수리 작업을 위해 일반에 폐쇄된다고 했으므로 (D) To announce a bridge closure가 정답이다.

2. 프로젝트 목표에 해당하는 것은?
(A) 도로 확장
(B) 보다 명확한 도로 표식
(C) 자전거 전용 도로 개설
(D) 신규 가로등 설치

해설 첫 번째 단락에서 그 과정 중에 도로 표식을 다시 칠하는 작업으로 운전자 가시성을 개선한다고 했으므로 (B) Clearer road markings가 정답이다.

3. [1], [2], [3], [4]로 표시된 곳 중, 다음 문장이 들어갈 위치로 가장 적절한 것은?
"이는 지난달에 있었던 폭풍으로 발생한 결과입니다."
(A) [1]
(B) [2]
(C) [3]
(D) [4]

해설 첫 번째 단락에서 작업에는 손상된 서스펜더 보수가 포함된다고 하여 주어진 문장이 뒤에 이어지기에 자연스러우므로 (B) [2]가 정답이다.

[4-6] 다음 보도 자료에 관한 문제입니다.

즉시 배포용

언론 연락 담당자: 에드 브라운
⟨ebrown@porchaentertainment.co.nz⟩

오클랜드 (⑤ 2월 13일) — [1] —. 뉴질랜드 내 최대 엔터테인먼트 기업이자, 히트작 ⟨공허한 공간⟩와 ⟨두 번째 기회⟩로 수많은 업계 상

을 수상한 포차 엔터테인먼트에서 목요일에 예상치 못한 발표를 했다. — [2] —. ④ 포차 엔터테인먼트의 회장인 제럴딘 애봇은 마이클 제닝스가 크리에이티브 디렉터 자리에서 물러날 것이라고 밝혔다. 창업부터 회사에 몸담아 온 제닝스 씨는 지난해 업계 콘퍼런스 자리에서 은퇴를 고려하고 있음을 시사했다. ⑥ 하지만 발표 시점은 모두를 깜짝 놀라게 했다. — [3] —. ⑤ 애봇 씨는 제닝스 씨가 다음 달 있을 회사의 비디오 게임 산업 진출을 지원하기 위해 고문직으로 남아있을 것이라고 알렸다. "이는 우리 회사에 중요한 기회이며, 앞으로 무슨 일이 일어날지 기대됩니다."라고 말했다. — [4] —.

어휘 entertainment 연예, 엔터테인먼트 | recipient 수령인 | numerous 수많은 | industry 업계 | award 상 | hit 히트작 | void 공허한 | unexpected 예상치 못한 | announcement 발표 | president 회장 | disclose 밝히다, 공개하다 | step down from ~에서 물러나다 | position 자리, 직위 | creative director 크리에이티브 디렉터 | inception 시작 | hint 암시하다, 넌지시 비치다 | consider 고려하다 | retirement 은퇴 | timing 시기 선택 | catch ~ off guard 깜짝 놀라게 하다 | stay on 계속 남아 있다 | consultant 고문, 상담역 | capacity (공식적인) 지위 | assist with ~을 돕다 | mark (중요 사건을) 기념하다 | momentous 중대한 | occasion 경우, 기회 | future 미래 | hold 잡고 있다 | note 언급하다

4. 보도 자료의 주제는 무엇인가?
(A) 제휴
(B) 은퇴
(C) 행사
(D) 광고

해설 포차 엔터테인먼트의 회장인 제럴딘 애봇은 마이클 제닝스가 크리에이티브 디렉터 자리에서 물러날 것이라고 밝혔다. 창업부터 회사에 몸담아 온 제닝스 씨는 지난해 업계 콘퍼런스 자리에서 은퇴를 고려하고 있음을 시사한다고 했으므로 (B) A retirement가 정답이다.

5. 보도 자료에 따르면, 포차 엔터테인먼트는 3월에 무엇을 할 것인가?
(A) 신규 사무실을 열 것이다
(B) 추가 직원을 채용할 것이다
(C) 시상식을 열 것이다
(D) 다른 분야로 진출할 것이다

해설 애봇 씨는 제닝스 씨가 다음 달 있을 회사의 비디오 게임 산업 진출을 지원하기 위해 고문직으로 남아있을 것이라고 알렸다고 했고, 작성일이 2월 13일이므로 (D) Expand into other areas가 정답이다.

6. [1], [2], [3], [4]로 표시된 곳 중, 다음 문장이 들어갈 위치로 가장 적절한 것은?
"그것은 내년으로 예정되어 있었다."
(A) [1]
(B) [2]
(C) [3]
(D) [4]

해설 '하지만 발표 시점은 모두를 깜짝 놀라게 했다'고 하여 주어진 문장이 뒤에 이어지기에 자연스러우므로 (C) [3]가 정답이다.

[7-9] 다음 웹 페이지에 관한 문제입니다.

https://www.medinastones.com/returns

메디나 스톤즈
반품 정책

— [1] —. **9** 당사 반품 규정에서는 30일 이내에 신청한 구매에 한해 적용됩니다. 반품은 처음 포장된 상태로 이루어져야 하며, 영수증이 있어야 합니다. **7** 포장이 심하게 훼손되거나 다른 포장을 사용한 경우, 10퍼센트의 수수료가 부과될 수 있습니다. 특별 할인 제품에 이루어진 구매는 반품될 수 없습니다. — [2] —.

8 반품을 원하시는 경우, 저희 웹 사이트를 방문하셔서 양식을 작성해 주세요. 저희 직원이 영업일 기준 3일 이내 연락 드려 반품 승인 번호를 알려드릴 것입니다. — [3] —. 이것을 받으신 후, 물품을 다음 주소지에 있는 저희 창고로 보내주세요: 25 핀치-해튼 드라이브, 섀와노, 위스콘신, WI 54950

저희가 물품을 수령하면 환불금을 지급해 드립니다. 환불이 처리되는 데는 최대 10영업일까지 소요될 수 있다는 점을 유의해 주십시오. — [4] —.

어휘 return 반품 | policy 정책, 규정 | cover 포함시키다 | purchase 구매 | as long as ~하는 한 | request 신청, 요청 | original 원래의 | packaging 포장(재) | receipt 영수증 | badly 심하게 | damage 훼손하다 | be subject to ~의 대상이다 | fee 수수료 | fill out 작성하다 | form 양식 | business day 영업일 | get back to ~에게 회신 연락을 하다 | authorization 승인, 인가 | warehouse 창고 | issue 발부[발행]하다 | up to 최대 | working day 근무일 | process 처리하다

---

7. 웹 페이지에 따르면, 메디나 스톤즈에서는 왜 반품 수수료를 청구하기도 하는가?
(A) 제품이 할인 중이라서
(B) 포장 상태가 좋지 않아서
(C) 회사에서 배송비를 부담해서
(D) 영수증이 포함되지 않아서

해설 첫 번째 단락에서 포장이 심하게 훼손되거나 다른 포장을 사용한 경우, 10퍼센트의 수수료가 부과될 수 있다고 했으므로 (B) Because the packaging is in poor condition.가 정답이다.

8. 메디나 스톤즈의 고객에 관하여 언급된 것은?
(A) 빠른 배송에 대한 비용 지불을 예상한다.
(B) 반품 제품을 매장 포인트로 교환할 수 있다.
(C) 메디나 스톤즈의 웹 사이트에 신분 증명을 제공해야 한다.
(D) 제품을 반품하기 전 연락을 받게 된다.

해설 두 번째 단락에서 반품을 원하는 경우, 웹 사이트에 방문해서 양식

을 작성하면 직원이 영업일 기준 3일 이내 연락해 반품 승인 번호를 알려줄 것이라고 했으므로 (D) They will be contacted prior to returning items.가 정답이다.

---

9. [1], [2], [3], [4]로 표시된 곳 중, 다음 문장이 들어갈 위치로 가장 적절한 것은?

"구매하신 제품이 마음에 들지 않는 경우, 전액 환불해 드립니다."

(A) [1]
(B) [2]
(C) [3]
(D) [4]

해설 첫 번째 단락의 당사 반품 규정에서는 30일 이내에 신청한 구매에 한해 적용된다고 한 문장보다 앞에 나와야 자연스러우므로 (A) [1]이 정답이다.

[10-13] 다음 안내문에 관한 문제입니다.

바바이어 항공 팀은 세계 전역에서 온 2만 5천 명이 넘는 각계각층의 사람들을 아우릅니다. **10** 저희는 일부 자리를 충원할 예정임을 알려드리게 되어 기쁩니다. — [1] —. 여러 부서에 공석이 있으니, 모두 지원해 주시기 바랍니다. — [2] —. 저희가 전 직원에게 제공하는 혜택에는 아주 적은 비용으로 세계 여행을 가능하게 하는 티켓 할인이 포함됩니다. — [3] —. **11B** 또한 유연한 근무 시간, **11C** 수강하는 모든 학습 및 개발 과정에 대한 비용 환불, **11D** 헬스 센터 및 카페테리아 무료 이용을 누리실 수도 있습니다. — [4] —. **13** 연간 유급 휴가를 활용해 일을 하면서 원하는 것을 성취하는 데 집중할 수 있습니다. **12** 바바이어 항공에서 일해야 할 이유가 더 많이 필요하다면, 5년 연속 '일하기 좋은 최고의 직장 10곳'에 당사를 지명한 팀 빌더 저널에 물어보세요.

어휘 encompass 아우르다, 포함하다 | all walks of life 각계각층 | announce 발표하다 | fill 채우다 | position 일자리, 직무 | opening 빈자리, 공석 | department 부서 | encourage 권장하다 | apply 지원하다 | perk (급여 외의) 특전 | discounted 할인된 | ticket 표를 발행하다 | fraction 일부, 부분 | cost 비용, 요금 | flexible 유연한 | working hours 근무 시간 | reimbursement 환급, 상환 | annual 연례의 | paid 유급의 | vacation 휴가 | focus on ~에 집중하다 | achieve 성취하다 | name 지명하다 | consecutive 연이은

---

10. 안내문은 누구를 대상으로 하는가?
(A) 바바이어 항공사 직원
(B) 바바이어 항공사 고객
(C) 현 구직자
(D) 저널 독자

해설 바바이어 항공이 일부 자리를 충원할 예정이며 여러 부서에 공석이 있으니, 모두 지원해 주시기 바란다고 했으므로 (C) Current job seekers가 정답이다.

11. 안내문에서 직원에게 제공되는 것으로 언급되지 않은 것은?

    (A) 무료 항공권

    (B) 변경 가능한 근무 시간

    (C) 교육비 지급

    (D) 체육관 이용

해설   유연한 근무 시간, 수강하는 모든 학습 및 개발 과정에 대한 비용 환급, 헬스 센터 및 카페테리아 무료 이용을 누릴 수도 있다는 것에서 (B), (C) (D)가 가능하지만, 무료 항공권은 언급하지 않았으므로 (A) Free airline tickets가 정답이다.

12. 바바이어 항공에 관하여 언급된 것은?

    (A) 최근 인력불 감축했다.

    (B) 업계 출간물에 언급되었다.

    (C) 경영진이 새로 바뀌었다.

    (D) 신규 사무실을 개장할 계획이다.

해설   바바이어 항공에서 일해야 할 이유가 더 많이 필요하다면, 5년 연속 '일할 만한 최고의 직장 10곳'에 바바이어 항공의 이름을 올린 팀 빌더 저널에 물어보라고 했으므로 (B) It has been mentioned in a trade publication.이 정답이다.

13. [1], [2], [3], [4]로 표시된 곳 중, 다음 문장이 들어갈 위치로 가장 적절한 것은?

    "성취하고자 하는 개인적인 목표가 있을 수 있음을 잘 알고 있습니다."

    (A) [1]

    (B) [2]

    (C) [3]

    (D) [4]

해설   주어진 문장은 연간 유급 휴가를 활용해 일을 하면서 원하는 것을 성취하는 데 집중할 수 있다고 한 문장 앞에 와야 자연스러우므로 (D) [4]가 정답이다.

UNIT 06. 동의어 문제

핵심 문제 유형

본서 p.263

1. (B)

[1] 다음 기사에 관한 문제입니다.

(5월 22일) 우스터 시가 축하할 거리가 하나 생겼다. 이 도시는 지난 해와 비교하여 시내 교통 체증을 25퍼센트 가량 감소시켰다. 교통 관계자들에 따르면, 통근은 아침 출근 시간대에 특히 안 좋지만, 지난 12월 시민들이 더 자주 지하철로 통근을 하게끔 하기 위해 시행된 이 현명한 계획 덕분에 상황이 상당히 개선되었다.

더 많은 시민들이 대중교통을 이용하게끔 하기 위해, 지하철 요금이 인하되었고, 시는 낡은 지하철을 새것으로 교체하고 더 자주 운행하기로 결정하였다. 우스터 시 거주자들을 대상으로 한 여론 조사에 따르면, 이러한 변화는 대중교통의 사용을 늘리고자 하는 그들의 결정에 중요한 요인이었다. "이 새로운 운행 시간표들이 큰 영향을 끼쳤습니다." 라고 한 주민이 말했다.

1 이 조치들은 일부 지하철 운영자들에게 재정적 실현 가능성의 측면에서 어느 정도 긍정적인 영향을 끼친 것으로 보인다. 예를 들어, 캐널가에서 퍼거스가로 운행하는 녹색 지하철 노선은 승객들이 거의 없었기에, 지하철 운영자들은 한때 이 노선을 폐지하는 것을 고려했었다. 하지만, 이 계획은 재정 안정성을 유지하기에 충분한 승객들이 이제 있기 때문에 더 이상 문제가 되지 않는다.

어휘   cause 원인 | manage 처리하다, 해내다 | cut 줄이다, 삭감하다 | traffic jam 교통 체증 | compared to ~와 비교하여 | transportation authority 교통 관계자, 교통 공무원 | rush hour (출·퇴근) 혼잡 시간대 | improve 개선하다, 향상시키다, 나아지다 | significantly 상당히, 중요하게 | thanks to ~덕분에 | initiative 계획 | implement 시행하다, 수행하다 | encourage 격려하다, 용기를 북돋우다 | commute 통근하다 | resident 거주민 | schedule 시간표; 일정 | measure 해결책, 조치 | in terms of ~면에서, ~에 관하여 | financial 금융의, 재정의 | viability 실행 가능성 | operator 운영자 | rarely 드물게, 좀처럼 ~하지 않는 | issue 문제, 쟁점 | maintain 유지하다, 지키다 | stability 안정(성)

1. 세 번째 단락, 첫 번째 줄의 단어 'measures'와 의미상 가장 가까운 것은

    (A) 거리

    (B) 조치

    (C) 기준

    (D) 성공

해설   세 번째 단락, 첫 번째 줄에 있는 measures를 찾아서 이와 바꿔 쓸 수 있는 보기가 무엇인지 해당 단어가 포함된 문장을 해석하고, 단어의 문맥적인 의미를 파악한다. 이러한 조치들이 재정 실현 가능성에 어느 정도 긍정적인 영향을 끼친 것으로 보인다는 뜻이므로 '조치'란 의미의 actions가 문장의 measures라는 어휘를 대신할 수 있다. 따라서 정답은 (B) actions이다.

Practice

본서 p.264

1. (A)	**2.** (C)	**3.** (D)	**4.** (D)	**5.** (A)
6. (B)	**7.** (D)	**8.** (A)	**9.** (B)	**10.** (A)
11. (B)	**12.** (D)	**13.** (C)		

[1-3] 다음 이메일에 관한 문제입니다.

수신: 매이블 핏먼 〈mablep@hmail.com〉

발신: 짐 린드스트롬 〈jlindstrom@travelogymag.com〉

날짜: **1** 7월 10일
제목: 구독 갱신

핏먼 씨께,

트레블로지 잡지에서는 작년 한 해 동안 귀하의 구독에 감사를 표하고자 합니다. 저희 트레블로지에서는 수상 경력이 있는 여행 저널리스트가 작성한 세계 각지의 목적지에 관한 양질의 기사를 제공해 드리는 것을 목표로 합니다.

1 귀하의 구독이 이번 달 말 종료됩니다. **2** 저희는 귀하의 구독을 아주 소중히 생각하며 계속해서 저희와 함께 하시길 바랍니다.

3 계약을 일 년 더 연장하실 경우, 앞으로 세 달 간(8월, 9월, 10월) 청구 요금에서 25퍼센트를 할인해 드립니다.

이 할인 혜택을 이용하고 싶으시면, 앞으로 2주 안에 저희에게 연락해 주시기 바랍니다. 귀하의 구독 및 휴가 패키지 핫딜에 관한 추가 정보는 저희 웹 사이트 www.travelogy.com를 방문해 주십시오.

진심으로,

짐 린드스트롬
고객 관리 매니저
트레블로지 잡지

어휘 subscription 구독 | renewal 갱신 | magazine 잡지 | aim ~를 목표로 하다 | provide A with B A에게 B를 제공하다 | quality 양질의 | article 기사 | destination 목적지 | award-winning 상을 받은, 수상한 | travel 여행 | journalist 기자, 저널리스트 | run out 더 이상 유효하지 않게 되다 | deeply 깊이 | value 소중하게 생각하다 | business (서비스 등의) 이용 | continue 계속하다 | remain 남다 | extend 연장하다 | contract 계약 | reduce 줄이다 | bill 청구서 | take advantage of ~을 이용하다 | reach out to ~에게 연락하다, ~에게 접근하다 | hot 유리한 | deal 계약, 거래 | vacation 휴가

1. 핏먼 씨의 현재 구독은 언제 만료되는가?
 (A) 7월에
 (B) 8월에
 (C) 9월에
 (D) 10월에

해설 메일의 발송일이 7월 10일이고, 두 번째 단락에서 귀하의 구독이 이번 달 말 종료된다고 했으므로 (A) In July가 정답이다.

2. 두 번째 단락, 첫 번째 줄의 단어, 'value'와 의미상 가장 가까운 것은?
 (A) 이익을 얻다
 (B) 경비로 청구하다
 (C) 소중히 여기다
 (D) 청구하다

해설 두 번째 단락의 귀하의 구독을 아주 소중히 생각하며 계속해서 저희와 함께 하시길 바란다에서 value는 '소중히 여기다'라는 의미로 쓰였으므로 같은 의미를 전달하는 (C) treasure가 정답이다.

3. 린드스트롬 씨는 핏먼 씨에게 무엇을 제공하는가?
 (A) 휴가 패키지
 (B) 1년 계약
 (C) 해외 여행 상품권
 (D) 월 요금 할인

해설 세 번째 단락에서 계약을 일 년 더 연장하실 경우, 앞으로 세 달 간(8월, 9월, 10월) 청구 요금에서 25퍼센트를 할인해 드린다고 했으므로 (D) A discount on monthly payment가 정답이다.

[4-6] 다음 이메일에 관한 문제입니다.

수신: 켄 샌토스 〈ksantos@velvetburger.com〉
발신: 커트니 페나 〈cpena@koboxworks.com〉
날짜: 6월 16일
제목: 담장 견적서
첨부: @벨벳 버거 프로젝트

샌토스 씨께,

4 벨벳 버거에 나무 담장을 설치하는 견적서를 첨부해 드립니다. 논의한 대로, 견적에는 현재 담장 제거 및 그 자리에 새로운 담장 설치가 포함됩니다. 작업에 착수하기 전에, 정부 기록에 따르면, 이웃인 더 호니 트리와 담장을 공유하고 있음을 유념해 주세요. **5** 따라서, 그곳 주인의 서명이 들어간 동의서를 받으셔야 할 겁니다.

전체 작업은 7일 내 완료될 것으로 예상합니다. 현재 일기 예보에 따르면, 악천후로 인한 지연을 피하고자 6월 23일에 시작하는 것을 권해 드립니다. 진행하고자 하신다면, 50퍼센트의 보증금을 요청 드린다는 점을 알아 두시기 바랍니다. **6** 프로젝트가 완료되면, 청구서가 정산되길 기대합니다.

문의 사항이 있으시면, help@koboxworks.com로 연락해 주시기 바랍니다.

감사합니다.

커트니 페나, 회계 담당
코복스 웍스

어휘 fence 울타리, 담장 | estimate 견적, 추정하다, 평가하다 | install 설치하다 | wooden 나무로 된 | removal 제거 | current 현재의 | installation 설치 | undertake 착수하다 | note 유념하다 | according to ~에 따르면 | government 정부 | record 기록 | consent 동의 | entire 전체의 | weather forecast 일기 예보 | avoid 피하다 | delay 연기 | due to ~때문에 | poor weather conditions 악천후 | proceed 진행하다 | deposit 보증금 | bill 청구서 | clear 처리하다, 정산하다

4. 설치되어야 할 담장에 관하여 언급된 것은?
 (A) 업체 두 곳에서 지불할 것이다.
 (B) 정부의 동의가 필요하다.
 (C) 금속으로 만들어질 것이다.
 (D) 다른 담장을 교체할 것이다.

해설 첫 번째 단락에서 벨벳 버거에 나무 담장을 설치하는 견적서를 첨부하며 논의한 대로, 견적에는 현재 담장 제거 및 그 자리에 새로운 담장

설치가 포함된다고 했으므로 (D) It will replace another fence.가 정답이다.

---

5. 페나 씨는 산토스 씨에게 무엇을 해달라고 요청하는가?
  (A) 건설 허가를 받아 달라고
  (B) 점검 일정을 잡아 달라고
  (C) 일부 자재를 구입해 달라고
  (D) 설문지를 작성해 달라고

해설 첫 번째 단락에서 그곳 주인의 서명이 들어간 동의서를 받으셔야 할 것이라고 했으므로 (A) Obtain permission to build가 정답이다.

---

6. 두 번째 단락, 네 번째 줄의 단어, 'cleared'와 의미상 가장 가까운 것은?
  (A) 보증되는
  (B) 전액 지불되는
  (C) 적법한
  (D) 반납되는

해설 첫 번째 단락의 '프로젝트가 완료되면, 청구서가 정산되길 기대합니다.'에서 cleared는 '정산되는'이라는 의미로 쓰였으므로 '전액 지불되는'이라는 의미를 전달하는 (B) paid in full이 정답이다.

[7-9] 다음 제품 후기에 관한 문제입니다.

> **훌륭한 세탁기!**
>
> 저는 항상 빨래방을 이용해 왔기에, 세탁기를 소유하려고 알아본 적이 없습니다. 새집으로 이사를 온 후, 동네에 빨래방이 없었기에 세탁기가 필요하게 됐습니다. 그러다가 우연히 크라이세어 250 광고를 몇 번 보게 됐어요. **7** 다른 모델들보다 더 비싸고 크기도 더 컸지만, 모든 후기에서 정말 오래간다는 내용을 언급하고 있었어요. 그 점이 저에게는 중요했기에, 그걸 사기로 했습니다. 현재 한 달 넘게 가지고 있는데, 정말 놀랍습니다. 제 옷은 매번 깨끗해지고 상쾌한 냄새가 납니다. **8** 게다가 기계가 정말 조용해서 작동하고 있다는 것을 잊을 때도 있습니다. 마지막으로, 저는 기계가 제 핸드폰으로 작동될 수 있는 점이 아주 마음에 듭니다. **9** 직장에서 상당한 시간을 보내는 사람으로서 저에게 시간은 아주 소중합니다. 어디에서든 세탁을 시작하도록 기계에 알릴 수 있다는 점이 정말 마음에 듭니다. 전반적으로 환상적인 구매이며 강력 추천합니다.
>
> — 레온 웰츠

어휘 washing machine 세탁기 | laundromat 빨래방 | own 소유하다 | area 지역 | come across ~을 우연히 발견하다 | advertisement 광고 | pricey 비싼 | review 후기 | mention 언급하다 | last 오래가다, 지속되다 | clothes 옷 | come out 나오다 | clean 깨끗한 | smell ~한 냄새가 나다 | fresh 상쾌한 | machine 기계 | forget 잊다 | run 작동하다 | control 조정하다, 제어하다 | valuable 소중한 | purchase 구매 | highly 매우 | recommend 추천하다

7. 웰츠 씨는 왜 크라이세어 250 세탁기를 선택했는가?
  (A) 할인가에 구입 가능했다.
  (B) 구입 가능한 가장 큰 모델이었다.

  (C) 평판이 좋은 브랜드에서 설계했다.
  (D) 내구성이 있다고 언급되었다.

해설 다른 모델들보다 더 비싸고 크기도 더 컸지만, 모든 후기에서 오래간다는 내용을 언급하고 있었다고 했으므로 (D) It was mentioned as being durable.이 정답이다.

---

8. 첫 번째 단락, 여덟 번째 줄의 단어 'running'과 의미상 가장 가까운 것은?
  (A) 작동하는
  (B) 연주하는
  (C) 조정하는
  (D) 이동하는

해설 '게다가 기계가 정말 조용해서 작동하고 있다는 것을 잊을 때도 있습니다.'에서 running은 '작동하는'이라는 의미로 쓰였으므로 보기 중 같은 의미를 갖는 (A) operating이 정답이다.

---

9. 웰츠 씨에 관하여 언급된 것은?
  (A) 새로운 회사로 옮겼다.
  (B) 시간 절약에 신경을 쓴다.
  (C) 가전제품을 전문적으로 리뷰한다.
  (D) 일 년 전에 세탁기를 구입했다.

해설 첫 번째 단락에서 직장에서 상당한 시간을 보내는 사람으로서 시간은 아주 소중하며 어디에서든 세탁을 시작하도록 기계에 알릴 수 있다는 점이 정말 마음에 든다고 했으므로 (B) He cares about saving time.이 정답이다.

[10-13] 다음 이메일에 관한 문제입니다.

> 수신: 에디스 가르자
> 발신: 조슈아 블레어
> 날짜: 1월 27일
> 제목: 긴급 및 기밀
>
> 에디스 씨께,
>
> **11** 새 회계연도부터 프레스티지 파트너스의 모든 정규직 직원을 대상으로 새로운 퇴직금 관련 옵션이 행사 가능합니다. 프레스티지 파트너스에서 직원의 퇴직 기금에 분담금을 지원하는 대신, 퇴직 포트폴리오에 예치하는 회사 주식의 형태로 수당을 받는 옵션이 이제 생겨납니다.
>
> **12** 이러한 변경 사항은 자사의 퇴직 관리 기업인 플레그스테프 펀드와 이미 논의되었습니다. 직원이 이러한 신규 옵션을 선택할 경우, 이 기업에서 전환 작업을 돕게 되며 계속해서 프레스티지 파트너스 직원에게 고객 지원을 제공할 것입니다. 플레그스테프 펀드의 연락 담당자는 아이린 카스티로이며, 이와 관련한 문의사항은 무엇이든 그녀에게 직접 해야 합니다. 연락 정보는 플레그스테프 펀드의 웹 사이트에서 찾을 수 있습니다.
>
> **10 13** 이러한 변경과 관련하여 전체 직원 연락망에 포함해야 할 필수 정보를 그에게 제공할 수 있도록, 인사팀장 커크 브래디에 협조해 주시기 바랍니다. 얼마나 많은 직원들이 주식 옵션을 선택하는지 최대한 빨리 자료를 수집하고 싶다고 최고 경영자께서 말씀하셨습니다.

감사합니다.

조슈아 블레어, CFO
프레스티지 파트너스

어휘 immediate 즉시의 | confidential 기밀의 | fiscal year 회계 연도 | regarding ~에 관하여 | retirement benefit 퇴직금 | exercise 행사하다 | full-time 정규직의 | employee 직원 | instead of ~ 대신에 | match [자금]을 ~에 지원하다 | contribution (연금 등을 위한) 개인 분담금, 기부금 | fund 자금 | compensation 보상(금), 보수 | form 형태 | stock 주식 | deposit 예치[예금]하다 | portfolio 포트폴리오 | management 경영, 관리 | firm 회사 | choose 선택하다 | transition 변화, 전환 | continue 계속하다 | provide 제공하다 | inquiry 문의 | related to ~와 관련 있는 | direct ~로 향하다 | head 책임자 | human resources 인사부 | state 말하다 | gather 모으다 | data 자료, 정보

10. 이메일의 목적은 무엇인가?
(A) **지침을 제공하는 것**
(B) 피드백을 수집하는 것
(C) 제안서를 수정하는 것
(D) 문제를 보고하는 것

해설 세 번째 단락에서 이러한 변경과 관련하여 전체 직원 연락망에 포함해야 할 필수 정보를 그녀에게 제공할 수 있도록, 인사팀장 커크 브래디에 협조해 주시기 바란다고 했으므로 (A) To provide instructions가 정답이다.

11. 첫 번째 단락, 두 번째 줄의 단어, 'exercised'과 의미상 가장 가까운 것은?
(A) 탐구되다
(B) **적용되다**
(C) 대체되다
(D) 작업되다

해설 첫 번째 단락의 '새 회계연도부터 프레스티지 파트너스의 모든 정규직 직원을 대상으로 새로운 퇴직금 관련 옵션이 행사 가능합니다.'에서 exercised는 '행사되다'라는 의미로 쓰였으므로 '적용되다'라는 의미를 전달하는 (B) applied가 정답이다.

12. 플레그스테프 펀드에 관하여 알 수 있는 것은?
(A) 자체 퇴직연금 제도를 제공한다.
(B) 프레스티지 파트너스와 같은 사무실에 위치한다.
(C) 회계 서비스를 제공한다.
(D) **어떤 문제로든 프레스티지 파트너스 직원에게 도움을 줄 것이다.**

해설 첫 번째 단락에서 이러한 변경 사항은 자사의 퇴직 관리 기업인 플레그스테프 펀드와 이미 논의되었으며, 직원이 이러한 신규 옵션을 선택할 경우, 이 기업에서 전환 작업을 돕게 되며 계속해서 프레스티지 파트너스 직원에게 고객 지원을 제공할 것이라고 했으므로 (D) It will help Prestige Partners employees with any issues.가 정답이다.

13. 누가 규정 변경 관련 전체 직원 공지를 담당하는가?
(A) 가르자 씨
(B) 카스틸로 씨
(C) **브래디 씨**
(D) 블레어 씨

해설 세 번째 단락에서 이러한 변경과 관련하여 전체 직원 연락망에 포함해야 할 필수 정보를 그녀에게 제공할 수 있도록, 인사팀장 커크 브래디에 협조해 주시기 바란다고 했으므로 (C) Mr. Brady가 정답이다.

UNIT 07. 문자 대화문과 화자의도

핵심 문제 유형   본서 p.269

1. (A)

[1] 다음 문자 대화문에 관한 문제입니다.

파커, 해롤드 (오전 10:09)
안녕하세요, 루시아. 오늘 테드 톰슨과 미팅이 있는데, 깜빡 잊고 수첩을 가져오질 않았네요. 그것 좀 확인해서 그분 주소를 제게 알려주실 수 있을까요?

스턴즈, 루시아 (오전 10:13)
방금 당신 책상을 봤는데, 수첩이 없는 것 같아요.

파커, 해롤드 (오전 10:14)
그럼 밑의 캐비닛 맨 위 서랍을 열면 거기 있을 거예요.

스턴즈, 루시아 (오전 10:15)
네, 찾았어요. 주소는 잭스 대로 57번지예요.

파커, 해롤드 (오전 10:17)
정말 고마워요. 괜찮다면 하나 더 요청해도 될까요? 제 책상에 있는 노란색 서류철을 캐이티 서머스에게 전달해 줄 수 있을까요?

스턴즈, 루시아 (오전 10:19)
❶ 이미 처리된 걸로 봐주세요. 제가 그녀를 곧 만날 예정이라서요.

파커, 해롤드 (오전 10:20)
정말 고마워요, 루시아. 이따 봐요.

어휘 Do you mind~? (허락·동의를 구하는 표현) 해 주시겠어요, ~하는 걸 꺼리나요? | look through ~를 살펴보다, 검토하다 | address 주소 | seem ~인 것처럼 보이다 | planner 계획표, 수첩 | drawer 서랍 | underneath ~의 밑에 | I've got it. 알았어요, 이해했어요, 받았어요. | request 요청 | mind 언짢아하다 | deliver 배달하다, 전달하다

1. 오전 10시 19분에 스턴즈 씨가 "이미 처리된 걸로 봐 주세요."라고 쓴 것은 무슨 의미인가?
(A) **서머스 씨에게 서류를 줄 것이다.**

(B) 파커 씨의 책상을 정리할 것이다.

(C) 캐비닛을 잠궈둘 것이다.

(D) 톰슨 씨에게 연락할 것이다.

해설 책상에 있는 노란색 서류철을 캐이티 서머스에게 전달해 줄 수 있는지 파커 씨가 물었고, 스턴즈 씨가 "Consider it done"이라고 답한 후, '그녀를 곧 만날 예정이라서요.'라고 한 것은 파커 씨의 요청을 들어줄 수 있다는 뜻이므로 정답은 (A) She will give a document to Ms. Summers.이다.

Practice

본서 p.270

1. (D)	**2.** (A)	**3.** (A)	**4.** (C)	**5.** (C)
6. (A)	**7.** (B)	**8.** (A)	**9.** (A)	**10.** (D)
11. (B)	**12.** (D)			

[1-2] 다음 문자 메시지 대화에 관한 문제입니다.

던컨 워너 (오후 12시 31분)
안녕하세요, 마크. 그 보고서 마무리 작업은 거의 끝났어요? 전 하루 종일 못 먹었어요.

마크 피니 (오후 12시 32분)
죄송해요, 던컨. **2** 아쉽게도 제가 오늘 당신이랑 힐 씨와 점심을 함께 하지 못할 것 같아요. 제가 막바지 변경 작업 업무를 맡았어요. 시간이 좀 걸릴 것 같아요.

던컨 워너 (오후 12시 35분)
아쉽네요. **2** 뭐 좀 갖다줄까요?

마크 피니 (오후 12시 39분)
1 돼지고기 부리토가 좋을 것 같아요.

던컨 워너 (오후 12시 40분)
1 알았어요. 잠시 후에 봐요.

어휘 finalize 마무리하다 I My apologies 죄송합니다 I unfortunately 아쉽게도 I task 과업을 맡기다 I last-minute 막판의 I bring 가져오다 I pork 돼지고기 I burrito 부리토 I lovely 아주 좋은

1. 오후 12시 40분에, 워너 씨가 "알았어요"라고 할 때 무엇을 의미하겠는가?

(A) 추가 변경이 필요할 수도 있다.

(B) 도움이 약간 필요할 수도 있다.

(C) 이미 요청 사항을 수행했다.

(D) 피니 씨에게 점심을 가져다줄 것이다.

해설 오후 12시 39분 ~ 12시 40분 대화에서 마크 피니 씨가 돼지고기 부리토가 좋을 것 같다고 한 말에 던컨 워너가 알았다고 말한 것이므로 (D) He will bring lunch for Mr. Finney.가 정답이다.

2. 다음으로 무슨 일이 일어날 것인가?

(A) 워너 씨와 힐 씨가 잠시 나갈 것이다.

(B) 워너 씨가 발표 자료 사본을 받을 것이다.

(C) 피니 씨가 전화를 걸 것이다.

(D) 힐 씨가 문서를 수정할 것이다.

해설 오후 12시 32분 ~ 12시 35분 대화에서 마크 피니 씨가 아쉽게도 오늘 당신이랑 힐 씨와 점심을 함께 하지 못할 것 같다고 한 말에 던컨 워너가 '뭐 좀 갖다 줄까요?'라고 말한 것이므로 (A) Mr. Warner and Mr. Hill will be out for a while.이 정답이다.

[3-4] 다음 문자 메시지 대화에 관한 문제입니다.

에반 제닝스 (오후 1시 25분)
안녕하세요, 시드니. **3** 켄톤 음악 그룹이 다음 달에 콘서트를 열어요. 직원 감사의 밤에 적합한 선택이 될 것 같아요.

시드니 카스틸로 (오후 1시 27분)
좋아요. 어떤 종류의 음악을 연주할 예정이에요?

에반 제닝스 (오후 1시 29분)
보통은 현대 클래식을 연주해요. **4** 공연하는 모습을 보고 싶으시면, 토요일 밤에 도시 광장에서 짧은 콘서트를 열 예정이에요.

시드니 카스틸로 (오후 1시 32분)
4 이번 주말에는 부모님이 오세요.

에반 제닝스 (오후 1시 33분)
그렇다면, 제가 웹 사이트 링크를 보내드릴게요. 거기에 공연을 일부 올려요.

어휘 suitable 적합한, 적절한 I choice 선택 I employee 직원 I appreciation 감사 I modern 현대의 I rendition 연주, 공연 I classical music 클래식 I perform 공연하다 I host 개최하다, 주최하다 I upload 올리다 I performance 공연

3. 제닝스 씨와 카스틸로 씨에 관해 암시된 것은?

(A) 회사 행사를 계획하고 있다.

(B) 도시 광장 근처에 산다.

(C) 다른 사무실에서 근무한다.

(D) 곧 출장을 갈 것이다.

해설 오후 1시 25분에 에반 제닝스가 켄톤 음악 그룹이 다음 달에 콘서트를 열고, 직원 감사의 밤에 적합한 선택이 될 것 같다고 했으므로 (A) They are planning a company event.가 정답이다.

4. 오후 1시 32분에, 카스틸로 씨가 "이번 주말에는 부모님이 오세요"라고 할 때 무엇을 의미하겠는가?

(A) 계획이 변경되어 답한다.

(B) 제닝스 씨가 세부사항을 확인해 주기를 원한다.

(C) 음악 공연에 참석할 수 없다.

(D) 다음 주에 사무실에 없을 것이다.

해설 오후 1시 29분 ~ 1시 32분 대화에서 제닝스 씨가 공연하는 모습을 보고 싶으면, 토요일 밤에 도시 광장에서 짧은 콘서트를 열 예정이라고 한 말에 카스틸로 씨가 이번 주말에 부모님이 오신다고 말한 것이므로 (C) She cannot attend a musical performance.가 정답이다.

[5-8] 다음 온라인 채팅 대화문에 관한 문제입니다.

future bakery owner가 정답이다.

크리스 샌도벌 (오후 2시 11분)

안녕하세요, 아이삭. 제가 진을 이 대화방에 초대했어요. 아시다시피, 그녀는 이 프로젝트에 많은 노력을 들였어요.

진 램지 (오후 2시 12분)

고마워요, 크리스. **6** 수리 기간 동안 일부 작업자들이 옛날 메뉴를 발견했다고 들었어요. 200년도 더 된 물건을 발견한다는 게 정말 신기해요.

아이삭 배렛 (오후 2시 13분)

6 맞아요. 믿기지 않아요.

크리스 샌도벌 (오후 2시 14분)

그래서 말인데요. 아이삭과 제가 그 건물에 관해 더 알아보기로 했어요. 그 건물에 약국이 있었던 건 알고 있었는데, 베이커리에 관해서는 전혀 몰랐어요. **5** 어쩌면 언젠가 우리 제빵사들이 고객들을 위해 메뉴에 있는 항목들 중 일부를 재현할 수도 있지 않을까 하는 바람이 있어요.

아이삭 배렛 (오후 2시 15분)

역사를 맛보며 과거 속으로 한걸음 발을 내딛을 수 있게 될 거예요.

진 램지 (오후 2시 16분)

7 최신 소식을 들을 수 있도록 이 대화방에 하청업자를 추가했어요. 안녕하세요, 로리. 모두 제대로 진행되고 있나요?

로리 윌리암스 (오후 2시 17분)

모두들 안녕하세요. 배선 및 배관을 비롯한 주요 공사 작업은 대부분 완료됐습니다. 지금은 주방 마무리 작업을 진행 중이에요. 납품업체와 이야기해 봤는데요, 냉장 진열장이 다음 주 월요일에는 도착할 거예요.

진 램지 (오후 2시 18분)

8 그러면 2월 개장에 맞춰 문제없이 진행되고 있다는 말인가요?

로리 윌리암스 (오후 2시 19분)

8 물론입니다.

어휘	**put in an effort** 노력하다 | **effort** 노력 | **fascinating** 대단히 흥미로운, 신기한 | **unbelievable** 믿기 힘든 | **aware** 알고 있는 | **pharmacy** 약국 | **property** 부동산, 건물 | **baker** 제빵사 | **recreate** 재현하다, 되살리다 | **step** 발을 내딛다 | **past** 과거 | **taste** 맛 | **add** 추가하다 | **contractor** 하청업자 | **on track** 제대로 진행되고 있는 | **major** 주요한 | **construction** 공사 | **wiring** 배선 | **plumbing** 배관 | **complete** 완료하다 | **finishing touches** 마지막 작업 | **supplier** 공급업자[체], 납품업체 | **refrigerated** 냉장의 | **display case** 진열장

5. 샌도벌 씨는 누구겠는가?

(A) 역사 고고학자

(B) 건물 설계자

(C) 미래 베이커리 주인

(D) 인테리어 디자이너

해설 어쩌면 언젠가 우리 제빵사들이 고객들을 위해 메뉴에 있는 항목들 중 일부를 재현할 수도 있지 않을까 하는 바람이 있다고 했으므로 (C) A

6. 오후 2시 13분에, 베렛 씨가 "믿기지 않아요"라고 할 때 무엇을 의미하겠는가?

(A) 최근의 발견에 크게 놀랐다.

(B) 추가 조사 없이는 재정적인 결정을 내릴 수 없었다.

(C) 공사 현장에서 약국 관련 물품을 찾게 될 줄은 예상하지 못했다.

(D) 하청업체의 견적에 관해 의구심을 갖고 있다.

해설 오후 2시 12분 ~ 2시 13분 대화에서 진 램지가 수리 기간 동안 일부 작업자들이 옛날 메뉴를 발견했다고 들었고, 200년도 더 된 물건을 발견한다는 게 정말 신기하다고 한 말에 아이삭 베렛이 믿기지 않는다고 말한 것이므로 (A) He was astounded by a recent discovery.가 정답이다.

7. 램지 씨는 무엇에 관해 물어보는가?

(A) 사업체의 정확한 위치

(B) 개조 프로젝트의 상황

(C) 향후 회의 안건

(D) 건물 설계도

해설 오후 2시 16분에 장 램지가 최신 소식을 들을 수 있도록 이 대화방에 하청업자를 추가했다고 했으므로 (B) The state of a remodeling project가 정답이다.

8. 2월에는 무슨 일이 있겠는가?

(A) 업체가 문을 열 것이다.

(B) 새로운 프로젝트가 시작될 것이다.

(C) 채용 전략이 재고될 것이다.

(D) 일부 장비가 배송될 것이다.

해설 오후 2시 18분 ~ 2시 19분 대화에서 진 램지가 2월 개장에 맞춰 문제없이 진행되고 있는지 물었고 로리 윌리암스가 물론이라고 말했으므로 (A) A business will open.이 정답이다.

[9-12] 다음 온라인 채팅 대화문에 관한 문제입니다.

데이비드 로우 (오전 9시 12분)

9 모두 안녕하세요. 저희 전 제품 라인업을 포함한 프레젠테이션이 다음 주에 매장으로 전달되어야 해요. 그쪽에서는 우리 신제품들이 어떤 평가를 받는지 뿐만 아니라 가장 많이 판매한 게 뭔지 알고 싶어 할 거예요.

피트 홈즈 (오전 9시 13분)

언제 보여요?

데이비드 로우 (오전 9시 15분)

아직 안 끝났어요. 일부 정보를 기다리는 중이에요.

니나 피어스 (오전 9시 17분)

10 저희가 출시할 새 시계에 대한 평가가 필요해요. 시범 사용을 막 마쳤고, 사용자 통찰도 좋아요. **11** 연구 개발실에서 하는 말로는 늦어도 목요일까지는 받을 거라고 해요.

피트 홈즈 (오전 9시 20분)

🔟 그럼요. 그걸 무시하면 안 되죠. 1️⃣1️⃣ 수요일까지 보고서를 받으시 못하면, 크리스탈 무어한테 연락해서 보고서 요약본을 보내달라고 합시다.

데이비드 로우 (오전 9시 22분)

요약본을 받아서 슬라이드에 그 정보를 추가할 경우, 1️⃣2️⃣ 전체 프레젠테이션을 다 함께 검토해야 할 것 같아요. 목요일이나 금요일에 두 분 시간 되세요?

피트 홈즈 (오전 9시 23분)

1️⃣2️⃣ 저는 목요일에는 사무실을 비워서요. 금요일 오후에 가능하세요?

니나 피어스 (오전 9시 25분)

1️⃣2️⃣ 전 괜찮아요. 제가 지금 회의실을 예약할게요.

어휘 contain 담고 있다, 포함하다 | line-up 라인업 | sell 팔다 | finish 끝내다 | information 정보 | watch 시계 | release 출시하다 | complete 완료하다 | test run 시험 운행[사용] | user 사용자 | insight 통찰 | research 연구 | development 개발 | at the latest 늦어도 | absolutely 전적으로; 그럼, 물론 | discount 무시하다 | contact 연락하다 | summary 요약, 개요 | slide 슬라이드 | entire 전체의 | together 함께 | possible 가능한 | book 예약하다

9. 프레젠테이션에 관하여 언급된 것은?

(A) 가장 잘 팔리는 제품을 보여줄 것이다.
(B) 연구 개발 팀으로 보낼 것이다.
(C) 몇몇 매장의 도움을 받아 만들어질 것이다.
(D) 참석자들에게 직접 선보일 것이다.

해설 오전 9시 12분에 데이비드 로우가 전 제품 라인업을 포함한 프레젠테이션이 다음 주에 매장으로 전달되어야 하고 그쪽에서는 우리 신제품들이 어떤 평가를 받았는지 뿐만 아니라 가장 많이 판매한 게 뭔지 알고 싶어 할 거라고 했으므로 (A) It will indicate the best-selling product.가 정답이다.

10. 오전 9시 20분에, 홈즈 씨가 "그걸 무시하면 안 되죠"라고 할 때 그가 내비친 것은?

(A) 추가 연구가 실시되어야 한다.
(B) 파일이 더 많은 사람의 검토를 받아야 한다.
(C) 제품 가격이 너무 높게 책정됐다.
(D) 사용자 피드백이 아주 중요하다.

해설 오전 9시 17분 ~ 9시 20분 대화에서 니나 피어스가 저희가 출시할 새 시계에 대한 평가가 필요하다며 시범 사용을 막 마쳤고, 사용자 통찰도 좋다고 한 말에 피트 홈즈가 '그럼요. 그걸 무시하면 안 되죠.'라고 말한 것이므로 (D) Feedback from users is very important.가 정답이다.

11. 무어 씨는 누구겠는가?

(A) 영업 관리자
(B) 제품 연구원
(C) 상점 주인

(D) 마케팅 관리자

해설 오전 9시 17분 ~ 9시 20분 대화에서 니나 피어스가 연구 개발실에서 하는 말로는 늦어도 목요일까지는 받을 거라고 한 말에 피트 홈즈가 수요일까지 보고서를 받지 못하면, 크리스탈 무어한테 연락해서 보고서 요약본을 보내달라고 하라고 했으므로 (B) A product researcher 가 정답이다.

12. 작성자들은 슬라이드 프레젠테이션 검토를 위해 언제 만날 계획인가?

(A) 월요일에
(B) 수요일에
(C) 목요일에
(D) 금요일에

해설 오전 9시 22분 ~ 9시 23분 대화에서 데이비드 로우가 전체 프레젠테이션을 다 함께 검토해야 하며 목요일이나 금요일에 시간이 되는지 묻는 말에 피트 홈즈가 목요일에는 사무실을 비우고 금요일 오후에 가능하냐고 물었고 니나 피어스가 괜찮다고 했으므로 (D) On Friday가 정답이다.

UNIT 08. 편지·이메일

핵심 문제 유형

본서 p.276

1. (A) **2.** (D) **3.** (C)

[1-3] 다음 편지에 관한 문제입니다.

박 씨에게,

1️⃣ 2월 3일 앤젤라 장 씨로부터 받으신 매우 훌륭한 서비스에 대해 자세히 적어 주신 서신에 감사드립니다. 편지 사본은 장 씨의 인사과 파일에 보관되었습니다.

고객이 시간을 내서 직원이 제공한 훌륭한 서비스를 공식적으로 인정해 주시는 사례는 드뭅니다. 그래서 보답으로 고객님께 무언가 해 드리고 싶습니다. 2️⃣ 부디 동봉된 상품권을 받아주세요. 이 상품권은 앞으로 저희 매장 어디서든 고객님이 원하시는 어떤 상품이든 15% 할인을 받을 수 있도록 해드립니다.

진심으로,

3️⃣ 브라이언 배
고객 서비스 매니저
동봉물 재중

어휘 appreciate 감사하다 | describe 설명하다 | exceptionally 유난히, 매우 | good service 좋은 서비스 | copy 한 부 | personnel 인사과 | rare 드문 | formally 정식으로, 공식적으로 | acknowledge 인정하다 | in return 보답으로, 답례로 | accept 받아들이다, 수락하다 |

enclosed 동봉된 I voucher 상품권 I entitle 자격을 주다 I
discount 할인, 할인하다 I item 상품 I location 지점, 위치 I
in the future 미래에, 추후에 I gratitude 고마움, 감사 I
upcoming 다가오는, 곧 있을 I prepaid 선불된

1. 편지의 목적은 무엇인가?

(A) 감사를 표현하기 위해

(B) 곧 있을 세일을 소개하기 위해

(C) 불만에 응대하기 위해

(D) 새 지점을 알리기 위해

해설 편지의 목적을 묻는 문제이다. 편지의 목적은 주로 글의 앞부분에 위치한다. 첫 번째 단락 첫 번째 줄에서 고객이 직원에게서 받은 매우 훌륭한 서비스에 감동해 편지를 보낸 것에 대한 감사를 표하고 있다. 따라서 정답은 (A) To express gratitude이다.

2. 편지와 함께 동봉된 것은 무엇인가?

(A) 카탈로그

(B) 선지불된 우편 라벨

(C) 제품 샘플

(D) 할인권

해설 세부 사항을 묻는 질문이므로 키워드 enclosed가 지문에 언급된 부분을 찾아본다. 두 번째 단락 세 번째 줄에서 15% 할인을 제공하는 상품권을 동봉한다고 하였으므로 정답은 (D) A coupon이다.

3. 배 씨는 누구인가?

(A) 회사 간부

(B) 공장 관리자

(C) 고객 서비스 매니저

(D) 취재 기자

해설 세부 사항 질문이므로 키워드 배 씨가 언급된 맨 마지막 부분에서 Customer Service Manager라는 직책을 확인할 수 있다. 따라서 정답은 (C) A customer service manager이다.

Practice

본서 p.278

1. (A)	2. (B)	3. (A)	4. (D)	5. (A)
6. (C)	7. (A)	8. (B)	9. (C)	10. (B)
11. (D)				

[1-2] 다음 이메일에 관한 문제입니다.

수신: 전 직원 〈allstaff@sudima.com〉
발신: 클린턴 우드 〈cwood@sudima.com〉
제목: 통신망 문제
날짜: 11월 7일

직원 여러분께,

1 오늘 아침 전사적인 통신 장애가 발생했습니다. 많은 분이 느린 접속, 간헐적인 접속, 이메일 송수신에 어려움을 겪었다고 알려왔습니다. 우리 엔지니어들이 문제를 해결했으며, 모든 것이 다시 순조롭게 돌아가고 있는 것을 확인했습니다. 문제를 계속 겪게 되는 경우, 시스템 부서에 도움을 요청하기 전에 컴퓨터를 다시 시작해 보세요.

2 오늘 오전 9시에서 10시 30분 사이에 이메일을 보냈다면, 전송되지 않았을 가능성이 있다는 점에 유의해 주시기 바랍니다. 다행히도 보낸 메일함으로 들어가서 전송 여부를 확인할 수 있습니다. 성공적으로 전송된 모든 이메일은 거기에 표시됩니다.

감사합니다.

클린턴 우드
시스템 관리자, 수디마

어휘 experience 겪다 I company-wide 전사적인, 회사 전반의 I
failure 장애, 실패 I report 알리다 I connection 연결, 접속 I
intermittent 간헐적인 I resolve 해결하다 I verify 확인하다 I run 작동하다 I smoothly 순조롭게 I restart 다시 시작하다 I chance 가능성 I go through 성사되다, 통과되다 I
fortunately 다행히 I successfully 성공적으로 I deliver 배달하다 I show up 나타나다, 표시되다

1. 우드 씨는 왜 이메일을 보냈는가?

(A) 기술적인 문제에 대한 세부 내용을 제공하려고

(B) 알 수 없는 웹 사이트를 방문하지 말라고 직원에게 경고하려고

(C) 회사의 이메일 시스템에 대한 피드백을 요청하려고

(D) 최근 업데이트에 대해 직원에게 알려주려고

해설 첫 번째 단락에서 오늘 아침 전사적인 통신 장애가 발생했다고 했으므로 (A) To provide details on a technical problem이 정답이다.

2. 우드 씨는 직원들에게 무엇을 해달라고 요청하는가?

(A) 회사 웹사이트에 로그인해 달라고

(B) 일부 이메일이 제대로 전송됐는지 확인해 달라고

(C) 시스템 부서로 연락해 달라고

(D) 곧 있을 인터넷 보안에 관한 회의에 참석해 달라고

해설 두 번째 단락에서 오늘 오전 9시에서 10시 30분 사이에 이메일을 보냈다면, 전송되지 않았을 가능성이 있으며 보낸 메일함으로 들어가서 전송 여부를 확인할 수 있다고 했으므로 (B) Check that some e-mails were correctly sent가 정답이다.

[3-4] 다음 편지에 관한 문제입니다.

알트리아 은행
8291 Berry 가
새크라멘토, 캘리포니아 92671
555-8993
12월 8일

허프 씨에게,

3 저희 기록에 의하면 고객님의 당좌예금계좌가 초과 인출되었습니다. 고객님은 12월 3일에 연방 우체국에 81달러 29센트의 수표를

쓰셨습니다. 그러나 당시 고객님의 잔고는 67달러 5센트였습니다. 유감스럽게도 고객님의 계좌는 당좌 대월 보호가 되어있지 않으므로, 오늘 현재 고객님의 잔고는 -20달러 24센트입니다. **4** 당좌 예금계좌에서 초과 인출이 되면 매일 1달러의 수수료가 있음을 유의해 주십시오. 이 문제를 처리하기 위해 가능한 빨리 저에게 연락 주십시오.

진심으로,

Jeanie Chitalli

지니 치탈리
새크라멘토 지점 매니저
알트리아 은행
555-8993

어휘 **record** 기록 | **indicate** 나타내다 | **checking account** 당좌예금계좌 | **overdrawn** 초과 인출한 | **check** 수표 | **Federal Postal Service** 연방 우체국 | **account balance** 계좌 잔고 | **overdraft** 당좌 대월, 마이너스 통장 설정 | **fee** 수수료 | **take care of** ~을 처리하다 | **branch** 지점 | **convey** 전달하다, 전하다 | **gratitude** 사의, 감사 | **performance** 실적 | **seek** 구하다, 찾다 | **benefit** 혜택 | **promote** 홍보하다 | **loyal customer** 단골고객 | **request** 요청 | **compromise** 타협하다 | **charge** 청구하다

3. 이 편지의 주된 목적은 무엇인가?
   (A) 고객에게 계좌의 문제를 알리기 위해
   (B) 최근 실적에 대한 감사를 표하기 위해
   (C) 계좌 혜택에 대한 정보를 찾기 위해
   (D) 단골고객에게 더 가까운 지점을 홍보하기 위해

해설 편지의 처음 부분에서 계좌에서 초과 인출된 문제를 알리기 위해 고객에게 연락했음을 알 수 있다. 따라서 정답은 (A) To inform a customer of an issue with an account임을 알 수 있다.

4. 알트리아 은행에 관하여 언급된 것은 무엇인가?
   (A) 많은 고객들이 계좌에서 초과 인출한다.
   (B) 요청하지 않아도 당좌 대월 보호를 제공한다.
   (C) 고객과 기꺼이 타협할 의향이 있다.
   (D) 초과 인출된 계좌에 대해 수수료를 청구한다.

해설 편지의 중간 부분에서 이 은행은 초과 인출된 당좌예금 계좌에 대해 매일 1달러의 수수료를 청구함을 알 수 있다. 따라서 정답은 (D) It charges a fee for overdrawn accounts.이다.

[5-7] 다음 이메일에 관한 문제입니다.

수신: 영상 프로젝트 그룹 목록
발신: 조쉬 베가
날짜: 3월 21일
제목: 영상을 위한 정보

영상 프로젝트 그룹 구성원 여러분께,

저희 웹 사이트에 올릴 30초짜리 영상 제작에 협조해 주셔서 감사합니다. 저희는 이 영상들이 중요한 기능을 하게 될 단일영상으로 합치길 바랍니다. 보다 폭넓은 독자층에 여러분의 역할을 보여주고 그것이 우리 기관의 비전에 어떻게 연관되는지 보여주게 될 겁니다. **5** 저희는 이것으로 저희 기관의 인지도를 높이고 보다 광범위한 투자자를 유치하여 더 많은 자금 지원을 확보하게 되기를 바랍니다.

6 오늘 오후 중으로 모든 분은 최종 대본이 담긴 이메일을 받게 되실 겁니다. 꼼꼼히 읽어주시고 여러 번 소리 내어 읽는 연습을 해 주시기 바랍니다. **7** 내일은 함께 스튜디오에 갈 예정인데요. 그곳에서 촬영 감독님이 무엇을 해야 하는지 자세히 설명해 주실 겁니다. 사무실에서 오전 10시에 출발할 예정이니, 시간을 지켜주시기 바랍니다. 당연한 말이지만, 단정하고 보기 좋은 모습으로 보여야 합니다.

진심으로,

조쉬 베가
바이베틱 주식회사

어휘 **co-operation** 협조, 협력 | **produce** 제작하다 | **second** 초 | **combine** 합치다 | **serve** 기여하다, 제공하다 | **function** 기능 | **show** 보여주다 | **audience** 독자층, 관객 | **role** 역할 | **relate to** ~과 관련되다 | **organization** 기관 | **vision** 비전, 미래상 | **secure** 확보하다 | **funding** 자금 지원 | **raise** 올리다 | **visibility** 가시성, 남의 눈을 끄는 것 | **attract** 끌어 모으다 | **a range of** 다양한 | **investor** 투자자 | **finalize** 마무리하다 | **script** 대본, 원고 | **read through** 꼼꼼히 읽다 | **practice** 연습 | **round** 한 차례 | **read out** 소리내어 읽다 | **camera operator** 촬영 감독 | **walk ~ through** …(익힐 수 있도록 차례차례) ~에게 …을 보여주다 | **on time** 제시간에 | **go without saying** 말할 필요도 없다 | **neat** 깔끔한, 단정한 | **presentable** (차림이) 보기 싫지 않은

5. 영상 프레젠테이션의 목적은 무엇인가?
   (A) 잠재 투자자들을 끌어 모으는 것
   (B) 제품의 장점을 광고하는 것
   (C) 회사의 연혁을 설명하는 것
   (D) 신입 사원을 교육하는 것

해설 첫 번째 단락에서 저희는 이것으로 저희 기관의 인지도를 높이고 보다 광범위한 투자자를 유치하여 더 많은 자금 지원을 확보하게 되기를 바란다고 했으므로 (A) To attract potential investors가 정답이다.

6. 그룹 구성원들은 무엇을 받게 되는가?
   (A) 비디오 카메라
   (B) 위치 지도
   (C) 소리 내어 읽을 문서
   (D) 일정표

해설 두 번째 단락에서 오늘 오후 중으로 모두 최종 대본이 담긴 이메일을 받게 될 예정이며 여러 번 소리 내어 읽는 연습을 해 달라고 했으므로 (C) A text to read aloud가 정답이다.

7. 베가 씨가 동영상에 관하여 언급한 것은?

(A) 스튜디오에서 녹화될 것이다.

(B) 오전 10시에 녹화를 시작할 것이다.

(C) 제한 시간을 넘길 수도 있다.

(D) 텔레비전에 나올 수도 있다.

해설 두 번째 단락에서 내일은 함께 스튜디오에 갈 예정이며, 그곳에서 촬영 감독님이 무엇을 해야 하는지 자세히 설명해 주실 거라고 했으므로 (A) They will be recorded at a studio,가 정답이다.

[8-11] 다음 편지에 관한 문제입니다.

누발리스 가구

오브리 톰슨
총책임자, 스태너즈 실내장식
테라스 가 1400번지
11 브리즈번 4000, 호주

7월 3일

톰슨 씨에게,

이 서신은 누발리스가 곧 이전한다는 것을 알려드리기 위한 것입니다. 7월 17일 화요일부로, 브리즈번에 있는 저희 가게는 문을 닫습니다. **10** 8월 2일 화요일부터 저희는 골드코스트, 플래니건 가 250번지에서 영업을 할 것입니다. **8** 저희의 새 지점은 훨씬 더 넓은 공간을 가지고 있는데, 이것은 저희가 더 다양한 종류의 가구를 들여놓을 수 있도록 해줄 것입니다.

9 저희가 이전 작업을 수행하는 동안, 7월 17일부터 8월 1일까지는 문을 열지 않으니 유념해 주세요. **10** 재개점일 당일 날, 저희는 최신 제품들 중 일부를 소개하고 경품이 걸린 추첨 행사를 열 것입니다. '당신의 가구를 알아라' 대회에도 참가해 주실 것을 요청 드립니다.

저희가 새 시설을 짓는 데 상당한 투자가 있었기 때문에 저희 제품과 배달 서비스에 약간의 가격 인상이 있을 것임을 알려 드리게 되어 송구스럽습니다. 하지만, **11** 귀사는 10년이 넘게 저희의 단골 고객이셨기 때문에, 일 년 동안 상기의 가격 인상에서 제외될 것입니다. 게다가, 8월달에는 귀사가 구매하는 모든 제품들에 대해 15퍼센트를 할인해 드리겠습니다.

또한, 8월 2일자로, 저희의 새 전화번호는 07-843-9526이 됩니다. 귀사의 거래에 감사드리며 후에 또 서비스를 제공할 수 있기를 고대하겠습니다.

진심을 담아,

Lydia Perkins

리디아 퍼킨스
운영 책임자, 누발리스 가구

어휘 inform 알리다 | relocate 이전하다 | raffle 추첨식 판매법, 복권 판매 | invite (정식으로) 요청하다 | participate in 참가하다 | modest 별로 많지 않은 | invest 투자하다 | exclude 제외하다 | expand 확장하다 | inventory 재고품 목록 | remove 제거하다 | reconsider 재고하다 | accomplish 이루다, 성취하다 | lift 올리다, 들어올리다 | enter a contest 대회에 참가하다 | survey 설문조사 | operate 영업하다; 작동되다, 가동되다 | price cut 가격 인하

8. 누발리스 가구에 대해 암시된 것은 무엇인가?

(A) 현재 지점이 두 개 있다.

(B) 품목을 확대할 것이다.

(C) 다른 회사를 인수했다.

(D) 배달 기사들을 추가로 고용할 것이다.

해설 새 지점은 훨씬 더 넓은 공간을 가지고 있는데, 이것은 더 다양한 종류의 가구를 들여놓을 수 있도록 해줄 것이라고 했으므로 정답은 (B) It will expand its inventory.이다.

9. 두 번째 단락, 첫 번째 줄의 단어 'carry out'과 의미상 가장 가까운 것은

(A) 제거하다

(B) 재고하다

(C) 수행하다

(D) 들어 올리다

해설 carry out이 언급된 문장을 확인한다. while we carry out the move는 '이전 작업을 수행하는 동안'이라는 의미이므로 carry out과 의미상 가장 가까운 것은 (C) accomplish이다.

10. 누발리스 가구 고객은 8월 2일에 무엇을 할 수 있는가?

(A) 브리즈번에 있는 공장을 견학할 수 있다

(B) 대회에 참가할 수 있다

(C) 특별 할인을 받을 수 있다

(D) 제품 설문조사에 참여할 수 있다

해설 8월 2일 화요일부터 영업할 것이라고 했으므로 8월 2일은 매장을 이전하여 재개업하는 날이다. 다음에 나오는 내용에 '당신의 가구를 알아라' 대회에도 참가해 주실 것을 요청 드립니다.'라고 했으므로 정답은 (B) Enter a contest이다.

11. 스태너즈 실내장식에 대해 언급되지 않은 것은 무엇인가?

(A) 최소 10년 동안 영업을 해 왔다.

(B) 브리즈번에 위치해 있다.

(C) 다음 달에 누발리스 가구에서 구매 시 할인을 받을 것이다.

(D) 누발리스 가구에서의 주문을 늘릴 예정이다.

해설 '귀사는 10년이 넘게 저희의 단골 고객이셨기 때문에'를 통해 (A)를 소거한다. 편지 윗부분의 브리즈번 주소를 보고 (B)를 소거한다. 편지를 보낸 날짜가 7월 3일인데 8월에는 귀사가 구매하는 모든 제품들에 대해 15퍼센트를 할인해 준다고 했으므로 (C)도 소거한다. 지문에 언급되지 않은 (D) It plans to increase its orders from Nuvallis Furniture.가 정답이다.

UNIT 09. 광고

핵심 문제 유형

본서 p.284

1. (B)   **2.** (B)   **3.** (D)

[1-3] 광고에 관한 문제입니다.

채용 공고: 수학 강사

포웰 기술 대학은 기술과 비즈니스, 그리고 보건과학 분야에서 학위와 수료 프로그램을 제공하는 선두적인 사립 대학입니다. 포웰 기술 대학의 강사들은 학생들이 선택한 진로를 준비할 때 학생들을 훈련시키고 감독하는 책임을 맡고 있습니다. 수학 강사는 실제 교실 수업을 제공하고 승인된 수업 계획안을 준비하고 활용하며 학생의 학업 진척도와 성적 보고를 준비할 책임이 있습니다.

1 지원자들은 반드시 이전 교수 경력이 있어야 합니다. 수학 석사 학위, 그리고 탁월한 구술 및 문서상 의사소통 능력이 필요합니다. 지원자들은 적어도 5년 이상의 교수 경력이 있어야 합니다. 저희는 경쟁력 있는 급여와 풍부한 복지 혜택을 제공합니다.

2 3 자기소개서와 추천 3부와 함께 귀하의 이력서 한 부를 8월 23일까지 다음 주소로 보내주세요:

앤 루쏘, 인사부 부장
포웰 기술 대학
컬럼비아, 사우스캐롤라이나

어휘 leading 선도하는, 일류의 | certification 수료 | responsible 책임이 있는, 책임을 져야 할 | supervision 감독, 관리 | hands-on 실제의, 직접 손으로 만지는 | utilize 활용하다 | approved 공인된, 정평 있는 | candidate 지원자 | competitive 경쟁의, 경합하는 | generous 많은, 풍부한, 인심 좋은 | outstanding 뛰어난 | letter of recommendation 추천서

1. 그 일자리에 대한 필수 조건이 아닌 것은 무엇인가?
(A) 학위
(B) 관리 능력
(C) 교수 경력
(D) 뛰어난 구술 능력

해설 세부 사항 문제이므로 키워드 requirement가 언급된 부분을 지문에서 찾아 선택지와 대조하며 소거한다. 채용 조건은 두 번째 단락 첫 두 문장에 must와 required가 있는 부분에 언급되어 있다. 필수 요건 세 가지는 교수 경험, 수학과 석사 학위, 구술 및 문서상 의사소통 능력이다. 관리 능력은 언급되지 않았으므로 정답은 (B) Management skills이다.

---

2. 지원자는 8월 23일까지 무엇을 제출해야 하는가?
(A) 연봉에 관한 정보
(B) 추천서
(C) 이전 고용주의 연락처

(D) 온라인 지원서

해설 세부 사항 문제이므로 키워드 by August 23가 지문에 언급된 부분을 찾아본다. 세 번째 단락에서 언급된 세 가지 제출해야 할 서류는 이력서, 자기소개서, 추천서이다. 따라서 정답은 (B) Letters of recommendation이다.

---

3. 지원자는 그 직책에 어떻게 지원해야 하는가?
(A) 전화로
(B) 이메일로
(C) 팩스로
(D) 우편으로

해설 지원 방법을 묻는 세부 사항 문제이다. 세 번째 단락에서 지원 서류를 보내는 방법을 언급하며 우편 주소를 알려주고 있으므로 정답은 (D) By mail이다.

Practice

본서 p.286

1. (D)   **2.** (D)   **3.** (B)   **4.** (A)   **5.** (D)
6. (A)   **7.** (C)   **8.** (D)   **9.** (A)   **10.** (C)

[1-2] 다음 광고에 관한 문제입니다.

퀼하우스 출판사의 신규 출판물이 출시됩니다!

1 퀼하우스 출판사의 마케팅 시리즈 최신작 ≪마케팅 혁명: 인터넷을 활용해 판매 증진하기≫가 5월 27일부터 구입 가능합니다. 12달러라는 저렴한 가격에 여러 형태로 출간됩니다. **2** 지금부터 5월 25일까지 이루어지는 선주문에는 15퍼센트 할인이 적용됩니다. 자세한 내용은 웹 사이트 www.quillhouse.com를 방문해 주세요.

어휘 publication 출판(물) | title 출판물, 제목 | on one's way ~오는[가는] 중인 | latest 최신의 | addition 추가(된 것) | marketing 마케팅 | revolution 혁명 | boost 북돋우다, 증진시키다 | sale 판매, 매출 | available 이용 가능한 | purchase 구입 | release 출시하다 | multiple 다양한, 다수의 | format (서적 등의) 형태, 형식 | affordable (가격이) 알맞은, 저렴한 | price 가격 | advance 사전의 | order 주문 | place (주문을) 하다 | detail 세부 내용

1. 무엇이 광고되고 있는가?
(A) 웹 브라우저
(B) 인터넷 공급업체
(C) 컴퓨터
(D) 서적

해설 퀼하우스 출판사의 마케팅 시리즈 최신작 ≪마케팅 혁명: 인터넷을 활용해 판매 증진하기≫가 5월 27일부터 구입 가능하며 12달러라는 저렴한 가격에 여러 형태로 출간된다고 했으므로 (D) A book이 정답이다.

---

2. 선주문에 관하여 사실인 것은?
(A) 매장에만 놓일 수 있다.

(B) 5월 25일에 출고될 것이다.

(C) 가격은 12달러다.

(D) 할인가에 판매될 것이다.

해설 지금부터 5월 25일까지 이루어지는 선주문에는 15퍼센트 할인이 적용된다고 했으므로 (D) They will be sold at a discount.가 정답이다.

[3-4] 다음 광고에 관한 문제입니다.

이번 주 히조에서 어마어마한 비용을 절약하세요!

3 날씨가 추워지기 시작하지만, 히조의 뜨거운 가격이 당신을 따뜻하게 만들어줄 겁니다. **3** 다음 주 한 주 동안, 히조에서 여름 티셔츠, 신발, 비치웨어의 가격을 대폭 인하합니다. 또한 가정용 운동기구 및 보충제가 새로 입고됐습니다. 운동을 더 하는 것이 여러분의 목표에 해당한다면, 저희 매장에 오셔서 피트니스 전문가에게 말씀하세요. 또한 저희는 월간 뉴스레터를 출시할 예정입니다. **4** 오늘 등록하시고 다음번 구매 시 10퍼센트 추가 할인을 받아보세요.

전국에 있는 저희 매장을 방문해 주세요. 또는 www.hijolook.com 에서 온라인으로 쇼핑하시고 까지 무료 가정 배송의 혜택을 받아 보세요.

어휘 massive 어마어마한, 거대한 | savings 절약된 금액 | warm up 따뜻하게 만들다 | slash 대폭 줄이다, 낮추다 | beachwear 비치웨어 | in addition 게다가, 또한 | shipment 배송(품) | exercise 운동 | equipment 장비 | supplement 보충제 | goal 목표 | fitness expert 피트니스 전문가 | release 출시하다 | monthly 월간의 | newsletter 소식지, 뉴스레터 | sign up 등록하다 | purchase 구매 | nationwide 전국에 | alternatively 또는 | take advantage of ~를 기회로 활용하다 | delivery 배송

3. 광고의 목적은 무엇인가?

(A) 운동 장비 신규 라인을 광고하는 것

(B) 이월 제품 할인 판매를 홍보하는 것

(C) 신규 온라인 배송 서비스를 소개하는 것

(D) 대회 결과를 발표하는 것

해설 첫 번째 단락에서 날씨가 추워지기 시작하지만 이라고 하면서 다음 주 한 주 동안, 히조에서 여름 티셔츠, 신발, 비치웨어의 가격을 대폭 인하한다고 했으므로 (B) To promote an end-of-season sale of merchandise가 정답이다.

4. 고객이 히조의 뉴스레터에 등록하면 무엇을 받게 되는가?

(A) 추가 할인

(B) 무료 제품

(C) 무료 가정 배송

(D) 폭넓은 선택권

해설 첫 번째 단락에서 오늘 등록하시고 다음번 구매 시 10퍼센트 추가 할인을 받아보라고 했으므로 (A) An additional discount가 정답이다.

[5-7] 다음 광고에 관한 문제입니다.

행사 기획자 및 회의 주최자 여러분 주목하세요!

5 이제 여러분의 무역 박람회, 컨퍼런스, 컨벤션에 서몬드 홀을 이용할 수 있습니다. 지금 예약하셔서 여러분의 참석자들에게 큰 감동을 선사할 완전 새로운 시설을 이용해 보세요.

6 저희 시설은 유명한 원야드 쿼터에 위치하며 이용 가능해진 지 이제 겨우 한 달 되었습니다. **7D** 230,000 평방미터의 공간은 수천 명의 참석자를 동시에 수용할 수 있으며, 최첨단 장비로 매끄러운 프레젠테이션과 인터넷 스트리밍이 가능합니다. **7B** 무역 박람회를 보다 수월하게 실시할 수 있도록 본관은 작은 구역 10곳으로 분할도 가능합니다. 또한 위층에는 개별 회의실이 많이 있으며, 야외 발코니를 이용할 수 있습니다.

7A 서몬드 홀 주변에는 여러 고급 호텔, 편리한 식사 옵션, 쇼핑 번화가가 있습니다.

오늘 reservations@thurmandhall.com으로 이메일을 보내셔서 이용 가능 여부를 문의해 주세요.

어휘 attention 주목 | event planner 행사 기획자 | conference organizer 회의 주최자 | available 이용 가능한 | trade show 무역 박람회 | take advantage of ~를 이용하다, 기회로 활용하다 | brand-new 완전 새로운 | premises (건물이 딸린) 부지 | wow 큰 감동을 주다 | attendee 참석자 | locate (특정 위치에) 두다 | prestigious 유명한, 명망 있는 | square metre 평방 미터 | space 공간 | play host to ~ 의 개최 장소[수용처]가 되다 | simultaneously 동시에 | state-of-the-art 최첨단의, 최신식의 | equipment 장비 | allow 허용하다 | seamless 아주 매끄러운 | divide 나누다 | area 구역 | facilitate 가능하게 하다 | additionally 또한 | upper 위쪽의 | floor 층 | include 포함하다 | plethora 과다, 과잉 | access 입장, 이용 | outdoor 야외의 | balcony 발코니 | situate 위치시키다 | next to ~옆에 | upscale 고급의 | convenient 편리한 | bustling 북적거리는 | district 구역 | availability 이용 가능성

5. 서몬드 홀은 어떤 종류의 건물인가?

(A) 대학 기숙사

(B) 쇼핑몰

(C) 콘서트 홀

(D) 컨벤션 센터

해설 첫 번째 단락에서 이제 여러분의 무역 박람회, 컨퍼런스, 컨벤션에 서몬드 홀을 이용할 수 있다고 했으므로 (D) A convention center가 정답이다.

6. 광고에 따르면, 서몬드 홀이 문을 연 지 얼마나 오래됐는가?

(A) 1개월

(B) 4개월

(C) 1년

(D) 2년

해설 첫 번째 단락에서 저희 시설은 유명한 원야드 쿼터에 위치하며 이용 가능해진 지 이제 겨우 한 달 되었다고 했으므로 (A) One month가 정답이다.

---

7. 서몬드 홀에 관하여 주어진 정보가 아닌 것은?
(A) 위치
(B) 설계
(C) 비용
(D) 크기

해설 지문의 단서와 보기를 매칭시키면, 두 번째 단락에서 '230,000 평방미터의 공간은 수천 명의 참석자를 동시에 수용할 수 있으며'에서 (D)를 '무역 박람회를 보다 수월하게 실시할 수 있도록 본관은 삭은 구역 10곳으로 분할도 가능합니다. 또한 위층에는 개별 회의실이 많이 있으며, 야외 발코니를 이용할 수 있다.'에서 (B), 세 번째 단락의 서몬드 홀 주변에는 여러 고급 호텔, 편리한 식사 옵션, 쇼핑 번화가가 있다에서 (A)와 일치하지만, 비용에 대한 내용은 언급된 바 없으므로 (C) Its cost가 정답이다.

[8-10] 다음 광고에 관한 문제입니다.

배이건 피트니스 레크리에이션 센터

7 배이건 피트니스 레크리에이션 센터는 지난달에 개장했으며, 버몬트 카운티에 굉장한 새로운 운동 시설을 가져왔습니다. 큰 언덕 꼭대기에 위치한 이 8천 제곱피트의 센터는 모든 사람들을 위한 다양한 운동 선택권을 제공합니다. 올림픽 규모의 10레인 실내 수영장부터 4개의 실내 농구장까지, 이곳은 모든 운동시설을 갖추고 있습니다!

8 또한 배이건 피트니스 레크리에이션 센터에는 보육·놀이센터가 있습니다. 그러므로 운동하러 방문한 부모님들은 어린 자녀들을 능숙하고 잘 보살피는 직원들에게 맡기실 수 있습니다. 그리고 아이들도 많은 운동을 할 것입니다! 놀이센터에는 아이들이 정말 좋아하는 볼풀이 있습니다. 또한 정글짐, 푹신한 암벽등반 인공벽, 장애물 코스가 있습니다.

배이건 피트니스 레크리에이션 센터에 대한 전반적인 정보를 보시려면, 저희 웹사이트 www.bagancenter.com을 방문해 주십시오. **9** 가격 정책이나 길 안내를 받으시려면, 저희 안내 데스크 800-718-1000으로 연락 하십시오.

어휘 bring 가져오다 | spectacular 장관인, 훌륭한 | exercise facility 운동 시설 | on top of ~위에 | hill 언덕 | a multitude of 다수의 | indoor 실내의 | daycare 보육 시설 | play center 놀이 센터 | parents 부모 | workout 운동 | leave 맡기다 | skillful 숙련된, 능숙한 | caring 배려하는, 돌보는 | plenty of 많은 | ball pool 볼 풀 | jungle gym 정글짐 | padded 쿠션 처리된 | climbing wall 암벽 등반 벽 | obstacle course 장애물 코스 | general 일반적인 | information 정보 | pricing 요금 정보 | directions 길 안내 | contact 연락하다 | front desk 안내 데스크

---

8. 배이건 피트니스 레크리에이션 센터에 관하여 언급된 것은 무엇인가?
(A) 곧 문을 열 것이다.

(B) 수영 강습을 제공한다.
(C) 운동 경기를 주최할 것이다.
(D) 버몬트 카운티에 위치해 있다.

해설 광고의 앞부분에서 피트니스 레크리에이션 센터는 지난달에 개장했으며, 버몬트 카운티에 굉장한 새로운 운동 시설을 가져왔다는 것을 알 수 있으므로 정답은 (D) It is located in Belmont County.이다.

---

9. 배이건 피트니스 레크리에이션 센터에서 무엇을 이용할 수 있는가?
(A) 보육
(B) 농구 강습
(C) 테니스 코트
(D) 무료 주차

해설 광고의 중간 부분에서 배이건 피트니스 레크리에이션 센터는 보육 / 놀이센터가 있다고 했으므로 정답은 (A) Child care임을 알 수 있다.

---

10. 이 광고에 의하면, 요금에 관한 정보를 어떻게 받을 수 있는가?
(A) 웹사이트에 방문함으로써
(B) 임원에게 이메일을 보냄으로써
(C) 안내 데스크에 전화함으로써
(D) 소책자를 읽음으로써

해설 광고의 마지막 부분에서 가격 정책이나 길 안내를 받으려면, 안내 데스크 800-718-1000으로 전화 달라고 했으므로 정답은 (C) By calling a front desk임을 알 수 있다.

UNIT 10. 공지·회람

핵심 문제 유형
본서 p.292

1. (A)   2. (B)

[1-2] 다음 공지에 관한 문제입니다.

도시 지하철 서비스
전 승객을 위한 공지

1 지하철 노조가 7월 18일 오늘 저녁 8시부터 시작해서 7월 20일 저녁 8시에 끝나는 도시 지하철 철도 노선의 48시간 파업을 선언했습니다. **2** 정상 운행은 7월 21일에 재개될 것입니다. 이 파업은 상당한 혼란을 일으킬 것이며 이 기간 동안 어떤 열차도 운행되지 않을 것이라 예상됩니다. **1** 따라서 저희는 승객 여러분께 다음 사항을 권장합니다: 시티 공항에 도착하시는 승객분들은 시내로 이동하실 수 있습니다. (지하철 노선에 포함되지 않는) 도시 급행열차는 전면 운행할 것이며 파업 기간 중에는 이 노선으로 운행하는 열차 수를 두 배로 늘릴 예정입니다.

시내에서 이동하시는 승객을 위해서는 여러분들의 도시 주변 이동을 돕기 위해 많은 추가 서비스가 제공될 것입니다. 벅슬리 다리에서 펜 스탯톤 제방을 지나 강을 가로질러 이동하는 무료 운행 서비스를 비롯하여 추가 버스 및 선박 서비스가 제공될 것입니다.

좀 더 자세한 정보를 원하시면, www.citytransportation.org를 방문해 주세요.

어휘 subway service 지하철 운행 서비스 | workers' union 노조 | announce 발표하다, 알리다 | strike 파업 | network (도로·신경 등의) 망, (인간·기업체의) 망, 관계 | resume 재개하다, 다시 시작하다 | cause 일으키다, 야기하다 | significant 커다란, 상당한 | disruption 혼란, 피해 | expect 예상하다 | operational 운영의, 가동되는 | period 기간 | passenger 승객 | downtown 시내로, 도심지로 | fully 완전히 | plan to ~할 계획이다 | double 두 배로 만들다 | a large number of 다수의, 많은 | move around ~를 돌아다니다 | including ~를 포함하여 | embankment 제방 | notify 알리다, 통지하다 | publicize 알리다, 홍보하다 | fare (교통) 요금

1. 공지의 주요 목적은 무엇인가?
(A) 승객들에게 대체 서비스를 알리기 위해
(B) 여행객들이 공항까지 버스를 탈 것을 장려하기 위해
(C) 파업의 이유를 설명하기 위해
(D) 도시 급행열차의 새 책임자를 알리기 위해

해설 글의 목적을 묻는 문제의 단서는 주로 지문 앞부분에서 찾을 수 있다. 첫 단락의 앞부분에서 지하철 노조의 파업이 있을 것을 알리며 파업으로 인한 혼란을 피하기 위해 승객들에게 대책을 알리고 있다. 따라서 정답은 (A) To notify riders of alternate services이다.

2. 7월 21일에 무슨 일이 일어날 것인가?
(A) 벅슬리 다리가 폐쇄될 것이다.
(B) 시 지하철 시스템이 정상적으로 운영될 것이다.
(C) 버스 요금이 인하될 것이다.
(D) 기차의 수가 두 배가 될 것이다.

해설 세부 사항을 묻는 질문이다. 키워드는 July 21이다. 첫 번째 단락에서, 지하철 노조가 7월 18일부터 20일까지 파업을 선언했다고 하면서 정상 운행이 7월 21일에 재개될 것이라고 했으므로 정답은 (B) The city subway will run normally.이다.

Practice

본서 p.294

1. (B)	2. (C)	3. (C)	4. (C)	5. (C)
6. (B)	7. (C)	8. (A)	9. (B)	10. (A)
11. (B)				

[1-2] 다음 공지에 관한 문제입니다.

더럼시
건축 허가 사무소

더럼에서 일하는 개인, 회사, 시공사를 위한 공지 사항

■ 9월 1일 월요일부터 선셋 로 918번지에 위치한 더럼시 건축 허가 사무소는 더이상 금요일과 토요일에 문을 열지 않습니다. 월요일부터 목요일까지의 영업시간은 변동되지 않았습니다. 이는 허가 신청서가 금요일부터 일요일까지는 접수 또는 처리되지 않는다는 의미입니다. 허가증 처리 기간은 3영업일로 유지됩니다. 불편하시겠지만, ■ 이는 더럼 시민에게 필요한 서비스 제공을 계속하면서 운영비 절감을 위해 필요한 조치입니다.

어휘 building 건축 | permit 허가(증) | notice 공지 사항 | individual 개인 | contractor 시공사 | effective 시행되는 | locate 위치시키다 | hours 영업시간 | application 신청서 | accept 받아주다, 수락하다 | process 처리하다 | remain 계속 ~이다 | business day 영업일 | inconvenient 불편한 | measure 조치 | reduce 줄이다 | operating 운영상의 | expense 비용 | continue 계속하다 | citizen 시민

1. 건축 허가 사무소에 어떤 변화가 생기는가?
(A) 다른 부서와 합병할 예정이다.
(B) 영업일을 줄일 예정이다.
(C) 허가 신청 절차를 간소화할 예정이다.
(D) 새로운 장소로 이전할 예정이다.

해설 9월 1일 월요일부터 선셋 로 918번지에 위치한 더럼시 건축 허가 사무소는 더이상 금요일과 토요일에 문을 열지 않으며, 월요일부터 목요일까지의 영업 시간은 변동되지 않는다고 했으므로 (B) It is reducing the days it is open.이 정답이다.

2. 공지에 따르면 왜 변화가 일어나는가?
(A) 서비스를 향상하려고
(B) 제안에 응답하려고
(C) 비용을 줄이려고
(D) 더 많은 신청을 권장하려고

해설 이는 더럼 시민에게 필요한 서비스 제공을 계속하면서 운영비 절감을 위해 필요한 조치라고 했으므로 (C) To reduce costs가 정답이다.

[3-4] 다음 회람에 관한 문제입니다.

수신: 전 직원
발신: 마빈 그린웰 이사
일자: 4월 5일
제목: 도로 작업

■ 여러분이 대부분 매일 제임스 몬로 가를 거쳐서 출근하기 때문에, 매리랜드 교통부가 이 노선 및 출구에 도로공사를 할 예정이라는 것을 알고 계시는 게 중요합니다. 이 프로젝트는 4월 12일에 시작될 것입니다. 그때 도로 표면 작업을 다시 하는 동안 도로의 1마일 구간이 한 차선으로 좁혀질 것이다. 이로 인해 상당한 지연이 야기

될 가능성이 높으므로 미리 준비해 주십시오. **4** 게다가 4월 19일에는 우리 회사 쪽 출구인 4A 출구가 폐쇄될 것입니다. 이 기간 동안 여러분은 5A 출구로 나온 다음 챈틸리 가를 이용하여 동쪽으로 3마일 운전하여 회사로 와야 할 것입니다. 모든 작업은 4월 30일에 완료될 예정입니다. 교통부는 이 프로젝트가 교통 혼잡을 야기할 것임을 인정하지만, 작업이 진행되는 동안 인내심을 가져줄 것을 요청하고 있습니다.

3. 무엇이 발표되고 있는가?
(A) 최근의 교통량 증가
(B) 새로운 노선의 개장
(C) 도로의 일부 보수
(D) 보고서의 지연

해설 회람의 처음 부분에서 대부분의 사장들이 매일 제임스 몬로 가를 거쳐서 출근하기 때문에, 매리랜드 교통부가 이 노선 및 출구에 도로공사를 할 예정이라는 것을 알고 계시는 게 중요하다는 내용이 나오므로, 도로 공사에 대해 직원들에게 알려주고 있음을 알 수 있다. 따라서 정답은 (C) Some repairs to a road이다.

4. 직원들은 언제 우회해야 하는가?
(A) 4월 5일
(B) 4월 12일
(C) 4월 19일
(D) 4월 30일

해설 메모의 중간 부분에서 4월 19일에는 우리 회사 쪽 출구인 4A 출구가 폐쇄될 것이며, 이 기간 동안 5A 출구로 나온 다음 챈틸리 가를 이용하여 동쪽으로 3마일 운전하여 회사로 와야 할 것이라는 내용이 나오므로, 4월 19일에 우회하여 출근해야 함을 알 수 있다. 따라서 정답은 (C) On April 19이다.

[5-7] 다음 공지에 관한 문제입니다.

5 이곳에 계신 모든 분이 오늘 공연에 저희와 함께 해주셔서 정말 기쁩니다. — [1] —. 시간 내어 안내 지침을 읽어주시고 이를 준수해 주시기 바랍니다. 이렇게 하면 모든 참석자가 공연을 즐길 수 있게 됩니다.

행사장 내부에 계실 때에는 모든 전자 기기의 전원을 완전히 꺼 주시기를 요청 드립니다. — [2] —. 기기에서 나오는 소리 및 빛은 모두에게 엄청난 방해가 될 수 있습니다. 기기를 무음 모드로 바꾸기만 하면 어두운 공간에 매우 잘 보이는 빛을 발산할 수 있습니다. 또한 당사 약관에서는 허가 없이 공연의 어떤 부분이든 녹화하는 것이 엄격히 금지된다고 명시하고 있습니다.

7 화재 시 통로에 있는 가방 및 기타 물품은 관객들이 비상구로 가는 데 방해가 될 수 있습니다. — [3] —. **6 7** 가방이 너무 커서 좌석 아래 들어가지 않는 경우 3달러로 이용하실 수 있는 사물함이 밖에 있습니다. — [4] —. 필요하신 분은 저희 안내원에게 알려 주시기 바랍니다.

감사합니다.

PART 7 UNIT 10

어휘 thrilled 신이 난 | guideline 지침 | adhere to ~을 충실히 지키다, 준수하다 | attendee 참석자 | venue 장소 | turn off 끄다 | electronic 전자의 | device 기기 | completely 완전히 | incredibly 엄청나게 | distracting 산만하게 하는 | switch 바꾸다 | silent 조용한 | give off 발산하다 | highly 매우 | visible 눈에 보이는 | dark 어두운 | additionally 또한 | terms and conditions 약관, 조건 | state 명시하다 | record 녹화하다 | performance 공연 | permission 허가 | strictly 엄격히 | forbid 금지하다 | in the case of ~경우 | aisle 통로 | hinder 방해하다 | audience 관객 | fire exit 비상구 | locker 물품 보관함 | available 이용할 수 있는 | attendant 안내원

5. 공지는 어디에 게시되겠는가?
(A) 강의실에
(B) 공항에
(C) 공연장에
(D) 경기장에

해설 첫 번째 단락에서 이곳에 계신 모든 분이 오늘 공연에 저희와 함께 해주셔서 정말 기쁘다고 했으므로 (C) In a concert hall이 정답이다.

6. 큰 가방에 관하여 언급된 것은?
(A) 안내원들이 수거해갈 것이다.
(B) 비용을 내고 안전한 상자 안에 넣을 수 있다.
(C) 행사장 앞쪽에 놓아야 한다.
(D) 도난 방지를 위해 명확하게 라벨을 부착해야 한다.

해설 세 번째 단락에서 가방이 너무 커서 좌석 아래 들어가지 않는 경우 3달러로 이용하실 수 있는 사물함이 밖에 있다고 했으므로 (B) They can be put inside a secure box for a fee.가 정답이다.

7. [1], [2], [3], [4]로 표시된 곳 중, 다음 문장이 들어갈 위치로 가장 적절한 것은?
"모든 소지품은 좌석 아래에 놓아 주십시오."
(A) [1]
(B) [2]
(C) [3]
(D) [4]

해설 세 번째 단락에서 화재 시 통로에 있는 가방 및 기타 물품은 관객들이 비상구로 가는 데 방해가 될 수 있다고 하면서 가방이 너무 커서 좌석 아래 들어가지 않는 경우 3달러로 이용하실 수 있는 사물함이 밖에 있다고 하는 말 앞에 주어진 문장이 들어가야 문맥상 연결이 자연스러우므로 (C) [3]이 정답이다.

[8-11] 다음 공지에 관한 문제입니다.

프라이머베라 테크 직원 여러분께 알려 드립니다.

알고 계시겠지만, **8** 7월 1일에 유로파 센트럴에서 신규 웨스트게이트로 데이터 플랫폼을 옮겨갈 예정입니다. 8월 1일에는 전 직원의

유로파 센트럴에의 접속이 막히게 되며, 사내 커뮤니케이션, 파일 공유, 회의실 예약 같은 모든 프라이머베라 관련 작업은 웨스트게이트를 통해 이루어집니다.

웨스트게이트에 접속하려면 직원 여러분은 우선 primavera.westgate.com에 계정을 등록해야 합니다. 그다음으로는 보안상의 이유로 인증 단계가 진행됩니다. **9** 먼저 부서 코드 뿐만 아니라 직원 식별 번호를 제공하라는 안내가 나옵니다. 이러한 내용을 입력한 후 회사 비밀번호를 이용해 로그인하게 됩니다. **11** 일단 이 작업이 완료되면, 여러분의 계정을 설정하고 웨스트게이트 플랫폼 이용을 시작할 수 있게 됩니다. **10** 전체 과정은 15분 정도밖에 소요되지 않습니다. 플랫폼에 접속할 때까지 파일 전송 과정이 완료되어야 하니, 모든 파일을 가지고 있는지 확인하시기를 권장 드립니다. 파일이 제대로 전송되지 않은 것을 발견한 경우, 가능한 한 빨리 기술 팀원에게 알려 주시기 바랍니다.

어휘 attention 주목 | employee 직원 | aware 알고 있는 | migrate 이동하다, 옮기다 | data 데이터 | platform 플랫폼 (사용 기반이 되는 컴퓨터 하드웨어, 소프트웨어) | access 접속 | disable 기능을 억제하다 | related 연관된 | sharing 공유 | booking 예약 | take place 일어나다, 열리다 | gain access to ~에 접속하다 | register for ~에 등록하다 | account 계정 | security 보안 | reason 이유 | verification 인증 | step 단계 | supply 제공하다, 공급하다 | identification 식별 | department 부서 | direct ~로 향하다 | sign in 로그인하다 | complete 완료된 | set up 설정하다 | entire 전체의 | process 과정 | take (시간이) 걸리다 | around 약 | transfer 옮기다, 이동하다 | correctly 제대로, 정확하게 | as soon as possible 가능한 한 빨리

8. 프라이머베라 테크에 관하여 언급된 것은?
(A) 데이터 플랫폼을 변경할 예정이다.
(B) 새로운 사무실로 이사할 예정이다.
(C) 근무 규정을 일부 수정할 예정이다.
(D) 신제품 출시를 준비하는 중이다.

해설 첫 번째 단락에서 7월 1일에 유로파 센트럴에서 신규 웨스트게이트 데이터 플랫폼으로 바꿀 예정이라고 했으므로 (A) It is changing its data platform.이 정답이다.

9. 공지에 따르면, 직원에게 필요한 것이 아닌 것은?
(A) 직원 번호
(B) 승인서
(C) 비밀번호
(D) 부서 코드

해설 지문의 단서와 보기를 매칭시키면, 두 번째 단락에서 먼저 부서 코드 뿐만 아니라 직원 식별 번호를 제공하라는 안내가 나온다에서 (D)와 (A), 이러한 내용을 입력한 후 회사 비밀번호를 이용해 로그인하게 된다에서 (C)라고 했지만, 승인서는 언급하지 않았으므로 (B) An approval form이 정답이다.

10. 과정에 관하여 언급된 것은?
(A) 많은 시간이 걸리지 않을 것이다.
(B) 웨스트게이트에서 코드를 받는 것을 포함한다.
(C) 기술 팀의 도움이 필요할 것이다.
(D) 7월 1일 전에 완료되어야 한다.

해설 두 번째 단락에서 전체 과정은 15분 정도밖에 소요되지 않는다고 했으므로 (A) It should not take much time.이 정답이다.

11. 두 번째 단락, 다섯 번째 줄의 단어 'Once'와 의미상 가장 가까운 것은?
(A) ~까지
(B) 하자마자
(C) 마침내
(D) 그 경우에

해설 두 번째 단락에서 일단 이 작업이 완료되면, 여러분의 계정을 설정하고 웨스트게이트 플랫폼 이용을 시작할 수 있게 된다에서 once는 '~하자마자'라는 의미로 쓰였으므로 보기 중 같은 의미를 전달하는 (B) As soon as가 정답이다.

UNIT 11. 기사

핵심 문제 유형

1. (A)   2. (C)   3. (A)   4. (C)

[1-4] 다음 기사에 관한 문제입니다.

합병하려는 센츄리 커뮤니케이션즈와 오람 인터네셔널

그린빌, 10월 10일 – **1** **2** 센츄리 커뮤니케이션즈와 오람 인터네셔널은 자신들이 곧 합병하게 될 것이라고 발표했다. 예전에 웨스트 버지니아주의 마틴스버그와 노스캐롤라이나주의 윈스턴세일럼에 본사를 두었던 **3** 두 회사는 그 지역에서 가장 큰 인터넷 서비스 제공업체를 형성할 예정이다.

3 새로운 회사의 이름은 센츄리-오람이고 반드시 대단한 일을 할 것이다. 두 회사는 이미 대규모의 고객층을 확보하고 있다. 그래서 이 합병 이후 경쟁사와의 경쟁은 거의 없을 것이다. **4** 센츄리-오람의 새로운 업무 중심지는 버지니아주의 로아노크에 있는 센츄리-오람 타워라는 이름으로 새롭게 건설된 고층 건물에 자리잡을 예정이다.

센츄리-오람은 내년 연말까지 켄터키와 남부 오하이오주로 확장할 계획이다. 이 움직임은 그쪽 시장들에서 강력한 입지를 가진 회사가 아무도 없기 때문에 성공할 것으로 보인다.

어휘 merge 합병하다 | previously 이전에 | be headquartered in ~에 본부를 두다 | merger 합병 | competition 경쟁 | rival 경쟁자 | operation 운영, 가동 | skyscraper 고층 건물 |

expand 확장하다 | strong 튼튼한, 견고한 | presence 존재감, 입지 | market trend 시장 동향

1. 이 기사의 목적은 무엇인가?
(A) **합병을 알리기 위해**
(B) 신규 서비스를 설명하기 위해
(C) 매출액을 보고하기 위해
(D) 시장 동향을 기술하기 위해

해설 기사의 목적을 묻는 문제이다. 기사의 주제와 목적은 기사의 제목과 앞부분에 제시되는 경우가 많다. 기사의 제목에서 두 회사가 합병한다는 것을 알리고 있고, 첫 단락의 첫 문장에서도 두 회사가 곧 합병할 예정임을 밝히고 있다. 따라서 정답은 (A) To announce a merger 이다.

2. 이 기사는 어디에 나오겠는가?
(A) 연예
(B) 여행
(C) **경제**
(D) 스포츠

해설 기사가 등장할 섹션을 묻는 추론 문제이다. 이 기사는 어느 한 부분에 정답 단서가 있는 것이 아니고 회사의 합병, 본사 위치, 사업 분야, 향후 전망 등을 다루고 있으므로 비즈니스 관련 기사라는 것을 파악할 수 있어야 한다. 따라서 정답은 (C) Business이다.

3. 센츄리-오람은 어떤 회사인가?
(A) **인터넷 서비스 제공업체**
(B) 컴퓨터 소매업체
(C) 휴대전화기 제조업체
(D) 광고 대행업체

해설 세부 사항을 묻는 문제이다. 질문의 키워드 센츄리-오람이 언급된 부분을 지문에서 찾아본다. 두 번째 단락에서 새로 합병될 회사의 이름이란 것을 알 수 있고 바로 앞인 첫 번째 단락 마지막 부분에서 합병될 회사는 가장 큰 인터넷 서비스 제공업체가 될 것이라고 했으므로 정답은 (A) An Internet service provider이다.

4. 센츄리-오람의 본사는 어디에 위치할 예정인가?
(A) 그린빌에
(B) 윈스턴 세일럼에
(C) **로아노크에**
(D) 마틴스버그에

해설 세부 사항을 묻는 문제이다. 두 번째 단락 마지막 부분에 headquarters가 center로 패러프레이징되었고 뒤에 신사옥의 위치가 언급되어 있다. 따라서 정답은 (C) In Roanoke이다.

Practice
본서 p.300

1. (A) **2.** (D) **3.** (D) **4.** (B) **5.** (C)
6. (B) **7.** (C) **8.** (B) **9.** (A) **10.** (A)
11. (C) **12.** (A)

[1-2] 다음 기사에 관한 문제입니다.

1 앵글라스 워프 부근의 마리타임 웨이에 위치한 넵튠스 바운티가 10년 전에 문을 열어 포틀랜드의 최고급 해산물 레스토랑으로 빠르게 자리 잡았습니다. 넵튠스 바운티는 신선한 해산물로 준비된 다양한 요리를 선보이고 있으며, 그것들 중 많은 것들이 이 지역에서 잡아 올린 것입니다. **2** 가장 신선한 재료만을 고집하고 있기 때문에, 메뉴는 계절에 맞는 해산물 종류에 따라 바뀌고 있습니다. 레스토랑은 지난 두 달 동안 수리를 위해 휴업했으나, 지난주에 다시 문을 열었습니다. 현재 내부는 오래된 목조 범선 내부처럼 보입니다. 또한 살아 있는 가재와 물고기, 다른 해산물이 들어 있는 수족관을 선보입니다. 그들의 재오픈 기념으로, 넵튠스 바운티는 모든 식사 손님에게 무료로 전채 요리를 제공할 것입니다.

어휘 maritime 바다의 | swiftly 신속히 | establish (입지를) 확고히 하다 | premier 최고급의 | seafood restaurant 해산물 레스토랑 | offer 제공하다 | a large selection of 다양한 선택의 | prepare 준비하다 | locally 지역적으로 | insistence 고집 | ingredient 재료 | renovation 수리 | interior 내부 | wooden sailing ship 목조 범선 | lobster 바닷가재 | creature 생물 | free appetizer 무료 전채 요리 | advertise 광고하다 | compare 비교하다 | throughout the year 일 년 내내

1. 이 기사의 목적은 무엇인가?
(A) **사업체를 광고하기 위해**
(B) 요리 수업을 홍보하기 위해
(C) 다른 레스토랑들을 비교하기 위해
(D) 관광 명소를 설명하기 위해

해설 기사의 도입부에서 포틀랜드에서 자리 잡은 지 10년이 된 레스토랑을 소개하고 있다. 따라서 이 기사의 목적으로 가장 적절한 답은 (A) To advertise a business이다.

2. 넵튠스 바운티에 관해 언급되지 않은 것은 무엇인가?
(A) 지난주에 다시 문을 열었다.
(B) 내부를 새롭게 꾸몄다.
(C) 메뉴가 일 년 내내 바뀐다.
(D) **새로운 장소로 옮겼다.**

해설 기사의 내용과 선택지의 내용을 비교 또는 대조하여 기사의 내용과 일치하지 않는 정보를 찾는 문제이다. 먼저 지난주에 다시 문을 열었다 해서 (A)를, 두 달간의 수리 후에 현재 내부는 오래된 목조 범선 내부와 같다고 했으므로 (B) 역시 지문의 내용과 일치한다. 마지막으로 메뉴가 계절에 따라 바뀐다고 했으므로 (C) 역시 사실임을 확인할 수 있다. 레스토랑을 이전했다는 정보는 기사 어디에서도 찾을 수 없으므로 정답은 (D) It has moved to a new location.이다.

[3-5] 다음 기사에 관한 문제입니다.

신선하고 과일 향이 풍부한

화이트 플레인즈 (6월 17일) — 레오나드르 마틴은 현지인들에게 기쁨을 주는 곳이 되겠다는 소박한 바람으로 과일 샐러드 가게를 열었다. 자신의 과일 샐러드가 전국을 휩쓸게 될 것이라고 상상한 적은 단 한 번도 없었다. 신선한 과일과 풍미 좋은 드레싱의 독특한 조합 덕분에 고객들은 레오나드르 마틴의 과일 샐러드가 어느 날씨에나 더할 나위 없이 큰 즐거움이 된다는 데 동감한다. **3** 문을 연 지 4년 만에 마틴은 이제 오레스테스에 다른 지점 개장을 앞두고 있다.

마틴의 사업체인 트로피프루트에서는 전 세계에서 공수한 신선한 과일을 조합해 유명한 과일 샐러드를 만드는 것으로 유명하다. 이것도 쉬운 일처럼 들릴 수 있으나, 결코 그렇지 않다는 것을 마틴 씨는 상기시켜준다. "과일에 관한 한 제대로 된 공급업체와 소매 협력업체를 찾는 일이 가장 중요합니다."라고 마틴 씨가 설명했다. "고품질 재료를 확보하기 위해 저희는 농부들을 신중하게 심사하며, **4** 저희 과일 샐러드를 판매할 레스토랑과 상점을 선택합니다. 저희는 프리미엄 브랜드를 유지하고 싶은 만큼 선택에 신중을 기합니다."

5 마틴 씨는 매일 화이트 플레인즈 지점을 운영했으나, 최근 그 업무를 자신의 3년차 사업 파트너인 에밀리 커닝햄에게 넘겨줬다. 이로써 마틴 씨는 더 많은 협력업체를 양산하고 오레스테스 지점 개장에 집중할 수 있게 된다. 개장일은 8월 22일로 정해졌다.

어휘 fresh 신선한 | fruity 과일 맛[향]이 나는 | fruit 과일 | salad 샐러드 | aspiration 열망, 포부 | treat 큰 기쁨[만족]을 주는 것, 한 턱, 대접 | local 현지인 | imagine 상상하다 | sweep 휩쓸다 | nation 국가 | owing to ~때문에 | unique 독특한 | combination 조합 | flavorful 풍미 있는, 맛 좋은 | dressing 드레싱, 소스 | weather 날씨 | location 지점 | business 사업체 | be known for ~로 유명하다 | blend 섞다, 조합하다 | create 만들어내다 | sound ~처럼 들리다 | remind 상기시키다 | anything but 결코 그렇지 않은 | when it comes to ~에 관한 한 | supplier 공급업자[업체] | retail 소매 | partner (사업) 파트너, 협력업체 | explain 설명하다 | carefully 신중하게 | vet 심사하다, 면밀히 조사하다 | farmer 농부 | ensure 보장하다 | high quality 고품질의 | ingredient 재료 | choose 선택하다 | selective 조심해서 고르는 | remain 계속 ~이다 | premium 고급의 | run 운영하다 | recently 최근 | pass A onto B A를 B에게 넘겨주다 | duty 업무, 직무 | set 정하다

3. 기사는 주로 무엇에 관한 내용인가?
(A) 업계 최신 동향
(B) 신규 광고 전략의 적용
(C) 건강한 식사의 중요성
(D) 사업체 확장

해설 첫 번째 단락에서 문을 연 지 4년 만에 마틴은 이제 오레스테스에 다른 지점 개장을 앞두고 있다고 했으므로 (D) The expansion of a business가 정답이다.

4. 트로피프루트에 관하여 언급된 것은?
(A) 정부의 자금 지원을 받았다.

(B) 지역 상점을 통해 제품을 판매한다.
(C) 텔레비전 프로그램에서 소개됐다.
(D) 여름철에만 운영된다.

해설 두 번째 단락에서 저희 과일 샐러드를 판매할 레스토랑과 상점을 선택한다고 했으므로 (B) It sells its goods through local stores.가 정답이다.

5. 커닝햄 씨에 관하여 알 수 있는 것은?
(A) 8월 22일에 계약서에 서명할 것이다.
(B) 과거에 농부로 일했었다.
(C) 트로피프루트에서 3년간 일했다.
(D) 오레스테스로 이사할 예정이다.

해설 세 번째 단락에서 마틴 씨는 매일 화이트 플레인즈 지점을 운영했으나, 최근 그 업무를 자신의 3년 차 사업 파트너인 에밀리 커닝햄에게 넘겨 줬다고 했으므로 (C) She has worked at TropiFruit for three years.가 정답이다.

[6-8] 다음 기사에 관한 문제입니다.

로리타 퍼디의 삶을 기리며

잉글우드 (6월 14일) - 모든 잉글우드 주민은 지역 후원자인 로리타 퍼디의 업적을 기념하는 자리에 초대된다. — [1] —. **6** 그녀의 은퇴를 기념하는 연회는 6월 22일 오후 6시부터 오후 9시 30분까지 파이아웃 호텔에서 열릴 예정이다.

7D 로리타 퍼디는 자신의 광고 회사인 퍼디 크리에이티브로 유명해졌다. 회사는 상당한 성공을 거뒀고, 퍼디 씨는 수익을 지역 사회에 다시 투자했다. **7A** 그녀는 학생들에게 기업가가 되는 법을 가르쳐주는 방과후 프로그램을 잉글우드 고등학교에 만드는 데 있어 필수적인 역할을 했다. — [2] —. **7B 8** 또한 몬로 마을 회관 개조에 핵심 후원자였으며, 지역 기업가를 지원하는 비스타 펀드를 설립했다. — [3] —.

행사는 오후 6시에 시작하며, 저녁 식사는 한 시간 후에 제공된다. 잉글우드 시립 관현악단이 행사 내내 음악을 연주한다. 현재 티켓은 15달러에 판매되고 있으며, www.englewoodcity.org에서 구입할 수 있다. — [4] —.

어휘 celebrate 기념하다, 축하하다 | resident 주민, 거주자 | achievement 업적, 성취 | local 지역의, 현지의 | benefactor 후원자 | banquet 연회, 만찬 | commemorate 기념하다 | retirement 은퇴 | hold 개최하다 | prominence 명성, 유명함 | advertising 광고 | firm 회사 | achieve 성취하다 | considerable 상당한 | success 성공 | invest 투자하다 | profit 이익 | community 지역 사회 | integral 필수적인 | creation 창조 | after-school 방과후의 | entrepreneur 기업가 | sponsor 후원자 | renovation 보수, 개조 | establish 설립하다 | support 지지, 지원 | serve (음식을) 제공하다 | currently 현재 | on sale 판매되는 | purchase 구입하다

6. 행사는 어디서 열리는가?
(A) 잉글우드 고등학교에서

(B) 파이우트 호텔에서

(C) 몬로 마을 회관에서

(D) 퍼디 크리에이티브 본사에서

해설 첫 번째 단락에서 그녀의 은퇴를 기념하는 연회는 6월 22일 오후 6시 부터 오후 9시 30분까지 파이우트 호텔에서 열릴 예정이라고 했으므로 (B) At the Piute Hotel이 정답이다.

---

7. 퍼디 씨에 관하여 언급되지 않은 것은?

(A) 방과후 프로그램을 도왔다.

(B) 개조 프로젝트에 돈을 기부했다.

(C) 자신의 학업을 위해 잉글우드로 이사했다.

(D) 자기 사업을 시작했다.

해설 지문의 단서와 보기를 매칭시키면, 두 번째 단락에서 로리타 퍼디는 자신의 광고 회사인 퍼디 크리에이티브로 유명해졌다에서 (D), 그녀는 학생들에게 기업가가 되는 법을 가르쳐주는 방과후 프로그램을 잉글우드 고등학교에 만드는 데 있어 필수적인 역할을 했다에서 (A), 또한 몬로 마을 회관 개조에 핵심 후원자였으며, 지역 기업가를 지원하는 비스타 펀드를 설립했다에서 (B)와 일치하지만, 자신의 학업을 위해 이사했다는 내용은 언급된 바 없으므로 (C) She moved to Englewood for her studies.가 정답이다.

---

8. [1], [2], [3], [4]로 표시된 곳 중, 다음 문장이 들어갈 위치로 가장 적절한 것은?

"수업은 지역 기업가들이 가르친다."

(A) [1]

(B) [2]

(C) [3]

(D) [4]

해설 두 번째 단락에서 그녀는 학생들에게 기업가가 되는 법을 가르쳐주는 방과후 프로그램을 잉글우드 고등학교에 만드는 데 있어 필수적인 역할을 했다고 하였으므로 주어진 문장이 이어지기에 자연스러우므로 (B) [2]가 정답이다.

[9-12] 다음 기사에 관한 문제입니다.

레이세스터 헤럴드
지역 뉴스—7월 7일

9 세계적인 식품 제조업체 페이턴 피셔에서 레이세스터에 연구 개발 센터를 연다는 계획을 발표했다. 구 글렌필드 쇼핑 플라자 건물을 사용하게 될 센터는 10월 초 문을 열 예정이다.

신규 센터의 재개발은 여러 차례 지연되었다. 인접한 앤스테이 의료 센터 공사로 인해 일부 진입로가 임시 폐쇄되었다. **10** 레이세스터 시 의회는 수많은 도시 계획 정책 문제도 다뤄야 했다.

"개발은 저희 측에 상당한 인내심을 요했습니다."라고 **11** 회사의 최고 마케팅 책임자인 엘비라 하예스가 말한다. "하지만 몇 달 후 마침내 문을 열게 되면 이 모든 게 가치를 발하게 될 겁니다."

12 행정 및 관리 직원에 더해 신규 센터의 식품 과학자, 맛 전문가, 포장 개발자 모집을 위해 페이턴 피셔는 앞으로 몇 달간 지역 곳곳

에서 취업 박람회를 개최할 예정이다.

어휘 global 세계적인 | manufacturer 제조업체 | announce 발표하다 | occupy 차지하다 | be set to ~할 예정이다 | redevelopment 재개발 | push back 미루다 | access road 진입로 | temporarily 임시로 | construction 공사, 건설 | adjacent 인접한 | address 다루다 | urban 도시의 | planning 계획 | policy 정책 | issue 문제 | patience 인내심 | end 부분, 한쪽 편 | worthwhile 가치 있는, 보람 있는 | organize 개최하다 | job fair 취업 박람회 | throughout the region 지역 곳곳에 | recruit 모집하다, 뽑다 | flavor 맛, 풍미 | packaging 포장 | developer 개발자 | administrative 행정의 | maintenance 유지, 관리

---

9. 기사의 목적은 무엇인가?

(A) 시설 개조에 대해 알리는 것

(B) 새로운 식품을 광고하는 것

(C) 레이세스터의 사업 동향을 평가하는 것

(D) 쇼핑 플라자의 개장을 발표하는 것

해설 첫 번째 단락에서 세계적인 식품 제조업체 페이턴 피셔에서 레이세스터에 연구 개발 센터를 연다는 계획을 발표했다. 구 글렌필드 쇼핑 플라자 건물을 사용하게 될 센터는 10월 초 문을 열 예정이라고 했으므로 (A) To report on the remodeling of a facility가 정답이다.

---

10. 두 번째 단락, 네 번째 줄의 단어, 'address'와 의미상 가장 가까운 것은?

(A) 다루다

(B) ~하에 떠맡다

(C) 구성하다

(D) 응원하다

해설 두 번째 단락의 레이세스터 시 의회는 수많은 도시 계획 정책 문제도 다뤄야 했다에서 address는 '다루다'라는 의미로 쓰였으므로 같은 의미를 전달하는 (A) deal with가 정답이다.

---

11. 하예스 씨는 누구겠는가?

(A) 건설 관리자

(B) 의료 센터 담당자

(C) 페이턴 피셔의 임원

(D) 레이세스터 시의회 의원

해설 세 번째 단락에서 회사의 최고 마케팅 책임자인 엘비라 하예스라고 했으므로 (C) A Peyton Fisher executive가 정답이다.

---

12. 기사에 따르면, 페이턴 피셔는 무엇을 할 계획인가?

(A) 다양한 직무에 직원을 채용할 계획이다

(B) 시의회에 기한 연장을 요청할 계획이다

(C) 센터의 로비를 개조할 계획이다

(D) 도로 폐쇄에 대해 공식 불만을 제기할 계획이다

해설 네 번째 단락에서 행정 및 관리 직원에 더해 신규 센터의 식품 과학

자, 맛 전문가, 포장 개발자 모집을 위해 Peyton Fisher는 앞으로 몇 달간 지역 곳곳에서 취업 박람회를 개최할 예정이라고 했으므로 (A) Hire employees for various positions가 정답이다.

UNIT 12. 양식

핵심 문제 유형

1. (A)   2. (C)

[1-2] 다음 청구서에 관한 문제입니다.

더 스타 호텔
3815 그랜드라이버 가

청구인: 수, 킴   날짜: 4월 20일
　　　이스트 랜싱, MI 48825   청구서 번호: 314

5월 28일에 열릴 일일 컨퍼런스를 위한 청구서

항목	가격	합계
1 일반실 회의 공간 (300명의 손님들을 위한)	200달러 / 하루	200달러

시청각 장비 대여

1 무선 마이크 2개	40.00달러/개당	80달러
프로젝터 1개	100.00달러/개당	100달러
프로젝션 스크린 1개	70.00달러/개당	70달러
1 아침 식사	10.00달러/한 사람당	3000달러
1 점심 식사	15.00달러/한 사람당	4500달러

소계 7750달러
세금 620달러
합계 8370달러

2 *위에 언급된 모든 서비스를 예약하기 위해선 5월 4일까지 이 금액을 보내주세요.

어휘   invoice 청구서 | standard 일반적인, 보통의, 기준 | rate 요금, 가격, 속도, 비율 | audiovisual 시청각의 | wireless 무선의 | microphone 마이크 | amount 양, 금액, 액수 | reserve 예약하다 | overnight 하룻밤 동안, 야간의, 일박(용)의 | hotel stay 호텔 숙박 | rental 임대(료), 대여 | make a payment 지불을 하다

1.   행사 비용에서 포함되지 않은 것은 무엇인가?
　　(A) 하룻밤 동안의 호텔 숙박
　　(B) 마이크
　　(C) 참가자들을 위한 식사

(D) 회의실 대여

해설   행사 비용에 포함되지 않은 것을 물어보는 문제로 지문과 대조하여 오답을 소거한다. (B)는 청구서의 시청각 장비 대여 표에 무선 마이크가 언급되어 있으므로 소거한다. (C)는 청구서의 시청각 장비 대여 표에 아침과 점심이 언급되어 있으므로 소거한다. (D)는 청구서의 일반실과 회의 공간에서 회의실 대여가 가능함을 알 수 있으므로 소거한다. 따라서, 청구서 내역에는 언급된 적이 없는 (A) Overnight hotel stay가 정답이다.

2.   김 씨가 하라고 요청받은 것은 무엇인가?
　　(A) 예약을 확인한다
　　(B) 시청각 장비를 반환한다
　　(C) 돈을 지불한다
　　(D) 메뉴에서 아이템을 고른다

해설   김 씨가 요청받은 것을 물었으므로 양식을 받는 사람이 부탁이나 요청을 받은 것이 무엇인지 파악한다. 마지막 부분에서 돈을 지불하라는 내용이 나오므로 이를 make a payment로 패러프레이징한 (C) Make a payment가 정답이다.

Practice

1. (C)   2. (A)   3. (A)   4. (A)   5. (D)
6. (C)   7. (A)   8. (A)   9. (C)

[1-2] 다음 영수증에 관한 문제입니다.

그레빌 주유소
S15 고속도로
래이스톤 그린 17번지
032-555-3286
1 9월 17일

1 USB 핸드폰 충전기	8.00달러
1 검정색 컵 거치대	7.00달러
1 방향제	6.50달러
세금	3.30달러
총액	24.80달러

2 그레빌의 단골 고객 멤버십 카드에 가입하세요. 오늘 구매로 24 그레빌 포인트를 쌓으실 수 있었습니다.

포인트를 사용하여 식품 및 휘발유에 할인을 받으실 수 있습니다. 또한 회원에게만 부여하는 경품 응모에도 참여하실 수 있게 됩니다.

어휘   gas station 주유소 | highway 고속도로 | charger 충전기 | cup holder 컵 거치대 | air freshener 방향제 | tax 세금 | sign up for ~에 등록하다, 가입하다 | loyal customer 단골 고객 | rewards card 멤버십 카드 | transaction 거래, 매매 | earn 얻다, 받다 | discount 할인 | petrol 휘발유 | eligible 자격이 있는 | enter 참가하다, 들어가다 | exclusive 전용의, 독점적인 | giveaway 증정품, 경품

100   파고다 토익 기본 완성 RC

1. 9월 17일에 무엇이 구매되었는가?

(A) 스낵

(B) 휘발유

(C) 차량용 액세서리

(D) 청소용품

해설 USB 핸드폰 충전기, 검정색 컵 거치대, 방향제를 구매했다고 나와 있으므로 (C) Car accessories가 정답이다.

2. 영수증에서 그레빌 주유소에 관하여 언급된 것은?

(A) 단골 고객 프로그램을 운영한다.

(B) 매달 대회를 개최한다.

(C) 휘발유 최저 가격 보상을 제공한다.

(D) 여러 지점이 있다.

해설 그레빌의 단골 고객 멤버십 카드에 가입하면 오늘 구매로 24 그레빌 포인트를 쌓으실 수 있다고 했으므로 (A) It has a customer loyalty program.이 정답이다.

[3-4] 다음 청구서에 관한 문제입니다.

청구서

주문일: 9월 16일

배송일: 9월 22일

출발지:

트레몬 전자제품점

콜러리즈 플레이스 391번지

그렌트, 미네소타 56531

도착지:

3 에바 제닝스

맨스필드 크레센트 18번지, 아파트 302호

더글라스, 위스콘신 54874

제품	설명	수량	가격
S6431	고화질 컴퓨터 모니터, 27인치	1	205달러

주문 소계: 205달러

세금: 10달러

배송: 6.50달러

총: 221.50달러

4 프로모션 / 할인 행사: −22.15달러

지불 금액: 199.35달러

어휘 invoice 송장, 청구서 | place of origin 출발지, 원산지 | electronics 전자제품 | place of destination 도착지 | quantity 수량 | high-definition 고화질의 | subtotal 소계 | tax 세금 | shipping 배송 | payment 지불(금) | due 지불해야 하는

3. 주문품은 어디로 배송되고 있는가?

(A) 집으로

(B) 소매상점으로

(C) 창고로

(D) 정부 청사로

해설 도착지에서 '에바 제닝스, 맨스필드 크레센트 18번지, 아파트 302호'라고 했으므로 (A) To a home이 정답이다.

4. 송장에서 나타내는 것은?

(A) 제품이 할인 대상이다.

(B) 배송이 무료다.

(C) 제품이 9월 16일에 도착할 것이다.

(D) 제품에 보증 기간 연장이 제공된다.

해설 프로모션/할인 행사에서 −22.15달러라고 했으므로 (A) The product is eligible for a discount.가 정답이다.

[5-6] 다음 표에 관한 문제입니다.

엑사버스터 시스템스

당신의 웹 사이트를 위한 호스트를 물색 중인데 당신에게 딱 맞는 플랜을 원하시나요? **5** 저희가 제공하는 플랜을 빠르게 비교해볼 수 있는 간편한 표가 있습니다.

5 특징	기본	프리미엄
전체 주문 제작 사이트	✓	✓
6B 신용 카드 및 직불 카드 처리 설치	✓	✓
6A 월간 분석 보고서	✓	✓
6D 사용자를 위한 비밀번호 암호화	✓	✓
무제한 데이터 저장		✓
6C 24/7 기술 지원		✓

어휘 look for 찾다 | convenient 편리한, 간편한 | chart 표 | quickly 재빨리 | compare 비교하다 | available 이용 가능한 | feature 특징, 특성 | fully 완전히 | customizable 주문 제작 가능한 | site 사이트 | built-in 붙박이의, 내장된 | processing 처리 | monthly 월간의 | analytics 분석 | password 비밀번호 | encryption 암호화 | user 이용자 | unlimited 무제한의 | storage 저장 | 24/7 연중무휴의 | technical 기술적인 | support 지원

5. 표에서 설명하는 것은?

(A) 고객 후기

(B) 특징 비용

(C) 개발 단계별 일정

(D) 플랜 비교

해설 첫 번째 단락에서 저희가 제공하는 플랜을 빠르게 비교해 볼 수 있는 간편한 표가 있다고 하면서 표에서 기본 및 프리미엄 간 특징을 비교하고 있으므로 (D) Plan comparisons가 정답이다.

6. 기본 옵션에 관하여 사실이 아닌 것은?

(A) 이용자가 고객에 관한 데이터를 볼 수 있게 한다.

(B) 온라인 구매를 가능하게 한다.

(C) 언제나 기술 지원을 제공한다.

(D) 이용자를 위해 비밀번호를 보호한다.

해설 기본 플랜의 특징으로 신용 카드 및 직불 카드 처리 설치에서 (B), 월간 분석 보고서에서 (A), 이용자를 위한 비밀번호 암호화에서 (D)가 해당하지만, 24/7 기술 지원은 프리미엄 플랜에만 포함됨을 알 수 있으므로 (C) It offers technical assistance at any time.이 정답이다.

[7-9] 다음 전단에 관한 문제입니다.

이제 막 런던으로 이사 오셨나요?
런던 거주민 위원회가 주최하는
'런던은 당신을 환영합니다' 오리엔테이션에 참가하세요.
5월 25일, 오전 10:30 – 오후 2:30
런던 타임즈 광장
빅 벤 센터
누구나 참석 가능합니다

발표 일정	
오전 10:30	**7** 다니는 방법: 이용 가능한 대중교통 (101호)
오전 11:30	런던에서 집 구하기 (103호) / 쓰레기 관리 조언과 옵션 (104호)
오후 12:30	런던의 현지 은행 시스템 이해하기 (105호) / 런던에서 현지 사업 창업하기 (104호)
오후 1:30	**7** 런던에서 할 것, 주민 모임과 오락 시설 안내 (101호)

두 행사가 같은 시간에 진행될 수도 있으니, 참석자들은 가장 관심이 있는 행사를 선택해야 합니다. **7** 게다가, 오락과 대중교통 세션에 대한 관심들이 높기 때문에 빨리 오셔서 자리를 확보하셔야 한다는 점을 유념하시기 바랍니다.

8 모든 발표는 영어로 진행되지만, 한국어, 스페인어, 프랑스어 팸플릿들이 준비되어 있습니다. 다과는 구매하실 수 있습니다.

9 마지막 발표 후에, 참가자들은 한 시간 동안 가이드가 안내하는 런던 시내 관광에 참여하실 수 있습니다. 이 무료 관광은 장기간 활동한 위원회 회원과 런던 거주민에 의해 제공됩니다.

이 행사와 관련하여 더 많은 정보를 원하면, www.welcometolondon.co.uk을 방문해 주시기 바랍니다.

어휘 **attend** 참석하다 | **host** 개최하다, 주최하다 | **resident** 거주자, 주민 | **open** 열려 있는 | **get around** 돌아다니다 | **public transportation** 대중교통 | **housing** 주택 | **waste** 폐기물, 쓰레기 | **advice** 조언, 충고 | **comprehend** 이해하다 | **local** 지역의, 현지의 | **gathering** 모임 | **facility** 시설 | **choose** 선택하다 | **match** 어울리다, 맞다 | **interest** 관심, 흥미 | **in addition** 게다가 | **aware** 자각하고 있는 | **due to ~** 때문에 | **secure** 얻어 내다, 확보하다 | **refreshments** 다과 | **provide** 제공하다 | **following** 그 다음의 | **participant** 참석자 | **join** 함께하다, 가입하다 | **detail** 세부 사항 | **regarding** ~에 관해 | **committee** 위원회 | **upcoming** 다가오는

7. 가장 인기 있는 발표는 어디서 진행될 것인가?
(A) 101호에서
(B) 103호에서
(C) 104호에서
(D) 105호에서

해설 가장 인기 있는 발표에 대해 언급된 내용을 찾는다. 오락과 대중교통 세션에 대한 관심이 높으므로 자리 확보를 위해서는 일찍 와야 한다고 했는데 대중교통 관련 세션과 오락 관련 세션 모두 101호에서 진행함을 알 수 있으므로 정답은 (A) In Room 101이다.

8. 런던 거주민 위원회에 관하여 언급된 것은 무엇인가?
(A) 여러 언어로 자료를 제공한다.
(B) 새로운 서비스를 제공하기 시작할 것이다.
(C) 회비를 요구한다.
(D) 월간 행사를 주최한다.

해설 런던 거주민 위원회의 활동과 제공 서비스 등에 대한 정보에 주목한다. 여러 언어로 된 팸플릿을 제공한다고 했으므로 정답은 (A) It provides materials in several languages.이다.

9. 전단에 의하면, 참석자들이 발표 후에 할 수 있는 것은 무엇인가?
(A) 무료 음식과 음료를 즐긴다
(B) 다가오는 행사의 좌석을 예약한다
(C) 시내 관광을 한다
(D) 회원으로 등록한다

해설 발표 이후의 활동에 대해 언급된 것을 찾는다. 발표 이후에 참가자들은 가이드가 딸린 런던 시내 투어에 참가한다고 했으므로 정답은 (C) Go on a tour of the city이다.

UNIT 13. 이중 지문

핵심 문제 유형
본서 p.312

1. (A) **2.** (C) **3.** (A) **4.** (D) **5.** (B)

[1-5] 다음 이메일들에 관한 문제입니다.

수신: 고객 서비스⟨customerservice@georgetownelectric.com⟩
발신: 지니 시푸⟨j.syfu@speedmail.org⟩
날짜: 9월 15일
제목: **1** 청구서 발급 건

담당자께,

제 최근 전기 요금 청구서에 문제가 있는 듯합니다. 새로운 청구서를 받기 시작한 후로 저는 한 달에 50달러의 정액 전기료를 지불해 왔습니다. 하지만 지난달 청구서는 73달러였습니다. **2** 저는 전기요금을 절약하고자 정액 요금 서비스를 신청했습니다. **3** 그런데 이 청구서는 제 계약이 명시한 금액보다 23달러 높게 나왔습니다. **1** 이를 검토하시고 문제가 무엇인지 알려주세요.

감사합니다.

지니 시푸

어휘 electricity bill 전기 요금 청구서 | fixed rate 고정 금액, 정액 요금 | sign up for ~를 신청하다 | contract 계약(서) | look into ~을 검토하다 | call attention to ~에 ~의 주의를 환기시키다

수신: 지니 시푸〈j.syfu@speedmail.org〉
발신: 고객 서비스〈customerservice@georgetownelectric.com〉
날짜: 9월 16일
제목: 회신: 청구서 발급 건

친애하는 시푸 씨에게,

이 문제에 대해 저희에게 연락을 주셔서 감사합니다. 지난달 고객님의 청구서에 정말로 실수가 있었다는 사실이 조사에서 밝혀졌습니다. 고객님이 말씀하신 대로 고객님 메시지에 언급된 금액만큼 초과 청구되었습니다. **3** 저희는 이 실수를 수정했으며 나머지 금액은 다음 달 귀하의 청구서에 공제액으로 표시될 것입니다. 따라서 9월 귀하의 청구서는 27달러가 될 것입니다. 이 문제로 인해 야기된 모든 불편에 대해 사과드립니다. **5** 고객님께 더 보상해 드리기 위해, 10월 전력 사용에 대해 50퍼센트 할인을 해드리겠습니다.

저희 고객들이 높은 수준의 서비스를 받는다는 사실을 확인하기 위해, 이 문제의 해결안에 대해 **4** 간단한 설문조사 작성을 정중히 요청합니다. 고객님께서 이 링크로 방문하셔서 설문지를 작성하실 수 있습니다: www.georgetownelectric.com/customersurvey. 조지타운 전기회사의 단골 고객이 되어주셔서 감사드리며, 앞으로도 지속적인 이용을 기대합니다.

감사합니다.

존 베이츠
고객 서비스 담당
조지타운 전기회사

어휘 contact 연락하다 | regarding ~에 관하여 | matter 문제, 사항 | investigation 조사 | reveal 밝혀지다, 드러나다 | overcharge (금액을) 초과하여 청구하다 | amount 액수, 양, 총액 | indicated 표시된, 나타난 | correct 수정하다, 바로 잡다 | appear 나타나다 | apologize 사과하다 | inconvenience 불편, 애로사항 | compensate 보상하다 | further 더 | usage 사용량 | ensure 보장하다 | level 수준 | kindly 정중히 | request 요청하다 | survey 설문조사 | concerning ~에 관하여 | loyal customer 단골 고객 | look forward to ~하기를 고대한다 | continued 계속되는, 지속된 | business 거래 | in the future 미래에도 | renew 갱신하다 | fill out 기입하다, 작성하다 | questionnaire 설문지

1. 첫 번째 이메일의 목적은 무엇인가?
(A) 문제점을 환기시키기 위해
(B) 예약을 하기 위해
(C) 새로운 결제 방식을 알리기 위해
(D) 회사 방침을 설명하기 위해

해설 이메일 목적을 묻는 문제이다. 글의 목적은 제목이나 글의 앞부분 또는 맨 뒤에 제시된다. 이메일의 경우 제목(Subject:)을 확인해 본다.

제목은 '청구서 발급 건'이고, 이메일에서 이에 대한 문제를 제기하며 끝부분에서 문제를 빨리 해결해 달라고 요청하고 있으므로 정답은 (A) To call attention to a problem이다.

2. 시푸 씨에 대해 언급된 것은 무엇인가?
(A) 친구 중 한 명에게 조지타운 전기회사를 추천했다.
(B) 별도의 계정을 만들기를 원한다.
(C) 매달 같은 금액의 전기요금을 지불할 것을 기대한다.
(D) 조지타운 전기회사와의 계약을 취소했다.

해설 세부 사항을 묻는 문제이다. 시푸 씨가 키워드이므로 시푸 씨가 작성한 이메일에서 I로 언급된 부분과 선택지를 대조하며 소거한다. 친구에게 조지타운 전기회사를 추천했다는 언급이 없으므로 (A)를, 청구서 발급 전 문제를 해결해 줄 것을 요구했을 뿐이고 새로운 계정을 요청한 적은 없으므로 (B)를, 문제에 대한 시정을 요구했을 뿐이고 자신이 받는 서비스를 취소하겠다는 언급은 없으므로 (D)를 각각 소거 한다. 그녀는 정액제 요금 서비스에 가입되어 있으므로 매달 동일한 금액의 전기요금을 지불할 것을 기대하는 것이 타당하다. 따라서 정답은 (C) She expects to pay the same amount for electricity each month.이다.

3. 9월에 시푸 씨의 계정에는 얼마의 돈이 입금될 것인가?
(A) 23달러
(B) 27달러
(C) 50달러
(D) 73달러

해설 이중 지문 연계 유형 문제이다. 첫 번째 이메일에서는 23달러의 금액이 초과 청구되었다고 했고, 두 번째 이메일에서는 그 금액이 9월 청구서에 공제액으로 표시될 것이라고 했으므로 정답은 (A) $23이다.

4. 베이츠 씨는 시푸 씨에게 무엇을 하도록 권유하는가?
(A) 회계 사무실에 연락한다
(B) 그의 상사에게 연락한다
(C) 구독을 갱신한다
(D) 설문지를 작성한다

해설 세부 사항을 묻는 문제이다. 키워드 encourage가 지문에서 kindly request로 표현되고 있다. 두 번째 이메일의 세 번째 단락의 해결안에 대해 간단한 설문 조사 작성을 정중히 요청한다에서 베이츠 씨가 시푸 씨에게 간단한 설문조사에 응해 달라고 부탁하고 있으므로 정답은 (D) Fill out a questionnaire이다.

5. 베이츠 씨가 시푸 씨에게 제공한 것은 무엇인가?
(A) 한 달 무료 서비스
(B) 할인
(C) 잡지
(D) 새로운 전화기

해설 세부 사항을 묻는 문제이다. 키워드 offer가 지문에서 유사한 단어인 give로 패러프레이징되었다. 베이츠 씨가 시푸 씨에게 10월 전력 사용 요금을 50퍼센트 할인해 주겠다고 하므로 정답은 (B) A discount이다.

Practice

본서 p.314

1. (B)	2. (D)	3. (B)	4. (C)	5. (A)
6. (B)	7. (A)	8. (D)	9. (B)	10. (D)

[1-5] 다음 이메일들에 관한 문제입니다.

수신: hlawrence@jpcbank.com
발신: cwest@fleximail.com
날짜: 6월 12일
제목: 주택 수리 대출
첨부: @대출 신청서

안녕하세요,

저는 클리포드 웨스트이고, JPC 은행에 개인 대출을 신청하고자 메일을 드립니다. 설명서에 따라 작성한 대출 신청서 양식을 첨부해 드립니다.

1 보시면 아시겠지만, 저는 지난 5년간 자영업을 하며, 시장 조사 기관을 창업해 성공적으로 운영해 왔습니다. 매출액은 매년 증가했지만, 저는 항상 어떤 돈이든 사업에 다시 재투자하고 있습니다. **2** 하지만 내년에 주방을 수리해야 하는데, 선불로 대금을 지불할 자금이 충분치 않을 것 같아 대출을 신청합니다.

이 문제에 대해 함께 논의할 수 있다면 대단히 감사하겠습니다. **3** 제가 귀사의 온라인 예약 시스템을 통해 6월 23일로 회의를 요청했습니다. 이 날짜가 가능한지 여부를 확인해 주시겠어요?

감사합니다.

클리포드 웨스트

어휘 loan 대출 | application 신청(서) | attach 첨부하다 | complete 작성하다, 기입하다 | as per ~에 따라, 대로 | instruction 설명, 지시 | self-employed 자영업을 하는 | past 지난 | operate 운영하다, 경영하다 | successful 성공적인 | market research agency 시장 조사 기관 | start up 시작하다 | turnover 매출액 | rise 오르다 | re-invest 재투자하다 | apply for 신청하다 | renovate 보수하다 | enough 충분한 | on hand 구할 수 있는 | pay for 지불하다 | up front 선불로 | greatly 대단히 | appreciate 고마워하다 | request 요청하다 | via ~를 통해 | booking 예약 | confirm 확인하다 | available 이용 가능한

수신: cwest@fleximail.com
발신: hlawrence@jpcbank.com
날짜: 6월 25일
제목: 추가 조치 필요

웨스트 씨께,

귀하의 대출 신청 상담을 하러 와 주셔서 감사합니다. **3** 요청하신 날짜보다 하루 일찍 오시게 해서 다시 한번 사과의 말씀 드립니다. 그로 인해 생겨난 문제가 많지 않으셨기를 바랍니다.

귀하의 대출이 거의 마무리되었음을 알려드리게 되어 기쁩니다. **4** 하지만 회의 때 논의한 것처럼, 다음 항목을 발송해 주시기 바랍니다: 1) 지난 세 달간 은행 입출금 내역, 2) 귀하 사업체의 작년도 현금 흐름표, 3) 운전 면허증이나 여권 스캔본, 4) 수정된 대출 신청서 서명본.

저희가 6월 29일까지 이 서류를 받을 수 있으면, 도움이 될 것 같습니다. 그런 다음 저희가 귀하의 대출을 승인할 수 있습니다. **5** 요청하신 총금액이 귀하께 이체되며, 대출금은 약정 이율로 매월 분할하여 상환하시게 됩니다.

진심으로,

휴 로렌스
대출 담당자, JPC 은행

어휘 further 추가의 | action 조치 | apologize 사과하다 | cause 야기하다 | nearly 거의 | finalize 완결하다, 마무리 짓다 | send in 발송하다 | bank statement 입출금 내역 | cashflow statement 현금 흐름표 | sign 서명하다 | amend 수정하다 | approve 승인하다 | amount 총액 | transfer 이체하다, 옮기다 | repay 상환하다 | monthly 월간의 | installment 분할 불입(금) | agreed-upon 합의된, 약정한 | interest rate 이자율, 이율

1. 웨스트 씨에 관하여 언급된 것은?
   (A) 투자 은행가로 일한다.
   (B) 자기 사업을 운영한다.
   (C) 최근 직장을 옮겼다.
   (D) 은행에 근무한다.

해설 첫 번째 이메일, 두 번째 단락에서 보시면 아시겠지만, 지난 5년간 자영업을 하며, 시장 조사 기관을 창업해 성공적으로 운영해 왔다고 했으므로 (B) He runs his own business.가 정답이다.

2. 웨스트 씨는 왜 은행 대출을 신청하는가?
   (A) 지붕을 교체하려고
   (B) 차고를 지으려고
   (C) 난방기를 설치하려고
   (D) 주방을 수리하려고

해설 첫 번째 이메일, 두 번째 단락에서 내년에 주방을 수리해야 하는데, 선불로 대금을 지불할 자금이 충분치 않을 것 같아 대출을 신청한다고 했으므로 (D) To renovate a kitchen이 정답이다.

3. 웨스트 씨는 언제 로렌스 씨와 만났는가?
   (A) 6월 12일에
   (B) 6월 22일에
   (C) 6월 23일에
   (D) 6월 29일에

해설 클리포드 웨스트가 보낸 이메일, 세 번째 단락에서 제가 귀사의 온라인 예약 시스템을 통해 6월 23일로 회의를 요청했다고 했는데, 휴 로렌스가 보낸 이메일, 첫 번째 단락에서 요청하신 날짜보다 하루 일찍 오시게 해서 다시 한번 사과의 말씀 드린다고 했으므로 (B) On June

22가 정답이다.

---

4. 로렌스 씨는 웨스트 씨가 무엇을 해야 한다고 언급하는가?
(A) 회의를 준비해야 한다고
(B) 신규 카드를 신청해야 한다고
(C) 몇몇 서류를 보내야 한다고
(D) 집의 사진을 제출해야 한다고

해설 휴 로렌스가 보낸 이메일, 두 번째 단락에서 회의 때 논의한 것처럼, 다음 항목을 발송해 달라고 했으므로 (C) Send some documents 가 정답이다.

---

5. 두 번째 이메일에서 웨스트 씨의 대출에 관하여 알 수 있는 것은?
(A) 로렌스가 논의했던 이자율이 될 것이다.
(B) 여러 차례에 걸쳐 웨스트 씨에게 이체될 것이다.
(C) 대출을 보증해줄 사람을 요구할 것이다.
(D) 웨스트 씨가 요청한 것보다 더 높은 금액이 될 것이다.

해설 휴 로렌스가 보낸 이메일, 세 번째 단락에서 요청하신 총금액이 귀하께 이체되며, 대출금은 약정 이율로 매월 분할하여 상환하시게 된다고 하여 이자율에 대한 논의가 이루어졌음을 알 수 있으므로 (A) It will have the interest rate that Mr. Lawrence discussed.가 정답이다.

[6-10] 다음 이메일과 티켓에 관한 문제입니다.

수신: gordon.burgess@whereitout.com
발신: monica.kim@countent.com
날짜: 4월 14일
제목: 회신: 몇 가지 제안

버기스 씨께,

6 9 저희 작업장에 주문하신 물건을 가지러 오겠다고 제안해 주셔서 정말 감사합니다. 항공이나 열차 수송으로 발생하는 비용까지 지불하겠다고 하셨지만, 저는 귀하의 주문을 제가 직접 가든 하이츠로 배달해 드리고 싶습니다. **7** 때마침 제가 베이 파인즈에서 열리는 무역 박람회에 참석하러 그쪽으로 갈 예정이라 저에게는 전혀 부담되는 일이 아닙니다. 그곳으로 가는 길에 제가 귀하의 댁에 들러 주문하신 물건을 문 앞에 놓아 드릴 수 있습니다.

고객 만족은 제 사업에서 중심을 차지합니다. 저는 상당히 파손되기 쉬운 물품을 다루기에 운송 과정이 꽤 어려울 수 있습니다. 파손된 물품을 받아 언짢아하신 고객에 대한 경험이 너무 많았습니다. **8** 제 경험으로 볼 때, 지상이나 해상 운송 회사 모두 자체 사정이 있지만, 둘 다 흡족하지 않은 것 같습니다. 그래서 저는 제가 자청해서 수많은 제품을 직접 가져다드려 왔습니다.

저는 4월 27일에 가든 하이츠에 도착할 예정입니다. 그 날짜에 임박하여 다시 한번 메시지를 드려 제가 몇 시에 도착할 예정인지 알려 드리겠습니다.

진심으로,
모니카 김
카운텐트

어휘 suggestion 제안, 의견 | order 주문(품) | workshop 작업장 | pay 지불하다 | cost 비용 | incur (비용을) 발생시키다 |

transport 수송 | prefer 선호하다 | personally 직접, 개인적으로 | deliver 배달하다 | burden 부담, 짐 | happen to 우연히 ~하다 | head 향하다 | attend 참석하다 | trade show 무역 박람회 | stop by 들르다 | drop off 두고 가다 | satisfaction 만족 | deal with 다루다 | fragile 부서지기 쉬운 | transportation 수송 | damaged 파손된 | ground 지상 | courier 택배 회사 | sufficient 충분한, 흡족한 | take it upon oneself 자청하다

---

10 파인래스 철도 서비스

발행일: 4월 21일
승객명: 모니카 김

10 승강장 번호: 17

파크 폴즈 출발: 4월 27일 금요일 오전 10시 25분
10 가든 하이츠 도착: 4월 27일 금요일 오후 2시 5분

수하물: 여행용 가방(중) 1개, **9** 조각품 1개 (100cm x 30cm)

총 요금: 45달러

파인래스 철도 서비스를 선택해 주셔서 감사합니다. 즐거운 여행되십시오.

어휘 railway 철도 | issuance 발행 | passenger 승객 | platform (기차역) 승강장, 플랫폼 | depart 출발하다 | baggage 수하물 | suitcase 여행용 가방 | sculpture 조각품 | fare 요금

---

6. 이메일의 목적은 무엇인가?
(A) 불만을 제기하는 것
(B) 계획을 확정하는 것
(C) 신규 주문을 받는 것
(D) 배송일을 변경하는 것

해설 첫 번째 이메일, 첫 번째 단락에서 작업장에 주문하신 물건을 가지러 오겠다고 제안해 주셨지만 귀하의 주문을 제가 직접 가든 하이츠로 배달해 드리고싶다고 했으므로 (B) To confirm a plan이 정답이다.

---

7. 김 씨는 왜 배이 파인즈로 이동할 예정인가?
(A) 행사에 참석하려고
(B) 지원자를 면접하려고
(C) 친구를 방문하려고
(D) 물품을 배송하려고

해설 김 씨가 보낸 이메일, 첫 번째 단락에서 베이 파인즈에서 열리는 무역 박람회에 참석하러 그쪽으로 갈 예정이라고 했으므로 (A) To attend an event가 정답이다.

---

8. 이메일에서 언급된 것은?
(A) 버기스 씨는 전에 카운텐트에서 주문한 적이 있다.
(B) 버기스 씨는 철도 회사를 운영한다.

(C) 김 씨는 온라인 주문만 받는다.

(D) 김 씨는 어느 택배 회사에도 만족하지 않는다.

해설 첫 번째 이메일, 두 번째 단락에서 지상이나 해상 운송 회사 모두 자체 사정이 있지만, 둘 다 흡족하지 않아 수많은 제품을 직접 가져다 드렸다고 했으므로 (D) Ms. Kim is not satisfied with any courier services.가 정답이다.

---

9. 버기스 씨에 관하여 무엇이 사실이겠는가?

(A) 학회에서 김 씨를 만날 것이다.

(B) 최근 조각품을 구입했다.

(C) 주문을 배송받기 위해 요금을 지불했다.

(D) 업무상 출장을 자주 간다.

해설 버기스 씨에게 보내는 이메일, 첫 번째 단락에서 저희 작업장에 주문하신 물건을 가지러 오겠다고 제안해 주셔서 정말 감사하다고 했고, 두 번째 지문[티켓]의 수하물 항목에서 조각품 1개라고 했으므로 (B) He recently purchased a sculpture.가 정답이다.

---

10. 김 씨는 4월 27일에 가든 하이츠로 어떻게 이동할 예정인가?

(A) 비행기로

(B) 자동차로

(C) 배로

(D) 기차로

해설 두 번째 지문[티켓]에서 제목에 '파인래스 철도 서비스, 가든 하이츠 도착: 4월 27일, 승강장 번호: 17'이라고 되어 있으므로 (D) By train이 정답이다.

UNIT 14. 삼중 지문

핵심 문제 유형

본서 p.320

1. (B)   2. (A)   3. (B)   4. (B)   5. (C)

[1-5] 다음 광고, 온라인 양식, 그리고 이메일에 관한 문제입니다.

챈들러 미술 학교

당신은 자유 시간에 스케치를 하거나 그림을 그리거나 다른 종류의 미술 작품을 만드는 것을 즐깁니까? 아마도 당신은 더 개발할 필요가 있는 미술 **1** 소질을 지니고 있을 수도 있습니다. 또는 어쩌면 당신은 단지 미술에 대해 배우고 싶을 것입니다. 그러시다면, 당신은 챈들러 미술 학교의 수업을 듣는 것을 고려해 보세요.

챈들러 미술 학교는 현재 가을 학기 지원서를 받고 있습니다. 각 수업은 3달 동안 진행되고, 일주일에 한두 번 만납니다. 당신의 바쁜 일정을 수용하기 위해, **2** 수업은 월요일부터 토요일까지 아침과 오후 저녁에 이용 가능합니다. 다음은 우리의 가장 인기 있는 몇몇 수

업들입니다. 전체 목록을 보시려면, chandlerfa.com/fallschedule을 방문하세요.

강의명	강의 번호	강사
유화 입문	53	팀 헤이븐
조각에 관한 모든 것	44	리사 아츠
3 고급 수채화	87	마리아 고메즈
5 르네상스 화가처럼 그림 그리는 법	42	**5** 엔리코 에코

학기는 9월 2일에 시작합니다. **3** 모든 수업은 비용이 250달러이지만 일부 수업은 추가 재료비가 있습니다.

어휘 fine arts 미술 | artwork 미술품 | aptitude 소질, 적성 | perhaps 어쩌면, 아마 | currently 현재 | semester 학기 | last 지속하다 | the following 다음, 아래 | popular 인기 있는 | listing 목록 | instructor 강사 | oil painting 유화 (그림, 화법) | sculpture 조각품, 조각, 조소 | watercolor painting 수채화 | cost 비용이 들다 비용 | material 재료, 자료

챈들러 미술 학교
온라인 등록 신청서

이름: 프레드 토마스

주소: W. 톰슨 가 45번지, 챈들러, 애리조나 85214

전화번호: 393-2396

이메일 주소: fred_t@privatemail.com

날짜: 8월 27일

강의(들):

강의명	강의 번호	비용
회화의 역사	31	250달러
고급 수채화	87	**3** 315달러

지불 방법:

4 현금 [✓]   수표 [ ]   신용카드 [ ]

챈들러 미술 학교에 등록해 주셔서 감사합니다. 당신은 24시간 이내에 확인 이메일을 받게 될 것입니다.

어휘 registration 등록 | history 역사 | advanced 고급의, 발전된 | watercolor painting 수채화 | cash 현금 | check 수표 | register 등록하다 | confirmation 확인

수신: 프레드 토마스 〈fred_t@privatemail.com〉

발신: 티나 포웰 〈tpowell@chandlerfa.com〉

날짜: 8월 28일

제목: 등록

토마스 씨에게,

챈들러 미술 학교 수업에 등록해 주셔서 감사합니다. 저희는 저희 학교에 신입생들을 맞이하게 되어 항상 기쁩니다.

저는 귀하의 시간표에 한 가지 변경 사항이 있음을 알려드리고 싶습니다. 귀하는 강의 번호 31번 **5** 회화의 역사에 등록하셨습니다.

5 그 수업의 강사가 바뀌었습니다. 카르멘 후퍼 씨는 더 이상 그 과목을 가르치지 않을 것입니다. **5** 대신 엔리코 에코 씨가 강의할 것입니다. 그는 재능 있는 강사라서 저는 귀하가 그에게서 배우는 것을 즐기시리라 확신합니다.

늦어도 수업이 있는 첫 번째 주의 말까지 수업료를 전액 지불하셔야 한다는 점을 유의하시기 바랍니다.

감사합니다.

티나 포웰
챈들러 미술 학교

어휘 welcome 맞이하다, 환영하다 | institute 기관, 협회, 학원 | talented 재능 있는 | positive 확신하는, 긍정적인 | in full 완전히, 전부

---

1. 광고 글에서, 첫 번째 단락 두 번째 줄의 'aptitude'와 의미상 가장 가까운 것은

(A) 욕망

(B) 재능

(C) 관심

(D) 분위기

해설 동의어 찾기 문제이다. aptitude는 '소질, 적성'이라는 뜻으로 의미상 가장 가까운 단어는 talent '재능'이다. 따라서 정답은 (B) talent이다.

---

2. 챈들러 미술 학교의 수업들에 대해서 사실인 것은 무엇인가?

(A) 하루 종일 열린다.

(B) 자리가 빨리 마감된다.

(C) 전문 예술가들이 수업을 가르친다.

(D) 수업들은 숙련된 개인들에게만 열린다.

해설 첫 번째 광고 지문, 두 번째 단락을 보면 수업이 월요일부터 토요일까지 하루 종일 진행된다는 사실을 알 수 있다. 정답은 (A) They are held throughout the day.이다.

---

3. 강의 번호 87번에 관하여 언급된 것은 무엇인가?

(A) 지역 미술가가 가르친다.

(B) 학생들은 제공품에 추가 비용을 지불해야 한다.

(C) 오후에 수업이 있다.

(D) 제한된 수의 학생들이 수강할 수 있다.

해설 사실 확인 유형의 문제이면서 두 개의 지문을 연계해서 봐야 답을 찾을 수 있는 문제이다. 키워드 class number 87이 지문에 나온 부분을 찾아본다. 온라인 등록 신청서에 강의 번호 87번은 수강료가 315달러이다. 첫 번째 지문인 광고 말미에 모든 강좌의 수업료는 동일하게 250달러이지만 일부 과목에 재료비가 추가될 수 있다고 하였으므로 정답은 (B) Students must pay extra for supplies.이다.

---

4. 토마스 씨는 수업료를 어떻게 지불하고자 하는가?

(A) 수표로

(B) 현금으로

(C) 신용카드로

(D) 은행 이체로

해설 세부 사항을 묻는 문제이다. 온라인 등록 신청서 마지막 부분에서 원하는 지불 방식으로 cash에 체크를 했으므로 정답은 (B) With cash 이다.

---

5. 에코 씨에 관하여 알 수 있는 것은 무엇인가?

(A) 다음 학기에 은퇴할 것이다.

(B) 수십 년간 가르쳐왔다.

(C) 한 과정 이상을 가르칠 것이다.

(D) 학생들 사이에서 인기가 많다.

해설 신청서를 통해 프레드 토마스가 등록한 과정은 31번(회화의 역사)과 87번(고급 수채화)임을 알 수 있는데, 이메일 두 번째 단락에서 '회화의 역사' 강사가 변경되었다고 하면서 새 강사로 엔리코 에코를 소개하고 있다. 광고를 보면 시간표에 강사 엔리코 에코가 가르치는 강의명이 '르네상스 화가처럼 그림 그리는 법'이므로 엔리코 에코가 두 과목을 강의할 거란 사실을 알 수 있다. 따라서 정답은 (C) He will teach more than one course.이다.

Practice
본서 p.322

1. (D)	2. (A)	3. (C)	4. (C)	5. (A)
6. (B)	7. (A)	8. (B)	9. (D)	10. (D)

[1-5] 다음 안내판들과 후기에 관한 문제입니다.

오피스 딜라이트
----
129 오넬 거리, 이브아르, 나뮈르
0482 555 9302

인기 서비스:
복사, 인쇄, 스캔, 코팅, 명함, 데이터 복구, 기술 지원

1 운영 시간

월요일	폐점
화요일	오전 8시 – 오후 8시
수요일	오전 7시 – 오후 9시
3 목요일	오전 8시 – 오후 8시
금요일	오전 8시 – 오후 9시
토요일	오전 7시 – 오후 7시
일요일	오전 7시 – 오후 5시

어휘 popular 인기 있는 | hours of operation 운영 시간 | photocopy 복사하다 | print 인쇄하다 | laminate 코팅하다 | business card 명함 | recovery 회복, 복구 | tech 기술상의 | support 지원

100% 진짜 가죽, 수제, 장인이 만든 지갑

제품	모델	유로	달러
마하나니 (검정색)	2648 (정사각형)	68.98	71.36
메그나 (갈색)	2535 (직사각형)	82.98	85.85
4 탑티 (베이지색)	2722 (정사각형)	106.98	110.68

어휘 genuine 진짜의 | leather 가죽 | artisan 장인, 공예가 |
wallet 지갑 | square 정사각형 | rectangle 직사각형 |
brown 갈색

---

https://www.travelforbiz.com
여행 후기

실페스타 딕슨 작성

등급: ★★★★★
7월 16일

벨기에 방문은 처음이었고, 저는 학회 참석차 나뮈르에 있었습니다. **2** 저는 비행기에서 내리자마자 핸드폰 충전기를 집에 놓고 온 것을 알아챘습니다. 재빨리 제가 찾을 수 있는 가장 가까운 사무용품점으로 달려갔는데, 그곳이 오피스 딜라이트였습니다. **3** 다행히 목요일 밤에도 문이 열려 있었고, 저는 정확히 폐장 시간에 도착했어요. 그곳 직원들은 아주 친절하고 상냥했으며 저에게 다양한 핸드폰 충전기를 보여줬습니다. 저는 나가는 길에 거기서 팔고 있는 수제 지갑을 우연히 발견했어요. **4** 심플하지만 효과적인 디자인 때문에 제 시선을 사로잡았고, 품질이 아주 좋아 보였어요. 저는 결국 탑티를 선택했습니다. **5** 계산하는 동안 사장님이 지갑 디자이너가 여행광이고 자신이 방문한 강의 이름을 따서 제품의 이름을 지었다고 말해줬어요. 그 지역에 가게 되면 오피스 딜라이트에 방문해서 직접 살펴보기를 강력 추천합니다!

어휘 rating 평가, 등급 | realize 깨닫다 | leave 두고 오다 | charger 충전기 | quickly 재빨리 | rush 급히 서두르다 | closest 가장 가까운 | office supply 사무용품 | thankfully 다행스럽게도 | exactly 정확히 | friendly 우호적인, 친절한 | show 보여주다 | a range of 다양한 | happen to 우연히 ~하다 | come across 우연히 발견하다 | sell 팔다 | yet 그렇지만 | effective 효과적인 | quality 질 | amazing 놀라운 | end up -ing 결국 ~하다 | go with 고르다 | check out 계산하다 | owner 주인 | avid 열렬한 | traveler 여행자 | name after ~를 따서 이름 짓다 | river 강 | highly 매우 | recommend 추천하다

1. 첫 번째 안내판에서 오피스 딜라이트에 관해 언급한 것은?
(A) 장비 대여 서비스를 제공한다.
(B) 호텔 옆에 위치한다.
(C) 나뮈르 전역에 매장이 여러 개 있다.
(D) 주 6일 영업한다.

해설 첫 번째 안내판, 운영 시간에서 월요일 폐점을 제외하고 다른 요일에는 모두 운영한다고 했으므로 (D) It operates six days a week.가 정답이다.

2. 딕슨 씨는 왜 오피스 딜라이트에 방문했는가?
(A) 깜빡하고 안 가져온 장비를 대체하려고
(B) 동료에게 이메일을 보내려고
(C) 불량품을 수리하려고
(D) 학회용 전단을 스캔하려고

해설 세 번째 지문에서 비행기에서 내리자마자 핸드폰 충전기를 집에 놓고 온 것을 알아챘고, 찾을 수 있는 가장 가까운 사무용품점으로 달려갔는데, 그곳이 오피스 딜라이트였다고 했으므로 (A) To replace equipment he forgot to bring이 정답이다.

3. 딕슨 씨는 언제 오피스 딜라이트에 도착했는가?
(A) 오전 7시
(B) 오전 8시
(C) 오후 8시
(D) 오후 9시

해설 세 번째 지문[후기]에서 다행히 목요일 밤에도 문이 열려 있었고, 정확히 폐장 시간에 도착했다고 했는데, 첫 번째 지문[첫 번째 안내판], 운영 시간에서 목요일 오전 8시 – 오후 8시라고 했으므로 (C) At 8:00 P.M.이 정답이다.

4. 딕슨 씨가 구입한 지갑에 관하여 언급된 것은?
(A) 모델번호 26480이다.
(B) 직사각형이다.
(C) 베이지색이다.
(D) 매장에서 가장 저렴한 제품이다.

해설 세 번째 지문[후기]에서 심플하지만 효과적인 디자인과 품질이 좋아 보여서 탑티를 선택했고 두 번째 지문[두 번째 안내판]에서 Tapti '베이지색'이라고 했으므로 (C) It is beige.가 정답이다.

5. 후기에 따르면 각 지갑은 무엇의 이름을 따서 지어졌는가?
(A) 강
(B) 도시
(C) 숲
(D) 호수

해설 세 번째 지문[후기]에서 사장님이 지갑 디자이너가 여행광이고 자신이 방문한 강의 이름을 따서 제품의 이름을 지었다고 말해줬다고 했으므로 (A) A river가 정답이다.

[6-10] 다음 일정표, 이메일, 광고에 관한 문제입니다.

〈홈 어디션즈〉 용 이니오스마트 포토그래피 촬영 일정표

날짜 및 장소	프로젝트	내용
3월 9일 수요일 태부키 웍스 스튜디오	벽에 페인트칠하기	페인트칠 방법 사진
3월 11일 금요일 홈 어디션즈 작업장	목재 측정 및 절단	목재 절단 도구 및 과정을 보여주는 사진
6 3월 15일 화요일 킨 호텔	**6** 벽에 난 구멍 보수하기	플라워즈 씨가 킨 호텔에 난 구멍을 수리하는 사진
3월 17일 목요일 홈 어디션즈 작업장	카펫에 관한 모든 것	카펫 오염 없애는 사진
3월 21일 월요일 델코 커뮤니티 센터	정원 가꾸기	플라워즈 씨가 식물 관리 방법을 보여 주는 사진

7 3월 24일 목요일	가구 복원하기	복원 전후 가구 사진
이니오스마트 스튜디 오 3호실		

어휘 photography 사진 촬영 | schedule 일정 | venue 장소 | paint 페인트를 칠하다 | wall 벽 | photo 사진 | technique 기법, 기술 | measure 측정하다, 재다 | cut 자르다 | wood 목 재 | show 보여주다 | tool 도구 | process 과정, 절차 | fix 수리하다, 고치다 | hole 구멍 | carpet 카펫 | clean 청소하다, 닦다 | stain 오염 | tend to 돌보다, 보살피다 | restore 회복 시키다, 복원하다 | furniture 가구 | restoration 복원

수신: ethel_flowers@tinkermail.com
발신: n.barber@iniosmart.com
날짜: 3월 14일
제목: 〈홈 어디션즈〉 도서용 최종 사진 촬영

플라워즈 씨께,

7 **8** 〈홈 어디션즈〉용 촬영 일정에 막바지 조정이 있었음을 알려 드리게 되어 대단히 죄송합니다. 저희 스튜디오에서 3월 24일에 귀 하의 가구 사진을 촬영할 예정이었습니다. 하지만 저희는 지속되는 조명 문제를 고치기 위해 해당 공간에 수리가 필요하다는 통보를 받 았습니다. 4월에야 공사가 시작되기 때문에 이 촬영을 거기서 계속 할 수 없습니다. **9** 11월 29일인 출간일에 맞추려면 3월 24일까지 전체 사진이 필요하실 테니, 제가 태부키 웍스측에 그 날짜에 스튜 디오를 사용할 수 있는지 문의해 놓았습니다. 저희가 그곳에 모든 장비를 설치하고 필요한 촬영을 하는 데는 문제되지 않을 겁니다.

태부키 웍스의 주인에게 회신이 오면 필요한 모든 내용을 알려드리 겠습니다.

불편을 끼쳐드려 다시 한번 사과드립니다.

노먼 바버
이니오스마트 포토그래피

어휘 final 마지막의 | last minute 막판의 | adjustment 조정, 수정 | shoot 촬영하다 사진 촬영 | shot 사진 | undergo 겪다 | repair 수리 | persistent 끊임없이 지속되 는, 끈질긴 | lighting 조명 | continue 계속하다 | meet 맞추 다 | launch 출시 | set up 설치하다 | equipment 장비 | owner 소유자, 주인 | get back to ~에게 회신 연락하다 | necessary 필요한 | apology 사과 | inconvenience 불편

---

9 《홈 어디션즈》 도서 출간 행사
9 11월 29일 오후 7시
10 델코 룸, 리버티 홀
39 에크톤 가, 에딘보로

● **10** 저자 에델 플라워즈와의 질의응답 시간을 즐기세요.
● 《홈 어디션즈》를 한 부 구입하시고 플라워즈 씨에게 사인을 받으 세요.

● 플라워즈 씨가 특별히 고른 다양한 도구를 시험해 보세요.
● 다과 및 음료가 제공됩니다.

더 자세한 내용을 알아보시거나 행사 자리를 예약하시려면 조이 샌 티애고에게 348-555-6483로 연락 주십시오.

어휘 launch 출시 | Q&A session 질의응답 시간 | author 저자 | purchase 구입하다 | sign 서명하다 | test 시험하다 | a range of 다양한 | specially 특별히 | pick out 고르다, 선발하다 | refreshment 다과 | reserve 예약하다

---

6. 어떤 프로젝트가 3월 15일에 촬영됐는가?
(A) 정원 가꾸기
(B) 벽에 난 구멍 보수하기
(C) 벽에 페인트칠하기
(D) 가구 복원하기

해설 첫 번째 지문[일정표]에서 3월 15일 프로젝트에 '벽에 난 구멍 보수하 기'라고 했으므로 (B) Fixing holes in walls가 정답이다.

---

7. 어떤 장소에서 촬영 일정이 취소되었는가?
(A) 이니오스마트 스튜디오 3호실
(B) 태부키 웍스
(C) 킨 호텔
(D) 델코 커뮤니티 센터

해설 두 번째 지문[이메일], 첫 번째 단락에서 3월 24일에 귀하의 가구 사진 을 촬영할 예정이었으나, 지속되는 조명 문제를 고치기 위해 해당 공 간에 수리가 필요하다는 통보를 받았다고 했고 첫 번째 지문[일정표] 에서 3월 24일 촬영 장소가 이니오스마트 스튜디오 3호실임을 알 수 있으므로 (A) Iniosmart Studo 3이 정답이다.

---

8. 이메일에서 바버 씨는 어떤 문제를 언급했는가?
(A) 일부 직원이 도움을 줄 수 없다.
(B) 일부 보수가 실시되어야 할 것이다.
(C) 공간이 잘못 예약되었다.
(D) 장비 한 개가 없어졌다.

해설 두 번째 지문[이메일], 첫 번째 단락에서 지속되는 조명 문제를 고치기 위해 해당 공간에 수리가 필요하다는 통보를 받았다고 했으므로 (B) Some repairs will have to be conducted.가 정답이다.

---

9. 바버 씨에 관하여 결론 지을 수 있는 것은?
(A) 11월 29일 행사에 참석했다.
(B) 델코 룸에서 수리를 했다.
(C) 플라워즈 씨와 책을 공동 집필했다.
(D) 프로젝트 마감일에 맞출 수 있었다.

해설 두 번째 지문[이메일], 첫 번째 단락에서 11월 29일인 출간일에 맞추려 면 3월 24일까지 전체 사진이 필요하실 거라고 했는데, 세 번째 지문 [광고], 첫 번째 단락에서 11월 29일 오후 7시라고 하여 일정에 맞춰 진 행되었음을 알 수 있으므로 (D) He was able to meet a project's deadline.이 정답이다.

10. 델코 룸 행사 방문객은 무엇을 할 수 있을 것인가?

(A) 일부 특수 도구를 주문할 수 있을 것이다

(B) 일부 수업에 등록할 수 있을 것이다

(C) 실시간 시연에 참여할 수 있을 것이다

(D) 저자에게 질문을 할 수 있을 것이다

해설 세 번째 지문[광고], 첫 번째 단락에서 델코 룸, 리버티 홀이라고 했고, 두 번째 단락에서 저자 에델 플라워즈와의 질의응답 시간을 즐기라고 했으므로 (D) Ask an author some questions가 정답이다.

REVIEW TEST

본서 p.326

1. (B)	2. (C)	3. (A)	4. (C)	5. (B)
6. (C)	7. (A)	8. (C)	9. (A)	10. (D)
11. (B)	12. (C)	13. (D)	14. (C)	15. (B)
16. (A)	17. (C)	18. (C)	19. (B)	20. (D)
21. (B)	22. (A)	23. (B)	24. (D)	25. (B)
26. (A)	27. (C)	28. (C)	29. (D)	30. (D)
31. (A)	32. (C)	33. (C)	34. (B)	35. (C)
36. (A)	37. (B)	38. (C)	39. (A)	40. (C)
41. (B)	42. (C)	43. (A)	44. (D)	45. (C)
46. (A)	47. (B)	48. (D)	49. (B)	50. (B)
51. (C)	52. (A)	53. (D)	54. (D)	

[1-2] 다음 양식에 관한 문제입니다.

노스티모 레스토랑에 오신 것을 환영합니다!

높은 수요로 인해 저희는 예약제로 전환하였습니다. 아래에 인원수 및 성함을 적어 주시기 바랍니다. 저희가 이름을 부를 때 자리에 안 계시는 경우, 귀하의 일행을 목록에서 어쩔 수 없이 삭제해야 합니다. 기다리시는 동안 메뉴를 살펴보면서 음료를 주문하실 수 있습니다. **1** 메뉴는 레스토랑 앞쪽 창문에서 보실 수 있습니다. **2** 저희는 현금 결제 방식만 받는다는 점에 유의해 주세요. 감사합니다.

1. 매티 홀로웨이, 일행 3명
2. 파블로 콜맨, 일행 2명
3. 미리암 그레고리, 일행 4명
4. 진호 홍, 일행 2명
5. 신시아 젠슨, 일행 1명
6.
7.
8.
9.
10.

어휘 due to ~로 인해ㅣdemand 수요, 요구ㅣtransition 이행하다, 옮겨가다ㅣreservation 예약ㅣparty 일행ㅣbelow ~아래에ㅣcall 부르다ㅣbe forced to 어쩔 수 없이 ~하다ㅣremove 제거하다ㅣwait 기다리기ㅣlook through 살펴보다ㅣavailable 이용 가능한ㅣfront 앞쪽의ㅣnote 유념하다, 주

의하다ㅣaccept 수락하다ㅣpayment 지불ㅣform 형태ㅣcash 현금

1. 고객은 어디서 메뉴를 찾을 수 있는가?

(A) 입구 옆에 인쇄된 간판에서

(B) 앞쪽 창문에 올린 게시문에서

(C) 양식 가까이에 있는 의자 위에서

(D) 레스토랑 웹 사이트에서

해설 메뉴는 레스토랑 앞쪽 창문에서 보실 수 있다고 했으므로 (B) Posted on the front window가 정답이다.

2. 노스티모 레스토랑에 관하여 언급된 것은?

(A) 온라인 주문을 받지 않는다.

(B) 음료를 제공하지 않는다.

(C) 신용 카드를 받지 않는다.

(D) 점심 시간에는 운영하지 않는다.

해설 현금 결제 방식만 받는다는 점에 유의해 달라고 했으므로 (C) It does not accept credit cards.가 정답이다.

[3-4] 다음 안내문에 관한 문제입니다.

https://www.monetatimes.com

독자 편지 작성 지침

독자 편지란의 목적은 지역 사회 구성원에게 발언권을 드리는 것입니다. **3** 저희는 매 발행호에 7~10통 사이로 편지를 선정하며, 웹 사이트에 올리기 위해 추가로 10통을 더 선택합니다.

이상적으로는 저희가 수령하는 모든 편지를 인쇄하겠지만, 저희가 받는 분량으로 인해 이는 불가능합니다. 저희가 어느 것을 인쇄할 지 선정하는 데 적용하는 지침은 다음과 같습니다.

1. 바로 요점으로 들어가세요. 이상적으로는 편지 길이가 150자 미만이어야 합니다.
2. **4** 시사성을 유지하세요. 바로 전주에 모네타 타임즈에서 다룬 주제를 언급해야 합니다.
3. 전문 지식이나 자격증, 경력이 있는 분들의 의견을 환영합니다.

어휘 guideline 지침ㅣeditor 편집자ㅣpurpose 목적ㅣsection 부분ㅣvoice 목소리, 발언권ㅣcommunity 지역 사회ㅣselect 선택하다ㅣletter 글자ㅣprint 인쇄하다, 발행하다ㅣedition (간행물의) 호ㅣchoose 선택하다ㅣadditional 추가의ㅣpost 게시하다, 올리다ㅣideally 이상적으로ㅣvolume 양ㅣimpossible 불가능한ㅣquick 빠른ㅣcurrent 현재의ㅣissue 주제, 문제ㅣcover 다루다ㅣopinion 의견ㅣexpertise 전문 지식ㅣqualification 자격ㅣwork experience 경력ㅣwelcome 환영하는

3. 안내문에서는 독자 편지에 관하여 무엇을 언급하는가?

(A) 온라인에서 볼 수 있다.

(B) 실명으로 서명해야 한다.

(C) 그 분야 전문가가 작성해야 한다.

(D) 최소 글자수는 150자다.

해설 첫 번째 단락에서 매 발행호에 7-10통 사이로 편지를 선정하며, 웹 사이트에 올리기 위해 추가로 10통을 더 선택한다고 했으므로 (A) They are available online.이 정답이다.

------

4. 기사에 관한 의견을 보내는 권장 기한은 무엇인가?

(A) 1일

(B) 4일

(C) 7일

(D) 10일

해설 세 번째 단락, 2번에서 바로 전 주에 모네타 타임즈에서 다룬 주제를 언급해야 한다고 했으므로 (C) Seven days가 정답이다.

[5-7] 다음 광고에 관한 문제입니다.

파스칼 세일즈 시스템즈

파스칼 세일즈 시스템즈(PSS)가 간편하면서 직관적인 포스 기기로 당신의 결제 시스템을 단순하게 만들어드립니다. 당신의 상점에 PSS가 있으면, 고가의 판매 기기와 높은 거래 수수료의 부담을 내려놓을 수 있습니다. 저희 기기와 지원 팀의 도움을 이용하시면, 당신은 오로지 사업 운영에만 전념하고 결제는 저희가 처리해 드릴 수 있습니다.

저희 시스템은 여러 상을 수상했습니다. **5** 상점에서든, 웹 사이트로든, 전화를 통해서든 판매할 때, PSS는 상시 전문 기술 지식을 지원해 드리면서, 이를 간편한 과정으로 만들어 드립니다. 저희 기기는 **6D** 신용 카드용 칩 리더기를 비롯해 **6A** 수표용 내장 스캐너, **6B** 웹 결제 서비스용 모바일 앱까지 다양한 결제 형태를 수용하도록 만들어졌습니다.

저희 웹 사이트로 가셔서 양식을 작성하시어 PSS에 가입해 주세요. 양식을 제출하시면, 저희 팀에서 당신의 사업체에 관한 세부 정보를 수집하기 위해 연락을 드릴 것입니다. **7** 당신의 사업체에 대한 저희 승인이 완료되면, 환영 선물로 30일 동안 무료로 PSS를 이용해 보실 수 있습니다. 오늘 www.pascalsolutions.com를 방문하셔서 이 혜택을 누려 보세요!

어휘 **simplify** 단순화[간소화]하다 | **payment** 결제, 지불 | **intuitive** 직관적인, 사용하기 쉬운 | **point-of-sale** 포스의 (판매시점 정보 관리 시스템) | **device** 기기, 장치 | **burden** 부담, 짐 | **expensive** 값비싼 | **sale** 판매, 매출 | **transaction** 거래 | **fee** 수수료 | **focus on** ~에 주력하다 | **solely** 오로지 | **run** 운영하다 | **handle** 처리하다 | **recipient** 수령인 | **several** 몇몇의 | **award** 상 | **conduct** 실시하다 | **painless** 괴롭지[힘들지] 않은 | **process** 과정 | **support** 지원하다 | **24-7** 언제나, 24시간 7일 내내 | **technical** 기술적인 | **expertise** 전문 지식[기술] | **equip** 장비를 갖추다 | **accommodate** 수용하다 | **a variety of** 다양한 | **chip reader** 판독기 | **built-in** 내장된 | **scanner** 스캐너 | **check** 수표 | **mobile** 모바일의, 핸드폰의 | **app** 앱 | **ensure** 보장하다 | **miss** 놓치다 | **potential** 잠재적인 | **sign up for** ~에 가입하다, 등록하다 | **head to** ~로 향하다 |

fill out 기입하다, 작성하다 | **submit** 제출하다 | **gather** 모으다 | **detail** 세부 정보 | **welcoming** 환영하는 | **gift** 선물 | **approve** 승인하다 | **try out** 시험 삼아 이용해 보다 | **at no cost** 무료로 | **take advantage of** ~를 기회로 활용하다

5. 두 번째 단락, 세 번째 줄의 단어, 'supporting'과 의미상 가장 가까운 것은?

(A) 확인하다

(B) 도와주다

(C) 발전시키다

(D) 종속시키다

해설 두 번째 단락에서 상점에서든, 웹 사이트로든, 전화를 통해서든 판매를 할 때, PSS는 전문 기술 지식을 상시 지원해 드리면서 이를 괴롭지 않은 과정으로 만들어 드린다의 supporting은 '지원하다'라는 의미로 쓰였으므로 '도와주다'라는 의미를 전달하는 (B) backing이 정답이다.

------

6. 어떤 지불 방법이 광고에 언급되지 않는가?

(A) 수표

(B) 모바일 앱

(C) 현금

(D) 신용 카드

해설 지문의 단서와 보기를 매칭시키면, 두 번째 단락에서 수표용 내장 스캐너는 (A)와, 웹 결제 서비스용 모바일 앱은 (B)와, 신용 카드용 칩 리더기는 (D)와 일치하지만, 현금에 대한 내용은 언급된 바 없으므로 (C) Cash가 정답이다.

------

7. PSS에서 판촉 활동으로 무엇을 제공하고 있는가?

(A) 30일 무료 체험

(B) 새 노트북

(C) 무료 교육

(D) 기기 할인

해설 세 번째 단락에서 당신의 사업체에 대한 저희 승인이 완료되면, 환영 선물로 30일 동안 무료로 PSS를 이용해 보실 수 있다고 했으므로 (A) A thirty-day free trial이 정답이다.

[8-9] 다음 문자 메시지 대화에 관한 문제입니다.

켄 스트릭랜드 (오전 9시 03분)

8 그린 씨, 제가 얼마 전에 곧 있을 배구 토너먼트에 관한 문의를 몇 개 받았는데, 일부 세부 사항에 관해서 당신에게 물어봐야 할 것 같아요. 기금은 변함없이 공영 수영장에 쓰일 예정인가요?

캐샌드라 그린 (오전 9시 04분)

8 자금은 학교 방학 기간 동안 안전 요원을 고용하는 목적으로 공영 수영장에 사용될 예정이에요. 이때가 수영장이 가장 혼잡한 시기라, 안전 요원을 추가로 고용해서 아이들 증가를 감당해야 해요.

켄 스트릭랜드 (오전 9시 05분)

바람직한 자금 사용처네요. 토너먼트 우승자들은 트로피 같은 걸 받게 될까요?

캐샌드라 그린 (오전 9시 06분)
트로피 같은 건 없을 거예요. 하지만, 저희가 상을 마련하긴 해야 할 것 같아요. 특히 우승자들을 위해서요. 대단한 걸로 할 필요는 없어요. 예쁜 컵과 접시 정도요? **9** 선물 쇼핑 좀 해주실래요?

켄 스트릭랜드 (오전 9시 07분)
9 잠깐만요. 지역 사업체에서 사용할 쿠폰을 구입하는 건 어때요? 동시에 지역 경제를 지원할 수 있어요.

어휘 inquiry 문의 | recently 최근 | upcoming 곧 있을 | volleyball 배구 | tournament 경기, 토너먼트 | run ~ by ~ (의견을 구하기 위해) ~를 ~에게 물어보다 | detail 세부 사항 | fund 기금, 자금 | go towards ~에 쓰이다 | public 공공의 | swimming pool 수영장 | hire 고용하다 | lifeguard 안전 요원 | accommodate 수용하다 | increase 증가 | trophy 트로피 | prize 상 | especially 특히 | winner 우승자 | amazing 대단한 | plate 접시 | mind 꺼리다 | shop 사다, 쇼핑하다 | gift 선물 | hold that thought 잠시만요 | voucher 쿠폰, 바우처 | local 지역의 | business 사업체 | support 지원하다 | economy 경제 | at the same time 동시에

8. 배구 토너먼트에 관하여 알 수 있는 것은?
(A) 수영장 직원들에 대한 보상이다.
(B) 아이들을 위해 열릴 예정이다.
(C) 공영 시설을 위한 돈을 모금한다.
(D) 지역 주민들 사이에 열리는 연례 행사다.

해설 오전 9시 03분 ~ 9시 04분 대화에서 켄 스트릭랜드가 얼마 전에 곧 있을 배구 토너먼트에 관한 문의를 몇 개 받았는데, 기금은 변함없이 공영 수영장에 쓰일 예정인지 묻는 말에 캐샌드라 그린이 자금은 학교 방학 기간 동안 안전 요원을 고용하는 목적으로 공영 수영장에 사용될 예정이라고 했으므로 (C) It is raising money for a public facility.가 정답이다.

9. 오전 9시 07분에, 스트랙랜드 씨가 "잠깐만요"라고 할 때 무엇을 의미하겠는가?
(A) 그린 씨의 의견에 더 나은 대안이 있다고 믿는다.
(B) 너무 바빠서 요청을 들어줄 수 없다.
(C) 작년의 선물 아이디어가 더 마음에 든다.
(D) 날짜를 재고해야 한다고 생각한다.

해설 오전 9시 06분 ~ 9시 07분 대화에서 캐샌드라 그린이 선물 쇼핑을 해달라는 말에 켄 스트릭랜드가 지역 사업체에서 사용할 쿠폰을 구입하는 건 어떤지 말한 것이므로 (A) He believes he has a better alternative to Ms. Green's suggestion.이 정답이다.

[10-11] 다음 이메일에 관한 문제입니다.

발신: 플로라 엘리어트 〈felliott@advancenow.com〉
수신: 넬슨 살라자르 〈nsalazar@urushine.com〉
날짜: 5월 18일
제목: 교육 워크숍

살라자르 씨, 안녕하세요.

저희 어드밴스나우 교육 팀이 3월 25일 저희 사무실에서 교육 워크숍을 진행하기 위해 우루샤인 서포트 팀을 초청할 예정임을 확인해 드립니다. **11** 교육은 프레젠테이션으로 시작해 귀하의 팀에 전기 자동차의 흔한 문제를 진단 및 수리하는 최상의 방법을 가르쳐드립니다. 또한, 고액의 수리 청구서를 피하도록 고객에게 차량을 제대로 관리하는 법을 알려주는 데에 중점을 둘 예정입니다.

프레젠테이션 후에는 다뤘던 문제들 중 일부로 실습 활동이 진행됩니다. **10** 여러 그룹으로 나눠, 각 그룹에서 서로 다른 차량을 살펴보게 될 것입니다. 그 다음으로 그룹 구성원들이 함께 문제를 정확하게 진단하고 해결할 것입니다.

궁금한 점이 있으시면 저에게 알려 주세요.

진심으로,

플로라 엘리어트
어드밴스나우 회장

어휘 confirm 확인하다, 확정하다 | host 주최하다, 개최하다 | support 지원 | deliver 진행하다 | teach 가르치다 | diagnose 진단하다 | fix 고치다 | common 흔한, 공동의 | issue 문제 | electric vehicle 전기 자동차 | additionally 또한 | focus 집중, 초점 | take care of 돌보다, 관리하다 | proper 제대로 된, 적절한 | avoid 피하다 | expensive 비싼 | bill 청구서 | be followed by ~로 이어지다 | hands-on 직접 해 보는 | activity 활동 | divide 나누다 | correctly 정확하게

10. 설명된 교육 워크숍의 특징은 무엇인가?
(A) 화상 회의
(B) 공장 견학
(C) 고객 미팅
(D) 단체 활동

해설 두 번째 단락에서 여러 그룹으로 나눠, 각 그룹에서 서로 다른 차량을 살펴보게 될 것이라고 했으므로 (D) A group activity가 정답이다.

11. 우루샤인에 관하여 무엇이 사실이겠는가?
(A) 전자 기기를 제조한다.
(B) 자동차 수리 서비스를 제공한다.
(C) 고객의 주택 수리를 도와준다.
(D) 사무용 가구를 판매한다.

해설 첫 번째 단락에서 교육은 프레젠테이션으로 시작해 귀하의 팀에 전기 자동차의 흔한 문제를 진단 및 수리하는 최상의 방법을 가르쳐드리며 고액의 수리 청구서를 피하도록 고객에게 차량을 제대로 관리하는 법을 알려주는 데에 중점을 둘 예정이라고 했으므로 (B) It provides automotive repair services.가 정답이다.

신입 직원 체크리스트

12 관리자 여러분께서는 신입 직원들이 제대로 근무 준비를 갖출 수 있도록 이 목록을 참고하셔야 합니다.

□ **업무 공간 / 노트북 설치**

신입 직원이 채용되면, 관리자는 www.yalyn.com/itrequest에서 신규 업무 공간 및 노트북을 신청해야 합니다. **13** 신입 직원은 자신의 첫 근무일에 노트북을 제공받고 자신의 업무 자리를 안내받는 것이 예상됩니다.

□ **얄린 자격 인증**

신입 직원은 사용자 이름과 비밀번호를 받게 됩니다. 로그인해서 새로운 비밀번호를 만들어야 합니다.

□ **출입 카드**

얄린 건물에 입장하려면 출입 카드가 필요합니다. **14D** 출입 카드는 4층 인사팀에서 수령할 수 있습니다. **14B** 출입 카드는 부서에 따라 달라지니, 제대로 된 카드를 받았는지 반드시 확인해 주세요. **14A** 이는 직원이 어떤 시설을 출입할 수 있는지를 결정하게 됩니다.

□ **사무실 전화 설치**

모든 업무 공간에는 전화기가 설치되어야 합니다. 반드시 직원이 음성 사서함을 설치하고 부재중 메시지를 설정하도록 해주세요. **15** 편의를 위해 전화기 옆에 방법에 관한 안내를 놓아 주세요.

□ **얄린 메신저 서비스**

신입 직원은 각자의 해당 부서 대화방뿐만 아니라 전사 대화방에도 추가되어야 합니다. 부서 대화방에는 각 팀의 팀장이 직원들을 추가할 수 있지만, 전사 대화방에는 인사팀에서 직원들을 추가해 드릴 수 있습니다.

어휘 new hire 신입 직원 | supervisor 관리자, 감독관 | refer 참조[참고]하다 | ensure 보장하다 | appropriately 적절히 | onboard (신입사원을) 일할 수 있는 상태로 준비시키다 | workstation (사무실 등에서 근로자에게 주어지는) 작업 공간 | setup 설치 | put in a request 신청하다 | start 시작 | credential 자격 | username 사용자 이름 | entry 출입, 입장 | gain access to ~에 입장[접속]하다 | human resources 인사부 | fourth 네 번째의 | differentiate 구별 짓다 | based on ~에 근거한 | department 부서 | correct 올바른 | determine 결정하다 | facility 시설 | equipped with ~를 갖춘 | voice mail box 음성 사서함 | out-of-office 부재중의 | place 놓다 | direction 사용법, 지시 | next to ~옆에 | convenience 편리함 | add 추가하다 | company-wide 전사적인 | respective 각각의

12. 누가 체크리스트를 사용하겠는가?
(A) 얄린 입사 지원자
(B) 얄린 고객
(C) 신입 직원의 관리자
(D) 인사팀원

해설 첫 번째 단락에서 관리자 여러분께서는 신입 직원들이 제대로 근무 준비를 갖출 수 있도록 이 목록을 참고하셔야 한다고 했으므로 (C) A new employee's supervisor가 정답이다.

13. 직원들은 얄린에서의 첫째 날 무엇을 받는가?
(A) 계약서
(B) 축하 메시지
(C) 설문지
(D) 컴퓨터

해설 두 번째 단락에서 신입 직원은 자신의 첫 근무일에 노트북을 제공받고 자신의 업무 자리를 안내받는 것을 예상한다고 했으므로 (D) A computer가 정답이다.

14. 얄린의 ID 카드에 관하여 언급되지 않은 것은?
(A) 일부 구역에 입장을 제공한다.
(B) 부서에 따라 상이하다.
(C) 표면에 Yalyn의 로고가 있다.
(D) 4층에서 받을 수 있다.

해설 지문의 단서와 보기를 매칭시키면, 네 번째 단락의 출입 카드는 4층 인사팀에서 수령할 수 있다에서 (D)를, 출입 카드는 부서에 따라 달라진다에서 (B)를, 직원이 어떤 시설을 출입할 수 있는 결정한다에서 (A)와 일치하지만, 로고가 있다는 내용은 언급된 바 없으므로 (C) They feature Yalyn's logo on them.이 정답이다.

15. 체크리스트에 따르면, 유용한 안내는 어디에 놓여야 하는가?
(A) 우편함에
(B) 전화기 옆에
(C) 책상 서랍 안에
(D) 웹 사이트에

해설 다섯 번째 단락에서 편의를 위해 전화기 옆에 방법에 관한 안내를 놓아 달라고 했으므로 (B) By a telephone이 정답이다.

10월 17일

쿠퍼 피어슨, 시설 관리자
인슈라 솔루션즈
81 머튼 은행
매컬로크, 텍사스 76836

쿠퍼 씨께,

귀하께서 매컬로크 사업 협회의 사업 관행 우수상에 후보자로 지명되셨음을 알려드리게 되어 기쁩니다. — [1] —. **16** 이는 지역 사업체들의 업무 관행 및 절차 향상에 도움을 주신 귀하의 공로를 인정해 드리는 것입니다. 이 회사들이 순조로운 출발을 하는 데 큰 도움이 되었습니다. — [2] —.

18 시상식은 12월 7일에 열리며, 간단한 시작 연설 후 수상자를 발표할 것입니다. — [3] —. **17** 지명자이시기에 최대 두 명의 손님을 데려 오실 수 있습니다. 빠른 시일 내에 행사 참석 여부 및 손님의 수를 저희에게 알려주시기 바랍니다.

수상자가 되시면 상금 5,000달러를 받게 됩니다. — [4] —. 행사장에는 기자들도 일부 있을 예정으로, 귀하를 인터뷰해서 기사를 낼 수도 있습니다.

이 훌륭한 업적을 축하 드립니다.

진심으로,

에블린 오스본
매컬로크 사업 협회 회장

어휘 facility 시설 | pleased 기쁜 | announce 발표하다 |
nominate (수상 후보자로) 지명[추천]하다 | business
사업(체) | association 협회 | excellence 우수, 탁월함 |
practice 관행 | award 상, 수여하다 | in recognition
of ~를 인정하여 | improve 향상시키다 | process 절차 |
instrumental 도움이 되는 | get off the ground 순
조롭게 출발[시작]하게 하다 | ceremony 의식 | take
place 열리다, 개최되다 | winner 우승자 | brief 간단한 |
commencement 시작, 개시 | speech 연설 | nominee
지명자 | bring 데려오다 | up to 최대 | guest 손님 | at
one's earliest convenience 빠른 시일 내에, 가급적
빨리 | attend 참석하다 | cash prize 상금 | reporter
기자 | interview 인터뷰하다 | article 기사 | terrific
훌륭한 | achievement 업적, 성취

16. 쿠퍼 씨는 왜 이 상에 지명되었는가?

(A) 사업체들에 도움이 돼서
(B) 학회를 조직해서
(C) 교육 프로그램을 만들어서
(D) 업무 장비를 제공해서

해설 첫 번째 단락에서 이는 지역 사업체들의 업무 관행 및 절차 향상에 도
움을 주신 귀하의 공로를 인정해드리는 것이라고 했으므로 (A) For
assisting some businesses가 정답이다.

17. 오스본 씨는 쿠퍼 씨에게 무엇을 요청하는가?

(A) 최신 이력서
(B) 연설 준비
(C) 초대에 대한 응답
(D) 행사 일정

해설 두 번째 단락에서 지명자이시기에 최대 두 명의 손님을 데려 오실 수
있으며 빠른 시일 내에 행사 참석 여부 및 손님의 수를 저희에게 알려
달라고 했으므로 (C) A response to an invitation이 정답이다.

18. [1], [2], [3], [4]로 표시된 곳 중, 다음 문장이 들어갈 위치로 가장 적절
한 것은?

"다음으로 출장 연회 만찬이 이어집니다."

(A) [1]
(B) [2]
(C) [3]
(D) [4]

해설 두 번째 단락에서 시상식은 12월 7일에 열리며, 간단한 시작 연설 후
수상자를 발표할 것이라고 하여 주어진 문장 뒤에 이어져야 자연스러
우므로 (C) [3]이 정답이다.

[19-21] 다음 기사에 관한 문제입니다.

아멜리아즈, 에머슨에 문을 열다

(12월 22일) — **21C** 지난 몇 년간 에머슨시의 상업 구역에는 상당한
재개발이 이루어졌다. 결과적으로, 지역내 수많은 새로운 사업체가
생겨났는데, **19** 어린이 장난감 소매점 더 플레이 캐슬과 악기상 톰
가르자, 여성용 평상복 및 정장 의류를 판매하는 패션 부티크 크레
센도도 여기에 포함된다.

아멜리아즈는 부상하는 상업 구역에 진입한 최신 사업체다. 소유주
의 이름 아멜리아 워렌을 딴 사업체에서는 향 비누, 소이 왁스 양초,
향유, 송진으로 만든 예술품처럼 세상에 단 하나뿐인 수공예품 선물
을 제공한다.

왜 에머슨에 사업체를 차리기로 선택했는지 묻자 워렌 씨는 "저는
인생의 대부분을 오크 브룩에서 살았는데, 그곳은 상당히 조용한 곳
이었어요. 저는 언제나 **21A** 부산한 도시에 살며 제 소유의 선물 가
게를 차리겠다는 평생의 꿈을 이루고 싶었어요."라고 답했다.

"작년 초, 우연히 에머슨 상업 구역의 재개발에 관한 뉴스 보도를 본
순간, 저 도시야말로 제 가게를 차려서 살기에 이상적인 장소가 되
겠다고 바로 알아차렸어요."라고 워렌 씨가 말을 이어나갔다. "그래
서 지금 여기에 있네요."

20 워렌 씨는 다음과 같이 말하며 자신의 이야기를 끝냈다. **21D** "에
머슨에는 오크 브룩과 다른 장거리 도시 및 소도시들을 자주 오가는
철도 체계가 아주 훌륭해서 제가 원하는 만큼 많이 가족과 친구들을
보러 갈 수 있어요. 결과적으로, 에머슨을 저의 새로운 고향으로 선
택해서 정말 기쁩니다."

어휘 commercial 상업의 | district 구역 | significant 상당한,
의미 있는 | redevelopment 재개발 | consequentially
결과적으로 | business 사업체 | spring up 갑자기 생겨나
다 | area 지역 | toy 장난감 | retailer 소매업체 | musical
instrument 악기 | dealer 상인, 중개인 | fashion
boutique 패션 부티크 | sell 팔다 | casual 평상시의 |
formal 격식을 차린 | look 모습, 스타일 | thriving 번성하는 |
handcrafted 수공예인 | one-of-a-kind 독특한, 세상에
단 하나뿐인 | scented 향기가 나는 | soap 비누 | soy wax
소이 왁스 | candle 양초 | fragrance 향 | resin 송진, 수지 |
art piece 예술 작품 | low key 주목 받지 않는, 억제된 |
bustling 부산한, 북적거리는 | fulfill 성취시키다, 이행하다 |
life-long 일생의 | own 소유하다 | happen to 우연히
~하다 | right away 곧바로 | ideal 이상적인 | launch 시작
하다 | frequent 잦은 | connection 연결 | distant 먼 | all
in all 결과적으로

19. 쇼핑객은 어디서 드럼 세트를 구입할 수도 있겠는가?

(A) 더 플레이 캐슬에서
(B) 톰 가르자에서
(C) 크레센도에서
(D) 아멜리아즈에서

해설 첫 번째 단락에서 악기상 톰 가르자라고 했으므로 (B) At Tom Garza
가 정답이다.

20. 기사의 목적은 무엇인가?

    (A) 서로 다른 두 도시의 생활비 비교하기

    (B) 독자에게 프로젝트 진행 상황 알려주기

    (C) 소상공인이 직면한 어려움 알리기

    (D) 결정에 대해 설명하기

해설 다섯 번째 단락에서 워렌 씨는 다음과 같이 말하며 자신의 설명을 끝냈다고 했으므로 (D) To provide an explanation for a decision가 정답이다.

---

21. 에머슨시에 관하여 언급되지 않은 것은?

    (A) 빠르게 돌아가는 도시다.

    (B) 오크 브룩에서 한 시간 거리에 있다.

    (C) 상업 구역의 규모가 커지고 있다.

    (D) 기차로 진입할 수 있다.

해설 지문의 단서와 보기를 매칭시키면, 첫 번째 단락에서 상업 구역에는 상당한 재개발이 이루어졌다는데서 (C)를, 세 번째 단락의 부산한 도시에서 (A)를, 다섯 번째 단락에서 (D)와 일치하지만, 오크 브룩에서의 거리에 대한 내용은 언급된 바 없으므로 (B) It is an hour away from Oak Brook.가 정답이다.

[22-25] 다음 이메일에 관한 문제입니다.

수신: jfields@reverber.com
발신: khopkins@southernlife.com
날짜: 8월 12일
제목: 주문 번호 219636

필즈 씨께,

22 주문 번호 219636 건으로 연락 주셔서 감사합니다. — [1] —. **23** 저희가 새로운 창고에서 작업을 이제 막 시작하여, 저희 팀이 밤낮없이 근무하며 배송 시스템에 통합하는 작업을 하고 있습니다. 그 결과, 주문 출고에 지연이 일부 발생했습니다. 불편을 끼쳐드려 진심으로 죄송합니다. **25** 저희 기록에 따르면, 귀하의 주문은 지난주 출고되어, 월요일에 주문을 받아 보시게 됩니다. — [2] —.

이로 인해 상당히 당황스러우셨을 겁니다. 지연을 받아들일 수 없으셔서 환불을 원하실 경우, 얼마든지 그렇게 처리해 드리겠습니다. 저희 쪽에 알려만 주시면, 바로 환불 처리해 드리겠습니다. — [3] —.

다시 한번 죄송하다는 말씀 드립니다. 저희는 고객 경험이 얼마나 중요한지 잘 알고 있으며, 고객 만족을 보장해 드리기 위해 끊임없이 노력합니다. **24** 지속적인 성원에 대한 감사의 표시로, 다음 번 주문 시 'VALUED' 코드를 사용하셔서 저희 로고가 들어간 재활용 자재로 만든 재사용 가능한 가방을 수령해 주시기 바랍니다. — [4] —.

어휘 get in touch with ~와 연락하다 | regarding ~에 관하여 | operation 작업, 운영 | warehouse 창고 | work around the clock 밤낮없이 일하다 | integrate 통합하다 | delivery 배송 | as a result 그 결과 | delay 지연 | ship out 발송하다 | sincerely 진심으로 | apologize 사과하다 | inconvenience 불편 | cause 야기하다 | considerable 상당한 | frustration 불만, 좌절감 | unacceptable 받아들일 수 없는 | request 요청하다 | refund 환불 | arrange

(일을) 처리하다 | process 처리하다 | right away 곧바로 | tirelessly 끊임없이 | ensure 반드시 ~하게 하다, 보장하다 | as a token of ~의 표시로 | appreciation 감사 | ongoing 계속되는 | support 응원, 지원 | reusable 재사용할 수 있는 | recycled 재활용된 | material 자재 | bear ~를 지니고 있다 | logo 로고

---

22. 홉킨스 씨는 필즈 씨에게 왜 연락하는가?

    (A) 문의에 답하려고

    (B) 환불 요청에 응하려고

    (C) 피드백을 요청하려고

    (D) 신제품을 홍보하려고

해설 첫 번째 단락에서 주문 번호 219636 건으로 연락 주셔서 감사하다고 했으므로 (A) To respond to an inquiry가 정답이다.

---

23. 서던 라이프에 관하여 언급된 것은?

    (A) 직원을 추가 채용 중이다.

    (B) 최근에 창고를 열었다.

    (C) 해외 배송을 하지 않는다.

    (D) 가격을 낮출 예정이다.

해설 두 번째 단락에서 새로운 창고에서 작업을 이제 막 시작하여, 저희 팀이 밤낮없이 근무하며 배송 시스템에 통합하는 작업을 하고 있다고 했으므로 (B) It recently opened a warehouse.가 정답이다.

---

24. 쇼핑백에 관하여 알 수 있는 것은?

    (A) 7일 후 발송될 것이다.

    (B) 개별 판매되지 않는다.

    (C) 플라스틱으로 만들어졌다.

    (D) 회사 로고가 붙어 있다.

해설 세 번째 단락에서 지속적인 성원에 대한 감사의 표시로, 다음 번 주문 시 'VALUED' 코드를 사용하셔서 저희 로고가 들어간 재활용 자재로 만든 재사용 가능한 가방을 수령해 주시기 바란다고 했으므로 (D) It has a company's logo on it.가 정답이다.

---

25. [1], [2], [3], [4]로 표시된 곳 중, 다음 문장이 들어갈 위치로 가장 적절한 것은?

    "추가 지연이 발생하는 경우, 저희에게 바로 알려주세요."

    (A) [1]

    (B) [2]

    (C) [3]

    (D) [4]

해설 첫 번째 단락에서 기록에 따르면, 귀하의 주문은 지난주 출고되어, 월요일에 주문을 받아 보시게 된다고 하여 주어진 문장이 뒤에 이어지는 것이 자연스러우므로 (B) [2]가 정답이다.

[26-29] 다음 온라인 채팅 대화문에 관한 문제입니다.

셰릴 존스톤 [오전 11시 21분]
안녕하세요, 이안, 클레어. **26** 대학교 카풀 프로그램이 드디어 시작돼서 너무 좋아요. 이 순간을 오랫동안 기다렸어요. **27A** 올 한 해 연료비에만 350달러 정도 절약할 수 있을 거예요.

이안 로우 [오전 11시 23분]
저도 그래요. **27D** 게다가 캠퍼스로 진입하는 카풀 전용 차선을 이용할 수 있게 되는 것도 생각났어요. 그렇게 되면 이동 시간이 줄어들 거예요.

셰릴 존스톤 [오전 11시 24분]
제 차는 정비소에 있어서, 2주는 지나야 준비가 될 거예요. **28** 다음 주에는 다른 분이 운전을 해줘야 할 것 같아요. 저희 태워줄 수 있으세요, 클레어?

클레어 장 [오전 11시 27분]
28 죄송한데, 제가 이제 월요일에는 못할 것 같아요. 제 남편이 지방 출장이 있어서 그 요일에 차를 사용할 예정이에요.

셰릴 존스톤 [오전 11시 29분]
28 이안, 당신이 우리 마지막 희망이에요!

이안 로우 [오전 11시 30분]
문제 없어요. 다음 주에 제가 태워드릴 수 있어요. 요즘 부쩍 운전하고 싶어서 몸이 근질거렸던 참이에요. 그런데 수요일에는 제가 3일 짜리 학회에 참석할 예정이에요.

클레어 장 [오전 11시 32분]
네, 말씀하셨던 거 기억나요. 디지털 사생활에 관한 거죠. **29** 월요일 빼고는 제가 캠퍼스로 태워다 드릴 수 있을 테니, 괜찮아요. 아, 그러고보니 지질학과의 수지가 우리 셋에 합류할 수 있는지 물어봤어요.

셰릴 존스톤 [오전 11시 34분]
물론 환영이죠. 그렇다면, 최적의 픽업 순서를 파악할 수 있게 어딘가에 우리 주소를 적어둬야 해요. 제가 작성할 종이를 돌릴게요.

클레어 장 [오전 11시 36분]
좋아요. 그럼 저는 오늘 캠퍼스 보안실에 들러서 카풀 이용자용 주차권을 받아 올게요. **27B** 공지에 따르면, 최소 3명이 있으면 중앙 주차장을 이용할 수 있어요.

어휘 carpool 카풀을 하다, 합승하다 | finally 마침내, 드디어 | launch 시작하다 | save 절약하다 | fuel cost 연료비 | remind 상기시키다 | allow 허용하다 | lane 차선 | cut down on ~을 줄이다 | travel time 이동 시간 | out-of-town 도시 외곽의, 다른 곳에서 일어나는 | trip 출장 | last 마지막의 | hope 희망 | itch (~하고 싶어 몸이) 근질거리다 | attend 참석하다 | except for ~를 제외하고 | geology 지질학 | department 학과 | address 주소 | figure out 파악하다 | optimal 적절한 | order 순서 | send around 돌리다 | fill out 작성하다 | stop by 들르다 | security 보안 | parking pass 주차권 | carpooler 카풀을 하는 사람 | central 중앙의 | carpark 주차장 | at least 최소한, 적어도

26. 글쓴이들에 관하여 알 수 있는 것은?
(A) 대학교에서 근무한다.
(B) 서로 이웃이다.

(C) 학회에 함께 참석할 것이다.
(D) 모두 이 도시에 새로 왔다.

해설 오전 11시 21분에 대학교 카풀 프로그램이 드디어 시작돼서 너무 좋다고 했으므로 (A) They are employed at a university.가 정답이다.

---

27. 직원 프로그램의 혜택으로 언급되지 <u>않은</u> 것은?
(A) 차량 관련 비용을 줄여준다.
(B) 주차장을 이용할 수 있다.
(C) 공기의 질을 향상시켜준다.
(D) 출근 시간을 줄여준다.

해설 지문의 단서와 보기를 매칭시키면, 올 한 해 연료비만 350달러 절약할 수 있다는 데서 (A)를, 카풀 전용 차선을 이용하면 이동 시간이 줄어들 거라는 데서 (D)를, 최소 3명이 있으면 중앙 주차장을 이용할 수 있다는 데서 (B)와 일치하지만, 공기 질 향상에 대한 내용은 언급된 바 없으므로 (C) It improves the air quality.가 정답이다.

---

28. 오전 11시 29분에, 존슨 씨가 "당신이 마지막 희망이에요"라고 할 때 무엇을 의미하겠는가?
(A) 로우 씨가 업무 행사를 취소해야 한다.
(B) 로우 씨가 양식을 작성해야 한다.
(C) 로우 씨가 동료를 초대해야 한다.
(D) 로우 씨가 운전할 수 있는 유일한 직원이다.

해설 오전 11시 24분 ~ 11시 30분 대화에서 '다음 주에는 다른 분이 운전을 해줘야 할 것 같아요. 저희 태워줄 수 있으세요, 클레어?'라고 하고, 클레어 장이 월요일에는 불가하다고 했으며, 셰릴 존스톤이 이안에게 당신이 마지막 희망이라고 말한 것이므로 (D) Mr. Lowe is the only employee available to drive.가 정답이다.

---

29. 월요일에는 얼마나 많은 사람들이 함께 출근하겠는가?
(A) 1
(B) 2
(C) 3
(D) 4

해설 첫 번째 단락에서 월요일 빼고는 제가 캠퍼스로 태워다 드릴 수 있을 테니, 괜찮아요. 아, 그러고보니 지질학과의 수지가 우리 셋에 합류할 수 있는지 물어봤다고 했으므로 (D) Four가 정답이다.

[30-34] 다음 안내 책자와 이메일에 관한 문제입니다.

노다웨이 커뮤니티 센터 임대 공간

30 이제 주민 여러분은 비즈니스 회의 및 사적인 행사를 목적으로 최근 완공된 노다웨이 커뮤니티 센터(NCC)에 공간을 대여할 수 있습니다. 세부 내용은 아래와 같습니다.

공간	시간당 요금	수용 인원 (좌석/입석)
아래층 회의실	75달러	15/30
위층 회의실	100달러	71/131
식당	130달러	52/98
콘퍼런스 룸	200달러	103/207

* **32** 학교 및 자선 단체에는 할인 요금을 제공합니다.
* **31** 방에는 스크린, 프로젝터, 마이크, 탁자, 의자가 갖춰져 있습니다.
* **34** 예약 시 보증금 50달러를 지불해야 합니다. 최소 30일 전 예약 취소 시, 보증금 50퍼센트가 환불됩니다. 예약일 30일 이내 취소 시 보증금은 돌려드리지 않습니다.

문의 사항은 bookings@nodawaycommunitycenter.org으로 이메일을 보내주세요.

어휘 recently 최근 | complete 완료하다 | available 이용 가능한 | citizen 주민, 시민 | hire out ~를 빌려주다 | private 사적인 | function 행사 | cost 요금 | per ~당 | hour 시간 | capacity 수용력 | seated 앉은 | standing 서 있는 | lower 아래쪽의 | upper 위쪽의 | dining room 식당 | offer 제공하다 | discounted 할인된 | rate 요금 | charitable 자선의 | organization 단체, 조직 | be equipped with ~을 갖추고 있다 | screen 화면 | projector 프로젝터 | microphone 마이크 | deposit 보증금 | pay 지불하다 | reservation 예약 | booking 예약 | cancel 취소하다 | at least 적어도 | in advance 미리, 사전에 | refund 환불하다 | cancellation 취소 | less than ~보다 적은 | book 예약하다 | result in ~를 야기하다 | forfeiture 몰수, 박탈 | inquiry 문의

수신: bookings@nodawaycommunitycenter.org
발신: w.martin@bastropcitymission.com
34 날짜: 8월 16일
제목: 취소 통지

관계자 분께,

33 힘겨운 회계 연도로 인해 베스트롭 시티 미션 (BCM)에서는 연례 자원 봉사자 감사 만찬을 계획대로 주최할 수 없게 되었음을 알려드리고자 합니다. **34** 따라서 9월 8일에 대해 취소 통지를 드립니다.

33 **34** 저희 자선 단체는 지난 6년간 한결같이 지역 사업체로부터 강력한 지원을 받아왔습니다. **33** 하지만 불황은 예상보다 더 심하게 사업체에 타격을 주었습니다. 이에 올해에는 상황이 나아질 때까지 보다 소규모 행사로 알아볼 예정입니다. 내년에는 저희가 NCC에서 연례 감사 행사를 주최하게 되기를 바랍니다.

진심으로,

웨인 마틴
BCM 회장

어휘 financial year 회계 연도 | inform 알리다 | unable 할 수 없는 | host 주최하다 | volunteer 자원봉사자 | appreciation 감사 | as planned 계획대로 | put in 제기하다, 제출하다 | notice 통지 | cancellation 취소 | charity 자선 | support 지지, 지원 | past 과거의 | recession 불경기 | hit 타격을 주다 | business 사업(체) | look into 살펴보다 | scale 규모 | condition 상태 | improve 나아지다, 개선되다 | celebration 기념 행사

---

30. 안내 책자에서 NCC에 관하여 알 수 있는 것은?
(A) 주차 시 추가 요금을 청구한다.
(B) 대중 교통 역 옆에 위치한다.
(C) 최대 150명을 수용한다.
(D) 최근 지어졌다.

해설 첫 번째 지문[안내 책자], 첫 번째 단락에서 주민 여러분은 비즈니스 회의 및 사적인 행사를 목적으로 최근 완공된 노다웨이 커뮤니티 센터(NCC)에 공간을 대여할 수 있다고 했으므로 (D) It was recently constructed.가 정답이다.

---

31. NCC의 공간 임대 요금에 포함되어 있는 것은?
(A) 시청각 장비
(B) 음식 공급
(C) 대리 주차
(D) 청소 서비스

해설 첫 번째 지문[안내 책자], 두 번째 단락에서 방에는 스크린, 프로젝터, 마이크, 탁자, 의자가 갖춰져 있다고 했으므로 (A) Audiovisual equipment가 정답이다.

---

32. BCM에 관하여 알 수 있는 것은?
(A) 전세계 기업의 지원을 받는다.
(B) 주로 지역 학교와 협업한다.
(C) NCC의 할인 대상에 속할 수 있었다.
(D) 5년 전에 시작됐다.

해설 첫 번째 지문[안내 책자], 두 번째 단락에서 학교 및 자선 단체에는 할인 요금을 제공한다고 했는데, 두 번째 지문[이메일], 두 번째 단락에서 저희 자선 단체는 지난 6년간 한결같이 지역 사업체로부터 강력한 지원을 받아왔다고 했으므로 (C) It was eligible for a discount at the NCC.가 정답이다.

---

33. 이메일에 따르면, BCM은 왜 예약을 취소해야 하는가?
(A) 행사를 연기할 예정이다.
(B) 특수 장비가 필요하다.
(C) 충분한 자금지원을 받지 못했다.
(D) 더 큰 장소를 선호한다.

해설 두 번째 지문[이메일], 첫 번째 단락에서 힘겨운 회계 연도로 인해 베스트롭 시티 미션 (BCM)에서는 연례 자원 봉사자 감사 만찬을 계획대로 주최할 수 없게 되었음을 알려드리고자 한다며, 두 번째 단락에서 지난 6년간 한결같이 지역 사업체로부터 강력한 지원을 받아왔습니다. 하지만 불황은 예상보다 더 심하게 사업체에 타격을 주었다고 했으므로 (C) It did not receive sufficient funding.이 정답이다.

---

34. BCM은 취소 수수료로 얼마를 지불해야 할 것인가?
(A) 25달러
(B) 50달러
(C) 75달러
(D) 100달러

해설 첫 번째 지문[안내 책자], 두 번째 단락에서 예약 시 보증금 50달러를 지불해야 합니다. 최소 30일 전 예약 취소 시, 보증금 50퍼센트가 환

불됩니다. 예약일 30일 이내 취소 시 보증금은 돌려드리지 않는다고 했는데, 두 번째 지문[8월 16일에 발송한 이메일], 첫 번째 단락에서 따라서 9월 8일에 대해 취소 통지를 한다고 하여 예약일 30일 이내 취소했음을 알 수 있으므로 (B) $50가 정답이다.

[35-39] 다음 이메일들에 관한 문제입니다.

수신: service@eminencehotel.com
발신: wgarcia@snoopmail.com
날짜: 3월 19일
제목: 호텔 숙박

관계자 분께,

35 이번 달 초 에미넌스 호텔 파타스칼라 지점을 이용해서 아주 즐거웠습니다. 제가 다른 에미넌스 호텔에도 가봤지만, 파타스칼라 지점에서의 숙박은 저한테 강한 인상을 남겼습니다.

저희는 호텔에 도착한 순간부터 귀한 고객 대접을 받았습니다. 체크인 하는 날 저희가 호텔에 제때 도착하도록 직원이 저희와 연락을 주고 받았습니다. 도착해서는 훌륭한 서비스를 제공받았습니다. **38** 접수 직원인 칸데스 로저스는 관광지를 모두 보여주면서 왕복 교통 수단을 마련하는 것을 도와줬습니다. 저희는 부모님인 프리맨 부부와 함께 여행하는 중이었는데, 전 세계를 여행해 본 분들입니다. **36** 그분들조차 에미넌스 호텔에서의 경험이 타의 추종을 불허한다고 여겼는데, 이게 바로 그들이 귀사의 체인 내 다른 호텔의 단골 고객이 된 이유입니다.

게다가 저희는 꼭대기 층에 있는 호텔 레스토랑에 깊은 인상을 받았습니다. **37** 저희가 파타스칼라로 여행 간 건 훌륭한 음식으로 유명해서입니다. 귀사의 레스토랑은 예외가 아니었기에, 저희는 그곳에서 두 번이나 식사를 했습니다.

감사드리며,

웬디 가르시아

어휘 absolute 완전한 | pleasure 기쁨, 즐거움 | location 지점 | impression 인상 | valued 소중한, 귀중한 | communicate with ~와 연락하다 | on time 제때, 정시에 | exceptional 우수한, 탁월한 | receptionist 접수 담당자 | tourist spot 관광지 | excursion 짧은 여행 | unrivaled 타의 추종을 불허하는, 비할 데 없는 | frequent guest 단골 고객 | highly 대단히, 크게 | be impressed with 감명을 받다 | floor 층 | travel 여행하다 | be known for ~로 알려져 있다, 유명하다 | no exception 예외가 아니다 | end up ~ing 결국 ~하게 되다 | dine 식사하다

수신: wgarcia@snoopmail.com
발신: cdouglas@eminencehotel.com
날짜: 3월 21일
제목: 감사합니다!

38 대단히 친절하신 말씀 감사드립니다. 귀하의 의견은 저희 접수 담당자에게 전달했습니다.

---

39 또한 저희는 귀하의 의견에 크게 감동 받았기에 저희 웹 사이트에 귀하의 의견을 게시하고자 합니다. 괜찮으시다면, 이 이메일에 답장으로 그렇게 하도록 허락해 주시겠어요?

감사합니다.

크레이그 더글라스, 매니저
게스트 서비스

어휘 pass on to ~에게 넘겨주다 | comment 의견, 코멘트 | publish 게재하다, 싣다 | touch 감동시키다 | reply 답장을 보내다 | permission 허락

35. 첫 번째 이메일의 목적은 무엇인가?
(A) 예약 세부 정보를 요청하는 것
(B) 새로운 서비스를 홍보하는 것
(C) 최근의 숙박에 대한 피드백을 제공하는 것
(D) 제공품이 변경되어야 한다고 제안하는 것

해설 첫 번째 지문[첫 번째 이메일], 첫 번째 단락에서 이번 달 초 에미넌스 호텔 파타스칼라 지점을 이용해서 아주 즐거웠다고 했으므로 (C) To provide feedback on a recent stay가 정답이다.

36. 첫 번째 지문, 두 번째 단락, 여덟 번째 줄의 단어, 'chain'과 의미상 가장 가까운 것은?
(A) 가맹점
(B) 주문
(C) 팀
(D) 링크

해설 첫 번째 지문[첫 번째 이메일], 두 번째 단락에서 그분들조차 애미넌스 호텔에서의 경험이 타의 추종을 불허한다고 여겼는데, 이게 바로 그들이 귀사의 체인 내 다른 호텔의 단골 고객이 된 이유라고 한데서 'chain'은 '체인점'이라는 의미로 쓰였으므로 '가맹점'이라는 의미를 갖는 (A) franchise가 정답이다.

37. 가르시아 씨가 파타스칼라의 요리에 관하여 언급한 것은?
(A) 추천자가 바로 그녀의 부모님이다.
(B) 그것에 관한 훌륭한 예시들을 호텔에서 이용 가능하다.
(C) 현지 재배한 재료를 포함한다.
(D) 여행 다큐에 소개된다.

해설 첫 번째 지문[첫 번째 이메일], 세 번째 단락에서 '저희가 파타스칼라로 여행간 건 훌륭한 음식으로 유명해서입니다. 귀사의 레스토랑은 예외가 아니었기에, 저희는 그곳에서 두 번이나 식사를 했다고 했습니다'라고 했으므로 (B) Good examples of it were available at the hotel.이 정답이다.

38. 더글라스 씨는 가르시아 씨의 이메일을 누구에게 전송했는가?
(A) 가르시아 씨
(B) 에미넌스 호텔 주방 직원
(C) 로저스 씨
(D) 프리맨 부부

해설 첫 번째 지문[첫 번째 이메일], 두 번째 단락에서 접수 직원인 칸데스 로저스는 관광지를 모두 보여주면서 왕복 교통 수단을 마련하는 것을 도와줬다고 했는데, 두 번째 지문[두 번째 이메일], 첫 번째 단락에서 대단히 친절하신 말씀 감사드리며, 귀하의 의견은 저희 접수 담당자에게 전달했다고 했으므로 (C) Ms. Rodgers가 정답이다.

---

39. 더글라스 씨는 가르시아 씨에게 무엇을 해달라고 요청하는가?

(A) 후기를 게시하도록 허락해 달라고
(B) 새로운 방문 날짜를 예약해 달라고
(C) 숙박 사진을 보내 달라고
(D) 미사용 바우처를 찾아가라고

해설 두 번째 지문[두 번째 이메일], 두 번째 단락에서 저희는 귀하의 의견에 크게 감동 받았기에 저희 웹 사이트에 귀하의 의견을 게시하고자 합니다. 괜찮으시다면, 이 이메일에 답장으로 그렇게 하도록 허락해 주시겠냐고 물었으므로 (A) Give permission to publish a review가 정답이다.

[40-44] 다음 설문조사 응답, 이메일, 구인 광고에 관한 문제입니다.

고객 만족도 조사

귀하께서 가장 최근에 경험하신 알바니 샤이닝 모터스의 서비스에 대해 전반적으로 얼마나 만족하셨습니까?
(1 = 완전 불만족, 5 = 완전 만족)

1	2	3	4	5
○	○	○	●	○

귀하의 평가에 대한 의견을 알려주세요:
제가 받은 서비스는 훌륭했습니다. 정비사는 아주 친절하고, 박식했으며, 자신이 수리한 모든 내용을 설명해 줘서 고마웠습니다. 40 42 43 하지만 제가 차를 돌려받아 보니 청소가 되어 있지 않더군요. 지역 정비사들의 이러한 주의 부족에 익숙한 편이긴 하지만, 우수한 서비스로 높은 평가를 받는 샤이닝 모터스에서 차량 내부 세차 및 진공 청소를 포함해 주면 좋았을 것 같습니다.

어휘 overall 전반적으로 | satisfy 만족시키다 | experience 경험 | completely 완전히 | dissatisfied 불만스러운 | satisfied 만족한 | comment 견해를 밝히다 | rating 평가 | mechanic 정비공 | friendly 친절한 | knowledgeable 아는 것이 많은 | explain 설명하다 | repair 수리 | notice 알아차리다 | clean 청소하다 | be accustomed to ~에 익숙해지다 | lack 부족 | attention 관심, 주의 | local 지역의 | rate 평가 | include 포함하다 | wash 씻다 | vacuum 진공 청소기로 청소하다 | interior 내부

수신: 카리사 폴란코
발신: 셰인 가드너
날짜: 9월 17일
제목: 설문조사 응답 논의
첨부: @설문조사 응답

폴란코 씨, 안녕하세요.

제가 전화로 논의 드린 설문조사 응답 분석 본을 보내드립니다. 참고하실 수 있게 응답 본을 첨부해 드립니다.

42 저희가 최고 수준의 서비스를 찾는 고객들을 만족시키는 데 있어 이 고객이 중요한 지적을 해주신 것 같습니다. 프리미엄 브랜드로서의 입지를 유지하려면, 우리가 이 부분을 우선시해야 한다고 생각해요. 43 이렇게 하려면 추가 인력 뿐만 아니라 장비에도 투자를 해야 한다는 점을 강조드립니다. 41 의사 결정 과정에 도움이 된다면, 제가 대략적인 견적을 내드릴 수 있습니다. 알려주시면 바로 시작하겠습니다.

인부를 드리며,

셰인 가드너
고객 경험부, 알바니 샤이닝 모터스

어휘 analysis 분석 | reference 참고 | bring up (화제를) 꺼내다 | valid 타당한, 정당한 | cater to ~를 충족시키다, 영합하다 | seek 찾다 | retain 유지하다 | premium 고급의 | brand 브랜드 | prioritize 우선적으로 처리하다 | point out 지적하다 | invest in ~에 투자하다 | equipment 장비 | additional 추가의 | personnel 직원들 | come up with ~를 마련하다 | rough 대강의 | estimate 견적 | decision-making adj 의사 결정 | right away 바로

알바니 샤이닝 모터스에서 전 지점에서 근무할 신입 세차 직원을 모집합니다. 모든 교육이 제공되므로 이전 경험은 필요하지 않습니다. 업무는 다음과 같습니다.

- 44 작업장에서 자동 세차장까지 차량 운전
- 차량 내부 표면 청소
- 43 진공 청소기로 바닥 매트 및 좌석의 먼지 및 쓰레기 제거
- 고객 픽업을 위해 청소된 차량을 전방으로 이동

jobs@shiningmotors.com에서 온라인으로 지원하거나 매장으로 오셔서 신청서 양식을 요청하세요.

어휘 entry-level 입문의, 초보자의 | car wash 세차 | attendant 종업원 | prior 이전의 | responsibility 책임, 의무 | workshop 작업장 | automated 자동의 | clean off 닦아내다 | surface 표면 | floor 바닥 | mat 매트 | dirt 먼지 | debris 쓰레기 | deliver 배달하다 | front 앞부분

---

40. 설문 응답에서는 샤이닝 모터스의 서비스 부서에 관해 무엇을 언급하는가?

(A) 요금이 비정상적으로 높다.
(B) 예약 절차가 너무 번거롭다.
(C) 꼼꼼함에 대한 주의 부족이 개선되어야 한다.
(D) 정비사가 시간을 너무 낭비한다.

해설 첫 번째 지문[설문 조사 응답], 두 번째 단락에서 차를 돌려받아 보니 청소가 되어 있지 않더군요. 지역 정비사들의 이러한 주의 부족에 익숙한 편이긴 하지만, 우수한 서비스로 높은 평가를 받는 샤이닝 모터

스에서 차량 내부 세차 및 진공 청소를 포함해 주면 좋았을 것 같다고 했으므로 (C) Its attention to detail should be improved.가 정답이다.

---

41. 가드너 씨의 이메일의 목적에 해당하는 것은?

(A) 폴란코 씨에게 다가올 점검을 알리는 것

(B) 제안된 변경 사항의 비용 견적을 제공하는 것

(C) 프로모션 행사 진행을 제안하는 것

(D) 프로젝트용 추가 부품을 주문하는 것

해설 두 번째 지문[이메일], 두 번째 단락에서 의사 결정 과정에 도움이 된다면, 제가 대략적인 견적을 내드릴 수 있다고 했으므로 (B) To offer to estimate the cost of a proposed change가 정답이다.

---

42. 가드너 씨가 이메일에서 언급하는 서비스는 무엇이겠는가?

(A) 임시 차량 제공하기

(B) 연료 탱크 채워주기

(C) 고객 차량 청소하기

(D) 대기 구역에 다과 제공하기

해설 첫 번째 지문[설문 조사 응답], 두 번째 단락에서 차를 돌려받아 보니 청소가 되어 있지 않더군요. 지역 정비사들의 이러한 주의 부족에 익숙한 편이긴 하지만, 우수한 서비스로 높은 평가를 받는 샤이닝 모터스에서 차량 내부 세차 및 진공 청소를 포함해 주면 좋았을 것 같다고 했는데, 두 번째 지문[이메일], 두 번째 단락에서 저희가 최고 수준의 서비스를 찾는 고객들을 만족시키는 데 있어 이 고객이 중요한 지적을 해주신 것 같다고 했으므로 (C) Cleaning customers' vehicles가 정답이다.

---

43. 폴란코 씨에 관하여 무엇이 사실이겠는가?

(A) 비용을 승인했다.

(B) 알바니 샤이닝 모터스의 소유주다.

(C) 정비사로 근무해왔다.

(D) 고객 설문조사를 실시했다.

해설 첫 번째 지문[설문 조사 응답], 두 번째 단락에서 차를 돌려받아 보니 청소가 되어 있지 않더군요. 지역 정비사들의 이러한 주의 부족에 익숙한 편이긴 하지만, 우수한 서비스로 높은 평가를 받는 샤이닝 모터스에서 차량 내부 세차 및 진공 청소를 포함해 주면 좋았을 것 같다고 했고, 두 번째 지문[이메일], 두 번째 단락에서 이렇게 하려면 추가 인력 뿐만 아니라 장비에도 투자를 해야 한다는 점을 강조 드린다고 했는데, 세 번째 지문[구인 광고], 두 번째 단락에서 진공 청소기로 바닥 매트 및 좌석의 먼지 및 쓰레기 제거라고 하여 추가 직원 채용에 대한 비용을 승인했음을 알 수 있으므로 (A) She approved an expense.가 정답이다.

---

44. 샤이닝 모터스에 광고된 직무의 요건은 무엇이겠는가?

(A) 고객 응대 경험

(B) 주말 근무 가능

(C) 기술 자격증

(D) 운전 면허증

해설 세 번째 지문[구인 광고], 두 번째 단락에서 작업장에서 자동 세차장까

지 차량 운전이라고 하여 운전 면허증이 필요하다는 것을 알 수 있으므로 (D) A driver's license가 정답이다.

[45-49] 다음 안내, 양식, 이메일에 관한 문제입니다.

https://www.wennunderairlines.com/baggageclaims
분실 또는 파손 수하물

수하물이 분실되거나 파손된 경우, 도착 3일 이내 수하물 보관소에 이를 신고해야 합니다. **45 46** 귀하의 수하물을 최대한 빨리 찾거나 추적하는 데 더 나은 도움을 드릴 수 있도록 수하물 영수증, 티켓, 탑승권의 전자 스캔본을 준비해 주세요.

때로는 이러한 과정에 시간이 걸려 수하물 안에 있는 필수품을 필요로 하실 수도 있다는 점을 잘 알고 있습니다. **48** 당사 규정은 세면도구와 의류 같은 필수품 비용을 배상해 드리는 것입니다. 당사 규정에서는 전자 기기까지 포함하지는 않는다는 점에 유의해 주시기 바랍니다.

수하물이 분실되거나 파손된 경우, www.wennunderairlines.com/baggageclaims/claim_form으로 가셔서 세부 내용을 작성해 주십시오. **45** 양식을 제출하기 전, 영수증 스캔본을 포함했는지 확인해 주시기 바랍니다. 온라인으로 양식을 작성할 수 없는 경우에는 양식을 출력해 작성하신 후 영수증 원본과 함께 다음 주소로 우편으로 보내주셔야 합니다.

웨넌더 항공 수하물 서비스
2195 Colonial Lane
히코리, 노스캐롤라이나 (NC), 28601

어휘 **delay** 지연하다 | **lose** 잃어버리다 | **baggage** 수하물 | **report** 알리다, 신고하다 | **arrival** 도착 | **ready** 준비가 된 | **digital** 디지털 방식의 | **scan** 스캔한 것 | **receipt** 영수증 | **boarding pass** 탑승권 | **flight** 비행 | **assist** 도움이 되다 | **locate** 찾다 | **trace** 추적하다 | **quickly** 빨리 | **necessity** 필수품 | **policy** 규정, 정책 | **reimburse** 배상하다 | **cost** 비용 | **toiletry** 세면도구 | **clothing** 의류 | **note** 주의하다 | **electric device** 전자기기 | **submit** 제출하다 | **unable** 할 수 없는 | **complete** (서식을) 작성하다, 완료하다 | **print out** 출력하다 | **along with** ~과 함께 | **original** 원래의 | **mail** 우편

---

www.wennunderairlines.com/baggageclaims/claim_form
웨넌더 항공 수하물 신청서

수하물 영수증 번호	0736532
46 분실 신고일	**46** 2월 11일 오후 4시 30분
수하물 총 가방 수	1
분실 또는 파손 총 가방 수	1
첨부 영수증	**46** jhammes_영수증
항공편 번호	WU320
출발지	엘 파소, 텍사스
연결편 정보	직행

도착지	산호세, 캘리포니아
46 도착 날짜 및 시간	**46** 2월 11일 오후 8시 15분
승객 이름	줄리아 햄즈
승객 주소	906 허밍버드 드라이브, 산호세, 캘리포니아 95125
승객 이메일 주소	jhammes@qwikmail.com
승객 핸드폰 번호	310-555-9725

어휘 loss 분실 | total 총, 전체의 | check (수하물을) 부치다 | attach 첨부하다 | departure 출발 | location 위치, 장소 | connection (교통) 연결편 | information 정보 | nonstop 직행편 | arrival 도착 | passenger 승객

수신: 웨넌더 항공 수하물 서비스
〈baggageservice@wennunderairlines.com〉
발신: 줄리아 햄스 〈jhammes@qwikmail.com〉
날짜: 2월 20일
제목: 수하물 신청서 영수증 번호 0736532

안녕하세요.

저는 2월 11일 착륙하자마자 귀사 사무실에 분실 수하물 신청서를 제출했습니다. **47** 며칠 후 제 가방이 발견되어 2월 13일에 제 호텔 방으로 배송됐습니다. 하지만 저는 가방이 없는 이틀 동안 몇 가지 제품을 구입해야 했습니다. 제가 2월 14일에 지출한 모든 비용에 대한 영수증을 제출했지만, 제가 받아야 할 배상액을 전액 지급받지 못한 것을 발견했습니다. 제가 신청한 물품 목록은 아래와 같습니다. 물품들 중 문제 있는 부분이 있다면 알려주세요.

구입 제품	가격
1. **49** 칫솔 및 치약	6.00달러
2. **49** 샴푸	4.00달러
3. 양말	5.00달러
4. **48** 헤어 드라이어	29.00달러
5. 수건	10.00달러
6. 재킷	40.00달러
총	94.00달러

진심으로,

줄러마 햄스

어휘 file 제출[제기]하다 | missing 분실된 | shortly 곧, 바로 | land 착륙하다 | suitcase 여행 가방 | find 찾다 | expense 비용 | incur (비용을) 발생시키다 | notice 알아차리다 | reimbursement 배상, 상환 | be entitled to ~에 대한 자격이 있다 | purchase 구입하다 | toothbrush 칫솔 | toothpaste 치약 | sock 양말 | hairdryer 헤어 드라이어 | towel 수건 | jacket 재킷

45. 웹 페이지에 따르면, 고객은 신청서를 작성할 때 무엇을 해야 하는가?
(A) 수하물 보관소를 방문해야 한다
(B) 직원에게 말해야 한다

(C) 모든 영수증의 사본을 포함해야 한다
(D) 반환되는 보증금을 지불해야 한다

해설 첫 번째 지문[안내], 첫 번째 단락에서 귀하의 수하물을 최대한 빨리 찾거나 추적하는 데 더 나은 도움을 드릴 수 있도록 수하물 영수증, 티켓, 탑승권의 전자 스캔본을 준비해 달라고 하면서, 세 번째 단락에서 양식을 제출하기 전, 영수증 스캔본을 포함했는지 확인해 주시기 바란다고 했으므로 (C) Include copies of all receipts가 정답이다.

---

46. 햄스 씨에 관하여 알 수 있는 것은?
(A) 항공사의 분실 수하물 신청 요건을 충족했다.
(B) 과거에 웨넌더 항공을 이용한 적이 있다.
(C) 여행 가방을 분실해서 연결 항공편을 놓쳤다.
(D) 가족 행사를 위해 텍사스로 여행했다.

해설 첫 번째 지문[안내], 첫 번째 단락에서 귀하의 수하물을 최대한 빨리 찾거나 추적하는 데 더 나은 도움을 드릴 수 있도록 수하물 영수증, 티켓, 탑승권의 전자 스캔본을 준비해 달라고 했으므로 (A) She fulfilled the airline's requirements for filing for lost baggage.가 정답이다.

---

47. 이메일에 따르면, 햄스 씨는 언제 수하물을 받았는가?
(A) 2월 11일에
(B) 2월 13일에
(C) 2월 14일에
(D) 2월 20일에

해설 세 번째 지문[이메일]에서 며칠 후 제 가방이 발견되어 2월 13일에 제 호텔 방으로 배송됐다고 했으므로 (B) On February 13이 정답이다.

---

48. 햄스 씨의 목록에서 어떤 물품이 배상되지 않는가?
(A) 물품 1
(B) 물품 2
(C) 물품 3
(D) 물품 4

해설 첫 번째 지문[안내], 두 번째 단락에서 당사 규정은 세면도구와 의류 같은 필수품 비용을 배상해 드리는 것입니다. 당사 규정에서는 전자 기기까지 포함하지는 않는다는 점에 유의해 주시기 바란다고 했는데, 세 번째 지문[이메일], 표에서 4번 항목에 헤어 드라이어는 전자 제품임을 알 수 있으므로 (D) Item 4가 정답이다.

---

49. 이메일에서 햄스 씨는 무엇을 언급하는가?
(A) 모든 물품을 같은 날 구입했다.
(B) 세면용품을 구입했다.
(C) 백화점을 방문했다.
(D) 자신이 구입한 재킷을 환불했다.

해설 세 번째 지문[이메일], 표에서 칫솔 및 치약, 샴푸라고 했으므로 (B) She purchased some toiletries.가 정답이다.

[50-54] 다음 웹 페이지와 이메일들에 관한 문제입니다.

https://www.upscaleliving.com/ourpromise

| 홈 | 제품 | 저희가 드리는 약속 | 블로그 |

모든 고객은 행복합니다

저희는 모든 고객이 완전히 만족하실 수 있도록 최선을 다합니다.
50 주문에 만족하지 않으시거나 잘못된 부분이 있는 경우 교환 또는
환불을 제공해 드립니다. 반품 배송비도 저희가 부담합니다.

배송

150달러 이상 주문에 무료 배송을 제공합니다.

누구에게 연락해야 하나요?

• 제품 관련 문의는 저희 제품 전문가 팀으로 전화 (151) 555-1358
또는 이메일 products@upscaleliving.com으로 연락해 주십시오.

• 매장 포인트나 특별할인 관련 문의는 계정지원팀으로 전화 (151)
555-1359 또는 이메일 accounts@upscaleliving.com으로 연
락해 주십시오.

• **53** 반품의 경우 고객서비스팀으로 전화 (151) 555-1363 또는 이
메일 customerhelp@upscaleliving.com으로 연락해 주십시오.

• 기업 계정 및 도매가격 관련 문의는 기업 영업부로 전화 (151)
555-1364 또는 이메일 sales@upscaleliving.com으로 연락해
주십시오.

어휘 promise 약속 | ensure 보장하다 | completely 완전히 |
satisfied 만족한 | wrong 잘못된 | provide 제공하다 |
replacement 교환 | refund 환불 | cover (비용을) 대다 |
cost 비용 | return 반품 | shipping 운송, 수송 | delivery
배송 | contact 연락하다 | product-related 제품에 관련
된 | query 문의 | specialist 전문가 | related to ~에 관
련된 | in-store 매장 내의 | offer 할인 | account 계정 |
corporate 기업의 | wholesale 도매의 | pricing 가격
책정

수신: customerhelp@upscaleliving.com
발신: 크리스터 코헨 〈c.cohen@airmail.com〉
날짜: 4월 13일
제목: 주문 229562
첨부: @영수증

관계자 분께:

51 52 저는 올해 2월 14일에 구입한 인체공학 사무용 의자 관련 문
제를 신고했습니다. 2월 16일에 의자를 받았으나 의자가 계속해서
삐거걱려 작업에 집중하는 것이 어렵다는 것을 바로 발견했습니다.
이 문제를 완화하기 위해 가능한 모든 방법을 시도해 봤습니다. 하
지만 의자 자체의 결함인 것 같습니다. 업스케일 리빙에서 구입한
다른 모든 제품에 만족했기에 실망스럽습니다.

53 저는 3월 초에 웹 사이트에 나와 있는 반품 번호로 전화해서 환
불을 요청했습니다. 그 팀에서는 4월 2일까지 송장을 받게 될 거라
고 저한테 알려줬습니다. 하지만 저는 아직까지 아무것도 받지 못했
습니다. **54** 제가 환불을 진행할 수 있도록 반품 송장을 받을 수 있을
까요? 편의를 위해 이 이메일에 제 영수증을 첨부해 드립니다.

감사합니다.

크리스터 코헨

어휘 attachment 첨부 | receipt 영수증 | report 알리다, 보
고하다 | issue 문제 | ergonomic 인체공학적 | office
chair 사무용 의자 | immediately 즉시 | notice 알
아차리다 | constantly 끊임없이 | squeak 삐거걱거리
다 | concentrate 집중하다 | mitigate 완화시키다 |
defect 결함 | disappointing 실망스러운 | request 요
청하다 | refund 환불 | list 열거하다 | inform 알리다 |
shipping label 송장 | proceed with ~를 처리하다 |
convenience 편의

수신: 크리스터 코헨 〈c.cohen@airmail.com〉
발신: customerhelp@upscaleliving.com
날짜: 4월 14일
제목: 회신: 주문 229562
첨부: @라벨

코헨 씨께

이 문제가 제때 해결되지 못한 것에 사과의 말씀 드립니다. **54** 요청
하신 서류 사본을 이 이메일에 첨부해 드렸습니다. 다시는 이런 일
이 발생하지 않도록 귀하께서 더 빨리 받아보지 못한 이유에 대해서
도 후속 조치를 취할 것입니다.

추가 문제가 발생하면 저희에게 알려 주시기 바랍니다. 최근 구매하
신 제품에 완전히 만족하지 못하셨다는 소식을 듣게 되어 안타까운
마음입니다. www.modernliving.com/survey에서의 설문조사를
통해 저희에게 피드백을 제공해 주시면 다음 구매 시 10퍼센트 할인
을 받으실 수 있습니다.

감사합니다.

윌슨 콕스

어휘 label 라벨 | apologize 송장 | resolve 해결하다 | on
time 제때 | follow up on ~에 대해 후속 처리하다 | earlier
더 일찍 | happen 일어나다, 발생하다 | further 추가의, 더
이상의 | fully 완전히 | latest 최근의 | purchase 구입 |
provide 제공하다

50. 웹 페이지에 따르면, 업스케일 리빙에서는 무엇을 제공하는가?

(A) 대량 주문 시 빠른 배송

(B) 모든 구매에 무료 반품

(C) 대량 주문 시 할인

(D) 일부 제품에 대한 시즌 할인

해설 첫 번째 지문[웹 페이지], 첫 번째 단락에서 주문에 만족하지 않으시
거나 잘못된 부분이 있는 경우 교환 또는 환불을 제공해 드립니다. 반
품 배송비도 저희가 부담한다고 했으므로 (B) Free returns on any
purchases가 정답이다.

51. 코엔 씨가 구매한 의자에 관하여 알 수 있는 것은?

(A) 공간 절약을 위해 접을 수 있다.

(B) 할인가에 구입했다.

(C) 업무 목적으로 사용되도록 설계되었다.

(D) 더 이상 구입할 수 없다.

해설 두 번째 지문[크리스티 코헨이 보낸 이메일], 첫 번째 단락에서 저는 올해 2월 14일에 구입한 인체공학 사무용 의자 관련 문제를 신고했다고 했으므로 (C) It was designed to be used for work purposes.가 정답이다.

....

52. 코엔 씨는 언제 주문했는가?

(A) 2월 14일에

(B) 2월 16일에

(C) 4월 2일에

(D) 4월 13일에

해설 두 번째 지문[크리스티 코헨이 보낸 이메일], 첫 번째 단락에서 저는 올해 2월 14일에 구입한 인체공학 사무용 의자 관련 문제를 신고했다고 했으므로 (A) On February 14가 정답이다.

....

53. 코엔 씨는 업스케일 리빙의 어떤 사무실로 전화했는가?

(A) 계정 지원 팀

(B) 제품 전문가 팀

(C) 기업 영업 팀

(D) 고객 서비스 팀

해설 두 번째 지문[크리스티 코헨이 보낸 이메일], 두 번째 단락에서 저는 3월 초에 웹 사이트에 나와 있는 반품 번호로 전화해서 환불을 요청했다고 했는데, 첫 번째 지문[웹 페이지], 세 번째 단락에서 반품의 경우 고객 서비스 팀으로 전화 (151) 555-1363 또는 이메일 customerhelp@upscaleliving.com으로 연락해 달라고 했으므로 (D) The Customer Service team이 정답이다.

....

54. 콕스는 코엔 씨에게 무엇을 보냈겠는가?

(A) 조립 설명서 세트

(B) 승인된 물류 회사 목록

(C) 업스케일 리빙 사무실 위치 지도

(D) 송장 사본

해설 두 번째 지문[크리스티 코헨이 보낸 이메일], 두 번째 단락에서 환불을 진행할 수 있도록 반품 송장을 받을 수 있을지 물었고, 세 번째 지문[Wilson Cox가 보낸 이메일], 첫 번째 단락에서 요청하신 서류 사본을 이 이메일에 첨부해 드렸다고 했으므로 (D) A copy of a shipping label이 정답이다.

MEMO

파고다
토익 RC
기본 완성 | 해설서